Exchange Server 5.5
and Outlook
Complete

SYBEX® ▸ San Francisco ▸ Paris ▸ Düsseldorf ▸ Soest ▸ London

Associate Publisher: Guy Hart-Davis

Contracts and Licensing Manager: Kristine O'Callaghan

Acquisitions & Developmental Editor: Maureen Adams

Compilation Editor: Donna Crossman

Editors: Susan Berge, Andy Carroll, Donna Crossman, Emily K. Wolman, Grace Wong

Compilation Technical Editor: Melissa Koslosky

Technical Editors: Tina Burden, Donald Fuller, James Howe, Will Kelly, Joshua Konkle

Book Designer: Maureen Forys, Happenstance Type-O-Rama

Graphic Illustrator: Tony Jonick

Electronic Publishing Specialists: Robin Kibby, Nila Nichols

Project Team Leader: Leslie Higbee

Proofreaders: Jennifer Campbell, Molly Glover, Dave Nash, Patrick J. Peterson, Nancy Riddiough, Suzanne Stein

Indexer: Nancy Guenther

Cover Designer: DesignSite

Cover Photographer: Steven Hunt, Image Bank

Library of Congress Card Number: 01-00111

ISBN: 0-7821-2705-3

Manufactured in the United States of America.

10 9 8 7 6 5 4 3 2 1

ACKNOWLEDGMENTS

This book incorporates the work of many people, inside and outside Sybex.

Guy Hart-Davis and Maureen Adams defined the book's overall structure and contents.

A large team of editors, developmental editors, and technical editors helped to put together the various books from which *Exchange Server 5.5 and Outlook Complete* was compiled. Maureen Adams and Sherry Bonelli handled developmental tasks. Susan Berge, Andy Carroll, Donna Crossman, Emily K. Wolman, and Grace Wong all contributed to editing; and the technical editors were Tina Burden, Donald Fuller, James Howe, Will Kelly, Joshua Konkle, and Missy Koslosky.

Thanks to Patrick J. Peterson, Susan Berge, and Kelly Winquist for chipping in on the editing to keep this project moving along.

The production team of electronic publishing specialists Robin Kibby and Nila Nichols; project team leader Leslie Higbee; and proofreaders Jennifer Campbell, Molly Glover, Dave Nash, Patrick J. Peterson, Nancy Riddiough, and Suzanne Stein worked with speed and accuracy to turn the manuscript files and illustrations into the handsome book you're now reading. Dan Schiff, Lisa Duran, and Lee Ann Pickrell also helped in various ways to keep the project moving.

Finally, our most important thanks go to the contributors who agreed to have their work appear in this *Complete* title: Gini Courter and Annette Marquis, Barry Gerber, Joshua Konkle, Jim McBee, and Cynthia Randall. Without their efforts, this book would not exist.

CONTENTS AT A GLANCE

TABLE OF CONTENTS

INTRODUCTION

Exchange Server 5.5 and Outlook Complete is a one-of-a-kind computer book—valuable both for the breadth of its content and for its low price. This thousand-page compilation of information from four Sybex books provides comprehensive coverage of Exchange and Outlook. Microsoft Exchange Server 5.5 is the backbone of Windows NT's electronic mail and Internet access systems. It extends complete messaging and collaboration solutions to businesses of all sizes. Version 5.5 of Exchange Server includes enhanced Internet connectivity features, calendaring, scheduling, white-boarding software, videoconferencing, and a host of new multimedia features. Exchange Server interoperates with Outlook 98 and Outlook 2000, Microsoft's desktop information manager (DIM), to provide full-featured electronic messaging, calendaring, and scheduling. This book, unique in the computer book world, was created with these goals in mind:

- ▶ To offer a thorough guide covering all the important elements of both Exchange and Outlook at an affordable price

- ▶ To help you become familiar with Exchange and Outlook so you can use them with confidence

- ▶ To acquaint you with some of our best authors—their writing styles, teaching skills, and the level of expertise they bring to their books—so you can easily find a match for your interests

This sampler book is designed to provide all the essential information you'll need while at the same time inviting you to explore the even greater depths and wider coverage of material in the original books.

If you've read other computer "how-to" books, you've seen that there are many possible approaches to the task of showing how to use software and hardware effectively. The books from which *Exchange Server 5.5 and Outlook Complete* was compiled represent a range of the approaches to teaching that Sybex and its authors have developed—home and small business networkers, students, technicians, and network and system administrators should all be able to learn from this format. The source books range from Mastering series books, which are designed to bring beginner and intermediate level readers to a more advanced understanding, to the 24seven series, which is intended as an essential resource for experienced systems administrators. As you read through various chapters of this book, you'll see which type of material is most useful for you. You'll also see what these books have in common: a commitment to clarity, accuracy, and practicality.

You'll find in these pages ample evidence of the high quality of Sybex's authors. Unlike publishers who produce "books by committee," Sybex authors are encouraged to write in individual voices that reflect their own experience with the software at hand and with the evolution of today's personal computers. The books represented here are works of a single writer or a pair of close collaborators pulling from and sharing their own direct experience.

In adapting the various source materials for inclusion in *Exchange Server 5.5 and Outlook Complete*, the compiler preserved these individual voices and perspectives. Chapters were edited only to minimize duplication, omit coverage of non-related topics, and update or add cross-references so that you can easily follow a topic across chapters.

Who Can Benefit from This Book?

Exchange Server 5.5 and Outlook Complete is designed to meet the needs of Outlook end users and Exchange administrators. While you could read this book from beginning to end, all of you may not need to read every chapter. The Table of Contents and the Index will guide you to the subjects you're looking for.

How This Book Is Organized

Exchange Server 5.5 and Outlook Complete has six parts consisting of 30 chapters.

- ▶ Part I: Outlook 2000 Basics
- ▶ Part II: Outlook 2000 Advanced Topics
- ▶ Part III: Developing Outlook Forms
- ▶ Part IV: Exchange Server 5.5 Basics
- ▶ Part V: Exchange Server Advanced Topics
- ▶ Part VI: Exchange Server Command-Line Reference

On the Sybex Web site, you will also find two appendices.

- ▶ Appendix A: Installing Outlook 2000
- ▶ Appendix B: Installing Exchange Server 5.5

A Few Typographical Conventions

When an operation requires a series of choices from menus or dialog boxes, the ≻ symbol is used to guide you through the instructions, like this: "Select Programs ≻ Accessories ≻ System Tools ≻ System Information." The items the ≻ symbol separates may be menu names, toolbar icons, check boxes, or anyplace you can make a selection.

This typeface is used to identify Internet URLs and HTML code, and lines of programming. **Boldface type** is used whenever you need to type something into a text box.

You'll find these types of special notes throughout the book:

TIP

Denotes quicker and smarter ways to accomplish a task, as well as any helpful tidbits you should know.

NOTE

Notes usually offer some additional information that needs to be highlighted.

WARNING

In some places you'll see a Warning like this one. These appear when there is a possibility of goofing something up. If you see one, read it carefully to make sure you don't get into trouble.

YOU'LL ALSO SEE "SIDEBAR" BOXES LIKE THIS

These boxed sections provide added explanation of special topics, examples of how certain people or companies might handle a situation, or ways to perform a specific function. Each sidebar has a heading that announces the topic so you can quickly decide whether it's something you need to know about.

Where Can I Find the Appendices and More Information?

See the Sybex Web site, www.sybex.com, to learn more about all the books that went into *Exchange Server 5.5 and Outlook Complete*. Also available on the Sybex Web site are this book's appendices—Appendix A, "Installing Outlook 2000," and Appendix B, "Installing Exchange Server 5.5." From the home page, click the Catalog button to reach the Catalog page, enter the four-digit book number for this book—**2705**—in the search box, and click the Submit button. Follow the search result to get to the book's Web page, and click the Downloads button to get to the information you need. On the site's Catalog page, you'll also find links to other books you're interested in.

We hope you enjoy this book and find it useful. Good luck!

PART I

Outlook 2000 Basics

Chapter 1

GETTING ACQUAINTED WITH OUTLOOK 2000

When cooking up a fabulous dish, great chefs know that they need to start with quality ingredients. By themselves, ingredients won't satisfy even the hungriest guest. But when blended together, they can create a masterpiece. In much the same way a chef stocks his kitchen with only the finest goods, Microsoft Outlook 2000 supplies you with all the ingredients you need to get together, communicate, organize and view information, and share content with others. Best of all, this premier product works seamlessly with Microsoft Office 2000, a suite of applications you use to create documents, spreadsheets, databases, and more; Microsoft Exchange Server, a top-selling messaging server; and Microsoft Internet Explorer 5, Microsoft's Web browser.

Outlook's key ingredients are enhanced e-mail and information management products combined with innovative collaboration products. One bowl is all you'll need for this dish because Outlook blends nicely with Office 2000. For instance, you can write and

Adapted from *Microsoft® Outlook™ 2000: No Experience Required™* by Cynthia Randall

ISBN 0-7821-2483-6   452 pages $19.99

send messages directly from any Office 2000 program, which makes mailing a document or a workbook as easy as slicing and dicing vegetables. And if you need to satisfy a crowd, Outlook brings more than enough to the table. Using contact management features, such as contact activity tracking and the Distribution List, you can easily create mass e-mailings, Word mail merges, or group scheduling with all your correspondence, appointments, and journal entries at your fingertips.

Outlook 2000 garnishes the dish with endless ways to manage and share your calendar. Special features let you place the mouse pointer over a particular item, such as an appointment, to get a quick peek at the details. You can share scheduling information and set up appointments via the Internet with anyone who uses a program that is compatible with Outlook. And best of all, you can publish your calendar in Hypertext Markup Language (HTML) as a Web page to give colleagues, family, and friends who have Internet access an up-to-date view of your activities. To top things off, Outlook has an integrated Internet solution, which means you can surf the Web from its main window.

Outlook 2000 makes organizing and managing e-mail, calendars, scheduling, tasks, contacts, and documents as simple as pie, which is why you'll find it absolutely scrumptious.

STARTING OUTLOOK 2000

 In order to get cooking, you need to fire up Outlook. Like most other Microsoft Office products, you can start Outlook using several different methods. The quickest, easiest way to start Outlook is to double-click the Outlook icon that sits on your Desktop. But for those of you who don't like this approach, you can start Outlook by:

 ▶ Clicking the Start button on the Microsoft Windows taskbar, pointing to Programs, and then clicking the Microsoft Outlook icon.

 ▶ Clicking the Outlook button on the Microsoft Office shortcut bar.

NOTE

You can drag the shortcut bar to any location on screen. If the shortcut bar is docked or positioned to one side of your screen, you can hide it until you need it by clicking Auto Hide on the Office shortcut bar menu. When you're ready to use the shortcut bar again, show it by pointing to the side of the screen where it is docked, and then click anywhere on the bar to keep it visible.

When Outlook 2000 opens, you see the Information viewer, which is in the right-hand panel of Outlook. The Information viewer is the main Outlook window in which e-mail messages, contact and calendar items, tasks, and other information are displayed (see Figure 1.1). Within the Information viewer are column buttons that you can use to change the way the contents are organized. The Outlook bar, located to the left of the Information viewer, includes Outlook Shortcuts, My Shortcuts, and Other Shortcuts—three groups that provide you with quick access to the functions you use most often. The Folder bar, the long gray bar that appears above the Information viewer, displays the name of the current folder. Directly above the Folder bar is the Standard toolbar, which gives you one-click functionality for many tasks such as sending or printing an e-mail message. The top of the Outlook window contains menus that change on the fly according to the folder you use.

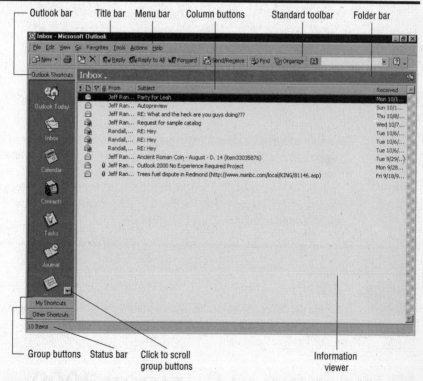

FIGURE 1.1: The Outlook window

RECEIVING DAILY TIPS FROM THE OFFICE ASSISTANT

You've probably noticed that when Outlook 2000 opens, a helpful little Office Assistant named Clippit appears on your Desktop. The Office Assistant can provide tips on how to use Outlook features more effectively, or you can have it automatically show Help information about a particular task that you're trying to accomplish. To have the Office Assistant provide you with daily tips when you start Outlook, follow these steps:

1. Right-click the Office Assistant, and select Option from the shortcut menu. The Office Assistant dialog box appears. If the Office Assistant isn't visible, choose Help ➢ Microsoft Outlook Help on the menu bar.

2. On the Options tab, click the Show The Tip Of The Day At Startup check box.

If a thin metal wire doesn't seem appealing, you can choose from several other Office Assistants, including a spunky little dog named Rocky. To check out the array of characters, right-click Clippit, and then click Choose Assistant from the shortcut menu. Scroll through the list of assistants using the Back and Next buttons, and when you've found a favorite character, click OK.

NOTE

To hide the Office Assistant and fly solo, simply right-click the Office Assistant, and click Hide from the shortcut menu.

NAVIGATING IN OUTLOOK 2000

To help you quickly access the information you need, Outlook provides two navigational tools that make moving around in Outlook as easy as a walk in the park. These tools, the Outlook bar and the Folder list, give you quick access to e-mail messages, calendar items, contacts, tasks, and more.

The Outlook bar, which is found along the left edge of the Outlook window, is divided into three groups: Outlook Shortcuts, My Shortcuts, and Other Shortcuts. The Outlook Shortcuts group provides you with one-click access to the most common Outlook features such as Inbox, Calendar, Contacts, Tasks, Journal, and Notes. The My Shortcuts group makes accessing Drafts, Outbox, Sent Items, Journal, and Outlook Update a breeze. The Other Shortcuts group helps you quickly access My Computer, locate a document, or open a file from Favorites.

The second navigational tool is the Folder list, which isn't visible until you click the Folder bar (see Figure 1.1). Once you can see the Folder list, click the push pin icon to keep it displayed. The Folder list displays to the right of the Outlook bar and to the left of the Information viewer and contains all of the folders in Outlook. The Folder list resembles the folder list you see when you're in Windows Explorer. If you haven't displayed the Folder list using the method described above, from the menu bar, choose View ➤ Folder List. Everything you can access from Outlook Shortcuts and My Shortcuts is available to you in the Folder list. You can use the Folder list to quickly find information in any Outlook folder.

TIP

You can use both the Outlook bar and the Folder list to navigate in Outlook. However, you may find it's easiest to use the Outlook bar for most tasks because it groups together the most frequently used shortcuts and is located right next to the Information viewer (provided the Folder list isn't in view), making it the quickest way to access the information you need.

Working with the Outlook Bar

The Outlook bar is located to the left of the Folder list (if it is visible) or the Information viewer and displays the: Outlook Shortcuts, My Short-cuts, and Other Shortcuts groups. When you click a group's label, such as My Shortcuts, the label moves to the top of the Outlook bar, and the shortcuts contained in that group display on the bar. You may notice that some e-mail shortcuts have a number in parentheses next to their name. It represents the number of unread messages in the folder. If a group contains many shortcuts, you'll notice a small down arrow at the bottom of the group's bar, as shown in Figure 1.1. Click the arrow to view additional shortcuts.

Using the Outlook Shortcuts Group

On the Outlook bar, the Outlook Shortcuts group is visible by default and contains shortcut icons to all the common planning, scheduling, organizing, and management features you need most. To open Outlook Today, Inbox, Calendar, Contacts, Tasks, Journal, Notes, or Deleted Items, click the appropriate shortcut on the Outlook Shortcuts bar. The name of the shortcut item appears in the Folder bar. If you're switching among several folders, the Folder bar can really help you keep track of the window you're working in.

Using Outlook Today   The Outlook Today window, shown in Figure 1.2, makes juggling a busy schedule, staying on top of e-mail, and tracking tasks just a wee bit easier. This window gives you a preview of your day, including an overview of any calendar events you've scheduled for the day, the number of unread messages in your Inbox, and a list of tasks that you have to perform. Begin your tour of Outlook by clicking the Outlook Today icon and taking a peek at the window.

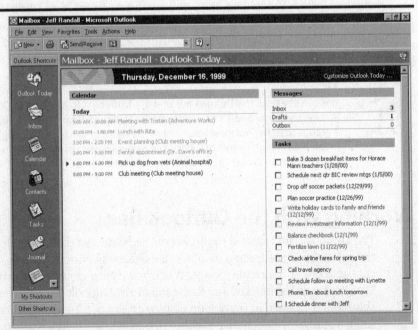

FIGURE 1.2: The Outlook Today window delivers your day or week at a glance.

Not only can you quickly prioritize your work using Outlook Today, but you can quickly jump to more detailed information by clicking the calendar, message, or task items that display in the Outlook Today window. Better still, you can customize Outlook Today to provide the information that best meets your needs. For example, you can have the Outlook Today window be the first thing you see when you start Outlook, which will help you prepare for your day or week. You can customize the following five elements of the Outlook Today window:

Startup   To start in the Outlook Today window rather than in the Inbox window, click the When Starting, Go Directly To Outlook Today check box.

Messages   You can select the folders for the messages you want to see in the Outlook Today window by clicking the Choose Folders button. Then in the Select Folder dialog box, click the check box next to the folder you want to display in the Outlook Today window, and click OK.

Calendar   Have the Outlook Today window display from one to seven days' worth of calendar items by selecting a number in the Show This Number Of Days In My Calendar drop-down list.

Tasks   Choose whether to display all of your active tasks or just the current day's tasks. You can also specify a primary and a secondary sorting order for your tasks. For example, you can choose to sort your tasks by priority and then by due date.

Styles   Choose a style for the Outlook Today window by selecting from a list of five different designs including Standard, Standard (two-column), Standard (one-column), Winter, and Summer. All styles are available from the Show Outlook Today In This Style drop-down list.

So if you're itching to get started with Outlook, try customizing the Outlook Today window by clicking the Customize Outlook Today button in the upper-right corner. Change any of the elements mentioned above, and then click the Save Changes button. You'll instantly see the changes in the Outlook Today window.

Using Inbox   Inbox contains your e-mail messages (see Figure 1.3). New messages appear as bold text and carry a closed envelope icon to the left of the sender's name. Messages you've already read appear as regular text and have an open envelope icon. Read messages remain in your Inbox until you delete or move them to another folder. The Information viewer, which contains the messages in your Inbox, has several columns that provide you with information about each message, including who sent the message, the subject of the message, when it was received, and additional details such as message importance, follow-ups, and attachments. You'll quickly find Inbox is the ideal place to create new e-mail messages and to read, forward, or reply to e-mail messages you receive. For more information on using Inbox, see Chapter 2, "Sending and Receiving E-mail Messages," and Chapter 3, "Managing and Organizing Your E-mail."

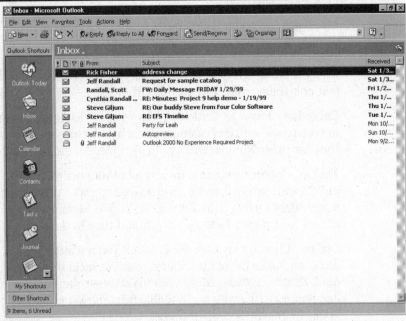

FIGURE 1.3: New messages are delivered to your Inbox.

Using Calendar   Calendar, as shown in Figure 1.4, eliminates the need for the familiar paper-based daily planner. It takes the work out of scheduling time for completing specific tasks, meetings, vacation, holidays, or any other activity. For instance, if you're scheduling a meeting and have several attendees, Calendar can help you locate a time that is convenient for everyone. And just like a regular planner, appointments, meetings, and events can be set up many months in advance. This electronic planner displays a calendar showing the appointments you've made in a typical daily planner format or in list format. Depending on how you've arranged the window, you may also see a list of tasks you've recorded.

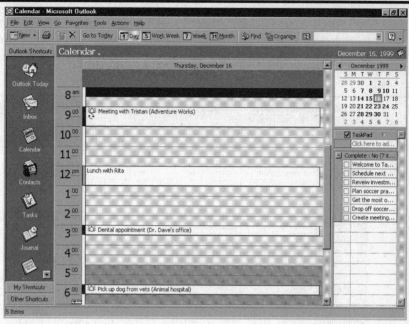

FIGURE 1.4:   Calendar displays your schedule in a typical daily planner format or in a list format.

Using Contacts   Keeping track of business cards and personal cards can be a job in itself. They either get lost in a drawer or fall out of your wallet every time you open it up. Get rid of all those paper-based business cards with Contacts, which lets you enter several mailing addresses, various phone and fax numbers, and e-mail addresses and Web sites for a single contact (see Figure 1.5). You can store all this data and more, so you'll never forget a business associate's job title or miss a friend's birthday or anniversary. Outlook organizes your contacts in alphabetical order so it's easy to locate just the person you need. You will also find that the alphabetical tabs on the far right of the Contacts window are very helpful in tracking down an important contact. Better still, you can use the Find feature, which puts directory assistance to shame.

Using Tasks   Tasks makes the paper-based to-do list a thing of the past (see Figure 1.6). You can use it to compile a list of projects and the tasks that are involved in each project. You can describe and categorize each task, record its due date, and track its status. You can also organize and sort tasks by category or by the name of the person assigned to the task. You can also delegate a particular task to someone else by sending them a task request with a deadline and related attachments. The subject and date for each task shown in the Tasks list are also displayed in the Outlook Today window.

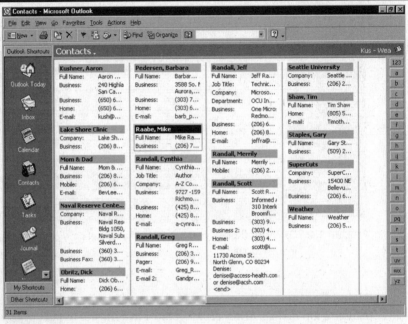

FIGURE 1.5: Contacts is the place for storing the names, phone numbers, and addresses of the people with whom you correspond and work.

Using Journal Journal makes it easy to keep records of your daily activities (see Figure 1.7). (If Journal doesn't display in your Outlook Shortcuts group, click the My Shortcuts label to find it there.) Each entry is organized on a timeline so you can see an overview of what you accomplished when and how long certain activities took. You can even sort the list of entries—by type, contact, category, entry list, last seven days, and phone calls—to better evaluate your records. Journal automatically records entries for your e-mail messages, task or meeting requests and responses, documents you've worked on, phone calls, and faxes. You can add new entries or existing Outlook items and documents to your journal.

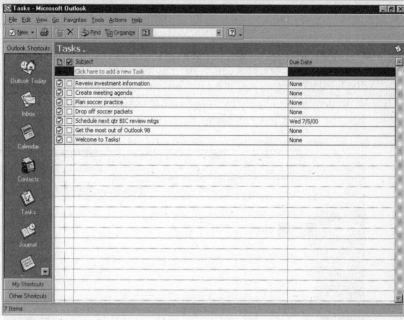

FIGURE 1.6: Keep track of all your projects in Tasks.

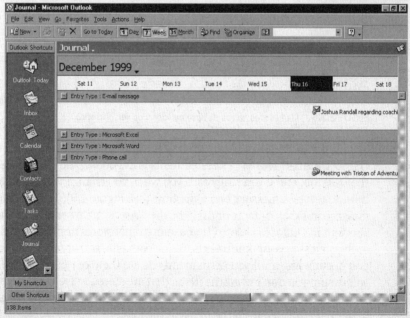

FIGURE 1.7: Keep a record of all your activities using Journal.

Using Notes   Sticky notes don't stick for long and scraps of paper tend to disappear at just the wrong time. Fortunately, Notes can remind you of an important meeting, make sure you remember to pick up supplies, and keep a question or thought at the tip of your tongue (see Figure 1.8). Unlike sticky notes, you can move a note anywhere on your screen and display it as long as you need it. You can even clip a note to a Microsoft Word document simply by dragging the note from Outlook to your document in Word. Click the Notes shortcut and discover its versatility.

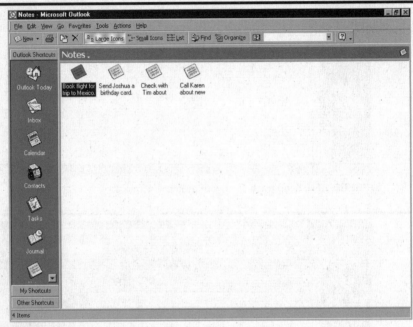

FIGURE 1.8:   Use Notes to jot down key ideas or reminders.

Using Deleted Items   Deleted Items is as good as the Recycle Bin on the Desktop, and it can really save you when you change your mind and want to review a message one more time (see Figure 1.9). You can open a message in Deleted Items or drag the message from its window to another shortcut in Outlook. Deleted Items temporarily stores items you've deleted, such as messages, appointments, tasks, contacts, activity records, notes, and documents, until you permanently delete them or quit Outlook. When you're sure you don't want the items that are stored in Deleted Items any longer, choose Tools ➤ Empty "Deleted Items" Folder from the menu bar to permanently delete all the items in the folder.

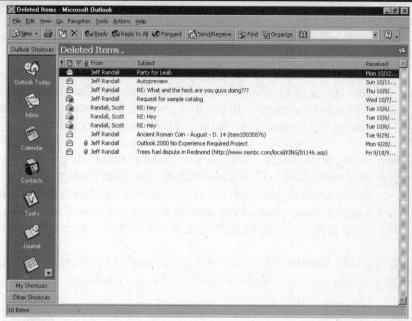

FIGURE 1.9: Keep your Outlook folders clean by sending old items to Deleted Items.

Using the My Shortcuts Group

When you click the My Shortcuts group label on the Outlook bar, you see five shortcuts in the group: Drafts, Outbox, Journal, Sent Items, and Outlook Update. After you begin working with Outlook, you'll quickly discover these shortcuts offer several benefits such as storing your mail until you're ready to deliver it and keeping a record of every message and meeting item you've sent to others.

Using Drafts   Drafts lets you store messages that you are not yet ready to send. So the next time you get interrupted in the middle of composing an e-mail, or need a few quick figures from another person before putting the finishing touches on a message, you can save it and Outlook will automatically store it in Drafts for you. Then, when it's convenient or when you finally receive those figures from your business associate, you can open the message in Drafts, complete it, and send it to your recipients.

Using Outbox   Just like putting paper-based mail in the mailbox outside your house, Outbox holds e-mail messages that you've created but that have not been sent from your computer to your e-mail server for delivery. This happens primarily when you work *offline,* or when you are not connected via a modem to your Internet Service Provider (ISP) or to your company's network server via a network tap. The Outbox holds your completed messages until you're connected. Once online, messages quickly depart from your Outbox to their assigned destinations.

 Using Sent Items   With so much information coming and going, it's sometimes hard to remember what you said. Don't worry, Sent Items stores copies of the e-mail messages you send. You can keep these messages as records and refer to them whenever you need. You can also delete items in the Sent Items folder just as you would any item in your Inbox.

 Using Journal   See the previous description of this feature in the "Using the Outlook Shortcuts Group" section earlier in this chapter.

 Using Outlook Update   This shortcut displays a Web page that provides you with up-to-date information about changes to Outlook. The page opens in the right pane of the Outlook window (Information viewer), so you don't have to open another browser application to get the latest news on Outlook.

Using the Other Shortcuts Group

The Other Shortcuts group label of the Outlook bar contains a miscellaneous group of folders. The setup for your computer will determine the folders you see when you click this label. For instance, you may see My Computer, which displays the same folders and files as the My Computer icon on the Windows Desktop when clicked. It's also likely that you'll see My Documents, Personal Folders (if these folders are set up in Outlook), Favorites, and Public Folders. For instance, prior to having Outlook, you may have used Word to create letters to friends and family and stored them in a special folder. If you want to quickly access your last letter to your parents to remind yourself of the new things you should share in your next e-mail to them, add the folder to the Other Shortcuts group. You can add folders from other drives and Outlook folders to the Other Shortcuts group. You'll learn how to add a shortcut to the Outlook bar in the following section.

Using My Computer   You can access the other computer drives and all the items you normally see in the My Computer folder by clicking the My Computer shortcut in the Other Shortcuts bar. With this folder you're never more than a click or two away from your computer's hard disk—which contains anything and everything you've created and stored on your computer, additional drives, printers, the features in the Control Panel, dial-up networking functionality, and more. The My Computer shortcut in Outlook turns locating and opening any folder, file, or document into child's play.

Using My Documents   My Documents makes it easy to access the My Documents folder on your computer's hard disk. Many people use the My Documents folder to keep the documents they create and to store the documents they frequently refer to and use. If you don't have a shortcut to your My Documents folder, you can easily add one to the Outlook bar. Then, when someone sends you a file in an e-mail message, you can simply drag it to the My Documents icon on the Other Shortcuts group. My Documents is handy for those times when you're composing a message and want to quickly review a document to be sure you have your facts right. It's also ideal for when you want to copy a section from a document and paste it in your message rather than sending the entire file.

Using Personal Folders   If you plan to work offline, then Personal Folders is a must. Personal Folders contains duplicates of your four mail folders—Inbox, Deleted Items, Sent Items, and Outbox—and stores these folders on your computer's hard disk. If you plan to use Outlook for Remote Mail, you'll need to install Personal Folders in order to access any existing items in any of your mail folders. Remote Mail makes it easy to retrieve your e-mail messages while you're on the road. Using this feature, you can briefly connect to your server to retrieve message headers, work offline to decide which messages you want to see in detail, and then make another brief connection to retrieve or send specific messages. Remote Mail is ideal if you have to pay high connection fees while connected to a server or ISP.

Using Favorites   Everybody has a favorite Web site, application, graphic, or document—you might have several. Use Favorites to store shortcuts to your favorite items on the Desktop, such as Internet addresses, disk folders, files, or applications.

Customizing the Outlook Bar

Outlook lets you create a unique Outlook bar to suit your needs. If you right-click the Outlook bar, a shortcut menu will appear. This menu contains several options that let you customize how the Outlook bar is displayed. For instance, you can rename an icon and change it to Large Icons or Small Icons using the shortcut menu. You can also add and remove shortcuts from the bar, which you'll learn how to do in a moment. You can also select Outlook Bar from the View menu to get rid of the Outlook bar altogether. The shortcut menu is also where you go to hide the Outlook bar. If you need the Outlook bar at a later time, select Outlook Bar from the View menu and it will display.

Adding a Shortcut to the Outlook Bar

Now that you've gotten to know the shortcuts on the Outlook bar, you might want to add a few of your own. To add a shortcut to a group on the Outlook bar, follow these steps:

1. Click the group label on the Outlook bar to which you want to add the shortcut.

2. Right-click an empty area of the Outlook bar, and click Outlook Bar Shortcut from the shortcut menu. The Add To Outlook Bar dialog box appears.

3. In the Look In list, select Outlook to locate a folder in Outlook or select File System to locate a folder stored on your computer's hard disk.

4.   In the Folder Name list, either type the shortcut name, select it from the list, or locate it from the box, and then click OK.

Removing a Shortcut from the Outlook Bar

To remove a shortcut from the Outlook bar, follow these steps:

1.   Click the group label on the Outlook bar from which you want to remove the shortcut.

2.   Right-click the shortcut you want to remove from the Outlook bar.

3.   Choose Remove From Outlook Bar from the shortcut menu.

4.   Click Yes to remove the shortcut.

Working with the Folder List

If groups and icons aren't your thing, then you'll appreciate the Folder list, which provides an alternate view of Outlook items. And even if the Outlook bar suits you fine, you may discover that if you have lots of folders, it's easier to move from one to another using the Folder list. The Folder list provides an at-a-glance preview of your primary folders, which you can expand or collapse to see the subfolders. To open the Folder list, follow these steps:

1.   On the Folder bar, click the Inbox button (see Figure 1.1 earlier in this chapter). The Folder list appears.

2.   Click the push pin icon to keep the Folder list open, as shown in Figure 1.10.

TIP

To close the Folder list, click its Close (x) icon.

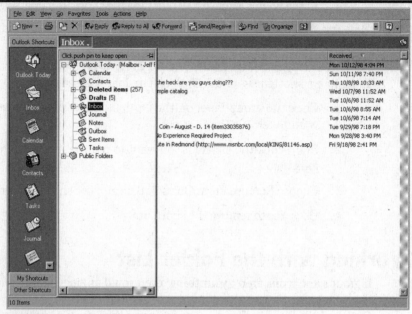

FIGURE 1.10:   Click the push pin to keep the Folder list open.

Creating a Folder

In addition to the default folders provided by Outlook, the Folder list can include any folders you create. To create new folders and add them to the Folder list, follow these steps:

1. On the menu bar, choose File ➢ Folder ➢ New Folder. The Create New Folder dialog box appears.

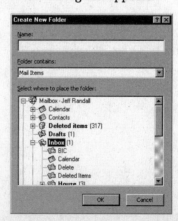

2. In the Name box, type a name for the folder.

3. In the Folder Contains drop-down list, select the type of information the folder will contain.

4. In the Select Where To Place The Folder list, click the folder where you want your new folder added. Click the plus (+) sign to show subfolders if necessary.

5. Click OK. The Add Shortcut To Outlook Bar? dialog box appears.

6. To add the folder to the Outlook bar, click Yes. If you don't want it added, click No. If you don't want to see this message displayed in the future when you create a new folder, click the Don't Prompt Me About This Again check box.

TIP

For quick and easy access to the folder commands, which let you create new folders among many other things, just right-click Inbox on the Folder bar.

Using the Menu Bar

NEW

Outlook menus logically group Outlook commands together, making it easy to perform a specific task. For instance, if you want to see the Folder list or the Preview pane, you can easily find the view commands grouped under the View menu. To access a particular menu, simply point to it on the menu bar and click. Initially, the most frequently used features are displayed as menu commands. However, if you leave the mouse pointer still for a moment, the menu expands and the full selection of commands is displayed.

You can also expand a menu by clicking the down arrows at the bottom of the short menu. Once a full menu is displayed on the menu bar, all other menus that you click display their expanded menus as well.

Customizing the Menu Bar View

Perhaps you decide that you don't like the way Outlook expands a menu when you leave your pointer over it for a moment. You want to be able to click the down arrows at the bottom of the menu yourself, or you might even decide that you don't want to use expanding menus at all. To turn off expanding menus and work in Outlook with full menus always displayed, follow these steps:

1. On the menu bar, choose Tools ➤ Customize. The Customize dialog box appears.

2. Click the Options tab.

3. Click the Menus Show Recently Used Commands First check box to clear the box, and then click the Close button to close the Customize dialog box.

4. On the menu bar, choose Tools. The Tools menu expands to show all commands.

Using Toolbars

Like all good programs with a graphical user interface, Outlook has toolbars in its windows to complement the menu bar. This means that toolbar buttons often have command equivalents on Outlook's menus. Toolbars are popular, and they will likely become one of your favorite window elements because they provide the easiest and most effective way to complete specific actions or perform common tasks.

If remembering every command name is challenging, take the easy route and choose a toolbar button instead. For instance, rather than trying to remember to choose File ➤ Print from the menu bar, all you have to do is find the Print button on the toolbar, which is easy to do because the button looks like a printer. In fact, all the toolbar buttons are graphic representations of the tasks they accomplish.

Figure 1.11 shows the Standard toolbar, which appears by default when you open Outlook. It displays directly beneath Outlook's menu bar. If you're not sure what a toolbar button does, hover the mouse pointer over the button for a moment to see a ScreenTip about the button or the button's name.

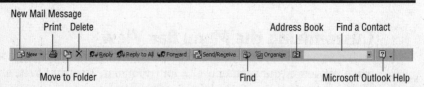

FIGURE 1.11: You'll save lots of work time if you know the functions of the toolbar buttons.

To use any of the toolbar buttons, simply click the button on the Standard toolbar. Outlook lets you do many things with toolbars. For instance, you can turn toolbars on and off, reposition them, and change the size of the buttons.

Adding Other Toolbars

Whether you're using Outlook for personal use, business use, or both, the Standard toolbar provides easy access to common Outlook functions that you'll likely need to stay in touch and on track, such as sending new e-mail or deleting messages. If you think you need a bit more than the standard model, but you don't want to customize toolbars, you can add "ready-made" toolbars. Besides the Standard toolbar, Outlook offers the following toolbars:

Advanced toolbar Contains an additional set of navigational buttons. For instance, the Previous Folder and Next Folder buttons let you quickly move from one folder to the next. The Preview Pane button lets you switch to the Information viewer so you can preview your messages without having to open them.

Clipboard toolbar Lets you easily copy and paste items. You can store up to 12 items on the Clipboard and paste each item individually or paste them all simultaneously.

Remote toolbar Contains buttons for running a remote mail session.

Web toolbar Brings a Web page or document right to your Inbox.

To add any of these toolbars, on the menu bar, choose View ➢ Toolbars, and select the name of the toolbar you want to add. Once you've added a toolbar, you can reposition it by dragging it left, right, up, or down.

WHAT'S NEXT?

This chapter showed you how to find your way around the Outlook tools, the Outlook bar, and Folder list to give you quick access to e-mail messages, calendar items, contacts, tasks, and more. It also explained how to customize Outlook Today and to add shortcuts to the Outlook bar. The next chapter shows you how to maximize correspondence using e-mail.

Chapter 2

SENDING AND RECEIVING E-MAIL MESSAGES

CREATING E-MAIL MESSAGES

Your mail carrier might pledge to deliver your mail in the rain and snow, but what about on Sundays and holidays, in the middle of the night, or during a strike? Whether you're sending e-mail across the street or around the world, Outlook is a convenient and effective way to communicate with others. For those who are unfamiliar with *e-mail*, it's an abbreviated term that stands for electronic mail. E-mail messages are the messages that people send from one computer to another. Unlike regular mail, e-mail messages can be delivered anytime, anywhere. Messages can include text, Web page addresses, e-mail addresses, pictures, charts, graphs, audio, video, and more. With e-mail, you can create a message anytime, have it delivered almost instantaneously, or save it so that you can finish it and send it

Adapted from *Microsoft® Outlook™ 2000: No Experience Required™* by Cynthia Randall

ISBN 0-7821-2483-6   452 pages $19.99

at a later time. In addition, e-mail software allows you to easily keep a record of your messages and the replies you receive.

Every day you communicate with numerous people about a variety of subjects. Your communication can take many forms, such as face-to-face or telephone conversations. For instance, you might need to update a committee member who was absent from your last meeting or want to share some exciting news about a new job with your best friend. Some forms of communication may require a more formal approach, such as a written letter or document; perhaps you need to address issues regarding changes to a community policy or provide a client with project status information. But in this fast-paced, ever-changing world we live in, the most direct and quickest form of communication always seems to work best, which is what Outlook 2000 is all about—enhancing your communication efficiency.

By now you're likely itching to begin sending and receiving lots of e-mail, but before you can do this, you'll need to get an Internet e-mail account. An *e-mail account* contains settings, or rules and conventions, that Outlook uses to pass e-mail messages to the Internet or to your company server, depending on how Outlook is optimized, or configured, during setup of the application. Setting up an e-mail account is very similar to setting up a bank account—except with an e-mail account, you exchange messages rather than money.

An Internet Service Provider (or ISP) can provide you with both an Internet connection via your telephone line and an Internet e-mail address. Outlook and the Internet use an e-mail address to uniquely identify you among the millions of other e-mail users, just like a mail carrier uses your home or business address to get your letters and packages to you. You can create messages when you're connected to the Internet and even when you're not connected, or *offline*. But to send or receive e-mail messages, you need to be connected to the Internet through a modem or network server that can process mail. Once you have your e-mail account set up, which means you have an e-mail name, e-mail address, and Internet connection, you can send a greeting to a long-lost friend, update your mother on your latest adventure, or begin building new opportunities with a business associate.

Opening and Addressing a New Message

It's easy to create a new e-mail message in Outlook. Simply choose File ➤ New ➤ Mail Message on the menu bar, or click the New Mail Message button on the Standard toolbar. The blank message form that appears serves as a template to help you write your message (see Figure 2.1).

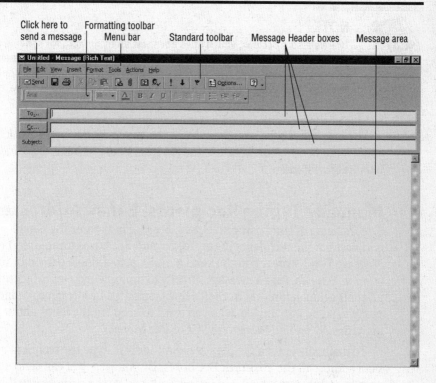

FIGURE 2.1: A blank message form appears when you click the New Mail Message button.

- ▶ The Standard toolbar, which is below the menu bar, allows you to send the message, cut and paste information, flag the message, access the Address Book, select options associated with your message, and more.

- ▶ The Formatting toolbar, which is below the Standard toolbar, lets you format your message, select a new font and font size, add bullets, and more.

- ▶ The Message Header area includes the To and Cc boxes, in which you enter the e-mail addresses of the recipients, and a Subject box, in which you can type a description of the message.

▶ The remainder of the message form is called the Message area, which you use to compose your message.

NOTE

There's also a Bcc box, which does not show up by default, for sending blind carbon copies. You might choose to send a blind carbon copy of an employee's review to the human resources manager of your company without the employee knowing. To add the Bcc box to the Message Header area, choose View ➤ Bcc Field on the menu bar.

You can either type e-mail names in the To, Cc, or Bcc boxes, which you'll learn about shortly, or use the Address Book, which is explained later in this chapter.

Manually Typing Recipients' E-mail Addresses

The first step of composing an e-mail message is to enter the e-mail addresses of the recipients in the To, Cc, and Bcc boxes located in the Message Header area. You can send a message to a single person or to several. You can send a message directly to multiple recipients by putting all their e-mail addresses in the To line (separated by a comma) or indirectly to some individuals, who you want to keep "in the loop" about your activities, by adding them to the Cc or Bcc boxes.

To manually enter a recipient's e-mail address, type the recipient's e-mail address in the To, Cc, or Bcc boxes. By doing so, you can send a message to an Internet e-mail address without having the address listed in your Address Book. If the address you type in the To box conforms to Internet standards, for example `cynthia_randall@hotmail.com`, a solid underline will appear under the address indicating that you used the correct syntax.

NOTE

You can also enter e-mail addresses by using the Address Book, which allows you to simply type the recipient's name; for instance, Cynthia Randall, as you'll learn in the next section.

Creating Your Own Address Book

The key to addressing a message is your Address Book. Outlook's Address Book is like the address book you might carry with you every day, only better. The Address Book is useful because it associates a friendly name, such as Tristan Randall, with an e-mail name, such as `tnrandall@hotmail.com`. So rather than having to remember an odd array of characters and numbers, all you have to do is type the names of friends, family, and colleagues in the To, Cc, or Bcc boxes of a message form and the Address Book will automatically know where to deliver the e-mail.

WHAT'S IN AN INTERNET E-MAIL ADDRESS?

An Internet e-mail address, such as `cynthia_randall@hotmail.com`, consists of a username (cynthia_randall) and a domain name (hotmail.com) separated by the @ sign. The *username* uniquely identifies you, and the *domain name* uniquely identifies a network to the Internet and its users. This is why an e-mail address includes both a username and an Internet domain name. Because the username and domain name are seen as separate items, you can use the same username with two different domain names. For instance, one e-mail address could be `cynthia_randall@hotmail.com` and another e-mail address could be `cynthia_randall@msn.com`. It's the combination of the two elements that form a unique e-mail address.

In addition to making it easier to enter e-mail names, the Address Book is a useful tool because it can store several unique address lists—such as personal addresses, global addresses, Outlook addresses, and contacts—all in one place. For example, you could have one list that contains your business associates and another list that contains your personal contacts—accessing either is quick and easy from within the Address Book. By creating multiple address lists, you can keep information about groups of people separate.

In short, the Address Book serves as the central location for storing all the names, e-mail addresses, and other pertinent contact information about the people to whom you send messages. Outlook has one Address Book, which contains several kinds of address lists that you can use. If Outlook has been optimized for Internet-only use, you'll see Personal, Outlook, and Contacts address lists. If Outlook has been optimized for workgroup use, you'll also see a Global address list. To begin building your Address Book, start adding names and their contact information to any of these address lists.

USING ADDRESS LISTS

The following list explains the best uses for each list within the Address Book:

Personal Address List   This is the best place to keep your frequently used e-mail addresses. This list is located on your computer's hard disk, provided Outlook is optimized for a corporate or workgroup environment.

Global Address List   This list contains e-mail addresses and contact information for members of your organization. This list is stored on a server and typically has numerous listings, including resources such as conference rooms and equipment.

Outlook Address List   If Outlook has been set up to run in a corporate or workgroup environment, you'll see this list. It automatically contains the entries in your Contacts folder, provided the entries have an e-mail address or fax number listed.

Contacts Address List   If Outlook has been set up to run in an Internet-only environment, this will serve as your personal address book in much the same way the Personal address list serves those who are using Outlook in a corporate or workgroup environment. Contacts lists all your contacts—even those without an e-mail address or fax number.

Adding a Name to the Address Book

It would be a daunting task to add every name from your Rolodex to the Address Book. Rather, you should begin by adding the people you'll likely be communicating with on a regular basis. Adding names will help you start to build a useful Address Book. Also, if you share your e-mail address with others and they send e-mail to you, you can add names to your Address Book using the messages you receive. You'll learn how to add names to the Address Book from e-mail messages later in this chapter.

To add a name to the Address Book, follow these steps:

1. On the Standard toolbar, click the Address Book button. The Address Book dialog box appears.

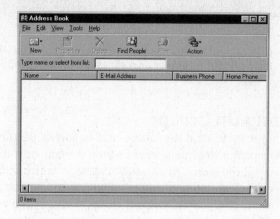

2. In the Address Book dialog box, click the New button on the toolbar, and then select New Contact. The Properties dialog box for the new contact appears.

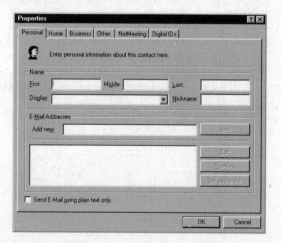

3. In the Name boxes on the Personal tab, type the contact's name information.

4. In the Add New box, type the contact's e-mail address, click the Add button, and then click OK.

TIP

If the recipient cannot read formatted messages, select the Send E-mail Using Plain Text Only checkbox on the Personal tab of the Properties dialog box.

Setting Up Groups

You may want to send the same e-mail to several people, such as members of a committee, members of a project team, or your sports team. You can type all the names in an e-mail message—which may take you some time—or you can create one or more groups in Outlook and then add members to it. Once you create a group, you can then e-mail all the members of the group by selecting the group name in the Address Book rather than the name of each individual recipient.

To create a group, follow these steps:

1. On the Standard toolbar, click the Address Book button. The Address Book dialog box appears.

2. Click the New button on the toolbar, and then select New Group. The Properties dialog box for the new group appears.

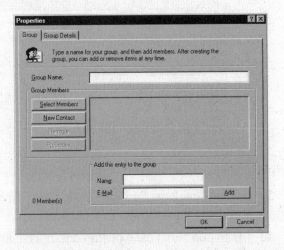

3. In the Group Name box, type a name for your group.

4. Click the Select Members button. The Select Group Members dialog box appears.

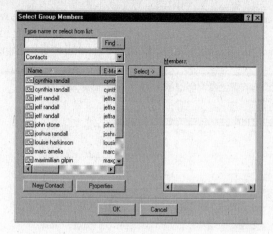

5. In the Type Name Or Select From List box, type a name to locate an individual, or scroll to locate a recipient's name.

6. Select the recipient's name, and then click the Select button. The name appears in the Members box.

7. Repeat steps 5 and 6 until all the members are added, and then click OK to close the Select Group Members dialog box.

8. Click OK twice to close the Properties dialog box and the Address Book dialog box.

NOTE

If your group meets at the same place every week and you have a designated phone or fax for your group, you can add this information in the Properties dialog box for the group. Simply select the Group Details tab and add address, phone and fax numbers, and other information, as needed. You can even add the address or *URL* (Uniform Resource Locator) for the group's Web site.

Checking an E-mail Address

Once you create an Address Book, Outlook uses it to automatically check the names you type in the To, Cc, and Bcc boxes before sending a message. By checking e-mail addresses before a message is sent, Outlook helps to ensure that your message can be delivered and that you're sending it to the person who you want to receive the message.

If your Address Book contains two or more people with the same name, such as Bob Smith, when you try to send your message, Outlook displays the Check Names dialog box, as shown in Figure 2.2.

FIGURE 2.2: The Check Names dialog box lets you select the correct e-mail address.

 You can select one of the names from the list in the Check Names dialog box or you can click the New Contact button to add a new contact who has the same username, but a different domain name. If you're not sure which name is correct, you can select a name from the list and then click the Properties button to display the Properties dialog box for the individual. You can also click the Show More Names button to display the Address Book, in which you can search for the recipient's name.

NOTE
You can also manually check whether a name is listed in your Address Book by clicking the Check Names button on the Standard toolbar.

When you type a name or an e-mail address and an exact match is found, the name is underlined. If multiple names are found that match what you type, for example, Bob S, a wavy red line appears under the name. You can select the correct name from a list of names by right-clicking the name and choosing a name from the list.

If you find the underline annoying, you can turn off this option and simply click the Check Names button before sending a message. To turn off automatic name-checking, follow these steps:

1.   On the menu bar, choose Tools ➢ Options. The Options dialog box appears.

2. On the Preferences tab, click E-mail Options, and then click the Advanced E-mail Options button. The Advanced E-mail Options dialog box appears.

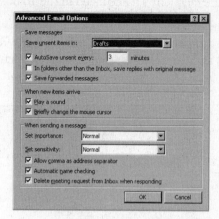

3. In the When Sending A Message area, click the Automatic Name Checking check box to clear it, and then click OK three times to close all open dialog boxes.

Using Your Address Book to Send an E-mail

No matter which window is visible in Outlook, the fastest way to send an e-mail message is to click the Address Book button on the Standard toolbar, which opens the Address Book dialog box. If you've optimized Outlook for a workgroup environment, before you type a name or scroll to find a name in the address list, you should select an address list. For example, you might select the Personal address list, which contains the names of friends and family members. Once you've selected an address list, or if Outlook is optimized for Internet-only, you can type a name in the Type Name Or Select From List box and Outlook will jump to the first name in the list that matches the letters you've typed. You can also scroll to locate a name listed in the box. So even if you don't know how to spell a recipient's entire name, you can type the first two or three letters and Outlook will get you close.

To send an e-mail message using the Address Book, follow these steps:

1. On the Standard toolbar, click the Address Book button. The Address Book dialog box appears.

2. Select a name from the box, and then on the menu bar, choose Tools, Actions, Send Mail. Or click the Action button on the toolbar, and then click Send Mail. A message form opens with the recipient's name listed in the To box.

If you already have a message form open and want to see a list of names you have in your Address Book, click the To or Cc buttons (see Figure 2.1) and the Select Names dialog box opens. This dialog box gives you access to all the names in your Address Book.

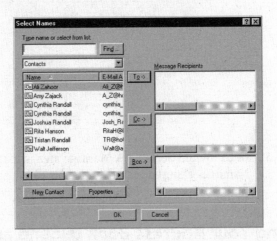

TIP

In the Type Name Or Select From List box in the Select Names dialog box, you can scroll the list and select a name, or select several names by pressing Ctrl while clicking each name you want. Then click the To, Cc, or Bcc buttons, and click OK to open a message form.

SETTING MESSAGE OPTIONS

You're in the driver's seat when you send e-mail messages using Outlook. The Message Options dialog box, which includes an array of exciting choices, lets you turn an ordinary e-mail message into a hot rod. You can control how or when your e-mail is sent, get notified when a recipient has received or read an e-mail message, set the importance of an e-mail message, and much more.

To open the Message Options dialog box, follow these steps:

1. On the menu bar, choose File ≻ New ≻ Mail Message, or select the New Mail Message button on the Standard toolbar. A blank message form appears.

2. On the Standard toolbar, click the Options button. The Message Options dialog box appears, as shown in Figure 2.3.

The settings you choose in the Message Options dialog box apply only to the message you're currently working on. The following sections describe in detail how each option in the Message Options dialog box works.

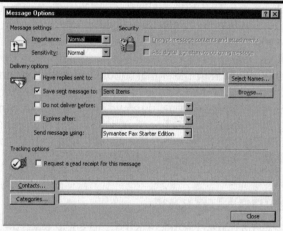

FIGURE 2.3: The Message Options dialog box gives you control over how your messages are sent and received and lets you specify the importance and sensitivity of a message.

Selecting Message Settings

The Message Settings option lets you mark the importance and sensitivity of a message. Importance levels help signal the recipient that a message should be read immediately or that it can wait. Important messages are flagged with an exclamation mark, which will stand out in a recipient's Inbox. Low priority messages are marked with a down arrow indicating they can be put off for a while. And just like an envelope stamped "confidential," your e-mail messages can be marked Normal, Personal, Private, or Confidential. This information helps the recipient determine how to handle your message. For instance, if you mark a message as Personal or Confidential, the recipient will know not to forward the message to others.

Specifying Delivery Options

The Delivery options let the replies to your message be sent to another person. This works well for times when you'll be away for a while or if you want any issues regarding the message to be handled by someone else. You can also specify the folder you want to store the sent message in.

You can use Delivery options if you don't want to deliver an e-mail message before a certain date. This is ideal for when you want to get an early jump in July on your holiday e-mail message, but don't want to deliver the 'ho, ho, ho' greetings until December. In addition, you can use Delivery options when you want an e-mail message to automatically expire. For instance, you can send an e-mail message regarding a friend's birthday party and specify that the e-mail should expire the day after the party. Recipients can still read messages even after they have expired. However, an expired message appears dimmed in the recipient's Inbox if the message has not been read. If it has been read and is still in the Inbox, it has a line through it. In addition, you can choose whether to send your message via the Internet or by fax.

Adding Tracking Options

You can opt to receive a delivery notice when the recipient reads the message. Actually, the notice only tells you that the recipient opened the mail—you might need to check your crystal ball to learn whether she has read it.

VOTING AND TRACKING OPTIONS IN A CORPORATE OR WORKGROUP ENVIRONMENT

Outlook brings the democratic process right to your Desktop with the Voting and Tracking options, provided Outlook is optimized for a workgroup environment. These options let you attach voting buttons to your message that allow the recipient to select one of several choices. This makes it easy to vote for a candidate or a favorite restaurant. When a recipient clicks a voting button, the message is sent back to you. You can read the e-mail to see the response and any additional comments. The Message tab of the message contains your original

CONTINUED ➡

message. The Tracking tab keeps a record of all recipients and the status and date of their replies. The voting results are immediately available to you, because Outlook automatically tallies the responses when messages are delivered. What you do with the results is up to you. To use voting buttons with Internet e-mail, the recipient's e-mail address must be set to use Microsoft Exchange Rich Text Format.

You can track what happens to an e-mail message after you've sent it using the Tracking option. To be sure that the person you're sending a message to receives it, you can set options so you receive a delivery notice when the recipient receives the message; this is just like sending a piece of certified mail via the U.S. Postal Service. When the recipient reads (opens) the message, you'll also receive a delivery notice.

NOTE

If you selected the Corporate or Workgroup mode when you installed Outlook 2000, you can use voting buttons.

Specifying Contacts

Contacts lets you associate a person or several persons with an e-mail message. For instance, a friend of yours gives you the name of a person to contact regarding a new position. You send that person an e-mail message, but before you send it off, you add your friend's name in the Contacts box of the Message Options dialog box. Then, when the person calls you for a job interview and asks from whom you got his name, you'll know just where to look for the contact information. You can type one or more contacts in the box, or click the Contacts button, and the Select Contacts dialog box will appear listing all the contacts you've entered.

Assigning Categories

You can group e-mails into categories to help keep your messages well organized. Categories let you match a message with other messages that belong to a specific project, an activity, a group, or any other designation. This makes reviewing and retrieving similar messages a breeze.

To assign a message to a category using the Message Options dialog box, follow these steps:

1. On the menu bar, choose File ➤ New ➤ Mail Message, or click the New Mail Message button on the Standard toolbar. A blank message form appears.

2. On the Standard toolbar, click the Options button. The Message Options dialog box appears (see Figure 2.3).

3. Click the Categories button in the Message Options dialog box. The Categories dialog box appears (see Figure 2.4).

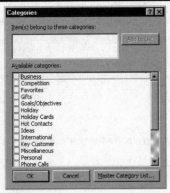

FIGURE 2.4:   Categories is a handy way to organize messages.

4. Click the check box next to the category name to assign the message to it (for instance, Business, Competition, or Favorites).

5. Click OK, and then click Close to close the Message Options dialog box and return to the message form.

NOTE

You can create a new category type by typing a new category name in the Items Belong To These Categories box in the Categories dialog box, and then clicking the Add To List button. You can also add additional new categories in the Master Category List by clicking the Master Category List button. In the New Category box, type a name, and then click the Add button.

FLAGGING A MESSAGE

You can mark, or flag, a message to remind yourself to follow up on an issue, or you can flag an outgoing message with a request for someone else. A message flag appears above the Message Header area (once you've flagged a message) and contains information about the reminder. If a solid red flag appears in the Flag Status column, the message is flagged. A message with a white flag indicates that someone has responded to the message. When a recipient receives a message with a flag, a comment on the purpose of the flag appears at the top of the message.

To flag a message for follow-up, follow these steps:

1. To flag an existing message, click Inbox from the Folder list, and then in the Information viewer, select the message you want to flag.

2. To flag a new e-mail message, on the menu bar, choose File ➣ New ➣ Mail Message.

3. On the Standard toolbar, click the Flag For Follow Up button. The Flag For Follow Up dialog box appears, as shown in Figure 2.5.

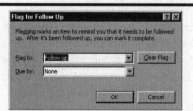

FIGURE 2.5: Flag a message to provide yourself or your recipient with additional information.

4. In the Flag To box, select the flag you want from the drop-down list, such as Call, Do Not Forward, Follow Up, or type your own.

5. In the Due By box, type a date or select a date that displays in the current month's calendar from the drop-down list. You can click any date on the calendar and it will be inserted in the box.

6. Click OK when you're done.

NOTE

If a message is currently flagged in your Inbox and you need to change the due date, double-click the message to open it. Then, on the Standard toolbar, click the Flag For Follow Up button. In the Due By box type a new date or select one from the drop-down list.

To remove a flag, right-click the flag, and then click Clear Flag from the shortcut menu. After you've addressed a flag comment, right-click the flag, and then click Flag Complete from the shortcut menu.

SAVING AN UNFINISHED MESSAGE

Right in the middle of composing an e-mail message the telephone rings. You manage to make it a quick call and you're back on track, right? Nope, now there's someone at the door. But you're able to tell the salesman "no" politely and return to your message. Then—and this is the one person too important to say no to—your seven-year-old begs you to help him with a puzzle. If you're using Outlook, you can say "sure" and not be worried that you'll lose all your hard work.

No matter where you're at in creating an e-mail message, you can save it by choosing File ➤ Save from the menu bar or closing the message window. When you close the message window, Outlook will ask you if you want to save the message. If you click Yes, the message will be saved to the Drafts folder.

When you have time to finish the e-mail, click the Drafts folder in the Folder list or click My Shortcuts on the Outlook bar and click the Drafts shortcut. Locate the message, and then double-click the message to open the e-mail.

CUSTOMIZING THE APPEARANCE OF E-MAIL MESSAGES

Outlook lets you design your e-mail message to match your personality, an occasion, or an audience. You can create many of the same effects in Outlook, such as bold text and bulleted lists, that you can create in a word processing program. You can make your e-mail message look similar to a Web page by changing the background color. If you're looking to create sophisticated, funny, or unusual e-mails, the built-in stationery samples can help. You can also create an electronic signature to use to sign your e-mail messages.

Formatting an E-mail Message

NEW

Outlook offers four mail editors you can use to format your e-mail message.

Using the HTML Editor

If you need to send someone a picture, animated graphic, or multimedia file, you should choose the HTML editor. But be sure that the recipient's e-mail editor supports HTML messages; otherwise, he'll only get a plain text version of your message. With the HTML editor, you can:

- ▶ Format text
- ▶ Create numbered and bulleted lists
- ▶ Align text
- ▶ Add horizontal lines and backgrounds
- ▶ Use HTML styles
- ▶ Insert Web pages

Using the Microsoft Outlook Rich Text Editor

This editor is ideal if you simply want to be able to spruce up your messages with a little bit of style, but don't want to slow things down with large graphics or media files. Outlook Rich Text is also a good choice because it's supported by Microsoft Exchange Server and many PC mail editors. Microsoft Outlook Rich Text allows you to:

- ▶ Format text
- ▶ Create bulleted lists
- ▶ Align text

Using the Plain Text Editor

If you're just looking for a plain vanilla envelope, then you'll want to use Plain Text, which is just that—no formatting.

Using Microsoft Word Editor

If you want a full-featured editor, use Microsoft Word, which allows you to:

- ▶ Use AutoCorrect to correct mistyped words
- ▶ Use Spell It to check spelling as you type
- ▶ Add bullets and numbers automatically
- ▶ Insert tables to present information such as schedules
- ▶ Use drawing tools such as WordArt and AutoShapes
- ▶ Highlight for emphasis
- ▶ Insert images and files into the body of the e-mail message
- ▶ Complete smart conversions of e-mail names and Internet addresses in which hyperlinks are automatically created from e-mail addresses and URLs

The HTML editor allows you to format e-mail with content as rich and compelling as content on the Web, so you can easily personalize your mail. Not only can HTML mail be exchanged reliably over the Internet, but it is readily supported by all leading e-mail applications, which means it's a good formatting choice if you plan to send lots of e-mail via the Web. Also, rich HTML mail can be easily exchanged between applications from different companies. If you often exchange messages back and forth with others, HTML may be the right choice for you. When you reply to a message that is enhanced with HTML, a border that is the same color as the reply appears down the left side of the original message. This helps you and others to easily track and read responses, particularly in long e-mail discussions.

The built-in Outlook Rich Text and Microsoft Word editors ensure that all your "i's" are dotted and your "t's" are crossed, so that others won't focus on grammar and spelling mistakes in your e-mail instead of the content of your message.

You can easily switch between HTML, RTF, or plain text editing in Outlook at any time.

To specify a format for your e-mail messages, follow these steps:

1. On the menu bar, choose Tools ➤ Options. The Options dialog box appears.

2. Click the Mail Format tab.

3. In the Message Format area, select one of the three options (HTML, Microsoft Outlook Rich Text, or Plain Text). To use Microsoft Word, select the Use Microsoft Word To Edit E-mail Messages check box.

4. Click OK.

NOTE

The Use Microsoft Word To Edit E-mail Messages option requires that you have Microsoft Word installed on your computer.

You can also compose your message in any Office application, and send the message as HTML, so the recipient can read your message without having the application.

Applying Basic Text Formats

Depending on the mail editor you choose, the appropriate options on the Formatting toolbar will be available. The Formatting toolbar is visible when you open a new message, but it isn't active until the cursor or text is in the Message area. To apply formatting to selected text in a message, click the buttons and boxes on the Formatting toolbar, as shown in Figure 2.6.

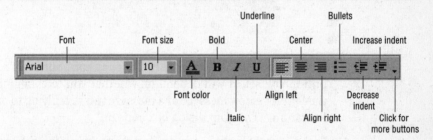

FIGURE 2.6: The Formatting toolbar lets you apply basic text formats to your e-mail messages.

Changing the Default Font

Outlook lets you change the default font for new messages, messages you reply to or forward, and messages you compose or read as plain text.

Outlook knows that everyone has a favorite font, and that's why it makes it easy to choose a font that matches your style or needs. If you primarily send e-mail to friends and family, you may want to choose a zany font that fits your personality. But if you plan on using Outlook as a professional tool to send e-mail to colleagues, you may feel more comfortable with a standard font like Times New Roman. You can make the default font the same for all three or choose a unique font for each. To change the default font, follow these steps:

1. On the menu bar, choose Tools ➤ Options. The Options dialog box appears.

2. Click the Mail Format tab, and then click the Fonts button. The Fonts dialog box appears.

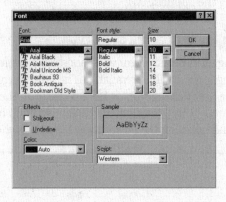

3. In the Fonts dialog box, click the Choose Font button. The button you select will depend on whether you're changing the font for a new message or a message you're replying to or forwarding. The Font dialog box appears.

4. In the Font dialog box, select a Font, Font Style, Size, Effects, Color, and Script option, as desired.

5. Click OK twice to return to the Options dialog box. Click OK or Apply to save your changes.

Using Stationery

Remember the boxes of nice stationery you got for your birthday when you were a child? Well if that's a fleeting memory, then how about the letter you received near the holidays? You know, the one that wished you joy and happiness and was printed on holiday paper. Outlook's stationery lets you design a message format, just like you would your company letterhead or office stationery, which you can use for one message or as the default design for all messages. Stationery includes an array of designs— everything from party balloons to formal announcements—a total of 24 in all. You can use stationery as is, edit the designs, or create your own. Add a bit of pizzazz to your next e-mail message by using stationery.

To use Outlook stationery, follow these steps:

1. On the menu bar, choose Action ➤ New Mail Message Using ➤ More Stationery. The Select A Stationery dialog box appears (see Figure 2.7).

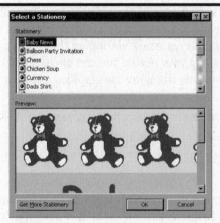

FIGURE 2.7: Use the Select A Stationery dialog box to choose a stationery design to use for a message.

2. Select a stationery design from the Stationery list, and then click OK.

A new e-mail message opens and displays the stationery you selected. Now you're ready to compose your e-mail message and send it.

Selecting Default Stationery

To select a stationery design to use as the default for all new messages, follow these steps:

1. On the menu bar, choose Tools ➤ Options. The Options dialog box appears.

2. Click the Mail Format tab, select HTML from the Send In This Message Format drop-down list, and then click the Stationery Picker button. The Stationery Picker dialog box appears.

3. In the Stationery Picker dialog box, select a stationery design from the Stationery list, and then click OK. The stationery you selected now displays in the Use This Stationery By Default box.

4. Click OK.

Creating Stationery

You can create your own stationery designs even if you're not so talented in the design department. By using an existing stationery file or an HTML file as a template, you can create new stationery that has a unique look designed specifically to meet your needs. You can make several changes to a stationery file, such as changing the graphics, color, or font used for its default text.

To create a new custom stationery file by modifying existing stationery, follow these steps:

1. On the menu bar, choose Tools ➤ Options. The Options dialog box appears.

2. Click the Mail Format tab, and in the Send In This Message Format drop-down list, select HTML, and then click the Stationery Picker button. The Stationery Picker dialog box appears.

3. Click the New button to create a new stationery file. The Create New Stationery dialog box appears.

4. Type a name for the new stationery in the Enter A Name For Your New Stationery box.

5. To choose a piece of stationery as a starting point, click Use This Existing Stationery As A Template. To pick an existing HTML file to start with, click Use This File As A Template. Then click Next. The Edit Stationery dialog box appears, and if you choose to base your stationery on an existing template, a sample of it appears in the Preview pane of the Edit Stationery dialog box, as shown in Figure 2.8.

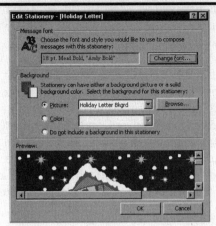

FIGURE 2.8: You can change the font and background of your stationery using the Edit Stationery dialog box.

6. To change the font for your stationery, click the Change Font button. The Font dialog box appears. Select a font, font size, and other options; then click OK.

7. To add a picture to your stationery, select the Picture option and then click the Browse button to locate the file.

8. To add a background color to your stationery, select the Color option, and then select a color from the drop-down list.

9. To remove the background from your stationery, select the Do Not Include A Background In This Stationery option.

10. Click OK to close the Edit Stationery dialog box. Click OK twice more to close all dialog boxes.

NOTE

If you create your own stationery, you can select either a picture or color for the background, but not both. If you select a picture it will be *tiled,* which means the picture will appear multiple times to completely fill the entire message background. For example, if your picture is one quarter the size of the background area, it will appear four times—once in the upper-right corner, once in the upper-left corner, once in the lower-right corner, and once in the lower-left corner.

The name of your new stationery will be listed with the other stationery and available from the Actions menu. You can use this stationery as your default stationery or on an individual basis.

Selecting Stationery Fonts   When it comes to fonts, you might like to keep it simple, so you choose Times New Roman or Arial. On the other hand, you might find that Comic Sans MS or Garamond keeps your creative juices flowing. Everyone has a favorite font, and Outlook makes it easy for you to match your favorite font with a design that's pleasing to you. To specify font selections for a stationery design, choose Tools ➤ Options from the menu bar, click the Mail Format tab, and then click the Fonts button to display the Fonts dialog box (see Figure 2.9). In the Stationery Fonts area, select the option that best suits you.

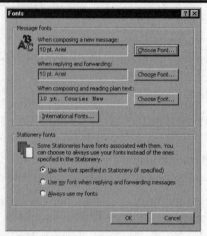

FIGURE 2.9:   Use the Fonts dialog box to specify fonts to use with stationery and when sending, replying, and forwarding e-mail.

Creating an Electronic Signature

Many people use stamps or labels that have their names and addresses on them to take the monotony and work out of placing a return address on envelopes. With this same idea in mind, Outlook lets you add an electronic signature to every e-mail message you send. You can include your name, job title, phone number, e-mail address, Web site address, or a favorite quote—whatever you want! You can even spruce up your signature by choosing a font that looks like handwriting—guaranteed to always look great and be readable. To create an electronic signature, follow these steps:

1. On the menu bar, choose Tools ➤ Options. The Options dialog box appears.

2. Click the Mail Format tab, and then click the Signature Picker button. The Signature Picker dialog box appears.

3. Click the New button. The Create New Signature dialog box appears.

4. In the Enter A Name For Your New Signature box, type a name for the signature.

5. Be sure that Start With A Blank Signature option is selected, and then click Next. The Edit Signature dialog box appears, as shown in Figure 2.10.

FIGURE 2.10: The Edit Signature dialog box lets you create a unique signature for all your e-mail messages. You can use it to share your favorite quote or to add your business title.

6. Click the Font button to open the Font dialog box, and then in the Font list, scroll to select a font. Select a font style and size, effects, and color, if desired. Then click OK.

7. Click the Signature Text area, and then type your name and message, if desired.

8. Click Finish. The Signature Picker dialog box appears and displays the new signature name in the box. Click OK to close the Signature Picker dialog box. Click OK again to close the Options dialog box.

NOTE

If you don't want to use the signature when replying or forwarding messages, click the Don't Use When Replying Or Forwarding box on the Mail Format tab (accessed through Tools ➢ Options on the menu bar).

Adding Objects

If grandma's still bugging you for pictures of the kids, or your friends can't wait to see your new puppy, give them what they want in an e-mail message. Of course you'll need to have a scanned photo before you can send the latest glossy to your loved ones. But if that's not handy, you can insert any number of other objects like clip art, a Microsoft Excel chart, a bitmap, media clip file, a video clip, and more. You can easily create a unique and special look for your e-mail messages by adding a graphic. And if you really want to liven things up, add an animated file that moves on the message, such as the animated GIF (Graphics Interchange Format) graphics common on the Internet. A GIF is just one of many popular graphics file formats available today.

To insert an object in a message, follow these steps:

1. On the menu bar, choose File ➢ New ➢ Mail Message, or on the Standard toolbar, click the New Mail Message button. The message form appears.

2. Click the Message area where you want the graphic to appear.

3. On the menu bar, choose Insert ➢ Object. The Insert Object dialog box appears.

4. Select the Create From File option, and then type the path and filename for the graphic or click Browse to locate it.

5. Click OK.

ADDING ATTACHMENTS TO MESSAGES

Every month most of us experience the joy of paying bills. We attach a check to a note, letter, or part of an invoice and stuff it all into an envelope, address it, add a stamp, and drop it in a mailbox. Just like you attach items to letters that you send through the post office, you can send attachments with e-mail messages. An *attachment* is a file on your disk that you want to send to the recipient of the e-mail. For example, you can attach a newsletter or meeting agenda created in Microsoft Word or an Excel spreadsheet containing everything from a budget to a roster for your soccer team. Just about any file type you can save to your disk drive, you can send in an e-mail message. When you attach a file, rather than copying and pasting the information into an e-mail message, the recipient can open the file and save it on her computer. This way, she can make changes to it, print it, or incorporate it into an existing file. When a recipient receives the e-mail message in Outlook, he knows the message contains an attachment because he sees a paper clip icon in the Attachment column of his Inbox. Recipients can open a file directly from e-mail or save it to their computers.

Attaching a File to a Message

You can attach files to a new message, a forwarded message, or a reply message. (You'll learn more about forwarding and replying to messages later in this chapter.) To attach a file to a new message, follow these steps:

1. On the menu bar, choose File ➤ New ➤ Mail Message, or on the Standard toolbar, click the New Mail Message button. The message form appears.

2. On the Standard toolbar, click the Insert File button. The Insert File dialog box appears.

3. In the Look In box, select the disk and the folder that contains the file.

4. Select the file or files you want to attach.

5. In the Insert As area, select the Attachment option, and then click OK.

Attaching an E-mail Message to Another E-mail Message

Let's say your sister calls and wants you to e-mail her the previous five cartoon messages that your brother sent to you. Rather than forwarding her all five, you can attach the original messages in a new message. This is a great shortcut, especially when sending related items, and it won't fill your recipient's Inbox with multiple messages. You create one message that includes your message and the five other e-mail messages. To insert existing e-mail messages into a new message, follow these steps.

1. On the menu bar, choose File ➢ New ➢ Mail Message, or on the Standard toolbar, click the New Mail Message button. The message form appears.

2. On the menu bar, choose Insert ➢ Item. The Insert Item dialog box appears (see Figure 2.11).

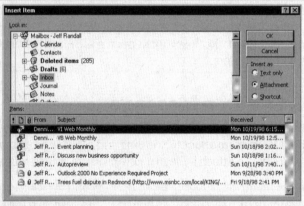

FIGURE 2.11: The Insert Item dialog box lets you attach a file as an e-mail message, text, or shortcut.

3. In the Look In list, click the folder containing the message you want to attach.

4. In the Items list, select the message you want to attach, and then click OK.

TIP

To select several messages at once, press Ctrl while selecting each message from the Items list.

Inserting a Hyperlink in an E-mail Message

More and more these days, people are using the Web to read the morning paper, purchase a car, or plan their next vacation. When you're browsing the Web, you may come across a site that you want to share with a friend or colleague. Although you can't copy and paste the Web page into an e-mail message, you can include a hyperlink, or shortcut, to the Web site. When the recipient receives the e-mail message, she can click the link and, assuming she has an Internet connection, view the Web page in a browser.

The quickest way to insert a hyperlink in an e-mail message is to type the Web site address in the Message area. When you type it using the correct syntax, and then press the Spacebar or Enter, the URL automatically becomes an active link indicated by the underline and blue color; for example, `http://microsoft.com`.

Sending a Business Card

Whether you have a business card for the company you work for or a personal card with your name, phone number, e-mail name and address, you've probably discovered how useful they are and how often others want one from you. Even if you have a business card and a personal card, you still don't have the right card for e-mail—but it's easy to get one. A *vCard* is a type of business card you attach to e-mail that includes information about yourself or a contact in your Address Book. You can include a vCard as a signature and recipients can read the information and add it to their address books with a single click, which makes a vCard superior to the paper-based cards.

To create and send a vCard with your own information, follow these steps:

1. Add yourself to the Contacts folder, if you aren't already listed.

2. In the Outlook bar, click the Contacts shortcut or click Contacts in the Folder list.

3. Scroll the list of contacts to locate your own listing. If you want to send a vCard for another person, locate his or her listing.

4. Right-click the listing, and choose Forward from the short-cut menu.

A new e-mail message opens with the Subject line filled in with the name of the vCard. The vCard, which has a .vcf extension and looks similar to an actual Rolodex card, is shown as an icon. Complete the remainder of the e-mail message and send it to your recipient.

SENDING E-MAIL MESSAGES

Depending on how your system is set up, sending e-mail may be instantaneous or it may require you to take an extra step. If you're using Outlook in a corporate or workgroup environment and are sending e-mail to recipients on your Exchange Server, all you need to do is click the Send button in your e-mail message and it's on its way. If you're sending mail to Internet recipients, messages are stored in your Outbox until you click the Send/Receive button on the Standard toolbar. Outlook then sends the mail in your Outbox and checks to see if anything new has arrived. If you want to send e-mail without checking your Outbox for new messages, choose Tools ➤ Send on the menu bar. Outlook will also dial up your Internet connection, send and receive messages, and disconnect from the Internet at an interval you set in the Mail Delivery tab of the Options dialog box. This feature can really come in handy when you're trying to reduce the cost of your Internet connection fees.

REVIEWING AND DELETING E-MAIL MESSAGES

The best thing about sending mail is that you'll receive mail in return. And to top it off, you won't have to trot out to your mailbox in the rain or snow to see what's been delivered. Instead, Outlook puts messages directly into your Inbox. You can preview messages, open and read them, respond to messages, forward them to others, and read or open attachments. The e-mail you receive can come from the neighbor next door, a colleague across town, or your parents who live 3,000 miles away. Although a message can only come from one person, it can contain many things, such as text, a picture, an attachment, a Web link, an e-mail response link, or voting buttons.

There are three primary ways to view messages or parts of messages in your Inbox.

► You can read a message in its own window by double-clicking the message line in the Inbox Message list.

► You can also read an e-mail message in the Preview pane, which allows you to view entire messages in a separate pane within the Information viewer.

► Or you can read the first three lines of a message directly in the Inbox Message list using AutoPreview. This is the default setting when you install Outlook.

Both the Preview pane and AutoPreview views provide a quick way to review e-mail messages without opening the messages, which saves you time. If you don't see the AutoPreview text, choose View ➤ AutoPreview on the menu bar.

The Information viewer contains icons to the left of the To column that provide additional information about an e-mail message. The icons tell you the importance of a message, its type, whether the message has been flagged, and if it has an attachment. In addition, the Information viewer also lets you know who sent the message, the subject of the message if the sender included one, the date you received the message, and its size. The most recent messages appear at the top of the list and unread messages display in bold text.

Previewing E-mail Messages

Outlook lets you preview messages so you can quickly scan through all your e-mail without having to open each one in a separate window. The Preview pane now includes full support for attachments, hyperlinks, HTML, and signed and encrypted mail, so you can easily access and work with all contents of a message without opening it. To easily read text messages using the Preview pane, follow these steps:

1. On the Inbox menu bar, choose View ➤ Preview Pane to display the Preview pane (see Figure 2.12).

2. Click a message in the Inbox Message list or any folder in the Information viewer.

3. If necessary, scroll through the Preview pane to read the entire message.

Part i

Viewing E-mail Attachments

How do you know if a message has an attachment? It's easy. Mail attachments appear as a paper clip icon in the Information viewer and display to the left of the From column, which shows the name of the sender. To view an e-mail attachment, follow these steps:

1. Double-click an e-mail message that has a paper clip icon in the Inbox Message list or in any folder in the Information viewer.

2. Double-click the paper clip. The attachment will open in the application in which it was created.

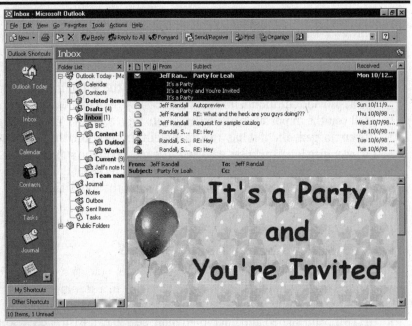

FIGURE 2.12: The Preview pane lets you quickly view all the messages in the Information viewer.

If you would rather open the attachment later, you can choose File ➤ Save Attachments from the menu bar of the message. In the Save Attachment dialog box, select the folder in which you want to store a copy of the file, and then click Save. The file remains attached to the e-mail message and can be opened later. It will be deleted when you delete the e-mail.

TIP

With the message open, you can also right-click the attachment and select Save As from the shortcut menu. If multiple files are attached, a Save All Attachments dialog box will display. You can simply click OK to save all the files or select individual files, and then click OK.

Printing E-mail Messages

You're planning to meet a friend for lunch at a great new restaurant she told you about when you exchanged e-mail. She sent you directions to the restaurant in the e-mail but you can't take your computer along for the ride. Rather than writing down the directions by hand, simply print the e-mail by selecting the message from the Information viewer and choosing File ➤ Print from the menu bar. Then in the Print dialog box, click OK. Alternately, locate the message, double-click it, and then click the Print button on the Standard toolbar. This process is best for when you want to first preview the message.

TIP

You can also print a message by selecting the message in the Information viewer and clicking the Print button on the Standard toolbar.

Deleting E-mail

So you've opened and read a message—now what do you do with it? Well, one option is to delete it. You can delete a message at any time. If the message is open, you can click the Delete button on the Standard toolbar. If the message is closed, select it in the Information viewer, and then click the Delete button on the Standard toolbar. Don't worry if you delete a message by mistake—you can retrieve it from the Deleted Items folder. To retrieve a message, double-click the Deleted Items shortcut on the Outlook bar. You can view the message or move it to another folder.

If the Deleted Items folder begins to look like an overstuffed wastebasket, you can empty it by clicking Empty "Deleted Items" Folder on the Tools menu. If manually dumping the trash seems like a chore, you can automatically delete e-mail from this folder by following these steps:

1. Choose Tools ➤ Options from the menu bar. The Options dialog box appears.

2. Click the Other tab.

3. Click the Empty The Deleted Items Folder Upon Exiting check box, and then click the Advanced Options button. The Advanced Options dialog box appears.

4. In the General Settings area, be sure that the Warn Before Permanently Deleting Items option is selected, and then click OK twice.

SETTING E-MAIL OPTIONS

Outlook knows that sending and receiving e-mail is just the first step to better communication. The second step is to define how e-mail is handled. You can have Outlook notify you when new mail arrives. When you're forwarding or replying to e-mail, Outlook can automatically enter your name in the Message area when you type comments in the original message text. There are three categories of options: Message Handling, Replies and Forwards, and Advanced. You can access E-mail Options by choosing Tools ➤ Options from the menu bar. Then on the Preferences tab, click the E-mail Options button. In the E-mail Options dialog box, select the options you want.

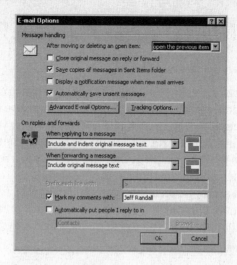

Table 2.1 summarizes the options:

TABLE 2.1: E-mail Options

OPTION GROUP	OPTIONS
Message Handling	Close a message after you reply to it or forward a copy of it
	Save a copy of a message in the Sent Items folder
	Display a notification when new mail arrives
	Automatically save unsent messages
	Specify the text format and annotations used for messages you reply to and forward
	Mark your comments with your name
Advanced	Set options for how and for when to save messages
	Set feedback options for when new mail arrives
	Set importance and sensitivity of new mail
	Set how addresses will be entered and checked
	Set what to do with meeting requests after responding
Tracking	Specify whether you'll be notified when your messages are delivered or opened
	Specify whether receipts and blank responses are to be automatically deleted after they have been processed

REPLYING TO AND FORWARDING E-MAIL MESSAGES

Replying to a message is even easier than sending one. You can direct your response to the person who sent the message or you can reply to the sender and the people listed in the Cc box. When you reply to a message, the title bar displays RE: and includes the text contained in the Subject box. This tells the recipient that the message is a reply to a previous message. When you type a reply in the Message area, the original message is indented and appended to your reply. If you modify the original message, you can have Outlook put your name in square brackets at the beginning of your changes to let the recipient keep track of your comments.

The next time a message provokes you to respond, follow these steps:

1. In the Inbox Message list (or folder containing the e-mail message), double-click the message you want to respond to. (You can also just select the message line in the Message list.)

2. To reply to the person who sent the message, click the Reply button on the Standard toolbar. To reply to the sender and others who received the original message, click the Reply To All button on the Standard toolbar (see Figure 2.13).

3. Type your response anywhere in the Message area.

4. Click the Send button on the Standard toolbar.

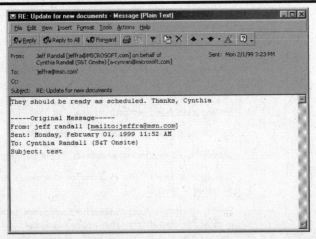

FIGURE 2.13:   Replying to a message is even easier than creating one.

A message that has been replied to appears different from a new or opened message in your Inbox; it displays an icon that's an opened envelope with a stamp on it and a sheet of paper attached to it.

Forwarding E-mail

Someone shares a great piece of news with you or sends you something really important or funny via e-mail. The first thing that pops into your head is how much someone else either would enjoy reading the message or needs to see it. Even though this person wasn't one of the original recipients, you can still share the message by forwarding the e-mail. Not only can you forward the e-mail message, but you can also forward any attachments.

To forward an e-mail message, follow these steps:

1. In the Inbox Message list (or folder containing the e-mail message), double-click the message you want to forward. (You can also just select the message line in the Message list.)

2. Click the Forward button on the Standard toolbar.

3. In the To box, type the names of those whom you want to receive the message.

4. If you want to add your own remarks to the message, type them anywhere in the Message area.

5. Click the Send button on the Standard toolbar.

NOTE

If you modify the original message, Outlook puts your name in square brackets at the beginning of your changes.

Once you've forwarded a message, the icon associated with original message changes to an envelope with an arrow, indicating that the message has been forwarded.

Part i

MINDING YOUR "P'S" AND "Q'S" AND OTHER E-MAIL ETIQUETTE

Here's some e-mail etiquette to help you remember that, even though your message is electronic, the recipient is a human being.

Do:

▶ Review your message before sending it. Attention to grammar and spelling will make you and your message more effective.

▶ Make the subject line meaningful. It should reflect your message's subject.

▶ Be polite.

▶ Use emoticons like :) or :(to convey your feelings. Non-verbal signals including facial expressions, eye contact, body language, and tone of voice don't come across in e-mail.

▶ Treat the security of your e-mail message the same as a message on a postcard. Anyone may see what you've written.

Don't:

▶ Type in all capital letters. This is SHOUTING and is considered RUDE.

▶ Reply to all recipients unless they all need to see your reply.

▶ Send e-mail when you're angry.

WHAT'S NEXT?

This chapter detailed the flexibility and versatility of using e-mail communication. It explained how to create and organize messages and how to customize your own e-mail using available options. In the next chapter, you will hone your e-mail skills as you learn to further manage and organize your e-mail.

Chapter 3
MANAGING AND ORGANIZING YOUR E-MAIL

SORTING AND FILTERING YOUR INBOX FOR FAST REVIEW

All the e-mail you receive stays in your Inbox until you decide to move or delete it. If you work in a busy office that relies on e-mail for communication, you probably receive lots of e-mail every day: memos from your manager, requests for meetings, invitations to events, and funny jokes. Even if you receive only five e-mails a day, in a week you will have 20 to 30 messages nestled in your Inbox. And what about the junk mail you don't want? If you're the "pack rat" type, then your Inbox could quickly begin to resemble an over-stuffed mailbox. Even if you aren't the type who saves every little message, you may send and receive lots of e-mail—and that alone can make managing an Inbox an overwhelming task.

Adapted from *Microsoft® Outlook™ 2000: No Experience Required™* by Cynthia Randall

ISBN 0-7821-2483-6   452 pages $19.99

Fortunately, Outlook 2000 has several powerful strategies that can help you tame the electronic beast and deal with the mail you do and do not want. By organizing your Inbox, you will be able to quickly find what you need, when you need it. Whether you choose to sort the Message list in the Information viewer, add a filter to screen only e-mail that meets a certain criteria, or organize your mail by adding fields to the Information viewer, Outlook makes it easy to group similar messages. You can create and use folders—such as Memos, Jokes, or Projects—to organize messages and set up rules that will automatically handle messages when they arrive without you having to do a thing. Add a splash of color to identify message attributes, such as messages that are sent only to you, and you'll be sure to spot them in your Inbox. Outlook also includes an array of features to help you manage or even delete junk e-mail, or *spam*, and adult content messages.

Sorting E-mail

You're running late for your 10:00 A.M. meeting, and, although you should already be on the road, you are frantically hunting through your e-mail to find the directions your colleague sent you last week. At this moment you've likely decided that locating e-mail that's buried in the list of messages is as impossible as finding a needle in a haystack. This thought will quickly fade from your mind when you learn how easy it is to sort mail in Outlook. Each Outlook folder can have different column buttons, also known as *fields*, so you can organize the contents of each folder in a different way. Outlook has a variety of fields that provide details of particular items, such as Mail, Tasks, and Contacts. You can add and remove fields from the different Outlook views. In views that list items in table format, such as the Inbox, fields are the columns of the table.

For instance, if you get lots of e-mail from several different people, you can set up your Inbox to display the name of the e-mail sender (From field) and the subject line (Subject field). You can set up another folder within the Inbox to display the date you received the e-mail (Received field) and the size of the file (Size field). This can be especially useful if you've created folders for a handful of people who frequently send you mail. Then, when the mail arrives in the Inbox, you can move it to the appropriate folder. Later, when you need to locate a message from the sender, you can open the folder and easily find the message based on the date the person sent it.

You can further organize your e-mail by clicking any of the column headings in a folder and applying a sort. You can sort items in either ascending or descending order. Ascending order is alphabetical, earlier time to later time, or lower number to higher number (for instance, file size); descending order is the reverse. You can quickly determine if a column is sorted in ascending order or descending order. Ascending-ordered columns have an up-pointing triangle; descending ones have a down-pointing triangle. Regardless of which folder you are in, the column headings are sorted the same way.

Outlook lets you sort by single column or multiple columns. For instance, if you select the column heading that is the exclamation mark (!) icon (located below the Folder banner), all your important messages will be listed at the top of the Message list. Or if you click the From button, the messages will be sorted in alphabetical order by first name of the person who sent you the message. To sort by more than one column, select the column headings in reverse order of how you want them sorted. For example, to sort e-mail first by date, then by sender, click the From button first and then the Received button.

In addition to sorting your e-mail using the column headings, you can sort e-mail using the Sort dialog box. This feature gives you more options for sorting than you have using the column headings. To sort e-mail using the Sort command, follow these steps:

1. Click the Inbox shortcut on the Outlook bar if the Inbox folder isn't already open.

2. On the menu bar, choose View ➤ Current View ➤ Custom Current View. The View Summary dialog box appears.

3. In the View Summary dialog box, click the Sort button. The Sort dialog box appears (see Figure 3.1).

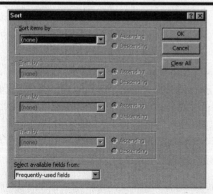

FIGURE 3.1: The Sort dialog box lets you select one or more fields to sort the contents of a folder.

4. In the Select Available Fields From drop-down list at the bottom of the dialog box, select the field set containing the fields that you want to use for sorting.

5. In the Sort Items By drop-down list, select an item from the list, such as From, Subject, or Received, and then choose either the Ascending or Descending option.

6. In the Then By drop-down lists, select a second, third, and fourth sort level, as desired, and then specify a sort order for each (Ascending or Descending).

7. Click OK twice to close the dialog boxes and see your changes.

TIP

To remove a sort, choose View ➤ Current View ➤ Custom Current View on the menu bar. In the View Summary dialog box, click the Sort button. Then, in the Sort dialog box, click the Clear All button.

NOTE

If a field that you want to sort by isn't visible, such as Sensitivity, Outlook will ask you if you want to display that field. If you click Yes, the field will display. If you click No, the field won't display, but Outlook will still sort the messages by that field. For instance, if your system administrator has put a limit on the size of your Inbox, and you receive a message that your Inbox exceeds the size limit, you could sort by Size to quickly identify messages that are very large. Then you could delete the large messages that you no longer need.

Filtering E-mail

Sometimes the easiest way to find something you need is to eliminate all the stuff you don't need. By using a filter, you can temporarily hide the items that don't matter and display only the ones that do. With fewer items in your folder, you can quickly find the message you need. When you remove a filter, the hidden items are visible again.

To set up a filter, follow these steps:

1. Click the Inbox shortcut on the Outlook bar if the Inbox folder isn't already open.

2. Open the folder you want to filter.

3. On the menu bar, choose View ➤ Current View ➤ Customize Current View. The View Summary dialog box appears.

4. In the View Summary dialog box, click the Filter button. The Filter dialog box appears (see Figure 3.2).

5. In the Search For The Word(s) drop-down box, type the words you want to locate. To look for two or more words or phrases, enclose the words in quotation marks.

6. In the In drop-down box, select a field to search. For the broadest search, select Frequently-Used Text Fields.

7. To find all the messages sent by one person, type the person's name in the From box. To find all the messages sent to you by more than one person, separate the names with commas. Click the From button to display a list of e-mail names to choose from.

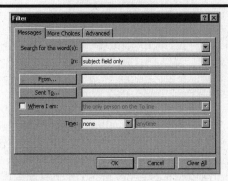

FIGURE 3.2: The Filter dialog box lets you display messages based on criteria you specify.

8. To find all the messages you have sent to a recipient, type the name of the person in the Sent To box. To find all the messages you have sent to more than one person, separate the names with commas. Click the Sent To button to display a list of e-mail names to choose from.

9. To find messages where your name is listed on a particular line, such as the To or Cc line, select the Where I Am check box, and then select an option from the drop-down box.

10. To locate a message based on a time criterion, select an option from the Time drop-down box, and then specify a time criterion in the drop-down box.

The Filter dialog box, shown above, includes three tabs: Messages, More Choices, and Advanced. The Messages tab lets you specify options to temporarily hide items that you are not interested in seeing. This limited view makes it easier to read relevant e-mail because it removes all the irrelevant messages until you decide to show them. For example, you could use the Messages tab to just display all Inbox messages sent by Joshua Randall concerning a customer issue.

The More Choices tab of the Filter dialog box gives you additional filtering options.

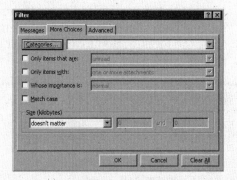

Categories   When you use categories as filter criteria, Outlook displays folder items that have been assigned to the categories you list. To filter by category, type the category name, or click the Categories button to select a category name in the Categories dialog box. If you use more than one category, separate each with a comma. This option is ideal when you are trying to locate all the messages that contain a particular type of category, such as business or personal.

Only Items That Are   To filter using this option, select the check box, and then select either Read (for e-mail that you have already read) or Unread (for e-mail that you haven't yet read) from the drop-down box. This option makes it a breeze to locate all your unread messages so you can quickly see if there are any important issues you need to attend to.

Only Items With   To filter using this option, select the check box, and then select One Or More Attachments (to filter for e-mails that contain attachments) or No Attachments (to filter for e-mails that have no attachments). This option is great if you need to locate a particular file that someone sent to you via e-mail.

Whose Importance Is   To filter using this option, which locates e-mails that have a specified level of importance, select the check box, and then select High, Normal, or Low from the drop-down box. Often, people mark joke messages as low priority. So the next time you need a quick pick-me-up, turn on this filter.

Match Case   You can turn on the Match Case option to display only those items whose uppercase and lowercase characters exactly match the uppercase and lowercase characters you type in the Search For The Word(s) box on the Messages tab. When you search for words, you can have Outlook check only the Subject box, the Subject box and Message area, or Frequently-Used Text fields. This option is especially useful when you are searching for an acronym, such as TEAM, and don't want every subject line that has the word 'team' to end up in your results.

Size   To filter for messages that match a certain size in kilobytes, select an option from the Size drop-down box. Options include Doesn't Matter, Equals (Approximately), Between, Less Than, or Greater Than. If you select any option other than Doesn't Matter, you'll need to specify size criteria in the Size boxes.

The Advanced tab of the Filter dialog box lets you make further refinements to the filter (see Figure 3.3). For instance, you may want to filter your messages to locate all e-mail that was received on or before a particular date. Although the Messages tab allows you to filter for received e-mail, it doesn't allow you to specify a value, such as on or before, which enables you to pinpoint an exact message or group of messages. On the Advanced tab, you can click the Field button to select a list of available fields, such as Frequently-Used Fields, and then select a specific field, such as Subject. The field name will display in the box below the Field button. Then, you'll need to specify a condition, such as Contains or Is (Exactly), and a value, such as Team Meeting, for the field.

To use options from the Advanced tab to control how Outlook filters items, follow these steps:

1. Click the Inbox shortcut on the Outlook bar if the Inbox folder isn't already open.

2. On the menu bar, choose View ➤ Current View ➤ Customize Current View. The View Summary dialog box appears.

3. Click the Filter button. The Filter dialog box appears.

4. Click the Advanced tab.

5. Click the Field button, point to an option in the list, and then select an item from the submenu.

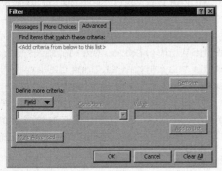

FIGURE 3.3:   The Advanced tab of the Filter dialog box helps you set up advanced filter criteria.

6. Select an option from the Condition drop-down list. If you select Is Empty or Is Not Empty, the Value box is not available.

7. Type a value in the Value box, and then click the Add To List button. The condition you create is displayed in the Find Items That Match These Criteria box. You can add additional filter criteria to further refine what you want Outlook to display.

8. Click OK twice to close the dialog boxes and see the results.

If you decide you no longer need a filter and you want to turn it off, follow these steps:

1. Click the Inbox shortcut on the Outlook bar if the Inbox folder isn't already open.

2. On the menu bar, choose View ➤ Current View ➤ Customize Current View. The View Summary dialog box appears.

3. Click the Filter button. The Filter dialog box appears.

4. Click the Clear All button.

5. Click OK twice to close all dialog boxes.

Adding Fields to the Information Viewer

The column headings in Outlook's Folder list are set by default and display fields that are frequently used. However, you can add or remove columns, and you can rearrange the order of the columns to make it easier to organize and manage your e-mail messages. To add columns to a Folder list, follow these steps:

1. Click the Inbox shortcut on the Outlook bar if the Inbox folder isn't already open.

2. Open the folder in which you want to add a column.

3. On the menu bar, choose View ➤ Current View ➤ Customize Current View. The View Summary dialog box appears.

4. Click the Fields button. The Show Fields dialog box appears, as shown in Figure 3.4.

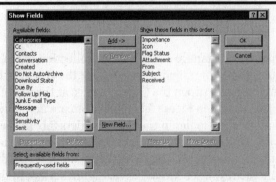

FIGURE 3.4: The Show Fields dialog box lets you add columns to the Information viewer.

5. In the Select Available Fields From drop-down list at the bottom of the dialog box, select the field set containing the fields that you want to add as a column button.

6. In the Available Fields list, click a field name, such as Categories, and then click the Add button.

7. To change the order of the field names, select the field name in the Show These Fields In This Order list, and then click the Move Up button or the Move Down button depending on where you want to position the field (column button) name.

8. Click OK twice to close the dialog boxes and to see your changes.

NOTE

To remove a field in the Show Fields dialog box, click the field name in the Show These Fields In This Order list, and then click the Remove button. If you can't remember how to get to the Show Fields dialog box, follow steps 1 through 4 in the procedure just described.

TIP

You can also change the order of the columns by dragging a column button to the left or right.

USING THE ORGANIZE PAGE TO MANAGE E-MAIL

 You can easily organize and manage e-mail using a collection of tools that Outlook keeps in one place—the Organize page. Click the Organize button on the Standard toolbar to open the Organize page at the top of the Information viewer, as shown in Figure 3.5. You can create new folders or move messages to an existing folder in the Using Folders tab. In the Using Colors tab, you can color-code e-mail messages, which will make them easy to identify in your Inbox. The Using Views tab lets you change Inbox views—one moment you see Message With AutoPreview, in the next you see By Sender—all with a single click. The Junk E-mail tool applies filters to weed out junk and adult content messages. You can also open the Rules Wizard and create a rule to automatically manage the messages you receive.

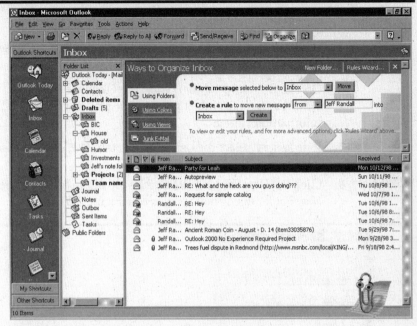

FIGURE 3.5: The Organize page offers several handy ways to manage your e-mail messages.

Creating a New Folder

Creating a new folder is a very simple task and one that you'll likely do often if you want to keep your Inbox manageable. Before you begin to add folders to your Inbox, you should consider what type of messages you will be receiving or who will be sending messages to you. For instance, if you exchange e-mail with your financial accountant, then you may want to create a folder called Investments. Or if you have a friend who sends you funny e-mail, you might want to store them in a folder called Humor.

Once you have a folder set up, you can create a *rule*, which is a procedure Outlook automatically carries out when an item arrives in your Inbox. For example, when a message arrives from your friend, Outlook can route it directly into the Humor folder. So, when you're having a bad day and need a quick pick-me-up, you can open the folder and find a message that will tickle your funny bone.

To create a new folder in Outlook using the Organize page, follow these steps:

1. Click the Inbox shortcut on the Outlook bar if the Inbox folder isn't already open.

2. On the Standard toolbar, click the Organize button. The Ways To Organize Inbox page will display at the top of the Information viewer.

3. If necessary, select the Using Folders tab. The Using Folders tab appears.

4. Click the New Folder button at the top of the box. The Create New Folder dialog box appears (see Figure 3.6).

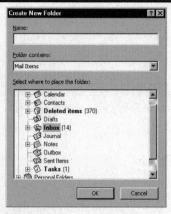

FIGURE 3.6:   You can create a new folder for messages in the Inbox or Personal folders.

5. In the Name box, type a name for the new folder.

6. Be sure the Folder Contains drop-down list shows Mail Items.

7. In the Select Where To Place The Folder list, select an existing folder in which you want to keep your new folder.

8. Click OK. The Add Shortcut To Outlook Bar dialog box appears.

9. To add a shortcut to the folder in My Shortcuts on the Outlook bar, click Yes.

TIP

You can also open the Create New Folder dialog box by choosing File ➤ Folder ➤ New Folder on the menu bar.

Organizing Your Messages in Folders

To move a message from the Inbox to your new folder, select the message(s) you want to move in the Information viewer. You can move more than one message by pressing Ctrl and then clicking each message. Messages don't have to be in any particular order when you select them. Once you've selected the message(s) you want to move, follow these steps:

1. In the Ways To Organize Inbox page, click Using Folders. The Using Folders tab appears.

2. In the Move Message Selected Below To drop-down list, select the name of the folder to which you want to move the message(s) (see Figure 3.7).

3. Click the Move button.

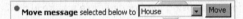

FIGURE 3.7:   You can move a message to a different folder by using the Move Message feature in the Organize page.

TIP

If the Organize page isn't visible, you can move e-mail messages from the Inbox to another folder by right-clicking the message and selecting Move To Folder from the shortcut menu. In the Move Items dialog box, select a folder, and then click OK. The message will be automatically moved to the folder you selected.

Creating Rules to Automatically Move Messages

Wouldn't it be great if every time a member of your family tossed a piece of clothing into the hamper, it would move to the hot, warm, cold, color, or whites pile in anticipation of laundry day? Well, that functionality may be far off for laundry but Outlook offers you similar functionality for incoming e-mail. Rather than having to handle each message manually, you can set up a rule to have Outlook automatically move the message to the folder of your choice.

To create a rule that automatically moves e-mail from a specific sender to a separate folder when it is received, follow these steps:

1. Click the Inbox shortcut on the Outlook bar if the Inbox folder isn't already open.

2. On the Standard toolbar, click the Organize button. The Ways To Organize Inbox page will display at the top of the Information viewer.

3. If necessary, click Using Folders. The Using Folders tab appears.

4. In the Create A Rule To Move New Messages drop-down list, be sure that From is selected in the first box, and in the second box, type the name of the sender (see Figure 3.8).

FIGURE 3.8:   Create a rule for e-mail using the Create A Rule feature in the Organize page.

5. In the Into drop-down list, select the folder where you want the mail moved to, and then click the Create button.

6. Outlook displays a message that says this rule will be applied as new messages are received. It then asks if you would like to run the rule on the current contents of the folder. If you click Yes, all existing messages from the sender will be moved to the specified folder. If you click No, all existing messages from the sender will remain in the current folder.

NOTE

To view or edit your rules, or to select more advanced options, click the Rules Wizard button at the top of the Organize page.

Part i

TIP

If the Organize page isn't visible, you can open the Rules Wizard dialog box by choosing Tools ➢ Rules Wizard on the menu bar.

Using Colors to Organize Messages

Outlook has 16 different colors you can use to color-code e-mail messages so that they are easy to find in your Inbox Information viewer. On the Organize page, you can apply a color to a message description based on who sent the message, who it was sent to, and if you are the only recipient. For instance, you may want to color-code messages from your broker or boss in red because these messages may require immediate action. You might also want to color-code all the messages you send to your mother's work e-mail so she can quickly find your message among her other work-related mail. However, your mother must also be using Outlook to see color-coded messages. And just because you receive a message doesn't mean it was sent directly to you. Often, you are receiving just a courtesy copy (Cc) of the e-mail message. To help identify messages sent directly to you from those messages in which your name appears in the Cc line, you can color-code all the messages sent only to you or all the messages in which your name appears in the To line.

To color-code e-mail messages based on the sender, follow these steps:

1. Click the Inbox shortcut on the Outlook bar if the Inbox folder isn't already open.

2. On the Standard toolbar, click the Organize button. The Ways To Organize Inbox page will display at the top of the Information viewer.

3. If necessary, click the Using Colors tab to select it. The Using Colors tab appears.

4. In the Color Messages box (see Figure 3.9), select From in the Color From drop-down list if it isn't visible, and in the second box, type the name of the sender. Or select a message from the sender in the Information viewer.

5. In the third Color Messages box, select a color from the drop-down list.

FIGURE 3.9: Color-code mail using the Color Messages feature in the
Organize page.

6. Click the Apply Color button to create the color rule.

TIP

To color-code all messages sent only to you, select a color from the Show Messages Sent Only To Me In drop-down list, and then click the Turn On button. Outlook displays a message confirming the rule.

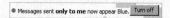

NOTE

You can also color-code all the messages you send to a particular person by selecting To in the first box of the Color Messages box and typing the recipient's name in the second box. The recipient must be using Outlook to see the color-coded message.

Setting Automatic Formatting Rules

You may have already noticed that various color rules are already applied by default in the mail folders. For example, unread messages appear as bold text, flagged messages that have passed the reminder date and time are red. You can change these rules and create new ones using the Automatic Formatting dialog box. By setting automatic formatting rules, you change the format used for messages that meet conditions set by you.

To change the default fonts for conditional message formatting, follow these steps:

1. Click the Inbox shortcut on the Outlook bar if the Inbox folder isn't already open.

2. On the Standard toolbar, click the Organize button. The Ways To Organize Inbox page will display at the top of the Information viewer.

3. If necessary, click Using Colors to select it. The Using Colors tab appears.

4. Click the Automatic Formatting button at the top of the Organize page. The Automatic Formatting dialog box appears, as shown in Figure 3.10.

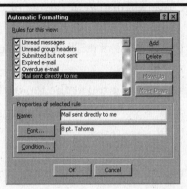

FIGURE 3.10:   The Automatic Formatting dialog box includes the default formats and any color rules you have created.

5. In the Rules For This View list, click the check box next to the item for which you want to change the default font setting.

6. Click the Font button in the Properties Of Selected Rule area. The Font dialog box appears.

7. In the Font dialog box, select a new font, font style, size, effects, or color.

8. Click OK twice to close all dialog boxes and to see your changes.

TIP

To turn off automatic formatting for an item in the list, click the check box next to the item to clear the check box, and then click OK. The formatting will revert to its default settings.

You can change the order in which your rules are applied by selecting the rule and then clicking the Move Up or Move Down buttons in the Automatic Formatting dialog box. If you don't see the rule you need, you can create a new rule in the Automatic Formatting dialog box or in the Organize page, depending on the rule.

To use the Automatic Formatting dialog box to add a new rule, follow these steps:

1. Click the Inbox shortcut on the Outlook bar if the Inbox folder isn't already open.

2. On the Standard toolbar, click the Organize button. The Ways To Organize Inbox page will display at the top of the Information viewer.

3. If necessary, click Using Colors to select it. The Using Colors tab appears.

4. Click the Automatic Formatting button at the top of the Organize page. The Automatic Formatting dialog box appears.

5. Click the Add button.

6. In the Name box of the Properties Of Selected Rule area, type a name for the rule.

7. Click the Font button. The Font dialog box appears.

8. Select a new font, font style, size, effect, or color.

9. Click OK twice to close all dialog boxes and to see your changes.

NOTE

To specify filter conditions for a new or existing rule you have created, click the Condition button in the Automatic Formatting dialog box. In the Filter dialog box, set the filter conditions, and then click OK to create the condition. For information on filtering, see the "Filtering E-mail" section earlier in this chapter.

Organizing Your E-mail by Topic

As the number of messages grows in Outlook, you'll want to be able to view related items. The Using Views tab of the Organize page lets you quickly change the view of messages. You can choose from 10 different views, including By Sender, Conversation Topic, and Message Timeline. When you select a new view, the messages in the Information viewer are reorganized to reflect your choice. Depending on the view you choose, some messages may be hidden or combined with similar messages. For instance, if you view messages By Sender, the name of each sender will appear on a separate line with a plus (+) sign next to the name. In addition, Outlook tells you how many messages the sender sent and the number of unread messages.

To choose a new view for your messages, follow these steps:

1. Click the Inbox shortcut on the Outlook bar if the Inbox folder isn't already open.

2. On the Standard toolbar, click the Organize button. The Ways To Organize Inbox page will display at the top of the Information viewer.

3. If necessary, click Using Views to select it. The Using Views tab appears (see Figure 3.11).

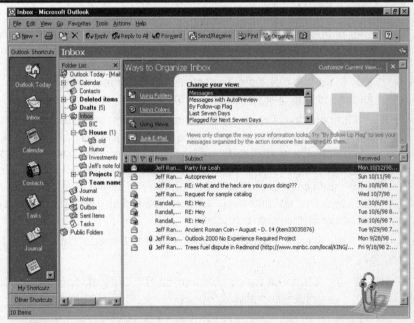

FIGURE 3.11: Using Views makes it easy to organize messages by sender, subject matter, and more.

4. In the Change Your View list, select a view. The messages in the Information viewer will display according to the view you select.

NOTE

If you select the By Sender view, your messages will be grouped by sender. To see individual message(s) sent by a particular person, click the plus sign to the left of the sender's name.

Identifying Junk and Adult Content Messages

You walk to your mailbox outside, open it, and see lots of mail. Instead of finding letters from friends and family, you discover an array of junk mail: advertisements, sales information, and direct mailings. Wouldn't it be nice if the mail carrier separated out this type of mail for you so that you could toss it into the garbage or recycle it without even having to open it? Better still, what if the mail carrier automatically removed the junk from your mail? You may not get that kind of service from the post office, but you can with Outlook. You can use the Junk E-mail tool in the Organize page to color-code junk e-mail. By color-coding these messages, you'll be able to quickly pick them out among the other messages in your Inbox folder and skip over them.

Outlook identifies junk e-mail and adult content messages based on a list of keywords likely to be in these types of messages. Outlook also lets you build a list of junk mail and adult content senders based on the e-mail addresses of persons or companies whose messages you identify. In addition to color-coding junk e-mail, you can assign a separate color to messages that contain adult content. You can also set up a rule to automatically delete these messages.

To display junk e-mail or adult content in a special color, follow these steps:

1. Click the Inbox shortcut on the Outlook bar if the Inbox folder isn't already open.

2. On the Standard toolbar, click the Organize button. The Ways To Organize Inbox page will display at the top of the Information viewer.

3. If necessary, click Junk E-mail to select it. The Junk E-mail tab appears.

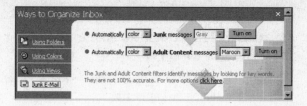

4. In the Automatically drop-down boxes, select Color for each type of e-mail (junk and adult content) that you want to color-code.

5. In the Junk Messages drop-down box and the Adult Content Messages drop-down box, select a color for each.

6. Click the Turn On buttons to activate each rule (junk messages and adult content messages).

NOTE

To delete names on the Junk E-mail or Adult Content list, select Click Here in the Junk E-mail box of the Organize page. Click the Edit Junk Senders button or the Edit Adult Content Senders button. Select a name from the list, click the Delete button, and then click OK.

TIP

To place a sender's address on the Junk E-mail list or the Adult Content list, right-click a message from the sender in the Information viewer. Choose Junk E-mail ➢ Add To Junk Senders List or choose Junk E-mail ➢ Add To Adult Content Senders List on the shortcut menu.

Deleting Junk Mail Automatically

Rather than using a special color to set junk e-mail apart from other e-mail, you can set up a rule to automatically delete these messages. You can create a rule based on a specific sender or subject matter using the Rules Wizard, which guides you step-by-step through the process of creating a rule. You can create standard or custom rules easily and add features to have a rule work the way you need it to. You can apply a rule to existing and future messages. By setting up a rule, you can control what happens to a message after it arrives in your Inbox.

To automatically delete junk mail, follow these steps:

1. Click the Inbox shortcut on the Outlook bar if the Inbox folder isn't already open.

2. On the menu bar, choose Tools ➤ Rules Wizard. The Rules Wizard dialog box appears.

3. Click the New button to create a new rule.

4. In the Which Type Of Rule Do You Want To Create set list, be sure Check Messages When They Arrive is selected (if it's not selected, click it to select it), and then click the Next button (see Figure 3.12).

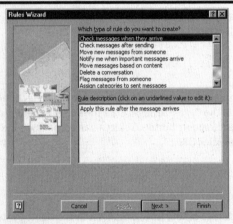

FIGURE 3.12: Use the Rules Wizard to automate message handling.

5. In the Which Condition(s) Do You Want To Check? list, select Suspected To Be Junk E-mail Or From Junk Senders check box, and then click the Next button. To have adult content messages automatically deleted, click the Containing Adult Content Or From Adult Content Senders check box before you click the Next button. The selected conditions will display in the Rules Description box at the bottom of the dialog box.

6. In the What Do You Want To Do With The Message set list, select the Delete It check box to move the message to the Deleted Items folder. Click the Permanently Delete It check box to instantly and permanently delete the message from Outlook. Then click the Next button.

7. In the Add Any Exceptions (If Necessary) list, select exceptions to the rule as desired, and then click the Next button.

NEW

8. In the Please Specify A Name For This Rule box, type a name for the rule. To activate the rule on existing mail in your Inbox, click the Run This Rule Now On Messages Already In (Inbox) check box.

9. Click the Finish button.

TIP

You can also set up a rule in the Junk E-mail box of the Organize page to automatically move junk mail to the Deleted Items folder or another folder you specify. In the Junk E-mail box, select Move from the first drop-down list, select Deleted Items from the second drop-down list, and then click the Turn On button.

USING THE OUT OF OFFICE ASSISTANT

Outlook has several tools to help you better manage your e-mail on a daily basis. But when you're not available to check your e-mail because you're taking a week-long vacation or you finally got approved for that extended sabbatical, who's going to keep up on all the e-mail messages you receive? Outlook's Out of Office Assistant, which is optimized for a corporate or workgroup environment, can automatically notify senders that you're not available for a while, which will reduce the number of e-mail messages they send and keep them happy knowing you're not simply ignoring their urgent requests. In addition to updating others on your status, the Out of Office Assistant can automatically perform specific actions on incoming items to keep you from drowning in a sea of e-mail messages when you return. The Out of Office Assistant is similar to the Rules Wizard in that you create a set of rules for performing actions on messages.

Setting Up the Out of Office Assistant

If your system is optimized for a workgroup environment, you can take advantage of the Out of Office Assistant. After you turn on the Out of Office Assistant, it will automatically send an out-of-office message to any corporate or workgroup member who sends you an e-mail message. You can create a personalized message to send to each person who sends you mail; however, this message will be sent only once to each person regardless of the number of e-mails the individual sends.

To set up the Out of Office Assistant to handle your e-mail while you're gone, follow these steps:

1. Click the Inbox shortcut on the Outlook bar if the Inbox folder isn't already open.

2. On the menu bar, choose Tools ➢ Out of Office Assistant. The Out Of Office Assistant dialog box appears (see Figure 3.13).

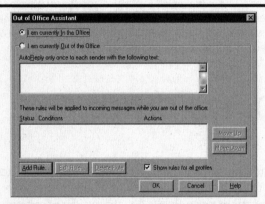

FIGURE 3.13: You can set up the Out Of Office Assistant in advance and then turn it on and off as needed.

3. Select the I Am Currently Out Of The Office option.

4. Click the AutoReply Only Once To Each Sender With The Following Text box, and type the message you'd like people to receive.

5. Click OK.

TIP

When you return, don't forget to open the Out of Office Assistant and select the I Am Currently In The Office option. Your out-of-office message will no longer be sent; however, the message will remain in the AutoReply Only Once To Each Sender With The Following Text box for future use.

Creating Rules for the Out of Office Assistant

You can easily set up rules to automatically process messages sent by workgroup members when you won't be checking your e-mail messages. For example, you can set up a rule to move messages to a specific folder or have the message forwarded to another person.

To set up a rule, follow these steps:

1. Click the Inbox shortcut on the Outlook bar if the Inbox folder isn't already open.

2. On the menu bar, choose Tools ➢ Out of Office Assistant. The Out Of Office Assistant dialog box appears.

3. In the Out of Office Assistant dialog box, click the Add Rule button. The Edit Rule dialog box appears (see Figure 3.14).

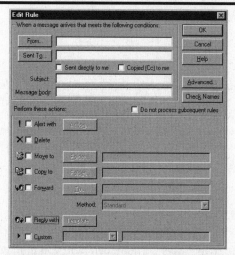

FIGURE 3.14: By adding a rule, you can have the Out of Office Assistant act on incoming items during your absence.

4. In the When A Message Arrives That Meets The Following Conditions area, type a name in the From box or click the From button to select a name from the Choose Sender dialog box to specify a condition for incoming mail. You can also type a name in the Sent To box or click the Sent To button to

select a name from the Choose Recipient dialog box to specify a condition for outgoing mail. To set up a condition for
mail sent directly to you, select the Sent Directly To Me check
box. To set up a condition for mail in which you are on the Cc
line, select the Copied (Cc) To Me check box. To set up conditions for content in the subject line or message body, type
text in the Subject box or Message Body box.

5. In the Perform These Actions area, select the appropriate
   check box option based on the condition specified in the
   When A Message Arrives That Meets The Following Conditions area.

6. Click OK twice to close all dialog boxes.

TIP

To check names listed in the From and Sent To boxes, click the Check Names
button in the Edit Rule dialog box.

NOTE

To further fine-tune your rule, click the Advanced button in the Edit Rule dialog
box. Even if you don't make any rules in the Edit Rule dialog box, you can still
choose settings in the Advanced dialog box. This dialog box allows you to specify rules based on the size of a message, when it was received, if it is unread, if
it has an attachment, its level of importance and sensitivity, and the displayed
properties of a message.

WHAT'S NEXT?

This chapter described the many ways Outlook can help you manage and
organize large volumes of e-mail. Among other options, you can sort, filter, automatically move, and color-code your e-mail message according to
your needs. In the next chapter, you will learn how Outlook's Calendar
helps you keep track of all of your important events, meetings, and tasks.

Chapter 4

GETTING TO KNOW YOUR CALENDAR

Keeping track of appointments, meetings, and tasks can be a job in itself, and Outlook 2000 can help. Outlook's Calendar folder, which is like the familiar paper daily planner, contains a calendar that shows all appointments, events, and tasks you or others have scheduled. You can look at your schedule in a number of ways to be sure you don't miss an important event today or overbook yourself in the future. In addition to looking at calendar information, you can go to any date in Outlook's date range and see consecutive dates or multiple nonconsecutive dates you specify. Outlook also lets you format TaskPad, which is the small task list you see in the lower-right corner of the Calendar window, to make identifying and accomplishing activities an easy task.

Adapted from *Microsoft® Outlook™ 2000: No Experience Required™* by Cynthia Randall

ISBN 0-7821-2483-6   452 pages $19.99

CHANGING CALENDAR VIEWS

Setting up a calendar so that you can easily find the information you need is the first step to making Calendar an effective tool for you. For instance, you may want to review detailed information about appointments and events that you've scheduled for the day or want to glance at next week's schedule to get a quick overview of what's coming up. If you need help scheduling items in your calendar, see Chapter 5.

To open Calendar, click the Calendar shortcut on the Outlook bar or click Calendar in the Folder list. When Calendar opens, your schedule displays in Day view by default. In addition to this view, Outlook lets you see your schedule using a five-day week, a seven-day week, or a monthly calendar. To look at your schedule using one of these views, click the appropriate button on the Standard toolbar or select a Calendar view option from the View menu.

You can also review Calendar items by Active Appointments, Events, Annual Events, Recurring Appointments, and By Category. All of these views are available by choosing View ➢ Current View from the menu bar and then selecting an option from the submenu.

In the Calendar window, the Folder banner displays the folder and the calendar date you're reviewing (see Figure 4.1). The Calendar button, which is located on the Folder banner, lets you open the Folder list. Below the Folder banner is the Display bar, which displays events scheduled for that day. If no events are scheduled, as shown in Figure 4.1, the bar appears as a solid gray area. Below this is the Appointments area in which you can see daily appointments and meetings.

The Date Navigator is displayed in the upper-right corner of the Calendar window. It shows the current calendar month and lets you quickly access the previous or following month by clicking the arrows to the right and to the left of the month heading. Using the Date Navigator, you can jump to different dates to add future appointments or to look at past events. If you click to the left of any week in the Date Navigator, that week will be highlighted and its schedule will display in the Appointments area. Or you can select a date in the Date Navigator to quickly see a listing of all your appointments and events for that date.

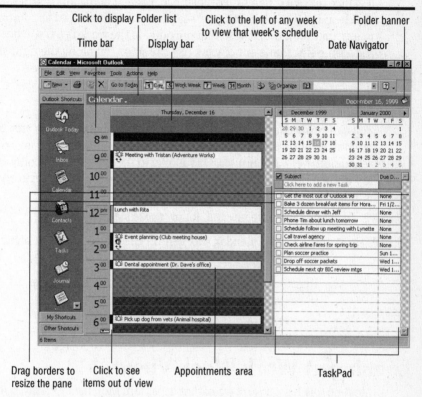

FIGURE 4.1: This calendar, in Day view, displays a 60-minute time interval.

Below the Date Navigator is the TaskPad, which you can use to keep track of tasks. Once you've completed a task, you check it off by clicking the check box, and the task is crossed out. You'll learn more about the TaskPad in the "Changing the TaskPad View" section later in this chapter.

Using Day View

Day view, which is the default view for Calendar, shows the workday (the unshaded area) starting at 8:00 A.M. and ending at 5:00 P.M. Each full-hour slot is further divided into 30-minute time slots by a line. Depending on the size of your Outlook window, the time intervals of your appointments, and the resolution of your monitor, the range of times that you can see at a glance may be different. For instance, instead of having 10 or 11 hours visible in the Time bar, you may see up to 15. You can add appointments to any time slot, even those that are outside the workday. If you need to see a time slot that's out of view, use the scroll bar along the right side of the Appointments area to scroll earlier or later times into view.

Changing Time Intervals

You can easily change the time interval for the Appointments area to better match your work. Perhaps you prefer to have shorter meetings that are scheduled every 20 minutes. Or you like to set appointments only at the top of the hour. You can change the default time interval from every 30 minutes to 5, 6, 10, 15, or 60 minutes.

To change the time interval, follow these steps:

1. Click the Calendar shortcut on the Outlook bar if Calendar isn't already open.

2. Right-click anywhere in the Time bar (see Figure 4.1 on previous page). A shortcut menu appears.

3. Click the interval you want to use.

Looking at Work Week View

Most people have a work week that goes from Monday to Friday, but what if your work week is Tuesday to Saturday? If you're using a paper-based daily planner you may be out of luck. But not so with Outlook, which makes it easy to change the work week to match the days you actually work. And for those of you who are parents—when every day of the week is a workday—Outlook has a seven-day view.

To look at your calendar one work week at a time instead of one day at a time, simply choose View ➢ Current View ➢ Day/Week/Month, and then click the Work Week button on the Standard toolbar. This view shows your schedule from Monday to Friday, which makes it easy to track all your appointments, meetings, events, and tasks for your work week.

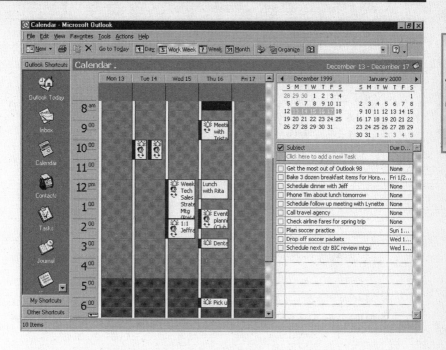

If you don't have a standard work week, you can set your calendar to reflect the days you're at work. Just follow these steps:

1. Click the Calendar shortcut on the Outlook bar if Calendar isn't already open.

2. Choose Tools ➤ Options. The Options dialog box appears.

3. Click the Calendar Options button. The Calendar Options dialog box appears, as shown in Figure 4.2.

4. In the Calendar work week area, clear the check boxes for the days you don't work by clicking the check box next to the day. Then select the check boxes for the days you do work by clicking them.

5. Click OK to close the Calendar Options dialog box.

6. Click OK to close the Options dialog box and see your changes.

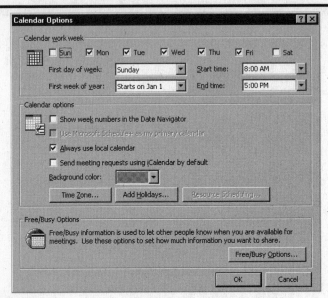

FIGURE 4.2: Use the Calendar Options dialog box to change your work week settings.

In addition to setting Calendar to display the days you work, you can also change the start and end times for your workday. Perhaps your work shift starts at midnight and goes until 9:00 A.M. Or maybe you simply like to beat the traffic and arrive at your office by 6:00 A.M. every morning. When you change the start and end times, the Time bar will change to match your work schedule. To set Calendar to reflect the time you start and end your workday, follow these steps:

1. Click the Calendar shortcut on the Outlook bar if Calendar isn't already open.

2. Choose Tools ➢ Options. The Options dialog box appears.

3. Click the Calendar Options button. The Calendar Options dialog box appears.

4. In the Start Time box, type a new time, or click the arrow and select a new time from the list.

5. In the End Time box, type a new time, or click the arrow and select a new time from the list.

Part i

6. Click OK to close the Calendar Options dialog box.

7. Click OK to close the Options dialog box and see your changes.

Reviewing Week View

Week view lets you see one full week of your calendar. The time slots are not available when all seven days are visible. Depending on how you've arranged the Calendar window and on the resolution of your display, you may be able to see the start and end times for calendar items, subject and location information, or other details, such as whether the item is recurring or private.

To display your calendar in Week view, choose View ➢ Current View ➢ Day/Week/Month, and then click the Week button on the Standard toolbar. Outlook shades any days you don't designate as workdays, such as Saturday and Sunday, but you can still add appointments to those days. This view is ideal if you often schedule appointments, meetings, or events on the weekend.

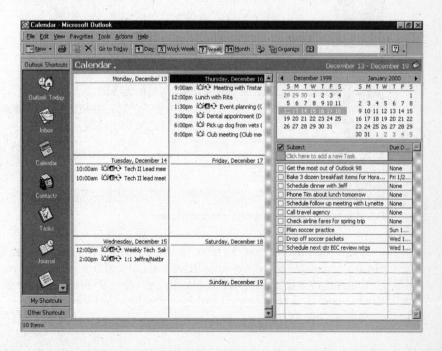

Using Month View

Most people keep a monthly wall calendar in their kitchen or office to help them keep track of the daily and weekly events they have scheduled for the month. This type of calendar is a very handy tool because it provides an at-a-glance view of all activities. Outlook brings the familiar wall calendar right to your Desktop and adds a level of versatility not possible with the paper-based version.

To view your schedule by month, choose View ➤ Month from the menu bar, or click the Month button on the Standard toolbar. The calendar displays in Month view as shown in Figure 4.3.

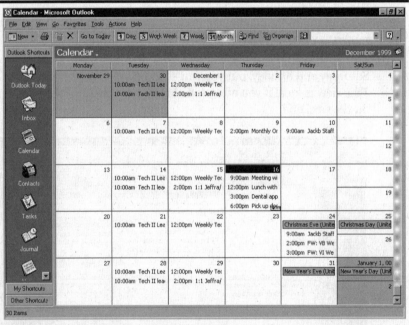

FIGURE 4.3: Calendar displayed in Month view

If you see a drop arrow for a particular date (see December 16 in Figure 4.3), it means there are more items out of view. If you click the arrow, all the items for that date will display in Day view. To return to Month view, simply click the Month button on the Standard toolbar.

TIP

When you look at your calendar by month, the Date Navigator and TaskPad are hidden by default. To display the Date Navigator and TaskPad in Month view, place the mouse pointer on the right window border. When it becomes a double vertical line with horizontal arrows, drag the border to the left toward the center of the Calendar window until both items display. The entire month is still visible, but you may not be able to read all the calendar items. To view a particular appointment, meeting, or event, position the pointer over the calendar item until the information appears in a ScreenTip.

Looking at an Individual Appointment

No matter which view you choose for your schedule, you won't be able to see every detail in the Appointments area. What you'll see is basic information about the appointment, such as its subject, location, and duration.

In addition, you'll be able to tell whether the appointment is:

▶ a group meeting or an online meeting

▶ scheduled just once or on a recurring basis

▶ private

▶ set with a reminder

To view all the details of an appointment, follow these steps:

1. Click the Calendar shortcut on the Outlook bar if Calendar isn't already open.

2. In the Appointments area, locate the appointment you want to view.

3. Double-click the appointment. Outlook displays a window that contains the appointment's details. To close this window, choose File ➢ Close from the menu bar or click the Close (x) icon in the upper-right corner of the window.

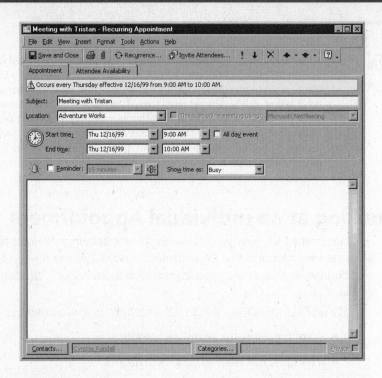

For more information about setting up appointments, see "Scheduling Appointments" in Chapter 5.

TIP

You can also view the details of an appointment by right-clicking it in the Appointments area and then selecting Open from the shortcut menu.

Looking at Recurring Appointments and Appointment Comments

You may have several appointments in your calendar that are recurring appointments. For instance, you may attend a class every Tuesday or a meeting every Friday. You can easily review recurring appointments and any comments associated with them because Outlook has built-in filters to group all your recurring appointments together.

The Recurring Appointments view displays only recurring appointments and meetings in a table format. Calendar items are grouped by recurrence status—daily, weekly, monthly, and yearly—along with any other recurrence pattern you may have specified. Unlike the Active Appointments view you'll soon learn about, this view also shows one-time appointments and meetings. There are eight column headings, which provide details about each calendar item. Headings include Icon, Attachment, Subject, Location, Recurrence Pattern, Recurrence Range Start, Recurrence Range End, and Categories. Similar to the Active Appointments view, each row is labeled and has a plus (+) sign next to it. If you click the plus sign it changes to a minus (−) sign and displays the contents of the group. To hide the detailed items within a group, click the minus sign.

To view your recurring appointments and appointment comments, follow these steps:

1. Click the Calendar shortcut on the Outlook bar if Calendar isn't already open.

2. On the menu bar, choose View ➢ Current View ➢ Recurring Appointments. The list of recurring appointments is displayed in the Information viewer, and it is divided into four categories: daily, weekly, monthly, and yearly.

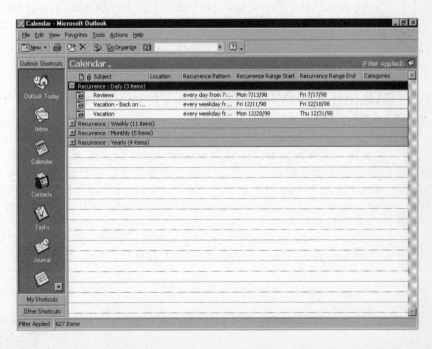

3. On the menu bar, choose View ➤ Preview Pane. The Preview pane opens at the bottom of the Information viewer so that you can view appointment comments.

4. To view a comment for a specific appointment, click the appointment.

NOTE
Click the Expand/Collapse button (the button with a plus (+) or minus (–) sign) to show or hide a list of recurring appointments.

Seeing the Calendar in Other Ways

You'll likely find that the Day, Week, and Month views are the preferred ways to look at your calendar. When you're in these views, you can also use the Date Navigator and TaskPad.

In addition to these views, Outlook offers five other ways to look at your Calendar folder. The Active Appointments view is ideal for keeping you current on upcoming activities, and the Day/Week/Month View or With AutoPreview view, will save you lots of time because you can view the details of your appointments, meetings, and events without having to open a single item. You can access these views by choosing View ➤ Current View from the menu bar. Then select one of the views described next.

Using Day/Week/Month View with AutoPreview

This view, which displays the same as the Day/Week/Month view, lets you see additional details of an appointment, a meeting, or an event. For instance, you can easily review time, subject and location information, and any comments that exist in the Message area of the Calendar item. You can see up to 256 characters of the item detail without having to open the item. To view most details of a calendar item, place your mouse pointer over the item until a ScreenTip displays the details. There is some information, such as the contents of the InfoBar, that isn't visible unless you open the item. Also, if you want to see attendee availability information, you must double-click the item, and then select the Attendee Availability tab.

Using Active Appointments View

This view lets you see all active appointments and meetings. *Active* means you'll only see current (today's) and future calendar items, not any past appointments or meetings.

The Active Appointments view displays calendar items in a table format with rows and columns. This format gives you a quick overview of all your appointments whether they are one-time or weekly activities. When you need to set up an appointment and aren't sure whether it should occur on a weekly or monthly basis, you can look at your active appointments to see the number of items already set up and then decide how to best schedule your time.

This view has four rows with headers, such as Recurrence: (none), which correspond to the type of calendar item. Rows are grouped by recurrence status: none (the item doesn't recur), daily, weekly, monthly, or yearly, or any other recurrence pattern an appointment might have. Next to each row label is a plus (+) sign. If you click the plus sign, it changes to a minus (–) sign and displays the contents of the group. To hide the detailed items within a group, click the minus sign. The column headings provide specific information about the calendar items. Column heading include Icon, Attachment, Subject, Location, Start, End, Recurrence Pattern, and Categories.

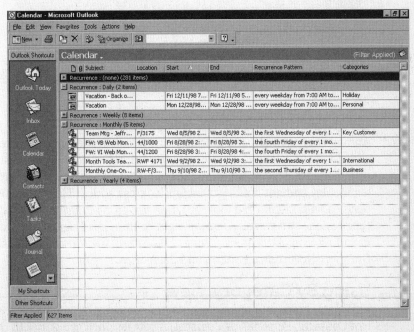

Using Events View

This view displays all the events (including annual events, such as holidays) that you add or Outlook adds to the calendar. Because you can add special events, such as birthdays, to your calendar, the Events view can be a handy tool to make sure you have plenty of time to plan for your next wedding anniversary or to purchase a gift for your nephew's upcoming graduation. Events display in a table format just like in the Active Appointments view and group by similar row and column headings. For more information about adding events to your calendar, see "Scheduling Events" in Chapter 5.

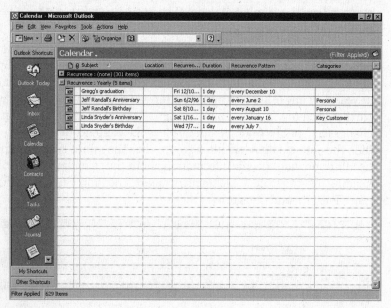

Using Annual Events View

Annual Events view is the quickest way to look at the events you've added to your calendar. This view shows only the annual events listed in your calendar. This means only the items that you've added to your calendar display and not holidays that Outlook has added. This view also displays calendar items in a table but does not group items together like in the previous two views. There are eight column headings in this view, including Icon, Attachment, Subject, Location, Recurrence Range Start, Duration, Recurrence Pattern, and Categories.

Using By Category View

This view shows your appointments and meetings by category, such as Hot Contacts, Personal, or Business, if you assigned categories to these calendar items when you created or edited them. If you assign more than one category to a calendar item, it will appear under more than one group. The By Category view has the same column headings as the Active Appointments view and the same functionality for showing and hiding items within a category.

TIP

In addition to using the View menu to display calendar items, you can use the Organize page to display appointments and meetings. When the Calendar folder is open, click the Organize button on the Standard toolbar. Click Using Views and then select a view from the Change Your View list.

Using the Organize Page to Review Your Calendar

Outlook offers you several ways to look at your calendar using the View menu. In addition, Outlook also lets you determine how the calendar is displayed using the Organize page. To use the Organize page to change the way your calendar displays, follow these steps:

1. Click the Calendar shortcut on the Outlook bar if Calendar isn't already open.

2. On the Standard toolbar, click the Organize button. The Ways to Organize Calendar page appears.

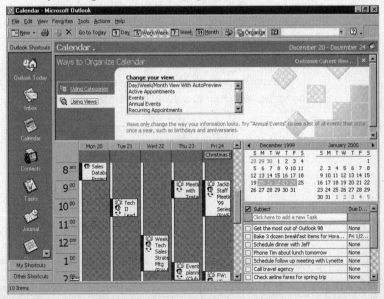

3. Click Using Views, and then select an option from the Change Your View list. Your calendar displays in the view you select.

GETTING A DATE

Although you'll spend most of your time in Outlook reviewing the appointments, meetings, and events you've scheduled for the day, if you need to schedule new appointments, you'll likely need to move around from one day to the next and from the current week to next month. You may also want move around in Calendar to plan for an upcoming meeting or to refresh your memory about an event that occurred last week. All of these desires will require you to jump ahead or jump back to other dates. Outlook makes it easy to move from one date to another with the Date Navigator or the Go To Date command.

Using the Date Navigator

Depending on what view you've selected and the resolution of your display, you may see one or more months in the Date Navigator. If you're in Day, Week, or Month view, you'll be able to see the Date Navigator. To jump to another date using the Date Navigator, use one of these methods:

▶ If the desired date is visible, click the date.

▶ If the date isn't visible, click the left or right arrow in the month heading to move to the previous or next month. Once the date is visible, click it.

▶ Click and hold the month heading to open a list containing the three months preceding it and the three months following it, as shown below. Drag to select the month you want to see.

TIP

When you open the list of months in the Date Navigator, you can drag the mouse pointer to the top or bottom border to scroll through many months of calendars.

Using the Go To Date Command

You may need to plan early for an event such as a wedding, a New Year's Eve party, or an annual business retreat. For these events, you'll probably want to use the Go To Date command, which can take you to any date within Outlook's date range. This method is ideal for when you need to track down or plan an event that occurs far in the future. Rather than scrolling through 8, 10, or 12 months' worth of calendar items, you can go directly to the date you need in just a few clicks.

To jump to any date, follow these steps:

1. Click the Calendar shortcut on the Outlook bar if Calendar isn't already open.

2. On the menu bar, choose View ➤ Go To ➤ Go To Date. The Go To Date dialog box shown in Figure 4.4 appears.

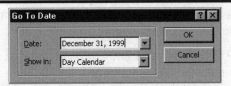

FIGURE 4.4: In the Go To Date dialog box, you can type the date you want to see in any standard date format.

3. In the Date box, type the date you want to jump to or click the arrow to display a calendar for the current month. The current month's calendar has arrows to the right and left of the heading, which allow you to scroll to previous or future months.

4. To change the view for the date to Day, Week, Work Week, or Month view, select the appropriate option from the Show In list. For instance, you may be in Week view, but you would like to see the date in Day view.

5. Click OK. The date displays in the Appointments area and shows the appointments and meetings you've scheduled for that day. The Date Navigator also changes to reflect the month of the new date.

NOTE

To open a date in a view other than your current view, select an option from the Show In list in the Go To Date dialog box.

TIP

You can also open the Go To Date dialog box by right-clicking anywhere in the Appointments area and selecting Go To Date from the shortcut menu.

There are a few rules you should follow when using the Go To Date command:

▶ Type dates using the following formats: 1/1/99, 1-1-99, Jan-1-99, or January 1-1999.

▶ If you type **69-99** for the two-digit year number for the year portion of a date, Outlook assumes that you mean 1969-1999. If you type **00-69**, Outlook assumes that you mean 2000-2069. But if you type **1/1/69**, Outlook will display January 1, 1969.

▶ Any date prior to 1970 or later than 2069 must be entered as month, date, and year—for example, **January 1, 2070**. The earliest date you can see in Calendar is April 1, 1601. The latest date you can see is August 31, 4500.

Returning to Today

`Go to Today` Whether you've ventured into the past or made a leap into the future, you may want to return to the present day. The fastest way to do this is to click the Go To Today button on the Standard toolbar. If this button isn't visible, you can jump back to today's date by choosing Go ≻ Go To Today from the menu bar. You can also right-click any empty appointment slot or any date label in the Appointments area, and then choose Go To Today from the shortcut menu.

NOTE

The Go To Today button is available in Day, Work Week, Week, and Month views. However, if you have a small display or a low-resolution display, you may have to widen the Outlook window or maximize it to see the Go To Today button. If your toolbar isn't large enough to display all the buttons available in Calendar, Outlook hides this button.

SELECTING MULTIPLE DATES

So you decide to blow out of town early this week and make it an extra long weekend. But before you finalize your plans, you need to check your schedule to see if you have any planned appointments, meetings, or events. Rather than checking each date separately, you can select a range of consecutive days in the Appointments area, or you can select a range of consecutive days or multiple nonconsecutive days in the Date Navigator.

To select a range of consecutive days using the Date Navigator, follow these steps:

1. Click the Calendar shortcut on the Outlook bar if Calendar isn't already open.

2. Display the calendar in Day, Work Week, Week, or Month view (be sure Date Navigator is visible if you choose Month view).

3. In the Date Navigator, drag over the dates you want to see. The dates in the calendar will change to reflect your selection. For instance, if you are using Work Week view and you select three consecutive days, your calendar changes to show only those three days rather than your standard five-day work week. The Date Navigator also highlights the days you select, as shown on the next page.

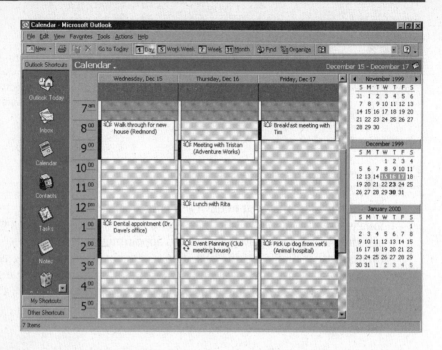

NOTE

After you've selected a range of dates, Outlook automatically retains the dates even if you scroll the calendar to a different month. For example, if you're in Week view and select the 8th, 9th, and 10th of January from the Date Navigator, those dates will display in the Appointments area. Then, if you use the Date Navigator to move to the month of February, the 8th, 9th, and 10th of February will be selected in the Date Navigator and will display in the Appointments area.

To select multiple (nonconsecutive) dates using the Date Navigator, follow these steps:

1. Click the Calendar shortcut on the Outlook bar if Calendar isn't already open.

2. Be sure the Date Navigator displays the month in which you want to select dates.

3. Click one of the dates you want to select, and then press Ctrl while you click the other dates you want to select. You can select up to 14 dates. As you click each date, it will be added to the Appointments area along with the other dates.

CHANGING THE TASKPAD VIEW

The TaskPad helps you keep track of tasks you need to do. Active tasks display with an unmarked checkbox, completed tasks are checked and have a line through them with a gray background, and overdue tasks appear in red text.

Today's Tasks is the default view for the TaskPad (see Figure 4.5). If you don't like this view, you can change it along with the formatting and arrangement of columns in TaskPad. To change the view, simply choose View ➤ TaskPad View from the menu bar, and then select your desired view.

☑ Subject	Due D...
Click here to add a new Task	
☐ ADCU/MSDN monthly online report	Fri 12/...
☐ Schedule dinner with Jeff	None
☐ Phone Tim about lunch tomorrow	None
☐ Schedule follow up meeting with Lynette	None
☐ Balance checkbook	Wed 1...
☐ Call travel agency	None
☐ Check airline fares for spring trip	None
☐ Fertilize lawn	Mon 1...
☐ Review investment information	Wed 1...
☐ Plan soccer practice	Sun 1...
☐ Drop off soccer packets	Wed 1...

FIGURE 4.5: The Today's Tasks view shows all tasks for "today."

The views available in TaskPad include:

All Tasks   This view lists every task you've set up, including completed tasks.

Today's Tasks   This is the default view for TaskPad and contains only the tasks that are active for "today." TaskPad considers "today" the current date that's indicated by your computer. Tasks include both active and overdue tasks.

Active Tasks For Selected Days   This view lets you display tasks that are active during specific days. Active tasks are those that you have not marked as completed. The active tasks that display depend on the dates you select in the Appointments area or in the Date Navigator. This is a good way to look at tasks when you know there will be several days when you'll be away from your home or office, perhaps while on vacation or in training.

Tasks For Next Seven Days   This view lets you see all the tasks you've listed for the coming week. You'll only see tasks with a due date that falls within the next seven days. To include tasks without a due date, choose View ➣ TaskPad View ➣ Include Tasks With No Due Date from the menu bar.

Overdue Tasks   This view lets you track down all the tasks you're behind on so you can work on getting them off your plate. You'll likely only want to see tasks with a due date. If you have turned on Include Tasks With No Due Date, choose View ➣ TaskPad View ➣ Include Tasks With No Due Date again from the menu bar to clear it.

Tasks Completed On Selected Days   This view gives you a quick overview of all the projects you've finished. You can display tasks that you've completed on specific dates by selecting them in the Appointments area or in the Date Navigator.

Include Tasks With No Due Date   This view lets you include or exclude tasks without a due date. By default, TaskPad includes tasks with no due date in its list of task item regardless of the view you choose. To exclude tasks without a due date, choose View ➣ TaskPad View ➣ Include Tasks With No Due Date from the menu bar. To change back to the default setting, select this same option from the menu bar.

Hiding and Restoring the TaskPad

If you don't have any tasks or simply need more space for either the Appointments area or Date Navigator, you can hide the TaskPad by following either of these steps:

▶ Drag the right border of the Appointments area to the right. This will also hide the Date Navigator.

▶ Drag the bottom border of the Date Navigator down. The current month and next two months of the Date Navigator will display.

Depending on your current Calendar view, you can restore the TaskPad by following either of these steps:

▶ If the Appointments area extends to the right Calendar window border, drag the right window border toward the center of the window.

▶ If the Date Navigator extends the length of the right Calendar window border, drag the bottom window border up toward the current month's Date Navigator.

Changing TaskPad Columns

By default, the TaskPad has three columns: Sort By Icon, Sort By Completed, Sort By TaskPad. You can change the view of TaskPad so that the items are sorted in ascending or descending alphabetical order or group by fields such as Completed. You can also remove columns, add new columns using the Customize Current View option, and format the view you use for the TaskPad. To change TaskPad settings, right-click a TaskPad column label to display a shortcut menu. Then choose an item from the shortcut menu to customize TaskPad to meet your needs (see Figure 4.6). If you go to another date or switch to another view, the TaskPad will retain your new settings.

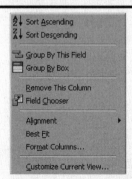

FIGURE 4.6:   The TaskPad shortcut menu lets you customize the way the TaskPad looks and the information you see.

WHAT'S NEXT?

This chapter detailed the numerous, helpful Calendar options. In the next chapter, you will learn to use these options to manage appointments, meetings, and events.

Chapter 5

PLANNING AND MANAGING APPOINTMENTS, MEETINGS, AND EVENTS

I t's Monday morning, and you're sure that you should be somewhere at 10:00 A.M. Or is it at 2:00 P.M.? Rather than trying to remember where you should be and when, use Outlook's Calendar to schedule your appointments and keep track of all the details related to each one. Unlike a meeting to which you invite one or more persons, you usually set appointments for yourself at a specified time on a given day: for example, you can make an appointment for a dental cleaning on Tuesday at noon, for your computer class on Thursday at 7:00 P.M., and for completing a budget on Friday at 3:00 P.M. You can set up a one-time appointment any time, day or night, or you can schedule affairs that regularly recur at daily, weekly, monthly, or yearly intervals.

Adapted from *Microsoft® Outlook™ 2000: No Experience Required™* by Cynthia Randall

ISBN 0-7821-2483-6   452 pages $19.99

When you add appointments to your calendar using Outlook, it helps you remember your commitments and can also let others know when you're unavailable. If you've given others permission to look at your schedule, they will be able to see the times that you're available, busy, tentatively tied up, or unavailable, so you won't end up double-booked. When your colleagues check your Outlook calendar and see your scheduled appointments, it's highly unlikely that they will select the same times. You'll learn more about scheduling meetings in Outlook later in this chapter.

If you've optimized Outlook for Internet-only, you can post your calendar to a Web site and provide friends, family, and colleagues with the URL so they can view your calendar. You'll learn more about how to save your calendar as a Web page later in this chapter. If you've optimized Outlook for a corporate or workgroup environment, others in your organization automatically will be able to look at your calendar.

SCHEDULING APPOINTMENTS

Calendar gives you two options for scheduling an appointment. You can choose to make the appointment in the Appointments area or use the Appointment form, which allows you to include more detailed information. Either way, you can easily edit the appointment or move it to a new time or date.

Adding Appointments Using the Appointments Area

The fastest way to set up an appointment is to use the Appointments area (see Figure 5.1). To quickly add an appointment to your calendar, follow these steps:

1. Click the Calendar shortcut on the Outlook bar if Calendar isn't already open, and be sure the Date Navigator is visible.

2. In the Date Navigator, click the date of your appointment. If the appointment date is several months ahead, choose View ➤ Go To ➤ Go To Date on the menu bar to select and jump to the date.

3. In the Appointments area, click the time slot of your appointment or drag until the time slot shows the duration of your appointment. For instance, if your appointment starts at 3:00 P.M. and ends at 5:00 P.M., you'll click the 3:00 P.M. time slot and drag through the 5:00 P.M. time slot to select it. After you're done selecting a time slot, those rows will appear highlighted in the Appointments area.

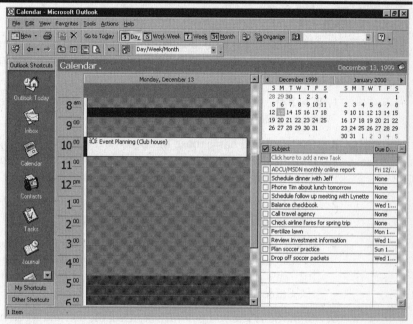

FIGURE 5.1: Add appointments quickly in the Appointments area, and Calendar won't let you forget.

4. Type a description; when you're finished, click anywhere outside the appointment time slot. The time slot is highlighted in blue on the left margin, indicating that the time period will show up as "busy" when others view your calendar. The bell icon indicates that a chime will ring, and a message box will display 15 minutes before the appointment is to take place.

TIP

Any time you add an appointment, schedule a meeting, or add an event in Calendar, you can quickly view the details of your engagement by pointing the cursor over the item.

Adding Appointments Using the Appointment Form

If you need to add details to an appointment, such as a comment or note, you should use the Appointment form. To schedule an appointment with details, follow these steps:

1. Click the Calendar shortcut on the Outlook bar if Calendar isn't already open.

2. On the menu bar, choose Actions ➢ New Appointment, or click the New Appointment button on the Standard toolbar. The Appointment form appears, as shown in Figure 5.2.

3. In the Subject box, type a description. This information will display in the Appointments area.

4. In the Location box, type the location of your appointment or select a previously entered location from the drop-down list. This information will display in parentheses right after the Subject information in the Appointments area.

5. In the Start Time drop-down box, select the text and type a new start date, or click the arrow and select a date from the calendar that appears. Then press Tab and type a new start time, or click the arrow and select a time from the drop-down list.

6. In the End Time drop-down box, select the text and type a new end date, or click the arrow and select a date from the calendar that appears. Then press Tab and type a new end time, or click the arrow and select a time from the drop-down list.

7. To have Calendar notify you prior to the start of the appointment, click the Reminder check box, and then select a time from the Reminder drop-down list.

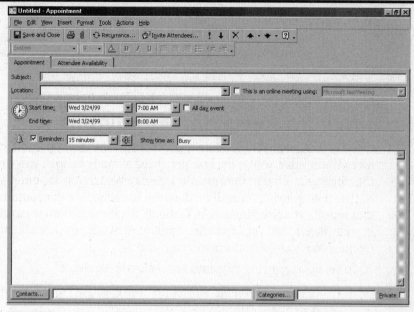

FIGURE 5.2: Use the Appointment form when you need to add detailed information about an appointment.

8. Select an option from the Show Time As drop-down list to let others who view your schedule know your availability.

9. Type any additional comments or notes in the Message area, and then click Save And Close on the Appointment form toolbar. Your appointment is now listed in your calendar. The information you typed in the Message area will only display when you open the appointment or print it. The information is simply there to help remind you about the appointment.

TIP

To make an appointment private so that others cannot see the details of your appointment, click the Private check box in the lower-right corner of the Appointment form. You may need to maximize the Appointment from to see this option. If you print your schedule, which you'll learn to do later in this chapter, any appointments you've marked as Private won't display a subject line or description.

NOTE

If you click the Attendee Availability tab on the Appointment form, Outlook converts the appointment item to a meeting. For more information on meetings, see "Scheduling Meetings" later in this chapter.

Scheduling a Recurring Appointment

If you're using a paper-based daily planner and have an appointment every Wednesday, you've likely experienced a hand cramp or two writing the same appointment information for every Wednesday in your planner. Rather than injuring yourself further, you can schedule an appointment that repeats at a fixed interval in Outlook. So, if there's still some life left in your fingers, add your recurring appointment once in Calendar and let Outlook duplicate the information for you.

To set up a recurring appointment, follow these steps:

1. Click the Calendar shortcut on the Outlook bar if Calendar isn't already open.

2. In the Date Navigator, click the date of your appointment. If the appointment date is several months ahead, choose View ➢ Go To ➢ Go To Date on the menu bar to select and jump to the date.

3. In the Appointments area, click the time slot of your appointment or drag until the time slot shows the duration of your appointment. For instance, if your appointment starts at 3:00 P.M. and ends at 5:00 P.M., you'll click the 3:00 P.M. time slot and drag through the 5 P.M. time slot to select it. After you're done selecting a time slot, those rows will appear highlighted in the Appointments area.

4. On the menu bar, choose Actions ➢ New Recurring Appointment, or right-click in the Calendar window and choose New Recurring Appointment from the shortcut menu. The Appointment Recurrence dialog box appears (see Figure 5.3). Note that the Appointment Time area automatically reflects the time slot you selected in the Appointments area.

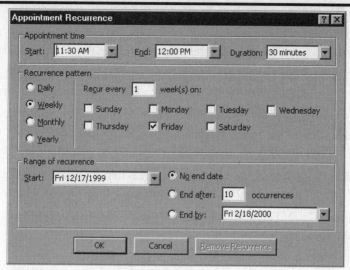

FIGURE 5.3: The Appointment Recurrence dialog box

5. For Recurrence Pattern, select the frequency of the appointment (daily, weekly, monthly, or yearly).

6. In the Recur Every box, type in the intervals for the appointment. This number tells Calendar how many time periods you want to have pass before repeating the appointment. Then select the options that tell Outlook when you want the appointment repeated.

7. In the Range Of Recurrence area, the date you specified is automatically inserted in the Start box. If you want to change the date, you can select the text and type a new date, or click the arrow and select a date from the calendar that appears. For instance, if you sign up for a class today, but it doesn't start for several weeks or even months, you can still add it to your calendar so you'll be ready to begin when it does. By default, Calendar does not specify an end date for the recurrence. To specify an end date, select the End After option, and then type a number to represent when you want the recurrence to stop, or select the End By option and type the last day of the recurrence.

8. Click OK. The Appointment Recurrence dialog box closes, and the Appointment form appears.

9. In the Subject box, type a description.

10. In the Location box, type the location of your appointment, or select a previously entered location from the drop-down list.

11. To have Calendar notify you prior to the start of the appointment, click the Reminder check box, and then select a time from the Reminder drop-down list.

12. Select an option from the Show Time As drop-down list to let others who view your schedule know your availability.

13. Type text in the Message area and then click Save And Close on the Appointment form toolbar. Your appointment is now listed in your calendar.

NOTE

You can also assign a recurring appointment or one-time appointment to a category by selecting the Categories button at the bottom of the Appointment form. You may need to maximize the Appointment form to see this option. By doing so, you can later view your appointments by category.

Moving Appointments

Making changes to appointments you've scheduled is just a part of life. No matter what the reason—whether it's because you're running late and won't be able to arrive at the destination on time or because you've found another great excuse not to keep your dental appointment—Outlook has the functionality to keep pace with your ever-changing, busy life.

There are several ways to move appointments you've scheduled in your calendar:

▶ Edit the appointment using the menu bar.

▶ Double-click the appointment, and make changes to the time and date in the Appointment form.

▶ Drag the appointment to another date in the Date Navigator.

No matter which method you choose, Outlook will move the appointment and any detailed information associated with the appointment, including reminders.

To move an existing appointment to a new date using the Outlook menu bar, follow these steps:

1. Click the Calendar shortcut on the Outlook bar if Calendar isn't already open.

2. In the Date Navigator, click the date of your appointment. If the appointment date is several months ahead, choose View ➤ Go To ➤ Go To Date on the menu bar to select and jump to the date.

3. In the Appointments area, click the appointment you want to move.

4. On the menu bar, choose Edit ➤ Cut.

5. In the Date Navigator click the new date for your appointment. If the new appointment date is several months ahead, choose View ➤ Go To ➤ Go To Date on the menu bar to select and jump to the date.

6. In the Appointments area, click (and drag) the time slot for the new appointment, and then on the menu bar, choose Edit ➤ Paste. The appointment will move to the new date.

TIP

If the date you want to move the appointment to is visible in the Date Navigator, you can select the appointment and drag it to the new date in the Date Navigator. After you've moved the appointment, Calendar will display the appointment for the new date in the Appointment list. Then, if you need to change the time slot for the appointment, select the appointment again and drag it to the new time.

You can also use this process to move recurring appointments. For instance, you may have a regularly scheduled appointment for every Tuesday at 3:00 P.M. But this coming Tuesday, you'll be out of town, and you need to change your appointment to Thursday. You can update your calendar with this change by using any of the methods described above. If you move a recurring appointment, Outlook will ask you if you want to change the date of all the occurrences, or just this one. If you only need to change this occurrence, click Yes when Outlook prompts you.

If you need to change all occurrences of a recurring appointment, follow these steps:

1. Locate the recurring appointment in the Appointments area and double-click the recurring appointment. The Appointment form opens.

2. In the Open Recurring Item dialog box, select the Open The Series option, and then click OK.

3. In the Recurring Appointment dialog box, make changes to the time and date.

4. Click OK.

Making Changes to Appointments

You may need to update the details of an appointment. For instance, you may want to add a comment to help you remember to bring paperwork to the appointment. To update the comments in an appointment, locate the appointment in the Appointments area, and double-click it. In the Appointment form dialog box, type new information in the Message area, and then click the Save And Close button on the Standard toolbar.

Deleting Appointments

Although it's often best to reschedule appointments, there are times when you simply need to cancel them. And when you do, the one thing you won't need is to be reminded of the appointment. Outlook knows that being able to remove appointments from your calendar is as important as being able to add them. Not only can you delete appointments or an instance of a recurring appointment, but you also can easily delete all occurrences of a recurring appointment.

To delete an appointment, follow these steps:

1. Click the Calendar shortcut on the Outlook bar if Calendar isn't already open.

2. In the Date Navigator, click the date of your appointment. If the appointment date is several months ahead, choose View ➢ Go To ➢ Go To Date on the menu bar to select and jump to the date.

3. In the Appointments area, click the appointment you want to delete.

4. On the menu bar, choose Edit ➢ Delete. Or click the Delete button on the Standard toolbar. The appointment is removed from the Appointments area.

TIP

To delete all occurrences of a recurring appointment, right-click the appointment, and select Delete from the shortcut menu. In the Confirm Delete dialog box, select Delete All Occurrences. If you select the Delete This One option in the Confirm Delete dialog box, only the recurring appointment you selected in the Appointments area will be removed.

SCHEDULING MEETINGS

Scheduling a meeting can often be a bigger hassle than actually conducting the meeting because you have to invite other people or reserve resources, such as a conference room or computer. If you try to set up a meeting without first calling everyone to check their availability, it could spell disaster. A better solution to this guessing game and scheduling madness is Outlook, which lets you quickly schedule meetings using Calendar.

You can send meeting requests to members of your workgroup or to someone over the Internet if they also use Outlook or another iCalendar-compliant application. The *iCalendar format* is the format Outlook uses when it is installed using the Internet Only mode. This format allows you and others to send, open, and respond to Outlook meeting requests via the Internet. By simplifying the process of scheduling meetings, Outlook gives you more time to focus on creating your meeting agenda and gathering supplies you might need.

In addition to sending meeting requests and reserving resources for face-to-face meetings, Outlook lets you schedule online meetings that use Microsoft NetMeeting or Microsoft NetShow. *NetMeeting* is a complete conferencing solution for the Internet and corporate intranet. You can communicate with others using both audio and video, collaborate on virtually any Windows-based application, exchange graphics on an electronic whiteboard, transfer files, use its text-based chat program, and more. *NetShow* is Microsoft's platform for streaming multimedia to enable both live and delayed audio and video broadcasts over the Internet.

NetShow broadcasts can range from simple audio to sophisticated interactive Web-based productions. You'll learn how to integrate these technologies with Outlook in the section "Setting Up an Online Meeting" later in this chapter.

Once recipients reply to your meeting message, you'll receive an e-mail in your Inbox. Reviewing these messages will help you track individual responses.

Outlook also makes it easy to add people to an existing meeting or to reschedule a meeting.

Setting Up a Meeting

Let's pretend you have just come from a meeting, and everyone has decided to get together a second time to complete unfinished tasks. You have talked to the attendees and know that everyone is available next Tuesday at 10:00 A.M. Since everyone has agreed to this time, you know they will show up, but if you schedule the meeting in Outlook, you can take advantage of several features that will help you get the most out of your meeting. These features include the abilities to set reminders, add comments regarding what topics still need to be addressed, and attach a document for review prior to the meeting.

To schedule a meeting in Outlook, follow these steps:

1. Click the Calendar shortcut on the Outlook bar if Calendar isn't already open.

2. In the Date Navigator, click the date of your meeting. If the meeting date is several months ahead, choose View ➤ Go To ➤ Go To Date on the menu bar to select and jump to the date.

3. In the Appointments area, click to select the time slot of your meeting or drag until the time slot shows the duration of your meeting. For instance, if your meeting starts at 3:00 P.M. and ends at 5:00 P.M., you'll click the 3:00 P.M. time slot and drag through the 5:00 P.M. time slot to select it. After you select a time slot, those rows will appear highlighted in the Appointments area.

4. On the menu bar, choose Actions ➤ New Meeting Request. The Meeting form displays, as shown in Figure 5.4.

5. Type the name(s) of the attendee(s) in the To box, or click To to open the Select Attendees And Resources dialog box. You can then select name(s) from your Address Book and click OK.

6. In the Subject box, type a description.

7. In the Location box, type the location for the meeting, or select a previous location from the drop-down list.

8. Select other options you want, and type comments in the Message area. To help attendees remember the meeting, click the Reminder check box, and select a time from the drop-down list.

9. On the Standard toolbar, click Send.

TIP

In Calendar, you can also schedule a meeting by dragging to select a block of time, right-clicking it, and then clicking New Meeting Request on the shortcut menu.

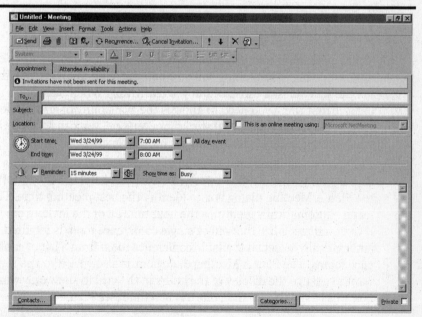

FIGURE 5.4: The Meeting form makes it easy to schedule a get-together with friends or business associates.

Attaching a Document to a Meeting Request

When you conduct a meeting, you often rely on an agenda to keep you on track or review documents prior to the meeting so that you're better informed. Outlook makes it easy to send a file along with your meeting request to attendees so that they can also prepare for the meeting. To attach a document to a meeting request, follow these steps:

1. Complete "Setting Up a Meeting," steps 1 to 7, in the previous procedure.

2. Select other options you want.

3. In the Message area, type comments, and then on the menu bar, choose Insert ➤ File. Or click the Insert File button on the Standard toolbar. The Insert File dialog box appears.

4. In the Look In box, locate the folder containing the file you want to send. When the file appears in the window below the Look In box, double-click it.

5. On the Standard toolbar, click the Send button.

Planning a Meeting

Unlike scheduling a meeting that you know everyone can attend, planning a meeting is something you do when you want to find a time that fits the schedules of those whom you're inviting. When planning a meeting, the first thing you need to know is the availability of all attendees. After you identify a time that works for everyone, you can schedule the meeting time and place and send the meeting request.

If you're beginning to wonder how you'll ever find the same hour free in everyone's schedule, don't worry; Outlook can help. Use the AutoPick in the Plan A Meeting dialog box to identify the best meeting time. This feature automatically identifies the next time all of the invitees are free. It can even recognize that only a single conference room is required and automatically select an available conference room from a list of conference rooms. The Plan A Meeting dialog box is also where you go if you want to change the display of the hours in the grid to show only working hours or to show more than one day at a time (see Figure 5.5).

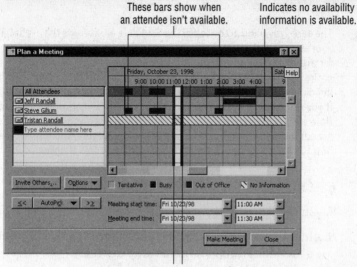

These bars show when
an attendee isn't available.

Indicates no availability
information is available.

Drag these bars to set the meeting time.

FIGURE 5.5: The Plan A Meeting dialog box lets you know when attendees are available and gives you one-click access to the Meeting form.

To plan a meeting, follow these steps:

1. Click the Calendar shortcut on the Outlook bar if Calendar isn't already open.

2. On the menu bar, choose Actions ➤ Plan A Meeting. The Plan A Meeting dialog box appears.

3. In the Plan A Meeting dialog box, click Invite Others. The Select Attendees And Resources dialog box appears.

4. In the Show Names From The drop-down list, select the relevant address book and then type a name in the Type Name Or Select From List box or select a name from the list. Click Required or Optional for each name you select, and then click OK. The names now appear in the All Attendees list of the Plan A Meeting dialog box, and the Schedule area shows each attendee's availability.

5. Select a time for the meeting by dragging the horizontal bars in the Schedule area or by typing a date and time in the Meeting Start Time and the Meeting End Time boxes (see Figure 5.5).

NEW

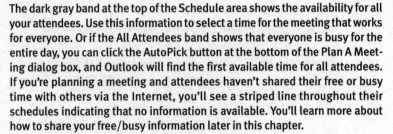

TIP

The dark gray band at the top of the Schedule area shows the availability for all your attendees. Use this information to select a time for the meeting that works for everyone. Or if the All Attendees band shows that everyone is busy for the entire day, you can click the AutoPick button at the bottom of the Plan A Meeting dialog box, and Outlook will find the first available time for all attendees. If you're planning a meeting and attendees haven't shared their free or busy time with others via the Internet, you'll see a striped line throughout their schedules indicating that no information is available. You'll learn more about how to share your free/busy information later in this chapter.

6. Click Make Meeting. The Meeting form appears.

7. In the Subject box, type a description.

8. In the Location box, type a location for the meeting or select a previous location from the drop-down list.

9. In the Message area, type agenda information, comments, or a note; add attachments if necessary.

10. On the Standard toolbar, click the Send button.

NOTE

If you want to check meeting details again, click the Attendee Availability tab in the Meeting form. On this tab, you can review and change the details of the meeting, review the schedules of the invited attendees, adjust the display of the schedule, and invite other attendees, if necessary.

TIP

You can also plan a meeting by choosing Action ➤ New Meeting Request on the menu bar. In the Meeting form, click the Attendee Availability tab to go to the Plan A Meeting dialog box.

In addition to inviting attendees, you can "invite" resources—such as conference rooms, equipment, or other materials you need for a meeting—if a global address list has been set up with rooms and equipment (usually done by your system administrator). You can schedule resources for your meeting in the same way that you schedule a person. In the Plan A Meeting dialog box, click Invite Others, and then select the resource from the list. When you send a meeting request that includes a resource, the message is delivered to the Inbox for the resource, which often belongs to a staff administrator.

NEW

Outlook also now lets you directly book resources, such as conference rooms, without having dedicated resource computers running. This feature is available to you if you have optimized Outlook for a corporate or workgroup environment. This means that if you have a resource without an e-mail address, such as a conference room or computer hardware, you can reserve the item as part of your meeting planning process, and then simply choose not to send the meeting request to the resource.

You can also choose to not send a meeting request to an attendee whom you've invited. For instance, you may have a list of key attendees and a list of alternate attendees. You can include all the names when you plan the meeting and choose to not send the request to the alternate attendees. To do so, in the Plan A Meeting dialog box, click the envelope icon to the left of the attendee's name or resource name, then click Don't Send Meeting To This Attendee. An X will appear over the envelope icon next to the attendee's name indicating that the person will not receive an invitation. Later, if you decide to include some of the alternate attendees, you can simply click the envelope icon next to the attendee's name and then click Send Meeting To This Attendee.

Verifying Attendee Responses

When you send a meeting request, the people you've invited to a meeting can accept, tentatively accept, or decline the request by clicking the appropriate button on the Standard toolbar in the e-mail message they receive. You can track the responses to the meeting request on Calendar's Attendee Availability tab. To verify who will be attending your meeting, follow these steps:

1. Click the Calendar shortcut on the Outlook bar if Calendar isn't already open.

2. In the Date Navigator, click the date of your meeting. If the meeting date is several months ahead, choose View ➤ Go To ➤ Go To Date on the menu bar to select and jump to the date.

Part i

3. In the Appointments area, double-click the meeting you want to verify. The Meeting form appears.

4. Click the Attendee Availability tab, shown in Figure 5.6.

5. Be sure Show Attendee Status is selected, and then check the Response column to see the status for each person whom you invited to the meeting.

6. Click the icon in the upper-right corner to close the Meeting form.

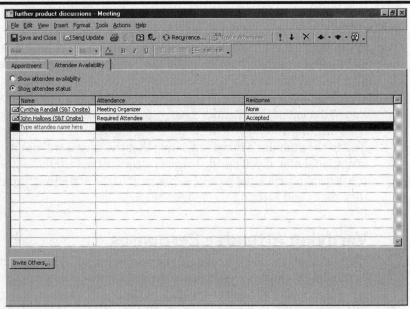

FIGURE 5.6:   You can quickly check the Attendee Availability tab to see who is planning to attend your meeting.

Adding and Removing Attendees

NEW

After you've organized and scheduled a meeting, you may sometimes decide that you need to invite additional people or remove some of the scheduled attendees. In Outlook, a meeting request or cancellation is automatically sent only to the people who have been added or removed. All you have to do to add an attendee is to open the Meeting form, add the person's name to the To line, and then click the Send Update button on the Standard toolbar. The Send Update To Attendees dialog box appears.

Depending on the option you choose, Outlook will send an update to only the new attendee (Send Updates Only To Added Or Deleted Attendees) or to everyone listed on the To line (Send Updates To All Attendees). After you select an option, click OK to close the dialog box and send the update.

TIP

To uninvite an attendee, simply delete their name from the To line, click the Send Update button, choose an option from the Send Update To Attendees dialog box, and then click OK.

Rescheduling a Meeting

Even the best-laid plans may not always work out. This is especially true when you're bringing several people together at the same time. Perhaps two or three of the attendees call and cancel, or you wake up on the morning of the meeting to find out your five-year-old has the chicken pox. These issues may cause you to change the date of a meeting, switch the time, move the location, or even cancel the meeting. When unexpected conflicts arise—and they will—you can quickly make changes to an existing meeting in Calendar and update attendees in a snap. To change the time for a meeting and notify attendees, follow these steps:

1. Click the Calendar shortcut on the Outlook bar if Calendar isn't already open.

2. In the Date Navigator, click the date of your meeting. If the meeting date is several months ahead, choose View ➤ Go To ➤ Go To Date on the menu bar to select and jump to the date.

3. In the Appointments area, double-click the meeting you want to reschedule. The Meeting form appears.

4. Make any necessary changes on the Appointment tab.

5. On the Standard toolbar, click the Send And Close button.

It's great when you're able to reschedule a meeting, but there will be times when you may simply choose to cancel a meeting. When you cancel a meeting, you must decide whether to send a cancellation notice. By sending a notice, attendees will be informed about the change and their schedules will be updated to reflect their new availability.

To cancel a meeting and send notification to your attendees, follow these steps:

1. Click the Calendar shortcut on the Outlook bar if Calendar isn't already open.

2. In the Date Navigator, click the date of your meeting. If the meeting date is several months ahead, choose View ➤ Go To ➤ Go To Date on the menu bar to select and jump to the date.

3. In the Appointments area, select the meeting, and then on the menu bar, choose Edit ➤ Delete. The Microsoft Outlook dialog box appears, as shown in Figure 5.7.

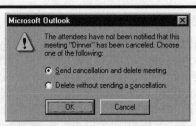

FIGURE 5.7: It's a good idea to send a cancellation notice when you have to cancel a meeting.

4. In the Microsoft Outlook dialog box, be sure Send Cancellation And Delete Meeting is selected, and then click OK.

TIP

You can also right-click a meeting in the Appointments area, select Delete from the shortcut menu, select a cancellation option, and then click OK.

Scheduling a Recurring Meeting

If you're a part of a committee that's planning an event, you may need to meet several times to share ideas and plan activities. Rather than sending out a separate meeting request for each meeting, you can easily schedule recurring meetings with the Outlook meeting planner. Scheduling becomes an easy task because you only have to send out one meeting request, which gets duplicated throughout an attendee's calendar.

To schedule a recurring meeting, follow these steps:

1. Click the Calendar shortcut on the Outlook bar if Calendar isn't already open.

2. In the Date Navigator, click the date of your meeting. If the meeting date is several months ahead, choose View ➢ Go To ➢ Go To Date on the menu bar to select and jump to the date.

3. In the Appointments area, click the time slot of your meeting or drag until the time slot shows the duration of your meeting. For instance, if your meeting starts at 3:00 P.M. and ends at 5:00 P.M., you'll drag from the 3:00 P.M. time slot through the 5:00 P.M. time slot to select it. After you select a time slot, those rows will appear highlighted in the Appointments area.

4. On the menu bar, choose Actions ➢ New Recurring Meeting, or right-click in the Calendar window and choose New Recurring Meeting from the shortcut menu. The Appointment Recurrence dialog box appears with the time slot you selected automatically inserted in the Appointment Time boxes.

5. In the Recurrence Pattern area, select the frequency of the meeting (daily, weekly, monthly, or yearly).

6. In the Recur Every box, type the intervals for the meeting. This number tells Calendar how many time periods you want to have pass before repeating the meeting. Then select the options that tell Outlook when you want the appointment repeated.

7. In the Range Of Recurrence area, the date you specified is automatically inserted in the Start box. To pick a new date, select the text in the Start box and type a new start date, or click the arrow and select a date from the calendar that

appears. By default, Calendar does not specify an end date for the recurrence. To specify an end date, select the End After option, and then type a number to represent when you want the recurrence to stop, or select the End Date option and type the last day of the recurrence.

8. Click OK. The Meeting form appears.

9. In the Subject box, type a description.

10. In the Location box, type the location of your meeting, or select a previously entered location from the drop-down list.

11. Select other options you want, and type comments in the Message area.

12. On the Standard toolbar, click the Send button. Your meeting request is sent, and the meeting is added to your schedule in the appropriate time slots (see Figure 5.8). If a recipient accepts the request, the meeting is also added to their schedule in the appropriate time slots.

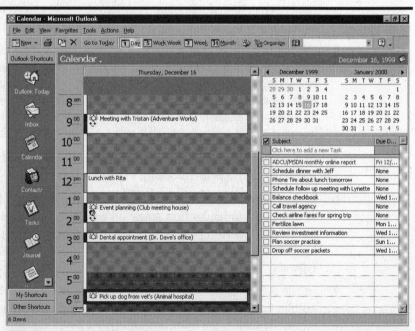

FIGURE 5.8: Recurring meetings are marked with an icon that looks like a circle with two arrow lines.

NOTE

You can check an attendee's free or busy time by clicking the Attendee Availability tab on the Recurring Meeting form, but you cannot change the meeting time or date from this tab. You must click the Recurrence button on the Standard toolbar and make changes in the Meeting Recurrence dialog box.

Scheduling a Meeting Over the Internet

Scheduling a meeting over the Internet can be ideal for people who work at home or travel and need to stay in touch with others via the Web. The Internet meeting feature only works if you have Outlook 2000 set up in an Internet-only environment. To send a meeting request and have attendees receive it, everyone must be using Outlook 2000 or another iCalendar-compliant application via the Internet and have e-mail access.

To schedule a meeting over the Internet, follow these steps:

1. Click the Calendar shortcut on the Outlook bar if Calendar isn't already open.

2. In the Date Navigator, click the date of your meeting. If the meeting date is several months ahead, choose View ➤ Go To ➤ Go To Date on the menu bar to select and jump to the date.

3. In the Appointments area, click the time slot of your meeting or drag until the time slot shows the duration of your meeting. For instance, if your meeting starts at 3:00 P.M. and ends at 5:00 P.M., you'll drag from the 3:00 P.M. time slot through the 5:00 P.M. time slot to select it. After you select a time slot, those rows will appear highlighted in the Appointments area.

4. On the menu bar, choose Actions ➤ New Meeting Request. The Meeting form appears.

5. In the To box, type the Internet addresses of the persons whom you want to have attend the meeting.

6. In the Subject box, type a description.

7. In the Location box, type the location for the meeting, or select a previous location from the drop-down list.

8. Select other options you want, and type comments in the Message area.

9. On the Standard toolbar, click the Send button.

10. On the menu bar, choose Tools ➣ Send/Receive, and then click Internet. You're prompted to log on to your Internet service, if you're not already connected.

11. After you log on to your Internet service, the meeting request is sent to the recipient(s) in the To line.

Setting Up an Online Meeting

A face-to-face meeting isn't always possible when attendees are located in different cities, states, or countries. Even when you're within close proximity to other attendees, schedule conflicts can sometimes make it seem nearly impossible to hold a meeting at a convenient time. In these situations, Outlook can help you plan an online meeting using Calendar. The participants can then communicate with each other via their computers using conferencing software, such as Microsoft NetMeeting.

You can schedule a NetMeeting for just yourself or invite others to see a live or taped broadcast. But instead of attending the meeting or presentation in person, attendees use NetShow Services to look at the meeting or presentation online. These types of one-way meetings are useful for when you need to present information to those who can't attend in person. To learn more about NetMeeting and NetShow Services, see the sidebar "Collaborating and Communicating Using Online Meetings."

Integrating Outlook with NetMeeting

NEW

If you've ever participated in a conference call or even three-way calling, you've likely experienced the ease with which people can "attend" a meeting without being in the same room. Participating in an online meeting is easy. All you need is a computer with an Internet connection and the same or compatible conferencing software. In addition to an Internet-based online meeting, you can also set up an intranet-based online meeting.

NOTE

Intranets, which are like private Internets, are often used within companies as a means of sharing company resources. Only the members of an intranet have access to information stored or shared on their intranet.

Regardless of which online medium you choose, once everyone is online, you can share computer files; talk to each other aloud or by interactive e-mail; see other participants via a video hookup; and even use a shared whiteboard, an onscreen chalkboard-like panel for sharing notes and drawings. Outlook 2000 has improved its NetMeeting integration by allowing you to associate an Office document with a meeting, which means you can collaborate with others on a single Office document. When you're collaborating on a document, NetMeeting does not support audio or video. Any verbal communication must be done over the phone or through other conferencing mechanisms (video conferencing or another computer running NetMeeting). So rather than scribbling on a document in a conference room, the attendees can edit online; when the meeting is over, the changes are already in the document.

Planning an online meeting is very similar to planning a meeting that everyone attends in your home, an office, or a conference room. The only difference in planning an online meeting and a regular meeting is that you use the Outlook Meeting Planner feature to set up the online connection.

To set up an online meeting using Microsoft NetMeeting (you must have NetMeeting 2.1 or later installed), follow these steps:

1. Click the Calendar shortcut on the Outlook bar if Calendar isn't already open.

2. On the menu bar, choose Actions ➤ New Meeting Request. A blank Meeting form appears.

3. Select the This Is An Online Meeting Using check box (next to the Location box) and then select Microsoft NetMeeting from the This Is An Online Meeting Using drop-down list (see Figure 5.9).

4. In the Subject box, type a description.

5. In the Location box, type a location for any users who might come to your location, or select a previously used location from the drop-down list.

6. In the Directory Server box, type in the name of the directory server that everyone will connect to for the online meeting. A directory server lists people who can be called using NetMeeting. If you log onto a directory server, people will see your name listed and you will see their names.

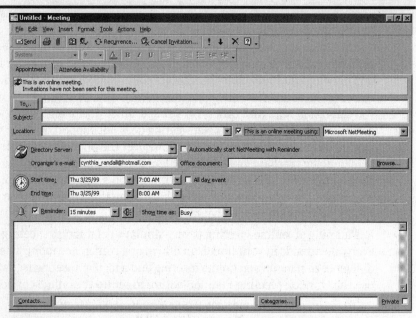

FIGURE 5.9: Planning an online meeting is a breeze with Outlook.

7. If you want to automatically start NetMeeting with a reminder, select the Automatically Start NetMeeting With A Reminder check box. If you select this option, Outlook will display a reminder notice for the meeting, and then the NetMeeting application will open automatically.

8. In the Organizer's E-mail box, type your e-mail address.

9. If you want to use an Office document during your Net-Meeting session, type the location of the Office document you want to use in the Office Document box, or click the Browse button to locate the file.

10. In the Start Time and End Time boxes, select the start and end dates and times for your meeting.

11. Select additional options, such as reminders, and type your comments in the Message area as needed.

12. Click the Attendee Availability tab. Then in the Type Attendee Name Here box, type the name of a recipient, and then press Enter. Continue this process until all attendees are added.

13. On the Standard toolbar, click the Send button.

14. On the menu bar, choose Tools > Send/Receive > Internet.

15. If prompted, log on to your Internet service. The meeting request is sent to the recipient(s) in the To line.

Part i

NOTE

NetMeeting only allows you to collaborate on Microsoft Office files, such as a Microsoft Word document, Microsoft Excel worksheet, Microsoft Access file, or a Microsoft PowerPoint presentation.

COLLABORATING AND COMMUNICATING USING ONLINE MEETINGS

Microsoft NetMeeting

NetMeeting 2.1 has several powerful features, such as data conferencing, which let you collaborate with a group of people from within any 32-bit Windows application. This means you can draw on a shared whiteboard, send text messages, and transfer files. In addition, NetMeeting offers wide-ranging support for video, so you can stay in touch with loved ones around the world without it costing you a fortune. With a microphone and video camera hooked to your computer, NetMeeting lets you experience the sights and sounds of any event—even when you're miles away. NetMeeting's real-time audio lets you talk to other people over the Internet, even if you use a 14.4Kbps modem. NetMeeting's video, audio, and data conferencing are all based on industry standards, so you can communicate with people using compatible products. To learn more about Microsoft NetMeeting, which is a free network conferencing program, check out the NetMeeting Web site at http://www.microsoft.com/netmeeting/.

Microsoft NetShow Services

Online meeting technology also includes Microsoft NetShow Services, which allows you to hold one-way meetings or presentations with attendees. By integrating audio and video with the Internet and intranets, NetShow Services makes it easy to take advantage

CONTINUED ➡

of online training, communications, customer and sales support, news and entertainment services, and product promotions. Net-Show Services 3 offers enhanced video and audio quality to ensure the best experience. You can use it to tune in to a meeting while sitting at your home office or to learn how to use the latest software from a multimedia presentation. NetShow Services is tightly integrated with Microsoft PowerPoint to deliver more effective multimedia presentations. And because it can be updated instantly, NetShow Services will quickly surpass CD-ROMs as the dominant means of accessing broadcast information. To learn more about Microsoft NetShow Services, check out the NetShow Services Web site at http://www.microsoft.com/ntserver/mediaserv/default.asp.

When recipients receive the online meeting request, it looks just like a normal Outlook Meeting request with the exception of the title bar, which displays "This is a NetMeeting." If recipients accept or tentatively accept the request, the meeting is added to their schedules. At this same time, the attendees can specify whether the application, such as NetMeeting or the Office application, starts automatically when the reminder appears.

When the meeting is about to begin, you (as the organizer) will see a reminder that asks if you want to start the NetMeeting. At the same time, attendees will receive a reminder. Click the Start NetMeeting button to begin, and attendees can join the meeting any time. Once NetMeeting launches, all attendees will see the document the group is collaborating on.

TIP

If you receive a NetMeeting request and have chosen not to have NetMeeting automatically start when you receive the meeting reminder, simply right-click the NetMeeting item in your Calendar, and then select Join NetMeeting Now from the shortcut menu.

Integrating Outlook with NetShow Services

NEW

Using NetShow Services, you can schedule an online meeting and deliver a presentation to colleagues or show grandma and grandpa slides from your recent trip to Brazil.

To schedule an online meeting with NetShow Services, follow these steps:

1. Click the Calendar shortcut on the Outlook bar if Calendar isn't already open.

2. On the menu bar, choose Actions ➤ New Meeting Request. A blank Meeting form appears.

3. Select the This Is An Online Meeting Using check box (next to the Location box), and then select NetShow Services in the drop-down list.

4. In the To box, type the names of the people who you want to invite to the broadcast. To select names from the Select Attendees And Resources dialog box, click To. After you have selected all attendees, click OK.

5. In the Subject box, type a description of the meeting.

6. In the Event Address box, type the address for the event.

7. To set a reminder and have NetShow start automatically, select the Automatically Start Broadcast With Reminder check box.

8. Enter times in the Start Time and End Time boxes.

9. Select any other options you want.

10. On the Standard toolbar, click the Send button.

11. On the menu bar, choose Tools ➤ Send/Receive ➤ Internet.

12. If prompted, log on to your Internet service. The meeting request is sent to the recipient(s) in the To line.

Part i

SCHEDULING EVENTS

You can use Outlook to schedule events just like you schedule appointments and meetings. *Events* are activities that last 24 hours or longer, such as multi-day business trips or vacations. Events can be annual like anniversaries or birthdays, or they may occur only once like a wedding. You can mark yourself available (free or tentative) or unavailable (busy or out of the office) to others during a scheduled event. You use the same dialog box to schedule an event as you do to schedule an appointment; the only difference is whether the All Day Event check box is selected or not. However, unlike appointments, events do not block out times in your schedule and cannot be reviewed by others.

To schedule an event, follow these steps:

1. Click the Calendar shortcut on the Outlook bar if Calendar isn't already open.

2. In the Date Navigator, click the date of your event. If the event date is several months ahead, choose View ➤ Go To ➤ Go To Date on the menu bar to select and jump to the date.

3. On the menu bar, choose Actions ➤ New All Day Event, or right-click the Appointments area, and select New All Day Event from the shortcut menu. The Event form appears (see Figure 5.10). Note that the date you have selected is automatically inserted in the dialog box.

4. In the Subject box, type a description.

5. In the Location box, type the location of the event, or select a previously entered location from the drop-down list.

6. Click the Reminder check box, and select a time from the drop-down list when you want to be notified by an alarm that the event is about to begin.

7. Select an option from the Show Time As drop-down list to notify others of your availability.

8. On the Standard toolbar, click the Save And Close button. The event notice is displayed in the gray box at the top of the Appointments area.

TIP

You can also open the Event form by double-clicking the gray bar at the top of the Appointments area under the date.

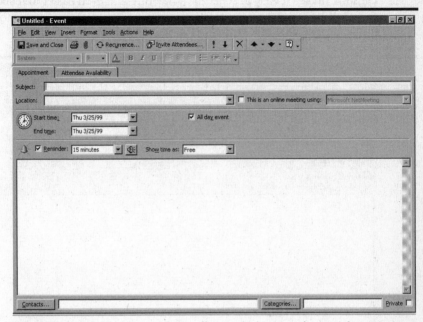

FIGURE 5.10:   An event is an all-day affair to which you might or might not invite others.

Creating an Annual Event

There are several events—birthdays, anniversaries, and even bulb planting—that all occur on an annual basis. You could add each of these as a separate event every year or create a recurring event that occurs once a year. Creating an annual event is just like creating an event, except that before you save and close the Event form, you click the Recurring button on the Standard toolbar (see the previous section on "Scheduling Events"). Then, in the Appointment Recurrence dialog box, select the Yearly option, and then click OK.

RESPONDING TO MEETING REQUESTS

Outlook makes it easy to schedule a meeting and even easier to respond to one. When someone sends you a meeting request or invites you to an event, you receive an e-mail message that looks like Figure 5.11.

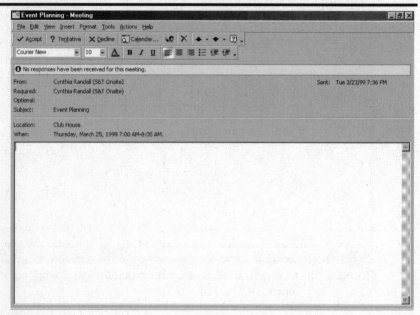

FIGURE 5.11:   Receiving a meeting request and responding to it

You can respond to the message by using the tools on the Standard toolbar:

▶ Click the Accept button to accept the invitation.

▶ Click the Tentative button to let the sender know you might attend.

▶ Click the Decline button to indicate that you can't attend.

- ▶ Click the Calendar button to look at your calendar before accepting or declining.

- ▶ Click the Forward button to forward the invitation to someone else.

If you choose to accept, tentatively accept, or decline the request, Outlook asks whether you want to send your response or add comments to it, as shown in Figure 5.12.

FIGURE 5.12:   It's a good idea to send a response to the meeting organizer, especially if you need to decline an invitation.

If you click the Edit The Response Before Sending option, you can add comments to the e-mail message and send it to the person organizing the meeting. If you click Send The Response Now option, your response will be sent to the meeting organizer without any comments. If you click Don't Send A Response, the organizer won't receive a response. If you accept or tentatively accept a request, the engagement is automatically added to your schedule.

TIP

To automatically delete meeting requests from the Inbox after responding, choose ToolsOptions on the menu bar. On the Preferences tab, click E-mail Options, and then click Advanced E-mail Options. Select the Delete Meeting Request From Inbox When Responding check box.

If you're a person who receives lots of meeting requests, you may wish you had an administrative assistant to help you process them. But you won't need to run an ad in the local paper to find just the right person, because Outlook can do the job for you. To have Outlook automatically handle meeting requests for you, follow these steps:

1. On the menu bar, choose Tools ≻ Options. The Options dialog box appears.

2. On the Preferences tab, click Calendar Options, and then click the Resource Scheduling button. The Resource Scheduling dialog box appears.

3. Click the Automatically Accept Meeting Requests And Process Cancellations option. This option will tell Outlook to automatically accept meeting requests, decline meeting requests that conflict with your existing schedule, and decline requests for recurring meetings.

4. Click OK to close the Resource Scheduling dialog box.

5. Click OK to close the Calendar Options dialog box, and then click OK to close the Options dialog box.

Dealing with a Reminder

After you have accepted a meeting or set up an appointment or meeting, Outlook will help you remember your scheduled engagements by displaying a reminder at a specified time on the appointed date, as shown in Figure 5.13.

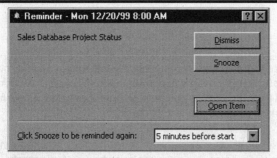

FIGURE 5.13:   Reminders make sure you get to your engagement on time.

When the reminder displays, you can click Dismiss to cancel further reminders. You can also click Snooze and select a delay interval to schedule a second reminder. Or you can click Open Item to review the calendar item. If you postpone the reminder past the start time of the engagement, the next reminder message displays the word Overdue in its title bar to let you know that the engagement has already started.

MAKING YOUR SCHEDULE WORK FOR YOU

By now, your schedule may be filled with important appointments and dozens of tasks to complete, so the last thing you want to do is spend time managing Outlook. Fortunately, Outlook was designed to help you, not hinder you, and you can activate several options to make it work even harder on your behalf. For instance, you can set free or busy time, specify holidays, and change time zone settings. You can also print a copy of your schedule to take with you so that when you're out and about, you can still keep track of where you need to be and when.

Sharing Free/Busy Information over the Web

NEW

If you've optimized Outlook for an Internet-only environment, you can easily allow others to check your availability (free or busy information) at a Web site in iCalendar format. Support for iCalendar, which is an emerging Internet standard that specifies the format and exchange of scheduling information, is growing. You and others can check the schedules of and exchange meeting requests with anyone who uses a program that also supports the iCalendar format. If Outlook has been optimized for a corporate or workgroup environment, your free and busy information can be concurrently made available to others using both Exchange Server and the Internet.

To share free or busy information on a Web site, follow these steps:

1. On the Tools menu ➤ Options. The Options dialog box appears.

2. Click the Calendar Options button. The Calendar Options dialog box appears.

3. Click the Free/Busy Options button. The Free/Busy Options dialog box appears.

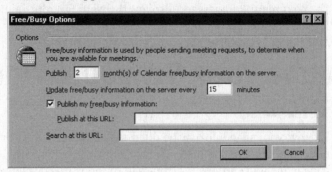

4. In the Publish box, type the number of months' worth of schedule information you want others to be able to see.

5. In the Update Free/Busy Information On The Server Every box, type the number of minutes you want your Calendar information updated for others.

6. Select the Publish My Free/Busy Information check box, and then type the location or path (URL) in the Publish At This URL box.

7. Click OK to close the Free/Busy Options dialog box.

8. Click OK to close the Calendar Options dialog box, and then click OK to close the Options dialog box.

NOTE

When blocks of time have been scheduled in your calendar or in someone else's calendar, Outlook highlights the time period with a color or pattern to indicate how the time is used. For example, no color indicates the time is marked as busy, light blue indicates the time is tentatively reserved for an appointment or meeting, purple indicates the person is out of the office, and diagonal lines indicate the person's availability is unknown.

Changing the Free/Busy Time of a Calendar Item

When others are scheduling a meeting, they can use the Attendee Availability tab to see when you're already booked with other engagements. Any appointment you have added to your calendar will show up as Busy by default, but there may be times when you want to exhibit greater scheduling flexibility. To change what others see when they view your schedule, double-click any negotiable calendar item, and specify one of the following choices in the Appointment form's Show Time As box:

Free   Although you have an activity scheduled for a specific time, you're willing to move it or cancel it to be available for an important meeting.

Busy   Typically when you create a new appointment, meeting, or event, you'll choose this option to let others know that you are not available.

Tentative   There may be times when you pencil in an engagement, because you're not sure it will happen or you want to be able to move or cancel the activity if something more pressing comes up.

Out of Office   If you know you'll be away from your office for a brief moment or extended period of time, you might want to make it clear to anyone planning a meeting that you can't be reached.

Depending on the option you select, Outlook will use the appropriate color on the Attendee Availability tab to show how you plan to spend your time.

Adding Holidays to Your Calendar

There are numerous holidays, but you may not celebrate all of them. You may get a vacation day for certain holidays and have to work on others. Rather than overload your calendar with every holiday, you can set or change the holidays the calendar displays at any time. Holidays are considered all-day events, so if you add a holiday, you'll see the name of the holiday displayed in the gray box at the top of the Appointments area just under the date.

To add a holiday to your calendar, follow these steps:

1.   Click the Calendar shortcut on the Outlook bar if Calendar isn't already open.

2.   On the menu bar, choose Tools ➤ Options. The Options dialog box appears.

3.   Click Calendar Options. The Calendar Options dialog box appears.

4. Click the Add Holidays button. The Add Holidays To Calendar dialog box appears.

5. Select the country or countries whose holidays you want to copy to your calendar, and then click OK. The Importing Holidays dialog box appears, and the selected countries' holidays are copied to your calendar.

6. Click OK twice to close the remaining dialog boxes.

Changing Time Zones

Unless you recently moved, you wouldn't want to change the time zone in your calendar, right? Although you might not want to change your time zone, it might be very helpful to add a time zone to the calendar. For instance, a second time zone is an ideal tool for people who frequently call or need to schedule meetings with people in another time zone. At a single glance, you'll know what time it is in the second time zone.

When you add a second time zone, the times are displayed in a gray band next to the current times in the Appointments area, as shown in Figure 5.14. It may not keep others from calling you at 4:00 A.M or midnight, but it will help you avoid making a 7:00 A.M call from the East Coast to someone deep in slumber on the West Coast.

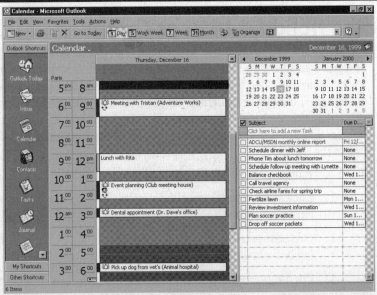

FIGURE 5.14: Even those who aren't world travelers can benefit by adding a second time zone to their calendar.

To add another time zone to your calendar, follow these steps:

1. Click the Calendar shortcut on the Outlook bar if Calendar isn't already open.

2. On the menu bar, choose Tools ➣ Options. The Options dialog box appears.

3. Click Calendar Options. The Calendar Options dialog box appears.

4. Click the Time Zone button. The Time Zone dialog box appears.

5. Click the Show An Additional Time Zone check box.

6. In the Time Zone list, select a time zone.

7. In the Label box, type a name for the time zone, and then click OK.

8. Click OK twice to close the remaining dialog boxes. The zone appears next to your first time zone in the Appointments area.

TIP

To remove a time zone, right-click the second time zone column in the Appointments area, and then select Change Time Zone from the shortcut menu. Select the Show Additional Time Zone box to clear it, and then click OK.

Printing Your Schedule

When you need a portable schedule you can carry with you throughout the day, your best bet is to print one. Outlook lets you choose from several print styles: daily, weekly, monthly, table, tri-fold, or calendar details. In addition, Outlook includes broad printing flexibility and support for leading paper calendar and binder sizes and formats. You can customize any of these print styles to meet your needs. You can also print appointments with detailed descriptions you may have added to the notes/comments area in the daily, weekly, and monthly print styles, and there's also an option to print monthly views on exactly one page per month.

To print your weekly schedule, follow these steps:

1. Click the Calendar shortcut on the Outlook bar if Calendar isn't already open.

2. On the menu bar, choose File ➤ Print, or click the Print icon on the Standard toolbar. The Print dialog box appears, as shown in Figure 5.15.

3. In the Print Style area, select Weekly Style.

4. In the Start box, type a start date, or click the drop-down arrow, and select a date from the calendar.

5. In the End box, type an end date, or click the drop-down arrow and select a date from the calendar. (When printing a weekly schedule, it isn't necessary to specify an end date.)

6. Click OK.

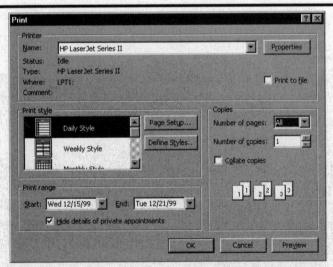

FIGURE 5.15: When you're on the go, print your schedule and take it with you to make sure you don't miss an important engagement.

NEW

> **TIP**
>
> If you're printing your schedule in the daily, weekly, or monthly style, you can hide the details of private engagements. Simply select the Hide Details Of Private Appointments check box in the Print Range area of the Print dialog box. If you select this option, only the time and the words Private Appointment will appear in your schedule.

ORGANIZING YOUR CALENDAR BY CATEGORIES

Organizing your calendar helps you to better manage your time. One way to gain a handle on all your calendar items is to categorize them. By assigning calendar items to categories, you can view all your appointments, meetings, and events grouped by category. To assign a calendar item to a category, follow these steps:

1. Click the Calendar shortcut on the Outlook bar if Calendar isn't already open.

2. Locate the item you want to categorize. Use the Date Navigator to locate it by date, or if the item is scheduled for several months later, choose View ➢ Go To ➢ Go To Date on the menu bar to select and jump to the date.

3. Double-click the item in the Appointments area. The appointment, meeting, or event item opens.

4. If you know the name of the category, you can type it in the box next to the Categories button. If you don't know the name of the category, click the Categories button. The Categories dialog box appears, as shown in Figure 5.16.

5. Select the category or categories you want to assign to the item by selecting the check box next to the category title. If you select multiple categories, Outlook will display the item under each category heading when you look at calendar items by categories, which you'll learn more about shortly.

6. Click OK, and then click the Save And Close button on the Standard toolbar.

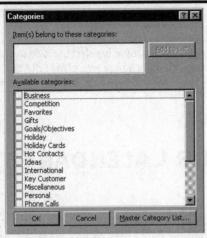

FIGURE 5.16: Assigning a category to a calendar item makes it easy to organize and sort all your appointments, meetings, and events.

NOTE

You can also assign categories to your appointments, meetings, and events when you create them by following Steps 4 through 6 in the previous procedure.

Reviewing Appointments by Category

Once you've added one or more categories to your calendar items, you can look at them in groups, by following these steps:

1. Click the Calendar shortcut on the Outlook bar if Calendar isn't already open.

2. On the menu bar, choose View ➣ Current View ➣ By Category. The headings for groups of calendar items display in the Information viewer.

3. In the Information viewer, click the Expand/Collapse buttons (plus (+) or minus (-) signs) next to the headers to display the list of calendar items contained in the group, as shown in Figure 5.17.

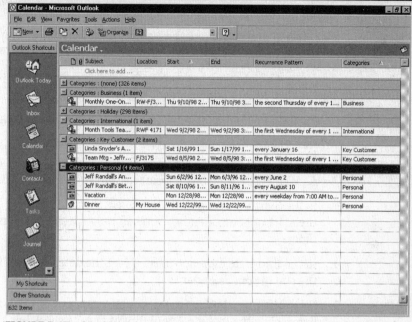

FIGURE 5.17:   It's easy to locate a specific calendar item or items, such as key customers, if you've assigned categories to your appointments, meetings, and events.

PUBLISHING YOUR CALENDAR ON THE WEB

NEW

Want to see your name in lights or at least in a colored font? You can have that and much more if you take advantage of Outlook's Web-based features. In fact, you can transfer all your Calendar meeting requests and appointments into a professional-looking HTML calendar and post it on the Web for yourself or for others to see. This is especially handy if you work or get together with people who don't use Outlook. You can let them know where to find the calendar on the Web and encourage them to check it frequently before organizing meetings and activities with you. If you can't imagine your personal appointments displayed before the world, then how about posting a monthly schedule of Cub Scout meetings so you don't have to keep calling everyone to let them know that the pack meeting has been changed to a new date? Or how about publishing a list of alumni events to keep school chums up-to-date on what's happening?

NOTE

If you plan to publish a calendar on the Web, you'll first need to secure some Web space from your Internet Service Provider. Contact your ISP for complete details regarding posting requirements.

To publish your calendar on the Web, follow these steps:

1. Click the Calendar shortcut on the Outlook bar if Calendar isn't already open.

2. On the menu bar, choose File ≻ Save As Web Page. The Save As Web Page dialog box appears, as shown in Figure 5.18.

3. In the Start Date drop-down list, select the date you want for the start of your calendar. You can only specify dates, not times.

4. In the End Date drop-down list, select the date you want for the end of your calendar.

5. To publish the details (notes, comments) of your calendar items, click the Include Appointment Details check box.

6. To add a background graphic to your calendar, click the Use Background Graphic check box, and then type the location of the file you want to use in the box. Or click the Browse button to locate the graphic file.

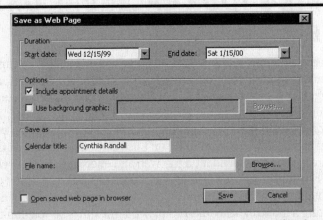

FIGURE 5.18: The Save As Web Page dialog box simplifies the process of turning your personal or group calendar into a Web page and makes it easy for others to keep up-to-date on your schedule.

7. In the Calendar Title box, type a title for your calendar. If it is your personal calendar, type your name.

8. In the File Name box, type the location or URL (for example: http:// server_name.com) where your calendar will be published. Or click the Browse button to locate the file.

9. To open the calendar in a browser, click the Open Saved Web Page In Browser check box.

10. Click Save. Your default browser opens, and your calendar appears as a Web page. This is a likely view of how others will see your calendar.

WHAT'S NEXT?

This chapter explained how to better manage your time using Calendar. You can now schedule one-time and recurring appointments, attach documents to calendar items, set up an online meeting, schedule annual events, publish your calendar on the Web, and more. Next, you will learn how to manage your contacts.

Chapter 6
MANAGING CONTACTS WITH OUTLOOK

O utlook is primarily a communication and organization tool and, as a result, your contacts form the foundation of your Outlook data. Contacts is the place to record name and address information, telephone numbers, e-mail addresses, Web page addresses, and a score of other information pertinent to the people with whom you communicate. If there is a piece of information you need to record about an individual, you can probably find a place for it in Contacts.

CREATING A CONTACT

In Outlook, a *contact* is an individual or organization you need to maintain information about. The information can be basic—a name and phone number—or include anniversary and birthday information, nicknames, and digital IDs. Outlook is, at its core, a contact management system. The other Outlook components are designed to work in conjunction with your contacts, so the more time you spend developing accurate and useful contact information,

Adapted from *Mastering™ Microsoft® Outlook™ 2000*
by Gini Courter and Annette Marquis
ISBN 0-7821-2472-0   787 pages $34.99

the easier it is to use Outlook to schedule meetings, send e-mail and faxes, and document time spent on the phone or visiting in person. You probably have an existing address and phone list in a contact management system, such as a Day Runner, Franklin Planner, or Rolodex. When you start using Outlook, entering data from your current system as Outlook Contacts is the best way to begin. While Outlook is robust enough to help you easily manage business and professional contacts, don't forget to take time to add personal contacts like friends and family members so all your important names, e-mail addresses, phone numbers, and addresses are in one place.

TIP

If you have contacts in a computerized contact manager like ACT or ECCO, or in a database like Microsoft Access, you don't have to reenter them.

You enter information about a contact in an Outlook Contact form. A blank form can be opened in several ways. If you're going to be entering a number of contacts, click the Contacts icon in the Outlook shortcut bar to open the Contacts component.

From the menu bar, choose File ➢ New ➢ Contact, or click the New Contact button on the toolbar to open a blank Contact form. If your hands are already on the keyboard, there's no need to grab the mouse: press Ctrl+Shift and the letter C to open a Contact form, shown in Figure 6.1.

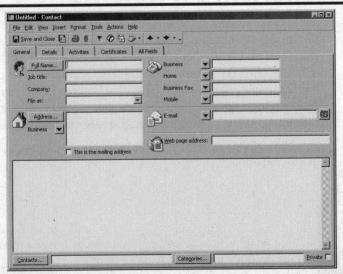

FIGURE 6.1: Use Outlook Contact forms to collect and manage information about business and personal contacts.

If you're working in another component (for example, the Outlook Calendar), you don't need to switch to Contacts to open a Contact form. You can choose File ➤ New ➤ Contact from the menu bar in any module—you'll just need to look a bit further down the menu selections to find Contact. The same list is attached to the toolbar; click the New Item button's drop-down arrow and select Contact from the menu.

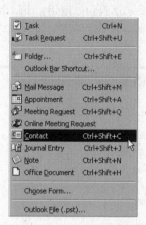

The Contact form is a multi-page form, with tabs labeled General, Details, Activities, Certificates, and All Fields. The form opens with the General page displayed, as shown in Figure 6.1. (To move to another page, simply click the tab for the page.) You'll use the text boxes on the General page to enter the kinds of information usually stored in an address or telephone book.

Entering Names, Job Titles, and Companies

Begin by entering the contact's name in the first text box on the General page, next to the Full Name button. If you just want to enter the contact's first and last names, that's fine, but you can also include their title, middle name (or initial), and suffix. For example, "Mary Smith," "Dr. Mary Smith," or "Smith, III, Mr. Richard M." are all acceptable ways of entering names.

You don't have to fill all the fields; on the other hand, you can't use information you don't enter. For example, Outlook provides an easy way to quickly create a letter to be sent to a contact. If you might need to send formal correspondence to your friend Bill Jones, take the time to enter Bill's title when you create the contact. You can always choose to omit the title on a specific piece of correspondence, but you can only include it easily if you've entered it in the Contact form.

When you've finished typing the contact's name, press Enter or Tab to move to the next field. Outlook will parse (separate) the name into parts for storing it. If Outlook can't determine how to separate the parts of the name, or if the name you entered is incomplete (perhaps you entered only a first name in the Full Name field), the Check Full Name dialog box, shown in Figure 6.2, opens so you can verify that Outlook is storing the name correctly.

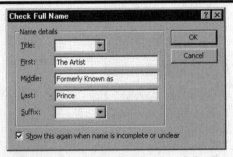

FIGURE 6.2:   The Check Full Name dialog box appears when you need to verify how a name should be stored in Outlook.

Outlook does a fairly good job of separating names appropriately. However, it doesn't handle some names and titles perfectly. If you enter the titles Dr., Miss, Mr., Mrs., Ms., or Prof., Outlook places them in the Title field. However, if you use other titles for example, Rev. for a minister, The Honorable for a judge, or Fr. for a priest Outlook will not recognize them as titles and places them in the First Name field. Names that are composed of two words, such as Jo Anne or von Neumann, may also not be separated correctly into first, middle, and last names. You can edit these fields manually by clicking the Full Name button to open the Check Names dialog box.

TIP

To instruct Outlook not to check incomplete or unclear names, clear the check box in the Check Full Name dialog box before clicking OK. To turn checking back on, open a Contact form, click the Full Name button to open the dialog box, turn the option back on, and then click OK.

In the Job Title text box, enter the contact's complete job title. If you don't know the contact's job title, simply leave the field blank. Enter the name of the contact's company in the Company field. If you've already entered another contact from the same company, make sure you spell and punctuate the company name the same way. Later, you'll probably want to sort your contacts by company. Outlook views each unique spelling of a company name as a separate company. If some of your contacts work for *Sybex* and others for *Sybex, Inc.*, Outlook won't group them together.

In the File As field, either select an entry from the drop-down list or type a new entry to indicate how the contact should be filed.

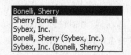

If you choose to file contacts with the first name first, you can still sort them by last name, so it's really a matter of personal preference. If you'll usually look up the company rather than the individual, it's a good idea to file contacts by company name. For example, ABC Graphics assigned Jim as the sales representative to your account, but it might be more useful to file the contact as *ABC Graphics (Jim)* than as just *Jim*, particularly if you have trouble remembering Jim's name.

You aren't limited to the choices on the File As drop-down list. Select the text in the File As text box, and then enter the File As text you'd like to use. This allows you to enter formal names for contacts, but store them in a way that makes them easy to retrieve; you can enter Dr. William Jones, III, as the contact name, but file your friend as Bill Jones so you can find him quickly.

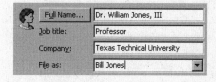

Entering Contact Addresses

Outlook allows you to store three addresses—Business, Home, and Other—for your contact and designate one of the three as the address you want to use as the contact's primary address. To choose the type of address you want to enter, click the drop-down arrow in the address section, and select the address type from the list. The address type will be displayed to the left of the arrow.

Click in the Address text box and type the address as you would write it on an envelope. Type the street address on the first or first and second lines, pressing Enter to move down a line. Type the city, state or province, country, and zip code or postal code on the last line. If you don't enter a country, Outlook uses the Windows default country.

NOTE

The Windows default country is set in the Windows Control Panel under Regional Settings.

When you press Tab to move to the next field, Outlook will check the address just as it did the contact name. If the address is unclear or incomplete, the Check Address dialog box opens, as shown in Figure 6.3. Make sure the information for each field is correct, and then click OK to close the dialog box.

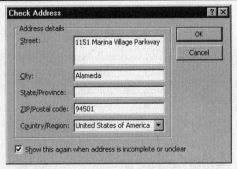

FIGURE 6.3:   The Check Address dialog box opens to allow you to verify an incomplete or unclear address.

In Outlook, the primary address for a contact is called the mailing address. The mailing address is the address displayed in most views, and is the address used when you merge a Word main document with your Outlook Contacts. By default, the first address you enter for a contact is set as the mailing address. To change the address used as the mailing address, make sure the address you want to use (Home, Business, or Other) is displayed in the Address text box; then click the This Is the Mailing Address check box to make the displayed address the mailing address.

Entering Contact Telephone Numbers

This is truly the age of connectivity. While three mail addresses are sufficient for nearly everyone you know, it isn't unusual to have five, six, or more telephone numbers to contact one person: home phones, work phones, home and work fax numbers, mobile phones, ISDN numbers, and pager numbers. With Outlook, you can enter up to nineteen different telephone numbers for a contact and display four numbers "at a glance" on the Contact form, as shown in Figure 6.4.

FIGURE 6.4: The Contact form displays four of the nineteen numbers you can enter for a contact.

When you create a new contact, the four default phone number descriptions displayed are Business, Home, Business Fax, and Mobile. To enter a telephone number for one of those four descriptions, simply click in or tab to the appropriate text box and type in the telephone number. You don't need to enter parentheses around the area code, hyphens, or spaces—just enter the digits in the telephone number, as shown here.

When you move out of the text box, Outlook will automatically format the digits, adding parentheses, spaces, and hyphens. If you enter a seven-digit telephone number, Outlook assumes the phone number is local and adds your area code to the number.

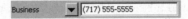

NOTE

International phone numbers get some rather convoluted treatment. Locate your contact, go to Actions ➤ Call Contact ➤ New Call, and click Dialing Properties. In the Dialing Properties dialog box, check the For Long Distance Calls, Use This Calling Card option and click the Calling Card button. Oddly enough, this does not mean you must have a calling card to make an international call—the default option is None (Direct Dial). Get your call information together and click the International Calls button. In the International Calls dialog box, you will be able to enter all of the information required to make a successful international connection.

NOTE

If you include letters in your telephone numbers (like 1-800-CALLME), you won't be able to use Outlook's automated dialing program to call this contact.

To enter another type of telephone number, click the drop-down arrow for any of the four text boxes to open the menu of telephone number descriptions.

The telephone number descriptions with checkmarks are those you've already entered. From the menu, choose the description of the telephone number you wish to enter; then enter the number in the text box. When you've finished entering telephone numbers for the contact, the numbers that are displayed in the four text boxes may not be the numbers you use most frequently. That's not a problem—just open the menu next to each text box and, from the menu, select the descriptions for the numbers you want to display. In Figure 6.5, we've displayed the four numbers we use most frequently to reach Bill Jones.

FIGURE 6.5:   You can choose to display any four telephone numbers in the Contact form.

Understanding E-mail Addresses

You can enter up to three e-mail addresses for a contact. The e-mail addresses are labeled E-mail, E-mail 2, and E-mail 3, rather than "Business" and "Home" like mail addresses and telephone numbers. You might think it would be easy to get a contact's home and work e-mail addresses confused, but the e-mail address itself usually contains the information you need.

Internet e-mail addresses have three parts: a username, followed by the "at" symbol (@), and a domain name. The domain name includes the *host name*, and may include a *subdomain name*.

Each e-mail account has its own *username*. In Windows NT, usernames include the owner's name, such as bjones, jonesb, or billjones. Many companies and e-mail providers also add a number to the usernames, so they look like bjones1, or they include the person's middle initial so that Bill Jones and Barbara Jones don't have to fight over who gets to be the "real" bjones.

The username and domain name are separated with the @ symbol. The *domain name* begins with the host name. The *host name* is the name of the server that handles the e-mail account. For example, in the address bjones@wompus.berkeley.edu, the host name is "wompus." (On one of the wompus server's hard drives, there's space for Bill Jones to keep his e-mail; the space is called his *mailbox*.) The *subdomain* is "berkeley"—the name or an abbreviated name of the organization that owns the server. The last part of the domain name, following the last period, is the *domain*, which describes the type of organization. Currently, there are six domains used in the United States, and seven additional domains may be added soon (if the politicians make some decisions). Table 6.1 lists the current domains.

TABLE 6.1: Current Domain Names

DOMAIN	TYPE	EXAMPLE
Com	Commercial: for-profit organizations	sybex.com
Edu	Educational: schools, colleges, and universities	berkeley.edu
Gov	Governmental: federal, state, and local governmental units	michigan.gov
Mil	Military: armed services	af.mil
Net	Network: network access providers	att.net
Org	Organization: non-profit businesses	uua.org

Outside of the United States, most domains are a two or three character abbreviation for the country: uk for the United Kingdom, ca for Canada, jp for Japan. An increasing number of educational organizations use us (United States) as their domain rather than edu; the domain name oak.goodrich.k12.mi.us describes a host at Oaktree Elementary in Goodrich Public Schools, a K-12 district in Michigan.

Entering E-mail Addresses

To enter an e-mail address, enter the entire address, including the username and the domain name. When you move out of the e-mail address text box, Outlook analyzes the address you entered to ensure that it resembles a valid e-mail address. Outlook does *not* check to make sure that the address is the correct e-mail address for this contact, or that the address exists. Outlook just looks for a username, the @ symbol, and a domain name. If all the parts aren't there, Outlook deletes the text you entered.

When you enter inappropriate characters, Outlook is a bit bolder in letting you know about it. Some addresses used within mail systems aren't compatible with the Internet. For example, many CompuServe addresses contain commas: 72557,1546. This is a valid e-mail address for a CompuServe member if you're also a CompuServe member and stay within the CompuServe system, using the CompuServe Information Manager to send your e-mail. However, it's not a valid *Internet* e-mail address. The only punctuation used in Internet addresses are periods and the @ symbol. If you want to send e-mail to this CompuServe address from Outlook or any other Internet mail system, the address must be modified for use on the Internet. (For CompuServe addresses, change the comma to a period and add the CompuServe domain name: *72557.1546@compuserve.com*.)

If you mistakenly enter the CompuServe address as the e-mail address for your contact, Outlook thinks it is two addresses, separated by a comma:

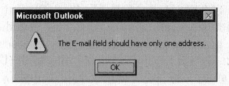

Outlook won't let you save this Contact until you either correct or delete the incorrect e-mail address.

All versions of Outlook support a file format called *Rich Text Format* (*RTF*). With RTF, you can format an e-mail message as you would a Word document, using boldface, italicized text, and different fonts and font colors to provide emphasis in the message. If you're using Outlook on a server at work, your colleagues running Outlook on the network will be able to open RTF messages and see your text in all its formatted glory.

However, not all e-mail services support RTF (and all of your colleagues may not be using Outlook). Services that don't support RTF support *plain text*. If your contact's e-mail service doesn't support RTF, the formatting of the message can make it harder to decipher the actual text of the message because it inserts funny codes. At best, the formatting doesn't appear, and you've spent time formatting for no good reason. If you know that your contact's e-mail service doesn't support RTF, check the Send Using Plain Text check box to send all messages to this contact in plain text. If you leave the check box disabled, messages will be sent in RTF if you choose RTF as your default e-mail format.

The Send Using Plain Text setting is for the Contact and affects all three of the contact's e-mail addresses. What happens when your contact's work e-mail service supports RTF, but their home service does not? In Outlook, you can change an individual e-mail message to plain text or RTF when you create the message. If one of the e-mail addresses you use for the contact doesn't support RTF, we suggest that you check the Send Using Plain Text check box.

Understanding URLs

When you're preparing for a visit, telephone call, or Internet meeting with a contact, you probably have a number of information sources you check. You'll look at your Calendar to see when you met last, check your Task list to ensure that all the tasks related to the contact are complete, and search online for recent news about the contact's organization. The contact's Web site is one of the places you'll want to search. Web sites often contain news about an organization, including recently announced products, promotions, legal actions, press releases, and other information of interest. By adding a *hyperlink* pointing to the URL of the General page on the Contact form, you can access the contact's Web site with one quick click of the mouse.

To find the contact's Web site, you must know the site's Internet address. An individual item you can find on the Internet is called a *resource*. Just as e-mail addresses are used to locate individuals, *Uniform Resource Locators*, or *URLs*, are Internet addresses that contain all the information needed to find a Web site or specific document.

The URL has two parts: the resource and a *protocol* that specifies the method used for retrieving the resource. The protocol for a page on the *World Wide Web* (*WWW*), the graphically based portion of the Internet, is *Hypertext Transfer Protocol* (*HTTP*). Most of the URLs you'll see begin with HTTP, but there are other protocols, including *File Transfer Protocol* (*FTP*), used on sites where you download files; *gopher*, a search and retrieve protocol used on university database sites; and *file*, used for files located on a local or network drive.

The protocol is followed by a colon and two slashes ":// " and then the resource, including directions to the file you want to retrieve. The resource includes the host name and may also include a filename and path.

Assigning a Web URL to a Contact

When you enter a World Wide Web URL in the Web Page Address text box, you don't need to enter the protocol. Enter the resource name (for example, www.disney.com), and when you leave the text box, Outlook will automatically add http:// to the beginning of the URL. However, if you're entering an address for another type of protocol, such as gopher, telnet, or ftp, you must enter the entire URL, including the protocol and the resource. If you don't, Outlook will still add http:// to the beginning of the URL, and it will be incorrect.

NOTE

If the URL you are pointing to includes standardized components, Outlook can handle things other than WWW links. For instance, ftp.uunet.com will become ftp://uunet.com and gopher.ucla.edu will become gopher://gopher.ucla.edu, which is nice if you need fast access to various, different resources. However, if an FTP site begins with a WWW prefix (this is how most ISPs allow access to personal Web space), then it will still be interpreted as a Web address.

To visit the user's Web site simply point to the URL, and the mouse pointer will change to the familiar browser-link hand shape. Double-click to launch your default browser and load the Web page. If the Contact form isn't open, select the contact in any view, and either choose Action ➤ Explore Web Page from the menu bar, or right-click the contact and select Explore Web Page from the shortcut menu.

Assigning a File URL

File URLs point to addresses on a local area network. A file URL begins with the file:// protocol, followed by the file path and filename. For example, file://k:\users\ BillJones.doc is a file on the K drive in the folder named "users." If there is a space anywhere in the filename or path, you must enclose the address in brackets, using the < and > symbols: for example, <file://c:\My Documents\News About Bill Jones.doc> is a valid URL. Without the < and > symbols, the URL is invalid. There are limitations to the usefulness of assigning URLs to files. You can only access files that you have network permissions for, and if another user moves or renames the files, the URL won't be correct.

Using Categories

A *category* is a key word or term that you assign to an item. Categories give you a way to sort, group, filter, and locate Contacts, Tasks, and other Outlook items. With the exception of e-mail messages, every type of Outlook item can be sorted and grouped by category. Outlook comes with 20 built-in categories, and you can delete categories or add other categories that reflect your work.

With categories, you can consistently organize items in all modules and use the categories as a way to relate items. If all the contacts, journal entries, tasks, and appointments related to Project XYZ are assigned to the Project XYZ category, you can use Advanced Find (see Chapter 11) or the newly added Categories button located in many forms to locate and display them. You can sort and filter Outlook items based on category within a module. Thoughtful use of categories is a key to Outlook organization.

For example, you can create a category for each department in your organization and assign staff to the appropriate department category. Sorting by category results in a list sorted by department. Print the view, and you've got an employee directory.

To assign a category to a Contact, either type a category description in the Categories text box or click the Categories button on the General page to open the Categories dialog box, shown in Figure 6.6.

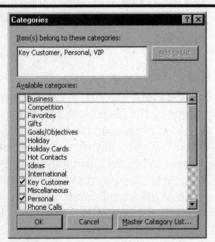

FIGURE 6.6:   Assign, add, and delete Outlook categories in the Categories dialog box.

You can add as many categories as you wish to a Contact. Click the check box in front of each category that you wish to assign. Some of the categories, such as Holiday and Time & Expenses, don't apply to Contacts. As you click the check boxes, the categories you select are listed in alphabetical order in the Items Belong to These Categories box at the top of the dialog box. When you close the dialog box, the categories are listed in the Categories text box on the General page.

WARNING

While Outlook allows you to assign multiple categories to items, many Outlook-compatible personal data assistants (PDAs) are more limited. If you intend to synchronize your Outlook Contacts with a PDA, see the owner's manual both for the PDA and the synchronization software before assigning multiple categories to contacts.

Adding and Deleting Categories

There are two approaches to changing categories: you can add them one at a time, as you need to use them, or do a bit of planning and add them all at once in the Master Category List. To add a category on the fly, click after the last category in the Items Belong to These Categories list, type a comma and the name of the category, and then click the Add to List button, shown in Figure 6.7. The new category is added to the alphabetized category list.

While you can add categories on a whim, we suggest a more planned approach. If you've already entered a hundred Contacts, creating a new category or deleting existing categories often means you'll have to open existing Contacts and change their categories. After you've looked at each of the Outlook components, but before you create too many Contacts, open the Categories dialog box and determine if the categories listed will meet your needs. Delete the categories you don't want to use, and add the categories you require to the Master Category List.

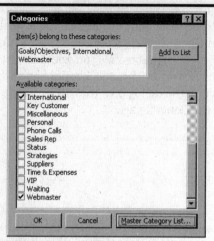

FIGURE 6.7: Click the Add to List button to add a new category to the Master
Category List.

To access the Master Category List from any Outlook form, click the
form's Categories button to open the Categories dialog box. Then click
the Master Category List button at the bottom of the Categories dialog
box. The Master Category List dialog box, shown in Figure 6.8, opens.

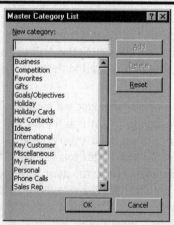

FIGURE 6.8: Use the Master Category List dialog box to add or delete Outlook
categories.

To remove a category from the list, select the category and click the Delete button. To add a category, type the category name in the New Category text box and then click the Add button. If you click the Reset button, Outlook returns the Master Category List to the 20 default categories, most of which are visible in Figure 6.8.

Deleting a category from the Master Category List does not delete it from the categories assigned to Contacts. In Figure 6.9, we've opened the Categories dialog box for a Contact after removing two categories, My Friends and Sales Rep, from the Master Category List. The two categories are still assigned to this Contact, but probably won't be assigned to another Contact because they're no longer choices in the list.

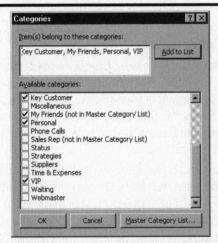

FIGURE 6.9: Categories that have been deleted from the Master Category List are indicated in the Categories dialog box.

This presents a minor problem. When you sort your Contacts by category, every category that's used in a Contact shows up, even after you delete the category from the Master Category List. If you don't want to see Contacts grouped under categories you've deleted from the list, you'll need to open each Contact and delete the category from the Contact.

TIP

The same category list is used in all the Outlook modules. So while it might not make sense to have a category for Phone Calls in Contacts, it can be very useful in categorizing Tasks. Create your category list with all the applications in mind.

Making a Contact Private

If you're using Outlook on a network, other users may have been given permission to share your Contacts folder, or you may place Contacts in a public folder. In the bottom-right corner of the General page, there's a check box marked Private. By enabling the Private setting, you prevent other users from seeing this Contact, even if they have access to your Contacts folder.

Entering Contact Comments

The large text box at the bottom of the General page is an open area for comments about the contact: anything from quick phrases to eloquent paragraphs. For example, if the contact is your sales representative, you might put your account number in the comments text box. Or you might note hobbies and favorite ice cream flavors. If your company hands out t-shirts, it's a perfect location for shirt sizes.

You can't sort, group, or filter on comments, so don't put information here that you'll want to use to sort views. For example, one Outlook user wanted to be able to organize lists of employees who participated in the company softball league, so they entered the contact's team name as a comment. After entering over seventy team members, they realized the contacts couldn't be sorted by team. (This would have been a good use for categories.)

NOTE

You can use Find to locate text in comments, but it's a time-consuming process.

Adding Details

On the Details page, shown in Figure 6.10, you'll record less frequently used information about your contacts. Remember that you can sort and filter your contacts on these fields, so try to use standard entries. If, for example, you want to be able to find all the vice presidents in your Contacts folder, make sure you enter **vice president** the same way for each contact.

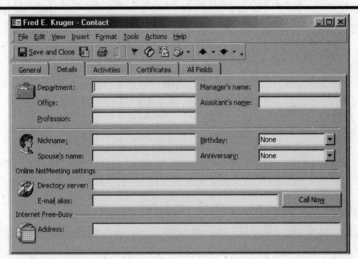

FIGURE 6.10: Use the Details page to record other information about your contact.

The Birthday and Anniversary fields have a drop-down arrow that opens a calendar. You can type dates in these fields using the *mm/dd/yy* format (03/08/57 for March 8, 1957), or you can select a date from the calendar. The Outlook calendar control is pretty nifty. Click the arrow and the calendar opens, displaying the current month.

To choose the current date, click the Today button on the bottom of the calendar. To enter a different date in the current month, just click the date. Click the arrows in the calendar's header to scroll to the prior month or the next month. This is fairly tedious if you're entering a contact's birthday (unless he was born yesterday!). To scroll more rapidly, point to the name of the month in the header and hold down your mouse button to open a list of calendar pages. Scroll up or down through the list to select the calendar for the month and year you want to display; then select the date from the calendar.

Entering NetMeeting Addresses

Microsoft NetMeeting is Internet-based collaboration software included with Outlook. With NetMeeting, you can work with one or more contacts "face to face" over the Internet, using video and audio as you would in a video conference call. Some hardware is required to support NetMeeting's high-end video and audio functions.

Even if you don't use these functions, though, NetMeeting has a lot to offer. You can use NetMeeting to send files directly to a meeting attendee, have open chat sessions for brainstorming ideas about projects, diagram ideas on a Net whiteboard, and work with other attendees in real time in shared applications. For information on scheduling online meetings with NetMeeting, see Chapter 12.

NetMeetings are held on an *Internet Locator Server (ILS)*; each meeting participant must log on to the server, which maintains a list of users so that other participants can find out who is available for a meeting. On the Details page, you can enter two NetMeeting settings. Enter the ILS used for meetings with the contact in the Directory Server text box, and the contact's E-mail Alias (usually their e-mail address), as shown in Figure 6.11.

FIGURE 6.11: Enter the ILS and alias the contact uses for NetMeetings in the Details page.

Accessing Your Contact's Schedule on the Internet

Free/Busy refers to the times that a user is available (for meetings, including NetMeetings) or unavailable, according to their Outlook Calendar. With Outlook, you can publish your free/busy times in two different ways: in Exchange Server on your local area network, or over the Internet using the iCalendar standard. With Exchange Server, the only people who can see your free/busy times are colleagues who can log on to your network. By publishing your free/busy times on an Internet server, you make the schedule of free time available to people outside your network.

Before users can access your free/busy schedule, you need to tell them where the file that contains the schedule is located. The file can be stored on a server, FTP site, or Web page. If your contact has given you the URL for their free/busy schedule, enter it in the Internet Free/Busy text box on the Details page.

NOTE

For more information on Internet Free/Busy, see Chapter 12.

Viewing Journal Entries

After you've entered a contact, Outlook's Journal module helps you track time spent working with or for the contact. Using the Journal, you can automatically record e-mail messages to a contact or manually record information during a phone call or after a meeting with the contact. The Activities page of the Contact form, shown in Figure 6.12, displays both automatic and manual entries related to the contact in a table.

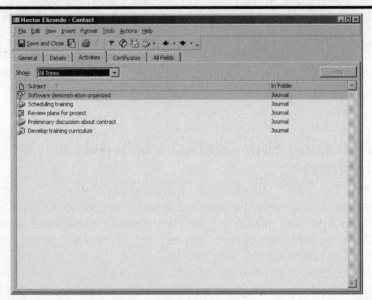

FIGURE 6.12: On the Activities page of the Contact form, you can see all the entries related to the contact.

The left column of the table has an icon for the type of entry, which is listed in the second column. The Start column is the start date of the entry; the Subject comes from the Subject line of the Activities form.

Previewing and Viewing Journal Entries

If you want to see more detail about each of the entries, right-click anywhere in the Journal window and select the AutoPreview option. The first three lines of the note in each entry will be displayed, as shown in Figure 6.13. It's easy to know if the preview shows all the text in the note, because the end of the note is marked <end>. If the note is longer than the preview, the preview ends with ellipses (...). To turn AutoPreview off, right-click and select AutoPreview again.

To see the entire entry, double-click the entry to open its Journal form.

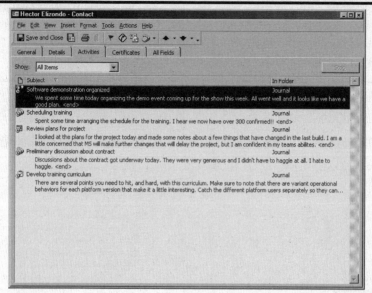

FIGURE 6.13: AutoPreview displays the first few lines of the note for the journal entry.

Sorting and Filtering Journal Entries

As with any Outlook view, you can click the heading of a column to sort the entries by the value in the column. For example, to arrange the entries by date and time, click the Start column heading. To filter the entries to show only phone calls, for example, click the drop-down arrow in the Show control to open the list of types of journal entries, as shown here.

Select a type of entry from the list, and Outlook will filter the list to only show the entry type you selected. In Figure 6.14, the journal entries have been filtered so that only Word files are displayed, and they're sorted with the most recent Word file opened first.

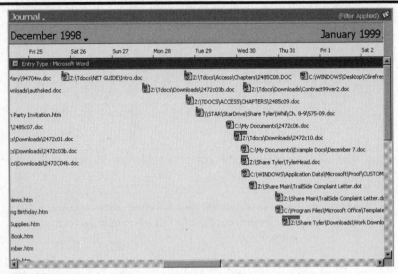

FIGURE 6.14: Use the Show drop-down list to filter entries by type.

Chapter 8 will give you all the details about manually and automatically recording journal entries.

Viewing Certificate Information

A *certificate*, or *Digital ID*, is used to verify the identity of the person who sent an e-mail message. Digital IDs have two parts: a *private key*, stored on the owner's computer, and a public key that others use to send messages to the owner and verify the authenticity of messages from the owner. The Certificates page of the Contact form shows Digital IDs that you've added for this contact. You can view the properties of the ID, and choose which ID should be used as the default for sending encrypted messages to this contact.

NOTE
In Chapter 12, you'll find out how to obtain a personal Digital ID.

Viewing All Fields

In the Contact form's All Fields page, you can display groups of fields in a table format. The default display is User Defined Fields in this page. Unless someone has customized your Outlook forms and added fields, there won't be any fields displayed—but don't assume that this page is totally useless. Choose Phone Number Fields from the Select From drop-down list, and you'll see all the phone numbers associated with the contact, as shown in Figure 6.15. If you print the form now, you'll get the contact's name and a list of their phone numbers.

Saving a Contact

When you've finished entering information in the Contact form, click the Save and Close button, or choose File ➤ Save and Close to save this contact's information and close the form.

 If you're going to be entering another Contact immediately, it's faster to click the Save and New button, or choose File ➤ Save and New to save the current Contact and open a blank form.

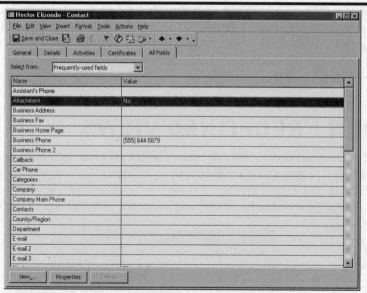

FIGURE 6.15:   The All Fields page displays the Frequently-Used Fields group of fields.

Adding a New Contact from the Same Company

Once you begin entering Contacts, you'll often have several contacts from the same organization. The contacts have the same business address and the same or similar e-mail addresses and business telephone numbers. Outlook lets you create a Contact based on an existing Contact, so you don't have to enter the business information again. When you've finished entering the first Contact, choose Actions ➤ New Contact from Same Company from the Outlook menu. The first Contact is saved, and the business information for the Contact is held over in the Contact form. Add the new Contact's personal information, and edit the business information as required.

If you've already closed the original Contact, right-click the Contact in the Contact List and choose New Contact from Same Company from the shortcut menu to create a new Contact at the selected Contact's company. When you've entered the last Contact, click Save and Close to close the Contacts form.

Deleting a Contact

To delete a Contact, select the Contact or open the Contact form. Then choose Edit ➤ Delete from the menu, or right-click and choose Delete from the shortcut menu, or press Ctrl+D. You will not be prompted to confirm the deletion. However, if you immediately notice that you've deleted a Contact erroneously, you can choose Undo Delete from the Edit menu to restore the Contact.

USING PREDEFINED VIEWS

The Contacts component has seven predefined views: Address Cards, Detailed Address Cards, Phone List, By Category, By Company, By Location, and By Follow Up Flag. To switch to another view, choose View ➤ Current View on the menu bar, and select the view you want to apply.

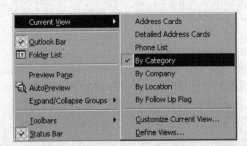

Card Views

The Address Card view, shown in Figure 6.16, displays basic information about the contact: File As name, mailing address, e-mail address, and telephone numbers. The Detailed Address Cards display additional data, including full name, job title, company name, and categories. Card views have a handy feature: an index on the right side that lets you quickly go to Contacts by the File By name. Clicking the *S*, for example, takes you to contacts whose File By name begins with the letter *S*. Many users choose either Address Cards or Detailed Address Cards as their default view for Contacts.

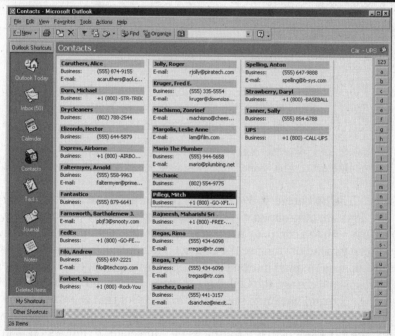

FIGURE 6.16:   The Address Card view is the default Contacts view for many users.

List Views

The remaining predefined views are list views: Phone List, By Company, By Category, By Location, and By Follow Up Flag. All the list views look and function like Excel worksheets. Field names appear at the top of the column, with records below in rows. You use the horizontal and vertical scroll bars to move up and down and pan side to side through the list. The Phone List, shown in Figure 6.17, shows Full Name, Company Name, File As Name, and telephone numbers for each contact.

	Full Name	Company	File As	Business Phone	Business Fax
	Click here to add a new C...				
		Ameritech Small ...	Ameritech Small Business Services	(800) 555-8959	
	Glenn Barton	Mission Health Care	Barton, Glenn	(810) 555-5659	
	Pamela Barton	Johnson' Electro...	Barton, Pamela	(508) 555-5656	
	Karla Browning	TRIAD Consultin...	Browning, Karla		(810) 555-2284
	Peggy Cartoni	Friend	Cartoni, Peggy	(810) 555-7845	
	Margaret Clinton	Carman-Ainswort...	Clinton, Margaret	(810) 555-8565	
	Amy Courter	Valassis Communi...	Courter, Amy	(800) 555-8959	(313) 555-8956
	Guy Courter	Flint Permanent ...	Courter, Guy	(810) 555-8959	
	Tom Crawford	Tom's Diner	Crawford, Tom	(800) 555-8956	(313) 555-8962
	Mary Rose Evans	PTR	Evans, Mary Rose	(248) 555-9856	
	Kent Fields	Sybex Books	Fields, Kent	(800) 555-5555	(510) 555-5555
	Jacklyn Flocker	Palatine Public S...	Flocker, Jacklyn	(517) 555-4141	
	Cindy Graystone	Church	Graystone, Cindy		
	Ingrid Guntner	Church	Guntner, Ingrid		
	Terrel F. Hatcher	Spring Valley Co...	Hatcher, Terrel F.	(616) 555-4151	(616) 555-4675
	David T. Holstein	Mission Communi...	Holstein, David T.	(616) 555-4545	(616) 555-1214
	Kimberly Mastersons	Mission Health Sy...	Mastersons, Kimberly	(549) 555-8959	(549) 555-5956
	Rosemary Walker		Walker, Rosemary		
	Gloria Wright	Genesee Interme...	Wright, Gloria	(810) 555-4545	(810) 555-7878

FIGURE 6.17: The Phone List shows contacts with their telephone numbers.

The By Category, By Company, By Location, and By Follow Up Flag views are all grouped views. When you open the By Company view, a dark bar with the company name separates contacts from each company. You can expand or collapse the Contact detail for each company. Click the Collapse (minus) button on the company bar to hide the company's contacts and change the Collapse button to an Expand (plus) button. Click the Expand button to see all the Contacts for that company. If you work in a field where employees begin mailing out resumes the second week on the job, Outlook has a feature you'll appreciate. To move a Contact from one company to another, select the Contact and drag it into the new company, as shown in Figure 6.18.

NOTE

You can create your own views, adding and deleting fields and setting up custom grouping.

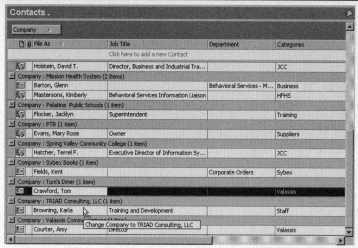

FIGURE 6.18:   In the By Company view, you can "transfer" employees from one company to another.

Locating a Contact

[Find] The easiest way to search through a long list of contacts is by using Find, which can help you quickly locate items in any view. Click the Find button on the Standard toolbar to open the Find pane at the top of the list, as shown in Figure 6.19. If you're looking for a contact, enter all or part of their name, company name, or address in the Look For text box. To search all the fields in the contact, including the Comments field, leave Search All Text in the Contact check box enabled. Disabling the check box limits the search to the fields displayed at the left and speeds up the search.

[Find Now] Click the Find Now button to find all the contacts that include the text you entered. Figure 6.20 shows the results obtained when searching for "Amy." When you find the contact you're looking for, just double-click the contact to open the Contact form.

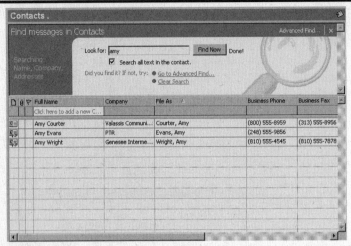

FIGURE 6.19:   The Find pane opens at the top of the Contact list.

Contacts .

Find messages in Contacts   Advanced Find... | x

Look for: amy   [Find Now] Done!
☑ Search all text in the contact.
Searching:
Name, Company,   Did you find it? If not, try: ● Go to Advanced Find...
Addresses   ● Clear Search

			Full Name	Company	File As		Business Phone	Business Fax	
			Click here to add a new C...						
			Amy Courter	Valassis Communi...	Courter, Amy		(800) 555-8959	(313) 555-8956	
			Amy Evans	PTR	Evans, Amy		(248) 555-9856		
			Amy Wright	Genesee Interme...	Wright, Amy		(810) 555-4545	(810) 555-7878	

FIGURE 6.20:   Use Find to locate a contact based on their name, address, or text anywhere in the Contact.

If you can't find the contact you're looking for in the Find pane, or if you're looking for text in specific fields or based on criteria other than text, consider using Advanced Find.

Advanced Find...   Click the Advanced Find button at the top of the Find pane to open the Advanced Find dialog box. On the Contact page of the dialog box, you can select the type of item, location, and fields to be searched. Open the topmost In drop-down list and select Name Fields Only; then click Find Now. Even if you just remember the person's first name or a part of their last name, Outlook will find every occurrence of those letters in the Name fields, without searching other fields.

Using the Time options, you can search for Contacts that were created or modified within a particular time frame. For example, you can find Contacts you created today or modified in the last week. In Figure 6.21, we're using Advanced Find to locate contacts modified in the last seven days with *Oak* in the company name.

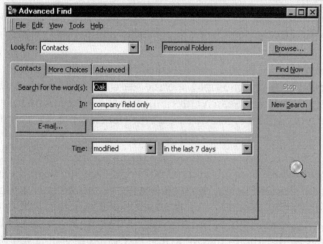

FIGURE 6.21:   Advanced Find lets you search for Contacts based on when they were created or modified.

Flip to the More Choices page by clicking its tab, and you can find Contacts by categories. Click the Categories button to open the Categories dialog box. Select the categories you want to search for. If you choose more than one category, Outlook treats the selection as a union and finds Contacts assigned to any of the categories you selected. Click OK to close the Categories dialog box, and then click Find Now to find the contacts who are assigned to the categories you chose. Figure 6.22 shows a search for Contacts with the Business or Ideas categories.

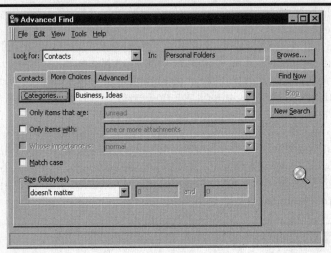

FIGURE 6.22: Use the More Choices page to search for contacts by category.

On the Advanced page of the Advanced Find dialog box, shown in Figure 6.23, you can enter multiple, specific search criteria based on the values in fields. To enter a search criterion, click the Field button to open a menu of Outlook field types. Choose a type (for example, All Contact Fields), and then select the field from the menu.

From the Condition text box, choose the appropriate operator. The operators in the list depend on the type of data that will be in the field you selected. For text fields, you'll choose between Contains, Is, Doesn't Contain, Is Empty, and Is Not Empty. Date fields have the same operators as the Time controls in the Contacts page: Anytime, Today, In the Last Seven Days, and so on. In the Value text box, enter the value you're looking for with Contains or Is, or not looking for if you use the Doesn't Contain operator. You don't have to enter a value for Is Empty or Is Not Empty. When you're finished building the criterion, click the Add to List button to add it to the Find Items list. To add another criterion, build it, and then add it to the list. When you've entered all the advanced criteria you need to conduct your search, click Find Now to find the contacts that match all the criteria you entered. In Figure 6.23, we're creating criteria to search for contacts with Vice President in their job title.

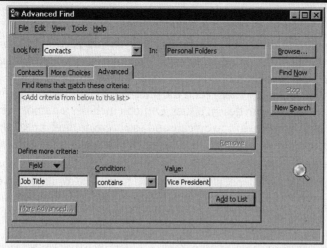

FIGURE 6.23:   Use the Advanced page to find contacts based on one or more specific fields.

New Search   You can enter search criteria on more than one Find page and find, for example, Contacts created in the last seven days in the Business category. If you're finished with one search and want to search for other Contacts, click the New Search button to clear the criteria you entered from all three pages of the dialog box.

When you're finished with Advanced Find, choose File ≻ Close or click the close button on the dialog box title bar to close Advanced Find and return to Contacts. To close the Find pane, click the close button at the top of the pane or switch to another view.

Sorting Contacts

Sorting is easy in any list view. To sort by a field in ascending order, click the heading at the top of the field. An upward pointing arrow is displayed in the field heading to remind you that it is sorted in ascending order.

Click the heading again, and you sort the list in descending order. When the list is sorted in descending order, the heading arrow for the sort-by column points down.

PRINTING CONTACTS

If you've ever been asked to create an employee directory for your organization, you know the potential pitfalls. Someone (probably you) has to enter data, choose a layout for the directory, format all the data, add headings. By the time you actually send the directory to your printer, you've invested a lot of time in design issues. Outlook includes a number of printing options that will help you quickly and easily create directories, phone lists, and other print resources that formerly took hours or days to create.

When you choose File ➤ Page Setup from the Outlook menu bar, you are presented with a list of styles to choose from. The available styles are dependent on the current view, so before you print, select the view that most closely resembles the printed output you want. For a simple employee telephone list, choose one of the list views. For complete names and addresses, choose a card view. Table 6.2 identifies the Contact views and their corresponding print styles.

TABLE 6.2: Page Setup Styles

STYLE	VIEW	DEFAULT PRINTED OUTPUT
Table	table	The view as it appears on the screen
Memo	table	Data for the selected contact(s), printed in portrait view, with your name at the top of each entry
Phone Directory	table	Two-column listing of names and phone numbers, with a heading for each letter of the alphabet (very slick)
Card	card	A two-column listing of names and contact information
Small Booklet	card	A multiple section listing of names and contact information prepared for two-sided printing
Medium Booklet	card	A two-column listing of names and contact information prepared for two-sided printing

Before you print, it's a good idea to look at each of the styles. Choose File ➤ Page Setup and select the style from the menu.

If you select the medium or small booklet style and your printer prints one-sided output, Outlook will ask if you wish to continue. Click OK to open the Page Setup dialog box, shown in Figure 6.24. The dialog box has three pages: Format, Paper, and Header/Footer.

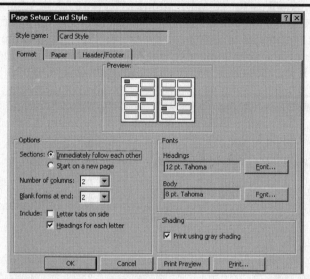

FIGURE 6.24: Use the Page Setup dialog box to set printing options for the style you selected.

In the Format page, choose the format options you would like to apply to the style:

Sections   To have each letter of the alphabet begin on a new page, choose Start on a New Page.

Number of Columns   As you increase the number of columns, Outlook decreases the font size.

Blank Forms at End   This option allows users to add new entries in the correct section.

Letter Tabs on Side   This check box will generate an index, like the index used in Address Card view, with the section's letters highlighted.

Headings for Each Letter   This feature gives you a highlighted letter at the beginning of each alphabetic section.

Fonts   These lists offer you choices of fonts for the letter headings and body.

Print Using Gray Shading   This check box enables or disables gray shading in the letter tabs, letter headings, and contact names.

After you make a change, you can click the Print Preview button to see how the change affects your printed output. In Figure 6.25, we're previewing a booklet with letter tabs on the side and headings for each letter. Click anywhere in the preview to zoom in on the detail; click again to zoom out. To close Print Preview and return to the Page Setup dialog box, choose Page Setup. If you click Close, you close both Print Preview *and* Page Setup.

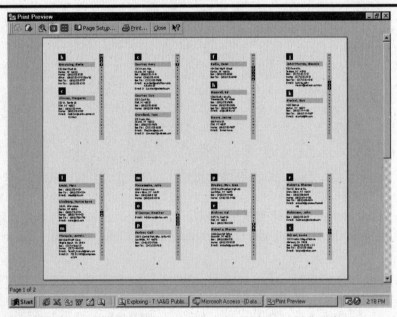

FIGURE 6.25:   Use Print Preview to see how your format change affects the printed document.

On the Paper page of the Page Setup dialog box (see Figure 6.26), choose the settings that describe the dimensions of the paper you're going to use.

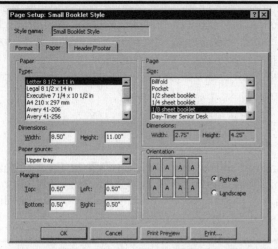

FIGURE 6.26: On the Paper page of the Print Setup dialog box, specify the size and location of the paper and size of the booklet.

On the Header/Footer page, shown in Figure 6.27, you can create a header and footer that contain text and document information. Headers and footers appear on each page of the finished product. If you're creating a ¼ page booklet, a header will appear four times on the printed sheet, so it will be at the top of each page after it is folded.

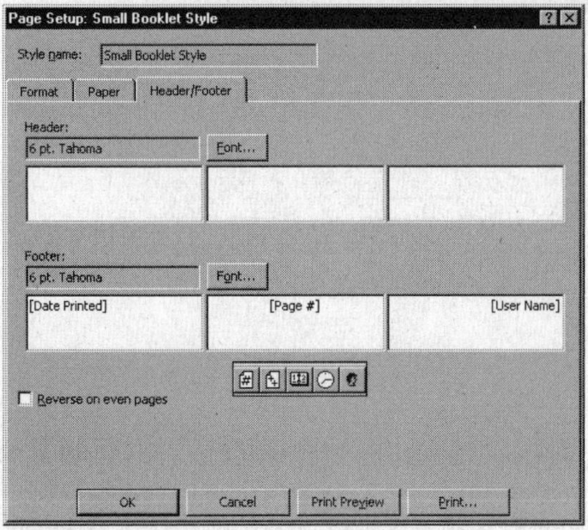

FIGURE 6.27: Create custom headers and footers in the Header/Footer page.

The header and footer each have a left-aligned, centered, and right-aligned section. To include text in the header or footer, just click in the appropriate section and begin typing. Use the five buttons on the toolbar below the header and footer sections to include the page number, total number of pages, date printed, time printed, or username in the header or footer.

When you've finished setting print options, click the Print button to open the Print dialog box, shown in Figure 6.28. Select a printer from the Name list, the range of pages to print, and the number of copies. Click the OK button to send the job to the printer.

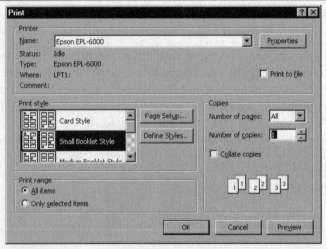

FIGURE 6.28: Change settings in the Print dialog box to specify the number of copies, range, and number of pages to print.

TIP

If you want to print a booklet with back to front pages and you have a one-sided printer, choose Odd in the Number of Pages drop-down list, and print all the odd-numbered pages first. Turn the sheets over and reinsert them into the printer. Choose Even to print the rest of the pages. Outlook will order the pages so they can be folded into a booklet when they're all printed.

The printing process is the same in all the Outlook components. Begin by selecting a view that supports the output you want. Preview the output in Print Preview. Change views, if necessary, and then adjust the Page Setup options to further define the final output. Finally, send the job to the printer, and think about how easy this was.

After you've entered your contacts into Outlook, and you can locate the data you need and print your Contact information successfully, you're ready to use Outlook's communication features to stay in touch.

WHAT'S NEXT?

This chapter showed how to enter contact information, including categories and other details, to make the most of the Contacts feature. It also described how this data can be used to quickly create a printed directory. An overview of the components of e-mail and Web addresses was also provided. In the next chapter, you'll learn how to maximize the Tasks feature.

Chapter 7

MANAGING TASKS IN OUTLOOK

Making a list of things you have to do is a time-honored tradition. Many people are great list makers, and some even accomplish the tasks on their lists. With the power of Outlook behind you, you now have the opportunity to become one of those people. However, Outlook's Task component is not just a place to type your to-do list. With Tasks you can actually manage your responsibilities by tracking when they are due, organizing related tasks, reminding yourself of recurring tasks, scheduling time to complete them, and evaluating the progress you are making. Making lists no longer becomes a futile attempt at organization with Outlook's Tasks, it's a real step toward task completion.

Adapted from *Mastering™ Microsoft® Outlook™ 2000*
by Gini Courter and Annette Marquis
ISBN 0-7821-2472-0   787 pages $34.99

CREATING A TASK

To create a task, you simply type the name of the task and its due date. You can also enter more detailed information about the task, taking full advantage of the power that Outlook has to offer.

To enter a task, click the Tasks icon on the Outlook bar. The default view in Tasks is the Simple List view, shown in Figure 7.1. The Simple List view has four columns:

Icon   An icon that changes if a task is assigned to someone else or was assigned by someone else

Complete   A check box indicating whether the task has been completed

Subject   A descriptive name for the task

Due Date   The date on which you expect or need to complete the task

You can enter a task directly into the Information Viewer by clicking in the Click Here to Add a New Task text box. The row turns blue, and the box that is active for editing is white. Type a subject in the Subject field. It's helpful if you make the subject descriptive but not too long less than 30 characters is best so the column doesn't have to be too wide to read it all.

NOTE

You must be in Simple List or Detailed List view to have the Click Here to Add a New Task text box. If you prefer to use another view, then create a new task by choosing Task from the New button.

Press Tab to move to the Due Date field (Shift+Tab will move you back to Subject); the text box will turn white. Because Outlook recognizes natural-language dates using its AutoDate feature, you have multiple options for entering dates in this field. Just about anything you type into the field that remotely resembles a date will be converted into a standard date format (Wed 8/18/99). You could type **8-18-99**; **aug 18**; **three weeks from now; a week from today; tomorrow; one month from next wed**. All are legitimate dates in Outlook (of course, they wouldn't all return the same date). Go ahead and try it it's fun to see what AutoDate's limits are.

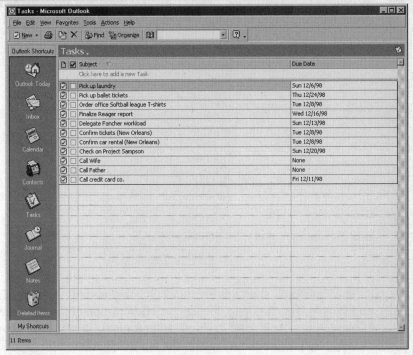

FIGURE 7.1: The Simple List view of Tasks

If your objective is just to get the task recorded and then come back to it later to add information, you're finished with this task. Click anywhere in the task list to move the task into the list. Where the task appears in the list depends on how the list is currently sorted. You can now enter another task. This is the quickest and easiest way to enter tasks.

Entering Details about a Task

To take advantage of the powerful features built into Outlook, you need to add more information about the task. The most direct way to do this is to enter a Task form. You can open the form for any existing task by double-clicking the task in the Information Viewer. To open a blank Task form, click the New button on the Standard toolbar (if Tasks is the active module in the Information Viewer); or click the down arrow to the right of the New button to open the New menu, and choose Task from the list.

The Task form, shown in Figure 7.2, is composed of two pages: Task and Details. The Task page focuses on a description of the task (see "Completing a Task" later in this chapter for more information about the Details page). Enter the subject in the Subject text box, and press Tab to move to the Due Date field. Click the down arrow to choose a date from the calendar, or enter a date in the text box. If the task is not scheduled to start right away, enter a Start Date to indicate when it should be started.

Setting Reminders

Click the Reminder check box to activate a reminder that will be displayed at a specified date and time.

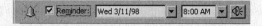

The Time drop-down list has a choice for every half hour around the clock, so be careful to select the correct A.M. or P.M. time. There's nothing like setting a reminder for twelve hours after something was supposed to be done! You can also type an entry in this box if you need a reminder at the quarter hour.

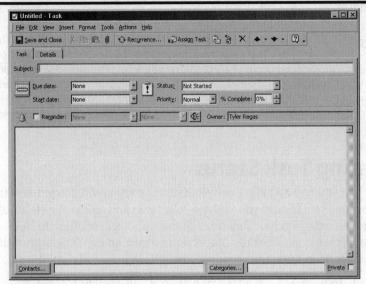

FIGURE 7.2:   The Task form

 Reminders come with a sound by default. You have the option of disabling the sound or changing the sound file it plays. Click the speaker icon to access the Reminder Sound options.

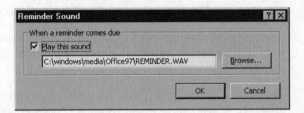

Clear the Play This Sound check box if you'd prefer your reminders appeared on your screen silently. If you would like to hear a sound but would prefer a different sound file, click the Browse button to locate the file you would like to use. Double-click the filename, and it will appear in the Play This Sound text box.

TIP

If you change the sound file within a task, it will only be in effect for that spe-cific reminder. To change the default sound file for Reminders, go to Sounds in the Windows Control Panel and change the sound assigned to Microsoft Office Reminders. Sound files, or wave files, are designated by a .wav extension. If you would like to record your own reminder message or sound that plays when it is time to do a task, you can do so using the Windows Sound Recorder.

Updating Task Status

When you enter a task, Outlook assumes you haven't started working on the task yet. To help you manage your tasks and assess the status of cer-tain projects, you have four other Status options in addition to Not Started available to you. Click the Status down arrow on the Task page of the Task form to open the list of choices:

In progress   If a task is in progress, you might also want to indicate the percentage that is complete in the % Complete text box. Use the spin box to change the percentage, or type the actual percentage directly in the box.

Completed   In addition to marking a task complete, you might also want to complete some additional fields on the Details page. See "Completing a Task" later in this chapter.

Waiting on someone else   It's helpful to set a reminder to yourself to call this person if you don't hear from them in a rea-sonable amount of time.

Deferred   You may want to change the start and end dates so this task doesn't show up on your list of active tasks.

Setting Priorities

By setting a priority level for a task, you can be sure that your most impor-tant tasks receive most of your attention. The default priority is set at Normal. You have additional options of High and Low. High priority items are designated by a red exclamation point in the Information Viewer, and Low priority items are designated by a blue downward-pointing arrow, as shown in Figure 7.3.

Owning a Task

The Task Owner is the person who creates the task, or the person to whom the task is currently assigned. When you create a task, you are the owner by default. To give up ownership, however, all you have to do is assign the task to someone else. As soon as that person accepts the task, they officially become the new owner.

Part i

☐ ☑ !	Subject	Due Date
		None
☑ ☐	Call Peggy	Fri 3/6/98
☑ ☐ !	Install MS Exchange Server	Mon 3/9/98
☑ ☐ !	Abby Referral letters and report changes	Tue 3/10/98
☑ ☐ !	Distribute paychecks	Tue 3/10/98
☑ ☐	Prepare month-end report	Thu 3/12/98
☑ ☐	Order bar code guns	Fri 3/13/98
☑ ☐ ↓	Create Educational Promotional Letter	Fri 3/20/98
☑ ☐	Survey DB Reports	Fri 3/27/98
☑ ☐	Order Company Polo Shirts	Thu 4/2/98
☑ ☐	EDD - English Wizard Dictionary	Fri 4/3/98
☑ ☐ !	Submit quarterly sales tax report	Fri 4/3/98
☑ ☐	Make Promotional Bookmarks	Fri 4/17/98
☑ ☐ ↓	Develop a "While We Were Here" form	Fri 4/17/98
☑ ☐ !	Database Natural language dictionary for O & Sat	Sun 5/10/98

FIGURE 7.3: Viewing the Priority field in the Information Viewer

Assigning Categories to Manage a Project

Categories are user-defined values that help to organize your data throughout Outlook. Chapter 6 provides a thorough discussion of how to create new categories and delete undesired categories. Despite the fact that you have the same list of categories available to you, categories serve a slightly different purpose in Tasks than they do in Contacts or the other Outlook modules.

Categories play a vital role in tracking tasks related to a single project. When you create a task, the more specific you can be, the easier it is to complete the task. For example, if the Task you enter is *Complete database for Goodrich*, you will have a difficult time demonstrating progress toward your goal. When is the database complete after the application is functioning or after the product is installed? Maybe it's not complete until employees are trained and using the product successfully.

It would be a lot more helpful to break down the various steps of the project into its logical components. In this case, you could list *Complete data analysis*, *Complete database structural design*, *Solicit feedback from client*, and so on as separate tasks in Outlook. Each could have its own description and due date. Status, priority, and % complete could also be assigned to each task.

Categories could then pull all these individual tasks together into one project. Just click the Categories button and assign each one to the same category from the Categories dialog box. (You can't do it as a group, so you have to open each task individually and make the assignment.) When you return to the Information Viewer, you can sort by category, group all the tasks in the same category together, or even filter out just those tasks related to a single category. Figure 7.4 is an example of a task list grouped by category (see "Viewing Tasks" later in this chapter).

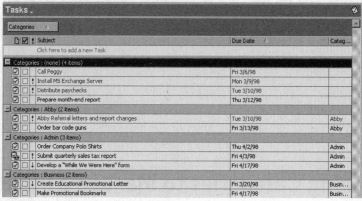

FIGURE 7.4:   Task list grouped by category

Making a Task Private

If your Outlook folders are shared on a network, there may be times when you don't want others to see information about a task. Click the Private button on the right-hand corner of the Task form to keep this task in your personal Outlook folders. The task will be hidden, and other users will not be able to view it.

SETTING UP RECURRING TASKS

A *recurring task* is a task that you must complete on a regular basis such as a monthly report, a weekly agenda, or a quarterly tax submission. Anything that you have to do periodically qualifies. In Outlook you can enter the task once, and then set a pattern for it to recur on your task list.

Outlook doesn't care if you've completed this month's report; when the time comes for next month's, it will add another copy of the task with a new due date to your list.

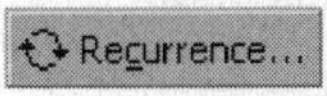

To set up a recurring task, enter the task as you would any other task that needs completion. When you have the data entered for the first occurrence of the task, click the Recurrence button on the Standard toolbar within the Task form. This opens the Task Recurrence dialog box, shown in Figure 7.5.

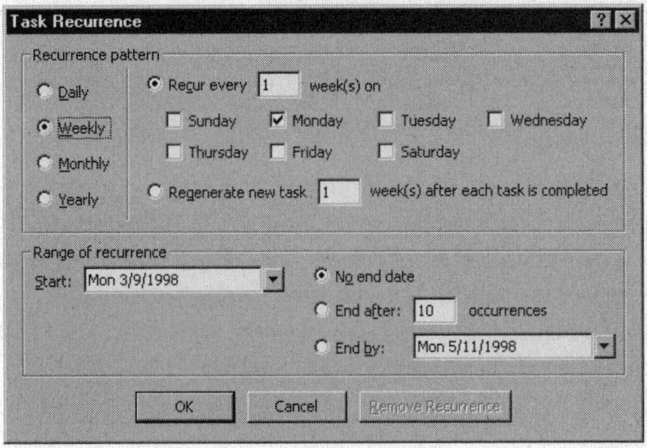

Part i

FIGURE 7.5: Task Recurrence dialog box

Here you can set the Recurrence Pattern and the Range of Recurrence. To set the Recurrence Pattern, indicate whether the task needs to be accomplished Daily, Weekly, Monthly, or Yearly. If the task needs to be completed every three days, choose Daily; every two months, choose Monthly; and so on. Each of the four options gives you different choices for defining the actual pattern. For each pattern, you are then asked to indicate how many days/weeks/months/years you want Outlook to wait after a task is marked as complete before it generates a new task.

Daily   Choose between Every *N* Days or Every Weekday.

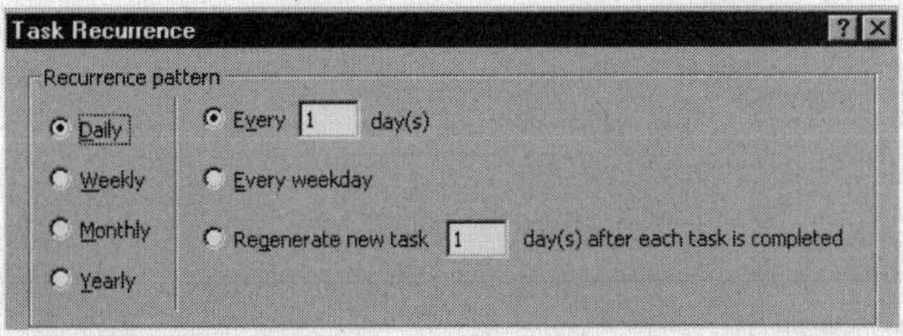

Weekly Indicate how often the task should occur: every week (1), every other week (2), every third week (3), and so on. This is the best option if the task needs to be completed every six weeks or every eight weeks (because some months have more than four weeks). Then mark on which day of the week the task needs to be accomplished.

Monthly Choose between specifying which date of each *N* month(s) or indicating the first, second, third, fourth, or last day of every *N* month(s); for example, the last Friday of every month or the third Thursday of every second month. You could also indicate the first weekday or the last weekend day of the month.

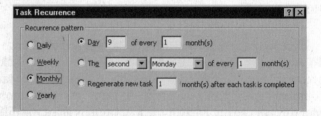

Yearly Indicate a specific date in a specific month (every May 5), or mark the first, second, third, fourth, or last day of a specific month (the first Friday in May).

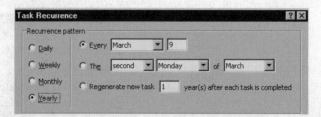

Sometimes you have to be creative to figure out how often a task really occurs. For example, if a task occurs two times a year on February 28 and August 31, do you use Monthly or Yearly? Because these dates are six months apart, you could use Monthly and indicate the last day of every six months (as long as the Start date was set to one of the two dates).

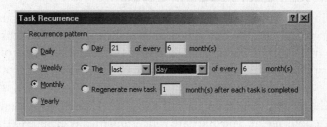

However, if this task is not so evenly spaced May 31 and August 31, for example you probably will have to enter two tasks: one for the May date every year, and one for the August date every year.

Defining the Range of Recurrence

The Range of Recurrence refers to when the first task in the series is due and how long the task will continue.

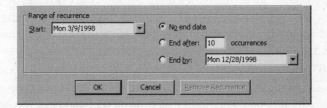

You have your choice of:

No End Date   The task will continue into eternity (or until you tell it to stop).

End after *N* Occurrences   You only need to complete the task a specific number of times, and then you are finished with it.

End By   You only have to do this task until a certain date, and then you are free.

Once you have set the Range of Recurrence, click OK to return to the Task form. Click Save and Close to save the task and return to the Information Viewer.

Editing Task Recurrence

To make changes to the recurrence pattern or range that you set, open the task and click the Recurrence Pattern button. Make your changes and then click Save and Close again. You may also edit the Subject of the task, but any changes you make will be made only to future occurrences of the task.

If you want to skip the next occurrence of a task but not interfere with the recurrence pattern, open the task and choose Skip Occurrence from the Actions menu. The due date will automatically change to the next date the task is due.

To delete the recurrence pattern without deleting the task, open the task, click the Recurrence button, and click the Remove Recurrence button on the bottom of the Task Recurrence dialog box. Close the Task Recurrence dialog box and Save and Close the task. The task will still be on your list, but it will be there for one time only.

ASSIGNING A TASK TO A CONTACT

If you work as a member of a team, or if you have people reporting to you, there are times when you may want to create a task for someone else to do. As long as the other person is running Outlook and you both have access to e-mail, you can assign tasks to each other.

To assign a task to someone else, create the task as you normally would, add task Recurrence, if appropriate, and click the Assign Task button on the Standard toolbar of the Task form. This opens a message form with the task included, as shown in Figure 7.6.

WARNING

When sending a task to another person through Internet e-mail, make sure the Properties for that person's e-mail address in Contacts is set to Always Send to This Recipient in Microsoft Outlook Rich-Text Format. This way, the recipient will be able to transfer the task directly into their task list using copy and paste. (See Chapter 6 for more information about Microsoft Outlook Rich Text format and address properties.)

Enter the person's e-mail address, or click the To button and choose the name from your address lists. You have two options related to this assignment:

Keep an Updated Copy of This Task on My Task List   Even though you have assigned the task to someone else, you may still want to know how the task is going. Every time the new owner of the task revises the task in any way, a message is sent to you indicating that the task was updated and the task is revised in your task list. This option is not available if the task is recurring.

Send Me a Status Report When This Task Is Complete   When the new owner marks the task as complete, you receive a message automatically informing you that the task is complete, and it is marked as complete on your task list.

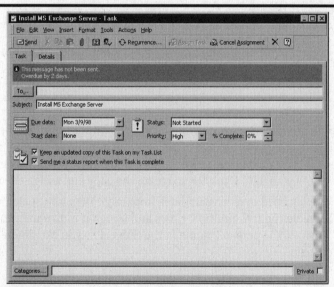

FIGURE 7.6:   Assigning a task to someone else

NOTE

Although you can assign a task to anyone who runs Outlook, if the person is not on your network, you will not receive automatic updates when that person makes revisions to the task.

If you would like to send a message along with the task assignment, enter the text in the message box. Click Send to transfer the message to your Outbox.

Assigning a Task to More than One Person

It's possible to assign the same task to more than one person, but if you do, you cannot keep an updated copy of the task in your task list. To assign the task to an additional person, open the task, click the Details tab, and click the Create Unassigned Copy button.

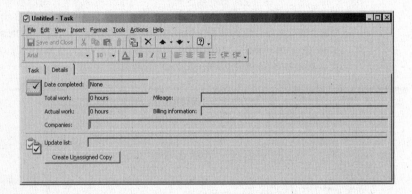

You will be warned that you will become the owner again (the person you originally assigned the task to took over ownership of the task when they accepted it) and will no longer receive updates (unless you want to write them to yourself). Click OK to create the copy and assign the task.

If you really need to receive updates from more than one person about the task, create the task multiple times and assign it individually to each person. Include the person's name in the Subject so you can differentiate the three tasks.

Receiving a Task Assignment

When someone sends you a task, you will receive an e-mail message labeled Task Request.

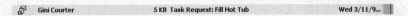

When you open the task, you can choose to accept the task or decline the task by clicking the appropriate button on the message form.

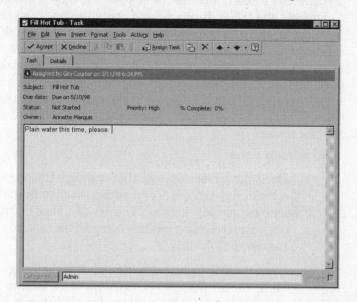

If you click Accept, the task is automatically added to your task list, and you become the owner of the task. If you click Decline, the person who sent you the task retains ownership. Either way, the person who originated the task is sent a message indicating your response. When you click Send, you are given the option of editing the response before sending it, or sending it without editing. If you want to explain why you're declining your boss's request, click Edit the Response Before Sending and enter your explanation in the message.

Even after you accept a task, you can change your mind and decline the task. Just open the task and choose Decline Task from the Actions menu.

Passing the Task Along

If you receive a task from someone, it's possible for you to accept the task assignment and then turn around and assign the task to someone else (commonly referred to as passing the buck). When you accept the task, you become the owner of the task, and changes and updates you make are returned to the task's originator. When you reassign a task to someone else, that person becomes the owner and future updates are returned to you. In order to keep the task's originator up-to-date, you will have to generate updated status reports when an update is returned to you from the new owner.

To reassign a task:

1. Open the e-mail message that contains the original task request, and click the Accept button to accept the task (if you have not already done so). This sends a Task Update to the originator indicating you have accepted the task. You are now the owner of the task.

2. Open the task in your task list and click the Assign button. Make sure the Keep an Updated Copy of the Task on My Task List and the Send Me a Status Report When the Task Is Complete options are both checked so you won't lose track of the task.

3. Enter the e-mail address of the person you want to assign the task to, and click Send to send the Task Request to them. They are now the temporary owner of the task. When they accept the task, they become the task's owner.

4. When you receive a task update from the new owner, click Actions ➤ Send Status Report from the Standard toolbar of the open task. Type in (or copy and paste) your status report. Enter the e-mail address of the task's originator, and click Send to send an update to them.

By following this process, you keep the task's originator informed, and you have someone else doing the work not bad work, if you can get it!

VIEWING TASKS

One way to stay on top of what you have to do is to review your tasks from different perspectives. The default view for tasks in the Information

Viewer is the Simple List (shown earlier in Figure 7.1). This view shows the Subject and Due Date of both active and completed tasks. It's quite simple to switch to another view that shows only active tasks or that organizes the tasks in some other meaningful way. To change to another view, click View ➤ Current View. This opens the list of available views displayed in Figure 7.7.

FIGURE 7.7: Available views in Tasks

The Detailed List and the Active Tasks are essentially the same view, except the Detailed List includes completed tasks while the Active Tasks includes only those tasks yet to be completed. The Detailed List is shown in Figure 7.8.

			Subject	Status	Due Date	% Complete	Categories	
			Click here to add a new Task					
☑			Make Promotional Bookmarks	Not Started	Fri 4/17/98	0%	Business	
☑	!		Abby Referral letters and report changes	In Progress	Tue 3/10/98	0%	Abby	
☑			Order bar code guns	Not Started	Fri 3/13/98	0%	Abby	
☑	↓		Develop a "While We Were Here" form	Not Started	Fri 4/17/98	0%	Admin	
☑			EDD - English Wizard Dictionary	In Progress	Fri 4/3/98	5%	JCC	
☑			Survey DB Reports	Not Started	Fri 3/27/98	0%	JCC	
☑			Order Company Polo Shirts	Not Started	Thu 4/2/98	0%	Admin	
☑	↓	0	Create Educational Promotional Letter	Completed	Fri 3/20/98	100%	Business	
☑	!		Submit quarterly sales tax report	Not Started	Fri 4/3/98	0%	Admin	
☑	!		Database Natural language dictionary for O & Sat	Not Started	Sun 5/10/98	0%	HFHS	
☑			Call Peggy	Not Started	Fri 3/6/98	0%		
☑	!		Distribute paychecks	Not Started	Tue 3/10/98	0%		
☑	!		Install MS Exchange Server	Not Started	Mon 3/9/98	0%		
☑			Prepare month-end report	Completed	Thu 3/12/98	100%		

FIGURE 7.8: Detailed List view

The Next Seven Days view displays the same fields as the Detailed List and Active Tasks views, but it filters the view to only show those tasks with Due Dates within the next seven calendar days.

When a task passes its Due Date, Outlook turns the task red to distinguish it from current tasks. You can then choose Overdue Tasks from the Current View menu to see only those tasks that require immediate attention.

The next three views allow you to examine your tasks by Category, by Assignment, and by Person Responsible. These views are especially helpful in managing the work on a particular project or managing the workloads of personnel, because they group tasks together that have something in common (see Figure 7.4 earlier in this chapter for an example of Tasks grouped by Category).

The final view, Task Timeline view, is designed to let you examine your tasks based on when they are due in relation to each other. Tasks are spread out along the timeline grouped together by due dates. This view, shown in Figure 7.9, can be used to plan your activities for particular days based on the tasks you have to accomplish.

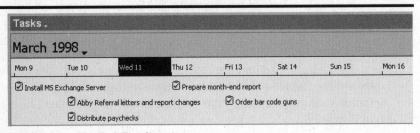

FIGURE 7.9: The Task Timeline view

CREATING TASKS FROM OTHER OUTLOOK ITEMS

Outlook's power comes from the incredible ease with which all of the components work together to make your life easier. How many times have you received an e-mail message asking you to do something? Unless you print the message and put it in the stack of papers on your desk and hope you run across it before it needs to get done, you may find yourself forgetting it was even asked of you. Outlook changes all that. The next time you receive an e-mail message asking you to do something, all you have to do is drag the message onto the Task icon on the Outlook bar.

Outlook will automatically open a Task form for you with the information already in it, including the actual contents of the e-mail message, as shown in Figure 7.10.

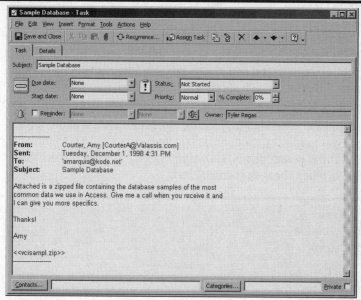

FIGURE 7.10: A Task form opens automatically from an e-mail message.

All you have to do is add Due Dates, assign the task to a category, and add any other details you want and your reminder is all set. (You will, however, have to actually do the task yourself.)

You can use this trick to create Outlook tasks with any other Outlook item, such as a Journal entry, a Calendar item, or a Note.

COMPLETING A TASK

When you've finally completed a task, there is nothing more satisfying than checking it off your list. Outlook wouldn't want you to miss out on this pleasure, so it has incorporated a check box into the Information Viewer for most of the standard views. To mark a task complete, just click the check box, as shown in Figure 7.11.

☑ ☐	Make Promotional Bookmarks	Fri 4/17/98
☑ ☐	Develop a "While We Were Here" form	Fri 4/17/98
☑ ☑	Submit quarterly sales tax report	Fri 4/3/98
	EDD - English Wizard Dictionary	Fri 4/3/98

FIGURE 7.11: Completing a task

The task is crossed off the list. If the view you are using does not include completed items, the item is actually removed from the list altogether. Of course, you can always see it by switching to a view such as Simple List view, which shows all Tasks. If you mistakenly check off a task as complete, just switch to Simple List view and clear the check box.

If you are interested in tracking more information about a completed task, you may want to open the task and click the Details tab of the Tasks form. It has several fields, shown in Figure 7.12, that are designed to be filled in when the task is completed.

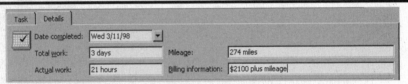

FIGURE 7.12: Tracking additional information about a completed task

On this page you can record the date the task was completed, the planned number of hours (Outlook will translate to days), the actual number of hours, and other billing information you may want to track, such as the number of miles traveled on the job. If you have to submit an expense or billing statement at the end of the month, this is a great way to track the information you need.

WHAT'S NEXT?

You know what you have to do and you make a to-do list, but this list can't complete the task for you. This chapter presented a realistic way to use Tasks to not only organize tasks but to actually complete them. Next, you will learn all about creating and relating Journal entries.

Chapter 8

USING THE JOURNAL AND NOTES

Let's face it: record keeping is not something that most people do well. Outlook 2000 may just change all that. Outlook has the ability to track items that you enter and also to record certain items automatically. Once you start using the Journal, it won't take long to discover the incredible power that comes with documenting your conversations, phone calls, and other interactions. All it takes is being able to go back and pull up your comments about one critical conversation to be hooked on what the Journal can do for you. And Notes gives you a way to organize every little tidbit of information that you currently have on those scraps of paper scattered all over your desk. With Journal and Notes together, you never knew you could be so organized.

Adapted from *Mastering™ Microsoft® Outlook™ 2000* by Gini Courter and Annette Marquis

ISBN 0-7821-2472-0   787 pages $34.99

UNDERSTANDING THE JOURNAL

To use the Journal effectively, it's helpful to have an understanding of what the Journal is designed to do. While Tasks and Calendar are intended to help you plan your upcoming activities, the Journal's purpose is to record the work you've done. You can make notes about telephone conversations, record your impressions after a meeting, organize e-mail communications to and from a contact, and track how long you spent developing an Excel spreadsheet. You can use the Journal to generate reports, to confirm conversations with your clients, and to keep a running history of your daily activities. If you need to prove to your manager that you're overworked, use the Journal to conduct time studies in which you document how you spend your days. You can even use the Journal to track your exercise program. The possibilities are endless.

If you've taken a class on using one of the popular day-planner systems, you probably have learned some things about the value of recording events in your planner. You may appreciate the importance of keeping all your notes in one place so you can refer to them when questions come up down the road. But paper-based systems can never compete with the organization and search utilities that electronic journaling can provide. The Journal has all the powerful tools that make Outlook such an incredible tool, such as Find, views, sorting, filtering, and integration with the other Outlook components and Office applications. These tools allow you to examine and organize your data in ways that have never been possible before.

NOTE
In order to use the Journal effectively, it's helpful to have a solid grasp of the other Outlook components, particularly Contacts. If you're a new Outlook user, we recommend that you spend some time working with Contacts before tackling the Journal. See Chapter 6 to learn all about Contacts.

MANUALLY RECORDING AN EVENT IN THE JOURNAL

To access the Journal, click My Shortcuts and then click the Journal icon on the Outlook bar. The Journal will open in its default view, Timeline view. The primary focus of the Journal is on how you've spent your time and what events have occurred on a particular day. Figure 8.1 shows one of this book's author's Journal pages while working on this book. In this example, you can easily see all the Word documents that were worked on during this time.

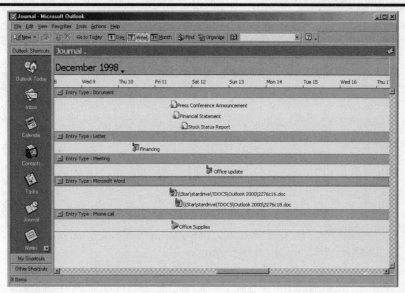

FIGURE 8.1: The Journal's Timeline view

To expand a particular Entry Type so you can see all of the entries underneath it, click the plus button to the left of the Entry Type label. To collapse a group that is already expanded, click the minus button.

NOTE

The first time you click the Journal icon on the Outlook bar, you may be surprised to find that there are already entries in the Journal. This is because the Journal is working behind the scenes automatically, recording work that you're doing in other Office applications. For a better understanding of these entries, and to learn how to change the automatic settings, see "Automatically Recording Journal Events" later in this chapter.

There are five Journal types visible in Figure 8.1: Document, Letter, Meeting, Microsoft Word, and Phone Call. In all, there are approximately 20 types of Journal entries that you can make. To create a new Journal entry, click the New button on the Standard toolbar and choose Journal Entry from the list. The Journal Entry form shown in Figure 8.2 will open.

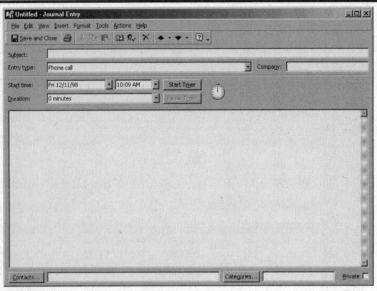

FIGURE 8.2: A Journal Entry form

The default entry type is Phone Call. Just click the down arrow in the Entry Type field to see the other available choices.

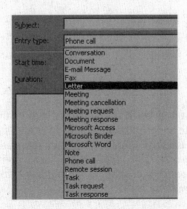

You are probably asking yourself, "Why would I want to record an e-mail message or task in a Journal entry? I've already got a record of that." The answer is simple: Journal entries can be linked directly to

Contacts. Instead of searching through all of your files, wouldn't it be nice if you could look in one place for all of your communications with an individual, including e-mail messages, phone conversations, faxes, and even tasks that were completed for this person? This is the power of the Journal.

Recording a Journal entry is really quite simple. If you've used Tasks and Calendar, you're already familiar with most of the fields on the Journal Entry form. Follow the steps below to create a Journal entry:

1. Choose Journal Entry from the New button to open a Journal Entry form.

2. Enter a Subject for the Journal entry and choose the Entry Type from the drop-down list.

3. To associate a Journal entry with an existing contact, click the Address Book button and choose a contact from the Select Contacts dialog box.

4. Enter a Company name, if desired.

> Start Timer

5. Enter a date and time in the Start Time fields or, if you're making a phone call, click the Start Timer button to have the Journal automatically time your conversation.

> Pause Timer

6. Record the length of the communication by selecting from the Duration drop-down list, or type in an entry of your own. If you clicked the Start Timer button, click the Pause Timer button when you've finished your phone call to have Outlook automatically record the call's duration.

7. Type your notes for this Journal entry in the open text box area.

8. Assign the Journal entry to a Category by clicking the Categories button at the bottom of the Journal Entry window.

9. If you'd like to make this Journal entry private, to prevent anyone who has access to your Outlook folders from reading it, click the Private check box at the bottom-right corner of the window.

10. Click the Save and Close button to record your Journal entry.

Part i

TROUBLESHOOTING THE COMPANY NAME FIELD

The Company field in the Journal is a different field from the Company field in Contacts. That's why when you associate a Journal entry with a contact, the Company field is not automatically filled in. (When you create a Journal entry from an e-mail message, the Company field *is* filled in. See "Creating Journal Entries from Other Outlook Items" later in this chapter.)

There is a reason for this apparently confusing behavior. You may want to enter a company name in the Journal that's completely different from the one you entered in Contacts. If, for example, you were calling a vendor on behalf of a client, you might associate the Journal entry with your contact at the vendor. On the other hand, you might want to organize your Journal entries by the client you were going to work for. Having separate fields allows you to do that.

If you are making cold sales calls, you might want to wait to add someone to Contacts until you get a positive response of some sort, rather than cluttering up your Contacts with people who are interested but not committed. You can still record the Company of the people you call, so you can track how many people within a company you have contacted.

When you start using the filtering features, it's important to remember that the Company field in Journal and the Company field in Contacts are distinct fields.

Inserting Files into Journal Entries

You can insert documents and Outlook items directly into Journal entries. For example, if you had a phone conversation about a proposal you were writing for a client, you could insert a copy of the Word document or a shortcut to the document directly into the Journal entry. In the future, when you want to review what you talked about, you could directly reference the proposal. Follow these steps to insert a file into a Journal entry:

1. Open the Journal entry.

2. Choose Insert ➢ File from the Journal Entry Standard toolbar. The Insert File dialog box opens.

3. Choose between Insert as Text Only, Attachment, and Short-cut (see the "Which Insert File Option Should I Choose?" sidebar, following).

4. Locate the file you want to insert, and select it.

5. Click OK to insert the file. The contents of the file (Text Only) or an icon representing the document (Attachment or Short-cut) appears in the Notes area of the Journal entry.

6. Double-click the icon to open the document.

WHICH INSERT FILE OPTION SHOULD I CHOOSE?

There are significant differences between inserting a file as Text Only, Attachment, or Shortcut; you should make a conscious choice each time you insert a file into an Outlook item. The default choice is Attachment. Be aware that when you insert an attachment, you are making a copy of the original document. When you double-click the icon in the Outlook item to open the document, you are opening and perhaps modifying the copy. The original document remains unchanged. Use this option with an e-mail message if you want to send a file to someone who can open a Word attachment.

The Shortcut option creates a pointer to the document on your local or network drive. Use this option if you are inserting the document for your own reference and do not plan to e-mail the item to anyone else. When you double-click the icon to open this document, you are opening and potentially modifying the original document in its original location.

The Text Only option is useful if you plan to send this item to someone who cannot open a Word document attached to an e-mail message. The actual text of the document (without formatting) is inserted into the Notes area of the item. If the document is formatted (font formatting, headers/footers, and so on), you may get a lot of unreadable characters, but somewhere in the midst of it all you should find your text. Saving the file as Rich Text Format (.rtf) or Text (.txt) before you insert it will eliminate the garbage characters.

Inserting Other Objects into a Journal Entry

To manually insert an object such as a bitmap image, Word document, or Access database into a Journal entry, follow these steps (you can also follow these steps to see which types of objects your computer will support, because each type is listed in the dialog box):

1. Open the Journal entry.

2. Choose Insert ➤ Object to open the Insert Object dialog box, shown in Figure 8.3.

3. Choose the type of object you would like to insert, and select either Create New or Create from File.

4. Click OK. If you chose to create a new file, the Journal entry window will be modified to show the tools necessary for creating the selected file type. If you chose to open an existing file, an Open File dialog will open.

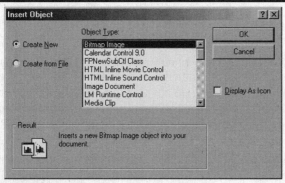

FIGURE 8.3: The Insert Object dialog box

Creating Journal Entries from Other Outlook Items

When an important e-mail comes through your Inbox, you may find it useful to record that e-mail in your Journal so you can easily find it again when you need it. You can drag items from any of the Outlook modules to the Journal, and Outlook will create a Journal entry from it. For example,

Figure 8.4 shows a Journal entry created by dragging an e-mail message to the Journal. Notice that it placed all the information from the message into the corresponding fields of the Journal Entry form.

WARNING

When you create a Journal entry from an existing item, Outlook places a shortcut in the Journal entry. If you move the original item, the shortcut will no longer be valid.

Relating Journal Entries to Contacts

Although you could easily find the entry from Figure 8.4 in the Journal, Outlook makes it even easier to track this communication by using the Activities page from the Contact form. Because the original e-mail message was from a contact, and because the Journal recognizes the relationship to your contacts, you can open the Contact form for that contact, switch to the Activities page, and see a list of Journal entries related to that particular contact. Figure 8.5 shows e-mail messages and other items on a typical Activities page of the Contact form.

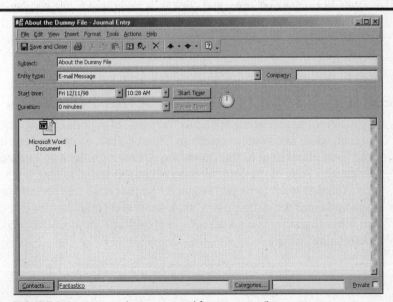

FIGURE 8.4: A Journal entry created from an e-mail message

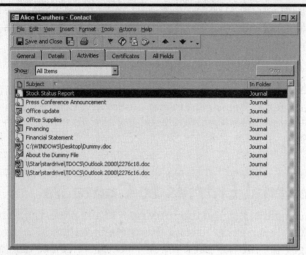

FIGURE 8.5: The Activities page of the Contact form

To manually record a Journal entry directly in a Contact form, open the Contact form and switch to the Activities page. Go to File ➤ New and select Journal Entry to open a Journal form.

Record the journal entry and click Save and Close to file it away. Next time you plan to contact this person, open their Contact form and the contents of the last contact will be right there in front of you. To view an existing entry in the Journal, double-click the entry to open it.

Creating a Task from a Journal Entry

If you agreed to take some action as the result of your discussion with a contact, you'll also want to create an Outlook Task. Open the Journal and drag the Journal item to the Tasks icon or folder. Outlook will create a Task with a copy of the Journal entry already included in the Notes section. You may want to revise the subject so that it is more specific to the Task and enter the details of the Task (start and end dates, for example), but other than that you are all set. (See Chapter 7 for more information about using Tasks.)

AUTOMATICALLY RECORDING JOURNAL EVENTS

Although you now know how to record e-mail messages in the Journal by dragging them to create a Journal entry, why not have Outlook do that for you automatically? You can set it up once and Outlook will do the rest for you behind the scenes. Any action associated with a contact, such as sending or receiving e-mail, a meeting response, or a task request, can automatically appear in the Journal for this contact.

1. Choose Tools ➤ Options from the menu and click Journal Options to open the Journal Options dialog box, shown in Figure 8.6.

2. Select the items you would like to automatically record from the list of choices, including:

   ► E-mail message

   ► Meeting request

   ► Meeting response

   ► Meeting cancellation

   ► Task request

   ► Task response

3. Mark the contacts for whom you want to record items automatically (this is an all-or-nothing proposition—f you want to record e-mail messages and task requests for one contact, you can't choose to record only e-mail messages for another).

4. Select the files you would like to record automatically from the list of application choices, including:

   ► Microsoft Access

   ► Microsoft Excel

   ► Microsoft Office Binder

   ► Microsoft PowerPoint

   ► Microsoft Word

   ► Other programs that are part of the Microsoft Office Compatible program

5. Choose if you want double-clicking a Journal entry to open the Journal entry or to open the item referred to by the Journal entry.

6. Click OK to save the Journal Options dialog box, and click OK again to close the Options dialog box.

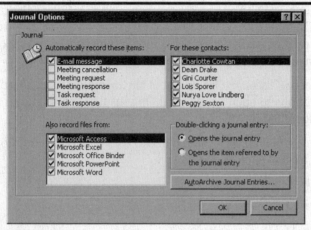

FIGURE 8.6: The Journal Options dialog box

After you have selected the Outlook items that you want to record automatically for a contact in the Journal Options dialog box, you can assign the item to a newly created contact from the referral's Contact form. Switch to the Activities page of the Contact form and click the Automatically Record Journal Entries for This Contact check box. Outlook will create Journal entries for this contact containing shortcuts to original Outlook items, as shown in Figure 8.7.

TIP

When you double-click a Journal entry, the Journal Entry form opens containing an icon for the referenced item. If you'd like to open the referenced item directly, go to Tools ➢ Options ➢ Journal Options, and choose Double-Clicking a Journal Entry Opens the Item Referred to by the Journal Entry.

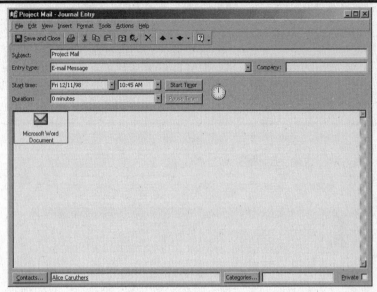

FIGURE 8.7: A Journal entry with a shortcut to a Word document

TIP

When you set the Journal to automatically record documents that you work on in any of the Office applications, Outlook records the author of the document as the contact it associates with the Journal entry. If you create the document, you are listed as the contact. However, if you open a document created by someone else, their name appears in the Contact field of the associated Journal entry. The author of the document is pulled from the Author field on the Summary page of the document's properties. (To get to the Summary page, open the document in the application, choose File ➤ Properties, and click the Summary tab.)

CHANGING JOURNAL VIEWS

Changing the way you look at something can open your eyes to connections and relationships that you previously couldn't see. Journal views let you both examine the minute-by-minute details of your day and step back to review the big picture. You can view your Journal entries according to when they were recorded and also organize them by type, by contact, or by category. This flexibility makes the Journal a tool that can help you analyze your activities, in addition to documenting them.

Viewing by Day, Week, or Month

The Timeline view is similar to the Day/Week/Month view of the Calendar in that there are three ways to view the timeline. Click the Day, Week, or Month button on the Standard toolbar to change the focus of the timeline. The Day view, shown in Figure 8.8, focuses on the time of day that the Journal events occurred.

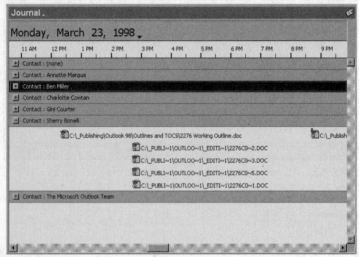

FIGURE 8.8:   The Day view of the Journal

There are several ways you can move quickly to a particular date:

▶ Select the date you want to see in Week or Month view by clicking the date in the Date row (the selected date will turn blue), and then switch to Day view.

▶ Right-click anywhere in the timeline (except right on an event) and choose Go to Date from the shortcut menu to open the Go to Date dialog box, shown here:

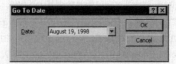

▶ Click the Month in the top row to open a date navigator.

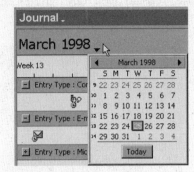

The Month view, shown in Figure 8.9, focuses on the big picture.

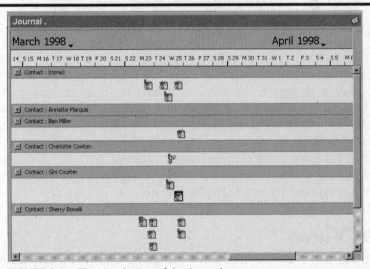

FIGURE 8.9: The Month view of the Journal

In both the Day view and the Month view, the Journal events are reduced to icons with no labels. Point to any of the icons to see what it represents.

Part i

To change the display in Day or Month view, use the Format Timeline View dialog box. You can open it by right-clicking the timeline and choosing Other Settings from the shortcut menu.

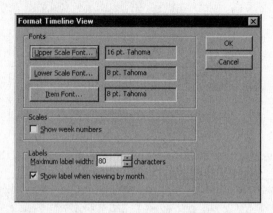

If you have a vision impairment and are having difficulty seeing the text that is displayed in the Timeline, use the Format Timeline View dialog box to change the font. To display the week numbers instead of the dates, click the Show Week Numbers check box. If you would like to display the icon labels in Day or Month view, click the Show Label When Viewing by Month check box (it turns the labels on for viewing by Days, too). You can also set the maximum number of characters to display in the labels, so they don't get too unwieldy. Click OK to save the new Format options and return to the Journal.

Other Views

In addition to the Timeline views that group data by entry type, the Journal has several other built-in views. Choose View ➢ Current View and choose from:

By Type   This Timeline view groups events and activities by their type.

By Contact   This Timeline view groups the events by contact (see Figure 8.8 and Figure 8.9 for examples).

By Category   This Timeline view shows events grouped by the assigned Category.

By Entry   This List view shows events in a list format, similar to the default Tasks view (see Figure 8.10). In this view, you can sort the events by clicking the column label.

Last Seven Days   This List view shows events from the last seven days exclusively.

Phone Calls   This List view displays phone calls only.

		Entry Type	Subject	Start	Duration	Contact	Categories
		Microsoft Word	C:_Publishing\Office 98\test docu...	Wed 3/25/98 1:...	0 hours	Ben Miller	
		Microsoft Word	C:_PUBLI~1\OUTLOO~1_EDITI~...	Wed 3/25/98 1:...	4 minutes	Sherry Bonelli	
		Microsoft Word	C:_Publishing\Outlook 98\Outlines ...	Wed 3/25/98 1:...	0 hours	Sherry Bonelli	
		Microsoft Word	C:_Publishing\Office 98\Office 98 ...	Wed 3/25/98 9:...	0 hours		
		Microsoft Word	C:_Publishing\Office 98\Office 98 ...	Wed 3/25/98 9:...	0 hours	Annette Marquis	
		Microsoft Word	C:_Publishing\Outlook 98\Outlines ...	Wed 3/25/98 9:...	0 hours	Gini Courter	
		Conversation	Developing next book project	Tue 3/24/98 9:...	15 minutes	Charlotte Cowtan	
		Microsoft Word	C:_Publishing\Outlook 98\2276c10...	Tue 3/24/98 6:...	236 minutes	Gini Courter	
		Microsoft Word	C:_Publishing\Outlook 98\Outlines ...	Tue 3/24/98 4:...	1 minute	Annette Marquis	
		Microsoft Word	C:_Publishing\Outlook 98\2276c09...	Tue 3/24/98 4:...	1 minute	Annette Marquis	
		Microsoft Word	C:_Publishing\Outlook 98\Outlines ...	Tue 3/24/98 4:...	4 minutes	Annette Marquis	
		Microsoft Word	C:_Publishing\Outlook 98\2276c09...	Tue 3/24/98 4:...	1 minute		
		Microsoft Word	C:_Publishing\Outlook 98\2276c09...	Tue 3/24/98 4:...	9 minutes	Annette Marquis	
		Microsoft Word	C:_Publishing\Outlook 98\Ch 09\c0...	Tue 3/24/98 4:...	3 minutes	Annette Marquis	
		Microsoft Word	A:\Auction item.doc	Tue 3/24/98 8:...	0 hours		
		Microsoft Word	A:\Auction item.txt	Tue 3/24/98 8:...	0 hours	Annette Marquis	
		Microsoft Word	C:\My Documents\Auction item.doc	Tue 3/24/98 8:...	20 minutes	Annette Marquis	
		Microsoft Word	C:_Publishing\Outlook 98_Editing ...	Mon 3/23/98 8:...	1 minute	Sherry Bonelli	
		Microsoft Word	C:_Publishing\Outlook 98\2276c09...	Mon 3/23/98 7:...	803 minutes	Annette Marquis	
		Microsoft Word	C:_PUBLI~1\OUTLOO~1_EDITI~...	Mon 3/23/98 2:...	0 hours	Sherry Bonelli	
		Microsoft Word	C:_PUBLI~1\OUTLOO~1_EDITI~...	Mon 3/23/98 2:...	0 hours	Sherry Bonelli	
		Microsoft Word	C:_PUBLI~1\OUTLOO~1_EDITI~...	Mon 3/23/98 2:...	0 hours	Sherry Bonelli	
		Microsoft Word	C:_PUBLI~1\OUTLOO~1_EDITI~...	Mon 3/23/98 2:...	0 hours	Sherry Bonelli	
		Microsoft Word	C:_Publishing\Outlook 98\2276c09...	Mon 3/23/98 2:...	5.5 hours	Annette Marquis	

FIGURE 8.10:   The By Entry view of the Journal

Grouping Data

Several of the built-in views group the events in the Journal in various ways: By Type, By Contact, By Entry, or By Category. You can easily change the grouping of any of the predefined Timeline views by right-clicking in the timeline and choosing Group By. This opens the Group By dialog box, shown in Figure 8.11.

Select the field you want to group by from the Group Items By drop-down list. You can choose up to four levels of grouping. For example, you could group by Contact, then by Date, then by Entry in either Ascending or Descending order.

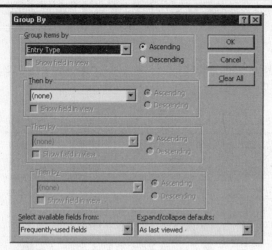

FIGURE 8.11: The Group By dialog box

If the field you want to group by is not in the list, click the Select Available Fields From down-arrow and choose All Journal Fields. Set the Expand/Collapse defaults to display the groups All Expanded, All Collapsed, or As Last Viewed. Click OK to display the new view.

To remove all grouping, open the Group By dialog box and click Clear All.

LOCATING EVENTS IN THE JOURNAL

If you are looking for a particular Journal entry, click the Find button on the Standard toolbar and type a key word or name into the Look For text box. Click the Find Now button to conduct the search. Outlook searches the Subject and Body of the entries for the text you entered and returns the results in a list view in the Information Viewer. Figure 8.12 shows search results for the name *Sherry*.

Click the Find button on the toolbar again to close the Find window.

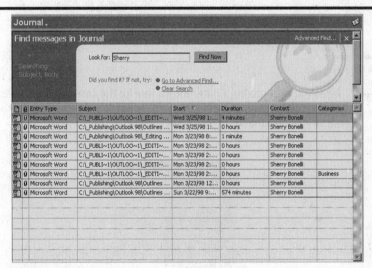

FIGURE 8.12: Using Find to search for key words or names

MAKING NOTES

Even after you are using Outlook to its fullest, you will still run across those odd pieces of information that have nowhere to go, or that you want to keep at your fingertips: your flight information, your sweetie's sizes, or information about your car insurance. They aren't related to a contact, they aren't events, so what do you do with them? Never fear; Outlook has a place for those, too. Outlook includes an easy way to computerize your notes. Choose Note from the New Item button (or hold

Ctrl+Shift and press N) to open a Note window. Enter your text in the
Note window.

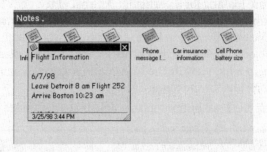

TIP

When you are entering a note, enter a title for the note and then press Enter
before entering the contents of the note. Otherwise, the entire text of the note
will be visible in the Notes Information Viewer.

Each note is automatically time and date stamped. Closing the window
automatically saves the note. To view a note, click the Notes icon on the
Outlook Bar to go to the Notes window. Double-click a note to open it.
Click the Note icon in the upper-left corner of the Note window to access
options for deleting, saving, and printing notes.

To make it easier to organize notes, Outlook 2000 brings the Categories
a simple right-click away. To apply a category (or two or three) to a note,
right click the target note, select Categories from the list, and make your
choices.

If a note grows up and it needs to become a task, a Journal entry, or an e-mail message, just drag the Note icon onto the appropriate icon on the Outlook bar or into the appropriate folder in the folder list.

Notes Views

Even though notes are small, you still have options for viewing them in different ways. Choose Small Icons, Large Icons, or List from the Notes Standard toolbar to change how the icons are displayed in the Information Viewer.

Choose View ➤ Current View to switch to a number of predefined views, such as Notes List view, shown in Figure 8.13, which shows you a list of your notes and gives a preview of the notes' contents.

Notes			
Subject ▽		Created	Categories
Phone message for Gini		Wed 3/25/98 3:42 PM	
Phone message for Gini Call your Dad <end>			
Network Logon information		Wed 3/25/98 3:42 PM	
Network Logon information Login in as user mtgrooms when working with Meeting rooms schedule information <end>			
Flight Information		Wed 3/25/98 3:44 PM	
Flight Information 6/7/98 Leave Detroit 8 am Flight 252			
Charlotte's Sizes		Wed 3/25/98 3:42 PM	
Charlotte's Sizes Pants 12 Blouses - med skirts 12 <end>			
Cell Phone battery size		Wed 3/25/98 3:41 PM	
Cell Phone battery size 10NT- 27 <end>			
Car insurance information		Wed 3/25/98 3:41 PM	
Car insurance information <end>			

FIGURE 8.13: Notes List view

Taking Your Notepad with You

To provide you with no excuse to continue using sticky notes, you can take a note with you to any application or even let it sit open on the Windows Desktop ready and waiting for you. To place a note on the Windows Desktop, restore the Outlook window (click the Restore button on the Outlook title bar) and drag the note to the Desktop.

Outlook does not have to be open for you to edit the note, make additions to it, or delete the contents. However, if you close the note you'll have to re-open Outlook to view the note again.

WHAT'S NEXT?

You now have an in-depth view of Outlook's basic components. The next section advances your Outlook knowledge. In the next chapter, you will learn how you can use advanced messaging techniques to meet your specific needs.

PART II

OUTLOOK 2000
ADVANCED TOPICS

Chapter 9

ADVANCED MESSAGE FORMATTING AND MANAGEMENT

Now that you know how to send and receive your e-mail messages, you'll want to make those messages look good for the right people. Outlook can help you make your messages and other contact material look, breathe, and feel professional. Also, although it's easy to let all of your incoming e-mail pile into one folder, after a while you'll find yourself searching in vain through several hundred messages for that really important one. Outlook can help you by drawing your attention to the important messages and filing the junk mail, all based on criteria that makes sense to you.

Adapted from *Mastering™ Microsoft® Outlook™ 2000* by Gini Courter and Annette Marquis

ISBN 0-7821-2472-0   787 pages $34.99

ADVANCED MESSAGE FORMATTING

One can only go so far with simple ASCII-based messages before one wants more. If you're this kind of person, or if your workflow dictates professionally delivered documents, electronic or otherwise, then Outlook can handle even the most complex formatting. Here, we'll discuss the ins and outs of formatting, including when *not* to do it.

TIP

Some Internet users, such as those who still use Pine (a Unix text-based e-mail program) for e-mail, will be annoyed by your neatly formatted messages, chock-full of HTML coding, embedded objects, and such. Formatted messages also cause similar problems when they are sent to some e-mail list servers that distribute in digest format (some know about this problem and strip out the offending HTML and MIME information). For these people (there are a lot more of them than you might think), we recommend avoiding unnecessary formatting. Remember: the larger the message, the larger the recipient's displeasure.

Formatting Messages

Outlook supports four distinct message formats: plain text, RTF, HTML, and Microsoft Word. The mail editor you select determines the tools you can use to format the text, paragraphs, and background of your mail message. You will select an editor before creating the message, and that editor is used for future new messages you create (until you change editors again).

- ▶ Plain text is the default format, created with a plain text editor. With plain text, the text appears in the computer's default e-mail font, usually Courier, and you can't apply formatting.

- ▶ Microsoft Outlook Rich Text format (RTF) lets you format fonts, align paragraphs, and use bulleted lists in your message.

- ▶ HTML (hypertext markup language) format is the language used to develop pages on the World Wide Web. The HTML format supports an incredibly wide range of formatting, including backgrounds, horizontal lines, numbered and bulleted lists, and any other formatting you expect to see on a Web page.

▶ Microsoft Word format uses Word as your e-mail editor and lets you apply any formatting that is valid in Word.

TIP

It's easy to confuse Microsoft Outlook Rich Text and HTML because Outlook refers to both as Rich Text. However, HTML is always listed as Rich Text (HTML); Outlook Rich Text does not include the HTML designation.

Depending on the editor you selected (or didn't select, in the case of the default plain text editor), various tools are available on the Format menu and Formatting toolbar in the message form. For information on choosing an editor, see "Setting a Format for New Messages" later in this chapter.

Formatting Plain Text Messages

The bottom line here is, you can't format Plain Text messages. When the default Plain Text editor is used to create a message, all the buttons on the Formatting toolbar and most of the items on the Format menu are disabled, as shown in Figure 9.1. You can switch between Plain Text and Rich Text (HTML) editors. To switch to HTML, choose Format ➤ Rich Text from the menu. This enables the buttons on the Formatting toolbar and the Format menu choices that let you change fonts, styles, alignment, and colors.

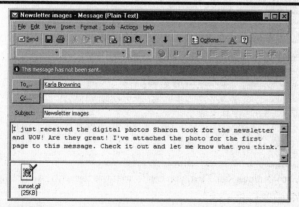

FIGURE 9.1: Plain text messages are exactly as described—plain.

Part ii

ADDING "CHARACTER" TO YOUR PLAIN TEXT MESSAGES

The plain text format has been in use for over three decades—long enough for enterprising users to invent ways to add meaning to messages using the characters on the keyboard. Precede and follow a word with an _underscore_ to indicate the word is underlined or italicized. Use asterisks *before and after* a word or words to indicate bold type. Insert emoticons—keystrokes that, when viewed from the side, resemble facial expressions :~)—to give recipients an idea of the emotion you're really trying to convey in your message.

Formatting Outlook Rich Text Messages

Outlook Rich Text Format is the default format for Microsoft Exchange. When the Rich Text editor is used to create a message, Outlook's Formatting toolbar is enabled, and two formatting choices appear on the Format menu: Font and Paragraph. Text can be bolded, underlined, and italicized; you can use different fonts, font sizes, font colors, and alignments to format your message, as shown in Figure 9.2.

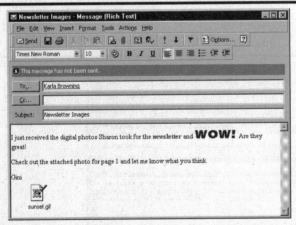

FIGURE 9.2: With Outlook Rich Text, you can format the text and paragraphs in your message.

Formatting HTML Messages

In the HTML editor, Font and Paragraph options are available, so you can format text as you would in an Outlook Rich Text format message. With HTML, you can also apply HTML styles—place horizontal lines, pictures, animated graphics, and multimedia files in the message—and apply a picture or color as a background, as shown in Figure 9.3. Anything that you can place in a Web page, you can include in an HTML message.

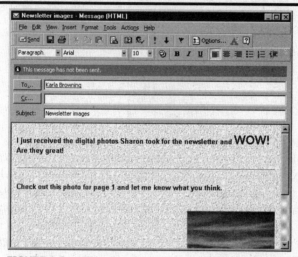

FIGURE 9.3:   HTML messages can include pictures as part of the message or as a background.

Adding a Horizontal Line   Horizontal lines can be an effective way to divide a message into parts. To add a horizontal line to an HTML message, place the insertion point where you want to insert the line in the message body. Then choose Insert ➤ Horizontal Line from the message form's menu bar to insert the line. To delete a line, place the insertion point directly above the line and press the Delete key.

Applying Paragraph Styles   HTML supports a number of paragraph styles, including bulleted and numbered lists and six levels of headings. To apply a style, select the paragraph(s) you want to format, and then choose Format ➢ Style to open a menu of paragraph styles. Choose the style you want to apply to the selected paragraphs.

Some aspects of the HTML styles are rigidly defined. For example, the Heading 1 style is bold. If you apply Heading 1 to a paragraph, you can't remove the bolding, but you can change the font. If Outlook won't let you change a text attribute in an HTML message, it's usually a limitation of HTML. You can try switching to the Formatted style and then applying your changes, but be aware that some browsers can't interpret the Formatted style and will simply substitute another font, size, and weight.

Adding Graphic Elements   To choose a background color, choose Format ➢ Background ➢ Color from the message form's menu and select a color from the palette. To use a picture as a background, choose Format ➢ Background ➢ Picture to open the Background Picture dialog box, shown in Figure 9.4. The dialog box list includes pictures suitable for use as backgrounds. Select from the list, or click the Browse button and select a picture from your local drive or a network drive.

FIGURE 9.4:   Use the Background Picture dialog box to apply a background to an HTML message.

To add a picture to the body of the message, choose Insert ➢ Picture from the message form menu to open the Picture dialog box, shown in

Figure 9.5. Click the Browse button to open the Open dialog box. There are two image formats widely used in Web pages—GIF and JPEG—so the Files of Type in the dialog box is set to these two formats. Change the Files of Type if you're looking for a picture saved in another image format. Select the image, and then click Open to return to the Picture dialog box.

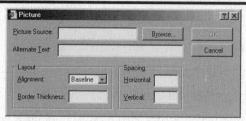

FIGURE 9.5:   In the Picture dialog box, select either a new file or an existing file to place in the body of the e-mail message.

If some of your recipients can't view HTML messages, you can enter text in place of the picture to let them know what they're missing. Enter the text that should be displayed in the Alternate Text box (see Figure 9.5). In the Layout section of the dialog box, select a position for the picture from the drop-down list. Borders and spacing around the picture are both entered in pixels. To add a border or additional space between a picture and surrounding text, enter a pixel value between 0 and 999. Click OK to close the Picture dialog box and place the image in the message.

NOTE

A `pixel` is the smallest displayable unit on a computer's screen. The relative size of a pixel is expressed in the screen's resolution setting; if the resolution setting is set to 640 × 480, there are 640 pixels horizontally on the screen, and 480 vertical pixels.

There is one more graphic element you can apply to Rich Text (HTML) messages. When you use the HTML format, you can use "stationery" to give your messages a distinct look. You can select stationery when you choose the default message format (see "Setting a Format for New Messages" later in this chapter).

Formatting Word Messages

The last format choice is Microsoft Word. When you install Outlook, you can choose Word as your default e-mail editor; you can switch editors for new messages at any point, so don't worry if you didn't make this choice during installation. Whenever you create a message, a Word session is opened, so you can utilize most of the formatting features available in Word, including:

▶ AutoCorrect, which corrects mistyped words and expands shortcuts

▶ Bulleted and numbered lists

▶ Drawing tools, including WordArt and AutoShapes

▶ Highlighting for emphasis

▶ Hyperlinks automatically created from e-mail addresses and URLs

▶ Images and files inserted into the body of the message

▶ Spelling and Grammar, which checks spelling and grammar as you type

▶ Tables, for presenting columnar material such as schedules

The mail message in Figure 9.6 was created in the Word format.

WARNING

Only use Word as your editor if you know that your recipient uses Word, too. When you use Word as your e-mail editor, it creates special formatting that is lost if you don't have Word on the other end. More importantly, if you open a Word document in a simple text editor, it's neither pretty nor very easy to read.

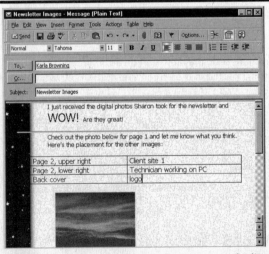

FIGURE 9.6: When you use Word as your e-mail editor, you have access to most of Word's formatting features.

Setting Mail Format Options

There are three types of mail format options: the default editor, which determines the Message Format; the Stationery and Fonts; and the customized Signatures you can add to your messages.

Setting a Format for New Messages

With all these choices, how do you choose a format for e-mail messages? The answer depends on a number of factors, including the e-mail editor and other software you and your recipients have. There are four steps to selecting an editor:

1. Choose Tools ➤ Options from the Outlook menu to open the Options dialog box.

2. Click the Mail Format tab.

3. Choose the text editor you wish to use in the Send in This Message Format text box.

4. Click OK to close the dialog box.

Table 9.1 summarizes the advantages and disadvantages of each format.

TABLE 9.1: Comparing Message Formats

FORMAT	ADVANTAGES	DISADVANTAGES
Plain Text	Messages can be read with any e-mail editor; supports MIME encoding.	Lack of formatting makes for boring-looking, but more universally readable, messages.
Outlook Rich Text	Allows font and paragraph formatting, supported by Microsoft Exchange and many PC mail editors.	No cross-platform support, so Unix and Macintosh users get plain text versions of messages.
HTML	Language is cross-platform; many users will eventually be able to read HTML messages. Provides support for encoding, graphics, formatting, and custom stationery.	Some e-mail editors don't support HTML messages yet, so a good number of your recipients will receive plain text, at best. Some of the e-mail clients that do support HTML are Eudora Pro and Eudora Light, Netscape's Messenger (a component of Communicator), and Microsoft's Outlook Express.

TABLE 9.1 continued: Comparing Message Formats

FORMAT	ADVANTAGES	DISADVANTAGES
Word	Lots of formatting options and support templates, and Word users see the message exactly as it appears on your screen. If a recipient doesn't have Word but their mail editor supports Rich Text format, most of the Word formatting is preserved.	You must have Word 97 or later to use this feature. Some of the best formatting features (like tables) are converted to plain text if the recipient doesn't have Word installed on their computer. Custom signatures must be created in Word templates; this format does not support digital signatures.

When you choose an editor, you're really choosing the potential formatting for new messages. For example, if you create and send an HTML message to a recipient whose e-mail system doesn't support HTML messages, they see the text of your message in plain text. Formatting and graphics are reduced to text strings that look like a lot of garbled text. On the other hand, if your recipient is using a mail editor that supports HTML messages, they get to see your message in all its glory. The potential is there, provided the recipient's mail editor can support the format you choose.

You can choose an editor in the Mail Format page of the Options dialog box. Choose Tools ➢ Options from the Outlook menu to open the Options dialog box, and then click the Mail Format tab, as shown in Figure 9.7.

FIGURE 9.7: Choose an e-mail editor and set message format options in the Options dialog box.

In the Send in This Message Format text box, select one of the e-mail editors. If you choose HTML or Microsoft Word, you will also be able to select a template or stationery. With HTML and Plain Text, you can automatically encode messages that are sent over the Internet.

TROUBLESHOOTING MESSAGE BACKUPS

Outlook keeps a backup of messages as you create them. If you close a message form after you've entered an address (for example, to change message formats), Outlook will prompt you to save or discard a draft of the message:

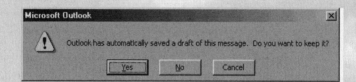

If you save the draft, you can open the message and continue working on it another time. The message will be saved in the Outlook Drafts folder.

If the power goes out while you're creating a message, check the Drafts folder when you restart your computer. The incomplete message may be there.

Encoding Messages

When you attach a Word document to a message, you're attaching more than just text. Applications add other information to files that is specific to the application. This information can't be translated by text editors—only by the application, in this case Microsoft Word. Encoding translates your message and its attachments into a binary code that your recipient's mail program must then decode. Many mail programs decode messages automatically; if a recipient's mail system does not, there are programs like WinZip that decode encoded messages.

Outlook supports two of the three primary encoding programs: uuencode and MIME. The third program, BinHex, was created for the Macintosh environment, and was not supported by Outlook 98 and is still not in Outlook 2000. To modify the default encoding settings, open a new message, select File ➢ Properties, and click on the Internet E-mail tab. You can either use the default setting or choose between MIME and uuencode. There are advanced settings for each encoding format, but the defaults for each are usually fine.

TIP

BinHex encoded files, designated by the `.hqx` or `.bin` extension, are pretty common when sharing files with Mac users. Don't feel out in the cold, though. Simply download the freeware Aladdin StuffIt Expander 2.0 for Windows from `http://www.aladdinsys.com` and you'll have access to a wide range of compressed file types that you may not have had before.

Uuencode (which originally meant Unix-to-Unix encode) was designed to allow users of different programs different word processors and operating systems to send information back and forth.

MIME (Multipurpose Internet Mail Extensions) was created by the Internet Engineering Task Force (IETF), and is the "official" standard for encoding Internet messages. Uuencode works well for text, but MIME was designed to support a wide range of file types: video, e-mail, audio, and graphics. Most mail programs automatically handle MIME encoding and decoding; other mailers, particularly freeware or shareware mailers, automatically handle uuencode.

TIP

Whether you use uuencode or MIME, your recipient must have the appropriate decoding software to decode and read your message. Unless you're sending audio or video files in your message, your best bet is uuencode. With audio and video attachments, use MIME, and choose base64 (an encoding protocol for non-text content) in the Encode Using drop-down list (in the message window, select File ➢ Properties and click the Internet E-mail tab to find this list). For more information and help using MIME, visit `http://www.hunnysoft.com/mime/`.

To encode your plain text or HTML messages, click the Settings button on the Mail Format page of the Options dialog box. Choose uuencode or MIME. If you choose MIME, you can also have your message encoded using base64. Click OK to return to the Options dialog box.

Choosing Stationery and Templates

If you use an HTML editor, you can personalize your e-mail messages by choosing HTML stationery, a scheme that includes a font and a background color or picture. You can create new stationery, or modify stationery by changing fonts and adding background colors or pictures.

To select stationery, you must select HTML as your mail editor in the Options dialog box (see Figure 9.7). Then, choose a stationery pattern from the Use This Stationery by Default drop-down list. To see what the various stationery patterns look like, click the Stationery Picker button on the Mail Format page of the Options dialog box to open the Stationery Picker dialog box, shown in Figure 9.8. Each stationery choice includes fonts and a background picture or color.

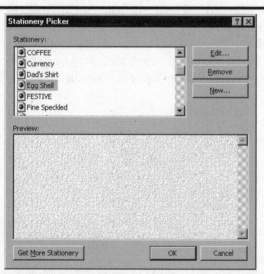

FIGURE 9.8: Select a background for HTML messages in the Stationery Picker dialog box.

WARNING

Not to spoil your fun, but the use of preformatted HTML stationery may not be appreciated by your recipient(s). Even though most people with e-mail also have a Web browser, this does not automatically mean they are willing to load each and every e-mail message from you into it for viewing. If the message requires the formatting of HTML stationery to get your point across and no other way will work, then by all means send it this way. Do try, though, to limit the number of messages you send in this fashion.

Select stationery from the scroll list, and you'll see a preview in the lower pane. Make your stationery choice; then click OK to close the Stationery Picker. Click OK again to close the Options dialog box.

TIP

Can't find stationery to meet your needs? Just click the Get More Stationery button in the Stationery Picker, and Outlook will launch your browser and visit the Microsoft Web site, where you can download more stationery patterns for free.

The stationery you selected will be the default stationery used for new messages created using the HTML editor. If you choose File ➢ New ➢ Mail Message or click the New Message button on the toolbar, the default stationery is applied. If you want to use other stationery for a specific message, choose Actions ➢ New Message Using to open the following menu:

Stationery that you've used recently is listed on the menu. You can choose a pattern, or No Stationery from the menu. Select More Stationery to open the Stationery dialog box and select stationery for this message. This does not change the default stationery, which will be applied to the next message you create.

Creating, Editing, and Deleting Stationery   You can create, delete, or edit stationery in the Stationery Picker. To create new Stationery, open the Stationery Picker and click the New button to open the Create New Stationery dialog box (which acts like a wizard). In the first page of the dialog box, shown in Figure 9.9, enter a name for your stationery and choose whether you want to create stationery from scratch or base it on existing stationery or an HTML file. To base your stationery on an existing HTML file, select the Use This File as a Template option, and click the Browse button to locate the file that you want to use. Click Next.

In the Edit Stationery dialog box (see Figure 9.10), click the Change Font button to open the Font dialog box and select a font to be used for message text in your stationery. Then, set the stationery background. Choose a picture from the list, browse to select another GIF or JPEG image, apply a color, or choose Do Not Include a Background in This Stationery. Click OK to create the new stationery and add it to the Stationery Picker.

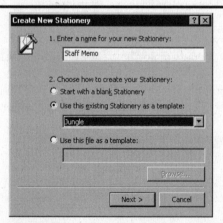

FIGURE 9.9:   To create new stationery, name the stationery and choose how you'd like to create it.

TIP

You don't have to be incredibly creative to have great stationery. Wait for one of your artistic friends to send you a well designed HTML message. Open the message, and choose File ≻ Save Stationery from the message form's menu bar. Enter a name for the stationery when prompted, and then click OK to save the stationery pattern. (Asking for your friend's permission is, of course, a good idea.)

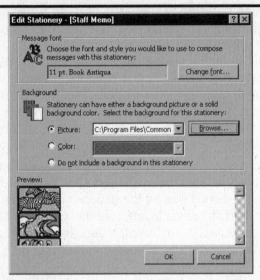

FIGURE 9.10: Select a font and background for the new stationery.

To edit existing stationery, select it in the Stationery Picker and click the Edit button. The Edit Stationery dialog box, shown in Figure 9.10, opens. Choose a font and background, and then click OK to save the edits. To delete stationery, select it in the Stationery Picker, and then click the Remove button. You'll be prompted to confirm the deletion:

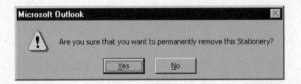

Selecting Templates If you've chosen Word as your e-mail editor, you can select a Word template to serve as the background for your messages. In the Options dialog box of Word itself (Tools ➤ Options ➤ General ➤ E-mail Options ➤ Personal Stationery), you can choose which theme is the default for your WordMail. Figure 9.11 shows the WordMail Themes section of the dialog box where you can choose a default Theme. To browse for other themes, click the Theme button to open the WordMail Theme dialog box.

NOTE

Keep in mind that all of the WordMail options are available in Word's Options dialog box and not in Outlook.

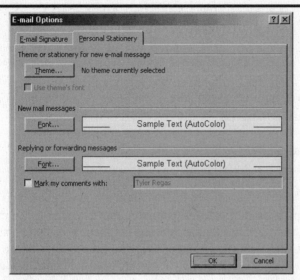

FIGURE 9.11: Select a WordMail theme in the Word E-mail Options dialog box.

NOTE

HTML message stationary is not the same as WordMail Themes (although they are included in the list), which gives you a wide range of graphical styles to choose from. If you have stationery selected in Outlook for HTML messages, it will not appear in WordMail.

TIP

You can't create new WordMail templates in Outlook; they must be created in Word. You'll find help creating templates in Word's Online Help.

Part ii

Designing Custom Signatures

A *custom signature* is text you add to the end of a message. Custom signatures are used to

▶ Identify the sender:

```
Gini Courter, TRIAD Consulting, 810-555-2221
```

▶ Reserve rights to your message:

```
The content of this message may be proprietary, and can-
not be reproduced or forwarded without my express writ-
ten consent.
```

▶ Pitch your products or services:

```
Annette Marquis, author of Mastering Outlook 2000, com-
ing soon to a bookstore in your neighborhood.
```

▶ Advertise your Web site:

```
For more information, visit us at www.sybex.com.
```

▶ Attach a digital ID to your message

Custom signatures have become commonplace e-mail features: ministers advertise their sermon topics, netizens list their favorite (or trash their least favorite) Web sites, managers add an inspirational quote for the week or month, and one of our friends includes a different bread recipe each month.

With Outlook you can create multiple custom signatures, and then select the signature you wish to use with each message you send. This lets you create a formal signature for business messages (like the "all rights reserved" signature in Figure 9.13) and a more friendly signature for messages to friends and family.

To create a custom signature or to choose a default signature for all messages, go to Tools ➤ Options ➤ General and click the E-mail Options button at the bottom of the dialog box. In the dialog box shown in Figure 9.12, type a name for your new signature in the topmost text box and, in the larger text box below, enter and format your signature. When you're finished, click the New button.

TIP

If you are using WordMail to compose your messages, the Signature Picker in Outlook is disabled. You can create and select your signatures in Word itself.

You may apply hyperlinks to parts of your signature that you want to make clickable, and you can also add pictures to your signature. Simply click the Picture or Hyperlink button, the two buttons at the right end of the toolbar in the E-mail Options dialog box, and enter a URL (for example, `http://www.microsoft.com` or `mailto:bgates@ microsoft.com`) or select a picture, respectively.

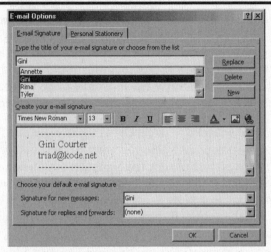

FIGURE 9.12: Create one or more custom signatures in the E-mail Options dialog box.

FIGURE 9.13: A formal signature for business messages

Part ii

WARNING

We strongly suggest that if you must put a picture in your signature, you keep it very, *very* small. Forcing people to wait while your signature-line graphics download can cause friends to become unfriendly. We suggest having a signature line of no more than five lines, the first line being three dashes (---). The dashes signify the end of the message to the mail server.

In the lower section of the E-mail Options dialog box, you can select which signatures to use for new messages and which for forwards or replies. You can choose to have no default signature or you can select another signature to insert in the message that will override your default selection. To select another signature while in WordMail, go to Insert ➤ AutoText ➤ Signature and select which signature you would like to use.

 Selecting a Custom Signature   To choose a custom signature for a message, place the insertion point where you want to insert the signature. Choose Insert ➤ Signature or click the Signature button and select a signature from the menu; if the custom signature you want to use isn't displayed on the menu, choose More to open the Signature dialog box. Select a signature, and then click OK to add the signature to the message.

MANAGING YOUR E-MAIL

Now that we've successfully covered special formatting of e-mail messages, we can move on to a more complex and important aspect of e-mail usage: what to do with it once you get it. There are many factors to successfully managing your incoming messages. You may receive mail from work, and you may need to access your work mail from home. This means you will need to synchronize the mail you get at work with the copies you have at home. And then there's your personal mail to deal with. This can get pretty complicated pretty quickly.

Now suppose you filled out a few forms for information on the Web, and you're starting to get a lot of spam (junk e-mail). You are subscribed to a number of helpful e-mail discussion lists, and you need to keep those messages separate so you don't miss important work messages. If Outlook wasn't at your beck and call to manage your mail for you, you'd spend the entire day filing messages by hand.

This section of the chapter will help you process your Inbox efficiently. In some cases you'll find it useful to flag messages for further action; in other cases you'll want to print them out. And you'll probably want to create e-mail filters to help you sort out your routine business messages from the important messages from friends. You'll learn how to use the Inbox Wizard to let Outlook handle your mail for you.

Flagging Messages for Further Action

You can't always reply to, forward, or even fully read and review a message when you receive it. You may be busy, need more information before you can reply, or require time to find out who should receive a forwarded message. However, if you let the message languish in your Inbox, it can get lost in the shuffle as new messages are delivered and grab your attention.

By flagging messages, you can ensure that they don't get lost, and it helps you stay organized. When you flag a message, you note the type of action that's required. You can even set a reminder so you don't forget to follow up on the message. The flag descriptions are

- ▶ Call
- ▶ Do Not Forward
- ▶ Follow-Up
- ▶ For Your Information
- ▶ Forward
- ▶ No Response Necessary
- ▶ Read
- ▶ Reply
- ▶ Reply to All
- ▶ Review

To flag an open message, choose Actions ➢ Flag for Follow-Up from the message menu or click the Flag for Follow-Up button on the message

Part ii

toolbar. If the message is not open, right-click on the message in the Inbox and choose Flag for Follow-Up from the shortcut menu.

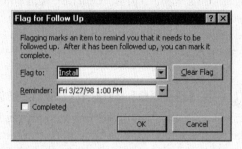

Choose a flag description from the Flag To drop-down list. You can also enter your own description of the action required; for example, Mail Application or Fax FAQ Sheet. You can sort the messages in any folder by flag description, so you should try to stick with the list and a small number of additions, or sorting won't be helpful.

Click the arrow in the Reminder text box to open the calendar control. Choose a date on which you want to be reminded about the message. If you want to be reminded at a specific time, edit the time in the text box. When you're finished entering flag information, click OK to close the dialog box.

TIP
You can flag messages that you're sending or forwarding, as well as those you receive.

 In the Inbox, a red flag is displayed in front of the message. In the message form, the flag description and date appear in an information box at the top of the message. The information bar for a flagged message is shown here—it includes a reminder to install the attached file by a specific date.

> ℹ Install by Friday, March 27, 1998 1:00 PM.

Clear Flag   When you've completed the follow-up, you can either clear the flag or mark the action complete. To clear the flag, open the Flag for Follow-Up dialog box, click the Clear Flag button, and then click OK. The message will no longer be flagged.

You may prefer to mark the flagged action as complete, which is indicated with a gray flag. When you mark the action as completed, you know that no further action is needed, but you are still keeping track of that action. To mark a flag as complete, open the Flag for Follow-Up dialog box, check the Completed check box, and then click OK to close the dialog box.

Printing Messages

To print an open message, choose File ➤ Print from the message form menu to open the Print dialog box, shown in Figure 9.14. Select a printer from the Name drop-down list. The default message print style is Memo Style; if you've defined other styles, you can select them from the Print Style list. If the message has attachments, you can print the attachments with the message by enabling the Print Attached Files with Items check box. In the Copies section, select or type a number of copies. Click the Preview button to preview the printed message before printing, or click OK to send the message to the printer.

Part ii

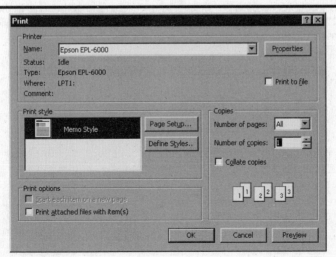

FIGURE 9.14: Set print options for your message in the Print dialog box.

To print the open message using the default Print settings, click the Print button on the message toolbar. If the message is not open, right-click the message in the list and choose Print. The message is sent directly to the printer. A message box appears briefly while the print job is being queued; you can click the Cancel button in the message box to cancel printing, but you've got to be quick.

To change formatting for messages, open the message and choose File ➤ Page Setup ➤ Memo Style (or another style that you've created) to open the Page Setup dialog box. Modify the settings on the Format, Paper, and Header/Footer pages as required.

Printing Multiple Messages and Message Lists

To print multiple messages, select the messages in the list, right-click, and choose Print from the shortcut menu. The Print dialog box opens. Select Memo Style to print all the text of each of the selected messages. Change the Print Options if you want to begin each memo on a new page or to print the attachments with each message.

Choose the Table Style to print the list view. In the Print Options, choose All Rows to print the contents of the folder, or Selected Rows to print or preview the selected messages in a table, as shown in Figure 9.15.

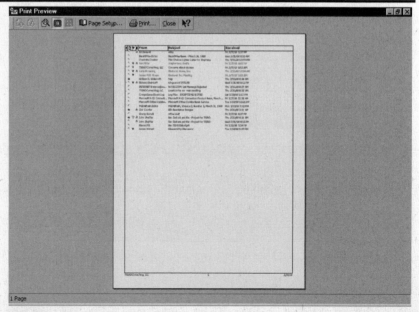

FIGURE 9.15: Use the Table style to print a list of the messages in a folder.

Setting E-mail Options

The hardest part of setting mail options is finding where to change the settings. Options for sending, receiving, securing, and formatting e-mail aren't in one central location. Options are set in the message form, Outlook Options, or one of the many dialog boxes Outlook provides to set mail management options. For example, you can choose to have a sound played or a message box displayed when new mail arrives at your desktop—but the two settings are found in totally different places. If you're having trouble locating a particular option that you know you've seen before, refer to Chapter 13. There you'll find a comprehensive list of mail options to help you wend your way through the maze of mail settings in Outlook.

Organizing E-mail Messages

One of the most persistent challenges facing the networked business is presented by electronic mail. In most organizations, even unpopular people receive a dozen messages a day. The truly connected may receive scores or hundreds of messages, and the messages compete for time with all the other important tasks in your work life. If you're reading your e-mail messages, you can't be visiting clients, participating in a meeting, building a prototype, or writing code.

Are all these messages important? Probably not. Recent studies indicate that when you advance in an organization, your e-mail volume increases—and so does the percentage of messages that are purely informational and require no action on your part. This makes sense, because, unless instructed otherwise, every person working for you will send you a courtesy copy of nearly every message they create to "keep the boss in the loop." You may like receiving all this information, but even the most controlling personalities can be overwhelmed by the sheer volume of messages hitting the Inbox every day.

[Organize] Outlook makes it easy for you to organize and manage your Inbox, and all the tools you need are in one place—the Organize page. Click the Organize button on the toolbar to open the Organize page at the top of the Inbox, shown in Figure 9.16. Using the Organize page, you can create folders for message management, create rules to color-code your messages, change Inbox views, or open the Rules Wizard and automate management of the messages you receive.

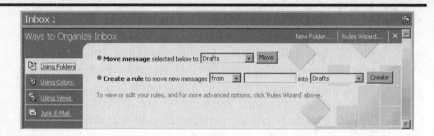

FIGURE 9.16: With the Organize page, all your message management tools are right at your fingertips.

The Organize page has four tabs: Using Folders, Using Colors, Using Views, and Junk E-mail. Find isn't included in the Organize page, but sooner or later you may need to find a message; for details on using Find, see Chapter 11.

Using Folders to Organize Messages

Outlook has a default set of personal folders, including the Inbox. E-mail messages continue to hang around in the Inbox, even after you've read them and dealt with their content. You can easily create additional personal folders to hold different types of messages. For example, you might create a new folder for a project you're working on, for each major client, for e-mail newsletters, or for updates you receive from vendors.

To create a new folder, click the New Folder button in the Organize page to open the Create New Folder dialog box, shown in Figure 9.17. Enter a name for the new folder and indicate the kind of items that will be stored in the folder. In the Select Where to Place the Folder pane, select a location for the folder. If you'll be using the folder for messages, we suggest you place it in the Inbox or directly in the Personal Folders. It gets confusing when you have mail messages stored in the Journal or Contacts. You can always move the folder later, using drag and drop in the Folder List.

When you create a folder, Outlook asks whether you want to add the folder to the shortcut bar. Click Yes if you want to create the shortcut.

NOTE

For more information on creating personal, public, and shared folders, see Chapter 11.

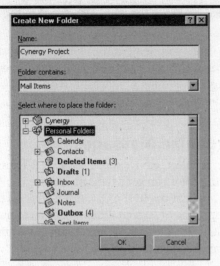

FIGURE 9.17: Creating a new folder for messages in the Inbox

To move a message from the Inbox to your new folder, select the message(s) you want to move in the list view. In the Move Message Selected Below To drop-down list, select the name of your folder, and then click the Move button to move the message.

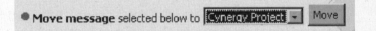

Creating Rules to Automatically Move Messages   In the Organizer, you create rules by example. If you want all messages from Karla Browning to be automatically placed in your new folder, select a message from Karla in the Inbox or any other mail folder.

Choose From or Sent To in the first Create a Rule drop-down box to indicate which type of messages should be moved. If you don't have a message from your recipient in any of your mail folders, enter the person's name or something else memorable in the text box. From the Into drop-down list, select the folder you want the messages to/from this person moved to, and then click the Create button to create the new rule.

Part ii

You'll know it worked because you'll see the word *Done* next to the Create button.

In Outlook 2000, the new rules you create can now be retroactively applied to messages you have already received, and to all of your new messages, incoming and outgoing. For more information on rules, see "Using the Rules Wizard" later in this chapter.

Using Colors to Organize Messages

Message information (sender, subject, etc.) is displayed in the Windows text color by default; this is the color you get when you choose the Automatic color in any Windows application. In the Organizer, click on the Using Colors tab. You can apply one of sixteen different colors to message descriptions based on who sent the message, who it was sent to, and whether or not you are the only recipient.

To set the color based on the sender or recipient, choose a message from the sender, or addressed to the recipient, in the list view. In the Color Messages drop-down lists, choose From or Sent To and a color you wish to apply. Click the Apply Color button to create the color rule.

When you receive a message, that doesn't mean it was "Sent To" you. If you're receiving a courtesy copy, then the message was sent to someone else. Messages that require your personal attention are often addressed directly to you, and you are the only recipient. Coloring these messages so they stand out in the Inbox separates personalized messages from courtesy copies or mail sent to groups. Choose a color in the Show Messages Sent Only to Me In drop-down list, and click the Turn On button to apply this rule.

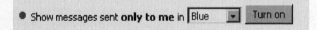

Some color rules are already applied in the mail folders; for example, unread messages are bolded, flagged messages that have passed the reminder date and time are red. To suppress these rules or change the format used for messages meeting different conditions, click the Automatic Formatting button located in the top-right corner of the Organize page to open the Automatic Formatting dialog box shown in Figure 9.18.

FIGURE 9.18: Change the default fonts for conditional message formatting in the Automatic Formatting dialog box.

This dialog box includes the default formats and any color rules you have created. To turn off automatic formatting for an item in the list, disable the item's check box. For example, to change the formatting used on unread messages, select Unread Messages in the list, and then click the Font button and select a new font for unread messages. Use the Move Up and Move Down buttons to change the order in which user-created rules are applied.

You can create a new Automatic Formatting rule in the Organize page, or here in the Automatic Forwarding dialog box. Click the Add button to create a rule named "Untitled." Type a descriptive name for the rule, click the Font button and choose a font, and then click the Condition button to open the Filter dialog box. In the three pages of the dialog box, set the filter conditions, and then click OK to create the condition. You can't change the conditions for the default items, only for rules you created.

Using Junk Mail and Adult Content Rules

Businesses have used direct mailing via snail mail to market to individuals and companies for years. What marketing companies call direct mailing, others call "junk mail." Now, direct marketing has moved to the Internet. Internet commerce is booming, with new retailers, wholesalers, and auctions arriving online every day. And while many users still don't purchase goods over the Internet, every Internet user purchases goods somewhere. Why not run a few commercials past us while we're surfing the Net? We can ignore them if we want to.

What users can't ignore is junk mail (spam) sent directly to their Inboxes: unsolicited e-mail messages advertising everything from low-cost hard drives to psychic NetMeeting sessions. For every directory service or Usenet group, there's a company that collects and sorts e-mail addresses, and then rents or sells the lists for use in e-mail–based advertising. If you or your company pay connect time charges, receiving junk e-mail is more than a nuisance, it's a quantifiable expense. While you can't avoid the connect charges, you can have Outlook automatically format junk mail messages so you don't waste your time opening them.

The other type of messages you can format based on content is adult content messages. To format junk e-mail or adult content messages, click the Junk E-mail tab on the Organize page. Choose a color for each type of message (you can apply the same color to both), and then click the Turn On buttons:

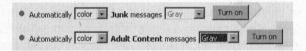

FILTERS FOR JUNK MAIL AND ADULT CONTENT MAIL

Outlook recognizes junk mail and adult content mail by filtering message content, searching for phrases commonly used in direct marketing messages and adult content messages. For junk mail, phrases include: "cards accepted," "extra income," "money-back guarantee," and "100% satisfied." Of course, this means that when a client e-mails "I am 100% satisfied with the way your staff handled our concerns," the message will end up in your designated junk mail folder.

With adult content mail, Outlook searches for phrases like "over 18," "adults only," "adult web," and "xxx." We're sure you can think of legitimate messages that would include some of these phrases.

It's worth knowing how Outlook and other programs with content filters determine which messages may be junk mail or have adult content. If you include phrases like "we're brainstorming ways to

CONTINUED ➡

generate extra income" or "there must be over 18 ways to complete this analysis" in a piece of regular business correspondence, don't be surprised if your recipient never reads the message. To see all the phrases Outlook uses to filter mail, open the file `filters.txt` in the folder where Outlook was installed.

There are other programs you can use to check incoming messages based on sender address that are compatible with Outlook. For more information, visit the Microsoft Web site.

Using the Rules Wizard

The Rules Wizard is a general-purpose tool to automatically deal with messages based on sender, category, content, or other criteria. You've been using a version of the Rules Wizard to create the folder, color, and content rules in the Organize page.

With the Rules Wizard, you can automatically move, forward, flag, color, or delete messages. As with the rules created in the Organize page, the Rules Wizard creates rules that are applied to messages you receive or send in the future. From the Outlook menu, choose Tools ➤ Rules Wizard to fire up the Wizard. If you have the Organize page open, switch to Using Folders and click the Rules Wizard button to open the Rules Wizard dialog box. Click the New button to start the Wizard. The first step of the Wizard is shown in Figure 9.19.

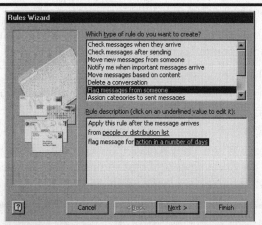

FIGURE 9.19: Use the Rules Wizard to automate message handling.

Rules have three parts: conditions that must be met for the rule to be applied, actions you want to occur when the conditions are met, and exceptions to the rule. The conditions are based on message attributes, and allow you to pinpoint exactly the types of messages you're interested in managing. Notify Me When Important Messages Arrive isn't an adequate description for a message management function this powerful because you can choose to be notified when a message meets one or more of these conditions:

▶ Sent directly to you or sent only to you

▶ Marked with a specified importance or sensitivity

▶ Your name is in the Cc box, the To or Cc box, or is not in the To box (therefore, Cc or Bcc)

▶ From or sent to specified people or distribution lists

▶ Contains specific words in the sender's or recipient's addresses, subject, body, subject or body, or message header

▶ Flagged for any action, or a specified action

▶ Assigned to one or more specified categories

▶ From out of office

▶ Created using a specific form or with values in form fields you select

▶ Contains attachments or is within a specified size range (in kilobytes)

▶ Received within a specified date range

▶ Suspected to be junk mail or from junk senders, adult content mail or from adult content senders

To create a rule, begin by selecting the primary action you want to occur in the rule. In the Which Type of Rule Do You Want to Create list, look for the action you want the rule to invoke—flag, move, notify—and choose one of the following:

Check Messages When They Arrive   Choose this option when none of the other types are what you're looking for and the rule you want to create is for incoming messages.

Check Message After Sending   Choose this one when none of the other types fit your requirements and the rule you want to create is for outgoing messages.

Move New Message from Someone   Like the Using Folders rules, this option moves incoming messages based on the attributes listed above.

Notify Me When Important Messages Arrive   Use this feature to receive notification on the arrival of a message based on attributes.

Move Messages Based on Content   This item works the same as Move New Message from Someone, but is based on content.

Delete a Conversation   This option deletes all messages based on attributes.

Flag Messages from Someone   Choose this option to apply a flag and set a reminder for *N* days from message receipt.

Assign Categories to Sent Messages   This item is for outgoing messages.

Assign Categories Based on Content   Use this option for incoming messages.

Move Messages I Send to Someone   This feature is the same as Move Messages Based on Content for outgoing messages.

Stop Processing All Following Rules   If a message meets the criteria here, this is the only rule processed.

After you select a rule, the rule description appears in the lower text box. In Figure 9.19, selecting Flag Messages from Someone inserts this rule description:

Apply this rule after the message arrives
from people or distribution list
flag message for action in a number of days

Each underlined term in the description is editable. Clicking People or Distribution List opens the Select Names dialog box, so you can choose the people or distribution list that will trigger this rule. Click Action in a Number of Days to open the Flag Message dialog box, so you can choose a flag and the number of days that should pass before you're reminded of the flag.

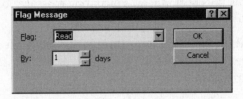

When you've finished this initial editing, each of the underlined terms will have been replaced with your choices.

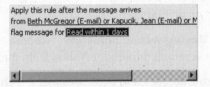

Click Next to continue to the second step of the Rules Wizard, shown in Figure 9.20. In this step, add more conditions to fine-tune your rule.

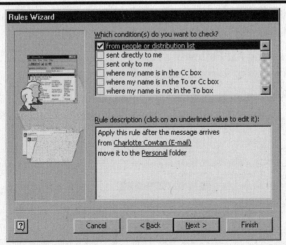

FIGURE 9.20: Select conditions to indicate when the rule should be applied.

To add a condition, click its check box. The condition is added to the rule description. If you choose a condition with an underlined term, click the underlined term in the rule description to add criteria to the condition. Here we've added two conditions: *with **planning** in the body*, and *received after 3/29/98 and before 4/19/98*.

> Apply this rule after the message arrives
> from Beth McGregor (E-mail) or Kapucik, Jean (E-mail) or N
> and with planning in the body
> and received after 3/29/98 and before 4/19/98
> flag message for Read within 1 days

Click Next to proceed to the third step of the Rules Wizard—selecting actions. The action you selected in the first step is already checked, as shown in Figure 9.21.

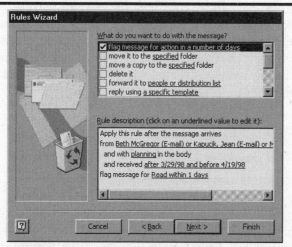

FIGURE 9.21:   Choose all the actions Outlook should take when the described message is delivered or sent.

Choose any other actions you want to happen when a message meets the conditions specified in the Rule Description:

- ▶ Flag or clear a flag, change the importance

- ▶ Move, copy, forward, or delete it

- ▶ Receive notification that it arrived with a message or sound

- ▶ Reply with a specific template

▸ Assign it to a category

▸ Perform a custom action (add-ins, not part of Outlook)

▸ Stop processing rules for the message

In the rule description below, the message is being flagged and forwarded. Flagging occurs first in the description, so the forwarded message will also be flagged.

> Apply this rule after the message arrives
> from <u>Beth McGregor (E-mail)</u> or <u>Kapucik, Jean (E-mail)</u> or M
>   and with <u>planning</u> in the body
>   and received <u>after 3/29/98</u> and before 4/19/98
> flag message for <u>Read within 1 days</u>
>   and forward it to Margaret A Sanders (E-mail)

In Outlook, every rule can have its exceptions. Now that you've constructed the rule, you can indicate conditions under which the rule should be ignored. Click Next to move to the next step of the Wizard, and note the conditions under which the rule should not be applied. In this example, we're not going to apply the rule if the specific person we were forwarding the message to already received the message. (This means the message won't be flagged, either.)

> from <u>Beth McGregor (E-mail)</u> or <u>Kapucik, Jean (E-mail)</u> (
>   and with <u>planning</u> in the body
>   and received <u>after 3/29/98</u> and before 4/19/98
> flag message for <u>Read within 1 days</u>
>   and forward it to <u>Margaret A Sanders (E-mail)</u>
> except if sent to Margaret A Sanders (E-mail)

In the last step of the Wizard, shown in Figure 9.22, enter a name for the rule. You don't have to turn the rule on when you create it you can create rules when you have time to create them and turn them on when you need them. Check the Run This Rule Now on Messages Already in X check box (where X is the folder group you are currently using) to apply the rule to existing messages. Click Finish to create the rule and return to the Rules Wizard dialog box.

WARNING

The Rules Wizard can be a little confusing. When you go to Tools ➢ Rules Wizard, it is actually a Rules Wizard manager dialog box that opens, even though it's called the Rules Wizard. You need to click New to get the "real" Rules Wizard, which walks you through the job of making a new rule to *add* to the Rules Wizard manager.

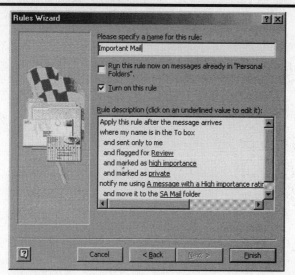

FIGURE 9.22: Name the rule and turn it on before you click Finish.

When a rule is turned on, messages that meet the conditions in the rule's description are acted on by Outlook as described in the rule. After you've created a rule, return to the Rules Wizard dialog box to turn the rule off or on, delete the rule, or rename the rule. You can copy the rule, and then modify the copy to create another rule with similar actions or conditions.

TIP

You can share your rules with other users. Click the Options button at the bottom of the Rules Wizard dialog box (the one that opens when you go to Tools ≻ Rules Wizard) to export rules to a floppy disk or shared folder. Other users can then open the Rules Wizard, click the Options button, and import the rules.

WHAT'S NEXT?

This chapter explained how you can make your e-mail do what you want it to. Outlook helps you to personalize your mail and organize large volumes of incoming messages. Next, you will learn to simplify your file-management chores by handling it all through Outlook.

Chapter 10

SETTING USER PREFERENCES

Much of Outlook's work behind the scenes is dictated by the settings in your user profile. A *profile* is a file that contains information about your Outlook configuration. The profile, stored on your local computer, links you to particular information services and address books.

An *information service* is a group of settings that tell Outlook how and where to send and receive messages, store and recall items, or connect to address books. Each of the following is an information service:

- ▶ Internet mail
- ▶ Microsoft Exchange mail
- ▶ CompuServe mail
- ▶ Personal address book
- ▶ Outlook address book

● ●

Adapted from *Mastering™ Microsoft® Outlook™ 2000* by Gini Courter and Annette Marquis

ISBN 0-7821-2472-0   787 pages $34.99

Each profile includes multiple information services. In order to configure a service that interacts with other computers, such as Microsoft
Exchange mail or Internet mail, you need to gather additional information. Depending on the specific service, this may include such things as
the server name, an access phone number, and your mailbox name.

CREATING A NEW PROFILE

If more than one person works on your computer, you should each have
your own profile. Profiles help keep your personal computer personal by
saving each user's mail and address book settings separately.

NOTE

Your profile is not the same as your Windows or Windows NT user account. A
workstation may have five different user accounts but only one profile, or *vice
versa*. However, when you're adding new profiles for current users, it's helpful
if you give it the same name as your Windows user account.

Each user can have more than one profile. For example, your notebook
computer might include one profile that you use when you're in your
office, connected to a mail server that delivers both internal and Internet
mail. A second profile, for use out of the office, could include dial-up
information services. You can designate a default profile or have Outlook
prompt you to select a profile when you launch Outlook. You create new
profiles, whether for yourself or another user, in the Windows Control
Panel.

Choose Start ➣ Settings ➣ Control Panel on the Windows taskbar to
open the Control Panel. Then double-click the Mail icon to open the Services page of the Properties dialog box, shown in Figure 10.1.

You'll be seeing this dialog box again—it shows the information services
included in the current profile. For now, though, click the Show Profiles
button to open the Mail dialog box, shown in Figure 10.2. On this workstation, there are two profiles: Microsoft Outlook Internet Settings and
Valued Acer Customer. (Guess what kind of PC this is!)

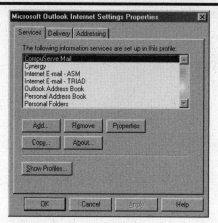

FIGURE 10.1: The Services page of the Properties dialog box displays information services for the active profile.

FIGURE 10.2: Open the Mail dialog box to see the profiles set up on the computer.

Click the Add button to launch the Inbox Setup Wizard to add a new profile. In the first step of the Wizard, shown in Figure 10.3, choose the information services you'd like the Wizard to configure for messaging on this workstation, or select Manually Configure Information Services. Manually Configure is the same as "do it later." You can add services to the profile at any time; don't add services until you intend to use them.

FIGURE 10.3:   Choosing services in the Inbox Setup Wizard

In the second step of the Wizard, you're prompted for a name for the profile. The default name is the username from Windows. If you're creating a profile for another user, enter their name. A second profile for your use might be called Alternate Profile, At Home, or any other descriptive name.

Configuring Services in the Wizard

If you chose information services in the first step, you're asked to configure each of the services you selected in order. You'll need information (and maybe a disk or CD) for each information service you selected. Windows will prompt you to provide configuration information. For Internet e-mail, for example, you will click a Setup Mail Account button in the Wizard, which opens the Mail Account Properties dialog box, shown in Figure 10.4.

In the General page (see Figure 10.4), you enter a friendly name for the service, which can be any text string you want to use to refer to the service. Enter the user's name, organization, e-mail address, and the address others use to reply to the user. In the other pages of the dialog box, things get a lot more specific. If you've configured your Internet e-mail account previously, you may know the name of the POP server and SMTP server and the server port numbers you need to use. If you don't, call your Internet service provider (ISP) and ask for this information.

When you're finished configuring services, the Services page of the Properties dialog box (see Figure 10.1) opens again, displaying the services you've just configured.

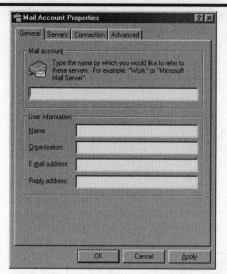

FIGURE 10.4: Configuring an Internet mail service in the Mail Account Properties dialog box

In the final steps of the Inbox Wizard, you can add Outlook to the Windows Startup group and then click Finish to close the Wizard. The Mail dialog box will still be open, displaying your PC's profiles, including the new profile you created.

ADDING SERVICES

To add a service to a profile, open the Mail dialog box (Start ➤ Settings ➤ Control Panel ➤ Mail ➤ Show Profiles). Select the profile you want to add services to in the Mail dialog box, shown in Figure 10.5.

Properties Click the Properties button to open the Properties dialog box for the service, shown in Figure 10.6.

Click the Add button to open the Add Service to Profile dialog box, shown in Figure 10.7. The dialog box has a list of services you can add. If the service you want to add is listed, select the service from the list and click OK.

If the messaging service you want to add isn't listed, you can insert the disk or CD for the service and click the Have Disk button. You'll be prompted to locate the setup file for the service on the disk or CD, and Windows will install the software for the service.

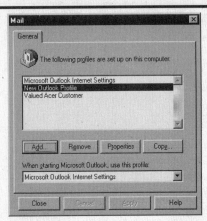

FIGURE 10.5: Selecting a profile to add new services

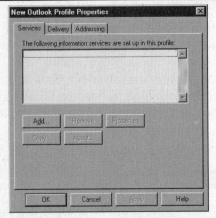

FIGURE 10.6: The profile's Properties dialog box displays the services—if any—configured for the profile.

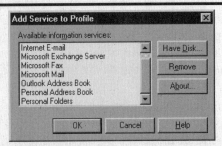

FIGURE 10.7: Select a service to add in the Add Service to Profile dialog box.

TIP

Contact your messaging service or visit its Web site to find out if you need additional software to install the service. For example, to install CompuServe mail, you need to add CompuServe and a driver for Outlook called `cismail.exe`, which is available from CompuServe, or you need to convert your CompuServe mailbox to a POP3 mailbox. While logged onto CompuServe, type **Go:PopMail** for instructions on how to activate your PopMail account.

Adding Personal Folders

At a minimum, a profile should include the Personal Folders service. Personal Folders is the *information store* (one type of information service) for the profile, which is the file where Outlook will keep the Contacts, Tasks, and other items associated with this profile. Personal folders have the `.pst` file extension.

To add a Personal Folders service, select Personal Folders in the Add Service to Profile dialog box (see Figure 10.7) and click the Add button to open the Create/Open Personal Folders File dialog box, shown in Figure 10.8. Select a file name and location for the `.pst` file, click Open to create the new `.pst` file. Choose a location for the `.pst` file. If you're creating personal folders for one of the users on your PC, consider creating the `.pst` file in the `Windows\Profiles\Username\Application Data` folder for the user. Outlook creates the `.pst` file and opens the Create Microsoft Personal Folders dialog box.

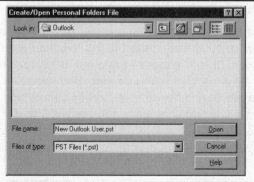

FIGURE 10.8: Configuring the personal folders for a new user

TIP

You can connect a profile to an existing set of personal folders by selecting the .pst file for the existing profile. The two profiles will share Outlook items.

The file path and name you entered has "read only" at the top of the dialog box. In the Name text box, enter the name that will appear for this service in the Information Services dialog box. Using part of the user's name, as well as Personal Folders, can help keep things straight when more than one person uses an information store.

Encrypting Personal Folders

Encryption stores the .pst file in a format that can't be read externally, keeping your data confidential. Choose No Encryption if you don't want to encrypt your data—for example, if you use a desktop computer on a secured network. Choose Compressible Encryption to encrypt your personal folders in the smallest disk space possible. Best Encryption chooses the most secure encryption, but will take up more disk space than Compressible Encryption. If you want to encrypt your files, this is the time to do it. You can't change this option later.

Assigning a Password to Personal Folders

You do not need to put a password on your personal folders. However, adding a password provides another level of security for your files. If other people use your computer and your .pst file is not password-protected, they can attach your personal folder file to their profiles.

If you add a password, you'll be prompted to enter the password when you either start Outlook or otherwise connect to your personal folders. You can save the password in your Windows password list and not be prompted by Outlook. Be aware that this is the computer version of putting all your eggs in one basket. Anyone who knows your Windows/Windows NT password can get into any application or folder that is protected with that password. If the password is saved, you're prompted to enter it only if you log on as another user or try to add the personal folders file to a profile.

Creating a Personal Address Book

In the Internet Only configuration, Contacts acts as your personal address book, and you create groups to use as distribution lists. If you want to create distribution lists in the Corporate/Workgroup configuration, you need a personal address book. Creating a personal address book, which has a `.pab` extension, is much like creating personal folders. In the profile's Properties dialog box, click the Add button, and then select Personal Address Book from the list in the Add Services to Profile dialog box.

The default name for a personal address book is `mailbox.pab`; a `.pab` file is often just called a "pab." You can choose an existing pab file to connect to your personal address book in another profile, or create a file with a different name for a new user's profile. Click OK to open the Personal Address Book dialog box, shown in Figure 10.9. Choose the default display for names in the pab, enter any notes about the pab on the Notes page, and then click OK to add the personal address book to the profile.

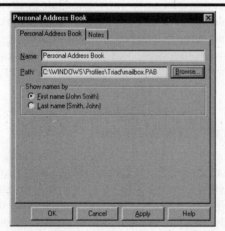

FIGURE 10.9:   Choose how names should be displayed in the personal address book.

Deleting Services

If you're no longer using a service, you should remove it from your profile. For example, if your workplace is routing your Internet mail, and you no longer need to connect to an ISP, you should remove the Internet mail service for the ISP from your profile for two reasons. Removing it as a service removes it from the Outlook menus and also ensures that it won't conflict with your other mail services.

To delete a service, open the Properties dialog box for the profile, select the service, and click Remove. You'll be prompted to confirm removing the service:

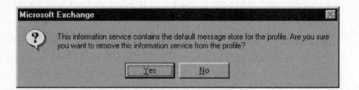

Modifying Service Properties

Occasionally, you'll need to modify your service properties. For example, your Internet service provider may add a new high-speed line (with a new telephone number) that you'd like to use. To change the properties of any service, open the profile's Properties dialog box (see Figure 10.1), select the information service you want to modify, and click the Properties button. Make the modifications you want in the service's dialog box, and click OK.

Copying Information Services

You already have a profile you use in the office, and you are creating a second profile for use on the road. You'll use the same personal address book in the new profile, so why re-create it? You can copy an information service to another profile. With complex services like Internet mail services, this increases the likelihood that the service will work in the new profile.

To copy a service, open the Properties dialog box for the profile that contains the service you want to copy. Select the information service and click the Copy button to open the Copy Information Service dialog box, shown in Figure 10.10.

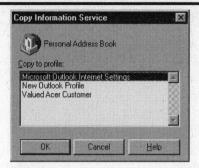

FIGURE 10.10: Use the Copy Information Service dialog box to copy a service to another profile.

Select the destination profile for the information service, and click OK to copy the service. You won't see a confirmation, but if you look at the properties for the destination profile, you'll see the copied information service on the list. You can't copy an information service that already exists in the destination profile.

SETTING PROFILE OPTIONS

The profile includes options for using the information services configured within it. You set these options in the profile's Properties dialog box. In the Control Panel, double-click the Mail icon to open the Properties for the active profile. (To make changes to a different profile, click Show Profiles, select the profile, and click Properties.)

Setting Delivery Options

On the Delivery tab of the Properties dialog box, shown in Figure 10.11, choose the information store where messages should be delivered in the Deliver New Mail to the Following Location drop-down list.

By default, mail is delivered to your Inbox in the Internet Only configuration, and to the mailbox on your server in the Corporate/Workgroup configuration.

FIGURE 10.11: Choose a location for mail and prioritize your mail services in the profile's Delivery options.

The Recipient Addresses list shows the messaging services in your profile in the order in which they process the mail you send. If you have more than one information service, you may want to change the order in which they process mail. For example, Microsoft Exchange can send Internet mail, so if Microsoft Exchange is higher in the list than an Internet mail service you have on your computer, Microsoft Exchange will handle all the Internet mail you send, as well as the Microsoft Exchange mail. To put the services in your order of preference, click to select the service that you want to use to process mail first. Use the Move Up arrow button to move your primary mail service into the first position. Select the other services in turn and use the Move Up and Move Down arrow buttons to rearrange them as required.

Setting Addressing Options

The Addressing options (see Figure 10.12) specify the default address book and the order in which address books are used in Outlook.

The address book you choose in the Show This Address List First drop-down list is the address book you'll see whenever you open the Select Names dialog box in Outlook or click the Address Book button in other Office applications. Select the address book you choose names from most often.

In the Keep Personal Addresses In drop-down list, you'll probably want to select your Personal Address Book or Outlook Address Book in the Corporate/Workgroup configuration, and Contacts in the Internet Only configuration.

FIGURE 10.12: Choose the default address book and address book processing order on the Addressing page.

The When Sending Mail list shows the address books in the order in which Outlook and other applications check them to find a name you enter for a message recipient. Use the Move Up and Move Down buttons so that the most frequently used address book is at the top of the list.

COPYING PROFILES

You don't have to create a new profile from scratch if you already have a profile with most or all of the services you want to add. In the Mail dialog box (Start ➤ Settings ➤ Control Panel ➤ Mail), choose the profile you want to copy, and click the Copy button. In the Copy Profile dialog box, enter a name for the copied profile and click OK. Then modify the profile by adding, removing, or modifying services.

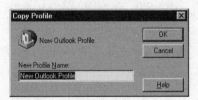

DELETING PROFILES

When someone quits using a workstation, you can delete their profile. Open the Mail dialog box (Start ➤ Settings ➤ Control Panel ➤ Mail), and then click the Show Profiles button. Select the profile you wish to delete, and click the Remove button. Windows will prompt you to confirm the deletion.

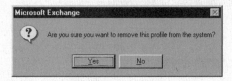

SELECTING A PROFILE

You set the default profile from the When Starting Microsoft Outlook, Use This Profile drop-down list in the Mail dialog box. When the computer is started, this is the profile that will be used:

But how do you get to the other profiles if this profile is always used? The setting to prompt for a profile is in Outlook. Choose Tools ➤ Options from the menu to open the Options dialog box, and click the Mail Services tab (see Figure 10.13). In the Startup Settings section, choose the Prompt for a Profile to Be Used option, and then click OK to close the dialog box.

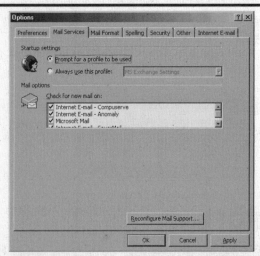

FIGURE 10.13:　Have Outlook prompt the user to select a profile.

The next time Outlook starts, you'll be prompted to choose a profile.

USING MULTIPLE COMPUTERS

In some companies, employees use more than one computer on a regular basis. With Outlook, you can receive mail at any computer you use. On one computer, make sure that your mail is being sent to your server mailbox, not your Inbox on the PC. (Do this on the Delivery page of the profile's Properties dialog box.) Next, create a user profile on another computer you use and connect it to your server mailbox.

Part ii

CUSTOMIZING COMMAND BARS

Outlook has four command bars: the menu bar; and the Standard, Advanced, and Remote toolbars. All command bars are fully customizable, and you can create your own command bars with features you use frequently.

To create a new command bar, choose View ➢ Toolbars ➢ Customize from the menu bar, or right-click any command bar and choose Customize from the shortcut menu, to open the Customize dialog box.

Settings in the Options page of the Customize dialog box, shown in Figure 10.14, affect not only all Outlook command bars, but the command bars in all Office applications. If you turn off toolbar ScreenTips in Outlook, they're gone in Excel as well. If you animate menus so they slither or slide here, then you'll have that added functionality in Word and PowerPoint. This is true throughout Office, so, for example, a change in Excel changes what you see in Outlook.

FIGURE 10.14: Change settings in the Options page of the Customize dialog box for all Office applications.

To change the items on a command bar, move to the Toolbars page of the dialog box, shown in Figure 10.15. You can reset an existing command bar to its default buttons and menu items by selecting the bar and then clicking the Reset button.

NOTE

Prior to Office 97, there were two different types of bars in Office applications: menu bars with text choices, and toolbars with buttons. Now you can place menus on toolbars and buttons on menus, so both are called command bars, although the customization dialog boxes refer to all of them as toolbars.

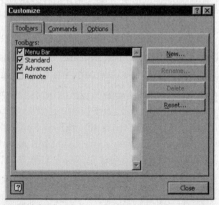

FIGURE 10.15: Create new command bars or reset existing bars on the Toolbars page of the dialog box.

Creating Toolbars

To create a new toolbar, click the New button to open the New Toolbar dialog box. Enter a name for the command bar and click OK. A tiny toolbar, just big enough to hold one button, will appear somewhere near the center of your screen.

Renaming and Deleting Toolbars

The default command bars can't be deleted or renamed. Custom toolbars that you (or other users) create are renamed or deleted on the Toolbars page. Select the toolbar, and click the Rename or Delete button.

Adding Commands to Toolbars

You add commands to new toolbars and to the default toolbars the same way. Click the Commands tab of the Customize dialog box to see the lists of available commands, shown in Figure 10.16. In the Categories list, select the type of command you want to add. For example, you might want to add a button for the Group By box to your new toolbar. In the Categories list, choose View, and then scroll through the list of commands to find the Group By button.

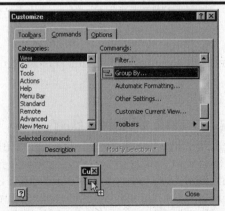

FIGURE 10.16: Drag commands from the list to a command bar to add a new button or menu option.

Drag the command from the Commands list and move it to the toolbar. A dark line appears. Move the mouse until the dark insertion line appears in the position where you want the new button, and then drop the button to place it (see Figure 10.16).

After you've added the button, you can click the Modify Selection button in the Customize dialog box to see a list of options for the button. For example, you can select a new image for the button by choosing Change Button Image, or display the name of the button as well as the Group By picture by choosing Image and Text.

Continue adding commands by selecting commands and dragging them onto the toolbar.

Adding Commands to the Menu Bar

When you add commands to the menu bar, be aware of one small difference in the process. You have to wait until the menu opens to place the command on the appropriate menu. For example, you can add the Group By button to the View menu. Drag the command from the Customize dialog box to the View menu, and wait for the menu to open. Drag the command to the desired location on the View menu before dropping it into place.

Rearranging Commands

Use drag and drop to move commands from one location on a toolbar or the menu bar to another (or from one toolbar to another). To copy a command, hold Ctrl while dragging it to its destination. To delete a command, drag the button off the toolbar. An X appears on the command; drop the button to delete it from the toolbar.

TIP

This may seem obvious, but if you rearrange the Outlook command bars too much, you'll have a hard time getting appropriate help from other users, your company's help desk, or Microsoft Technical Support. After the third or fourth time you reply "I don't have that there," you'll be on your own. If you want a specialized toolbar or menu, create a new toolbar or add a menu to the existing menu bar (with the New Menu command) and add commands to the new toolbar or menu.

As long as the Customize dialog box is open, you can add, delete, and rearrange commands. When you're finished customizing the command bars, click OK to close the Customize dialog box.

CONTROLLING OUTLOOK STARTUP OPTIONS

When Outlook launches, the file `Outlook.exe` runs. You can add command-line parameters to the shortcut you use to start Outlook and change what Outlook does when it opens. There are two approaches you can take:

- ▶ Add parameters to the default shortcut.
- ▶ Create a new Outlook shortcut on the Desktop with special parameters, and leave the default shortcut in place.

If you change the default shortcut, Outlook will always start with the command-line parameters, whether you launch it from the Programs menu, the Office shortcut bar, or the Start menu. If you create a Desktop icon, you can launch Outlook from the icon when you want the customized behavior, and from the Start menu, Programs menu, or Office shortcut bar otherwise. Table 10.1 lists the actions you can have Outlook automatically follow.

Part ii

TABLE 10.1: Outlook Startup Options

ACTION	PARAMETER
Create e-mail message	c/ipm.note
Create an appointment	c/ipm.appointment
Create a journal item	c/ipm.activity
Create a contact	c/ipm.contact
Create a note	c/ipm.stickynote
Open a folder	/select *"path and folder name"*

Changing the Default Shortcut

If you always want Outlook to open a folder or create an item, you can change the default shortcut. In Windows Explorer or My Computer, locate the shortcut to Outlook.exe. The shortcut to Outlook.exe is either in the same folder as Outlook.exe or up one folder level.

Microsoft
Outlook

Right-click the shortcut's icon and choose Properties to open the Microsoft Outlook Properties dialog box, shown in Figure 10.17. In the Target text box, click at the end of the target text, type a space, and add the command parameter you want to use from Table 10.1. The Target shown in Figure 10.17 will cause Outlook to open a new message form automatically.

Click OK to close the Properties dialog box. The next time Outlook is launched, it will behave according to the command parameters you entered.

In Figure 10.17, the Target and Start In paths are enclosed in quotes because there's a space in the path between *Microsoft* and *Office* and between *Program* and *Files*. In Windows, paths with spaces need to be enclosed in quotes.

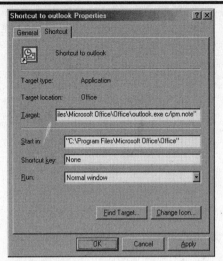

FIGURE 10.17: Add parameters to the Target to have Outlook automatically open a form.

Adding a New Shortcut

If you only want a new message form (or journal form, or whatever) some of the time, you're better off with a new shortcut that you can use when you want a new form, leaving the default shortcut for use at other times.

To create a new shortcut, find either Outlook.exe or the shortcut to Outlook.exe. Right-click and choose Create Shortcut from the menu to create a new shortcut in the current folder. Drag the shortcut onto the Desktop, and add the parameters you want to use to the new shortcut. You can rename the shortcut (right-click the icon and choose Rename) so that the Desktop shortcut is called Outlook E-mail, reminding you that it creates a new e-mail message when you use it to launch Outlook.

WHAT'S NEXT?

This chapter showed that you can simplify your file management chores by handling it all through Outlook, instead of switching to Windows Explorer or My Computer. In the next chapter, you'll learn how to create folders, move and copy files, and rename and delete files and folders without ever leaving Outlook. You'll also learn how to archive old data and back up those all-important Outlook folders.

Chapter 11

ORGANIZING YOUR OUTLOOK DATA

We have often referred to Outlook as a desktop information manager. Nowhere does it do a better job of living up to its name than in its folder- and file-management features. You never have to launch the Windows Explorer or My Computer again. All of your file-management needs can be accommodated from within Outlook. And to top it off, all of the features that make Outlook so exciting, such as views, integration, and the powerful new Find feature, give Outlook the edge over Windows as a file-management tool.

Adapted from *Mastering™ Microsoft® Outlook™ 2000*
by Gini Courter and Annette Marquis

ISBN 0-7821-2472-0   787 pages $34.99

MANAGING DATA AND FILES IN OUTLOOK

Whether you've realized it or not, all of the Outlook components are organized as folders, and they each have all of the properties of other folders on your hard drive or network. You can move them, copy them, rename them, create subfolders under them, and view them in different ways. The easiest way to grasp the Outlook folder structure is to choose Folder List from the View menu. This opens a third pane in the Outlook window that clearly shows the folders and subfolders that make up the Outlook components (see Figure 11.1).

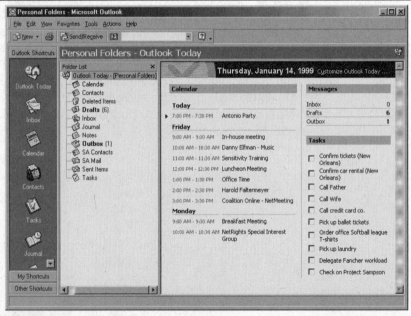

FIGURE 11.1: The Folder List view of Outlook

Another quick way to open the Folder List is to click the component name in the banner of the Information Viewer. This opens the Folder List temporarily so you can view it and move between folders. To keep it open, click the push pin in the top-right corner.

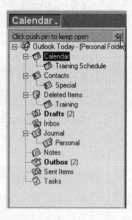

Part ii

At the top of the list is Outlook Today - [Personal Folders]. *Personal folders* is the Outlook information service that contains your personal information. Other information services may contain public folders on a Microsoft Exchange server or Internet folders for sharing information with others on the Internet. The personal folders information service contains your personal information store, Contacts, Calendar, Tasks, and so on. It's possible to have more than one set of personal folders available to you as part of your user profile, or to have a mixture of personal and public folders.

Click on any of the folders to display the contents of that folder. The minus sign or plus sign to the left of Outlook Today - [Personal Folders] (and of other folders, too) is a Collapse/Expand button. If it's a minus sign, you can click it and collapse the folder, so that all of the folders underneath it are hidden, as shown in Figure 11.2. The minus sign changes to a plus sign to indicate that this folder can be expanded to show the folders or files underneath it.

FIGURE 11.2: Click the Collapse button to collapse all the folders.

Clicking the plus sign expands the folder again. To change the width of the folder list, point to the right border and, when your pointer changes to a double-headed resize arrow, like the one in Figure 11.3, drag the border to the left or the right. Release the mouse button when you have the desired pane size.

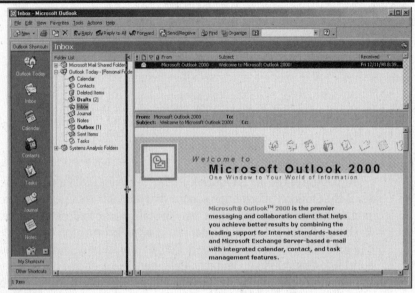

FIGURE 11.3: Change the width of the Folder List by dragging its border.

When the list is too narrow to display all of its contents, a scroll bar appears at the bottom of the list.

NOTE

If you prefer using the Folder List instead of the Outlook Bar, you can turn off the Outlook bar by choosing View ➢ Outlook Bar. Turn it back on again by repeating the process. See "Customizing the Outlook Bar," later in this chapter, for more about using the Outlook bar effectively.

Creating Folders

As your personal folders begin to fill up with information, you may find it valuable to create subfolders to store some of your information. This is especially useful in managing your incoming and outgoing e-mail. To create a subfolder, right-click on the main folder and choose New Folder from the shortcut menu.

You could also choose File ➤ New Folder or click the New button drop-down list and choose Folder. Any of these options opens the Create New Folder dialog box. The main folder you clicked will be highlighted; the Folder Contains option corresponds to that type of folder. In Figure 11.4, the Inbox is highlighted and the Folder Contains list box is set to Mail Items. You are not bound by these choices. Once the Create New Folder dialog box opens, you can select a different main folder altogether. If you do, however, the Folder Contains option will not change on its own, so you'll have to change it to match the folder type. For example, if you decide to create a Calendar folder instead, just click the Calendar in the Select Where to Place the Folder list, and choose Appointment Items from the Folder Contains list.

FIGURE 11.4: The Create New Folder dialog box

Part ii

When you have finished entering the folder type and selecting where it will go, enter a name for the new folder. In Figure 11.5, a new Calendar folder called Training is created.

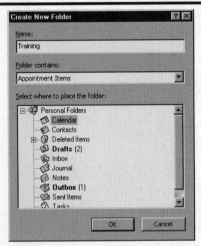

FIGURE 11.5:   Creating a new Calendar folder

When you click OK, you will be asked if you would like to create a short-cut to this folder on the Outlook bar.

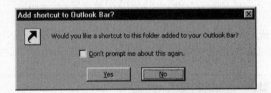

The Outlook bar is fully customizable—you can add to it and remove any of the items on it (see "Customizing the Outlook Bar," later in this chapter, for details). If you would like this folder to be available to you on the Outlook bar, click Yes; if you would prefer not to add this folder to the Outlook bar, click No. The only way you'll be able to access the folder if you choose No is to turn on the Folder List. If you plan to keep the Folder List visible and turn off the Outlook bar (View ➤ Outlook Bar), check the Don't Prompt Me About This Again check box and click No. Figure 11.6

shows the newly created Calendar folder (you may have to click the Expand button (+) to see it).

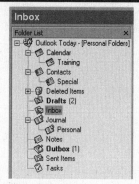

FIGURE 11.6: A subfolder is displayed under the Calendar folder.

NOTE

If you decide you'd like to add a folder to the Outlook bar after you've created it, just right-click the folder and choose Add to Outlook Bar from the shortcut menu.

Moving Items to Different Folders

Now that you have a new folder, it might be nice to have something in it. You can create new items to put in the folder by selecting the folder and clicking the New button. If you want to organize existing items into subfolders, just click on the item and drag it into the new folder. For example, Figure 11.7 shows a Calendar item, Publisher Training, which is highlighted on the right (note the thick border), being dragged to the Training folder. Dragging an item places a small, gray rectangle at the bottom of the pointer.

To copy an item instead of moving it, hold down the Ctrl key when you drag. The pointer will include a plus symbol below the Move Document icon.

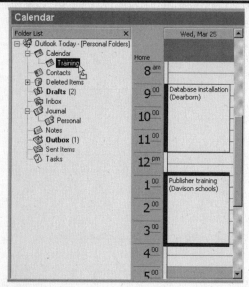

FIGURE 11.7: Dragging an item into a subfolder

Moving or Copying Multiple Items

To select more than one item in a folder for moving or copying, you can use the standard Windows selection techniques. Click on the first item and hold down the Ctrl key before clicking the next item. Keep the Ctrl key held down until you've selected all the desired items.

If you want to select several consecutive items in a list, click the first one and hold the Shift key down before selecting the last item in the list. This will select all the items in between. To select all the items in a list, choose Edit ➤ Select All.

You can move multiple items at once by clicking anywhere in the selected list and dragging them, as shown in Figure 11.8.

NOTE

If you're confused by whether you are moving or copying, you might find it easier to drag with the right mouse button. When you reach your destination, release the mouse button and a shortcut menu will appear that lets you choose among Move, Copy, or Cancel.

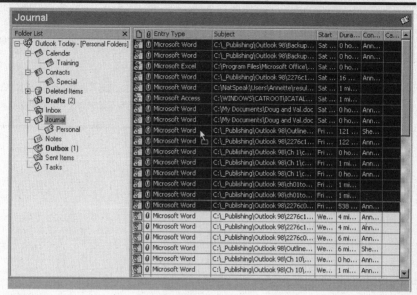

FIGURE 11.8: Dragging multiple items

Part ii

Moving and Copying Items to Folders Using Menus

If you're not proficient at dragging and would like to use menu options to move and copy files, Outlook has not forgotten you. Right-click on any item to open the shortcut menu and choose Move to Folder.

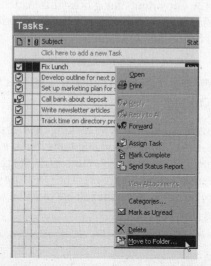

NOTE

The shortcut menu has different choices depending on what type of item you select.

Choosing Move to Folder opens the Move Items dialog box, shown in Figure 11.9. Select the folder you want to move the item to, and click OK.

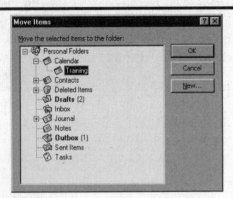

FIGURE 11.9:　The Move Items dialog box

If you want to create a new folder, click the New button in the Move Items dialog box to open the Create New Folder dialog box (shown previously in Figure 11.4).

To copy an item, you must choose Copy to Folder from the Edit menu. This opens the Copy Item dialog box (this is identical to the Move Items dialog box shown in Figure 11.9, except for the title) and creates a copy of the items in the designated folder.

Moving Items to Folders Using the Organize Page

The Organize page, opened by clicking the Organize button on the Standard toolbar, has options for moving some items, specifically contacts, tasks, notes, and mail items, to folders (this excludes using this option to move Calendar items or Journal entries). The Organize page is slightly different depending on which component you are in, but it closely resembles the Contacts version shown here.

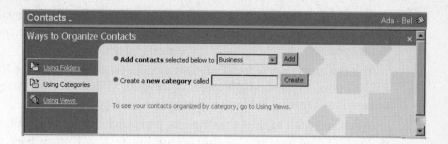

The Organize page has a Web-like interface, so instead of buttons it uses hyperlinks. Click the Using Folders hyperlink and click the down arrow on the Move Contact Selected Below To field to display the list of available folders.

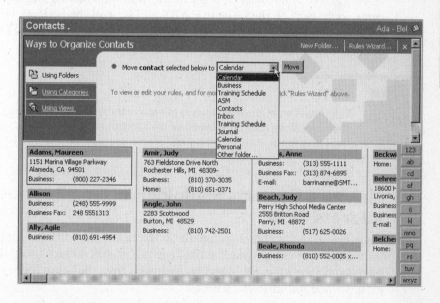

If the folder you want is visible from the Folder List, select it and click Move. If the folder you want is not visible, select Other Folder at the bottom of the list to open the Select Folder dialog box. Select the folder you want from this list and click OK to close the dialog box; then click Move to actually move the item.

Remember to only move an item into a folder that was created to accept it—a mail item into a Mail folder, a contact into a Contacts folder, and so on—unless you want to create another type of item. For example, you can schedule time to work on a task by moving a task into a Calendar folder.

When you do, a meeting form opens so you can schedule the task. If you move a contact into a Mail folder, it creates an e-mail message addressed to that person.

You can create a new folder on the Organize page by clicking the New Folder button in the top-right corner of the pane. Follow the same process outlined in "Creating Folders" earlier in this chapter.

When you want to close the Organize page, click the Organize button on the Standard toolbar, click the Close button on the Organize page, or switch to another component.

Moving and Copying Folders

Moving and copying folders is really no different from moving and copying items. Right-click on the folder in the Folder List, and choose Move Folder or Copy Folder. You'll find the same dialog box you saw in Figure 11.9. Select the folder and click OK.

NOTE

You cannot move the main folders of each of the Outlook components. The choice for Move Folder is dimmed on the shortcut menus of Contacts, Calendar, Tasks, Inbox, Journal, and Notes.

Making a Contacts Subfolder an E-mail Address Book

If you create a subfolder underneath Contacts, you have to let Outlook know that you want to make it available as an Outlook address book. This will let you access the e-mail and fax addresses from the Select Name dialog box when you are creating e-mail.

To make a folder available as an Outlook address book:

1. Right-click the new Contacts subfolder, and choose Properties from the shortcut menu.

2. Click the Outlook Address Book tab of the Special Properties dialog box, shown in Figure 11.10.

3. Click the Show This Folder as an E-mail Address Book check box.

4. Enter a different name for the address book if desired. This does not change the folder name, only the name of the address book.

5. Click OK to save the changes and close the Special Properties dialog box.

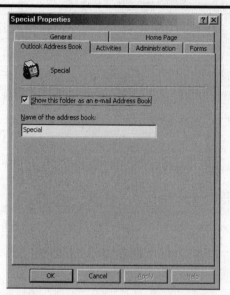

FIGURE 11.10:   The Outlook Address Book tab of a Contact folder's Special Properties dialog box

Opening Folders in New Windows

There may be times when you want to check something *now* while you're in the middle of something else. Maybe you're reading your e-mail and discover that your best friend has front row tickets to a Semisonic concert and is inviting you to go if you are available. You don't want to waste any time getting back to her, so, rather than switch from the Inbox to the Calendar and back again, you can just right-click on the Calendar icon on the Outlook bar (or the Calendar folder in the Folder list) and choose Open in New Window from the shortcut menu. The message automatically minimizes and the Calendar opens in a separate window. To double-check that you have the date right, just click the message on the Taskbar and you can easily see both windows at the same time, as shown in Figure 11.11.

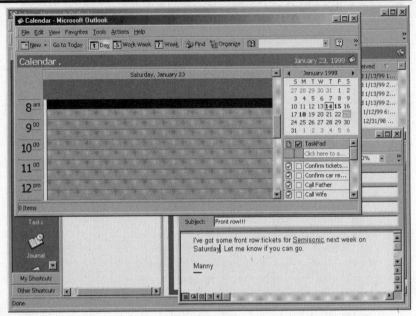

FIGURE 11.11: Choose Open in New Window to have two components open at once.

Renaming Folders

As long as you created the folder, you can rename it or delete it whenever you want. To rename a folder, follow these steps:

1. Right-click on the folder you want to rename from the folder list.

2. Choose Rename [Folder Name] from the shortcut menu.

3. The folder name is selected (it becomes blue with a black box around it), and a flashing insertion point appears at the end of the current name.

NOTE
If you select Rename from a right-click and start typing, you will replace the existing name. If you want to edit the current name, you must deselect the text before making any changes.

4. Enter the new folder name in the text box.

5. Press Enter to save the name or, if you change your mind about renaming the folder, press the Esc key.

Deleting Items and Folders

 To delete a folder, right-click on the folder and choose Delete [Folder Name] from the shortcut menu. To delete an item, right-click the item and choose Delete, or choose the delete button from the Outlook Standard toolbar or the Standard toolbar on the item's form. Don't worry if you delete something by accident—it doesn't go far.

 You'll find deleted material in the Deleted Items folder, which is accessible from the Outlook bar or the Folder List. Folders and items remain in the Deleted Items folder until you delete them from the Deleted Items folder. At that point, you are given a warning, like this one:

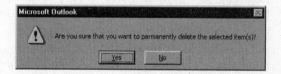

If you delete a folder from the Deleted Items folder, the warning is slightly different.

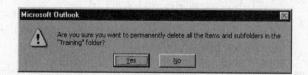

NOTE
You can also delete items and folders by dragging them to the Deleted Items folder on the Folder List or the Deleted Items icon on the Outlook bar. To recover them from the Deleted Items folder, just drag them back to their original locations.

Part ii

USING THE ADVANCED TOOLBAR

Whether you are an Outlook 97 user finally migrating to Outlook 2000 or a new Outlook user, there are buttons on the Advanced toolbar that will make your life easier. This is especially true in file management. The Advanced toolbar shown below, in addition to having an Outlook Today button and a New button, includes Back, Forward, Up One Level, Folder List, Undo, Current View, Group by Box, Field Chooser, and AutoPreview.

The Back and Forward buttons, which work like buttons on a Web browser, are particularly useful in navigating through your folder structure. The Up One Level button found in Windows Open and Save dialog boxes takes you up your directory tree to the folder above where you began. Undo is only useful in editing, so it doesn't serve much purpose here. Current View can be used to easily switch between views in any of the Outlook components. Group by Box opens a box above the file list that you can drag a field into to group by that field. For example, to see all of the files grouped by Type, drag the Type field into the Group by Box. Field Chooser lets you easily add and remove fields from your view. AutoPreview is most useful in the components where you can see the first couple of lines of e-mail messages, Journal entries, and notes.

To make the Advanced toolbar visible, choose View ➤ Toolbars and choose Advanced. Because the file-management Standard toolbar is so small, you can move the Advanced toolbar to the same row as the Standard toolbar (move it by pointing to the two parallel bars on the left side of the toolbar and dragging). When you move back to the Outlook components, the Advanced toolbar will move to a new position below the Standard toolbar.

If you think that having both toolbars on all the time is too much, refer to Chapter 10 to design a custom toolbar that meets your personal work habits.

Managing the Files and Folders on Your Computer or Network

In addition to the folders contained within Outlook, you can use Outlook to access all the folders and files on your computer and network drives. Click the Other Shortcuts button on the Outlook bar. There you'll find three icons: My Computer, Favorites, and My Documents, as shown in Figure 11.12.

FIGURE 11.12: The Other Shortcuts group on the Outlook Bar

Click the My Computer icon to see the drives available on your computer. Notice that the Standard toolbar changes rather dramatically to include icons related to file management, such as Map Network Drive and Disconnect Network Drive.

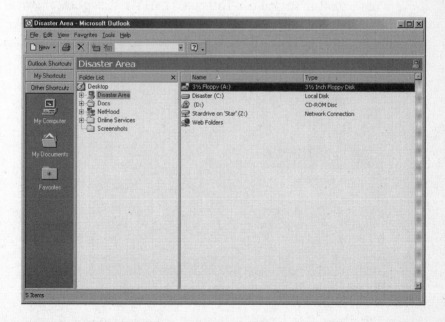

Click any one of the drives in the Information Viewer to see the folders and files on that drive. Right-clicking on any file or folder gives you the

same list of choices you get when you right-click on a file in the Windows Explorer.

Printing a List of Files and Folders

Choosing Print from the shortcut menu opens and prints the document. One of the more exciting things about using Outlook for file management is that you can print a list of the files on your drive or in any folder on your drive. This isn't possible with your traditional Windows file-management tools. To print the file list, choose Print from the File menu or click the Print button on the toolbar. This opens the Print dialog box, shown in Figure 11.13.

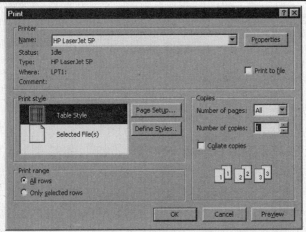

FIGURE 11.13:   The Print dialog box

The list prints in Table style. You can choose to print all rows of the list, or you can select only the rows you want to print. If you would like to see what the list will look like before you print it, click the Preview button in the Print dialog box. Figure 11.14 shows an example of what the Windows folder looks like in Print Preview.

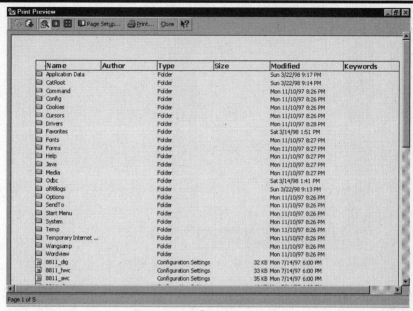

FIGURE 11.14: The Windows folder in Print Preview

Click the Page Setup button if you'd like to change the paper size, margins, or add a header or footer to identify the file list you are printing and the date you're printing it. Click the Print button to return to the Print dialog box, or click Close to return to Outlook without printing.

Taking a Quick Look at a Document

Rather than having to open a document to see what it is, wouldn't it be nice to be able to preview it first? Right-click any file and choose Quick View to open the document in a miniature application window, as shown in Figure 11.15.

Click the arrows in the top-right corner of the document to scroll through the pages of the document.

If you need to actually read the document to figure out if it's the one you want, click the Increase Font Size button. It's really more like a Zoom—it doesn't really increase the font size of the document, it only makes it look that way so you can read it. Click Decrease Font Size to return it to its full-page view.

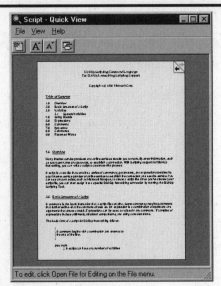

FIGURE 11.15: Viewing a document in Quick View

Another way to read the document is to click the View menu and click Page View to toggle Page View off. This makes the contents readable without having to click the Increase Font Size button repeatedly. Select View ➤ Page View again to return to the full-page view.

If you decide that this is the document you want to open, click the Open File for Editing button on the toolbar. This button represents the application the document was created in, so it changes depending on the document.

 If you'd like to view another document, you can choose to have the document displayed in the same window or have a new Quick View window opened with the new document. Click the Replace Window button to close the current document and open a new one in the same window. When the Replace Window button is depressed, click it again, and the next document you open will open in a new window.

NOTE

When you click outside the Quick View window to select another document, the Quick View window minimizes to the Taskbar. If you have chosen the Replace Window option, the window is restored when you select another document to Quick View. If you have chosen to open the document in a new window, the original window stays minimized on the Taskbar.

Click the window's Close button or choose File ➤ Exit to close the Quick View window.

NOTE

Quick View is a Windows component. If Quick View is not an option when you right-click on a file, the Quick View component was not installed with Windows. To install it, go to Add/Remove Program on the Windows Control Panel and click Windows Setup. You'll find Quick View in the Accessories group.

Moving and Copying Files and Folders

Moving and copying files and folders works the same as it does in Windows Explorer. The following lists outline your moving and copying options.

To move a file to a new location:

▶ Drag the file from one folder to another on the same drive.

▶ Use Shift+drag to move the file from one folder to another on a different drive.

▶ Right-click and drag, and then choose Move from the shortcut menu that appears when you release the dragged item.

▶ Right-click and choose Cut from the shortcut menu, open the new folder, and right-click again to choose Paste.

▶ Choose Edit ➤ Cut, open the new folder, and choose Edit ➤ Paste.

To copy a file to a new location:

▶ Drag the file from one folder to another on a different drive.

▶ Use Ctrl+drag to copy the file from one folder to another on the same drive.

▶ Right-click and drag, and then choose Copy from the shortcut menu that appears when you release the dragged item.

▶ Right-click and choose Copy from the shortcut menu, open the new folder, and right-click again to choose Paste.

▶ Choose Edit ➤ Copy, open the new folder, and choose Edit ➤ Paste.

Part ii

Creating New Folders

If you decide that having two hundred documents in your My Documents folder is getting a little unwieldy, you can create a new folder by choosing File ➢ New ➢ Folder. Enter the folder name in the Create New Folder dialog box that opens.

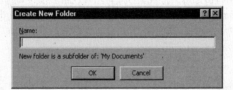

Renaming a File or Folder

To change the name of a file or folder, all you have to do is right-click it and choose Rename from the shortcut menu. This opens the Rename dialog box where you can type in the new name. Click anywhere in the existing name if all you want to do is edit that name.

Applying Outlook Views

One of the greatest file organization tools offered by Outlook is the ability to apply Outlook views to your files. In Windows Explorer, you have your choice of four views: Large Icons, Small Icons, List, and Details. You can also sort (arrange) your files by Name, Type, Size, and Date. Although those options have seemed adequate for years, Outlook views blow them out of the water.

The default view for My Computer in Outlook is Details view. In Details view, as shown in Figure 11.16, you can see the name of the file, what type of document it is, who created it, the size, when it was last modified, and any keywords that have been assigned to help locate it later.

One of the most helpful views that Outlook can offer (and which you can't get anywhere else) is the By File Type view. This organizes all the files in a folder of the same type so you can ignore those system files that just get in your way. The By File Type view is especially useful if you're looking for files in large folders, such as the Windows folder. To see all the files of one type, just click the Plus button next to the type, as shown in Figure 11.17.

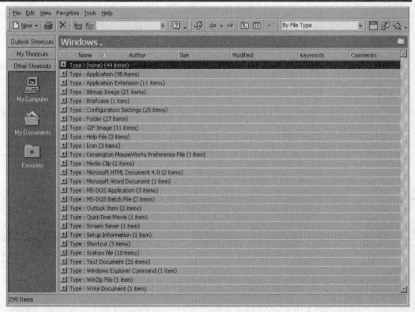

FIGURE 11.16: The default Details view

FIGURE 11.17: The Windows folder organized by file type

Another useful view is the Document Timeline view. This view is similar to the Timeline view in the Journal, but includes files that you didn't create or that weren't automatically recorded in the Journal (see Chapter 8 for more information about how to automatically record documents in the

Journal). If you'd like to display the document name in the Month view, right-click anywhere in the timeline (except on an icon) and choose Formal View. Click the Show Label when Viewing by Month check box and click OK. The results are shown in Figure 11.18.

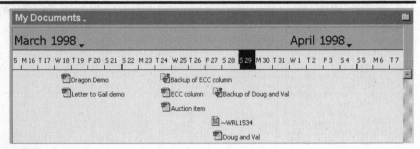

FIGURE 11.18:   The Document Timeline view

You can combine the Document Timeline view with By File Type by switching to the Document Timeline view and choosing View ➢ Current View ➢ Edit Current View, and selecting Group by File Type.

The other views in files and folders that are available to you include:

By Author   Groups files by author (as designated in the file's properties)

Icons   The familiar My Computer view of the world

Programs   Shows only folders and applications

Of course, if none of these views is exactly what you want, you can always design your own custom views.

Filtering Files and Folders

When you want to create a view that contains only files that meet certain criteria, you can set up a filter to select the files you want to see. You'll want to keep a few considerations in mind when applying filters to Windows folders.

1. You cannot apply a filter that will identify files in multiple folders—a filter can only be applied to one folder at a time.

2. Filter is not a menu option when you are in your Windows folders. You have to access it from the shortcut menu. Open the folder you want to filter, move to an empty space at the bottom of the file list, and right-click and choose Filter.

3. A filter can be saved with a view, but it will only apply to the current folder. You can't create a view that filters for a certain file type, for example, and then apply that view to other folders.

For the differences between filtering and finding files, see "Using Find to Locate Items" later in this chapter.

CUSTOMIZING THE OUTLOOK BAR

The Outlook bar, shown in Figure 11.19, is a relatively new tool in the Microsoft arsenal. Introduced in Outlook 97, this feature received positive responses from user groups, so it has started appearing in other applications. FrontPage 98, for example, uses a similar navigational feature in the FrontPage Explorer.

FIGURE 11.19: The Outlook bar

The concept behind the Outlook bar is simple. It holds shortcuts to the Outlook components and other folders on your computer, so with one click you can easily switch between folders. The Outlook bar is fully customizable, which means you can add shortcuts to your most commonly used folders, rearrange icons, rename icons, add new groups to organize your shortcuts, and, if you prefer, turn it off completely.

The shortcuts on the Outlook bar are divided into three groups:

Outlook Shortcuts   Shortcuts to all of the Outlook components, Outlook Today, and the Deleted Items folder

My Shortcuts   Shortcuts to the Drafts, Outbox, and Sent Items folders

Other Shortcuts   Shortcuts to the My Computer, My Documents, and Favorites folders

You may find that these groups meet your needs, or you may be itching to change them. Stayed tuned to learn more about how to make the Outlook bar more useful to you.

Customizing the Outlook Bar's Display

One of the first things you might want to do to the Outlook bar is change the size of the icons, so you don't have to scroll to access all of the icons in the Outlook group. To change the size of the icons, right-click anywhere in the Outlook bar (except on an icon), and choose Small Icons from the shortcut menu.

This lets you see all of the Outlook icons and leaves you plenty of room to add new icons.

Adding New Shortcuts to the Outlook Bar

Whenever you create a new folder, you are prompted to create a shortcut for it on the Outlook bar (unless you've told Outlook not to prompt you again; see "Creating Folders" earlier in this chapter). You can add a shortcut to any existing folder by right-clicking on the folder in the Folder List and choosing Add to Outlook Bar from the shortcut menu.

Outlook adds the shortcut to the bottom of the currently active group. Point to the icon and drag it if you would prefer having it in a different location. Figure 11.20 shows the Training Schedule icon being dragged to below the Calendar.

FIGURE 11.20: Moving an icon by dragging it

NOTE

To move an item to a new group, drag the icon to the group title. When the group opens, drop the icon into the new group. Be sure to move into the group itself before you drop it, or you'll get an error message telling you that you can't drag an icon to a group's title.

You can also click File ➢ New and choose Outlook Bar Shortcut from the list. This opens the Add to Outlook Bar dialog box. Just select the folder you want to add, and click OK.

Deleting an Icon from the Outlook Bar

To remove an icon from the Outlook bar, right-click the icon and choose Remove from Outlook Bar. Remember, this won't delete the folder—you're only removing a shortcut to the folder. Outlook gives you a friendly prompt to make sure you want to remove it and reminds you how to re-create if later if you change your mind and want it back.

Adding, Removing, and Renaming Groups

Groups help you organize your shortcuts so you can access them quickly and efficiently. Adding a new group is as simple as right-clicking on the Outlook bar and choosing Add New Group. Enter the name for the new group in the group box and press Enter.

To remove a group, right-click on the group's title and choose Remove Group. Renaming a group is just as simple. You guessed it—right-click again and choose Rename group. Type the new name in the title box and press Enter.

SIMPLIFYING THE OUTLOOK BAR

If you create too many groups, it becomes difficult to remember where you put the shortcut you want, which defeats the whole purpose of the Outlook bar. For one way of simplifying access to your folders, follow these steps:

1. Switch to Small Icons.

2. Move all the icons from My Shortcuts into the Outlook group.

3. Remove the My Shortcuts group.

4. Rename the Other Shortcuts group to My Computer.

5. Add additional commonly used folders to either of the appropriate groups.

This gives you just two groups—one that has all your Outlook folders in it and one that gives you access to the folders on your hard drive or network.

USING FIND TO LOCATE ITEMS

Although it may not happen right away, it won't be long before you have so many Outlook items that you can't easily find the one you want. You know you received two messages from your boss about a particular project, but you can only find one of them—the one that says the project is late. Don't panic. Outlook will scour through all of your folders, reviewing each item thoroughly until it comes up with the one you're looking for.

Outlook has a Find feature that lets you enter key words and phrases, like on a Web search page. Outlook will search the primary fields in a component or, if you prefer, it will search the entire text of the items to find what you're looking for.

 You can access Find by clicking the Find button on the Standard toolbar. This opens up the Find page shown in Figure 11.21.

Enter the text you want to search for in the Look For text box, and click Find Now. If you know that what you're looking for is in one of the primary fields indicated on the Find page, it will speed the search to clear the Search All Text in the Message check box.

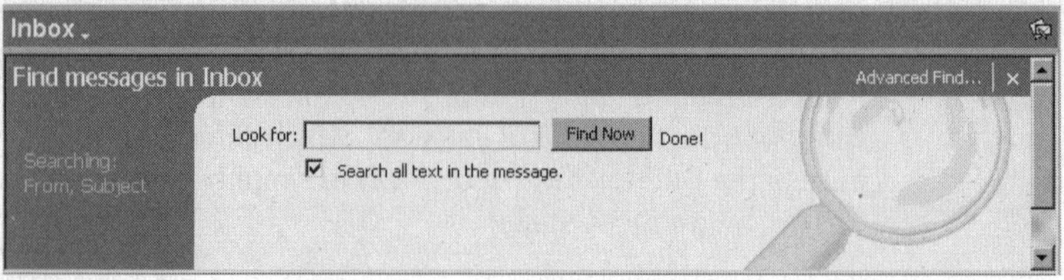

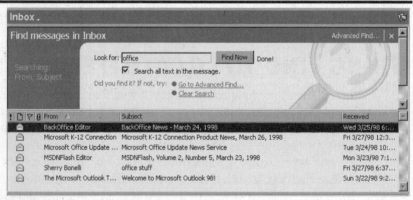

FIGURE 11.21:   The Find page

Your results are returned in a list format below the Find page. Figure 11.22 shows the result of a Find on the Inbox for the word *office*, searching all text in the message.

Click the Clear Search button if you want to conduct another search. If you didn't find the results you were looking for, or if you would like to refine the search more, click Go to Advanced Find.

To close the Find page, click the Find button on the Standard toolbar.

FIGURE 11.22:   The results of a search

Advanced Find

Finding something that you've lost is certainly a practical and worthwhile enterprise, but the uses of Find don't stop there. Advanced Find is really a powerful tool that is both similar to and different from Filter. The major differences can be summed up this way:

▶ While both Filter and Find let you establish criteria to search any single Outlook folder, Find lets you search all of the Outlook folders at once.

▶ You can save a filter with a view, so that you can apply it later. You can save a search (Find) as a file that you can reapply at another time or even send to coworkers who have the need to apply the same criteria to their data.

▶ Filters can only be applied to Outlook folders. By installing an Outlook add-on component called Integrated File Management, you can use Find within Outlook to search all your Windows files and folders as well.

For a practical example, let's say you need to know all the communications and all the work you've engaged in for a particular client or customer. You could create a search that showed you every mention of the customer's name in all of your Personal Folders. The results would include communications, meetings, notes, contacts that were related to the customer, and also those correspondences where you discussed the customer with a member of your team. As long as the customer's name was mentioned somewhere, the item would appear in the list.

To use Advanced Find, click the Find button on the Standard toolbar and click Advanced Find or choose Advanced Find from the Tools menu. The Advanced Find window, shown in Figure 11.23, looks almost identical to the Filter dialog box.

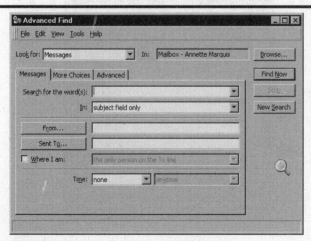

FIGURE 11.23: The Advanced Find dialog box

All the options for applying criteria to Filter work the same way in Advanced Find. There are only a couple of exceptions that are noted here.

▶ When you create a search, click the Look For list to choose from a list of all the Outlook components, from Any Type of Outlook Item or from Files.

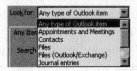

▶ If you are searching for Outlook items, the default folder to look in is Personal Folders. If you would like to narrow your search or choose a different folder altogether, click the Browse button next to the In field. This opens a Select Folders dialog box. Click the Plus button in front of Personal Folders to expand the list. Click any of the folders you want to include in the search. Clear the Search Subfolders check box if you want to search only the main folders.

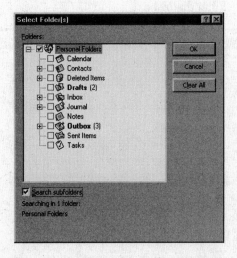

NOTE
You can only select individual folders that are part of the same information service.

indicate if you want to start each item on a new page and if you want to print the attached documents.

4. Use the Page Setup and Print Preview buttons to prepare your document for printing.

5. Click Print to send the document to the printer.

ASSIGNING CATEGORIES TO MULTIPLE ITEMS AT ONCE

After locating all the items related to a single customer or other search criteria that you establish, you may decide that you'd like to assign all the items to the same category for ease in grouping them in individual Outlook folders in the future. You can do this in one easy step. Just choose Select All from the Find Edit menu, and then select Edit ➢ Categories. Select the category you want to assign, and click OK. There are some items, such as messages in your Inbox, that cannot be assigned categories, but all the others will now roll up to a single category.

This technique can also be applied in any of the Outlook components. For example, you can use Ctrl+click to select several items in your Contacts folder. Choose Edit ➢ Categories and assign them all to the same category. Any of their original categories will be retained, and the new one you assign will be added, unless you clear all the existing categories in the Categories dialog box first.

nding Public Folders

If you work in a large company, the number of public folders on the Exchange Server may grow out of control, making it difficult to find the information you are looking for. With Outlook 2000's new Find Public Folders option, shown in Figure 11.24, you can quickly locate and open any public folder you need. To access this feature, follow these steps:

1. Select Tools ➢ Find Public folder.

2. Click Browse to open up a Select Folders list if you want to narrow your search.

3. Enter the text you are searching for in the Contains Text box.

Once you identify what you want to search and where you
you can establish your criteria for the search itself using the s
as you would to set up a filter.

- ▸ You can sort the search results table by clicking tl
  headings.

- ▸ Click View ≻ Current View and select from By Categol
  ject, or Detailed Items to change the table's view.

- ▸ Choose View ≻ Current View ≻ Edit Current View to
  the view the way you want it. You can't apply a Filtel
  results, but you can apply any of the other custom vie'

- ▸ Use Edit Features to move and copy items in the seal
  table to different folders. They will stay in the search re
  but will show up in a different location (the In Folder

- ▸ To move an item to the Deleted Items folder, select th
  choose Delete from the Edit menu (this does not delel
  from the search results—it only changes its In Folder l

Saving the Search Results

Save the search (but not the results) by choosing File ≻ Save
will save the search criteria and the view, but not the results
search file (.oss). You can re-run the search at any time by cl
Open Search and opening the search file.

If you want to save the actual items as a document, choos
As. You are only given the option of saving the document as
you can then open it in Word to format it.

Printing the Search Results

Depending on the purpose of your search, you can print the
table, or, if you are developing a report based on the search re
print the details of each item in memo form, even choosing to
documents if you want. To print the search results, follow th

1. Highlight the items you want to print. If you wal
   them all, choose Edit ≻ Select All.

2. Choose File ≻ Print.

3. Choose Table style and indicate if you want to print
   table or only the selected rows, or choose Memo

4. Indicate whether you would like to look for that text in the Name or Description, Internet Newsgroup Name, Folder path, Folder name, or Folder Description.

5. Specify a folder creation date if you want to search within a certain date parameter.

6. Click Find Now to conduct the search.

Outlook returns the name of the folder and the path where the folder is located. Just double-click the folder to open it in a separate window.

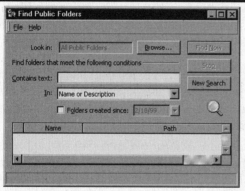

FIGURE 11.24: Use the Find Public Folders option to locate a public folder.

ARCHIVING ITEMS

How many times have you gone back and looked at your calendar from two years ago or at a to-do list you completed months before? If you're like most people, probably not very often. A time may arise, however, when you need one piece of information from one of those sources, so, just to be on the safe side, you probably haven't thrown them away just yet. Conceivably, you could keep all of your outdated information in Outlook forever. You'd have to have a lot of extra disk space to store the file, and Outlook would be running so slowly you'd need a fair amount of patience, but it could be done. It makes a lot more sense, though, to decide how long to keep your outdated data around, and store anything that exceeds that time period in another file. This is called *archiving* your data, and it's a built-in Outlook feature.

Calendar items, tasks, Journal entries, and e-mail messages can all be archived, and you can establish different archive schedules for each component. You may have a need to keep Journal entries available longer than completed tasks. If you're really daring, you can also choose just to delete items completely after a certain amount of time. Outlook lets you determine what makes sense to you.

AutoArchive

The process that governs archiving in Outlook is called *AutoArchive,* and you can guess from the name that it happens automatically (see "Archiving Items Manually" later in this chapter for details on manual archiving). Don't let this make you nervous—there are a number of controls that you can put on AutoArchive to make sure it doesn't do things without your approval. When Outlook archives data, it moves it to a personal folder on your hard drive called `archive.pst`. The default location for this folder is `C:\WINDOWS\Profiles\your profile name\Application Data\ Microsoft\Outlook\ archive.pst`. You can change this to any location you'd prefer when you set up the archive options. If you ever need any data that's been archived, you can restore the archive file, pull out the information you need, and send the file back to the attic until the next time.

Several Outlook folders have AutoArchive turned on and default archive periods established when they are originally set up. These folders are Calendar (6 months), Tasks (6 months), Journal (6 months), Sent Items (2 months), and Deleted Items (2 months). AutoArchive is not activated automatically for Inbox, Notes, and Drafts.

Setting Up AutoArchive

To set up AutoArchive, follow these steps:

1. Right-click on Calendar, Tasks, Journal, or any of the message folders, and select Properties.

2. Click the AutoArchive tab to open the AutoArchive page shown in Figure 11.25.

3. Click the Clean Out Items Older Than check box if it is not already checked.

4. Enter the number of Months, Weeks, or Days that you'd like to establish.

5. Choose the path and folder name you'd like to move items to (you can enter a name other than `archive.pst`, but retain the `.pst` file extension).

6. If you'd prefer to delete old items, select Permanently Delete Old Items.

7. Click OK to save the AutoArchive properties for that folder.

8. Repeat the process with each folder you want to archive.

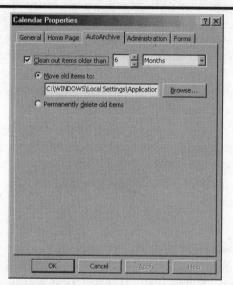

FIGURE 11.25: The AutoArchive Properties page

Setting AutoArchive Options

To control how AutoArchive actually works, there are several options you may want to adjust. To find them, click Tools ➤ Options, click the Other tab, and then click AutoArchive.

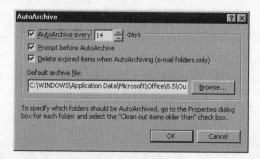

Indicate here how frequently you'd like Outlook to AutoArchive. The default is every 14 days, but you may want to change that to monthly or increase it to once a week, depending on the volume of Outlook items you process each week.

AutoArchive initiates when you log in to Outlook on the designated day. However, if you happen to need a phone number in a hurry that particular day, having to wait until AutoArchive is completed may not be what you want. If you'd prefer that Outlook notifies you before it begins its AutoArchive process, you can click the Prompt before AutoArchive option.

The third option deletes e-mail messages that have expired. This only applies to messages that have a specified expiration date.

The final option lets you designate a default folder for the `archive.pst` file. If you change the folder here, before setting the AutoArchive options in each component, you won't have to change it in each place.

Click OK to close the AutoArchive dialog box, save your settings, and click OK again to close Options.

Archiving Items Manually

If you'd rather Outlook left the driving to you, you can archive items when you are good and ready. Follow the steps below to archive items manually.

1. On the File menu, select Archive.

2. To archive all folders, click the Archive All Folders According to Their AutoArchive Settings option button (see "Setting AutoArchive Options" earlier in this section). To archive one folder only, click Archive This Folder and All Subfolders, as shown in Figure 11.26. Click the folder that contains the items you want to archive.

3. In the Archive File box, type a filename for the archived items to be transferred to, or click Browse to select from a list.

4. In the Archive Items Older Than box, enter a date. Items dated before this date will be archived.

5. Select the archive file if you want to change the default.

6. Click OK to begin the archiving process.

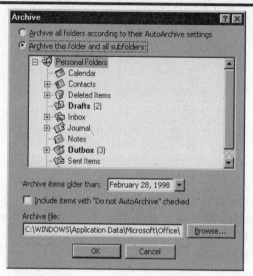

FIGURE 11.26: The Archive dialog box

Restoring Archived Items

There are two ways to recover items from `archive.pst`. You can:

- Import the items into their original files. If you choose to import the items, you can filter the archive file first to only retrieve the items that you want to recover.

- Open `archive.pst` in Outlook. If you are looking for multiple items in the archive file, you may prefer to open the Personal Folders file to find the items you're looking for. To open the `archive.pst` file, follow these steps:

  1. Choose File ➤ Open ➤ Other Outlook File (`.pst`).

  2. Locate the `archive.pst` file on your hard drive.

3. Click OK to bring the Archive folder into Outlook. It will appear as a separate folder above Outlook Today - [Personal Folders].

You can open the AutoArchive personal folders and work with them just as you do your regular personal folders. When you've found the information you're looking for, you can close AutoArchive by right-clicking on the folder and choosing Close ➢ AutoArchive.

NOTE

AutoArchive re-creates the folder structure of your personal folders that are being archived, even if the folders are empty. The Inbox may be created, for example, even if you're only archiving folders underneath the Inbox. This is so that Outlook can restore the folders to the same location if you choose to import them back into Outlook.

WHAT'S NEXT?

Organizing your Outlook data includes being able to use the data in other applications and being confident that your data is safely backed up in another file location. With help from this chapter, you can be that confident. In the next chapter, you will learn how Outlook works with the Internet. You will find out how to use vCards, newsreader, NetMeeting, security features, and more.

Chapter 12

Outlook
and the Web

O utlook 2000 continues the Microsoft Office tradition of supplying increasing levels of support for Internet tools and Web technologies. With Outlook, you can send Contacts and Calendar items and schedule online meetings in a format that crosses platforms and Personal Information Manager (PIM) products. As you increase your Internet use, Outlook's security features ensure that the Web remains a secure environment for all your messaging needs.

Adapted from *Mastering™ Microsoft® Outlook™ 2000*
by Gini Courter and Annette Marquis

ISBN 0-7821-2472-0   787 pages $34.99

OUTLOOK AND INTERNET EXPLORER

Outlook is part of the Internet Explorer (IE) family. When you install Outlook on Windows 95, setup checks to see if Internet Explorer is already on your system. If not, it adds it. If you were using Internet Explorer 3, it will be automatically upgraded. Do not remove Internet Explorer 4 from your computer—Outlook needs it.

When installing Outlook on a Windows 98 computer, setup checks the version of Internet Explorer 4.x you have (there are several incremental versions) and offers to install Internet Explorer 5. The installation of IE 5 simply updates all of the application files and doesn't touch any of your settings, favorites, or other modifications you have made to IE.

WARNING

If you choose to install IE 5 over IE 4 or another previous version, you may be in for a surprise when you first start it up. IE 5, just like IE 4, installs a small URL applet that only runs the very first time you start the application (C:\windows\system\runonce.exe). This applet takes you to a special Microsoft Web page. Don't worry, the next time you log on to the Net, your old home page will appear.

This doesn't mean you have to use Internet Explorer as your browser, but if you don't, Internet Explorer will nag you about it when it gets the chance. For example, let's say you use Netscape Navigator as your default browser. If you launch Internet Explorer, it will remind you that you leave it alone too often by asking you to select *it* as your default Web browser.

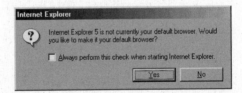

Clear the check box, and you won't see this message again.

TIP

If you're a system administrator or application developer, you'll be interested in another benefit of this integration—Outlook's support for Microsoft's Internet Explorer Administration Kit (IEAK). The kit, which you can download for free from the Microsoft Web site, can be used to automatically configure and upgrade workstation settings in Internet Explorer and Outlook over a network.

USING THE OUTLOOK NEWSREADER

Another feature of Outlook is its support for the Network News Transport Protocol (NNTP), a standard for transmitting news on the Internet. Internet newsgroups are like bulletin boards where users post messages—called articles—and download and read articles posted by other users. Outlook's implementation of NNTP is Outlook Express, which provides all of Outlook's mail and news handling capabilities, and it can be used to access Internet Usenet groups and newsgroups on your company's intranet.

The first time you use the newsreader, you'll need to configure it. The Internet Connection Wizard will open, and you'll be prompted to enter your name, e-mail account, and the name of the NNTP server you'll use to access news. Contact your Internet service provider (ISP) for the name of their news server.

After you finish the Internet Connection Wizard, the newsreader prompts you to download the list of Usenet groups available through your server. You only need to do this once. The download takes a few minutes; the length of time is testimony to the tremendous number of Usenet and alternative newsgroups—over 36,000 were available at last count. So far, there are already 15,000 in this download alone.

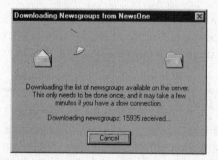

WARNING
The number of newsgroups you have available depends on your Internet service provider. In fact, some ISPs don't carry newsgroups at all. Check with your ISP to see if they carry newsgroups and how to access them.

Most users access a news server through their ISP. However, in a company setting, your Microsoft Exchange administrator can provide access to Internet newsgroups or create newsgroups on your network (intranet newsgroups). Figure 12.1 shows the Newsgroup dialog box with a list down-loaded from the Internet. If you download the newsgroup list from an Exchange server, the list you see may be shorter and only include company newsgroups or traditional Usenet groups.

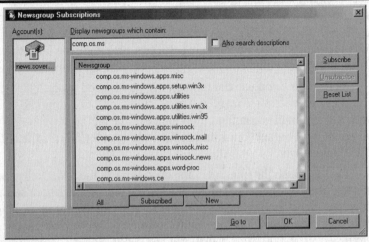

FIGURE 12.1: The Newsgroup Subscriptions dialog box displays the newsgroups available from your server.

To find a newsgroup for a particular topic, enter text in the Display Newsgroups Which Contain text box. The newsreader filters the list to display groups with names that include the text string you entered.

WHAT'S IN A NAME?

Traditional Usenet groups have a fixed naming structure. The group name begins with one of the seven Usenet categories: comp, news, rec, sci, soc, talk, or misc. Additional text in the name indicates an increased level of specialization: comp.mail is a newsgroup about computer mail services; comp.mail.mime is a discussion of mime encoding for computer mail. Members of the comp.mail group discussed and voted to create a more specialized Usenet group for MIME.

Alternative groups, beginning with alt and other nontraditional categories, don't always follow this structure. Alt names are often

CONTINUED ➥

more like friendly names, rather than being strictly hierarchical: `alt.this.is.a.test`. Humorous names abound in the alt groups. One of the first, familiar to fans of the Muppet Show, was `alt.swedish.chef.bork.bork.bork`, creating a kind of tradition for humorous naming where the final segment is repeated three times, for example, `hype.hype.hype`.

The groups with traditional names tend to be more long-lived; it took a group to create the subgroup. One individual can create a nontraditional Usenet group, so content often reflects the values of one person; in the nontraditional groups, there's something to offend everyone.

Finding the topic you're interested in can be difficult. Abbreviations are commonly used. If, for example, you enter **operating systems**, you won't find much. Enter **os,** and you're in the right area, but you'll see every name with "os," a common text string.

It helps to think categorically and look for the general heading that might contain the type of discussion you're looking for. A friend was looking for information on rotball, a type of offline baseball league, with no results. Entering **rot** brought up an extensive list, including an alt group on erotic relationships with collectible stuffed toys. Entering **fantasy,** the general category for fantasy baseball, provided an even steamier list, but she finally hit pay dirt—`alt.fantasy.sports`.

Part ii

To subscribe to a newsgroup, double-click the newsgroup name in the Newsgroup list, or select the name and click the Subscribe button. An icon appears next to the name, and it is copied to the Subscribed page of the dialog box. (Double-clicking a subscribed name removes your subscription.)

Reading Newsgroup Postings

Once you have subscribed to the lists you wish to read, you may now read messages from and post new messages to these lists. Groups you subscribed to are indented underneath the friendly name of the newsreader. Double-click on a newsgroup name to begin downloading headers from the newsgroup, as shown in Figure 12.2.

To view an individual posting, select the posting to see it in the preview pane, as shown in Figure 12.3. Double-click the posting to open it in a separate window.

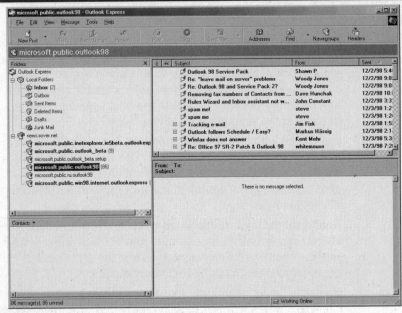

FIGURE 12.2: The news server and groups you've subscribed to are added to the folder view in the Outlook newsreader.

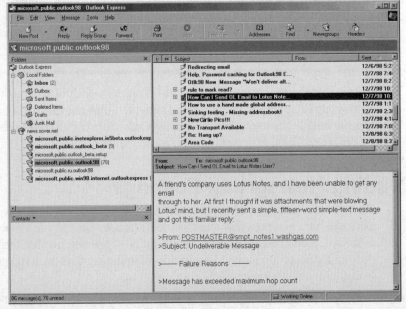

FIGURE 12.3: Select a posting to preview or open.

SPAM! SPAM! SPAM! @#!

If you've wondered what spam is, there's a quintessential example in Figure 12.3 (look at the fourth message from the bottom). Spam is an unwelcome, inappropriate message, advertisement, or other such mail, that is sent to a newsgroup or individual without their consent or prior request, and often without regard to who might read the message. Figure 12.3 shows a newsgroup about Outlook Express, and right there in the middle is a message advertising pornography that was sent to thousands of newsgroup readers. This didn't take a lot of effort on the part of the spammer; the messages were addressed with a spamming program: an electronic bulk mailer.

The message is irrelevant to this discussion; that's part of what makes it spam. If you really wanted to download stolen sex videos, you could find a newsgroup (several actually) to support this activity; you wouldn't need to find out about it in the middle of a newsgroup on Outlook Express.

Most netizens agree that spamming is beyond tacky, and there are several newsgroups dedicated to anti-spamming strategies. There are also several legal cases being fought. America Online recently won a large case against a commercial spammer and has provided its users with a number of options that can significantly reduce messages, either in e-mail or newsgroup posts, that are even remotely related to advertising, much less spam.

Part ii

Posting and Forwarding Messages

You can send a new post to the newsgroup, reply to all newsgroups that the selected message was addressed to, or reply to the individual who wrote the selected message. If you want to send the message to a mail recipient outside the newsgroup, you can forward the message. Click the appropriate button on the Newsreader toolbar to open a message form.

When you've finished composing your message, click the Post or Send button to post, send, or forward the message.

TIP

Outlook Express is filled with useful features. As with Outlook information services, you can configure the newsreader to retrieve messages or headers as you desire. You can filter newsgroup headers using the Newsgroup Filters dialog box, a stripped-down version of the Rules Wizard. For more information, choose Help ➢ Contents and Index on the Outlook newsreader menu.

Exchanging Internet Business Cards

It's your first face-to-face meeting with a client or vendor, and the big question is: do you shake hands or swap business cards first? While you can't shake hands over the Net, you can swap virtual business cards, or vCards, even when you don't meet face-to-face.

The vCard standard, created by a computer industry group called the Versit Consortium, was developed to allow users of contact management systems to receive text, images, and other contact information over the Internet. When your recipient has a vCard-compliant contact manager, they don't have to reenter your name, phone numbers, and other information. They simply drag the vCard into their contact manager to add your contact information; vCards are even easier to use than business card scanners. A large number of contact managers support vCards, including ACT! (Symantec) and Lotus Organizer (Lotus Development Corporation), so recipients don't have to use Outlook to use the vCard you send them. The Internet directory service Four11 also supports vCards.

NOTE

For more information regarding the vCard and vCalendar initiative and the nonprofit standards organization that manages vCard and vCalendar, Internet Mail Consortium, visit their Web site: http://www.imc.org.

Creating a vCard from a Contact

In Outlook, you create vCards from contact items. The contact's name is used as the vCard filename. vCards have the .vcf file extension and are stored by default in the Signature folder on your hard drive. You can attach a vCard file to a message or include a vCard file in an AutoSignature.

Follow these steps to create a vCard:

1. Select the contact you want to save as a vCard.

2. Choose File ➢ Save As from the menu bar, or right-click and choose Export to vCard File from the shortcut menu.

3. In the Save as Type drop-down list, choose vCard Files.

4. Select a location for the file.

5. Click Save.

Adding a vCard to a Mail Message

Creating and adding vCards to messages is much faster and more accurate than looking up a contact and typing that information into a message form. A vCard is a fast and helpful response to many of the requests you'll receive in the course of a business day:

▶ What cleaning service does your company use?

▶ Can you recommend someone to analyze our data needs?

▶ How do I get in touch with the person who worked part-time for us last summer?

Sending a vCard note delivers the information in a way that's convenient for the recipient as well as for you. You can also add a vCard to a mail message:

1. In the body of the message, choose File ➢ Insert from the menu bar.

2. Locate and select the contact's vCard file.

3. Click OK to insert the vCard.

TIP

You don't have to create the vCard in advance. To forward a contact as a vCard, select the contact, and then choose Actions ➢ Forward as vCard from the Outlook menu. Outlook will open a message form, create the vCard file, and attach it to the message. The vCard file will not be saved separately.

Creating an AutoSignature with a vCard

For contacts that you regularly forward, you should consider an Auto-Signature that includes a vCard. (For more information on creating AutoSignatures, see Chapter 9.) An obvious candidate is your own vCard, so this is a good time to add yourself as an Outlook contact.

TIP

The plain text, HTML, and Outlook Rich Text editors support vCards, but WordMail does not. If you want to use vCards, don't choose Word as your e-mail editor.

To create an AutoSignature with a vCard:

1. Choose Tools ➤ Options from the Outlook menu bar to open the Options dialog box.

2. Click the Mail Format tab.

3. Click the Signature Picker button to open the Signature Picker dialog box.

4. Click the New button to create a new AutoSignature.

5. Enter options in the first page of the New Signature dialog box. Click Next.

6. In the Edit Signature dialog box, enter any text you wish to include in your AutoSignature.

7. Click the New Contact as vCard button to open the Select Contacts to Export dialog box.

8. Choose the contact whose vCard you want to add to the AutoSignature, and click the Add button.

9. Click OK to close the Select Contacts dialog box and return to the Edit Signature dialog box. Finish creating your AutoSignature, and then click Finish.

10. Close the Signature Picker dialog box.

11. To use this signature as your default, select it in the Signature drop-down list. Click OK to close the Options dialog box.

Adding a vCard to Contacts

When you receive a vCard in a mail message, it looks a lot like it does when you send a vCard: a file with an attachment, as shown in Figure 12.4.

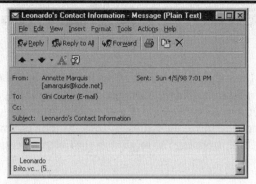

FIGURE 12.4: This message includes a vCard.

Drag the vCard from the message and drop it on a Contacts folder, as shown in Figure 12.5. Outlook will create and open the contact so you can add or correct any information. If you make changes or additions to the new contact, you'll be prompted to save the changes when you close the Contact form.

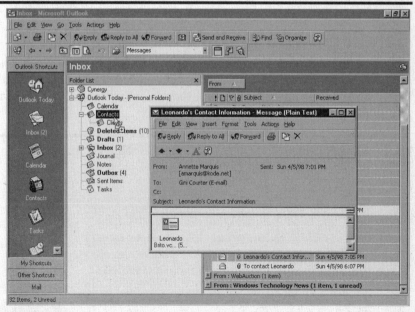

FIGURE 12.5: Drop the vCard into a Contacts folder to create a new contact from the vCard.

Part ii

USING vCALENDAR FOR MEETING REQUESTS

vCalendar is another brainchild of the Versit Consortium. vCalendar supports both calendaring (creating a calendar) and scheduling (comparing calendars) on the Internet. As with vCard, the recipient of the meeting invitation can drag the meeting request directly into Outlook or any vCalendar-compliant PIM. Dropping the request in the Calendar creates a new Calendar item.

TIP

As stated previously, both vCard and vCalendar are part of Versit's Personal Data Interchange (PDI) technology. The Versit companies—Apple Computer, IBM, Lucent Technologies, and Siemens—transferred their rights to PDI to the Internet Mail Consortium (IMC) in 1996. Developers can download PDI software development kits from the IMC's Web site at http://www.imc.org/pdi/pdiproddev.html.

Sending a vCalendar Meeting Request

Begin by creating the appointment or event request in Outlook. Choose Actions ➤ Forward as vCalendar from the Meeting menu, and Outlook opens a new message form with the vCalendar embedded, as shown in Figure 12.6.

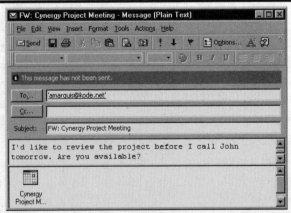

FIGURE 12.6: Sending a meeting request with a vCalendar item

When your recipient gets the meeting request, they can drag it into their electronic calendar.

TIP

You can save any appointment as a vCalendar item. Select the item, and then choose File ➤ Save As and choose vCalendar format from the Save as Type drop-down list. You can import vCalendar and vCard files using the Import and Export Wizard.

HOLDING MEETINGS ON THE INTERNET

Microsoft's NetMeeting online collaboration tool, included with Outlook, includes an entire toolkit for remote meetings:

- ▶ Chat, a text-based interface

- ▶ Whiteboard, for illustrating concepts

- ▶ NetMeeting Video, which lets you see other participants in their natural environment

- ▶ NetMeeting Audio, which lets you talk with other participants

- ▶ Sharing, which displays files in any open application

- ▶ Collaboration, which lets you work together on open files

You need a camera and video card in order to send video, but no extra hardware is required to see video sent by other participants. You'll need a sound card and speakers to use any of the audio capability of NetMeeting and a microphone to add your own voice to the discussion. But you can use NetMeeting even without video or audio. Meeting participants can work together on documents using Sharing and discuss them in a Chat window. NetMeeting was included with Internet Explorer 4, and a lot of people are comfortable using it to do group work when it isn't possible or convenient to gather at one location.

NOTE

If you didn't install NetMeeting with Outlook, you can download it from the Microsoft download site, http://www.microsoft.com/msdownload/. If you need more information about using NetMeeting after installing it, choose Help on the NetMeeting menu.

SETTING UP AN ONLINE MEETING

With Outlook, you can invite participants to an online meeting from the Calendar. In the Meeting Request form, enable the This Is an Online Meeting check box before sending the meeting request, as shown in Figure 12.7.

WARNING

If you send a meeting request over the Internet (even as a vCalendar item), This Is an Online Meeting gets turned off. Make sure you let Internet users know that it is an online meeting in the text of the message.

From the Appointment page of the Meeting Request form, as shown in Figure 12.8, select a Directory Server for the meeting from the drop-down list of servers. There is no charge for using these servers.

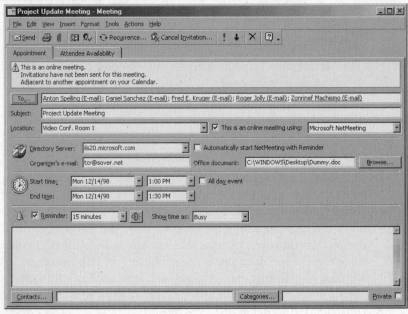

FIGURE 12.7: Inviting attendees to an online meeting

NOTE

You can start an immediate NetMeeting with a contact. Select the contact, and then choose Actions ➤ Call Using NetMeeting from the Outlook menu bar.

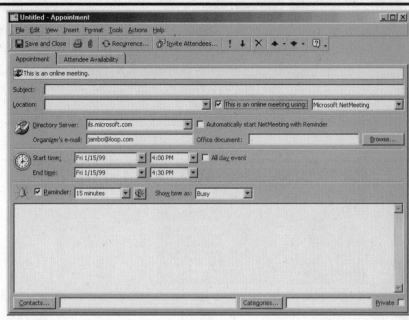

FIGURE 12.8: Setting the meeting location

If you haven't used NetMeeting before, the NetMeeting Wizard opens so that you can create a directory listing and test your sound card, speakers, and microphone. Work through the steps in the Wizard so you're prepared for the meeting.

Follow these steps to schedule an Online Meeting:

1. Open a new Meeting Request form.

2. Enter the meeting information on the Appointment page and enable the This Is an Online Meeting check box.

3. Enter the names of the invitees in the To, Cc, and Bcc text boxes.

4. Type the name of the meeting in the Subject text box.

5. Check the This Is an Online Meeting check box. The Net-Meeting-specific section will be added to the Appointment tab.

6. Choose a server from the list, or specify one for the meeting.

7. Enable the Automatically Start NetMeeting with Reminder check box to have Outlook automatically start NetMeeting.

Part ii

8. Click Save and Close.

9. If you have not previously used NetMeeting, the NetMeeting Wizard will open.

At the interval you set in the Reminder box, Outlook will remind you that you have a meeting, as shown in Figure 12.9. Choose Snooze to be reminded again in a few minutes. If you don't delay the reminder, be prepared for Outlook to fire up NetMeeting and connect to the server you selected.

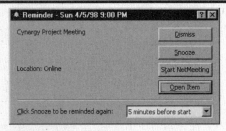

FIGURE 12.9: Outlook reminds you that the online meeting is about to begin.

MASTERING COLLABORATIVE WORK ON THE INTERNET

If you haven't used NetMeeting, the idea of holding a meeting on the Internet can be intimidating. When Internet workgroup tools first came out, only a few brave souls used them. Today, it isn't unusual for team members in separate cities to suggest meetings on the Internet as casually as they'd suggest a telephone conference call. It makes sense to practice ahead of time with a friend or colleague so you can participate smoothly in your first NetMeeting with clients or vendors.

Make a NetMeeting trial run as a product evaluation. You don't need additional hardware to give it a try. You can use Chat and the Whiteboard with the hardware required for Outlook. Once you've experienced a NetMeeting, you'll be able to evaluate its potential use in your business and decide whether you want to invest in video cameras, sound cards, microphones, and fast modems.

Sharing Calendars on the Internet

When you need to schedule a meeting with other users on your Microsoft Exchange network, you can easily check their free/busy times. Microsoft and Lotus developed an Internet free/busy standard called iCalendar, which has been submitted to the Internet Engineering Task Force (IETF). Outlook was one of the first applications to support this emerging standard, although there are many others now. With iCalendar, you can post your free/busy time on a Web page, allowing other Internet users to schedule meetings with you more efficiently. In an Internet Only configuration, you must specify the Web page URL and update frequency. When you use the Meeting Planner in the Calendar, it checks the attendees' free/busy information. (In an Exchange Server setting, the location for iCalendars is set by your system administrator, and you choose how often the settings on the server should be updated.)

To publish your free/busy information on the Internet, choose Tools ➢ Options to open the Options dialog box. Click the Calendar Options button, and then click the Free/Busy Options button to open the Free/Busy Options dialog box, shown in Figure 12.10.

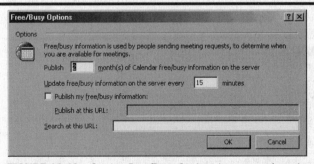

FIGURE 12.10: Setting Free/Busy Options in a network environment

Using Internet Security Features

The Internet is the modern equivalent of the Wild West, but with fewer marshals. No one polices the population, so there are scofflaws, criminals, and cutthroats sprinkled in with the law-abiding netizens. Fortunately, you can deputize Outlook to keep guttersnipes from invading your small portion of the Information Highway.

Part ii

Setting Warning Levels for Mail with Attachments

Plain old text can't contain viruses. For someone to send you a virus, either intentionally or accidentally, the virus code has to be included in a script, attachment, or link, either embedded in a document or sent as a freestanding program. Outlook can check incoming messages and warn you when they contain attachments or links that could potentially contain viruses. You can then choose to open the file, save it, or do neither if it is not from a trusted source.

Attachment security is an option. If you prefer, you can turn it off. Choose Tools ➤ Options to open the Options dialog box. On the Security page, shown in Figure 12.11, click the Attachment Security button to open the Attachment Security dialog box. Choose the security level you wish to employ, and click OK.

Attachment security is only a warning; Outlook cannot check files for viruses. You're fairly safe opening files created in Word, PowerPoint, and Excel if you have virus checking enabled in these applications, but Access and other applications do not check files before opening them. In addition to attachment security, you should have a good virus-checking program on your computer and download the virus update files regularly. You can find links to download evaluation copies of two antivirus programs on the Microsoft Web site (see Table 12.2 later in this chapter).

FIGURE 12.11: Set Outlook security options in the Options dialog box.

Setting Security Zones for HTML Messages

HTML is a page description language, so HTML itself cannot contain viruses; however, embedded scripts and active content components can, often producing disastrous results. *Security zones* let you control the way incoming HTML messages and Web pages that you access in your browser interact with your computer. Security settings in Outlook affect Outlook Express and Internet Explorer. The four different security zones are:

Local Intranet   Sites on your local intranet (default: Medium security)

Trusted Sites   For messages and pages from Web sites that you are confident are well protected against viruses (default: Low security)

Restricted Sites   For sites and messages that do not inspire your confidence (default: High security)

Internet   Any site not placed in one of the other zones (default: Medium security)

You set security levels of High, Medium, Low, or Custom for each zone, and then add Web sites and HTML messages to a zone. For information on adding Web sites to zones, see Security in Internet Explorer Help.

To set security levels for the zones, open the Options dialog box and click the Security tab. On the Security page, click the Zone Settings button. You'll be reminded that these settings are used by different applications:

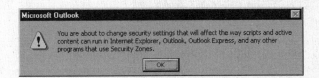

Click OK to open the Security dialog box, shown in Figure 12.12. Select a security zone by clicking on the appropriate zone icon, and its settings will be displayed below.

Choose High, Medium, or Low Security for the zone. With security set on High, potentially damaging content is summarily excluded. Potentially damaging content includes Java applets, scripts, and ActiveX components in Web pages and HTML messages. With Medium security, messages are checked for potentially damaging content, and you are warned before the message is opened so you can decide whether or not you want to proceed. With Low security, anything in the message is assumed to be safe.

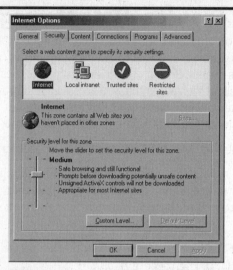

FIGURE 12.12:   Set security options for each zone, and then assign sites to the zones.

Customizing Security for a Zone

The Custom security level allows you to pick and choose between potentially damaging items. Choose the security zone you want to create custom settings for, and then click the Custom Level button to set a custom security level. Click the Settings button to open the Security Settings dialog box, shown in Figure 12.13.

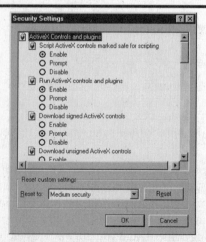

FIGURE 12.13:   Specify detailed security settings for a zone in the Security Settings dialog box.

For most of the items listed in the scroll box, there are three choices: Enable, Prompt, and Disable. Enable executes the action for the item; Disable rejects the action. With Prompt, you're always prompted to allow or disallow the content. The messages are very specific, as shown here:

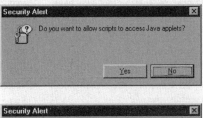

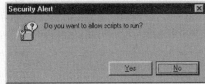

You might think, "Well, I'll just have Outlook and my browser prompt me about all active content." But on an active Web site, you'll receive frequent messages if you choose Prompt for too many settings. When browsing *Revealing Things*, the Smithsonian's first exhibit designed for the World Wide Web, prompting was incessant; as soon as we closed one message box, another opened. On the other hand, this is a great way to find out how each of the active elements in a good Web site was created.

TIP

Revealing Things can be found at http://www.si.edu/revealingthings/. If you're interested in what an incredibly well-implemented site looks like, check it out.

The list in the Security Settings dialog box includes both signed and unsigned active items. *Signed* means signed with a certificate. If you choose Prompt for Signed Items, the message box will let you know who digitally signed the item. For example, if you download an ActiveX component from the Microsoft Web site, the message box will indicate that the component is signed by Microsoft Corporation. Table 12.1 lists all of the security settings; some are only relevant in your browser, but you may want to change them while you're customizing the settings for messages.

TABLE 12.1: Security Settings for Zones

ACTION/FILE/PROGRAM/DOWNLOAD	CHOICES
Script ActiveX Controls Marked Safe for Scripting: allows scripting for controls that have been downloaded	Script ActiveX Controls Marked Safe for Scripting: allows scripting for controls that have been downloadedEnable, Prompt, Disable
Run ActiveX Controls and Plug-Ins: run controls from your computer	Enable, Prompt, Disable
Download Signed ActiveX Controls: download new signed controls	Enable, Prompt, Disable
Download Unsigned ActiveX Controls: download new unsigned controls	Enable, Prompt, Disable
Initialize and Script ActiveX Controls Not Marked as Safe: allows scripting for downloaded controls	Enable, Prompt, Disable
Java Permissions: groups of settings for signed and unsigned content, including scripting and file size limitations	Custom, Low Safety, Medium Safety, High Safety, Disable Java
Active Scripting	Enable, Prompt, Disable
Scripting of Java Applets	Enable, Prompt, Disable
File Download: with download enabled, you'll be prompted	Enable, Disable
Font Download	Enable, Prompt, Disable
User Authentication Logon: choose when you would like to be prompted for your name and password	Automatic Logon Only in Intranet Zone; Anonymous Logon; Prompt for Name and Password; Automatic Logon with Current Username and Password
Submit Non-encrypted Form Data: allow or disallow submission of your personal data in a non-secured Web user form	Enable, Prompt, Disable
Installation of Desktop items: from messages or a site	Enable, Prompt, Disable
Drag and Drop or Copy and Paste Files	Enable, Prompt, Disable
Software Channel Permissions	Low Safety, Medium Safety, High Safety

Choose the security option for each item for the selected security zone. When you've finished tweaking security for the zone, click OK to close the Security Settings dialog box.

To reset the security for all zones, click the Reset button in the Security dialog box. To reset security settings for a specific zone, choose the zone, open the Security Settings dialog box, and click Reset.

NOTE

If you choose Custom for Java Permissions, a Java Custom Settings button appears at the bottom of the Security Settings dialog box. Clicking the button opens another dialog box to customize Java settings. Combinations of the Java settings form the Low Safety, Medium Safety, and High Safety choices in the Security Settings dialog box, just as combinations of the settings in the Security Settings dialog box create the High, Medium, and Low levels in the Security dialog box. If you're not a Java programmer, don't choose custom Java permissions.

Obtaining a Digital ID to Secure Sent Messages

With a digital ID, you can open messages encrypted for your eyes only and add a digital signature to verify your messages to the recipients. This is the same type of certificate you trust to validate sites in the Security Settings. Digital IDs have two parts: the private key, stored on your PC, and the public key that you send to other people to validate your digital signature. You obtain your digital ID from a company that issues certificates, such as VeriSign. Your company's network administrator may also be able to issue your digital ID.

Personal digital IDs are inexpensive; you can obtain a free 60-day trial ID from VeriSign; a full-featured one-year subscription is less than $10. To get a digital ID from VeriSign, go to the Security page of the Options dialog box and click the Get a Digital ID button. Outlook will launch your browser and open a digital ID information page on the Microsoft site.

Click the VeriSign Get Your ID Now button to go directly to the VeriSign Web site and obtain either a full-featured or trial ID.

TIP

To add a digital signature to all of your messages, choose Tools ➢ Options from the Outlook menu to open the Options dialog box, and then click the Security tab. Enable the Add Digital Signature to Outgoing Messages check box.

OUTLOOK RESOURCES ON THE WORLD WIDE WEB

Most of the Outlook resources on the Web are, not coincidentally, on the Microsoft Web site. The site has add-ins that you can download for no charge other than what you pay your ISP for connect time. Additional resources are posted on a regular basis, so we encourage you to browse the site regularly to see what's available. Choosing Help ➤ Office on the Web will take you to the Outlook users download area. Table 12.2 is a list of other pages that include resources for deploying, using, and customizing Outlook.

NOTE

Some of the sites that follow did not have updated information regarding Outlook 2000 by the time this book went to press. Just keep in mind that some of these resources are for Outlook 97/98; these sites may be updated to cover Outlook 2000.

TABLE 12.2: Outlook Resources on the Web

SITE/PAGE	RESOURCES
http://www.microsoft.com/office/org/office97.htm	Decision-making and deployment information for Outlook and Microsoft Exchange Server for large organizations
http://198.107.140.12/office/sbe/v2/demo/welcome.htm	Decision-making and deployment information for small businesses
http://www.microsoft.com/office/000/viewers.htm	File viewers and converters for all Office products; training and certification information including Outlook Expert User certification
http://officeupdate.microsoft.com/	Microsoft Office Update page, with links to new Office Assistants, Office Sounds, and subscription to a monthly Office Update newsletter
http://www.microsoft.com/outlook/evalres.htm	Pre-implementation decision-making resources, including information on moving to Outlook from other mail services
http://www.microsoft.com/office/Outlook/outsolres.htm	Links to synchronization software (see Chapter 18), VeriSign, and third-party vendors, including virus-checking software

TABLE 12.2 continued: Outlook Resources on the Web

SITE/PAGE	RESOURCES
http://www.microsoft.com/exchange/ guide/papers/collabsolutions .asp?A=2&B=6	White paper on using Outlook with Exchange Server
http://www.mous.net and Office User certification programs	Facts about the Microsoft Outlook certification

You can create custom applications in Outlook to meet the particular needs of your office or business. If you don't want to start your new applications from scratch, Microsoft has created several customized applications that you can download for free and further customize.

Microsoft is constantly adding new goodies to their new Office Update Web site at http://officeupdate.microsoft.com/updates/ updOutlook.htm. Add it to your list of Favorites and check regularly to see what's new and exciting. These add-ons and information pages can significantly enhance your work with Outlook, allowing you to take advantage of new technology without having to buy additional software.

WHAT'S NEXT?

This chapter demonstrated how you can extend the value of Outlook beyond the confines of your office by sharing contacts and calendar events with people across the World Wide Web. Also, using Outlook between computers within your office makes it a powerful tool for managing your intraoffice communications. Although Outlook runs smoothly most of the time, its complexity and interaction with other applications will cause the occasional problem. In the next chapter, you will find solutions to these occasional unexpected problems.

Part ii

Chapter 13

TROUBLESHOOTING COMMON OUTLOOK PROBLEMS

Although you can expect Outlook to behave nicely most of the time, the complexity of the program and its interaction with other applications mean that you will probably encounter an occasional unexpected problem. In this chapter, you will find answers to many of the most common Outlook problems, organized by category. If you review this chapter before you spend much time working in Outlook, you can avoid a number of problems from occurring in the first place. However, if problems do pop up, you should be able to solve them quickly and easily. Just scan the list of questions until you find what you're looking for. If you can't find the answer here or in the Outlook Help files, check out Microsoft's online support. Choose Help ➢ Office on the Web. Microsoft maintains an extensive library of articles on every aspect of Outlook, from the obvious to the obscure.

Adapted from *Mastering™ Microsoft® Outlook™ 2000*
by Gini Courter and Annette Marquis

ISBN 0-7821-2472-0   787 pages $34.99

TROUBLESHOOTING COMMON OUTLOOK PROBLEMS

Q: Why can't I see all the items in my folder?

A: Look above the view list, and you'll see the words "Filter Applied." You can either customize the view to change or remove the filter, or switch to another view to show all your items.

Q: I just created a view; where is it?

A: You access custom views from the View menu. Click on the folder you created the view in and choose View ➤ Current View; then choose the view from the menu.

Q: I accidentally changed one of the predesigned views. How can I get the original view back?

A: Select the folder that contains the view you want to reset. Choose View ➤ Current View ➤ Design Views to open the Design Views dialog box. Select the view from the list and then click the Reset button.

Q: How do I change the default view on a folder?

A: Right-click on the folder and choose Properties; then select the view you want from the Initial View drop-down list.

Q: How do I restore the default settings for the Outlook toolbars?

A: Choose View ➤ Toolbars ➤ Customize to open the Customize dialog box. Select the toolbar and click the Reset button.

TROUBLESHOOTING OUTLOOK INSTALLATION

Q: How do I change my Outlook installation?

A: Go to Start ➤ Settings ➤ Control Panel ➤ Add/Remove Programs, and open the Microsoft Office 2000 item. Click on the Add or Remove Features button and you can make changes to Outlook from the hierarchical list of items under the Outlook 2000 item.

Q: I used to use Outlook with Microsoft Exchange Server. Now, I want to use it in Internet Only configuration. How do I change configurations?

A: Open Outlook and go to Tools ➢ Options ➢ Mail Services ➢ Reconfigure Mail Support and select your new configuration. Click OK and confirm the next dialog box. Outlook will close, but you can reopen it immediately afterward and begin using your new configuration.

TROUBLESHOOTING CONTACTS

Q: Why doesn't AutoDial work for some of my contacts?

A: If AutoDial functions properly for contacts in your area code, but not in other area codes, check the long distance dialing settings in the Dialing Properties dialog box. (Choose Actions ➢ Call Contact ➢ New Call and then click the Dialing Properties button in the New Call dialog box.) If the problem isn't related to area code, check the number to make sure it contains only numbers, not letters.

Q: Why doesn't my Contacts folder appear in the list of address books in the Select Names dialog box?

A: Right-click on the Contacts folder and choose Properties from the shortcut menu. On the Outlook Address Book page of the Properties dialog box, enable the Show This Folder as an E-mail Address Book check box to use Contacts as an address book.

Q: Why don't all my contacts appear in the Select Names dialog box?

A: In the Workgroup/Corporate configuration, only contacts with e-mail addresses or fax numbers appear when you use the Select Names dialog box to address mail and faxes.

Q: My current contact manager doesn't appear on the list in the Import/Export dialog box. How can I import my information into Outlook?

A: In your contact management program, save your contacts in a supported format, such as a text file. Then, import the text file using the comma separated value format in the Import/Export dialog box. You will have to map the fields in your old program to Outlook, but take the time to do this.

TROUBLESHOOTING THE CALENDAR

Q: Why does my appointment appear at the top of the Day view rather than at its scheduled time?

A: You created an event rather than an appointment. To convert the event to an appointment, double-click the event and then disable the All

Day Event check box. Verify the starting and ending times and save and close the appointment.

Q: Why did the times for all my appointments change?

A: When you switch time zones, Outlook automatically changes all your appointments to reflect the change. (This often happens when you import items to a new computer before setting the system clock. The default Windows time zone is Pacific time.) Double-click on the time in the Windows Taskbar, set the correct time zone, and return to Outlook. The correct time will appear for your Calendar items.

Q: How do I display the date navigator? It's not on the View menu.

A: The date navigator is displayed by default. If you resize other items in the Calendar (such as the TaskPad or the Appointment list), there may not be room to display the date navigator. Use the adjustment tool to narrow the display window for the other elements and create room for the navigator.

Q: How do I display the TaskPad in the Calendar?

A: Resize the items that are displayed to create space for the TaskPad display.

Q: Why do some holidays appear more than once in my Calendar?

A: Many holidays are repeated from country to country and between countries and religious groups. For example, Christmas Day is shared by Christians and people in the United States, Ireland, and numerous other countries. If you choose to add all of these holidays to your Calendar, you will have multiple occurrences of these shared holidays on your Calendar. Outlook has no way to remove the holidays once you've added them, except by selecting and deleting them each individually.

Q: Why don't I have a Delegates page in the Options dialog box?

A: If you aren't connected to a Microsoft Exchange Server, you can't add delegates for your Calendar, so the Delegates page isn't an option. If you are on an Exchange Server network and the Delegates tab doesn't appear, Delegate Access hasn't been installed. In the Options dialog box, go to the Other tab, click Advanced Options, and click the Add-In Manager button. Select Delegate Access from the list of choices and click Install. Choose Dlgsept.cgf from the list of available add-ins and click Open. If Dlgsept.cgf does not appear in the list, you must install it using the Office Setup program.

TROUBLESHOOTING TASKS

Q: When I send a task to another user, they receive text instead of the task item. How do I send the task item?

A: When sending a task to another person through Internet e-mail, make sure the properties for that person's e-mail address in Contacts is set to Always Send To This Recipient In Microsoft Outlook Rich-Text Format. This way, the recipient will be able to transfer the task directly into their Task List using copy and paste.

Q: When I assigned one of my tasks to someone else, it disappeared from my task list. How do I get it back?

A: You can't. If you cleared the Keep An Updated Copy Of This Task check box in the Task Request form, Outlook deleted the copy of the task from your list. You can have the assignee send you a copy of the task.

Q: The person I assigned to a task says they marked it as completed. Why didn't I receive a status report?

A: To receive status reports, the Send Me A Status Report check box must be enabled when you send the task. Also, the assignee must be on your network. Status reports don't work with Internet mail.

Q: Why isn't an assigned task being updated in Outlook?

A: To receive updates on assigned tasks, you must have a copy of the original task in your task list. If you disabled the Keep An Updated Copy Of This Task check box in the task request form, or have deleted the task from your list, you won't receive updates even if you re-create the task. Also, the assignee must be on your network. Status reports don't work with Internet mail.

TROUBLESHOOTING PRINTING OPTIONS

Q: Outlook doesn't print. How do I fix it?

A: First, make sure that you've selected a valid printer (File ➢ Print to open the Print dialog box). If you have selected a printer, the problem is in Windows, not in Outlook. See Windows Help for information on troubleshooting printers.

Q: Sometimes I can't find the print style I want to use. What am I doing wrong?

A: Remember that views and print styles are linked. If the current view is a table view, the print styles will be table print styles. Change to a view similar to the print style you want and choose File ➤ Print Preview again.

Q: Why can't I preview outbound mail messages before I print them?

A: HTML and WordMail don't support Print Preview. Change your mail format to Plain Text or Microsoft Rich Text Format if you want to preview messages.

Q: When I print the Calendar, long appointment descriptions are cut off. How do I get them to wrap?

A: Calendar items only wrap in Daily view. If you're printing a monthly or weekly calendar, items are truncated if they're too wide. You can change the font (File ➤ Print ➤ Page Setup) or switch to Day in one of the Day/Week/Month views.

Q: In the Calendar component, how do I set the range of days I want to print?

A: Choose beginning and ending dates in the lower-left corner of the Print dialog box.

Q: How can I print noncontiguous days; for example, just the weekends or weekdays in a month?

A: You can't do it as a single print operation. Print the first weekend, then the second, and so on.

TROUBLESHOOTING SERVICES AND MAIL OPTIONS

Q: Why can't I send and receive e-mail messages?

A: Outlook relies on a number of settings to send and receive e-mail messages. In the Internet Only configuration, you may have more than one e-mail service (for example, CompuServe and an ISP). Check each service by choosing Tools ➤ Send and Receive and then selecting the service you want to use. If one of them works, you can use that service to send mail. Try removing and reinstalling the service that does not work. Sometimes, walking through each step of a service configuration reveals a missing or misconfigured item.

NOTE

Remember, when Outlook is in Internet Only mode, the Services menu item is called Accounts.

If none of the services work, open the Windows Control Panel and check your modem. (It's also a good idea to make sure the phone line is plugged in!) Open the Dial-Up Networking folder in My Computer, and check the settings for the dial-up connection you're using. Launch the dial-up connection directly from the folder to see if it's the connection, rather than your Outlook settings, that's causing the problem. You'll find troubleshooting help for modems and dial-up connections in Windows Help.

In the Workgroup/Corporate configuration, your messaging is normally handled by a LAN-based mail server. When this mail server is down, you won't be able to send or receive messages. If other users on your network can send mail, check with your network administrator to see how your mail services should be configured.

Q: I can't find a mail message I received a couple of months ago. Where is it?

A: If you didn't move the message, there are three possibilities: you switched to another Inbox since you received the message, the message has been archived, or the message was automatically moved or deleted based on rules you created in the Rules Wizard. If you've installed a new set of personal folders, check the Inbox in the folders you used previously. The message should be there. To see if the message may have been archived, right-click on the Inbox, choose Properties, and see if Automatic Archiving is enabled on the AutoArchive tab. If you're using the Rules Wizard to move or delete items automatically, choose Tools ➤ Rules Wizard to change the rules so you don't move or delete messages accidentally.

Q: I AutoArchive my messages. Can I mark individual messages so they won't be archived?

A: Yes. Open the message and choose File ➤ Properties to open the message's Properties dialog box. On the General page, enable the Do Not AutoArchive This Item check box.

Q: Why are the voting options disabled in my mail message form?

A: You can't use voting in the Internet Only configuration. Voting options are only supported if you are using Microsoft Exchange as well as Outlook.

Q: Why don't all of my recipients see the voting options in my messages?

A: The voting options don't work for messages sent over the Internet.

Q: Why does an e-mail message stay in the Outbox after I click Send?

A: If you edit a message after it's in the Outbox, you must click Send again to send the message. If you simply close it, it remains in the Outbox. You can easily check to see if this is the problem. Messages that will be sent are italicized. If a message isn't italicized, open it and click Send.

Q: Why does it take more time to send and receive mail when I change editors?

A: You need to have a fair amount of memory to use Word as your e-mail editor; if you have less than 32MB of memory, it will take longer to send and receive Word mail messages. To speed things up, switch to Microsoft Rich Text Format or Plain Text mail format (Tools ➤ Options and change formats on the Mail Format page of the Options dialog box).

Q: Why is the Signature Picker disabled in the Mail Format dialog box?

A: You're using Word as your e-mail editor, so you can't create a custom signature in Outlook. You can create a template in Word that includes a custom signature, and then use that template for WordMail in Outlook. However, you can't include a digital signature in a WordMail template, so you might consider using one of the Outlook mail editors rather than Word.

Q: I'm trying to find a specific e-mail option. Where should I look?

A: Outlook's mail options are found in a number of locations. Table 13.1 lists the more frequently used e-mail options by type.

TABLE 13.1: E-mail Options

TYPE OF OPTION	PURPOSE/ACTION	LOCATION
Accounts	Set to check for mail, Internet Only configuration	Account Properties dialog box: Tools ➤ Accounts ➤ Properties
Address Separator	Allow comma	Advanced E-mail Options dialog box: Tools ➤ Options ➤ Preferences ➤ E-mail Options ➤ Advanced E-mail Options
Automatic Name Checking	Toggle on or off	Advanced E-mail Options dialog box: Tools ➤ Options ➤ Preferences ➤ E-mail Options ➤ Advanced E-mail Options

TABLE 13.1 continued: E-mail Options

TYPE OF OPTION	PURPOSE/ACTION	LOCATION
Automatic Processing	Complete processing of mail on arrival	Advanced E-mail Options dialog box: Tools ➤ Options ➤ Preferences ➤ E-mail Options ➤ Advanced E-mail Options
Comments	Add your name	E-mail Options dialog box: Tools ➤ Options ➤ Preferences ➤ E-mail Options
Custom Signatures	Select or create	Mail Format, Options dialog box: Tools ➤ Options ➤ Mail Format
Digital Signatures	Obtain Digital ID	Security, Options dialog box: Tools ➤ Options ➤ Security
Digital Signatures	Set defaults	Security, Options dialog box: Tools ➤ Options ➤ Security
Encoding	Default format for Internet mail	Internet E-mail, Options dialog box: Tools ➤ Options ➤ Internet E-mail or Mail Format, Options dialog box: Tools ➤ Options ➤ Mail Format
Encrypted Messages	Set defaults	Security, Options dialog box: Tools ➤ Options ➤ Security
Forwarded Messages	Default font	Mail Format, Options dialog box: Tools ➤ Options ➤ Mail Format
Forwarded Messages	Include or exclude original text	E-mail Options dialog box: Tools ➤ Options ➤ Preferences ➤ E-mail Options
Forwarded Messages	Save or discard	Advanced E-mail Options dialog box: Tools ➤ Options ➤ Preferences ➤ E-mail Options ➤ Advanced E-mail Options
Importance	Set default	Advanced E-mail Options dialog box: Tools ➤ Options ➤ Preferences ➤ E-mail Options ➤ Advanced E-mail Options
Importance	Set for this message	Message Options dialog box: View ➤ Options
Message Delivery	Automatically hang up when finished sending/receiving	Internet E-mail, Options dialog box: Tools ➤ Options ➤ Internet E-mail

Part ii

TABLE 13.1 continued: E-mail Options

TYPE OF OPTION	PURPOSE/ACTION	LOCATION
Message Delivery	Check for Internet messages at set interval	Internet E-mail, Options dialog box: Tools ➤ Options ➤ Internet E-mail
Message Delivery	Display a message box when new messages arrive	E-mail Options dialog box: Tools ➤ Options ➤ Preferences ➤ E-mail Options
Message Delivery	Play a sound or change cursor when new messages arrive	Advanced E-mail Options dialog box: Tools ➤ Options ➤ Preferences ➤ E-mail Options ➤ Advanced E-mail Options
Message Delivery	Prompt or don't prompt before connecting to ISP	Internet E-mail, Options dialog box: Tools ➤ Options ➤ Internet E-mail
Message Delivery	Warn before switching to dial-up connection	Internet E-mail, Options dialog box: Tools ➤ Options ➤ Internet E-mail
Message Format	Default stationery for HTML	Mail Format, Options dialog box: Tools ➤ Options ➤ Mail Format
Message Format	Set default	Mail Format, Options dialog box: Tools ➤ Options ➤ Mail Format
Original Message	Close on reply or forward e-mail	Options dialog box: Tools ➤ Options ➤ Preferences ➤ E-mail Options
Replies	Default font	Mail Format, Options dialog box: Tools ➤ Options ➤ Mail Format
Replies	Quote text, format quoted text	E-mail Options dialog box: Tools ➤ Options ➤ Preferences ➤ E-mail Options
Replies	Send replies to another person	Message Options dialog box: View ➤ Options
Sensitivity	Set default	Advanced E-mail Options dialog box: Tools ➤ Options ➤ Preferences ➤ E-mail Options ➤ Advanced E-mail Options
Sensitivity	Individual message	Message Options dialog box: View ➤ Options
Sent Messages	Delay delivery	Message Options dialog box: View ➤ Options

TABLE 13.1 continued: E-mail Options

TYPE OF OPTION	PURPOSE/ACTION	LOCATION
Sent Messages	Folder to save in	Advanced E-mail Options dialog box: Tools ➤ Options ➤ Preferences ➤ E-mail Options ➤ Advanced E-mail Options
Sent Messages	Save in location for individual message	Message Options dialog box: View ➤ Options
Sent Messages	Save or discard original	Advanced E-mail Options dialog box: Tools ➤ Options ➤ Preferences ➤ E-mail Options ➤ Advanced E-mail Options
Sent Messages	Save or discard copies	E-mail Options dialog box: Tools ➤ Options ➤ Preferences ➤ E-mail Options
Sent Messages	Set expiration for deletion of sent messages	Message Options dialog box: View ➤ Options
Services	Set expiration for deletion of sent messages	Mail Services, Options dialog box: Tools ➤ Options ➤ Mail Services
Spelling	General options	Spelling, Options dialog box: Tools ➤ Options ➤ Spelling
Spelling	Select custom dictionary, all other options	Spelling, Options dialog box: Tools ➤ Options ➤ Spelling
Tracking	Set defaults for Internet Only configuration	Tracking Options dialog box: Tools ➤ Options ➤ Preferences ➤ E-mail Options ➤ Tracking Options
Tracking	Set defaults for Internet Only configuration	Rules Wizard
Tracking	For this message, Corporate/Workgroup only	Message Options dialog box: View ➤ Options
Unsent Messages	AutoSave	Advanced E-mail Options dialog box: Tools ➤ Options ➤ Preferences ➤ E-mail Options ➤ Advanced E-mail Options
Unsent Messages	Save in drafts or discard e-mail	Options dialog box: Tools ➤ Options ➤ Preferences ➤ E-mail Options

Part ii

TABLE 13.1 continued: E-mail Options

TYPE OF OPTION	PURPOSE/ACTION	LOCATION
User Profile	Prompt or use default	Mail Services, Options dialog box: Tools ➤ Options ➤ Mail Services
vCard	Attach as signature	Mail Format, Options dialog box: Tools ➤ Options ➤ Mail Format
Voting	Corporate/Workgroup only	Message Options dialog box: View ➤ Options

Q: Why does an error message appear whenever I try to send digitally signed messages?

A: Class 1 digital signatures include your e-mail address. If you change addresses (or your system administrator changes your address), you will need to obtain a new or updated certificate from your ID provider to send digitally signed messages.

Q: Why can't I preview a message/an encrypted message?

A: The message is encrypted. You can open the message, but you can't preview it.

TROUBLESHOOTING ATTACHMENTS

Q: Why can't I open a file attached to a mail message?

A: To open an attachment, you must have a program that can read the file format of the attachment. For example, if someone sends you a drawing created in Visio, you must have Visio on your machine to open the file or an application that can import the file. Ask the sender to save the file in a format you can open and send it to you again.

Q: Why do some of my recipients receive a file called Winmail.dat attached to messages I send?

A: This happens when you send a message that uses Microsoft Rich Text formatting to someone whose mail program can't read RTF. To change the format used to send all mail messages, choose Tools ➤ Options to open the Options dialog box and choose Plain Text on the Mail Format page. If you're using plain text or HTML, open the Contact form for the recipient and double-click their e-mail address to open the Address Properties dialog box. Disable the Always Send To This Recipient in Microsoft Outlook Rich Text Format check box, and then click OK.

Q: Why can't message recipients open attachments I send as shortcuts?

A: The recipient must have permission to open the folder that contains the file that the shortcut points to. Consider attaching the file itself instead of a shortcut.

TROUBLESHOOTING CATEGORIES

Q: Why do categories I deleted from the Master Category list still appear in some items?

A: Deleting a category from the list does not delete it from the individual items that you'd already assigned to the category.

Q: How do I remove a category from multiple items?

A: Use Find to locate all items that use the category, and then select the items. Choose Edit ➤ Categories to open the Categories dialog box. In the Available Categories list, turn off the check boxes for the categories you want to remove from the selected items.

Q: Why do I have Categories that I didn't create?

A: Outlook includes default categories, so the category may have been on the default list. If other users send you mail messages or items with custom categories they created, the categories are added to your list of available categories. This is why it's a good idea to remove your custom categories from items you send to other users.

TROUBLESHOOTING FILES AND FOLDERS

Q: I created a custom view in a public folder. Why can't other users see it?

A: When you create a view, you can let everyone see it, or hide it from other users by choosing In This Folder, Visible Only To Me in the Create View dialog box. While you can't change this setting, you can copy the view and make it visible by choosing the In This Folder, Visible to Everyone option in the Copy View dialog box.

Q: Why can't I open a shared folder?

A: If you can see the folder, but not open it, there are two possibilities: the server that the folder is shared on isn't available, or you don't have permission to open the folder. For permission to open the folder, talk to the folder's owner or your network administrator.

Q: If I can open a public folder, why can't I create a new item in it?

A: You have permission to read the items in the folder, but you don't have permission to create new items. (Either your system administrator or the folder's owner can give you permission to create items.) If you have the appropriate permissions, you may need a customized form to post to the folder.

Q: Why can't I create a subfolder in a public folder?

A: Author, the default role for users of a public folder, doesn't have permission to create subfolders. If you need to create subfolders in an existing public folder, ask the folder's owner or the system administrator to create a new subfolder for you or to give you permission to do it yourself.

WHAT'S NEXT?

This chapter gave answers to common problems you may encounter with Outlook. In the next chapter, you will go beyond the boundaries of what you know about Outlook so far. You will learn how to customize Outlook to handle the more specialized data and communications requirements of your organization.

PART III

DEVELOPING OUTLOOK FORMS

Chapter 14

IMPROVING YOUR OUTLOOK

Outlook, today's best desktop information manager, is a general tool for use in a wide variety of organizations. But can Outlook handle the more specialized data and communications requirements of your organization? The answer is yes—with some help from you. In this chapter, you'll see how Outlook can be customized to track your critical information.

Adapted from *Mastering™ Microsoft® Outlook™ 2000* by Gini Courter and Annette Marquis

ISBN 0-7821-2472-0   787 pages $34.99

TYPES OF OUTLOOK APPLICATIONS

Outlook customization ranges from simple applications to complex office solutions using Microsoft Exchange and ODBC database connectivity. The amount of work required to create an Outlook application depends on the level of complexity. For example, you can:

- ▶ Add a few data fields to an existing component and create custom views that include the fields

- ▶ Construct new forms in existing components

- ▶ Build new forms from scratch

- ▶ Create an entirely different level of functionality in a public folder by adding new controls or modifying existing controls

Outlook is a robust tool for rapid development of user-friendly applications. If you want to let users view contact data in a number of combinations and sort orders in a traditional database (for example, Access), you can create queries and forms to display information or reports to print each data combination. With Outlook, you create and save one or more new views. There are four advantages to developing your projects in Outlook.

First, it's faster to create a view in Outlook than to create a good-looking tabular form in Access or another database tool. Second, the finished product is accessible. In a completed database application, users are kept at arm's length from the tools used to manipulate data. In Outlook, you can encourage users to customize views. The third benefit is a result of the second: because Outlook users can enhance the views you create, you don't have to anticipate and create every view users will ever need.

The fourth benefit is that Outlook automatically supplies a lot of the functionality that's the hardest to create in a programming language or database development tool. For example, an Outlook application that you base on a message form automatically supports forwarding, replying, and the other mail features. Use the form, and you get instant access to all the actions that belong to the form. Inherited functionality is a major reason increasing numbers of Office users and developers are creating office productivity tools in Outlook: you don't have to understand the ins and outs of messaging to create mail applications or be intimate with threading to create post and reply bulletin boards. Imagine building a mail application from scratch using a programming language, and you immediately recognize the massive head start Outlook provides.

Workgroup Applications Created in an Afternoon

If you create new views and forms for use on your desktop, you have a stand-alone application. Publish the forms and views in a Microsoft Exchange Server public folder and you have instant groupware. Collaboration is one of the strengths of Exchange that you can extend to your workgroup with Outlook. With Exchange public folder applications, you can set permissions to allow only specific people to add newsletter subscriber tasks or to schedule classes, so your application can be as open as you want it to be.

For example, say you're responsible for tracking subscriptions to your company's Office Tips newsletter. Three months before a subscription expires, you notify the Customer Service department, which contacts the subscriber about renewing. To make your job easier, you create an Outlook Contacts folder called Newsletter that contains contact information for subscribers and some new views. If you copy your Newsletter folder to a public folder, you can grant other users on your network access to the Newsletter folder. Instead of e-mailing contacts to the Customer Service Department, you can let your colleagues in the department access the information directly.

Collaborative Calendar applications are popular tools. Create a public folder for Calendar items, and you have a scheduling application for training classes, a speakers' bureau, or personnel development opportunities. Trainees can check to see when specific classes are available or see the entire schedule of opportunities, simply by changing Calendar views. If you're managing a project for your workgroup, create a public folder for the project's tasks. Team members can check the views in the folder to get an update as tasks are assigned, started, and completed.

Applications Based on Calendar, Contacts, and Tasks

If you need to track additional information that isn't included in an Outlook component, create a new form so users can collect and view the data. There are four types of forms you can create in Outlook:

- ▶ Calendar, Contacts, or Task forms
- ▶ Mail message forms

Part iii

▶ Post forms

▶ Office document forms

Before you create a form from scratch, see if you can identify an Outlook component that contains most of the fields you need and has the desired functionality. For example, if you want to keep track of people in a database type of application, consider simply adding fields to the default Contacts form. Figure 14.1 shows a newsletter form based on the Contact form. Two fields, Beginning Date and Ending Date, were added to the Contact form.

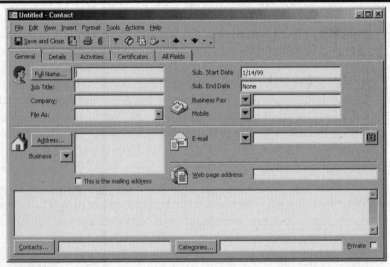

FIGURE 14.1:   The Newsletter Circulation form is based on the Contact form.

The form allows users to enter or view beginning and ending date information for individual contacts. The existing Contacts views didn't include the added fields, so two new views were created: Subscriber Since and Expiring Subscriptions (see Figure 14.2). Now users in the Customer Service Department can concentrate on reaching subscribers before their subscriptions run out. These modifications to the Contacts component took less than an hour to complete.

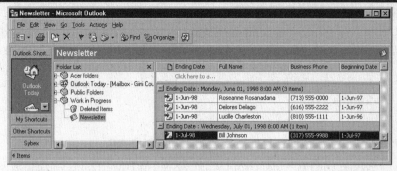

FIGURE 14.2: The Customer Service Department contacts customers whose subscriptions are expiring.

Mail Message Applications

Mail message applications are used for internal and external communications. Forms can be pre-addressed so that, for example, the Suggestion form is automatically delivered to the Quality Control Department and the Newsletter Subscription form is sent to Customer Service. Mail message items can be sent to a public folder or a distribution list as well as to an individual user. Figure 14.3 shows a customized message form used to send a training request to a company's training coordinator. The message is pre-addressed by the application.

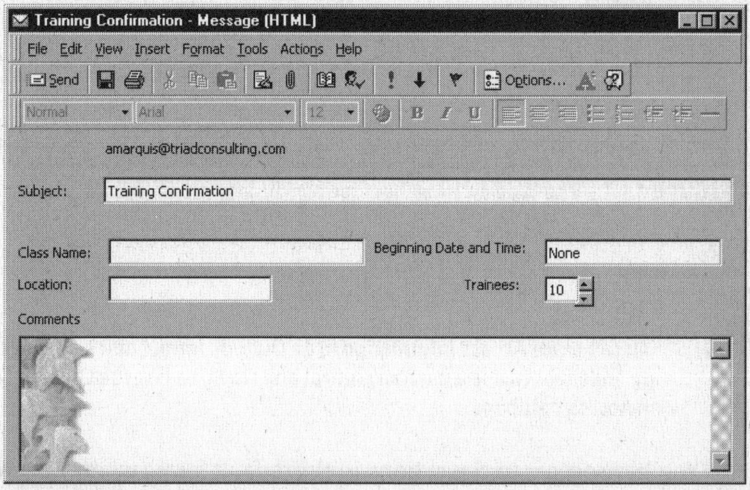

Part iii

FIGURE 14.3: Mail message applications send and receive customized mail forms.

Post Applications

A Post form is like a message form, but the recipient is a public folder. Other users can read a posted message and reply to the message in the same folder, creating a threaded discussion. Post applications are popular for internal bulletin boards, online brainstorming sessions, and other forums.

Office Document Applications

When you need tools from Word, Excel, or PowerPoint, you can rely on Outlook's integration with the other members of the Office family. Office document forms are containers that hold Office documents so they can be mailed or posted. The Weekly Timesheet application's main form, shown in Figure 14.4, includes part of a Microsoft Excel worksheet.

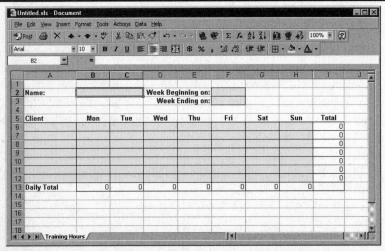

FIGURE 14.4: The Weekly Timesheet form includes part of an Excel worksheet.

TIP

You can place Access information in an Outlook form, but it's a more challenging endeavor to use a custom control and ODBC to link the Outlook form with an Access database.

You have access to the actions in the default forms when you create a new form based on one of the default forms. If you want to add other bells and whistles to your Outlook application, you can use Microsoft's popular Visual Basic programming language.

Don't worry if Visual Basic is not up your alley. Its use in Outlook makes the application much more powerful, but the changes are relatively simple. You don't need to prepare yourself for late nights and lots of coffee.

BEYOND THE BOUNDARIES OF OUTLOOK

It's easy to get excited by the ease of development and the professional look of Outlook applications. Eventually, you'll begin to wonder why you can't create anything you want in Outlook—why anyone would bother to develop applications using Access, Excel, Visual Basic, Java, or any of the other tools at hand. The answer is that there are a few things Outlook is *not* designed to do. Outlook isn't the only tool you'll need, for example, when you need to:

- ▶ Relate data entities. When your data application includes two or more types of entities (classes and students, customers and orders, employees and skills), you'll probably want to use Access, SQL Server, or both. Outlook databases are not relational databases.

- ▶ Sort and filter huge quantities of data. Outlook's Contacts component handles hundreds and even thousands of contact records with decent speed. But Outlook is not the place to store your company's 250,000 customers. For large-scale data storage, look to Access for desktop applications and SQL Server when multiple users need to access the data.

- ▶ Use form- or control-level permissions. In databases like Access, security is at the form or control level. You can, for example, give one user or group read-only permissions for data displayed in a particular database form and full permissions for a different form in the same database. In Outlook, permissions are set at the folder level, so a user who can delete one type of item in a folder can delete any item in the folder.

Outlook can't be the only solution in these scenarios, but it can be part of your customized solution. With the addition of user-defined form fields and Visual Basic, you can check to see who is editing or deleting an item and allow or disallow the edit or deletion. Or you can set permissions on groups of folders, and then add Visual Basic code to user forms to copy items from folder to folder.

You can connect customized Outlook forms to data stored in Access. For example, your users can view and enter data in an Access database from a form in Outlook. They will use the familiar tools from Outlook, but the data they're manipulating is stored in Access. Outlook and Microsoft Exchange Server connect to SQL Server for your larger databases.

WHAT'S NEXT?

This chapter provided an overview of the types of applications you can create using Outlook. In the following chapters, you'll find out how to create applications for yourself and other users in your office or workgroup.

Chapter 15
CREATING CUSTOM FORMS

In this chapter, we'll look at how to create, modify, and manage custom forms in Outlook. We'll begin by recapping what forms are. We'll then look at the three classes of forms that Outlook supports, and we'll discuss the reasons why creating custom forms is useful. We'll then go through the process of customizing forms and publishing them for use. Finally, we'll look at how to manage your forms and how to create a template for reuse.

Adapted from *Mastering™ Microsoft® Outlook™ 2000*
by Gini Courter and Annette Marquis
ISBN 0-7821-2472-0   787 pages $34.99

WHAT IS A FORM?

A form is essentially a window or container for working with information within Outlook. Each form contains a number of *controls*—interface elements such as text boxes, option buttons, and command buttons—that you use to interact with the form. You'll be familiar with most (if not all) of these controls from your work with other Windows applications and with the eight built-in forms that Outlook provides: the Appointment, Contact, Journal Entry, Mail Message, Meeting Request/Online Meeting Request, Note, Task, and Task Request forms.

As you've seen, the forms vary tremendously in complexity, with the Note form being the simplest. Most of the forms contain more than one *page*—different areas of the form that you reach by clicking the tabs at the top of the pages. For example, the standard Contact form, shown in Figure 15.1, contains five visible pages identified by the tabs General, Details, Activities, Certificates, and All Fields. The form also contains a number of other, hidden pages that you can reveal by customizing the form.

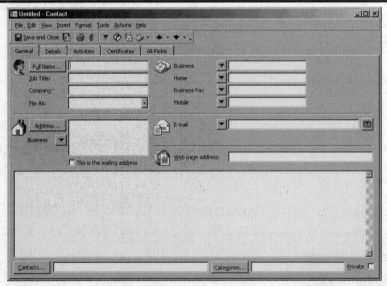

FIGURE 15.1: The standard Contact form contains five visible pages—General, Details, Activities, Certificates, and All Fields.

UNDERSTANDING THE THREE CLASSES OF FORMS

Outlook has three classes of forms: personal forms, organization forms, and folder forms. These forms are stored in different forms folders, also referred to as *forms registries* or *forms libraries*:

▶ Forms in the *personal forms folder* or *personal forms library* are personal to the current user of Outlook and can be accessed only by that user. Outlook stores personal forms in the individual user's mailbox.

▶ Forms in the *organizational forms folder* or *organizational forms library* are shared across the Exchange enterprise and can be accessed by anyone in the enterprise who has the appropriate permissions; by default, all users can access forms in an organizational forms library. Outlook stores organizational forms on the server. You can replicate organizational forms libraries between Exchange sites in an organization so that each site has access to the organizational forms.

▶ Forms in the *folder forms folder* or (more understandably) *folder forms library* can only be accessed from that folder, no matter whether the folder is a public folder or a private folder. The folder forms library is useful for attaching forms to public folders, so that those people with access to a public folder can use the forms associated with it.

As you'll see later in the chapter, you can copy or move forms from one forms library to another, which gives you flexibility regarding where you decide to store your forms. For example, you might initially create a form for your own use and store it in your personal forms library, and only copy it to the organizational forms library when you've established that your colleagues could use it, too.

WHY CREATE CUSTOM FORMS?

Outlook's built-in forms provide a great deal of flexibility and functionality straight out of the box. But for many business purposes, you will need to extend or modify their functionality. For example, if you work in sales, you might need to store extra information on your contacts, such as details on their recent orders, fulfillment, and payments. By using custom forms, you can do this easily. Likewise, you might be able to speed up the creation of frequent task requests and appointments by creating custom forms that already contain or automatically enter part of the information for you. If you need to create an application with solid mail or post functionality, Outlook is the place to do it. You can create an e-mail–based application in hours rather than days, because Outlook 2000 handles the mail features for you.

You can customize any of the forms except for the Note form, perhaps because it is too simple to be customized. Each built-in form, apart from the Note form, contains a number of extra, unused pages that are normally hidden from view; you can use these to extend the form. Each built-in form also contains one or more special pages, such as Actions and Properties, that are normally hidden as well. We'll look at how to use these pages later in the chapter, in "Setting Properties for the Form" and "Choosing Actions for the Form."

You can customize a form in several ways:

▶ Preset information in the form so that you don't have to fill it in each time you create an item based on the form. For example, if you regularly need to send a message to 15 different people, you can create a custom form that contains their addresses in the To box.

▶ Add fields to or remove them from the pages the form normally displays. For example, you might choose to add one or two extra fields to the standard Contact form so that you could include extra information with your contacts.

▶ Reveal hidden pages in the form (effectively, adding pages to the form) or hide existing pages (effectively, removing them from the form).

▶ Add fields to the new pages.

▶ Rename any page that does not have a default name assigned.

▶ Alter how the controls on the form work.

The main way of creating a custom form in Outlook is by basing it on one of the existing Outlook forms. For minor customizations, you can simply extend the existing components of a form by adding new pages, custom fields, and features. For more radical customizations, you can remove most of the existing components of a form, providing yourself with an almost clean slate for designing your own form.

You can also create a custom form in Outlook by basing it on an Office document, such as an Excel chart or worksheet, a Word document, or a PowerPoint presentation. The following are a couple of possible uses:

▸ Distributing interactive questionnaires with embedded Power-Point slides to employees for training purposes

▸ Automating departmental approval of budget expenditures by including spreadsheet views and Exchange Server voting features

These forms are less customizable than forms based on the existing Outlook forms. We'll look at how to create Outlook forms based on Office documents at the end of this chapter.

Opening a Form for Customization

To open a form for customization:

1. From the main Outlook window or from a form window, select Tools ➣ Forms ➣ Choose Form, or File ➣ New ➣ Choose Form, to display the Choose Form dialog box (see Figure 15.2).

NOTE

To open a form in Design mode from an open form, you can choose Tools ➣ Forms ➣ Design a Form to display the Design Form dialog box, which is the Choose Form dialog box in disguise. If you want to exploit a neat shortcut from an empty form, go to Tools ➣ Forms ➣ Design This Form and you will directly enter Design Mode for the form from which you chose this option.

2. In the Look In drop-down list, choose the forms library in which the form you want to use is stored. You can choose from the Standard Forms Library (which contains the standard Outlook forms: Appointment, Contact, Journal Entry, and so on), the Organizational Forms Library (which contains organizational forms available to you), the Personal Forms Library (which contains personal forms stored in your

mailbox), Outlook Folders, Templates in File System, Tasks, Calendar, Inbox, Mailbox, and Contacts.

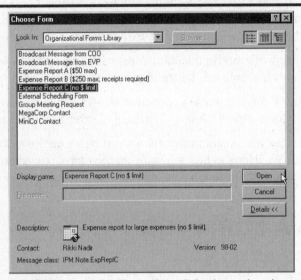

FIGURE 15.2:   In the Choose Form dialog box, select the type of form you want to create or customize and click Open. This view of the dialog box shows some custom forms available for use or modification.

If the folder you need to access is not displayed, click Browse to display the Go to Folder dialog box. Select the appropriate folder and click OK to display it. The Browse button is not available when one of the forms libraries is selected in the Look In drop-down list.

3. In the main list box, select the form you want to work with. The Choose Form dialog box has a number of features to help you locate the form you want:

> ▶ You can click Details to toggle the display of the details panel at the bottom of the Choose Form dialog box. This panel, which you can see in Figure 15.2, shows the Contact, Version, and Message Class information for this form.

► Description describes the purpose of the form. For example, the Description for the Meeting Request form is "This form is used to create meeting requests." For the forms you're familiar with, these descriptions may be too obvious to be useful, but for custom forms stored on an enterprise network, they can be helpful in identifying the precise purpose of each form.

► Contact specifies the designated contact for the form. This information is more useful for custom forms than for the standard Outlook forms, which have Microsoft listed as the contact.

► Version is the version number allotted to the form. Again, this is primarily useful for custom forms.

► Message Class shows Outlook's classification of the form. The message class controls the icon allotted to the form. Each class description starts with the letters IPM, followed by a period and the type of form on which the form is based (for example, Appointment or Contact), followed by another period and the file name of the form. As you'll see when you create a custom form, Outlook assigns the class description automatically; you cannot change it.

4. Click Open. Outlook will open a copy of the form in a new window.

5. Choose Tools ➤ Forms ➤ Design This Form to display this form in Design mode so that you can change its design. Figure 15.3 shows a Contact form open in Design mode.

When you display a form in Design mode, Outlook displays all the pages that the form contains—the pages that are normally displayed, the blank pages that are normally hidden, and the special pages (such as Properties and Actions). You can then change the form as discussed in the next section.

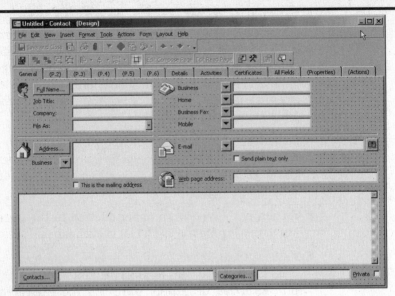

FIGURE 15.3:   A Contact form open in Design mode

Customizing a Form

In this section, we'll look at the ways in which you can customize a form: by adding, removing, and renaming pages; and by adding, removing, and altering controls on those pages.

NOTE

By design, Outlook prevents you from changing the first tab of a custom form based on the standard Appointment form, Journal form, or Task form. The only workaround for this limitation is to hide the first page of the form and use the second page in its stead.

Adding Pages to a Form

Each form contains a number of unused pages that are normally hidden when the form is displayed. You can activate any of these pages so that they are visible when the form is displayed.

When you display a form in Design mode, the names of pages that are hidden will appear within parentheses on their tabs: (P.2) and so on. The names of pages that are displayed will appear without parentheses.

To cause Outlook to display a page, select the page and choose Form ➤ Display This Page. The Display This Page menu item will display a checkmark to indicate that it is active, and Outlook will not display parentheses around the page's name on its tab.

Removing Pages from a Form

To remove a page from a form, you simply tell Outlook not to display it when it displays the form. Select the displayed page and choose Form ➤ Display This Page to remove the checkmark from the Display This Page menu item.

Renaming a Page

To rename a page, choose Form ➤ Rename Page to display the Rename Page dialog box. Enter the new name for the page in the Page Name text box, and then click OK. Page names can be up to 32 characters long (including spaces and punctuation), but usually you'll do better to keep them shorter for legibility—particularly in forms that use more than two or three pages.

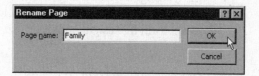

Adding Fields to a Form

As you've seen from the standard forms, Outlook has a bewilderingly large number of different fields available. You can add any of these fields to a form.

To add fields to a form:

 1. Display the Field Chooser window (see Figure 15.4) by clicking the Field Chooser button on the Form Design toolbar. Alternatively, you can right-click a blank space in the form and choose Field Chooser from the shortcut menu, or choose Form ➤ Field Chooser.

FIGURE 15.4: The Field Chooser provides access to all the fields that Outlook offers.

2. Use the drop-down list at the top of the Field Chooser to select the set of fields you want to use. This drop-down list offers a choice of field sets, depending on the form. The noteworthy field sets are the following:

    ▶ Frequently-Used Fields include Outlook's assortment of fields most frequently used for the form you're working on. A Message form in Design mode will have a different set of frequently used fields in the Field Chooser than a Contact form in Design mode.

    ▶ Address Fields, E-mail Fields, Date/Time Fields, and so on are self-explanatory.

    ▶ User-Defined Fields in Inbox/Folder include all user-defined fields available in the library or folder containing the form.

    ▶ The Forms item at the bottom of the drop-down list displays the Select Enterprise Forms for This Folder dialog box (see Figure 15.5). In the left-hand list box, select the form or forms that contain the field or fields you want to use, and then click Add to add the forms to the Selected Forms list box on the right-hand side of the dialog box.

(Use the Remove button to remove selected forms from the Selected Forms list box.) Click the Close button to close the Select Enterprise Forms for This Folder dialog box.

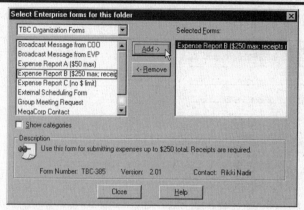

FIGURE 15.5: Use the Select Enterprise Forms for This Folder dialog box to select one or more forms containing fields you want to use.

3. To place a field on the form, click its button in the Field Chooser and drag it to where you want it to appear on the form, as shown in Figure 15.6.

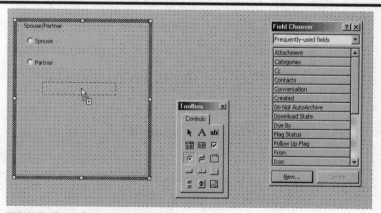

FIGURE 15.6: Dragging a field from the Field Chooser to a form

Part iii

Creating a New Field

If Outlook doesn't provide the type of field you need for your custom forms, you can easily create a suitable field. To do so:

1. Click New at the bottom of the Field Chooser to display the New Field dialog box (see Figure 15.7).

FIGURE 15.7: Creating a new field in the New Field dialog box

2. In the Name text box, enter the name for the field. Avoid reusing the name of an existing field (Outlook will stop you if you try to do this).

3. In the Type drop-down list box, choose the type of field this will be. The choices are:

Type	Contains
Text	A string of text
Number	A number in any of nine numeric formats
Percent	A percentage, rounded or unrounded
Currency	A dollar amount, in either of two currency formats
Yes/No	A two-position choice: Yes/No; On/Off; True/False; or Icon
Date/Time	A date/time, date, or time value in any of a number of formats
Duration	A length of time, specified in any of four formats

Keywords	A text string limited to certain words
Combination	A combination formula consisting of either fields and text fragments or the first non-empty field in a series of fields
Formula	A formula consisting of fields, functions, or both
Integer	An integer in any one of four formats (three computer formats, one conventional integer format)

4. In the Format drop-down list box, choose the format you want for the field. The formats available will depend on the field type. For example, a field of the Text type can have only the Text format, while a field of the Number type can be one of nine number formats (All Digits, Truncated, 1 Decimal, and so on).

5. Click OK to create the new field. Outlook will close the New Field dialog box and will add the new field to the User-Defined Fields in Inbox set.

You can now use the new field in your forms by selecting the User-Defined Fields set in the Field Chooser.

Deleting a Custom Field

To delete a custom field, select it in the Field Chooser and click Delete. Outlook will display the message box shown here to warn you that the field will be removed from the list of available fields but will remain in the items in which it has already been used. Choose Yes to delete the field.

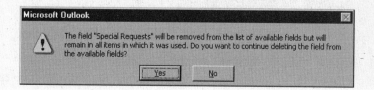

Part iii

NOTE
You cannot delete any of Outlook's built-in fields or change the type of any field.

WORKING WITH CONTROLS

In addition to Outlook's built-in standard fields and the new fields you create, you can also use custom controls to customize forms in Outlook. You'll be familiar with most, if not all, of these controls from your work with Outlook and other Windows applications.

In the following sections, we'll discuss how to add custom controls to a form, how to lay them out, how to change their properties to control their appearance and behavior, and how to connect controls to fields.

Adding Custom Controls to a Form

Like the Visual Basic Integrated Development Environment and the Visual Basic Editor for the Office applications, Outlook provides a Toolbox (see Figure 15.8) of custom controls that you can add to a form. To display the Toolbox, click the Control Toolbox icon on the Form Design toolbar.

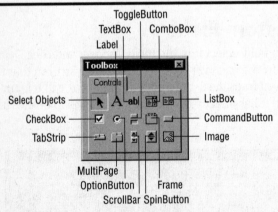

FIGURE 15.8:   The Toolbox provides custom controls that you can use on your forms.

As you can see, all except one of the buttons in the Toolbox represent controls. The odd one out is the Select Objects button, which restores the mouse pointer to Selection mode; you typically use it when you've selected a control and then find that you need to work with another control before placing the current one. Here's what the controls in the Toolbox are:

Control	Creates
Label	A label—text used to identify a part of a form or provide information on the form.
TextBox	A text box (also known as an edit box) for text entry or editing.
ComboBox	A combo box—a control that consists of a text box at the top of a list box. Use a combo box to present existing choices (in the list-box section) but also let the user enter a different value.
ListBox	A list box—a box control that lists a number of values.
CheckBox	A check box and a label to identify it.
OptionButton	An option button (also known as a radio button) and a label to identify it. Only one option button out of a group of option buttons can be selected at any one time (like a radio, which can be tuned to one station at a time).
ToggleButton	A toggle button—a button that shows whether an item is selected. A toggle button can have any two settings, such as On/Off or Yes/No.
Frame	A frame—an area of a UserForm or dialog box surrounded by a thin line, also called a group box—and a label to identify it. Use frames to group related elements in your dialog boxes.
CommandButton	A command button—a button used for taking action in a dialog box. Buttons such as OK, Cancel, Close, or Send are command buttons.
TabStrip	A tab strip for creating multipage dialog boxes whose pages share the same layout.

Part iii

MultiPage	A multipage control for creating multipage dialog boxes whose pages have different layouts.
ScrollBar	A stand-alone scroll bar for scrolling a custom control. (Combo boxes and list boxes have built-in scroll bars.)
SpinButton	A spin-button control for incrementing and decrementing the value of another control.
Image	An image control for displaying a picture on the form.

To add a control to a form:

1. If the Toolbox isn't displayed, display it by clicking the Control Toolbox icon on the Form Design toolbar.

2. Click the button for the control in the Toolbox. The mouse pointer will take on the icon for the item.

3. Place the control on the form:

   ▶ To place a standard-sized control, click where you want the upper-left corner of the control to appear.

   ▶ To place a custom-sized control, click where you want one corner of the control to appear, and then drag the mouse until the outline for the control is the size you want. Release the mouse button, and Outlook will create the control.

   ▶ To simply dump the control on the form (for example, if you're intending to use the alignment commands to arrange a number of controls), drag the control from the Toolbox to anywhere on the form.

4. For a control that has a text label, click in the control to place the insertion point, and then type the text for the label. Click outside the control or press the Enter key to accept the text.

You can customize the Toolbox by adding new pages and new controls to it. Briefly, to create a new page, right-click the tab of an existing page and choose New Page. Right-click the new page (which will be named New Page) and choose Rename from the shortcut menu to rename it. You can then drag custom controls (for example, controls with their properties set to suit you) from a form to the Toolbox, where they will be available for reuse.

Laying Out the Controls on a Form

Once you've placed a number of controls on a form, you'll typically need to work on their layout. Outlook provides a lot of help for laying out the controls on a form, with many layout commands accessible from both the Form Design toolbar and the Layout menu.

All the layout commands work on the active control or active group—the control or group with white selection handles on it. To select one control or group, click on it. To select a range of contiguous controls, select the first control, hold down the Shift key, and then select the last control in the range; Outlook will select all the controls in between as well. To select multiple noncontiguous controls, select the first control, hold down the Ctrl key, and then select the other controls one by one.

Here's what the buttons on the Form Design toolbar (see Figure 15.9) do:

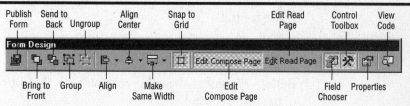

FIGURE 15.9: The Form Design toolbar

Publish Form Displays the Publish Form As dialog box, which you use for publishing a form for use by your workgroup.

NOTE
Keep in mind that users can't use your custom form until you publish it. Once you do, it's available for general use and can be reached by all people with the appropriate access.

Bring to Front Brings the selected control or controls to the front of the form (i.e., displays them on top of any controls they overlap).

Send to Back Sends the selected control or controls to the back.

Group Makes a group of the selected controls. This allows you to work with the group as one unit.

Part iii

Ungroup   Disbands the selected group of controls.

Align   Aligns the selected controls horizontally and vertically depending on your choice from the Align drop-down list, as described in the following list. The alignment in each case is relative to the active control—the control with the white selection handles around it.

- ▶ Left alignment aligns the controls with the left side of the active control.

- ▶ Center alignment centers the controls on the horizontal midpoint of the active control.

- ▶ Right alignment aligns the controls with the right side of the active control.

- ▶ Top alignment aligns the controls with the top of the active control.

- ▶ Middle alignment aligns the controls with the vertical midpoint of the active control.

- ▶ Bottom alignment aligns the controls with the bottom of the active control.

Align Center   Centers the selected controls either horizontally or vertically, depending on your choice from the drop-down list.

Make Same Width   Makes the selected controls the same width as the active control. The Height item in the Make Same Width drop-down list makes the selected controls the same height as the active control. The Both item in the drop-down list makes the selected controls the same width and height as the active control.

Snap to Grid   Toggles the Snap to Grid feature on and off. When the Snap to Grid feature is on, Outlook automatically aligns controls you place or move with the grid pattern in the form. This makes for quick and accurate alignment of controls, but can mean that you cannot place controls precisely where you want them. The Snap to Grid button appears highlighted (pushed in) when the Snap to Grid feature is active, and appears normal when Snap to Grid is not active.

TIP

To gain more control over the placement of controls when you're using the Snap to Grid feature in Design mode, you can change the spacing of the dots that form the grid. Choose Form ➤ Set Grid Size to display the Set Grid Size dialog box. Enter the width and height measurements in the Width and Height text boxes, and click OK to apply them.

Edit Compose Page   Displays the *compose page*—the page that the user will see when composing an item based on this form. The Edit Compose Page button is available only when you have chosen to create a separate read layout for the form (by choosing Form ➤ Separate Read Layout). We'll discuss creating forms with separate compose pages and read pages in "Creating Forms with Separate Compose Pages and Read Pages," later in the chapter.

Edit Read Page   Displays the *read page*—the page that the recipient of an item based on this form will see. As mentioned in the previous paragraph, you can create a separate read layout for a form.

Field Chooser   Toggles the display of the Field Chooser window.

Control Toolbox   Toggles the display of the Toolbox.

Properties   Displays the Properties dialog box for the selected control.

View Code   Displays the Script Editor for the current form.

The Layout menu offers many of these commands, together with the following:

Size to Fit command   Sizes the selected control or controls to fit its contents.

Size to Grid command   Sizes the control to the nearest gridline.

Horizontal Spacing submenu   Provides adjustments to the horizontal spacing of controls.

Vertical Spacing submenu   Provides adjustments to the vertical spacing of controls.

Part iii

Arrange submenu   Offers Right and Bottom options useful for arranging groups of command buttons.

AutoLayout command   Automatically places controls relative to existing controls as you drag them onto the form.

Changing the Properties for a Control

Each control has a number of *properties*—attributes—that govern its appearance and behavior. Different controls have different properties—for example, a list box needs different properties than a command button, though both share common properties such as Height and Width.

Outlook provides two ways of changing the properties for a control: by using the Properties dialog box and by using the Properties window. In the next two sections, we'll look at each way in turn.

Changing the Properties of a Control by Using the Properties Dialog Box

Here's how to use the Properties dialog box to change the most frequently used properties of a control:

1.   Right-click the control and choose Properties from the shortcut menu, or select the control and choose Form ➤ Properties to display the Properties dialog box (see Figure 15.10).

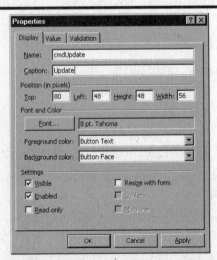

FIGURE 15.10:   Use the Properties dialog box to set the most commonly used properties for a control.

2. On the Display tab, choose settings for the properties that affect how the control appears. For different types of controls, different fields will be available in the Properties dialog box.

   ▶ In the Name text box, enter the name by which the control will be known by Outlook (and in your code). For example, if you added a command button that bore the text *Mortgage Payments*, you might use *cmdMortgage-Payments* as the Name property.

   ▶ In the Caption text box, enter the text that should appear on the control. For example, the command button mentioned in the previous point would have a Caption property of *Mortgage Payments*. To set an access key for the control, enter an ampersand (&) before the appropriate letter. (The *access key*, also known as the *accelerator key*, is the underlined letter that you can press to quickly access a control.) For example, to set an access key of *M* for the Mortgage Payments button, you would enter a Caption property of **&Mortgage Payments**.

   ▶ In the Position area of the Display tab, set the values of the Top, Left, Height, and Width text boxes to the measurements you want for the control. These properties give you fine adjustment over the size and placement of the control. It's usually easiest to place controls approximately where they belong by dragging them about the form with the mouse and using the options on the Layout menu (discussed earlier in this chapter), and then make fine adjustments as necessary in the Properties dialog box (or the Properties window, which we'll look at next).

   ▶ If you need to change the font used in or on the control, click the Font button to display the Font dialog box. Choose suitable font settings and click the OK button to close the Font dialog box. The grayed-out text panel to the right of the Font button will reflect your changes.

Part iii

WARNING

If you change the font on a control, be sure to use a font that will be available to all users of the form. For most purposes, you'll do best to stay with the default font on controls, both to ensure the font is available and to present a consistent and readable interface.

▶ If you want to change the foreground or background of the control, select the color you want in the Foreground Color drop-down list or the Background Color drop-down list.

▶ The Visible check box (which is selected by default) governs whether the control is visible when the form is displayed (in some situations, you may want to keep certain controls invisible until the need for them arises).

▶ The Enabled check box (which is selected by default) governs whether the control is enabled or disabled (if a control is disabled, it is displayed grayed-out, and the user cannot use it).

▶ The Read Only check box (which is cleared by default on most controls) governs whether the user can make changes to the control. If a control is read only, the user can select information in it and copy that information, but they cannot change the information.

▶ The Resize with Form check box (which is cleared by default) controls whether the control resizes itself when the user changes the size of the form.

▶ The Sunken check box (whose state varies by control) gives suitable controls (such as a text box) a sunken, 3-D appearance.

▶ The Multi-line check box, which applies only to text boxes, controls whether the text box can contain only one line (when the Multi-line check box is cleared) or multiple lines (when it is selected).

NOTE

To view the effect that the changes you have made will have on the form, click the Apply button.

3. On the Value tab, set the field to which the control is *bound*—the field whose information the control displays—as follows:

▶ To bind the control to an existing field, click the Choose Field drop-down list button and choose the field from one of the submenus on the drop-down list: Frequently-Used Fields, Address Fields, and so on.

▶ To bind the control to a field available in an enterprise form, select Forms from the drop-down list to display the Select Enterprise Forms for This Folder dialog box. In the left-hand list box, choose the form containing the field, and click Add to add the form to the Selected Forms list box. Click Close to close the dialog box. Outlook will add the form as a submenu to the drop-down list of available fields; click the Choose Field drop-down list button again and choose the field from the submenu for the form.

▶ To bind the control to a new field, click New to display the New Field dialog box. Create the field as discussed in "Creating a New Field" earlier in the chapter.

NOTE

The Properties dialog box for the Frame control and the MultiPage control has only a Display tab—it does not have a Value tab or a Validation tab.

4. The Value tab of the Properties dialog box will display the Type, Format, and List Type of the field as appropriate. If these are grayed-out, you cannot change them; if they are displayed in black on white, you can change them if necessary.

5. If necessary, change the property of the field to use by selecting a different property in the Property to Use drop-down list. If the Possible Values text box is available, check the possible values it displays.

Part iii

6. If the Initial Value section of the Value tab is available, you can set the initial value of the field when the form is created:

   ▶ Select the Set the Initial Value of This Field To check box.

   ▶ In the text box, enter the value for the field. To enter a function or a formula, click the Edit button and build the function or formula in the resulting dialog box.

   ▶ Choose the Calculate This Formula When I Compose a New Form option button or the Calculate This Formula Automatically option button.

7. On the Validation tab, choose the validation required for the field:

   ▶ Select the A Value Is Required for This Field check box if you need to have the user enter a value for the field. If the user tries to close, save, or send the form without having entered a value in the field, Outlook will prompt them to enter a value.

   ▶ To have Outlook validate the field, select the Validate This Field before Closing the Form check box and enter the validation formula in the Validation Formula text box. You can either type the validation formula or click the Edit button to display the Validation Formula dialog box, in which you can build the form using formulas or functions. In the Display This Message If the Validation Fails text box, enter the message that Outlook should display if the value fails the validation. Again, you can click the Edit button to display the Validation Text dialog box, in which you can build the text using formulas or functions.

   ▶ Select the Include This Field for Printing and Save As option if you want to include the field's information when the user prints or saves the form.

8. Click OK to apply your choices and close the Properties dialog box.

Changing the Properties of a Control by Using the Properties Window

To set properties that do not appear in the Properties dialog box, or to set a slew of properties all together, display the Properties window by right-clicking on the control and choosing Advanced Properties from the shortcut menu or by selecting the control and choosing Form ➤ Advanced Properties. Figure 15.11 shows the Properties window for a command button.

FIGURE 15.11: Use the Properties window to set less frequently used properties for a control, or to have quick access to all the properties for controls.

To change a property in the Properties window:

1. Click in the list of properties to select the property you want to change. The box at the top of the Properties window (to the right of the Apply button) will display any current value for the property. For a property with a predefined set of values (such as True or False, or a set of values regarding, say, scroll bars), the box will become a drop-down list box; for a user-definable property (such as the Caption property, which governs the text displayed on a control), the box will be a text box.

2. Choose the value you want for the property:

   ▶ For a property with a predefined set of values, choose the value from the drop-down list box.

   ▶ For a user-definable property, enter the value in the text box. For example, to set a Caption property, enter the appropriate text string in the text box.

3. Change other properties as necessary by repeating steps 1 and 2.

4. Click Apply to make the change.

You can now either click the close button on the Properties window to close it, or leave the Properties window open so that you can make further changes to this control or to other controls as you work.

Working with the Properties window rather than the Properties dialog box has three advantages:

▶ The Properties window presents all the properties for a form, rather than a subset.

▶ You can resize the Properties window to present more or less information to suit your needs.

▶ Because the Properties window is a window rather than a dialog box, you can keep it open on-screen as you work (at the expense of some screen real estate, of course). This gives you quick access to all the properties associated with the controls you're working with.

Creating Forms with Separate Compose Pages and Read Pages

You can create forms that display different pages to the sender (or creator of an item based on the form) and to the recipient. The *compose page* is the version of the form that the sender sees, and the *read page* is the version of the form that the recipient sees. You can create these separate *read layouts* page by page for each displayed page in the form. For example, if you customize a Contact form by adding a page named Contact History, you can choose to have separate read layouts for the Contact History page (so that your colleagues to whom you send the form will see a different layout than you) but share the read layout for the General page (so that your colleagues will see the same layout as you). The compose page and read page have the same name, but apart from that, the contents can be entirely different.

To create a separate compose page and read page for the form, select Form ➢ Separate Read Layout. Outlook will create the separate pages and will activate the Edit Compose Page button and the Edit Read Page button on the Form Design toolbar. You can then use these buttons to toggle between the read layouts.

TIP

When you use separate compose and read pages, the compose page is only displayed when the item is being composed—before it is posted or sent. If you add custom fields to the compose page, you will need to add the same fields to the read page if you want to be able to display the information later.

Viewing the Code on a Form

 To view the code on a form, click the View Code button on the Design toolbar or choose Form ➢ View Code. Outlook will display the Script Editor window containing the VBScript code for the current form.

Changing the Tab Order of a Form

The *tab order* of a form is the order in which you move through the fields by pressing the Tab key (to move forwards) or Shift+Tab (to move backwards). (Other forms let you use the Page Down key to move forward and the Page Up key to move backwards.) Most Windows dialog boxes have a tab order arranged in logical groupings starting at the upper-left corner of the dialog box and moving towards the lower-right corner (following the way we read in English and most Western languages).

In UserForms you create, you should try to arrange the controls in a tab order that allows the user to move through them in the most logical way and with the least effort. This usually means putting the controls that the user will need to work with first in the upper-left area of the form, where the user's eye will be drawn first.

The tab order of controls in a form is initially set in the order in which you place the controls on the form, but you can change the tab order at any time. To do so:

1. Choose Layout ≻ Tab Order to display the Tab Order dialog box (see Figure 15.12).

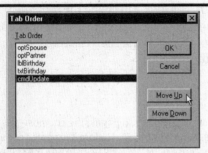

FIGURE 15.12:   Use the Tab Order dialog box to change the tab order of a UserForm.

2. In the Tab Order list box, select the control whose position in the tab order you want to change.

3. Click Move Up or Move Down until the control appears where you want it in the tab order.

4. Adjust the position of other controls in the tab order as appropriate.

5. Click OK to close the Tab Order dialog box.

SETTING PROPERTIES FOR THE FORM

The Properties page for the form contains a number of property settings that you can adjust to influence how the form behaves and the information that the user can access about it. Figure 15.13 shows the Properties page for a message-based form.

The following sections describe what you can do on the Properties page of a form. To access the Properties page of a form, click the Properties tab when the form is in Design mode.

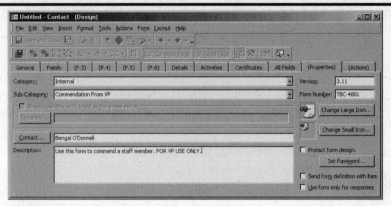

FIGURE 15.13: Use the Properties page of a form to set information about the form—and to protect it if necessary.

Setting the Category and Subcategory for the Form

The first choice to make on the Properties page is to assign the form to a category and subcategory by entering the information in the Category and Subcategory text boxes. Use the category and subcategory to manage your forms. For example, you might create several forms relating to business trips and group them in a Business Trip category, with subcategories such as Expenses, Contacts, Reports, and Authorizations.

Choosing the E-mail Editor

For a message-based form, deselect the Always Use Microsoft Word as the E-mail Editor check box (also on the Properties page) to prevent the user from using Word as the e-mail editor rather than Outlook. There are limitations to using Word (there's no guarantee that the recipient has Word installed; you're limited to the Word file format; and it is difficult to revert back to a non-Word-based form). You would have to completely redesign the form to use it anywhere else.

WARNING

If Word is not installed on the computer, Outlook will display an error message when the user starts a form with the Always Use Microsoft Word as the E-mail Editor property selected. Outlook will then default to the Outlook editor for the form.

Setting Information for the Form

You can set the following information for the form on the Properties page:

▶ Assign a contact name for the form—usually the person in charge of administering and troubleshooting the form. Either type the name of the contact into the text box; or click the Contact button to display the Select Contact dialog box, select the contact, and click OK.

NOTE

The icon, contact name, description, and version for a form appear in the Details panel of the Choose Form dialog box when the user selects a form to open. The contact name, form number, version, and description also appear in the About Form dialog box, which you can display by choosing Help ➤ About This Form. The Properties dialog box for the form (File ➤ Properties) includes the icon for the form, its type, and its location.

▶ Enter a description for the form in the Description text box. Your description should help the user identify the form, understand its purpose, and fill it in correctly with a minimum of effort.

▶ Enter the version number of the form in the Version text box and the form number in the Form Number text box.

▶ Choose a different icon for the form by clicking the Change Large Icon button or the Change Small Icon button. In the File Open dialog box, choose the icon to use and click Open.

Protecting the Form

The Properties page of a form is where you choose protection for the form. To protect the form against changes, first select the Protect Form Design check box on the Properties page. Then click the Set Password button to display the Password dialog box (shown here).

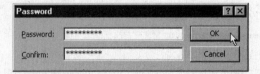

Enter a password in the Password text box, enter it again in the Confirm text box, and click OK. The password can be up to 32 characters long.

Once the password is set, Outlook will prompt for a password when the user tries to enter Design mode from the form. If the password is incorrect, Outlook will not switch the form to Design mode.

Sending the Form Definition

If you publish the form to your personal forms library rather than to the organizational forms library or a public folder, you will need to send the form definition information with the form so that the recipient can see all the components of the form. If you do not send the form definition information, the recipient will see a vanilla version of the form on which the customized form was based—without any of the customizations. To include the form definition information, select the Send Form Definition with Item check box on the Properties page of the form.

If you publish the form to the organizational forms library, other users will be able to see all of the components of the form without being sent the form definition information. You can still send the form definition information, but it increases the amount of information Outlook is sending and has no practical benefit.

Use Form Only for Responses

The final choice to make on the Properties page of the form is whether to use the form only for responses. Select the Use Form Only for Responses check box to have the form used only when a user chooses one of the Reply actions for a form.

Forms used only for responses are not listed in the forms library in which they are stored (to prevent users from choosing them in the Choose Form dialog box).

CHOOSING ACTIONS FOR THE FORM

The Actions page of a form lists the user actions that the form supports. You can use this list to check the actions, to adjust the actions, to enable and disable actions, or to create new custom actions for your forms. Figure 15.14 shows the Actions page of a form.

The Appointment, Contact, Mail Message, Meeting Request, Task, and Task Request forms support the Reply, Reply to All, Forward, and Reply to Folder actions by default. The Journal Entry form supports the Forward action and the Reply to Folder action by default. The Note form supports no actions.

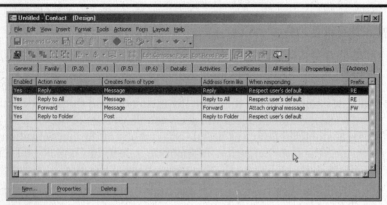

FIGURE 15.14:   Use the Actions page to customize the actions that the form supports.

Creating a New Action

To extend the use of a form beyond the standard actions available for it, you can create a new action for a form. For example, you might create a Broadcast action and form for forwarding a message to everyone on your Exchange system.

To create a new action:

1. Display the form in Design mode by choosing Tools ➣ Forms ➣ Design This Form when the form is open.

2. Click the Actions tab to display the Actions Page.

3. Click New to display the Form Action Properties dialog box (see Figure 15.15). Alternatively, double-click in a blank row in the table of actions.

4. In the Action Name text box, enter the name for the new action.

FIGURE 15.15: Use the Form Action Properties dialog box to adjust the actions supported by a form.

5. To enable the action, make sure the Enabled check box is selected.

6. Use the Form Name drop-down list to enter the name of the form to be used when the user chooses this action. Click the Form Name drop-down list button and select Form in the drop-down list to display the Choose Form dialog box. Select the form as usual, and click Open to return to the Form Action Properties dialog box. The Message Class text box will display the message class of the form you chose. You cannot change the message class from the Form Action Properties dialog box.

7. In the Characteristics of the New Form section, choose how the form created by the action should behave. In the When Responding drop-down list, choose how the original message should be handled: include the original message, attach it, prefix it, and so on. In the Address Form Like A drop-down list, choose Reply, Reply to All, Forward, Reply to Folder, or Response, as appropriate.

8. In the Show Action On section, decide how to present the action in the user interface of the form. To have the action appear, select the Show Action On check box. Select the Menu and Toolbar option button to have the action appear

on both the Actions menu and the item's toolbar. Select the Menu Only check box to have the action appear only on the Actions menu.

9. In the Subject Prefix text box, enter any text that should appear as a prefix for the message in the Subject line. For example, for a broadcast message, you might enter **BROAD-CAST** or an abbreviation for it.

10. In the This Action Will section, choose whether to open the form, send the form immediately, or prompt the user. Open the Form, the default setting, is the most widely useful; for procedural forms, such as acknowledgments or receipts, Send the Form Immediately comes in handy.

11. Click OK to close the Form Action Properties dialog box. Outlook will create the new action and enter it on the Actions page for the form.

Changing an Existing Action

You can also change an existing action for a form by using the Form Action Properties dialog box:

1. Display the form in Design mode.

2. Click the Actions tab to display the Actions page.

3. Select the action you want to change.

4. Click the Properties button to display the Form Action Properties dialog box. (Alternatively, you can press Enter or double-click the action.)

5. To disable the action, clear the Enabled check box. To enable the action, select the Enabled check box.

6. To change the type of form that the action creates, click the Form Name drop-down list button and choose Forms from the drop-down list. In the Choose Form dialog box, select the form to use and click Open.

7. To change the way the form behaves when the user responds, select another action from the When Responding drop-down list. The default setting is Respect User's Default, but you can also choose actions such as Do Not Include Original Message,

Attach Original Message, and Prefix Each Line of the Original Message. These enable you to override the user's choice of settings.

8. For a built-in action, you cannot change the Show Action On settings. For a custom action, you can change the Show Action On settings as necessary.

9. Change the Subject Prefix setting if you want.

10. Change the selection in the This Action Will section as necessary.

11. Click OK to close the Form Action Properties dialog box and apply your changes.

Deleting a Custom Action

To delete a custom action, select it in the table of actions on the Actions page and click Delete or press the Delete key. Click Yes in the confirmation message box that Outlook displays.

You cannot delete a standard action from a form—the best you can do is to disable it. If you try to delete a standard action, Outlook will ask if you want to disable it instead. Click Yes or No as appropriate.

USING THE ALL FIELDS PAGE

The All Fields page of a form (see Figure 15.16) presents a tabular view of all the fields of a particular type contained in the form. This is useful for getting quick information on the fields and checking their properties:

▶ Use the Select From drop-down list to choose which fields to display.

▶ To view the properties of a field, select it in the table of fields and click the Properties button to display the Field Properties dialog box.

▶ To create a new field, click New to display the New Field dialog box. Create the field as described in "Creating a New Field," earlier in this chapter.

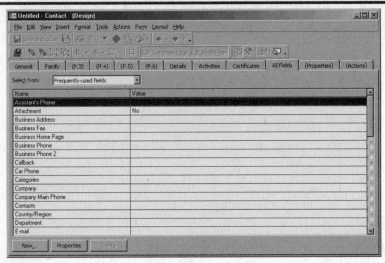

FIGURE 15.16: Use the All Fields page of a custom form to check the fields in the form and their properties.

PUBLISHING A FORM

Once you've created a form, you need to *publish* it to make it available for use. You can publish a form to any of the form folders available to you. Which folders are available will depend on the permissions set by your network or Exchange administrator.

To publish a form:

1. Click the Publish Form button on the Form Design toolbar, or choose Tools ➤ Forms ➤ Publish Form, to display the Publish Form As dialog box (see Figure 15.17).

2. In the Look In drop-down list, choose the location in which you want to store the form: the Organizational Forms Library, the Personal Forms Library, Outlook Folders, or one of the folders.

3. In the Display Name text box, enter the name by which the form will be identified (when the user opens it) and listed in forms-related dialog boxes (for example, in the Choose Form dialog box). Outlook will duplicate the name you enter in the Display Name text box in the Form Name text box.

4. In the Form Name text box, specify the name under which the form should be saved. You can leave the name that Outlook has automatically entered or enter a different name. For example, you might use a descriptive naming convention for the display names of forms so that users could easily identify them, but use a more formal or condensed naming convention for the form names. So a form might have a display name of `Meeting with Outside Company`, but a form name of `Mtg_Ext_2`. Outlook will add the text you enter in the Form Name text box to the end of the Message Class description at the foot of the Publish Form As dialog box.

5. Click the Publish button to publish the form to the location you chose.

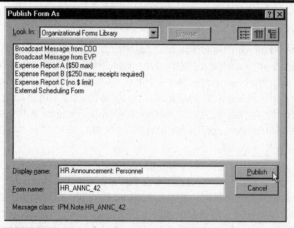

FIGURE 15.17: In the Publish Form As dialog box, specify the location in which to store the form, the display name for the form, and the form name.

Once you have published the form, you will be able to access it via the Choose Form dialog box (File ➤ New ➤ Choose Form).

To publish an already-published form under a different name, choose Tools ➤ Forms ➤ Publish Form As to display the Publish Form As dialog box. Specify the location, display name, and form name for the form, and click the Publish button.

"MY COLLEAGUES CAN'T SEE THE CUSTOM FIELDS IN MY FORMS"

If the three classes of forms cause your eyes to glaze over, read this sidebar. For one thing, it's easy to get confused about the results of having multiple forms libraries available. For another, there's a complicating factor: when designing a form, you can choose whether to send the *form definition*—the information about how the form is constructed and what customizations it contains—with the form. This ensures that the recipient will see all the customized parts of the form as well as the standard parts. But when sending an item based on a form, you cannot choose whether to send the form definition or not; Outlook simply applies the setting that the form's designer chose when designing the form. (By default, Outlook does not send the form definition. For details on how to include the form definition, look back at "Sending the Form Definition," earlier in this chapter.)

If you send an item based on a custom form to a colleague, and the form does not include its form definition, the recipient must have the form available in order to see the customized parts of the form. If you send an item based on a custom form to a colleague, and the form *does* contain its form definition, your colleague will see all the customized parts of the form whether or not the form is available to them.

The disadvantage to always including the form definition is that doing so significantly increases the size of the message you are sending. For small-office environments with plenty of network bandwidth and server power, this may not be a serious worry. But in enterprise environments in which the network and servers are handling many thousands of messages a day, transmitting the form definition with custom forms can degrade performance appreciably.

If you choose not to include the form definition when designing a form, you need to understand the interaction between the personal forms library and the organizational forms library. For example, say you create a custom e-mail message form with two extra pages, and choose to store it in your personal forms library. You then create a message based on the form and send it to a colleague. Here's what happens:

▶ If your colleague does not have the form available, they will see only the uncustomized parts of the form, so it will appear as a regular e-mail message.

CONTINUED ➡

- ▶ If your colleague has the same version of the form available in their personal forms library, they will see the same form as you sent.

- ▶ If your colleague has a *different* version of the form available in their personal forms library, they will see that version of the form rather than the form you sent. Under certain carefully coordinated circumstances, this behavior can be useful—for example, if the recipient needs to access sensitive areas of the form that the form's original sender should not see. But under most normal circumstances, this behavior is liable to cause confusion.

- ▶ If your colleague has a different version of the form available in their personal forms library *and* a version of the form available in the organizational forms library, they will see the version of the form stored in their personal forms library.

Generally speaking, it's seldom a great idea to have multiple copies of forms with the same name available. Here are our recommendations for where to store forms:

- ▶ Store forms that you share with your colleagues in the organizational forms library. For example, if you create a customized e-mail message or meeting request form that your colleagues need to use, store the form in the organizational forms library so that your colleagues can access it and see all the customizations to it.

- ▶ Store forms that you do not share with your colleagues in your personal forms library. For example, if you create a customized contact form that only you use, store it in your personal forms library.

- ▶ When creating and testing a form, store it in your personal forms library or in another location where your colleagues will not be able to access it unintentionally. Once the form is viable, move it into the organizational forms library.

- ▶ If, in your personal forms library, you keep copies of forms posted to the organizational forms library, keep the forms in sync. Otherwise, you may find yourself seeing a different version of a form than do people sending you items or receiving items from you.

CONTINUED ➡

Part iii

In most cases, with proper planning and management of your forms, you should not need to send the form definition. Under special circumstances, or for testing purposes, you may choose to send the form definition—preferably on a form-by-form basis.

Changing a Published Form

Once you've created and published a form, you may need to make changes to it. You may also need to create new forms based on a form. For example, say you need to create a dozen variations on a human resources form. You'll save a lot of time if you create a template form that you can use as a base for the other forms rather than creating each of the forms from scratch.

To change a form you've created and published, open it as usual: choose Tools ➢ Forms ➢ Choose Form, or choose File ➢ New ➢ Choose Form; then select the form in the Choose Form dialog box, and click Open. You can then modify the form as discussed earlier in this chapter. When you've finished modifying it, publish the form again to make it available.

WARNING

You can open two or more copies of the same form at the same time, make changes to each, and then publish both. The changes in the last-saved version of the form will overwrite changes in the previous version of the form—even if the previous version is still open.

Making a Form the Default Form

If you customize the standard Outlook forms, you may want to use them by default when you create new items. For example, if you customize the Task Request form, you may want to use the customized form rather than the standard form by default when creating a new task request.

To make a form the default form:

1. In the Outlook bar or the Folder List, right-click the folder for which you want to make the form the default, and choose Properties to display the Properties dialog box for the folder.

2. In the When Posting to This Folder, Use drop-down list, choose Forms to display the Choose Form dialog box.

3. Select the form that you want to make the default form for the folder and click Open. Outlook will enter the name of the form in the drop-down list. (If you choose an unsuitable form for the folder, Outlook will warn you to that effect and will refuse to enter the form's name in the drop-down list.)

4. Click OK to close the Properties dialog box for the folder.

When you create a new item based on this folder, Outlook will use the form you chose by default.

MANAGING YOUR FORMS WITH THE FORMS MANAGER

Outlook provides a Forms Manager dialog box for managing your forms. You can use this dialog box to perform the following tasks:

▶ Delete a form

▶ Check or change various properties of a form

▶ Save a form as a separate file (for example, to distribute it to other users)

▶ Install (add) a form to a forms library

▶ Copy a form from one forms library to another

▶ Move a form from one forms library to another

▶ Update a form with a newer version

To perform many of these actions—for example, updating or deleting a form—you need to have owner permission in the forms library that contains the form.

Part iii

Displaying the Forms Manager Dialog Box

To display the Forms Manager dialog box, you have to tunnel through several other dialog boxes as follows:

1. Choose Tools ➤ Options to display the Options dialog box.

2. Click the Other tab.

3. Click the Advanced Options button to display the Advanced Options dialog box.

4. Click the Custom Forms button to display the Options dialog box.

5. Click the Manage Forms button to display the Forms Manager dialog box (see Figure 15.18).

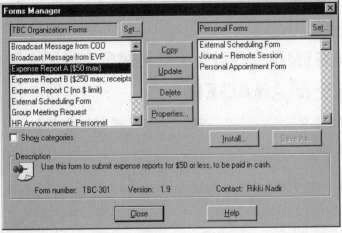

FIGURE 15.18:   Use the Forms Manager dialog box to manage your forms.

Changing the Forms Library Displayed in the Forms Manager Dialog Box

Before you can perform most operations with the Forms Manager dialog box, you need to display the appropriate forms library. To change the forms library displayed in the Forms Manager dialog box:

1. Click one of the two Set buttons to display the Set Library To dialog box (see Figure 15.19).

FIGURE 15.19: Use the Set Library To dialog box to change the forms library displayed in the Forms Manager.

2. Select the forms library you want to use from either the Forms Library drop-down list or the Folder Forms Library list box. Outlook will automatically select the Forms Library option button or the Folder Forms Library option button to suit your choice.

3. Click OK to close the Set Library To dialog box. Outlook will return you to the Forms Manager dialog box and will display the forms library you chose in the list box attached to the Set button.

The default view of the forms in the forms libraries displayed in the Forms Manager dialog box is by form name, but you can select the Show Categories check box to display the forms grouped by categories. You can then expand and collapse the categories and subcategories by clicking on the Expand (+) or Collapse (−) buttons next to them to display or hide the forms in them. Figure 15.20 shows the Forms Manager dialog box with categories and subcategories displayed.

Part iii

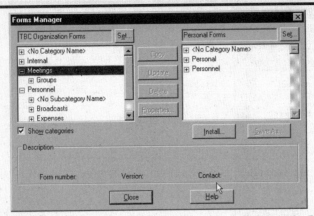

FIGURE 15.20: Select the Show Categories check box in the Forms Manager dialog box to display the forms in the forms libraries grouped by categories and subcategories.

Removing a Form from a Forms Library

To remove a form from a forms library, select the form in one of the list boxes in the Forms Manager dialog box and click Delete. Click Yes in the confirmation dialog box that Outlook displays.

Copying or Moving a Form to a Different Forms Library

To copy a form to a different forms library, select the form in the left-hand list box or the right-hand list box in the Forms Manager dialog box and click Copy. Outlook will copy the form to the selected forms library.

To move a form to a different forms library, copy the form as described in the previous paragraph, and then remove the form from the original forms library, as described in the previous section.

Updating a Form

When a form has changed, you will often need to update the older versions contained in different forms libraries. For example, you might change your personal copy of a form, test it, and then need to update the copy of the form stored in the organizational forms library or in a public folder on the network.

To update a form, select it in the left-hand list box or the right-hand list box in the Forms Manager dialog box. When you have selected the version of the form that requires updating, Outlook will make the Update button available. (If the version of the form you have selected cannot be updated, the Update button will be dimmed and unavailable.) Click the Update button. Outlook will update the form with the latest version of the original form.

Installing a Form

You can install (add) a form to a forms library from either a form configuration file or a form message file. Form configuration files have a .cfg extension, while form message files have an .fdm extension.

To install a form:

1. Select the forms library to which you want to install the form.

2. Click the Install button to display the Open dialog box.

3. Select the form file to install. (If necessary, change the selection in the Files of Type drop-down list from Form Setup Files to Form Message Files.)

4. Click Open. Outlook will display the Form Properties dialog box. If the forms library already contains a version of the form you are installing, Outlook will display a message box asking whether to replace the existing form. Click Yes if you want to replace the form.

5. Check the form's properties, and make changes and updates as appropriate.

6. Click OK to close the Form Properties dialog box. Outlook will install the form to the forms library and apply the properties you specified.

Saving a Form as a Separate File

You can save a form as a separate file, so that you can share the form with other users or install it in a different forms library. To do so:

1. Select the form in the left-hand list box or the right-hand list box in the Forms Manager dialog box.

2. Click Save As to display the Save As dialog box.

Part iii

3. Specify the name and location for the form message. Outlook will automatically add an `.fdm` extension to the name.

4. Click Save to save the form.

Changing the Properties of a Form

Using the Forms Manager dialog box, you can change the following properties of a form:

▶ Display name

▶ Category (under which the form is listed)

▶ Subcategory (under which the form is listed)

▶ Contact name

▶ Comment (which appears with the form to describe the form and its purpose)

▶ Whether the form is hidden or displayed in forms dialog boxes

You cannot change these properties:

▶ Version number

▶ Form number

▶ Platforms the form is available for

▶ Design tool (the program or tool used to create the form)

▶ Message class

To change the properties of a form:

1. Display the Forms Manager dialog box.

2. Select the form whose properties you want to display in either of the list boxes.

3. Click Properties to display the Form Properties dialog box (see Figure 15.21).

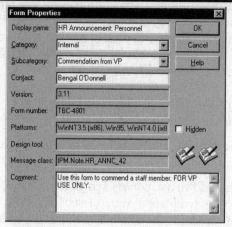

FIGURE 15.21: Use the Form Properties dialog box to check or change the properties of a form.

4. Check or change the properties of the form as appropriate.

5. Click OK to close the Form Properties dialog box.

6. Click Close to close the Forms Manager dialog box; then click the OK buttons of the Options dialog box, Advanced Options dialog box, and the main Options dialog box to close each in turn.

CREATING AND USING A TEMPLATE

As you saw earlier in this chapter, you can reuse a form by placing it in a suitable folder. Another way of reusing a form is to save it as a template. Not only can you then reuse it, but you can easily share a template with another Outlook user.

To save a form as a template:

1. Open the form (for example, by choosing File ➢ New ➢ Choose Form).

2. Choose File ➢ Save As to display the Save As dialog box.

3. Enter the name for the template in the File Name text box.

4. Make sure that Outlook Template is selected in the Save as Type drop-down list.

5. If necessary, specify a different drive or folder for the template by using the Save In drop-down list and list box. Often, you'll want to save the template in your \Templates\Outlook\ folder so that it is available via the Templates in File System selection in the Choose Form dialog box.

6. Click Save.

To create a new item based on the template:

1. Select File ➤ New ➤ Choose Form to display the Choose Form dialog box.

2. In the Look In drop-down list, choose Templates in File System if you stored the template in your \Templates\Outlook\ folder. (If you stored the template in a different folder, choose that folder from the Look In drop-down list, or use the Browse button to navigate to the folder.)

3. Choose the template in the list box and click Open.

CREATING A CUSTOM FORM BASED ON AN OFFICE DOCUMENT

Instead of creating a form based on an Outlook form or creating an Outlook form from scratch, you can also create a form based on an Office document, such as a Word document, an Excel spreadsheet or chart, or a PowerPoint presentation. By doing so, you can quickly leverage the capabilities of such a document. For example, if you need a form to contain spreadsheet information, you can save time by basing the form on an Excel spreadsheet rather than creating a new form from scratch in Outlook.

To create a custom form based on an Office document:

1. Click the New drop-down list button on the Standard toolbar and choose Office Document, or choose File ➤ New ➤ Office Document, or press Ctrl+Shift+H to display the New Office Document dialog box.

2. Choose the type of document on which you want to base the new form. Typically, you'll get the choice of Microsoft Excel Worksheet, Microsoft Excel Chart, Microsoft Word Document, and Microsoft PowerPoint Presentation. (These

choices will vary depending on the applications installed on your computer.)

3. Click OK to proceed. Outlook will display the Microsoft Outlook dialog box shown in Figure 15.22.

FIGURE 15.22:   In the Microsoft Outlook dialog box, choose the Post the Document in This Folder option button.

4. Choose the Post the Document in This Folder option button and click OK. Outlook will display a new window containing a new document of the type you chose. The window will display a mixture of the host application's toolbars and menus with the Outlook toolbars and menus. For example, the Excel window shown in Figure 15.23 contains a Standard toolbar that combines the Outlook Standard toolbar and the Excel Standard toolbar, along with the Excel Formatting toolbar. The menu bar displays an Actions menu instead of the Excel Window menu, and the menus themselves contain different commands from the regular Excel menus. The window will be identified as follows:

Untitled.xls - Document for an Excel chart or spreadsheet

Untitled.doc - Document for a Word document

Untitled.ppt - Document for a PowerPoint presentation

5. Choose Tools ➤ Forms ➤ Design This Form to enter Design mode. The window will display the Form Design toolbar and a tab strip identifying the different pages of information available in the form: Document for the document itself, (Properties) for the properties page, and (Actions) for the actions page. The title bar of the window will display (Design) in parentheses after the title. The title of a Word window will change from "Untitled.doc - Document" to "Untitled - Document," but Excel and PowerPoint windows will remain the same.

6. Set Properties and Actions for the form as described earlier in this chapter.

7. Enter information in the form as necessary.

8. Choose Tools ➢ Forms ➢ Publish Form to display the Publish Form As dialog box, and publish the form as described earlier in this chapter. The form will then be available for posting in the folder to which you published it.

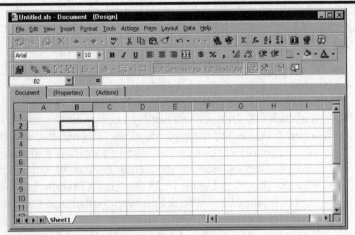

FIGURE 15.23: When you create a new form based on an Office document, Outlook displays a window with a mixture of the application's toolbars and its own.

WHAT'S NEXT?

In this chapter, you've seen how to create custom forms by modifying the standard forms that Outlook provides. The next step in creating custom forms is to use Visual Basic and VBScript to program them—automating actions and adding custom actions. In the next two chapters, we'll discuss what Visual Basic is and how it works.

Chapter 16

AN INTRODUCTION TO VISUAL BASIC

Automation has always been the promise of computers: get more work done as the computer toils away at repetitive tasks. However, in order to have your computer perform a series of actions when you click a button, you need to tell it what to do in words that it understands. What if your company has a need for a specialized contact sheet, or needs to speed up the budget approval system, or needs to collect disparate versions of a Word document and create a report on the changes as quickly as possible? You can't simply tell your computer to go do these things as you would tell an assistant. You need to write a program.

This is where Visual Basic and VBScript come in. Now, don't shy away. Microsoft has worked hard to make programming with these two languages relatively easy, using English language terms strung together to tell your computer what to do.

Adapted from *Mastering™ Microsoft® Outlook™ 2000* by Gini Courter and Annette Marquis

ISBN 0-7821-2472-0   787 pages $34.99

TIP

Computers are perfectly literal, so when writing a program, you have to tell the computer exactly what to do, where to find things, and what to do if something unexpected happens. If you've programmed in the past, you should find Visual Basic fairly easy to learn. If you haven't programmed before, the learning curve will be a little steeper because you also have to learn to think like a computer.

NEW

Throughout the next two chapters, we will be discussing Visual Basic and its offspring. The family is comprised of Visual Basic (VB), Visual Basic for Applications (VBA), and Visual Basic Script (VBScript). Prior versions of Outlook only supported VBScript. Outlook 2000 has both VBScript and VBA built in, allowing you to automate or accommodate most tasks that you need Outlook to perform. This allows you to add fields and forms that are specific to your business or the job at hand.

NOTE

VB and VBA are identical in syntax. Microsoft, however, felt it would be smart to ship VBA with a trimmed-down version of the VB programming interface, called the Integrated Development Environment (IDE), which focuses on augmenting the capabilities of a host application (in this case Outlook) rather than on creating freestanding applications, which it cannot do. We think they're right, but because of this we will refer to VB and VBA separately on occasion.

WHAT IS VISUAL BASIC?

To understand what VB is, we need to understand what it does. Within the scope of its abilities, VB will perform the tasks you ask of it. VB cannot be used to tell your computer to make coffee at 7:00 A.M. every morning *unless* your computer is actually capable of controlling a coffee maker. (No Java jokes, please.)

However, you will probably *not* be seeking a programming solution for coffee making unless you're spending time at a ubiquitous computing shop. You'll use VB to automate tasks and extend the capabilities of Outlook 2000. Outlook is already very good at a number of tasks, such as maintaining contacts, managing messages and other forms of communication, and offering access to informational services and archival data.

Microsoft realized, though, that there was no way they could anticipate the exact needs of all their users, so they allow you to do it. Most often you will do this by modifying an existing *form*.

NOTE

A *form* is very much like a window; forms are the basis of all programming in Visual Basic.

When you add a contact, send a message, or announce a meeting, you are using a form. Before we get into any programming, let's take a brief look at how Outlook lets you customize forms. As you'll see, the "visual" part of Visual Basic comes from the fact that most of the code is generated by *drawing* the controls onto a virtual canvas, the aforementioned form. Start up your computer and follow these steps:

1. Open Outlook and click Inbox.

2. Select File ➢ New ➢ Message. What appears is the New Message form. Take a brief look at the form to get a feel for it.

3. Now select Tools ➢ Forms ➢ Design This Form. What appears now is something that *looks* like the New Message form, but it has more tabs and a new toolbar. To the right of the form appears another window called the Field Chooser.

4. Choose Attachments from the top of the list in the Field Chooser and drag it to the New Message form. Note the small + sign that appears next to the mouse pointer. This indicates a copy operation, just like in Windows. You are simply copying the Attachments control to the Form.

When you drag the item over to the form, you'll see that the message area, the large blank area, moves and resizes on the form to accommodate the new control. You have just placed a new control on an existing form to modify it.

Part III

NOTE

A *control* is an object, like a button or a text field, that you add to a form and that can modify the form's behavior. For example, the OK buttons that show up in most dialog boxes are controls. When you place a control on a form, you must also add programming code to tell the control what to do. We will examine coding later in this and the next chapter.

Behind each control, you add code that makes the control do what you wish. If the control you placed on your form was a CommandButton (one of the control choices), you could, for example, program that button to open a Save dialog box to automatically let you retain an additional copy of outgoing documents in a folder of your choice.

An *event* is a user- or system-generated action, such as the user clicking a button or a CD-ROM activating the AutoPlay software. Visual Basic is called an event-driven programming language because it responds to events. You place control objects on your forms and then program them to handle specific events. In the case of a command button, you would program it to respond to a Click event: the event that happens when a user mouses over to and clicks a button. All of this is created in the Visual Basic Integrated Development Environment, or IDE, shown in Figure 16.1.

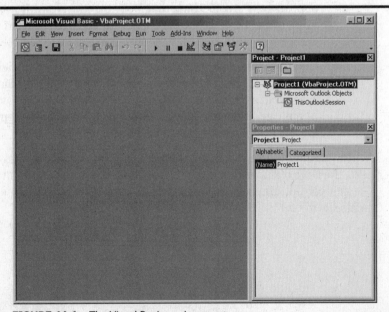

FIGURE 16.1: The Visual Basic environment

In essence, each control has its own capabilities and can be coded to operate independently of everything else on the form. As an example, we'll look at the ubiquitous OK button, present on most dialog boxes. To create an OK button in VB you would simply click on the CommandButton button in the toolbox, drag the cursor to the form, and drop. This procedure creates a button called *CommandButton1*, as shown in Figure 16.2.

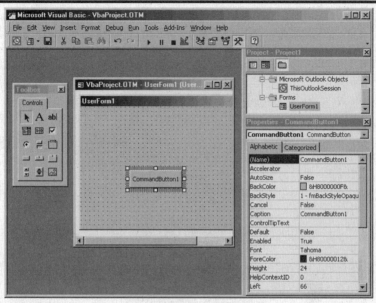

FIGURE 16.2:   A new CommandButton on a form

For each control there are *properties* that define how the control works. The properties for the CommandButton control are simple, and you use them to define the way the control presents itself. In Figure 16.3, the Default property of CommandButton1 is set to True, meaning that if you were to open this Form in an application and press the Enter key, this button would be clicked by default.

If we created a simple form, placed a CommandButton control and a TextBox control on it, and programmed it to put something in the TextBox control when the CommandButton is clicked, we would be looking at a simple example of programming in action. If, on the other hand, we only included the controls and omitted the code, nothing would happen. Why? Because there is no code to tell the button control what to do. You would click the button, and nothing would happen. It's safe to say that users don't really appreciate this type of form very much.

You can think of writing code as sending a letter of instructions to someone. Assuming we were in the VBA IDE, we would begin that letter by double-clicking the CommandButton control to open the Code Editor, which automatically adds the following code (which, in the world of programmers, is called a *snippet*):

```
Private Sub CommandButton1_click()
End Sub
```

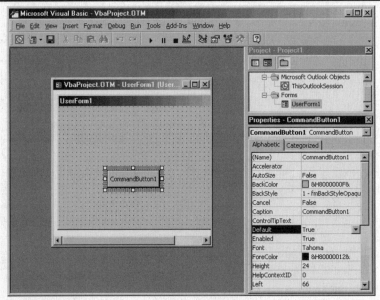

FIGURE 16.3: CommandButton showing the Default property to True

The IDE assumes that you want to add code to the control you just double-clicked to open. This snippet is a procedural framework, a structure that defines the beginning and the end of what is called a *procedure*.

NOTE

A procedure is a complete and independent piece of working code. Procedures can be triggered by an event or from other procedures.

In that code snippet, `Private` tells the control that this code will only be available to the form that it is being constructed in. `Sub` is short for subroutine and identifies the code as a procedure.

NOTE

Before confusion sets in, the terms *subroutine* and *function* both refer to types of *procedures* in VB. The difference is that a function returns information to a variable and subroutines do not.

CommandButton1_Click identifies the CommandButton by name and indicates what the procedure expects of the control: a click. Each control receives a unique name when it is created so it can be individually identified later. You can rename your controls anything you like, as long as each name is unique. It is also a good idea to make the names easily recognizable so that you can readily recognize their purpose when you go back to the code next year. End Sub indicates the official close of the procedure.

To get the command button to close the window when it is clicked, we just need to add one command between the Private Sub and End Sub lines: Unload Me. The whole completed procedure will look like this:

```
Private Sub CommandButton1_click()
    Unload Me
End Sub
```

If you were writing this as a letter of instructions in English, it might read something like this:

```
RE: Confidential To Do List

Dear CommandButton1,

If you get clicked, close the window you occupy.

Sincerely,
Programmer
```

 Now that we've added a command in language that VB can understand, it will perform the action we ask of it. Clicking the small blue arrow button on the toolbar causes the form to run. This is the same as selecting Run ➤ Run Macro. If we clicked the button, we would see that the form disappears.

NOTE

You can create code without first creating a button. To create a new macro, choose Tools ≻ Macro ≻ Macros and type a name for the macro. Make sure that the names you give macros are short, descriptive, and contain no spaces (you can, however, use underscores). If the name you enter meets these criteria and isn't already used in the current VBAmodule, the Create button will be enabled. Click the Create button to open the Visual Basic Editor.

Making Use of Visual Basic

We just took a quick look at what VB is and how easy it can be to use it. Now, we're going to examine what VB can be used for. To begin, let's further examine what VB can do as a language.

VB is a complete and powerful event-driven language, which means that each component, like our example button, can operate independently of the rest of the program. When an *event* occurs, VB responds by running the procedure that was defined for that specific event, if any; if no procedure was defined for the event, nothing happens. These event procedures are tied to the controls that you place on your forms to permit users to interact with the application (for example, the Common Dialogs control, which adds the ability to use system-based Open and Save dialog boxes with only a few lines of code).

Going back to our example in the previous section, we told Command-Button1 to execute the code related to it when it was clicked. The click was the event, and the code executed was the event procedure.

NOTE

Event-driven programming should not be confused with object-oriented programming languages. A programming language can be event-driven, object-oriented, or both. For example, programs like Visual C++ and Delphi are both. Those languages, which can be much more complicated to understand and use, allow programmers to create functions, or independent segments of code, and then make use of them across multiple applications. Those languages also allow objects to define the parameters of children objects through inheritance. VBA doesn't support this level of object-oriented functionality, but it is nevertheless a very powerful programming environment used to create commercial applications.

Generally, VB is considered a Rapid Application Development (RAD) tool, with which custom solutions can be prototyped, debugged, and built in a much shorter period of time than with other languages. One of the more common reasons VB is deployed is to provide fast development of database front-end applications. Here are two uses that specifically relate to Outlook:

▸ You can automate how forms work, specify customized handling of new data, or create new data.

▸ You can create customized Outlook forms and personalized applications.

▸ You can access data from Outlook while in other applications.

VBScript, included in Outlook 97, 98, and 2000, allows you to extend the functionality of Outlook forms. VBScripts are stored in the form, which makes them portable. This allows you to send custom functionality to another user merely by clicking the Send/Receive button. It's important to recognize the differences between VBScript and VBA, as it will help you determine which to use when faced with a problem to be solved. Let's look at that now.

WARNING

Code written for VBA will very likely not work in VBScript without significant alteration.

THE DIFFERENCES BETWEEN VBSCRIPT AND VBA

Sometime after Microsoft created Visual Basic, it created VBA, a subset of the original language geared toward complex and complete automation of Office applications.

When Microsoft recognized that the Internet was to become very important, it created *another* subset of VB called VBScript, a simplified programming language that they hoped would become the scripting language of the Internet, allowing Web browsers to do things HTML couldn't. VBScript was direct competition for Netscape's JavaScript programming language. VBScript can be used just about anywhere, but mostly appears in HTML files on some Web sites.

To create VBScript, Microsoft trimmed what was not necessary in VB and left only the most essential components. As a result, VBScript does not support all of the VB syntax, specifically I/O, financial and statistical functions, intrinsic constants, and intrinsic data types. In other words, VBScript is leaner, trimmer, and cannot access the host computer's files, which improves security.

Converting: Should I or Should I Not?

If you created customized solutions in Outlook 97 or 98, they were created using VBScript. Since VBScript is simply a version of VB, you can retain your existing code in VBScript form. However, in some cases it is better to convert the code to VBA. Here are some cases in which we *would* convert VBScript code to VBA:

- ▶ Your VBScript code is large and slow.

- ▶ You use VBScript to retrieve but cannot modify and save data from another application.

- ▶ You need access to the Windows Win32 API (application programming interface), or a way to talk directly to the operating system and tell it to do things.

Let's look at the reasons behind each one of these items.

Perhaps you've created a script that performs a number of actions that are very important to you, but it often slows down your system and can even slow traffic on the network. This happens at times when you have implemented a VBScript solution in a workgroup. The best way to solve this is to migrate it to VB.

VBScript is also not well suited to retrieving data to display in another application; it cannot perform true file I/O operations, so you've most likely worked around this limitation by publishing your data to a Web page and used VBScript to parse the data for the viewer. This is a cumbersome approach and VBScript is not well suited to this type of task.

If you need access to the local machine's files, VBScript is not very helpful. Since VBScript does not have all of the capabilities of VB or

VBA, it cannot perform certain tasks, specifically file I/O. If you need Outlook to access files on a local or remote disk, you should convert to and expand your code in VBA.

What's Next?

This chapter introduced programming with Visual Basic. In the next chapter, we'll look more closely at VBA as a language, gain a greater understanding of VBA by creating our first application, and point you to some valuable Visual Basic resources—both books and information that is available for free on the Web.

Chapter 17

A More Complete Introduction to Visual Basic

We realize that the example in the previous chapter was not quite enough to let you really show off your application development skills. In this chapter, we'll build and run a small Visual Basic application; small applications in any language are called *applets*. The applet is called Hello World! and has a long history in the world of programming as the first program many people create when learning a new language. Then we'll point you to some great VB resources that are available over the Internet and some books that can teach you everything you want to know about VB.

Adapted from *Mastering™ Microsoft® Outlook™ 2000* by Gini Courter and Annette Marquis

ISBN 0-7821-2472-0   787 pages $34.99

THE BIG PICTURE

Before we do anything at all with the computer, we need to determine exactly what we want the computer to do and how we are going to accomplish this using VB. Very few professional programmers sit down and start coding with no idea of what their goal is. If you want to develop a good program in the most efficient way, you need a process.

There are several steps in the program development process:

1. Define the application.

2. Define the programmatic requirements.

3. Define the interface.

4. Compose the application.

5. Debug and test the application.

6. Build and distribute the application.

Let's take a closer look at this to-do list, which is generally referred to as a development cycle. The term *cycle* implies that this process happens more than once, and it does in the course of developing a large application or improving an application. You finish testing your application, release it to users, and then begin planning extensions or improvements.

First we need to define the application. This is when you hammer out the most important details of your application and nail down just what your application will do. In this case, we've already decided what we're going to do.

For the purposes of this exercise, we'll be using the classic beginners program, Hello World! This little application performs a minor task, but provides an easy framework for understanding Visual Basic. The task is simple: create an application that displays a message when you click a button.

Second, we need to define the programmatic requirements. At this point we need to take inventory of our needs and trim them down to the most necessary. It's a cycle, so we can always go back and add functionality; initially, we want to separate the requirements from the fluff. For our project, our basic requirements are the following: display a button to click, a text box so users can view the message, and a window (form) to display them on.

Third, we need to define the *interface*, the part of the application that the user interacts with. Interface design is a critical component, so don't jump into it until you understand the concept behind the application. If you are not entirely clear on what your program will do, you can't be clear on an interface design. (Programs with an outstanding interface but no real functionality are referred to as "smoke and mirrors.") Our applet has a simple but easy to understand interface: a CommandButton control and a TextBox control.

The fourth step is to actually compose the application. Only after you've set down what you want your application to do, what programmatic components it should contain, and how the user will interact with it can you really start to create it. This is the step in which you'll create the interface that you decided on in the previous step. As you place each control, you will modify its properties to suit your needs. Once this is completed, you can create the operational code that makes the application work. For our project, we've included a step-by-step tutorial on the construction of the Hello World! program.

The fifth step is to debug and test the application. As you are working on your application, you will run it from time to time to make sure you have not missed anything or made an error. When you do this in VBA's IDE, you are not actually compiling the code (translating it into a form that the computer can read more easily) as you are required to do with many IDEs. The code you have written is actually interpreted as it's read by the computer. Interpreting the code allows the application to run without waiting for all of your code to compile. This also allows you to debug your source code while the application is running.

NOTE

When VB compiles your code, it actually strips out all formatting and comments and creates a more streamlined version of the program for the computer to run. The result is called P-Code. Unlike compiling in languages such as C/C++ or Pascal, this process does not convert the program code into another language.

Although this can be the end of the development process, that's only if your application is perfect the first time around—an unlikely event except in the case of very simple applications like Hello World! If you find a bug, you go back one or more steps depending on whether minor or major changes are needed to fix the problem. At a minimum, you need to repair the problem and run and test the application again. Some applications actually work with minor or occasional bugs in them until a user notes the combination of events that triggers the bug. Most commercial applications ship this way, despite exhaustive beta testing.

The bugs that affect operation or that damage files are the most important to fix. Then come the less problematic operational bugs, which make the application less usable but do not cause it to crash. Finally, you can deal with the relatively minor cosmetic bugs, which are unpleasant to look at but don't cause any actual programmatic problems.

Our Hello World! applet is small enough that an experienced programmer could create it with no bugs the first time round. However, we will slip a few deliberate errors into the code so you can see how VBA handles them and reports their activities to you. And no matter how experienced you become, you always need to test even simple programs.

Finally, we will build and distribute our application. The term *build* refers to the process of making a program ready for an end-user to use. In other languages, projects must be built before the user can even run them. In VB, however, the code is interpreted, as we mentioned previously, so when we talk about compiling VB code what we really mean is that the code is *pre*-interpreted, allowing it to run somewhat faster. Compiling will also identify any lingering syntax errors, because every line of code is interpreted and checked for syntactical accuracy.

NOTE
Until you compile the program, VBA runs an application interpretively. That means it only compiles the lines of code that it uses and nothing else.

HELLO, WORLD!

We're now ready to begin with the fourth step: composing the program, which will consist of a dialog box with a TextBox and a CommandButton control. When the button is clicked, the program will display a text string in the TextBox control.

We'll use the Visual Basic IDE to create our program. Visual Basic's integrated development environment is a programming environment in which you manage, create, and compile your projects. The IDE provides you with the windows and tools you need for programming. The VBA IDE is somewhat trimmed down from the full VB version, but it maintains most of the same functionality.

To get to the VBA IDE, follow these two steps:

1. Start up Outlook.

2. Select Tools ➣ Macro ➣ Visual Basic Editor.

This opens the VBA IDE as shown in Figure 17.1. To the right, there are two panes: the top one displays the Project Explorer, and the bottom one is the Properties window, which displays the selected object's properties and makes them available for editing. The large gray area is where you'll actually create your form, and the relatively familiar toolbars are just up above.

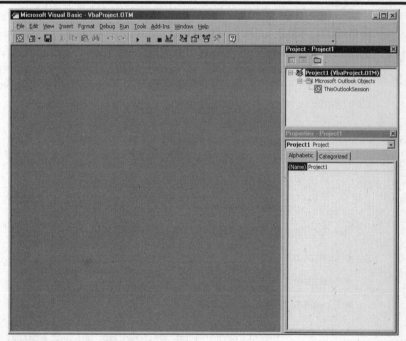

FIGURE 17.1: The VBA IDE for Outlook

NOTE

When you start a new project in VBA, you do so within the host application, in this case, Outlook. In the Project Explorer, you'll see an entry at the top called Project1 (VbaProject.otm) linked to Microsoft Outlook Objects and then to ThisOutlookSession. This simply indicates that whatever you create will be attached to Outlook.

Creating the Application Interface

Our project calls for a text box and a command button, but before we can create them, we have to create the UserForm that they will sit on. The UserForm is our canvas, onto which we will "paint" our controls.

Adding the UserForm

To add a UserForm, go to the toolbar and look at the second icon from the left, which is the Insert Object button. Click the pull-down menu attached to the button to see the objects you can add. These options are also available from the Insert menu.

The choices, as shown above, are the following:

▶ UserForm

▶ Module

▶ Class Module

▶ Procedure (currently unavailable)

We'll only be using the UserForm for our application, but here's a brief explanation of each of the types:

UserForm   A dialog box or window that is used to provide or collect information in an application's user interface.

NOTE

You can attach VB code to a UserForm; the code is stored in a form module built into the UserForm. This form module is not to be confused with modules or class modules, which are described below.

 Module   Modules are also known as standard modules. They are where procedures and declarations are stored for your project. In essence, this is a code stockpile.

 Class Module   This is the first hint of object-oriented programming (OOP) in Visual Basic. Class modules are used for complex applications and other operations that are only possible through Visual Basic code. For example, class modules are used to define functions that no control or add-in already provides or to call functions directly from the Windows 32-bit application programming interface (API).

 Procedure   Procedures are used to break VB code into components that perform specific functions so that repetitive tasks do not need to be written over and over again. Using procedures eases your coding work because each procedure can be written, tested, and debugged independently, rather than as one part of a much larger whole. You can also reuse your procedures in other applications if you keep the code homogenous (avoiding references or calls to application-specific variables).

NOTE

The Procedure item is only available when you have a UserForm code module, (standard) module, or class module window open.

Now that you've seen the options, select Insert ➤ UserForm from the VB Editor toolbar to create a UserForm for your application. The form will appear in the large gray area of the VB Editor. You'll notice that you get two windows: a UserForm object window and a window to hold it, as we see in Figure 17.2.

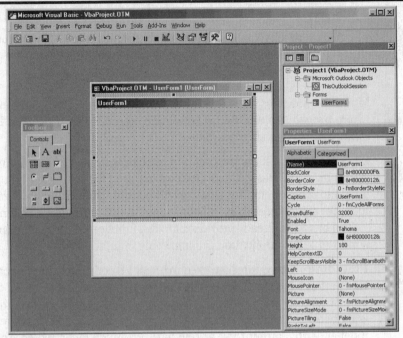

FIGURE 17.2: The default UserForm object

This form, as you can see from Figure 17.2, is named UserForm1. The Properties window shows the properties of the form and the current values of each property. And to the left of the UserForm, you can see the Toolbox. This Toolbox is where you select the controls to add to your UserForm, which we'll do next.

Adding the Controls

A control is a pre-programmed object that the user can interact with or get information from. Controls include buttons, pull-down lists, and check boxes. Every time you see a dialog box warning you of something and you click the OK button, you have used a control.

To add a CommandButton control to the form, follow these steps:

1. Click the CommandButton button on the Toolbox (the small, gray rectangle, shown here). The button remains depressed once you have clicked it, indicating that the CommandButton is selected.

2. Move your mouse pointer to the form area and point to where you would like the top-left corner of the button to be; then click and drag down and right until you've outlined a rectangle the size you want the button to be.

The other way of creating a CommandButton on your form is to click on the button in the Toolbox and drag it to the UserForm. The default size and shape of the CommandButton control will be illustrated by a gray box.

TIP

The best way to think of the interface design process is to equate it with painting a picture. If you've used Microsoft Paint or any of the Office drawing tools, you'll have a good idea of how this works. Just select a tool from the Toolbox and click and drag on the form to define its size.

3. Resize and relocate the control to look something like Figure 17.3 below. To resize a control, select it, point to one of the handles that appear around the control, and drag the handle. Moving the control is simple, too. Point near the center of the selected control and drag it to the new location.

This takes care of the first control, the CommandButton with its default name of CommandButton1. We'll change the name in a moment, but first we're going to add the TextBox control.

Part iii

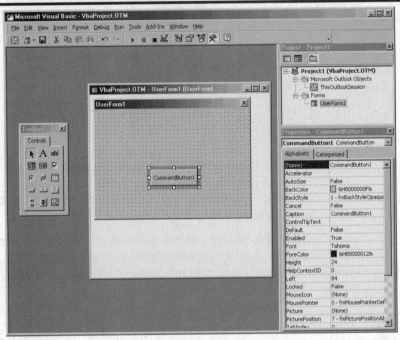

FIGURE 17.3: Congratulations, your first control!

 Go back to the Toolbox and select the icon with "ab|" on it. Follow the same steps that you used to create the CommandButton control, but place the TextBox *above* the button control. Your end result should look something like Figure 17.4.

After placing the TextBox, you can also resize and relocate it to meet your needs. You can do that by clicking the control and dragging the nodes around, as you did with the CommandButton, but the VB Editor can perform this task for you. There are two tools that can resize and relocate your controls so they look uniform. First, let's size our two new controls in relation to each other.

1. Select the two controls by clicking on the form and dragging across both of them to "lasso" them. Both controls will have handles when they're selected. In Microsoft products, you don't have to drag completely around controls to select them; any control that you drag across will be selected.

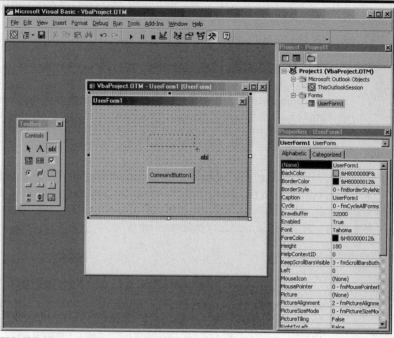

FIGURE 17.4:   Adding the TextBox control

2.   Select Format ➤ Make Same Size ➤ Height.

3.   Select both controls again.

4.   Select Format ➤ Align ➤ Centers to align the centers of the two controls.

5.   While the two controls are still selected, choose Format ➤ Center in Form ➤ Horizontal. Do not center them vertically in the form or you'll simply place one object on top of the other in the very center of the form.

Now that you've created the interface, we'll move on to setting properties and other options.

Changing Properties

It's one thing to add controls to your form, but it's another to make those controls *look and* act as you want them to. This is where properties come in. In this section, we'll look at the properties for each of our controls and examine what they can do for us.

NOTE

We're not going to list all of the properties for each control because there are a great number of them. If you're curious about a control's properties, place the control on a form following the steps we've outlined above, and look in the Properties window, which gives you access to all of the properties for the selected control.

First, we'll look at the properties for our UserForm. The Properties window, which is in the lower-right part of the VB Editor window, sorts the list alphabetically by default. You can also click the Categorized tab to see your control's properties organized by type.

NOTE

To select the UserForm itself, click any area on the UserForm that is not occupied by a control. When the object handles appear around the form itself, it is selected, and you can see and modify the UserForm's properties.

The left column of the list shows the name of the property; the right column shows the value for that property. There are two ways to change a property:

▶ Type a new value

▶ Select an option from a list

The UserForm

For our Hello World! project, we need to rename our UserForm. Locate the Caption property in the Properties window, and click the property name (Caption) to highlight it. When you begin typing, even though the text "UserForm1" is not selected, your new text will replace it. You will note that your new text also appears in the UserForm at the same time. Type **Hello World!** and press the Enter key to change the Caption property.

To add some individuality to our UserForm we'll also define its SpecialEffect property. Locate the SpecialEffect property near the bottom of the list and select its name. You'll note that a pull-down arrow appears in the value column. This property has preset values. You can choose from the following:

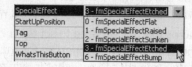

- ▶ fmSpecialEffectFlat
- ▶ fmSpecialEffectRaised
- ▶ fmSpecialEffectSunken
- ▶ fmSpecialEffectEtched
- ▶ fmSpecialEffectBump

Take a look at the form in each of these modes and decide which one you like better. We're particularly fond of the etched look, so we'll use that ourselves. You can choose what you like; choosing a different value will not affect the operation of the applet—it's only the caption, after all.

The CommandButton Control

Now we can move on to the next control, the CommandButton. We're going to do two things to the CommandButton control:

- ▶ Change the Caption property to "Hi, my name is World."
- ▶ Set the newly named CommandButton as the default button for the UserForm.

First, select the CommandButton in your form; then locate the Caption property in the list and select it by clicking on the word Caption. As with the UserForm, the Caption changes as you type the new caption. If your caption text is larger than the button itself, simply drag one of the side handles until the button is large enough to show all of the text in one line.

NOTE

If you resize your CommandButton, it will probably be out of alignment with the TextBox. Simply drag-select both controls and select Format ➤ Centers to fix it.

When that's done, go back to the Properties window and locate the Default property. From the pull-down list, select the True value. This sets the button to be the default when the UserForm is run, which allows it to be "clicked" with the Enter key or spacebar as well as the mouse.

There are no properties we need to set for the TextBox control, but it's helpful to be familiar with the properties for this very common control. Take a look at its properties to see what is available.

Writing the Code

Now that we have a pretty face on our project, we need to write some code so that clicking the CommandButton will cause a text string to appear in the TextBox control.

Here is the code for the CommandButton that will start our procedure when we click on it.

```
Private Sub CommandButton1_Click ()
    TextBox1.Text = "Hello World!"
End Sub
```

Once you've added the second line of code, your code window should look like Figure 17.5.

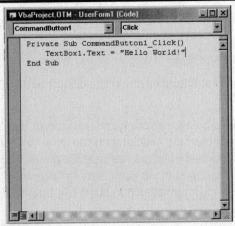

FIGURE 17.5: The code editor window showing our program code

The easiest way to add code to a control is to double-click the control. This opens the Code Editor window. As you can see when you try this yourself, most of your code is already there. All you have to do is add the second line of code. This is just one of the ways that VBA makes it easy for you to create applications.

TIP

There are a few conventions in programming that are accepted by most programmers. Your program will still work if you don't follow them, but most programmers follow these conventions because it makes code easier to read. When you add the new code above, you can add it without indenting the second line, but it would be harder to distinguish the subroutine from the surrounding statements. Adding tabs at the beginning of lines that are controlled by the previous line simply shows that the tabbed line is subordinate to the preceding one. It won't make much difference in this program, but in larger ones it makes your logic easier to follow and your bugs easier to find.

Let's look at each line of the code so we can get a better understanding of how it works. The first line reads like this:

```
Private Sub CommandButton1_Click ()
```

We already explained this code briefly in the previous chapter, but let's look at it again.

First, `Private` indicates that this procedure is available only to the form that it is on. If you want to make the procedure available to other forms in this application, you would substitute `Public` for `Private`.

Second, `Sub` indicates that the code following is a subroutine. Subroutines are the building blocks that make up programs. Our subroutine here, which includes a single line of code, performs a single task.

Third, `CommandButton1_Click` does two things. The first part of the name tells the subroutine which control is expecting an event; the `Click` part of the name tells the subroutine what *kind* of event to expect, in this case a Click event. When we run the application, we will see that clicking the button *does* cause the text "Hello World!" to appear in the TextBox control.

NOTE

You probably noted the lonely parentheses apparently doing nothing at the end of the first line. They are used to surround any values you need to pass into the procedure from another function, or to apply a static value that is always used. These values are called variables. You need the parentheses, even if you don't have any variables to pass into the procedure.

The next line, which is indented for easier reading, is a *statement*. A statement is a line that contains instructions for the program to follow.

The first item is `TextBox1`, which performs the same function as `CommandButton1` in the previous line. It is the name of the TextBox control we placed on our UserForm, and it was given the name TextBox1 for identification purposes. Its presence here indicates that when we click the button, the result will happen in the TextBox control.

The period (`.`) tells the program that the next item (`Text`) is a property of the first item, `TextBox1`. This sets up the Text property to be ready to accept input of some sort.

NOTE
The Text property of the TextBox control is used to set the default text in the control when the form opens. If you place nothing in the Text property field, the TextBox control will be empty.

You can probably already figure out how the rest of the line works. The equal sign (=) sets the Text property equal to the next bit of information. In this case the Text property is set to "Hello World!" When we run the program and click the button, the text string "Hello World!" will replace the existing text in TextBox1's Text property.

The last line, `End Sub`, simply tells the program that it has finished its subroutine and can return control to Windows. Every time you click the button, the program runs and puts the text string "Hello World!" into the TextBox control. You won't actually see this unless you change or delete the text in the TextBox.

Now that we understand how the program works, let's run it and see it in action.

Proof of Concept

 Click the Run Macro button on the toolbar and, unless an error exists, your form should appear on your screen. Click the CommandButton and watch as the phrase "Hello World!" appears in the TextBox control.

This was a very basic project, but it is indicative of the process required to add to or modify the functionality of Outlook with VBA. There are, however, a few things that can trip up even the simplest applications.

To Err Is Human

Computers take everything literally, so if you made a typing mistake, your program won't work properly. For example, if, instead of this line:

```
TextBox1.Text = "Hello World!"
```

you had entered this line:

```
TextBox1.Txt = "Hello World!"
```

the program would return an error. (Try it yourself and see what happens.)

To fix this problem, you simply need to fix the typing error. However, it's good to know what happens when VBA detects that something is not quite right. When we run the program with the error and click the button, we get an error dialog box with the following message:

```
Compile Error: Method or Data member not found
```

If we go and look at the code after dismissing this dialog box, we'll see that the first line of code is highlighted in yellow and that the text we changed is marked in blue. This tells us that the yellow line was the one that the compiler stopped on when it detected something wrong, and that the error comes from the misnamed property, Text.

Compiling and Distributing Your Program

Because VBA is dependant on the application it lives in to run (in this case Outlook), that is where the code you create is stored. If you don't *build* your project, VBA will compile your procedures from the code when the user runs a macro, which can be significantly slower, depending on the size of your application. To confuse the issue slightly, VBA refers to building a project as compiling it (though, as we mentioned previously, what it really does is pre-interpret it). To compile your project, go to Debug ≻ Compile Hello World!

This wraps up our VBA tutorial, but that's not all there is. The next section points you to some books and online resources for programming and Visual Basic.

Part iii

OUTLOOK VBA DISTRIBUTION QUIRKS

Outlook uses VBA a little differently than do other Office products. For example, in a Word document, you would distribute the application by distributing a copy of the document that contains the

CONTINUED ➡

macros—this is the way we distributed our VBScripts when we published a form (see Chapter 15). However, Outlook attaches the VBA macros to users' profiles, not directly to documents. To distribute our project we will have to export all the forms and modules from the project, and users will have to import them into their Profile project, a user's local code storage file. You can only export one file at a time.

To export a module or form, follow these four steps:

1. Open the Visual Basic Editor in Outlook.

2. Select a module or form in the Project Explorer by clicking it.

3. Select Tools ➤ File ➤ Export

4. Select the destination for the module and enter a filename for it in the dialog box.

To import a module or form follow these steps:

1. Open the Visual Basic Editor in Outlook.

2. Select Tools ➤ File ➤ Export

3. Select the file you want to import in the dialog box.

GOING FURTHER WITH VISUAL BASIC

Here is a list of some resources—print and Internet-based—that can help point you in the right direction if you're interested in going further with VB.

Visual Basic 6: In Record Time by Steve Brown

(Sybex)   Learn Visual Basic programming quickly and effectively. This book offers clear, practical coverage of the Visual Basic environment; insightful instruction in the principles of Windows programming; and tested, easy-to-follow tutorials that let you quickly learn the language's essential skills.

Visual Basic 6 Developer's Handbook **by Evangelos Petrout-sos and Kevin Hough (Sybex)**   Written by leading VB developers whose enterprise-level VB applications are used by COMPAQ, Exxon, Texas Instruments, and NASA, this book offers high-end coverage of the advanced topics you have to master in order to take your work and your career to the next level.

Visual Basic 6.0 Programmer's Guide **by Microsoft (Microsoft Press)**   This comprehensive and exhaustive guide to programming in Visual Basic 6.0 straight from the horse's mouth is a great help when learning the intricacies of this occasionally complex and powerful language. This book comes with the complete collection of programmer's guides for Visual Studio 6 from Microsoft Press.

Microsoft's Visual Basic Technical Resources site   Plenty of technical information, tutorials, and other helpful material that's freely available. `http:// msdn.microsoft.com/ vbasic/technical/default.asp`

Developer.Com   A large network of resources for developers from all walks and languages. They also cover Visual Basic very well. `http://www.developer.com`

Visual Basic Web Directory   An immense collection of pointers and links to a huge amount of information about VB. It is organized in categories, which makes it simple to find what you're looking for, including learning from the bottom up. `http://www.vb-web-directory.com/`

VBOnline Magazine   An online magazine with lots of helpful material and tutorials that can help get you up to speed with VB. `http://www.vbonline.com/ vb-mag/`

WHAT'S NEXT?

This chapter explained simple programming with VB and offered opportunities to practice this new skill. Exchange will be introduced in the next chapter and then expanded throughout the rest of the book. To start, you will learn Exchange basics and Exchange Server's key role in e-messaging.

Part iii

PART iV
EXCHANGE SERVER 5.5
BASICS

Chapter 18

INTRODUCING EXCHANGE

Microsoft's Exchange client/server electronic messaging system is a major player in what I call the "e-messaging decade." It lets people work together in a variety of productivity-enhancing ways. The Exchange system is one of the most exciting, innovative, and promising software products I've ever seen. I can't wait to get started, so let's go to it.

Adapted from *Mastering™ Microsoft® Exchange Server 5.5* by Barry Gerber

ISBN 0-7821-2658-8   916 pages $44.99

Exchange and the E-messaging Decade

Electronic messaging is more than e-mail. It is the use of an underlying messaging infrastructure (addresses, routing, and so on) to build applications that are based on cooperative tasking, whether by humans or computers. We can expect the years 1996 to 2005 to be the decade of electronic messaging *(e-messaging)*, when store-and-forward–based messaging systems and real-time interactive technologies will complement each other to produce wildly imaginative business, entertainment, and educational applications with high pay-off potential.

Microsoft's Exchange Server will play a key role in e-messaging. Exchange Server is one of the most powerful, extensible, scalable, easy-to-use, and manageable e-messaging back ends currently on the market. Combined with Microsoft's excellent Outlook clients, Internet-based clients from other vendors, and third-party or home-grown applications, Exchange Server can help your organization move smoothly and productively into the e-messaging decade.

In writing this book, I was guided by three goals:

▶ To share the excitement I feel about both the promise of electronic messaging and the Exchange client/server system

▶ To help you decide if there's a place for Exchange in your organization

▶ To provide the information and teach you the skills you'll need to plan for and implement Exchange systems of any size and shape

The rest of this chapter introduces you to the Exchange client/server system. We start with a quick look at several of the neat ways you can use Exchange for e-mail and more, then focus on some of Exchange's key characteristics and capabilities. This is just an introduction, so don't worry if you don't understand everything completely by the end of this chapter. There will be more details throughout the rest of this book.

By the way, when I use the word *Exchange* or the words *Exchange system* from here on, I'm talking about the whole Exchange client/server system. *Exchange Server* means just the server product, and an *Exchange server* is any computer running the Exchange Server product. *Exchange client* refers to any client that lets you access all the features of Exchange Server, for example, Microsoft's stable of Outlook clients. *Exchange client* does not refer to general-purpose clients like IMAP4 or POP3 clients or to Internet browser-based clients that provide limited access to Exchange Server's features. When I talk about these, I'll use either their commercial or generic names or both, for example, *the Eudora POP3 client*. Got that? Okay, explain it to me.

EXCHANGE APPLICATIONS

I dare you not to get excited about electronic messaging and Exchange as you read this section. Just look at what's possible and imagine what you could do with all this potential.

E-mail Is Only the Beginning

Together, Exchange Server and its clients perform a variety of messaging-based functions. These include e-mail, message routing, scheduling, and supporting several types of custom applications. E-mail is certainly a key feature of any messaging system. And the Outlook Calendar is far and away better than previous versions of Microsoft's appointment- and meeting-scheduling software. (Figures 18.1 and 18.2 show the Outlook 2000 client Inbox and Calendar for Windows in action.) Take a look at Figures 18.3, 18.4, and 18.5 for a glimpse of the Internet-based POP3, IMAP4, and Web browser clients you can use with Exchange 5 and above.

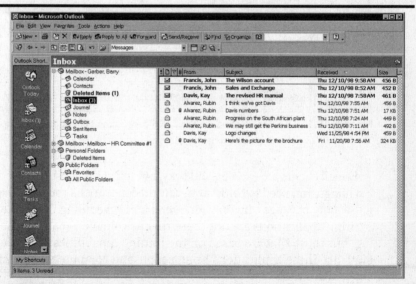

FIGURE 18.1: The Outlook 2000 client for Windows Inbox

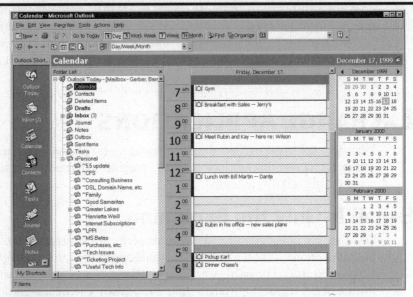

FIGURE 18.2:   The Outlook 2000 client Windows Calendar

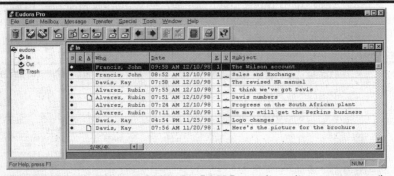

FIGURE 18.3:   Qualcomm's Eudora Pro 3 POP3-compliant client accesses mail stored on an Exchange server.

E-mail clients are exciting and sexy, but to get the most out of Exchange, you need to throw away any preconceptions you have that messaging packages are only for e-mail and scheduling. The really exciting applications are not those that use simple e-mail or scheduling, but those that are based on the routing capabilities of messaging systems. These applications bring people and computers together for cooperative work.

So what do these hot apps look like? Let's start with the simplest and move toward the more complex.

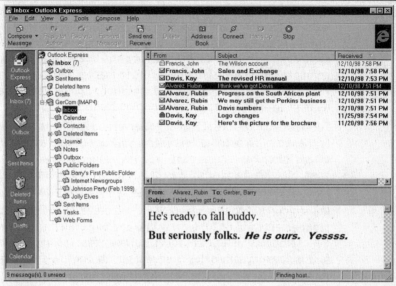

FIGURE 18.4:   Microsoft's Outlook Express IMAP4 client function accesses messages and folders on an Exchange server.

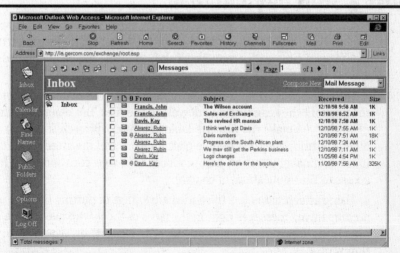

FIGURE 18.5:   Microsoft's Internet Explorer Web browser accesses mail stored on an Exchange server.

CHANGE IS THE NAME OF THE GAME

Some of the marvelous user interfaces you see in Figures 18.1 through 18.5 may look different by the time you read this book. Software development and marketing, especially in the world of electronic communications, is running at hyperspeed. Updates and even major revisions hit the market at a breakneck pace. The Internet makes it even easier for vendors to market and deliver their wares. New pieces and parts of applications appear almost daily for manual or totally automatic download and installation.

The basic architecture of Exchange Server and its clients is unlikely to change much over the next year or so. The outward appearance of user interfaces is much more likely to change. As far as Exchange goes, plan for change as a way of life. Keep an open mind and at least one eye on Microsoft's Exchange-oriented Web pages.

In the long run, all this hyperactivity will prove a good thing. Our requirements will find their way into and bugs will find their way out of products faster. I will admit, however, that I sometimes long for the days of yearly or less frequent updates on low-density $5^1/_4$-inch floppies.

Just a Step beyond Mail

You're probably familiar with e-mail *attachments*—those word processing, spreadsheet, and other work files you can drop into messages. Attachments are a simple way to move work files to the people who need to see them.

Sure, you could send your files on floppy disk or tell people where on the network they can find and download the files. But e-mail attachments let you make the files available to others with a click of their mouse button: They just double-click an icon, and the attachment opens in the original application that produced it (if your correspondent has access to the application, of course).

Using attachments has the added advantage of putting the files and accompanying messages right in the faces of those who need to see them. This leaves less room for excuses like "Oh, I forgot" or "The dog ate the floppy disk."

As great as attachments can be, they have one real weakness: The minute an attachment leaves your Outbox, it's out of date. If you do further work on the original file, that work is not reflected in the copy you sent to others. If someone then edits a copy of the attached file, it's totally out of sync with the original and all other copies. Getting everything synchronized again can involve tedious hours or days of manually comparing different versions and cutting and pasting them to create one master document.

Exchange offers several ways to avoid this problem. One of the simplest is the *attachment link* or *shortcut:* Instead of putting the actual file into a message, you put in a link to the file (see Figure 18.6), which can be stored anywhere on the network. The real kicker is that the file can also be stored in Exchange public folders (more about these later). When someone double-clicks an attachment link icon, the linked file opens. Everyone who receives the message works with the same linked attachment. Everyone reads and can modify the same file.

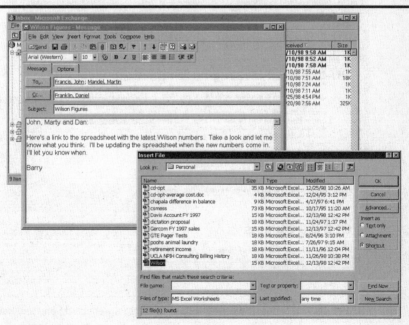

FIGURE 18.6: Exchange links keep attachments alive.

Off-the-Shelf Messaging-Enabled Applications

Here's another way to guard against dead work files: Microsoft Windows enables messaging in many word processing and spreadsheet applications. For example, when you install the Exchange client on your computer, Microsoft's Office products like Word and Excel are e-messaging enabled. You can select Send or Route options from the apps' File menu; this pops up a routing slip. You then add addresses to the slip from your Exchange client's address book, select the routing method you want to use, and assign a right-to-modify level for the route. Finally, you ship your work off to others with just a click of the Route button.

Figure 18.7 shows how all this works. Though it's simple, application-based messaging can significantly improve user productivity and speed up a range of business processes.

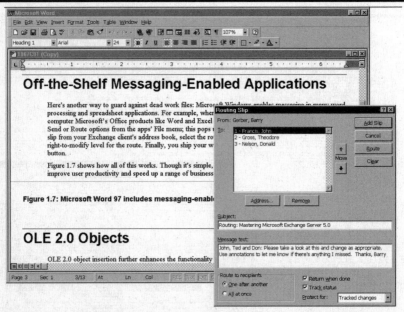

FIGURE 18.7:   Microsoft Word 97 includes messaging-enabled Send and Route functions.

OLE 2 Objects

OLE 2 object insertion further enhances the functionality of the Exchange messaging system. Take a close look at Figure 18.8. Yes, the message includes an Excel spreadsheet and chart. The person who sent the message simply selected Object from the Insert menu that appears on every Exchange message. The Exchange client then inserted a blank Excel spreadsheet into the message as an OLE 2 object. Having received the message, we can see the spreadsheet as an item in the message, as shown in the figure. When we double-click the spreadsheet, Excel is launched and Excel's menus and toolbars replace those of the message (Figure 18.9). In essence, the message becomes Excel.

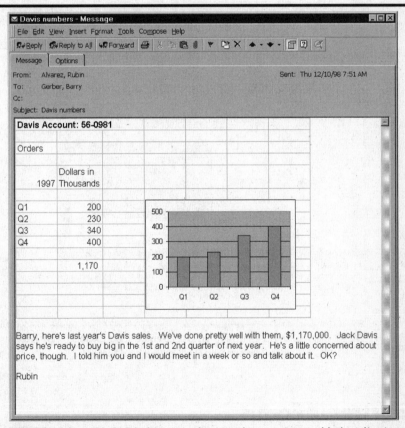

FIGURE 18.8: With OLE 2 objects, sophisticated messaging-enabled applications are easy to build.

The Excel spreadsheet is fully editable. Though Excel must be available to your recipients, they don't have to launch it to read and work on the spreadsheet. Even if your recipients don't have Excel, they can still view the contents of the spreadsheet, though they won't be able to work on it. (That is, even if they don't have the application, they can still view the object when they open the message.)

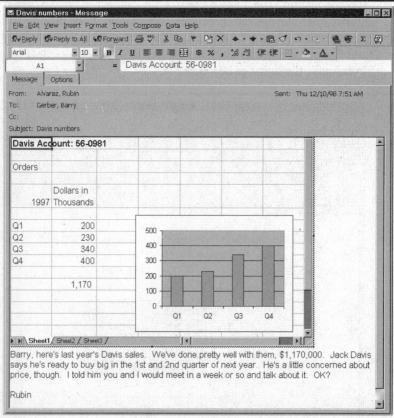

FIGURE 18.9:   Double-clicking an OLE 2-embedded Excel spreadsheet in a message enables Excel menus and toolbars.

Electronic Forms

Exchange Server 4 and 5 come with the Exchange Forms Designer (EFD) that is based on Microsoft Visual Basic. You can use the Forms Designer to build information-gathering forms containing a number of the bells and whistles you're used to in Windows applications. These include drop-down list boxes, check boxes, fill-in text forms, tab dialog controls, and radio buttons.

EFD, which is easy enough for nontechnical types to use, includes a variety of messaging-oriented fields and actions. For example, you can choose to include a preaddressed To field in a form, as shown in Figure 18.10, so users of the form can easily mail it off to the appropriate recipient. Once you've designed a form, it can be made available to all or select users, who can access the completed form by simply selecting it while in an Exchange client or Outlook (EFD forms work in both).

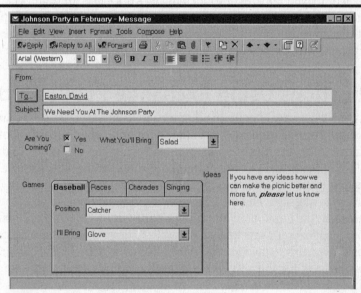

FIGURE 18.10:   Electronic forms turn messages into structured information-gathering tools.

Exchange 5.5 adds Outlook Forms Designer (OFD). This Visual Basic Script-capable application opens many new doors, especially when linked with Exchange 5.5's groupware-enabling server scripting features. OFD forms work only with Outlook clients.

Applications Built on APIs

If all this functionality isn't enough, you can go to the heart of Exchange Server and use its Application Program Interface (API). Exchange Server supports both the Simple and Extended versions of Microsoft's Windows-based Mail Application Program Interface (MAPI). It also supports the X.400-oriented, platform-independent Common Mail Call (CMC) APIs, which have functions similar to those of Simple MAPI. Using Simple MAPI or CMC, you can build applications that use e-messaging addresses behind the scenes to route data between users and programs. Extended MAPI lets you get more deeply into Exchange's storage and e-messaging address books to create virtually any messaging-enabled application you can imagine.

These custom-built applications may involve some level of automation, such as regular updates of your company's price lists for trading partners or sending a weekly multimedia message from the president to employees at your organization. Building apps based on MAPI or CMC requires someone with programming skills in languages like Visual Basic or C++.

Applications Using Exchange Public Folders

As you'll discover later in this chapter and chapters to come, Exchange Server supports mailboxes, private folders, and public folders. All of these can hold messages and any kind of computer application or data file. Mailboxes and private folders are where Exchange users store and manage their messages and files. Public folders are used for common access to messages and files. Files can be dragged from file access interfaces like the Explorer in Microsoft's Windows 95/98/NT 4 and dropped into mailboxes, private folders, or public folders. If you begin thinking of mailboxes, private folders, and public folders as a messaging-enabled extension of Explorer, you'll have a fairly clear picture of Microsoft's vision of the future in regard to how an operating system organizes and displays stored information.

You can set up sorting rules for a mailbox, private folder, or public folder so that items in the folder are organized by a range of attributes, such as the name of the sender or creator of the item or the date the item arrived or was placed in the folder. Items in a mailbox, private folder, or public folder can be sorted by conversation threads. You can also put applications built on existing products like Word or Excel or with Exchange or Outlook Forms Designer, server scripting, or the API set into mailboxes and private or public folders. In mailboxes and private folders these applications are fun for one, but in public folders, where many people access them, they can replace the tons of maddening paper-based processes that abound in every organization.

If all this isn't already enough, Exchange is very much Internet-aware. With Exchange 5.*x*, you can publish all or selected public folders on the Internet where they become accessible with a simple Internet browser. You can limit Internet access to public folders to only those who have access under Exchange's security system or you can open public folders to anyone on the Internet. Just think about it: Internet-enabled public folders let you put information on the Internet without the fuss and bother of Web site design and development. Any item can be placed on the Internet by simply adding a message to a public folder. Figure 18.11 shows a public folder-enabled price list for the one product produced by my favorite fictitious company, GerCom, which you'll learn more about later.

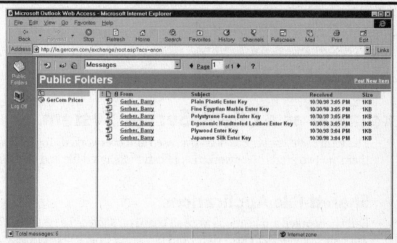

FIGURE 18.11: Using Exchange public folders to publish a price list on the Internet

Before we leave public folder applications, I want to mention one more option. Exchange Server 5 and later lets you bring any or all of those devilishly delightful USENET Internet newsgroups to your public folder environment. With their Outlook clients, users then can read and reply to newsgroup items just as though they were using a standard newsgroup reader application. Exchange Server comes with all the tools you need to make it so. All you need is an Internet connection, access to a newsfeed provider, and a set of rules about which groups to exclude. Remember, this is where the infamous alt.sex newsgroups live.

Part iv

SOME EXCHANGE BASICS

It's important to get a handle on some of Exchange's key characteristics and capabilities. Once you do, you'll better appreciate the depth and breadth of Microsoft's efforts in developing Exchange, and you'll be better prepared for the rest of this book. In this section, we'll take a look at the following items:

- ► Exchange as a client/server system

- ► The Exchange client

- ► Exchange Server's dependency on Microsoft's Windows NT Server

- ► Exchange Server's object orientation

- ► Exchange Server scalability

- ► Exchange Server security

- ► Exchange Server and other e-messaging systems

Exchange as a Client/Server System

The term *client/server* has been overused and overworked. To put it simply, there are two kinds of networked applications: shared-file and client/server.

Shared-File Applications

Early networked applications were all based on *shared-file* systems. The network shell that let you load your word processor from a network server also allowed you to read from and write to files stored on a server. At the time, it was the easiest and most natural way to grow networked applications.

Microsoft Mail for PC Networks is a shared-file application. You run Windows, OS/2, DOS, or Macintosh front ends, which send and receive messages by accessing files on a Microsoft Mail for PC Networks post office that resides on a network file server. The front end and your PC do all the work; the server is passive. Figure 18.12 shows a typical Microsoft Mail for PC Networks setup.

Easy as it was to develop, this architecture leads to some serious problems in today's networked computing world:

- ► Changing the underlying structure of the server file system is difficult, because you have to change both the server and the client.

- ▶ System security is always compromised, because users must have read and write permissions for the whole server file system, which includes all other users' message files. Things are so bad that a naive or malicious user can actually destroy shared-file system databases in some cases.

- ▶ Network traffic is high, because the front end must constantly access indexes and hunt around the server's file system for user messages.

- ▶ Because the user workstation acts directly on shared files, these can be destroyed if workstation hardware or software stop functioning for some unexpected reason.

Shared-file applications are in decline. Sure, plenty of "legacy" (that is, out of date) apps will probably live on for the data processing equivalent of eternity, but client/server systems have quickly supplanted the shared-file model. This is especially true in the world of electronic messaging.

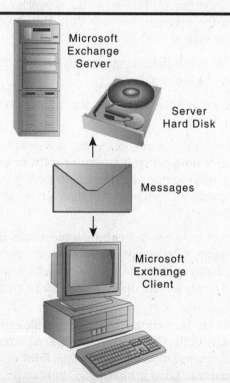

Microsoft
Exchange
Server

Server
Hard Disk

Messages

Microsoft
Exchange
Client

FIGURE 18.12: Microsoft Mail for PC Networks is a typical shared-file e-messaging system.

Client/Server Applications

Today, more and more networked applications are based on the client/server model. The server is an active partner in client/server applications. Clients tell servers what they want done, and if security requirements are met, servers do what they are asked.

Processes running on a server find and ship data off to processes running on a client. When a client process sends data, a server receives it and writes it to server-based files. Server processes can do more than simply interact with client processes. For example, they can compact data files on the server or—as they do on Exchange Server—automatically reply to incoming messages to let people know, for instance, that you're going to be out of the office for a period of time. Figure 18.13 shows how Exchange implements the client/server model.

Client/server applications are strong in all the areas in which shared-file apps are weak:

▶ Changing the underlying structure of the server file system is easier than with shared-file systems, because only the server processes access the file system.

▶ System security can be much tighter, again because only the server processes access the file system.

▶ Network traffic is lighter, because all the work of file access is done by the server, on the server.

▶ Because server processes are the only ones that access server data, breakdowns of user workstation hardware or software are less likely to spoil data. With appropriate transaction logging features, client/server systems can even protect against server hardware or software malfunctions.

As good as the client/server model is, it does have some general drawbacks. Client/server apps require more computing horsepower, especially on the server side. With Exchange, plan to start with very fast Pentium machines, lots of RAM, and plenty of hard disk capacity—and expect to grow from there.

Client/server applications are more complex than shared-file apps. This is partly due to the nature of the client/server model and partly due to the tendency of client/server apps to be newer and thus filled with all kinds of great capabilities you won't find in shared-file applications. Generally, you're safe in assuming that you'll need to devote more resources to managing a client/server application than to tending a similar one based on shared files.

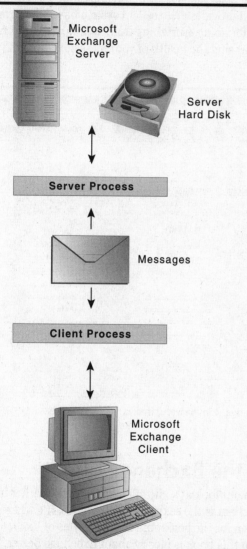

FIGURE 18.13: Microsoft Exchange is based on the client/server model.

The good news is that Microsoft has done a lot to reduce the management load and to make it easier for someone who isn't a computer scientist to administer an Exchange system. I've looked at many client/server messaging systems, and I can say without any doubt that Exchange Server is absolutely the easiest to administer. Exchange Server's administrative front end, called the *Exchange Administrator,* organizes the management processes very nicely and provides an excellent system based on a graphical user interface (GUI) for doing everything from adding users and network connections to assessing the health of your messaging system (see Figure 18.14).

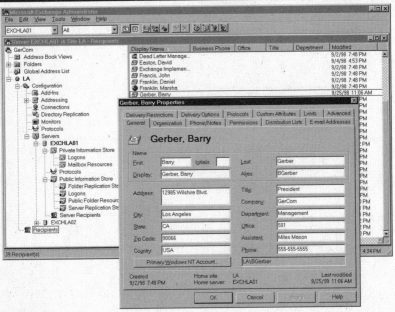

FIGURE 18.14:   The Exchange Administrator makes management easier.

A Quick Take on the Exchange Client

As should be clear from our look at some of its applications earlier in this chapter, the Exchange client is the sexy part of Exchange. It's where the action is—the view screen for the backroom bits and bytes of Exchange Server. While the rest of this book is mostly about Exchange Server, you can't implement an Exchange system without the clients. So we'll spend some time on the Exchange client, currently incarnated under the rubric *Outlook,* and some client basics.

Information Storage

The client stores information in one of two places—private and public information containers. Each has a different purpose and function.

Private Information Containers   Though you can share some of their contents with others, private information containers generally hold items that you and you alone have access to. There are two basic kinds of private information stores: mailboxes and personal folders. You access mailboxes and personal folders using an Exchange client or Internet-based clients such as the POP3 and IMAP4 clients built into Outlook Express.

Mailboxes can send and receive messages. You can add folders to a mailbox to help you organize your messages. If you have the rights to other mailboxes, you can open them in your Exchange client as well.

Personal folders may or may not have the send and receive capabilities of mailboxes. You can create as many personal folders as you desire. A private folder can hold as many subfolders as you wish. Like the folders you add to mailboxes, personal folders help you organize information. You can drag and drop messages between folders. Using *rules* (discussed below), you can direct incoming mail into any of your personal folders.

The contents of mailboxes are stored inside the Exchange Server database. Personal folders are stored outside of Exchange Server on private or networked disk space.

Public Information Containers   Public information containers are often called *public folders*. Let's use that term here. Public folders hold items that you want others to see. Users whom you authorize can create public folders and drag and drop anything they wish into them. Public folders can also be nested and rules can be applied to them.

Public folders are stored inside the Exchange Server database. They are key to the organization-wide implementation of Exchange. Some, all, or none of an Exchange server's public folders can be automatically replicated to other Exchange servers. This lets you post items to public folders on one Exchange server and have them quickly and painlessly appear on any combination of the Exchange servers in your system. Even without replication, users all over your organization can access public folders.

Part iv

Sharing Information

You can share information with others by sending it to them or placing it in public folders for them to retrieve on their own. You can drop messages, word processing documents, and other work files—even whole applications—into public folders. You can use public folders to implement many of the kinds of applications I talked about at the beginning of this chapter.

For example, instead of electronically routing a draft of a word processing document to a bunch of colleagues, you can just drop it into a public folder. Then you can send e-mail to your colleagues asking them to look at the document and even to edit it right there in the public folder.

Organizing Information

Creating a set of personal and public folders and dropping messages in them is a simple way to organize information. More sophisticated approaches include the use of rules, views, and the Exchange client's Finder.

Rules As a user, you can set up a range of *rules* to move mail from your Inbox into personal or public folders. For example, you might want to move all the messages from your boss into a folder marked URGENT. Rules can be based on anything from the sender of a message to its contents. Depending on its type, a rule may run on the Exchange server or on the client. The Exchange client doesn't have to be running for server-based rules to execute.

Views Exchange messages can have numerous attributes. These include the obvious, such as sender, subject, and date received, as well as less common information, including sender's company, last author, and number of words. You can build views of messages using any combination of attributes and any sorting scheme. Then you can apply a particular view to a folder to specially organize the messages it contains.

The Finder You can use the Exchange client Finder to search all folders or a single folder for messages from or to specific correspondents, messages with specific information in the subject field or message body, and even messages received between specific dates or of a specific size.

Exchange Server's Dependency on NT Server

Exchange Server is a component of the Microsoft BackOffice suite. Like Microsoft's SQL Server and Systems Management Server, Exchange Server runs only with Windows NT Server. It won't run on top of NT Workstation or on Windows 95/98; even though both are 32-bit operating systems, they can't host Exchange Server.

Among operating systems, NT is the new kid on the block. As a long-time Novell NetWare user, I initially faced NT with not just a little fear and foreboding. That was then. Now I am a confirmed NT user and supporter. My personal workstation is an NT-based machine, and all my servers but one run NT. (The one holdout is a NetWare server I use to ensure that NT- and Windows-based software works with Novell's IPX/SPX.)

It took me two weeks to get comfortable with NT and a month to become totally productive with it. What sets NT off from all other operating systems for workstations and servers is Microsoft Windows. NT, whether the workstation or server version, *is* Microsoft Windows. If you can use Windows, you can use NT. Networking with NT is a breeze, and running apps on top of NT Server is a piece of cake. Figure 18.15 shows one of my NT/Exchange server desktops with some NT and Exchange management applications running. This shouldn't be foreign territory for any Windows aficionado.

NT is chock-full of features that make it an especially attractive operating system. One of these is its very usable and functional implementation of Microsoft's domain-based security system. Domains have names—one of mine is called LA for my hometown, Los Angeles—and include NT servers, NT workstations, and all flavors of Windows- and DOS-based machines. Though there are a number of domain security models, the general rule is that the members of a domain can use any resource they have been given permission to use—disk files, printers, and so on—in the domain without having to enter a password for each. Exchange Server depends on NT domain security for a good deal of its security.

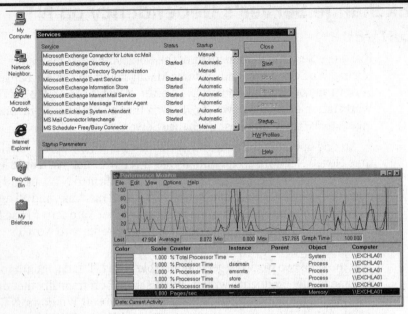

FIGURE 18.15: On the surface, NT Server is just plain old Microsoft Windows.

Exchange Server's Object Orientation

Exchange is a classic example of an *object-oriented* system. Take another look at Figure 18.14. See all those items on the tree on the left-hand side of the Exchange Administrator menu, such as GerCom, LA, EXCHLA01, EXCHLA02, and Recipients? Each of these is an *object*. Each object has attributes and can interact with other objects in specific ways. Exchange objects can hold other objects, serving as what Microsoft calls *containers*.

GerCom is the name of the fictitious organization I created for this book; it is the equivalent of a company name like IBM or TRW. (People often ask if I'm related to the baby-food Gerbers. I'm not, but GerCom at least lets me dream. Want to buy some stock?) Microsoft refers to this object as the *organization*. The GerCom organization contains all the objects below it.

LA is the name of a physical site in the GerCom corporate hierarchy, Los Angeles. It is also a home for Exchange servers. The GerCom/LA hierarchy has two servers, named *EXCHLA01* and *EXCHLA02*.

The Recipients object way down at the bottom of the hierarchy is a container for Exchange Server recipients. *Recipients* are objects that can send or receive messages. Among other things, recipients include user mailboxes and distribution lists. Each recipient object can contain a large number of attributes. The tabbed Properties dialog box in Figure 18.14 should give you some idea of the breadth of attributes that can be assigned to a mailbox.

Notice that the Recipients container is a part of the LA site hierarchy. *Sites* are the most important containers in Exchange. They hold configuration information about recipients and how to reach them, as well as information about servers and other Exchange objects. This information is stored in what Microsoft calls the *Exchange Server directory*. Though specific instances of the directory are stored on the servers in a site, any instance of the directory actually contains information about all the servers in an organization.

Object orientation makes it easy for Microsoft to distribute Exchange Server's functionality and management, and it makes it easy for you to administer an Exchange Server environment. For example, based on my security clearances I can manage any set of recipients—from those in only a single site to all the recipients in my organization.

Exchange Server Scalability

Exchange Server scales very well both vertically and horizontally. NT runs on top of computers based on single and multiple Intel and DEC Alpha processors, so it's very easy to scale an Exchange server upward to more powerful hardware when increased user loads make additional computing power necessary. Since you'll be taking both Exchange Server and NT with you, you really won't have to learn much more about your new machine than the location of its power switch.

If vertical scalability isn't what you need, horizontal scaling is also a breeze with Exchange Server. You can set up a new Exchange server and quickly get its directory and public folders in sync with all or some of your other servers. You can even move mailboxes between Exchange servers in a site with a few clicks of your left mouse button.

How do you know if it's time to scale up or out? Microsoft has an answer for this, too: You can use the LoadSim application included with Exchange Server to simulate a range of different user loads on your server hardware. By analyzing the results of your LoadSim tests, you'll get some idea of the messaging loads you can expect a server to handle in a production environment.

Exchange Server Security

Exchange Server security starts with NT's security system. Several different NT security models are available; the one that's right for you depends mostly on the size and structure of your organization and the department that supports Exchange Server. In all cases, the idea is to select a security model that puts the lightest burden on users and system administrators while still appropriately barring unauthorized users from messaging and other system resources. (More on this in Chapter 21.)

NT also audits security. It can let you know when a user tries to add, delete, or access system resources.

The security of Exchange Server is enhanced in several ways beyond the NT operating system's security. Access to Exchange Server objects such as public folders can be limited by the creator of the folder. Data encryption on the server and client protects messages and other Exchange resources from eavesdropping by those with server or workstation access. Digital signatures prove the authenticity of a message. Even traffic between servers can be encrypted.

Exchange Server and Other E-messaging Systems

The world of electronic messaging is far from a single-standard nirvana. A good e-messaging system must connect to and communicate with a variety of other messaging systems. Microsoft has done a nice job of providing Exchange Server with key links, called *connectors,* to other systems. The company has also built some cross-system message-content translators into Exchange Server that work automatically and are very effective. With these translators, you're less likely to send a message containing, say, a beautiful embedded image that can't be viewed by some or all of the message's recipients.

In the case of Microsoft's legacy messaging systems—Microsoft Mail for PC Networks and Microsoft Mail for AppleTalk Networks—you have an option beyond connectivity. You can choose to migrate users to Exchange. Migration utilities for other messaging systems like Lotus cc:Mail are also provided with Exchange.

X.400

A fully standards-compatible X.400 connector is built into Exchange Server and can be used to link Exchange sites. The 1984 and 1988 standards for X.400 are supported. The connector also supports attachment to foreign X.400 messaging systems.

SMTP

As with the X.400 connector, a Simple Message Transfer Protocol (SMTP) connector is built into Exchange Server. Unlike the old Microsoft Mail for PC Networks SMTP gateway, it is a full-fledged SMTP host system capable of relaying messages and resolving addresses, while supporting several Enhanced SMTP (ESMTP) commands. UUencode/UUdecode and MIME (Multipurpose Internet Mail Extensions) message-content standards are also supported. So, once you've moved your users from MS Mail for PCs to Exchange, you won't hear any more of those vexing complaints about the meaningless MIME-source attachments users get because the SMTP gateway was unable to convert them back to their original binary format.

Microsoft Mail for PC Networks

A built-in connector makes Microsoft Mail for PC Networks 3.x (MS Mail 3.x) post offices look like Exchange servers to Exchange clients and vice versa. If connectivity isn't enough, you can transfer MS Mail 3.x users to Exchange with a supplied migration tool. If all this is too much, Exchange clients can directly access MS Mail 3.x post offices. So you can keep your MS Mail 3.x post offices, at least until you've got Exchange Server running the way you want and have moved everyone off the legacy mail system.

Microsoft Mail for AppleTalk Networks

Connectivity for Microsoft Mail for AppleTalk Networks systems is also provided by a connector built into Exchange. When connectivity isn't enough, Mail for Apple-Talk users can be migrated to Exchange Server.

cc:Mail

If Lotus cc:Mail is running in your shop, you'll be happy to hear that Exchange 5.x comes with tools to connect and migrate users to Exchange. Never let it be said that Microsoft doesn't care about users of IBM/Lotus products. At least there's a way to pull them into the MS camp.

Part iv

Lotus Notes

Exchange 5.5 adds a connector for Lotus Notes. With this connector, Exchange and Notes clients can see each other's address directories and exchange mail.

Other Messaging Systems

Gateways are available for links to other messaging systems such as Notes, PROFS, SNADS, fax, and MCI Mail. Both Microsoft and third parties build and support these gateways. You can even extend the benefit of these gateways to your MS Mail users.

WHAT'S NEXT?

In this chapter you learned about some of the exciting things you can do with Exchange. You also had a first look at some key aspects and characteristics of the system. The next chapters will help you understand Exchange—how it works and how you can implement some of the nifty applications I've only hinted at in this chapter. Next you will see both a conceptual view and a practical view of the Exchange hierarchy; Exchange organizations, sites, servers, and recipients; and how Exchange hierarchy design affects server administration and e-messaging addressing.

Chapter 19
THE EXCHANGE HIERARCHY

Microsoft has built Exchange around a set of four key elements:

- ▶ Organizations
- ▶ Sites
- ▶ Servers
- ▶ Recipients

The relationship between these elements is hierarchical. The organization is at the top of the hierarchy, and recipients are at the bottom. The Exchange hierarchy imposes an organizational structure on both the real world and the Exchange world. The hierarchy also determines at least the defaults used to construct e-mail or, even better, e-messaging addresses for Exchange users.

Adapted from *Mastering™ Microsoft® Exchange Server 5.5*
by Barry Gerber
ISBN 0-7821-2658-8   916 pages $44.99

A Conceptual View of the Hierarchy

The four key elements in the Exchange hierarchy stand for two conceptually different but related realities. First, the elements represent real people, places, and things. An *organization* is a collection of people who have some reason for associating with each other. An organization can be a business, an academic institution, a club, or some other entity. A *site* is a sub-organizational unit like a geographical location or a department. *Servers* are computers running Exchange Server software. And *recipients* are the people and things that can send or receive mail. In the real world, each of these elements includes all the elements below it: Organizations include sites, which include servers, which include recipients.

The four key Exchange elements represent a second set of realities: Exchange *objects*. Remember when I talked about Exchange's object orientation in Chapter 18? I noted that each of the four Exchange objects serves as a container for the objects below it. Organizational objects include site objects, which include server objects, which include recipient objects.

In this latter case, the language of object orientation replaces the language of social organization, but the effect is the same. The Exchange hierarchy orders the way we think about both the real world and Exchange itself. Take a look at Figure 19.1 to see how the Exchange Administrator brings these two conceptual views together in a single, easy-to-use interface.

While there are four key elements in the Exchange hierarchy, other significant elements are contained within each of the four elements. We'll talk about these later in this chapter.

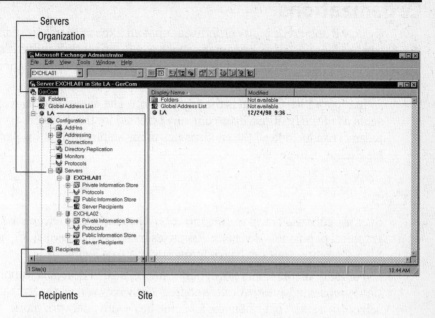

Servers

Organization

Recipients   Site

FIGURE 19.1: The Exchange Administrator makes it easy to deal with Exchange's hierarchy.

A MORE PRACTICAL VIEW OF THE HIERARCHY

Concepts are important, and I'll assume you're comfortable with the ones presented above. However, we "systems" types can't live by concepts alone. We need to move quickly from concepts to designing, installing, and running systems.

So let's look at the four elements in the Exchange hierarchy from a more practical perspective. As you read on, you'll begin to see where you'll have to make some very specific design decisions related to the four elements before you can even think about installing an Exchange server. You'll also begin to see just how central the Exchange hierarchy is to setting up and managing an Exchange environment.

Part iv

Organizations

By now it should be pretty clear to you that an Exchange organization can be all or part of a company, a school, a club, or another entity; it's the master container in the Exchange hierarchy. Examples of organizational names include IBM, IBMUSA, and IBMENG.

In Figure 19.1, GerCom is the organization. The name GerCom represents *all* of the fictitious little company I created for this book. That means I can include all the subdivisions of my empire within this particular Exchange hierarchy.

Sites

Sites are subdivisions of the organization. Generally, they encompass geographical or business divisions. Examples include Engineering, NY, and SFO. Currently, GerCom has only one site, LA (see Figure 19.1).

For fault tolerance and faster performance, a good deal of key information is replicated automatically and frequently between all the Exchange servers in a site. That can make for some heavy-duty network traffic. Sites should be geographically contiguous enough that Exchange servers within them can be connected at reasonable cost by higher-bandwidth (128Kb/sec or greater) wide area networks (WANs).

Sites are usually connected by slower WANs, since replicating information between sites is usually done in a more selective way and at a more leisurely pace. Sites include a range of sub-elements or objects. For example, Exchange connectors let you link sites together and to the outside world. Exchange contains tools for setting up and administering these objects, including tools for administering and managing Exchange connectors. Figure 19.2, another view of the Exchange Administrator, shows the tool for the Internet Mail Service (IMS), which links my LA site to the Internet mail system and can even be used to link my LA site to other sites in my Exchange hierarchy through the Internet.

The IMS tool has a number of what Microsoft calls *property pages*—so called because this is where you set the attributes, or *properties,* of the service. Figure 19.2 shows the Internet Mail property page of the IMS tool, as you can see from the tab at the top of the page. The IMS tool has a total of 12 property pages, as indicated by the 12 tabs. Each tabbed page covers a different set of properties required to administer and manage an Internet mail link.

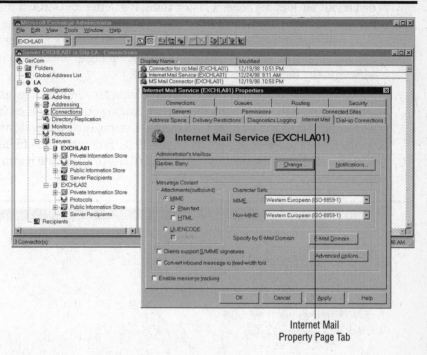

Internet Mail
Property Page Tab

FIGURE 19.2: Working with the Internet Mail Service in a site

Servers

Servers are the physical Exchange servers within a site. At the moment, there are two Exchange servers in the LA site. They're called EXCHLA01 and EXCHLA02, which stand for "Exchange [Server] in Los Angeles #1" and "Exchange [Server] in Los Angeles #2." You'll find the servers toward the bottom of the Exchange hierarchy tree in Figure 19.1; notice that they are in the Servers container.

Some organizations like to base their Exchange server names on departments, such as engineering or marketing, within a geographical site (for example, site = LA; server = Marketing). Working with my imaginary MIS department, I've decided to use a different naming scheme for GerCom. To start, I put all my LA employees on one server, EXCHLA01. As I ran out of capacity on EXCHLA01, I added EXCHLA02. As GerCom grows—and I know it's going to grow—I'll add more servers, called EXCHLA03, EXCHLA04, and so on. (There's nothing inherently good or bad about my naming scheme; I just think it's better for GerCom than a scheme based on department names. My company is relatively small right now, so two servers are enough for all employees. I don't want to pop for servers for each department, and I'm willing to tolerate Exchange servers with "meaningless" names. So there!)

As with sites, a number of tools are available for administering and managing server-based Exchange objects. Among other things, each server has tools for managing local message storage and for replicating public folders between servers. In Figure 19.3, the Exchange Administrator is used to set some default limits for EXCHLA01's private information storage area.

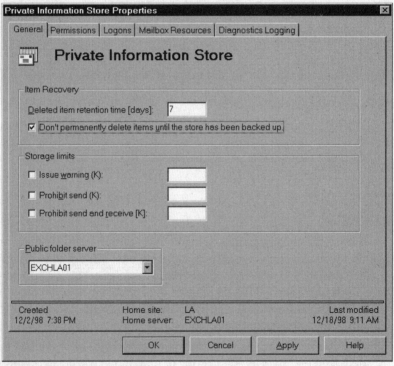

FIGURE 19.3: Exchange servers include tools for managing private information storage areas.

Recipients

Exchange has four major types of recipient objects: mailboxes (the most widely used of which is the primary mailbox), public folders, custom recipients (essentially aliases for addresses outside an Exchange organization), and distribution lists. Each of these plays a different role and can be used to good advantage depending on the needs of your organization. As with other entities in the hierarchy, Exchange has tools for administering and managing recipient objects.

MAILBOX AGENTS: RECIPIENT OBJECTS THAT SERVE THE SYSTEM

There is a fifth kind of recipient object, though it's one you have little control over. It's called a *mailbox agent*. Mailbox agents are generally created by the system and used to support system-level information passing. Developers can write programs that implement mailbox agents. I'll talk in a bit about one of these mailbox agents, the Schedule+ Free/Busy mailbox agent.

Recipients live in recipients containers. In Figure 19.4, which is a view from the Exchange Administrator, recipients containers show up five times in the GerCom tree. The Folders container near the top of the hierarchy holds, among other things, public folders. The Global Address List, down a bit from the Folders container, holds *all* recipients for an organization. Each of the two servers in the LA site has a recipients container named *Server Recipients*. And there is a site-level recipients container, named *Recipients*, at the bottom of the hierarchy.

Each of the four types of recipients containers—Folders and the Global Address List at the organization level, Server Recipients at the server level, and Recipients at the site level—plays a special role in Exchange Server.

▶ The Global Address List holds all the recipients in an organization. It is used by Exchange clients to address messages and can be used by Exchange administrators to administer and manage recipients. For reasons of corporate policy or for the purpose for which they were created, some recipients may be hidden from the Global Address List and other address books. Exchange administrators with the proper rights can readily access hidden recipients and even unhide them if necessary.

Part iv

▶ The Public Folders container holds all the public folders in an organization. Even hidden public folders are visible in the Public Folders container, which is available only to Exchange administrators with the proper access rights.

▶ The messages in each Exchange mailbox are stored on one and only one Exchange server. However, the attributes of the mailbox (for example, the name and street address of the mailbox user) are, or can be, replicated on other Exchange servers in the site and organization.

▶ Site-level recipients containers hold all mailboxes on all servers in a site, as well as the three other types of recipients for a site. A good deal of recipient administration and management is done in site-level recipients containers.

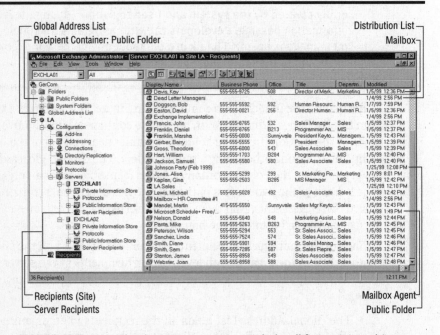

FIGURE 19.4: A site-level recipients container includes all five recipient object types.

Figure 19.4 shows what's in the site-level recipients container for GerCom. As you can see, all five of the recipient object types are included in this container. Distribution lists, public folders, and custom recipients appear only at the site level. That little icon marked *Microsoft Schedule+ Free/ ...* is a mailbox agent. It represents the Microsoft Schedule+ Free/ Busy Connector for the LA site. The connector lets users of Schedule+ for Exchange Server see the schedules of users of Schedule+ for Microsoft Mail for PCs, and vice versa.

Now, just to verify that server-level recipients containers hold only mailboxes and, to be totally correct, mailbox agents, take a look at Figure 19.5. There's not a distribution list, custom recipient, or public folder to be seen—just a sea of mailboxes. Well, almost. Our old friend the Schedule+ Free/Busy Connector is there, too. It's there because, although it serves the whole LA site, it lives on my server EXCHLA01 or, in Microsoft-speak, it is *homed* on EXCHLA01. (That is, mailbox agent recipients appear in the Server Recipients container of the server they're homed on.)

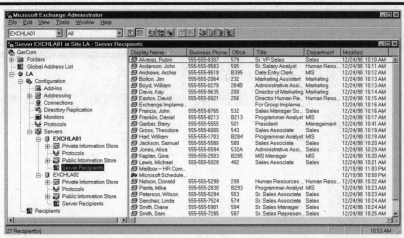

FIGURE 19.5: A server-level recipients container includes only mailboxes and mailbox agents.

Let's take a closer look at each of the four major Exchange recipient objects.

Mailboxes

Mailboxes hold private messages and other objects, such as word processing documents or spreadsheets, that belong to individual Exchange users. Any mailbox may contain folders created by the system or users. There are four system-created folders in Exchange: Inbox, Outbox,

Deleted Items, and Sent Items. Generally, messages are received in the Inbox folder, sent from the Outbox folder, moved into the Sent Items folder after transmission, and held in the Deleted Items folder after deletion.

Other folders may be created in an Exchange mailbox by a specific Exchange client. For example, the Outlook 2000 client creates Calendar, Contacts, Drafts, Journal, Notes, and Tasks folders in an Exchange mailbox when it initially accesses the mailbox.

Users can create as many folders in a mailbox as they wish and can give the folders any name they choose. Users can delete folders they create, but they cannot delete system-created folders. Any folder, whether system- or user-created, can have folders nested below it.

All mailboxes are stored on the user's Exchange server in an Exchange database called the *private information store.* You must be connected to your Exchange server to access your mailbox on Exchange Server. Figure 19.6 shows my own Exchange client and its mailbox; my Inbox is open.

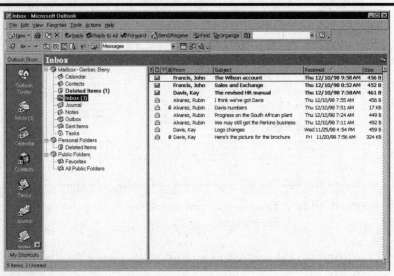

FIGURE 19.6: An Exchange client with its mailbox

You can give others access to your mailbox. This lets them see and, if you wish, respond to your messages, as a secretary might do for a boss. You can also create mailboxes just to support specific activities or projects. By assigning certain people the rights to these kinds of mailboxes, groups can work cooperatively without turning to the public folders I'll discuss later. If you have rights to multiple mailboxes, they can all be made available simultaneously in your Exchange client. Figure 19.7 shows that my colleagues and I are using a shared mailbox to plan our Exchange system.

Notice that the shared mailbox has not been accessed by an Outlook 2000 client. You can tell this because the mailbox only has Deleted Items, Inbox, Outbox, and Sent Items folders.

Shared Mailbox to Plan Exchange Server System

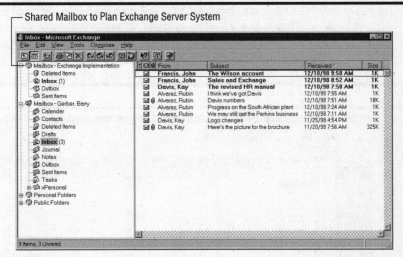

FIGURE 19.7: An Exchange client with access to multiple mailboxes

PERSONAL FOLDERS

To hold messages outside the Exchange server environment, Exchange users can create personal folders. Unlike mailboxes, which are stored in a specific Exchange database called the *private information store*, personal folders are stored, at least initially, as standard files on a local or networked disk. When created, personal folders have only one system-created folder, Deleted Items. Personal folders can help you organize information in special ways. As Figure 19.8 shows, I'm using a personal folder named *Exchange Book* to isolate and manage messages and other information related to this book. In the folder named Chapter 1, I've dragged

CONTINUED ➡

Part iv

and dropped the items with .TIF and .DOC extensions into the folder using the Windows NT Explorer. The item from Rubin Alvarez, which is flagged with an envelope icon, is a message I dragged and dropped into the folder from my mailbox's Inbox.

You can tell that my Exchange Book personal information store is stored on a local or network disk (and not inside the Exchange private information store database) because it's not in either of the two mailboxes in my Exchange client. To move folders or items in the personal information store into my Exchange server, all I have to do is drag them into one of the two mailboxes.

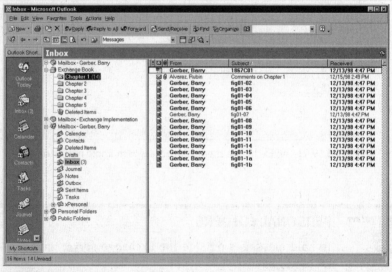

FIGURE 19.8: An Exchange client with a personal information store for a special project

Public Folders

Though public folders can originate messages, most of the time you'll use them to receive messages. They're created by users and allow groups of users to share data. When you create a public folder, you can choose who has access to it—all users or only some. When you use a public folder, you can mail or directly post messages or files to it or simply drag and drop them into the folder. (Remember that messages can be anything from simple text to application files.)

Custom Recipients

When Exchange Server users need to communicate with people outside your Exchange system, you can add these "foreigners" to your directory as custom recipients. Then Exchange users can pick them from directory lists just as they would select any internal Exchange recipient. You'd do this, for example, with someone who has an SMTP mail account on another system.

You don't have to create a custom recipient for every foreigner, however. If only a few Exchange users need to access a particular outsider, they can create an address for that person in their own contacts lists or address books or do "one-off" addressing on a per-message basis (one-off addressing is a one-time, manually typed address).

Distribution Lists

Distribution lists let you group together recipients, including other distribution lists. They make it easy to send a message to lots of people and places using a single address.

Hiding Recipients

You can hide any of the four recipient objects. Hidden recipients can send and/or receive mail, but they don't show up in address books. You can use them, for example, to protect the anonymity of specific recipients or to support applications.

REASONS TO BE CAREFUL ABOUT EXCHANGE HIERARCHY DESIGN

The Exchange hierarchy does a nice job of imposing an organizational structure on both the real world and Exchange's own little world. If that were all it did, we could stop right here. But the hierarchy plays two more significant roles: It shapes the way you manage your Exchange system, and it defines the default e-messaging addresses of everyone inside it.

Part iv

The Exchange Hierarchy and Exchange Management

Look at Figure 19.1 once more. No matter how much GerCom grows as a real company, I'll always be able to easily think about and manage all the sites, servers, and recipients inside it from the same Exchange Administrator session.

Furthermore, if I had more than one Exchange organization, I'd have to treat the organizations as foreign to each other when I linked them together. That could significantly increase the networking and administrative cost of operating my Exchange system. For example, I'd have to set up and manage separate Internet links for each organization.

It's not all that easy to fix problems like the one I'd create by dividing my company into a bunch of sub-organizations. You'll welcome the ability to bring together Exchange organizations when your real-world organization changes—for example, when it merges with another organization. Still, it's better not to rely on futures. Define your organization as broadly as you can from the start, unless you've got some social, political, or economic reason for doing otherwise.

The Exchange Hierarchy and E-messaging Address

In Figure 19.9, you can see how my default cc:Mail, Microsoft Mail for PC Networks, SMTP, and X.400 addresses are dependent on the way I've named the first two elements—organization and site—in my Exchange hierarchy. Server names are not included in addresses. Once a message gets to its destination site, the servers in the site are "smart" enough to get the message to the appropriate server, wherever it is located in the Exchange organization.

It's quite easy to change the default addresses that Exchange Server assigns to one or more recipients or even to add more addresses of a given type for any recipient. This way you're not trapped by your original Exchange hierarchy naming scheme. Still, it's best to get everything as right as possible from the get-go.

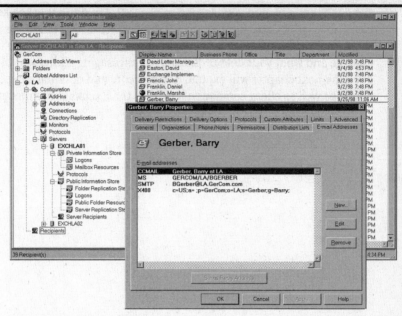

FIGURE 19.9: The Exchange hierarchy defines everyone's default e-mail addresses.

Although a variety of social and political barriers can get in the way of doing so, it's best to make your Exchange organization as all-inclusive as possible. Try to include the whole company, university, club, or whatever. If you don't, you may end up with a bunch of folks running around with addresses like jones@marketing.*acmela*.com and smith@marketing.*acmeny*.com.

One of the few times that centralized MIS or general management should rear its sometimes ugly head is in the early stages of Exchange hierarchy design. If yours is a decentralized organization, you can get back on your own horse as soon as this phase of the design process is finished.

WHAT'S NEXT?

In this chapter, you learned about the Exchange hierarchy. You saw how the objects in the hierarchy organize both the real world and Exchange itself. You learned key terms that you'll see again and again throughout

Part iv

the next chapters, and you learned to be careful in designing the key elements of your Exchange hierarchy. How you define and name these elements will determine both how easy your Exchange system will be to manage and what your default Exchange e-messaging addresses will look like. The next chapter will explain Server's core and optional components, as well as client components, within the Exchange architecture.

Chapter 20

THE ARCHITECTURE OF EXCHANGE

Exchange is a client/server electronic messaging system. In this chapter, we'll take a close look at the architectures of both the Exchange server and client. We'll also see how the Exchange client and server interact from an architectural perspective, as illustrated in Figure 20.1.

This is an important chapter. It exposes you to a range of Exchange terminology that you'll find useful later on, and it gives you a sense of how the whole Exchange system hangs together and works. Remember that virtually all of the architectural components we discuss here are, in whole or in part, real program code running somewhere on an Exchange server or client machine.

Adapted from *Mastering™ Microsoft® Exchange Server 5.5*
by Barry Gerber
ISBN 0-7821-2658-8   916 pages $44.99

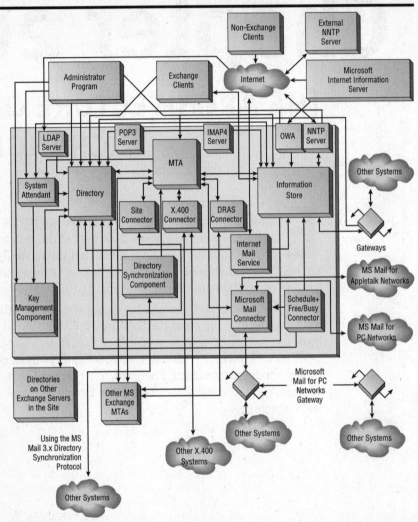

FIGURE 20.1: The architecture of Exchange

No, Figure 20.1 isn't a bird's-eye view of a spaghetti factory; rather, it's more or less a complete diagram of the Exchange hierarchy based on a diagram originally developed by Microsoft. It shows the components in the hierarchy and how they relate to each other. Everything inside the large, heavy-lined rectangle is part of a single Exchange server running all the required and optional Exchange Server components. Everything outside the rectangle is external to the server itself. The lines indicate communications between components. All communications are two-way; where there is only one arrowhead, the arrowhead points away from the Exchange component that initiates communications. A line with an arrowhead at each end indicates that either of the two components can initiate communications at different times, depending on the function being carried out.

Don't get too hung up with the details of Figure 20.1. It's here partly to give you a sense of the complexity of Exchange and partly to get you thinking about Exchange as a set of real processes that do real work. We won't go through every line and arrowhead of the figure in gory detail. However, when you come to the end of this chapter you should have a pretty good idea of how the various components in the Exchange hierarchy work, both alone and in league with their fellow components.

EXCHANGE SERVER'S CORE COMPONENTS

Exchange Server cannot provide messaging services to users unless all its core components are up and running. Core components include:

- ▶ The Directory
- ▶ The Information Store
- ▶ The Message Transfer Agent
- ▶ The System Attendant

Let's take a closer look at each of the core components.

The Directory

The Exchange Server directory functions as both a database and a service. The directory is a container holding information about all of a site's objects that are required to send and receive messages within and to the site. These include recipients (as defined in the previous chapter) as well as servers and all kinds of message-routing information. Copies of the directory for a site are stored on all Exchange servers in that site. If an organization includes multiple sites, information for all sites is included in every site directory.

The directory service (DS) is the access point for the directory database. Other processes on the Exchange server and on Exchange clients talk to the DS to provide and obtain information.

One of the key functions of the DS is to send and receive directory update information. Within an Exchange site, the DS sends this information directly to and receives it directly from the DSs on other Exchange servers. Across Exchange sites, the DSs send and receive directory update information as standard messages through the message transfer agent (MTA) on each Exchange server. The Exchange Server directory uses this update information for regular intrasite and intersite replication of directories across an Exchange organization. The DS can also exchange directory update information with "foreign" e-messaging systems. The optional directory synchronization component does this.

Note that I use the term *replication* to describe the directory update process inside an Exchange organization, while I use *synchronization* to describe updates with foreign e-messaging systems. Though the processes are similar, Microsoft has chosen to use different terms to describe them. Remembering the differences in meaning between the two words will make your hands-on experience with Exchange Server much easier.

In addition to cross-server and cross-system updates, the DS is responsible for such tasks as managing and presenting system address books to Exchange users and enforcing security on all recipient objects. Figure 20.2 shows how the directory and the DS work together to present address information to users. Figure 20.3 shows some of the major functions of the directory in graphical form.

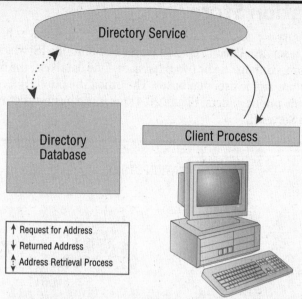

FIGURE 20.2:   The directory service process accesses the directory database.

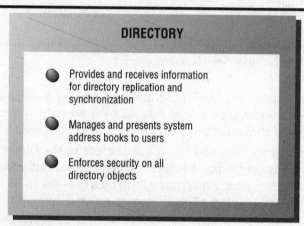

FIGURE 20.3:   Major functions of the directory

The Information Store

Like the directory service, the information store (IS) functions as both a database and a service. Each Exchange server contains one IS, which can, at your pleasure, contain one or two databases. One database, the private information store, holds user mailboxes. The other, the public information store, holds public folders. Figure 20.4 shows the basic structure of the Exchange Server IS.

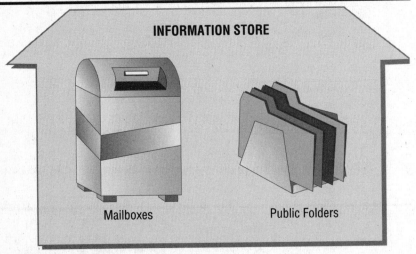

FIGURE 20.4: The Exchange Server information store

Incoming messages are placed in the Inbox, which, as I noted in Chapter 19, is a special folder in a mailbox. Public folders are used to give all or some recipients in an Exchange system access to specific messages.

To balance network loads and reduce access costs, public folders can be replicated in whole or in part to other Exchange servers, either in the same site or in remote sites. Additionally, to lighten the load on servers with mailboxes, you can place public folders on separate Exchange servers and direct clients to those servers when they need access to public folders.

The *IS service* is a buffer between the IS databases and other components of Exchange Server. It performs a number of functions. Among other things, it receives incoming mail from and delivers outgoing mail to the message transfer agent, notifies clients of the arrival of new mail, looks up addresses in the directory, and creates directory entries for public folders. Figure 20.5 shows some of the major functions of the IS service.

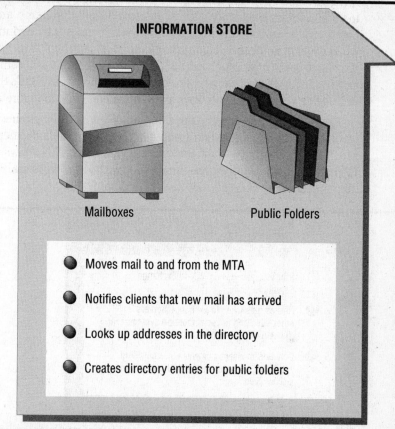

INFORMATION STORE

Mailboxes   Public Folders

● Moves mail to and from the MTA

● Notifies clients that new mail has arrived

● Looks up addresses in the directory

● Creates directory entries for public folders

FIGURE 20.5:   Major functions of the IS service

The Message Transfer Agent

The message transfer agent (MTA) routes messages between its server's IS and other Exchange systems. Within a site, the MTA routes messages directly to the MTAs on other Exchange servers. When it routes messages to Exchange servers located in different sites in the same organization, the MTA gets help from other Exchange components called *connectors*. Back in Figure 20.1, you can see three of these connectors—Site, X.400, and DRAS (Dynamic Remote Access Server)—directly below the MTA. I'll discuss these in more detail later in this chapter.

The MTA also routes messages to certain foreign e-messaging systems, including legacy Microsoft Mail 3.x systems, Internet systems, and those based on the X.400 standard. As with intersite and intrasite routing, when routing to these foreign systems the MTA gets help from special Exchange connectors, such as the Microsoft Mail and X.400 connectors, and the Internet Mail Service. For other systems such as IBM's SNADS or Novell's GroupWise, gateways are used. (Refer back to Figure 20.1.)

The MTA has one other major function: When X.400 systems are involved, the MTA converts messages in Exchange's default Microsoft MAPI format to native X.400 format, and vice versa. This allows Exchange Server to readily trade messages with X.400 systems. Figure 20.6 presents the MTA's major functions graphically.

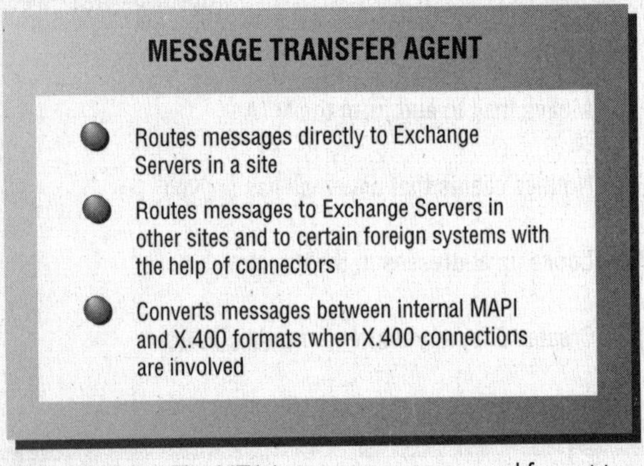

MESSAGE TRANSFER AGENT

- Routes messages directly to Exchange Servers in a site
- Routes messages to Exchange Servers in other sites and to certain foreign systems with the help of connectors
- Converts messages between internal MAPI and X.400 formats when X.400 connections are involved

FIGURE 20.6: The MTA is a message router and format translator.

The System Attendant

Other Exchange Server components cannot run without the system attendant (SA); it's the first Exchange component to activate on start-up and the last to stop on shutdown. The SA performs a range of functions, six of which are key to Exchange Server's operation. Let's take a closer look at each of these functions, as shown in Figure 20.7.

The SA Helps Other Servers Monitor Network Connections to Its Server

The system attendant receives and replies to network link integrity messages from other Exchange servers. These servers know that something is wrong—either with the network link or the system attendant's own server—if they fail to receive these replies.

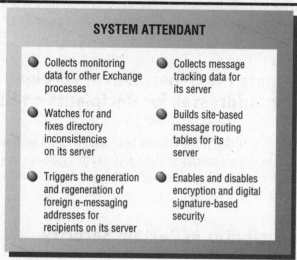

FIGURE 20.7: The system attendant performs six key functions for Exchange Server.

The SA Monitors for and Corrects Directory Inconsistencies on Its Server

The SA automatically checks the consistency of its copy of the directory against those of other Exchange servers in its site. If it finds inconsistencies, the SA attempts to reconcile and fix them.

The SA Collects Message-Tracking Data for Its Server

The SA logs data about sent messages, which can be used for tracking a message's status and the route that it traveled once sent. This capability is especially useful when used in conjunction with similar data gathered by the SAs on other Exchange servers.

The SA Builds Site-Based Message Routing Tables for Its Server

Like any network, an Exchange Server network needs *routing tables,* which are used specifically for routing messages. The SA interacts with the directory to build tables that the MTA uses to route messages to servers in its site.

The SA Triggers the Generation of Foreign E-messaging Addresses for Recipients on Its Server

The SA generates X.400, SMTP, Microsoft Mail, and cc:Mail addresses by default. When gateways are installed, the SA generates gateway-specific e-mail addresses for users. When creating addresses, the SA interacts with the directory.

The SA Participates in Certain Security Functions

Security in Exchange is very good. An Exchange mailbox can use both digital signatures and encryption. The SA is involved in enabling and disabling these two components of Exchange security. To do this, it interacts with the *Key Management Component,* which is discussed later in this chapter.

OPTIONAL EXCHANGE SERVER COMPONENTS

Exchange Server comes with all the following optional components except gateways. These components are "optional" not because you always have to pay extra for them, but because Exchange Server can run without them. Optional components include:

- ▶ The Exchange Administrator program
- ▶ The Directory Synchronization Agent

- ▶ The Key Management Component
- ▶ Exchange Internet protocol servers:
  - ▶ Web Service
  - ▶ Post Office Protocol 3 (POP3)
  - ▶ Internet Message Access Protocol V4 (IMAP4)
  - ▶ Network News Transfer Protocol
  - ▶ Lightweight Directory Access Protocol
- ▶ Exchange connectors:
  - ▶ Site Connector
  - ▶ X.400 Connector
  - ▶ Dynamic RAS Connector
  - ▶ Internet Mail Service
  - ▶ Microsoft Mail Connector
  - ▶ Schedule+ Free/Busy Connector
  - ▶ cc:Mail Connector
- ▶ Exchange gateways

You might find it helpful to refer back to Figure 20.1 as I discuss each component.

The Exchange Administrator Program

You've seen examples of the Exchange Administrator program in action in Chapters 18 and 19, and you'll get to know it very well as we move along. The main point I want to make here is that the Exchange Administrator is *home*. It's where you go whenever you need to do almost anything with Exchange Server—from creating and managing users to linking with other Exchange servers or foreign mail systems to monitoring the activities on your server. The Administrator is the single point from which you can manage anything, whether it's one Exchange server or your entire Exchange organization.

The Administrator is home in another way, too: It's easy. Soon after you start using the Administrator, you'll feel about it the way you feel about that comfortable old chair in the den. Really!

Part iv

The Directory Synchronization Agent

The Directory Synchronization Agent (DXA) lets you create address books that include addresses from outside your Exchange system. It also allows you to send Exchange Server address information to other e-messaging systems. It sends directory update information to and receives it from Microsoft Mail for PC Networks 3.x and Microsoft Mail for AppleTalk Networks systems.

The DXA uses the Microsoft Mail 3.x Directory Synchronization Protocol, so any foreign, non-Microsoft e-messaging system that is compatible with this protocol is fair game for cross-system directory synchronization.

The Key Management Component

Exchange supports RSA public key encryption and digital signatures within an Exchange organization. These help ensure the authenticity of a message and the person sending it. Exchange Server's Key Management Component supports these services. With this component in place and running, Exchange client users can create secure messages.

Exchange Internet Protocol Access Components

Exchange 5.5 comes with a set of five Internet protocol servers. These let you extend the reach of Exchange users beyond Microsoft's very good but proprietary electronic messaging protocols. The five components are Outlook Web Access (OWA), the Post Office Protocol (POP3) server, the Internet Message Access Protocol (IMAP4) server, the Network News Transfer Protocol (NNTP) server, and the Lightweight Directory Access Protocol (LDAP) server. If you try really hard, you'll find all five of these in Figure 20.1's spaghetti factory.

Outlook Web Access

Outlook Web Access (OWA) lets users access everything in their Exchange or Outlook mailboxes as well as items in public folders using a Web browser like Microsoft's Internet Explorer or Netscape's Navigator. Outlook Web Access components work in conjunction with the Active Server (AS) subsystem of Microsoft's Internet Information Server.

POP3 SERVER

Exchange Server's POP3 server gives users with standard POP3 e-mail clients, like Eudora or the mail clients in both Microsoft's Internet Explorer and Netscape's Navigator, limited access to their Exchange mailboxes. Users can download mail from their Exchange Inboxes, but that's all. Users have no direct access to other personal or public information stores or to their schedules. This is due to limitations in the POP3 protocol itself, and not in Microsoft's implementation of the protocol.

IMAP4 Server

The Exchange IMAP4 server goes POP3 one better, adding access to folders in addition to the Exchange Inbox. With IMAP4, folders and their contents can remain on the Exchange server.

NNTP Server

The NNTP server lets you bring all those exciting USENET newsgroups into your Exchange server's public folders where your users can read and respond to them with the same e-mail clients they use to read other public folders.

LDAP Server

Exchange Server supports the Lightweight Directory Access Protocol (LDAP), a protocol that works with X.500-compatible directories. Exchange Server security willing, any client with LDAP capability can access information in the directory on an Exchange server via the Internet. Thus, users of non-Exchange e-mail clients can use the Exchange directory to find the addresses of people they wish to send mail to. LDAP also opens the Exchange directory to other exciting things like communications applications (e.g., Web browser–based paging or faxing apps) that use the directory to get the information they need to reach a particular Exchange user. LDAP is a neat way to open the Exchange directory to the non-Exchange world. Exchange 5.5 provides full LDAP version 3 compatibility.

Part iv

Exchange Connectors

You use Exchange connectors to link Exchange sites to each other and to connect them to foreign e-messaging systems. You link Exchange sites to each other so that they can exchange user messages and cross-replicate their directories and public folders. You link Exchange sites to foreign systems primarily so that Exchange users can trade messages with users of those systems and/or synchronize directories with them. As an added bonus, you can also use connections to foreign sites to link Exchange sites to each other; more on this in just a bit.

Exchange connectors run on—surprise!—Exchange servers. You can run one or more instances of any Exchange connector within a site; one instance can service all the Exchange servers in a site or even all the sites in an organization.

Before we dive into the connectors themselves, we need to talk a bit about an impressive feature of Exchange Server, *indirect site links*. When Exchange servers connect sites, they conduct their business using standard messages; that is, they move user-to-user communications as messages. And they replicate directories and public folders by means of system-generated messages. Users generate user messages, but directory and public folder replication messages are generated by the Exchange Server system itself. Directory and folder replication messages are marked as system messages to indicate their special content. Figure 20.8 shows how this works.

When an Exchange server sees a system message, it treats the message differently from a user message, using it to update directory or public folder information.

Because site links are message-based, you can connect Exchange sites *directly* (point-to-point) and/or *indirectly* (through foreign e-messaging systems). Direct site links are easy to understand: You just run a connector on an Exchange server in each of two sites and tell the connectors to link to each other. Direct site links are done in real time without any intervening systems between the Exchange servers. (Figure 20.8 shows a direct site link.)

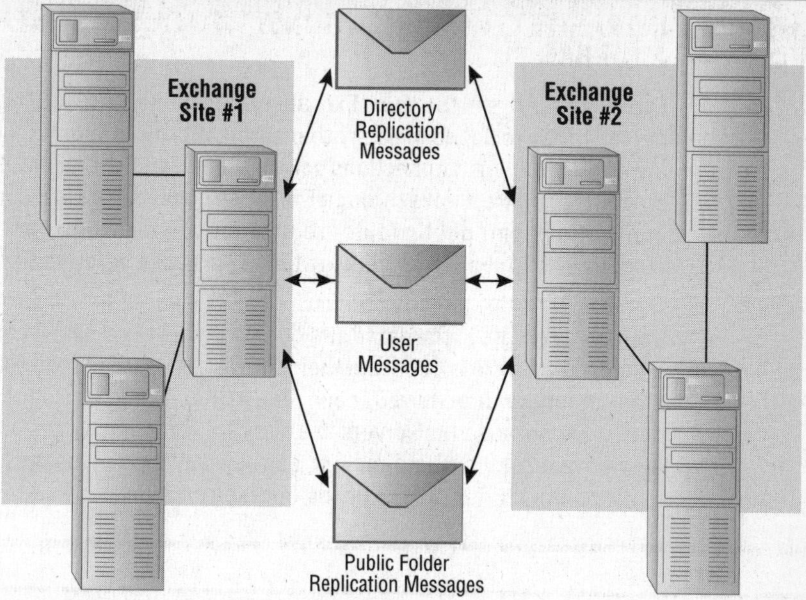

FIGURE 20.8: Site links are based on the exchange of messages.

Indirect site links are a bit less self-evident. When two or more Exchange sites are connected to a foreign e-messaging system such as the Internet or a public X.400 system, not only can users trade messages, but the servers in the sites can also exchange system messages that let them cross-replicate directories and public folders. Indirect site links are not done in real time. An Exchange server in one site sends its user and system messages to an intervening e-messaging system such as the Internet. The intervening system then passes these messages on to the Exchange server in the other site. The effect is the same as a direct link, though the process is different.

That wasn't so bad, was it? Take a look at Figure 20.9 if you're still a bit in the dark.

Okay, now we can talk about the Exchange connectors. There are a number of different Exchange connectors, including Site, X.400, Dynamic RAS, Internet Mail Service, Microsoft Mail, cc:Mail, and Schedule+ Free/Busy. Let's look at each of these connectors.

Part iv

INTRASITE COMMUNICATIONS: TWO OUT OF THREE AIN'T BAD

Exchange servers in the *same* Exchange site require no special connectors. They're linked to each other automatically as soon as they are up and running. Connections *between* sites require that you set up direct or indirect links through Exchange connectors. User communications and public folder replication are message based, whether two Exchange servers are talking intrasite or intersite.

However, as we've already noted when talking about the directory, Exchange servers in the same site don't use message-based communications to cross-replicate their directories. Instead they communicate more directly with each other. Direct communication is necessary because the servers in a site can't send messages until they have a copy of the directory, so they can't use messages to replicate directories. It's a chicken-and-egg problem.

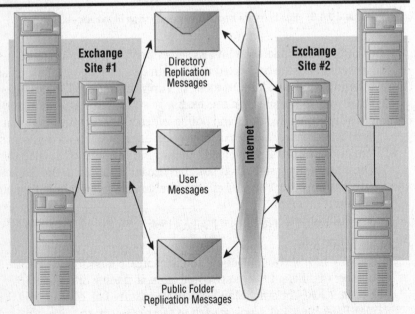

FIGURE 20.9:   Linking Exchange sites indirectly through foreign e-messaging systems

Site Connector

The Site Connector is used for direct links only. It requires synchronous (continuous) connections between sites. The Site Connector is the fastest, least complicated route to intersite connectivity.

X.400 Connector

Despite its name, the Site Connector is not the only way to directly link Exchange sites; the X.400 Connector also performs this function. Again, you need a synchronous network connection for direct links. In addition, the X.400 Connector can indirectly link Exchange sites through foreign X.400 systems and it can be used to link Exchange sites to foreign X.400 systems just for user message exchange. Indirect or mail exchange–only links can be implemented with either a synchronous or an asynchronous (non-continuous) connection. The X.400 Connector is fully compliant with all the 1984 and 1988 X.400 transport and message content standards.

Dynamic RAS Connector

You'll learn more about NT's Remote Access Server (RAS) in the next chapter. Exchange's Dynamic RAS Connector (DRASC) lets you set up direct links between Exchange sites in a way similar to the Site Connector, but it operates over cheaper, lower-bandwidth voice, ISDN, and X.25 lines. An asynchronous connection is all you need for a DRAS connection.

Internet Mail Service

The Internet Mail Service (IMS) is your Exchange server's link to SMTP mail systems. It can issue and respond to SMTP and several ESMTP commands and can do both MIME encoding and decoding and uuencoding/ uudecoding of messages. The IMS can be used only to exchange mail with Internet mail users or to directly or indirectly link Exchange sites.

Microsoft changed the IMS a bit in version 5 of Exchange Server. Its original name, *Internet Mail Connector*, was changed along with the way you install the IMS. There are also a number of improvements in the IMS, like its ability to route Internet mail from non-Exchange clients or servers.

Microsoft Mail Connector

You have two post office–wide options for dealing with legacy systems running Microsoft Mail 3.*x* for PC Networks and Microsoft Mail 3.*x* for

AppleTalk Networks. Either you can move entire post offices and their user mailboxes to Exchange Server using migration tools that come with Exchange Server or you can link the legacy systems to Exchange Server, providing recipients on all sides with transparent access to each other. The Microsoft Mail Connector (MMC) supports the latter option.

The MMC creates and interacts with a shadow (emulated) Microsoft Mail post office on the Exchange server. Exchange sends and receives mail through the MMC using this shadow, which looks like an Exchange server to users on the Exchange side and looks like a Microsoft Mail 3.*x* post office to users on the MS Mail side. Microsoft Mail's EXTERNAL .EXE program or a version of EXTERNAL .EXE that runs as an NT service is used to transfer mail between the shadow and the real MS Mail post office. Connections can be either synchronous or asynchronous. If it can bear the traffic, you need only one MMC to link all your MS Mail post offices to the Exchange world.

Users of Microsoft Mail 3.*x* for AppleTalk Networks are linked in a similar manner. Once the connection is in place, the MMC gives AppleTalk Mail recipients full access to Exchange recipients, and vice versa.

Before we leave the MMC, I want to be sure you're aware of a third option for users of legacy Microsoft Mail for PC networks systems. This one requires neither whole post office migration nor use of the MMC. On a user-by-user basis, you can connect a user's Exchange client directly to both the user's Microsoft Mail and Exchange mailboxes. This lets the user send and receive messages from both the Microsoft Mail and Exchange systems. This option is best when you haven't got the time or other resources to migrate everyone in a Microsoft Mail post office to an Exchange server or to deal with the intricacies of the MMC.

cc:Mail Connector

The cc:Mail Connector works a lot like the Microsoft Mail Connector. It allows Exchange Server users to continue accessing messages in their Lotus/IBM cc:Mail post office. Like the Microsoft Mail Connector, the cc:Mail Connector is ideally suited to keeping access to a legacy mail system alive during migration to Exchange Server.

Schedule+ Free/Busy Connector

Microsoft Schedule+ lets users set up meetings with each other. It uses a graphical user interface to show, in aggregate fashion, the times available to users selected for a meeting. This information is available on Exchange servers and in Microsoft Mail for PC Networks post offices. The Free/Busy Connector, which is an extension of the MMC, lets Exchange servers and Microsoft Mail post offices share schedule information. You *can't* use the Free/Busy Connector for Exchange site connections, either directly or indirectly.

Exchange Gateways

Exchange Server supports X.400 and SMTP mail natively; to access other systems, you'll need *gateways*. Exchange Server gateways don't resemble the clunky DOS gates used with Microsoft Mail 3.*x*. Like the rest of Exchange Server, they run as processes on NT Server. As long as gateway developers know what they're doing (and that's sometimes a big assumption), gateways tend to be stable, robust, and fast.

Gateways are available for such services as Notes, PROFS, SNADS, and fax, as well as for pagers and voicemail. Microsoft produces some gateways, and third parties offer others. Keep in touch with Microsoft and the trade press for details.

EXCHANGE CLIENT COMPONENTS

As I've noted before, the real fun of Exchange is on the client side. That's where you get to see the business end of Exchange—from "simple" e-mail to complex, home-grown messaging-enabled applications. Exchange client components include:

- The Exchange client (currently incarnated as the *Outlook client*)
- POP3 and IMAP4 clients from Microsoft
- Schedule+
- The Microsoft Exchange and Outlook Forms Designers
- Microsoft Exchange and Outlook Forms Designer forms
- Other client-based applications

Here's a quick look at the Exchange client components from an architectural perspective. Figure 20.10 shows the clients and their functions graphically.

The Exchange Client

You receive, transmit, and access messages in the *Exchange client*. It's your window to your mailbox and to personal and public folders. The Exchange clients work with all versions of Exchange Server up to and including 5.5.

Exchange Server ships with clients for Macintosh, Microsoft/PC DOS, Windows 3.1x, and Windows NT and with an upgrade for the Exchange client that ships with Windows 95 (aka the Inbox or Windows Messaging). The upgrade adds a range of new features to the Windows 95 Exchange client, including out-of-office messaging, auto-signatures, and free-form rules.

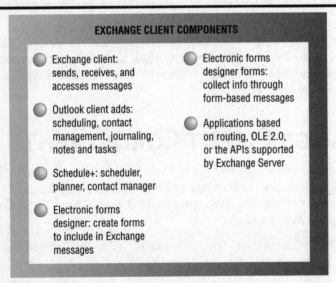

EXCHANGE CLIENT COMPONENTS

● Exchange client: sends, receives, and accesses messages

● Outlook client adds: scheduling, contact management, journaling, notes and tasks

● Schedule+: scheduler, planner, contact manager

● Electronic forms designer: create forms to include in Exchange messages

● Electronic forms designer forms: collect info through form-based messages

● Applications based on routing, OLE 2.0, or the APIs supported by Exchange Server

FIGURE 20.10: Exchange client components

TIP

Don't try to use the original Windows 95 client to access Exchange Server. It doesn't work. Upgrade to the Exchange Server version of the Windows 95 client. Trust me, it'll save you a lot of grief.

The Outlook clients are Microsoft's most current Exchange clients. They ship with Microsoft Office 97 and 2000 and, for some operating systems, with Exchange Server. Outlook nicely integrates electronic messaging, scheduling, and contact and task management with a whole bunch of other functions (like electronic journaling of every message you read or file you open). Take a look at Figures 18.1 and 18.2 in Chapter 18 for a refresher on Outlook's user interface. Outlook accesses the same directory and information store as the Exchange client. It does modify your Exchange mailbox, adding new folders for things like your schedule, contacts, and tasks. More important, it uses a differently structured schedule database, so you have to decide whether you're going to use the older Schedule+ or Outlook for scheduling and contact/task management.

POP3 and IMAP4 Clients from Microsoft

Microsoft Internet Explorer 4 and later come with Outlook Express. This lighter-weight client supports both POP3 and IMAP4 server access. Outlook 2000 includes support for both POP3 and IMAP4.

Schedule+

Schedule+ is a messaging-enabled application that includes scheduling, planning, and contact-management features. Version 7.5, the version that comes with Exchange Server, is a serious update of the original version, which was labeled "version 1.0" (Microsoft has a knack for skipping version numbers). Most of the improvements lie more in the way it handles features such as schedule viewing, printing, and to-do lists, and less in the program's already pretty decent collaborative-scheduling function.

TIP

Again, don't try to use the 7.0 version of Schedule+ that comes with Microsoft Office 95. Upgrade!

The Microsoft Exchange and Outlook Forms Designers

Users and developers can create forms with the Microsoft Exchange or Outlook Forms Designers. Forms created with the Designers can be used for a range of tasks, including the collection of data, and can have drop-down pick lists, multiple-choice selections, action buttons, and other useful attributes.

Microsoft Exchange and Outlook Forms Designer Forms

Forms created in the Microsoft Exchange and Outlook Forms Designers can be stored on servers and made available to all or select users, who can send them to specific recipients as messages or post them in folders for others to access. Users can manually collate data collected in forms; or, with the right programming, data can be automatically extracted from forms and processed. (Look back at Figure 18.10 in Chapter 18 for a glimpse into the wonderful world of electronic forms.)

Other Client-Based Applications

Aside from the Microsoft Exchange and Outlook Forms Designers, there are a variety of ways to build client-based applications using Exchange Server's messaging capabilities:

▶ Microsoft's version 95 and 97 stable of applications (Word, Excel, and so on) include some nice collaborative tools and easy-to-use routing-slip capabilities based on Exchange messaging. Applications from other vendors also incorporate these capabilities.

▶ You can turn an Exchange message into any OLE 2–compliant application just by inserting an object from the app into the message.

▶ You can write programs that use Simple and Extended MAPI or the X.400-oriented Common Mail Call APIs supported by Exchange Server.

NOTE

Exchange is a complex product. The cost of an Exchange installation will, of course, depend heavily on licensing fees imposed by Microsoft. Check with the company for all pricing details.

WHAT'S NEXT?

In this chapter, you got a grounding in the architecture of Exchange. You learned about the core and optional components on both the Exchange server and client sides. You also had a chance to learn how the components interact with each other. The knowledge you've gained here has more than theoretical value: It will help immensely as you move toward installing and managing a real-world Exchange environment. Chapter 21 focuses on Windows NT Server and how it integrates with Exchange Server.

Chapter 21

EXCHANGE AND WINDOWS NT SERVER

E xchange Server is part of Microsoft's BackOffice suite of products. Like other BackOffice applications—SQL Server and Systems Management Server, for example—Exchange Server runs only on top of Microsoft Windows NT Server. You can install Exchange Server's very nice Administrator program on an NT Workstation, but not Exchange Server itself. Windows 95? Windows 98? Forget it!

Adapted from *Mastering™ Microsoft® Exchange Server 5.5* by Barry Gerber

ISBN 0-7821-2658-8   916 pages $44.99

WHY NT SERVER?

NT Server has two key features not available in other Microsoft operating systems. The lack of these features does not make it impossible to run Exchange Server on, say, NT Workstation or Windows 95/98. Together, however, these features make NT Server the best platform for Exchange Server and Microsoft's other BackOffice products.

The key features? First, NT Server is optimized for lots of users. Second, it has some nice extended tools for ensuring the integrity of your disk system. Let's look at these features in more detail.

WHAT ABOUT WINDOWS 2000?

As I write, Microsoft's Windows 2000 is going through beta testing. 2000 is an exciting and innovative operating system with all the features of NT 4 and lots more. However, I strongly urge you to stick with NT 4 until Windows 2000 has had a complete version 1 shakedown. I remember with much dismay those scary blue screen crashes that killed NT 4 when Service Pack 2 was installed and a SCSI disk or tape device was accessed. If e-mail is a mission-critical application for your organization, don't tempt fate by using a brand new OS.

NT Server Can Handle Heavy Multiuser Loads

Servers tend to support lots of users. Server users make major demands on CPU, disk, and network resources. NT Server is optimized to move data within and between these resources even under heavy loads.

Because of this optimization, NT Server can handle a large number of simultaneously connected users—just how many is limited only by your hardware configuration and the number of connect licenses you've bought.

Because it lacks server-oriented optimization and because it *is* optimized for workstation functionality, NT Workstation is limited to a maximum of ten users. Some claim that this limitation is artificially low and designed to force users to buy NT Server so that Microsoft can make more money. I have to disagree. The price difference between NT Server and NT Workstation isn't great enough to justify such an argument.

Windows 95 and 98 are also optimized for workstation functionality, but I'm uncomfortable with their continued reliance on MS-DOS to support older hardware technologies. Windows 95/98 are great for user workstations running newer hardware and faster, more stable 32-bit applications; however, they do not have the stability to function as a platform for critical applications such as e-messaging.

NT Server Supports RAID Levels 1 and 5

Systems using redundant arrays of inexpensive disks (RAID) protect data by writing all or part of it to two or more drives. This ensures that the data can be recovered in case of a drive failure. When the bits in a byte of data are written to two or more drives, data is said to be *striped across* the drives.

There are at least five levels of RAID:

- ▶ *Level 1* mirrors data stored on one disk onto another disk and provides 100 percent duplication of data. The system usually has to be shut down to replace a failed mirrored drive with the mirroring drive; however, a shutdown isn't required with NT's level 1 RAID.

- ▶ *Level 2* uses data disks and extra check drives; data bits are striped across these drives *(bit-striped)*, along with information that allows 1-bit data errors to be fixed and 2-bit errors to be detected (though not fixed) on the fly. Level 2 RAID offers the best performance with large data blocks.

- ▶ *Level 3* uses a single redundant check disk for a group of data drives. Data is bit-striped across the data disks, and XORed (exclusive ORed) parity information for the data is stored on the check disk. If any drive fails, its data can be reconstructed from the remaining drives and the check disk.

▶ *Level 4* is similar to RAID level 3, but data is block- or sector-striped—instead of bit-striped—across disks. Level 4 is best for transaction processing.

▶ *Level 5* doesn't use dedicated check drives; rather, it distributes regular and check data over the drives in the array, based on an algorithm that allows data to be recovered when a failed drive is replaced. Level 5 RAID allows for simultaneous reads and writes of data to disks and is most efficient when handling small amounts of information.

If you show just about anyone these definitions of the various RAID levels, they'll probably tell you I'm all wet. But actually I'm quite dry; the problem is that specific RAID implementations never fully adhere to all the details of these general definitions. Don't worry, though: These definitions are more than adequate to help you understand how NT Server handles RAID.

RAID can be implemented in hardware or software. NT Server supports software-based disk mirroring and disk duplexing (RAID level 1), and disk striping with parity (RAID level 5).

Under *disk mirroring* you create a constantly updated copy of all or part of one hard drive on another drive; both drives are connected to the same disk controller. The copy lets you recover from a drive failure. With *disk duplexing* you do the same thing, but the drive being copied is connected to a different disk controller than the drive holding the copy. This eliminates the single point of controller failure you have with disk mirroring.

Disk striping with parity involves creating stripes on up to 32 drives, preferably connected to multiple disk controllers. Data is written in ordered bits across the stripes. Parity information lets you recover data stored on a failed drive using the remaining good drives. Depending on hardware, you can often swap out a bad drive with a good one without even turning off the computer's or drive system's power.

Another benefit of RAID, especially level 5, is better disk performance. A RAID system can improve disk access speeds by splitting reads and writes over multiple drives and multiple disk controllers. (In fact, Microsoft recommends using RAID level 5 disk striping to improve Exchange Server performance. More about this later.)

CONSIDER A STAND-ALONE HARDWARE RAID SYSTEM

You can purchase stand-alone hardware RAID systems for NT from a variety of third-party vendors. Third-party hardware RAID solutions won't let you run Exchange Server on top of NT Workstation or Windows 95/98, but they might give you better performance than NT Server's built-in software-based RAID functionality. This is especially likely if you run NT Server on a single-processor computer. Stand-alone hardware RAID systems don't eat up your computer's CPU time doing RAID.

Exchange is likely to be considered a critical application in your organization. You probably won't want to run it without the benefits of at least RAID level 1.

NOTE

You manage NT disks in general and RAID systems in particular using NT's Disk Administrator, which is located in NT's Administrative Tools program group. For more on the Disk Administrator, see the Sybex book *Mastering Windows NT Server 4*. And for more on mastering Windows NT Server 4, see the sidebar in this chapter brilliantly titled—yep—"Mastering Windows NT Server 4."

NT SERVER IS A PIECE OF CAKE

If you haven't had much (or any) experience with NT Server, don't let that bother you. It is quite simple to install—not much harder than installing Windows 95/98, in fact.

Once installed, NT Server is very easy to use. It comes outfitted with the complete Microsoft Windows graphical user interface (GUI) suite that is the spitting image of Windows 95/98. If you're comfortable with Windows 95/98, you'll be just fine with NT Server. Trust me.

Applications for NT—Exchange Server included—tend to build on the Windows GUI. Remember the neat GUI administrative front end for Exchange Server we looked at back in Chapters 18 and 19? With their GUI front ends, NT apps let you focus on the substantive task in front of you. That way, you don't have to spend all your time editing cryptic text files or cobbling together makeshift system monitoring or administration commands in the wide-open spaces of the operating system. (If it's not obvious, that last sentence was referring to UNIX.)

NT SPECIFICS FOR THE EXCHANGE SERVER CROWD

NT Server is a bundle of nifty components. To understand how NT Server and Exchange Server work together, you'll need a basic grounding in eight of these components:

- ▶ NT services
- ▶ NT networking
- ▶ Microsoft network domains
- ▶ NT User Manager for Domains
- ▶ NT Server Manager
- ▶ NT and multiprocessing
- ▶ NT Event Viewer
- ▶ NT Performance Monitor

Some of the eight key NT Server components are also available in NT Workstation. That's a nice plus. If you're not already an NT aficionado, by the time you're finished setting up NT Server and Exchange Server, you'll probably be ready to make NT Workstation your desktop operating system. I've even gone a step further. My office, home, and laptop workstations run NT Server. I'll wait while you get back up off your knees after paying homage to yours truly. Anyway, for you NT converts-in-the-making, the following detailed discussion of the eight components is a kind of two-for-one deal: It'll help you get comfortable with both NT Server and your future NT Workstation machine at the same time. And just so you know when a particular component is available only in NT Server, I'll use the words *NT Server* as opposed to *NT* when discussing it. (I'm just loaded with brilliant ideas.)

MASTERING WINDOWS NT SERVER 4

The eight NT Server components discussed in this chapter are far from all you'll ever want or need to know about NT. For the definitive word on NT Server, get a copy of Sybex's *Mastering Windows NT Server 4*. The authors—Mark Minasi, Christa Anderson, and Elizabeth Creegan—manage to make learning about a complex operating system both relatively painless and, believe it or not, fun.

I decided to have Sybex publish my book partly because I liked *Mastering Windows NT Server 4* so much. The deal was cinched when the company assured me that I'd have the same stylistic freedom given to Minasi, et al. I got that freedom, and I hope you'll like this book as much as I enjoyed *Mastering Windows NT Server 4*.

NT Services

NT is a full-blown, preemptive, multitasking, multithreaded operating system that's able to run many tasks or processes simultaneously. Many of the processes that run on NT are called *services*. Services can run all the time the computer is on, or they may be started and stopped manually as needed by those with the appropriate rights. Network protocol services, the computer's login services, and many applications, such as client/server databases and tape backup and virus protection programs, run as NT services. And—you guessed it—Exchange Server is a set of NT services as well.

The NT Control Panel includes a little Services icon. When you double-click it, an applet starts up with a window that displays all available NT services. Within this window you can check to see if a service is running, stop and start services, and set a service's default configuration (that is, whether it starts on boot-up, can be manually started, or is disabled). Figure 21.1 shows the Services applet in action on the GerCom Exchange server.

Don't worry about how services get created or integrated into the operating system; it's the responsibility of the application provider to make sure this happens. And don't get the idea that the NT Services applet is the only way to monitor Exchange Services. No way. As you'll see, Exchange comes with a bunch of its own service monitoring tools.

Part iv

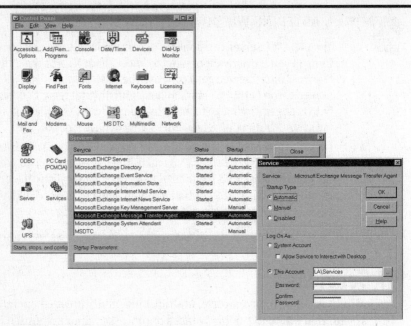

FIGURE 21.1: The NT Services applet is used to monitor and control Exchange Server components.

NT Networking

NT provides support for a range of networking protocols. These include IPX/SPX, NetBEUI, TCP/IP, and (with optional software) SNA networks. Third parties provide other networking protocols for NT Server, including DECnet and XNS.

NT also supports a set of standard remote procedure calls (RPCs) that enable client/server communications between programs running on the same or different computers. RPC-based communications move with equal ease across hardware platforms, operating systems, and networking protocols.

All Exchange client-to-server communications and some Exchange server-to-server communications—intrasite directory replication, for example—are based on the RPCs. The RPCs support only direct links between Exchange servers (as *direct* was defined in Chapter 20). The RPCs can run on top of IPX/SPX, NetBEUI, TCP/IP, or SNA. The RPCs can also work over other network layers that are not transport protocols—for example, Named Pipes or Sockets. In Figure 21.2 you can see how the RPCs work in an Exchange system and use the networking protocols supported by NT. See the sidebar "NT's RPCs and Exchange" for more on this RPC set, which is so central to Exchange.

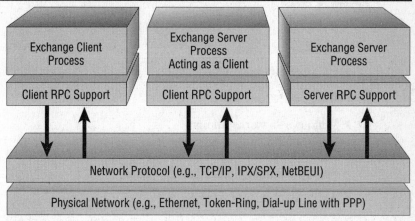

FIGURE 21.2: How NT's RPCs and Microsoft networking support Exchange Server

One of the really impressive parts of NT networking is the Remote Access Server (RAS). The RAS supports client-to-server and server-to-server links based on slower connect options. It works with standard phone lines, ISDN, X.25, and RS-232C null modems. Key supported protocols include NetBEUI, TCP/IP, and IPX/SPX—all on top of the Point-to-Point Protocol (PPP). One NT Server can have up to 256 RAS connections. (For the record, NT Workstation supports only one RAS connection.) As you'll see later, the RAS is a key part of Exchange's connectivity options.

NT networking, like Microsoft networking in general, is quite simple. If you've got a network adapter in your computer, you're asked what kind of networking you want when you install NT Server. If you understand basic networking concepts—for example, how to set up a TCP/IP node—you'll have little, if any, trouble with NT networking.

Part iv

Microsoft Network Domains

Microsoft network domains both organize and provide centralized administration and security for groups of resources. Resources include computers, the programs running on them, and the peripherals attached to them. Windows and DOS workstations integrate best into Microsoft networks.

Computers in Microsoft networks can include

- ▶ Windows NT servers

- ▶ Novell NetWare servers

- ▶ Windows NT workstations

- ▶ Windows 95 workstations

- ▶ Windows 3.11 workstations

- ▶ MS-DOS workstations

- ▶ Apple Macintoshes

Peripherals include disk drives and the files on them, as well as printers.

NT'S RPCS AND EXCHANGE

Exchange relies heavily on Microsoft's implementation of the OSF's DCE RPC API. Talk about alphabet soup! Translation: Exchange depends on Microsoft's version of the Open Software Foundation's (OSF's) Distributed Computing Environment (DCE) remote procedure call (RPC) application programming interface (API). That's quite a mouthful, so I'll use the term "OSF RPCs" from here on to avoid drowning you in a sea of acronyms.

In general, remote procedure calls support client-server computing. The OSF RPCs aren't suitable for all client-server applications, because to work they require direct, synchronous (continuous) connections between clients and servers. You can't use the OSF RPCs in a situation where you want to assign a task to a server, disconnect from the server, and then go about your work until the server contacts you to return the results of the task you assigned it. You've got to remain linked to the server during the entire process. So the OSF RPCs are not well suited to things like client-server databases; in fact, Microsoft uses other RPCs to support its SQL Server database.

CONTINUED ➡

There are OSF RPCs for clients as well as servers. NT Server, NT Workstation, and Windows 95/98 support both the client and server RPC sets. The other Microsoft operating systems support only the client RPC sets.

Client and server versions of the OSF RPCs are available for a wide range of operating systems, which means that Microsoft can more easily write Exchange clients and servers for non-Microsoft operating systems. This is key to the company's development of Exchange clients for the Apple Macintosh.

NOTE

Microsoft's NT Server Enterprise Edition adds new stability and reliability to NT. Servers can be clustered so that if one fails, the other can take over.

Microsoft networks are built around *domains.* A Microsoft network can have one or many domains, each of which is a logically separate entity. A resource in a Microsoft network can belong to one and only one domain.

Generally, domain users log in to domains, not to the individual machines in a domain. Domains can make life easier both for users and for system managers. Users don't have to remember more than one password to access any resource in the domain (unless it is protected by a special password). System managers can centrally create and administer user accounts for the domain.

Domains also make interserver communications easy. If servers live in the same domain, each has to log in to the domain only once in order to communicate with all other servers in the domain—unless, of course, a special password is required for specific communications.

Domains require *domain controllers,* which is where

▶ NT administrators:

　▶ Create and manage accounts for domain users

　▶ Set access rights for domain resources

▶ The NT Server operating system:

　▶ Stores user account information for the domain

Part iv

▶ Stores resource access rights for the domain

▶ Authenticates domain users

▶ Enforces access rights for domain resources

Of all the resources in a Microsoft network domain, only NT servers can be domain controllers; while every NT server needn't be a domain controller, every domain controller *must* be an NT server. Exchange Server can optionally be installed on an NT server that is a domain controller. That way, you can set up a simple Exchange system using just one NT server.

It's considered good practice to have at least one backup controller in each domain. Backup domain controllers stay in sync with the primary controller and take over if the primary controller fails. They can also perform authentication in parallel with the primary and other backup domain controllers. This helps balance the load in systems with large numbers of users.

As you'll see later, domains are key to using and administering Exchange. Domain and Exchange security are tightly integrated—to see just how tightly, take a look at Figure 21.3, which shows the Exchange Administrator being used to create both a new Exchange mailbox and a new domain user account for the mailbox.

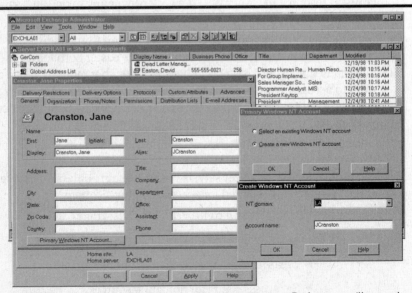

FIGURE 21.3:   The Exchange Administrator creates a new Exchange mailbox and domain user.

Cross-Domain Trusts

When one domain (called the *trusting* domain) trusts another (the *trusted* domain), it accepts the other domain's authentication of a user or server. The user or server doesn't have to log in to the trusting domain to access its resources; one login to a trusted domain is enough to access all available resources in a trusting domain, unless access to a resource is specifically limited by a special password.

Figure 21.4 shows how cross-domain trust relationships make it easier for users and servers to access resources across a network. The users and servers in domain B (the trusted domain) can access resources in domain A (the trusting domain) without using additional passwords. Note that the figure's arrowhead points to the trusted domain and away from the trusting domain.

Trusts are not only good for users, they're just what the doctor ordered for busy system administrators as well. Trusts expand the reach of administrators in creating and maintaining user accounts. After setting up a trust relationship between domains, an administrator can, in one fell swoop, create a user in one domain and give that user access to all other trusting domains.

Trust relationships have all kinds of implications for the way users and systems managers operate day to day. For example, with the right kind of trust relationship and security rights you can administer Exchange not on a domain-by-domain basis, but from a multidomain or network-level perspective.

Also, trust relationships are key to cross-domain interaction between Exchange servers. With the appropriate trust relationships and rights in place, Exchange servers in different domains can interact to Exchange messages and cross-replicate directories and public folders.

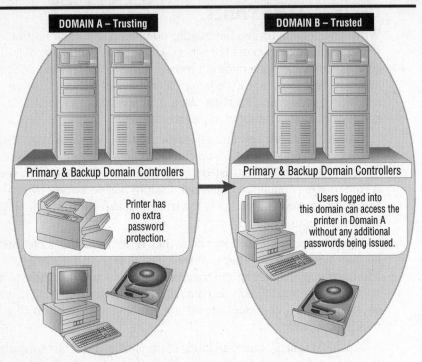

FIGURE 21.4:   Trust relationships open a network to users.

Domain Models

There are four domain models for Microsoft networks:

- ► Single-domain model
- ► Master-domain model
- ► Multiple-master domain model
- ► Complete-trust domain model

Let's look at each model in detail.

The Single-Domain Model

Single-domain systems have no need for trust relationships because there is only one isolated domain. See Figure 21.5 for a graphical depiction of a network with a single domain.

The single-domain model is best in situations that have no organizational or technical need for a segmented network. The maximum number of users in a domain is limited pretty much by the hardware your domain controller runs on. The more users you have, the larger your domain security tables become; in addition, you'll need more powerful hardware (CPU, RAM, and disks) to plow through the tables when authenticating users. Depending on the hardware you use and based on hardware capabilities current as of December 1999, you can expect to support up to 26,000 users if all users are using NT Workstation and/or NT Server in a domain.

Once you're running your primary and backup domain controllers on the most powerful hardware you can find or afford, the only way to support more users is by moving either to the multiple-master domain model or the complete-trust domain model. I'll discuss these two in just a bit, but first let's look at the master-domain model.

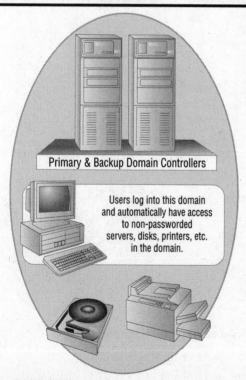

Primary & Backup Domain Controllers

Users log into this domain
and automatically have access
to non-passworded
servers, disks, printers, etc.
in the domain.

FIGURE 21.5: A network based on the single-domain model

The Master-Domain Model

Master-domain systems include one administrative domain and one or more resource domains where servers and workstations are located. The master domain handles all security tasks. It is a trusted domain, while all other domains are trusting. See Figure 21.6 for a diagram of a master-domain system.

The master-domain model is most appropriate in organizations that need to segment resources (say, by department or geographically) and that have a centralized MIS department. Each department or geographical unit can have its own domain, while MIS administers from the master domain. Note that even though this model has multiple domains, there is only one administrative domain—so you're still limited to 15,000 to 40,000 users per domain.

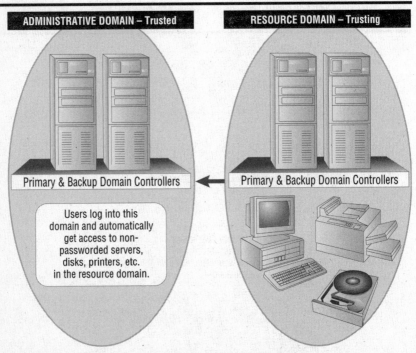

| ADMINISTRATIVE DOMAIN – Trusted | RESOURCE DOMAIN – Trusting |

Primary & Backup Domain Controllers ← Primary & Backup Domain Controllers

Users log into this domain and automatically get access to non-passworded servers, disks, printers, etc. in the resource domain.

FIGURE 21.6: A network based on the master-domain model

The Multiple-Master Domain Model

Multiple-master domain systems have two or more master domains and two or more resource domains. Each master domain is responsible for some portion of users based on a logical segmenting factor—for example, the first letter of the user's last name, or the geographical breakdown of the company. Each resource domain trusts all the master domains. Figure 21.7 depicts the multiple-master domain model. Here the master domains trust each other and are trusted by both of the resource domains. This is not required, however; each master domain can be trusted by either one or a set of resource domains. In the figure, for example, Administrative Domain #1 could be trusted only by Resource Domain #1, while Administrative Domain #2 could be trusted by both resource domains.

In many cases, you'll also want two-way trusts between the master domains. That way, system administrators with appropriate rights can create new users, and so on, in any master domain as needed.

The multiple-master domain model works best for larger organizations that need to segment both resources and MIS administration. Resource domains are often based on departmental divisions.

Multiple-master domains are a way around limits on the maximum number of users per domain. So if your domain controller hardware limits you to 40,000 users per domain, *each* master domain can handle up to 40,000 users. With two domains you're up to 80,000 users, and so on.

Multiple-master domains also allow MIS administration to divide the task of managing domains into smaller units. This tends to reduce the likelihood of error and lets large multinational organizations spread the management tasks across geographical and sociopolitical boundaries.

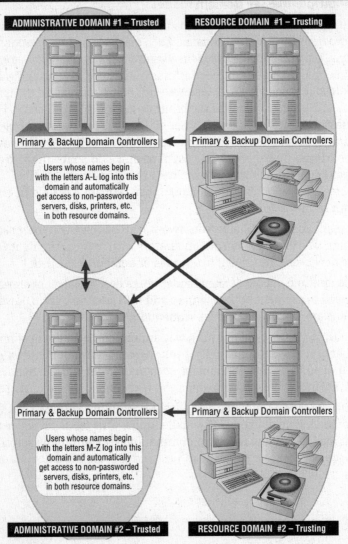

FIGURE 21.7:   A network based on the multiple-master domain model

The Complete-Trust Domain Model

Complete-trust domain systems consist of several domains; each domain handles its own security administration. Since this model has no master domains, all domains must be both trusted and trusting. Figure 21.8 shows a system based on the complete-trust domain model.

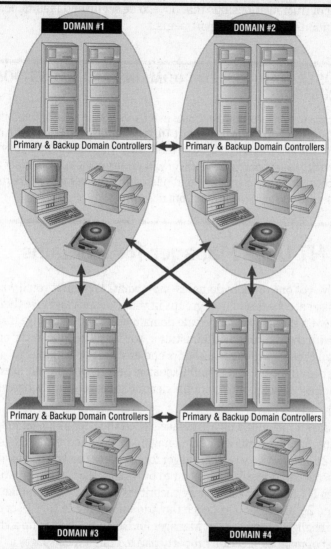

FIGURE 21.8: A network based on the complete-trust domain model

Complete-trust domain systems are appropriate when an organization lacks central MIS administration and is segmented in some way—by department, for example. Each department is a domain, and control of the domain is in the hands of the department. Each domain can have up to the maximum number of users its domain controller hardware will support. The major drawback of complete-trust domain systems is the number of trust relationships that have to be set up and maintained in organizations with lots of departments.

USER MANAGER FOR DOMAINS AND CROSS-DOMAIN TRUSTS

You set up cross-domain trusts in NT's User Manager for Domains. From the Policies menu, select Trust Relationships. From there it's a no-brainer, as long as you've really got other domains and they're on the same continuous local or wide area network. You can set up both trusted and trusting relationships for the domain you're running the User Manager for Domains from.

The NT User Manager for Domains

So you've got one or more domains—now what? Well, first you'll want to create user accounts and user groups in your domains and give them rights. Even though you can create domain users and Exchange mailboxes with the Exchange Administrator, you'll still need to know how to create and manage domain accounts and groups. For example, as you'll see later—even before you install Exchange Server—you'll want to create a domain-based user group to administer and manage your Exchange servers.

NT Server includes a nice interface, called the User Manager for Domains, for administering and managing domain accounts and groups. Figure 21.9 shows how User Manager for Domains can be used to add a new user account to a domain. Just to prove that the tight integration between NT Server and Exchange security is a two-way street, take a look at Figure 21.10. As soon as I click the Add button in the New User dialog box, Exchange—through User Manager for Domains—brings up a standard set of mailbox-creation property pages. I fill in these pages as needed, then click OK in the mailbox's Properties dialog box, and I've created a new domain user and an Exchange mailbox all at once.

Though the actual domain account information is stored on an NT server, you can run the User Manager for Domains on an NT Workstation as well. (I'm running it on my NT Workstation in Figures 21.9 and 21.10.) This is just one of the ways you can manage an NT server remotely. As you'll find out later in this chapter, Exchange Server also supports a lot of remote management functions. In fact, remote management is one of the most impressive features of both products.

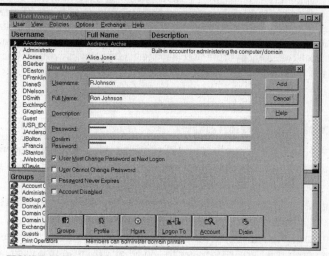

FIGURE 21.9: Adding a user to a domain with the User Manager for Domains

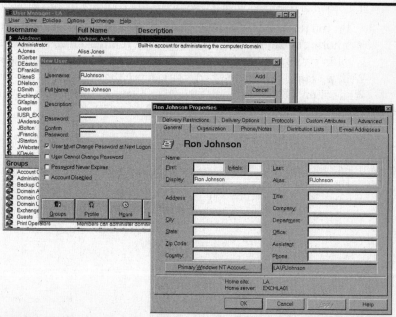

FIGURE 21.10: The User Manager for Domains lets you set up an Exchange mailbox for a new user.

> **NOTE**
>
> Although it runs on NT Workstation machines, User Manager for Domains comes only with NT Server. You can borrow it from one of your NT servers, or you can use the copy of the User Manager for Domains that's included in Microsoft's optional NT Resource Kit. The kit, worth its purchase price even if you don't need a copy of the User Manager for Domains, is available from a variety of sources. Check with Microsoft for more information.

The NT Server Manager

The Server Manager is another one of those wonderful NT management tools that can run remotely. It lets you see what's happening on other servers and allows you to make certain changes on those servers.

In Figure 21.11, I'm running the Server Manager from my NT Workstation. You'll notice that we're looking at the domain LA; the servers and workstations in LA are listed on the upper left-hand side of the screen. Here I'm using the Server Manager to see what's up resource-wise on my Exchange server, EXCHLA02. You'll notice that I have the option of disconnecting one or more of the shared resources. I might choose to do this if a problem occurred with a resource that I couldn't fix any other way.

Do you remember our earlier discussion of the Control Panel applet for monitoring and administering the services running on an NT machine? Wouldn't it be neat if we could use the applet for remote computers, too? Well, we can't. But not to worry: We can use the Server Manager instead. While at my NT Workstation (shown in Figure 21.12), I can stop an Exchange Server process on EXCHLA02. I love it!

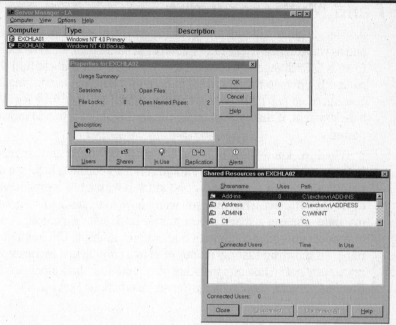

FIGURE 21.11: Using the Server Manager to remotely monitor shared resources

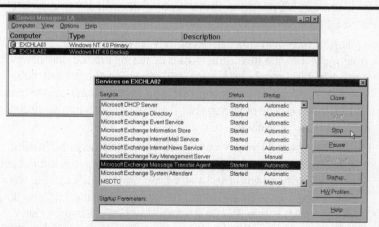

FIGURE 21.12: Remotely administering Exchange Server services using the
Server Manager

NT and Multiprocessing

As users begin to take advantage of the great features built into Exchange and as you add new users and tasks—an Exchange connector, for example—to an NT/Exchange server, you'll find yourself scrambling to find the computing horsepower you need to keep everyone and everything happy. You can often pep up a server by adding more RAM and/or a RAID level 5 disk system. If that isn't enough, the next best bet is to add processing power.

When you know the load on an Exchange server will grow significantly in the span of a year or so, you should seriously consider buying a multi-processing system, even if you don't outfit it with a full complement of CPUs at the outset. That way, you won't have to upgrade to a whole new machine—you can just add processors when demands increase. A number of vendors now offer computers that support multiple-CPU configurations. To show you that my money or at least my clients' money is where my mouth is, I've taken to insisting on a minimum dual-processor Pentium machine for the Exchange Server installations I set up.

The NT Event Viewer

Like all good operating systems, NT logs a variety of things that happen as it runs. In NT parlance, these "things" are called *events*. Event *logging* is just another NT service.

Three kinds of events can occur in NT: system, security, and application. *System events* include activities centering around disk drives, network adapters, serial ports, mice, and other peripheral hardware. *Security events* are attempts by users and NT processes to enter the system. *Application events* can be anything that the authors of an application that runs on an NT machine choose to log.

You use the NT Event Viewer, which you can find in NT's Administrative Tools program group, to look at events. You pick the kind of event—system, security, or application—that you want to look at from the Event Viewer's Log menu. To see details about a particular event, you double-click the event. Figure 21.13 shows the Application Log for the NT/Exchange server EXCHLA01.

Each event shown in the Event Viewer is given what might be called an "attention level." Events included solely for informational use are flagged with a little blue icon that has a lowercase letter *i* inside it. Events that require some attention are marked with a yellow exclamation-mark icon. Events that have failed or for some other reason require serious attention are flagged with a red stop-sign icon. Events marked with a little key concern application-level security. Figure 21.13 shows the successful loading of a component of Exchange Server's Web service, which lets users access their mailboxes and schedules with a Web browser.

You can do lots of other useful things with the Event Viewer, such as applying filters to check only some events. For now, though, we'll focus on another of the Event Viewer's great capabilities: You can use it to look at other computers in domains you have access to. In fact, although we're viewing the NT server EXCHLA01 in Figure 21.13, the Event Viewer is actually running on my NT Workstation.

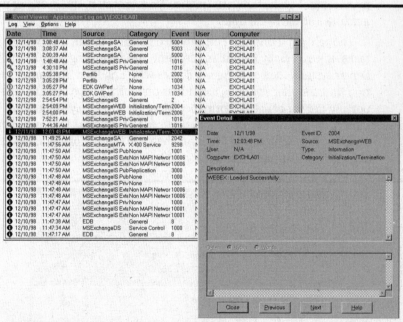

FIGURE 21.13: The Event Viewer shows the Application Log for an NT/Exchange server.

KEEP THOSE ICONS IN VIEW

I keep shortcuts for User Manager for Domains, Server Manager, Event Viewer, and Performance Monitor on my desktop. A shortcut for Exchange Administrator also occupies a place of honor on my desktop. I use these five apps so often that it's a pain to have to navigate NT 4's Start menu to find them.

The NT Performance Monitor

NT's Performance Monitor is a graphically oriented application that lets you monitor hundreds of activities on an NT machine. Like other NT management tools, the Performance Monitor can monitor one or more machines at the same time.

Though you'll find the Performance Monitor useful for a variety of tasks, it's especially helpful in planning and managing your Exchange Server system. Exchange Server comes with LoadSim, a planning application that simulates various user loads on an Exchange server and a supporting network. The Performance Monitor is one way to measure the impact of these loads. Load-measurement parameters for e-messaging are added to the Performance Monitor when you install LoadSim. Figure 21.14 shows the Performance Monitor and LoadSim in action.

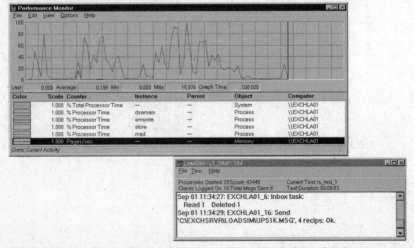

FIGURE 21.14: The Performance Monitor and LoadSim help in planning an Exchange system.

Exchange Server also adds several measurement parameters of its own to the Performance Monitor, letting you monitor certain aspects of the performance and health of an Exchange server. For the record, you'll also use the Exchange Administrator program for some monitoring tasks.

What's Next?

In this chapter you learned why Exchange Server runs only on top of NT Server and how easy NT Server is to use. You also had a chance to become familiar with a number of NT Server components and to see how important they are to Exchange Server. This information, combined with what you've learned in previous chapters, will help you in planning and implementing your Exchange system. In the next chapter, you will learn how to design your Exchange system using an 11-step process and detailed examples.

Chapter 22

DESIGNING AN EXCHANGE SYSTEM

Whether your system will be based on a single Exchange server in a single site or hundreds of Exchange servers spread out over multiple sites, you need to consider a number of design issues before implementation. This chapter presents a planning model based loosely on an 11-step process developed by Microsoft. Tracking and re-tracking through these steps will help your organization decide where it wants to go with electronic messaging and how it can get there with Exchange. I can tell you from lots of experience that the 11-step process really works. Generally, I've found I can gather any required information and generate a fairly complex first-draft plan, complete with a most convincing executive summary in a week or less.

This chapter isn't just about design, though. It also offers practical information about Exchange and how it works. Here, for example, you'll find detailed information about Exchange's seemingly endless network connection options: what they do and which networking topologies and protocols support them. Information like this is central to designing and implementing an Exchange system. If you're going to skip a chapter, please—not this one. This is a long chapter covering a great deal of information in detail. Just as you wouldn't try to implement a complex Exchange system in one day, you shouldn't try to plow through this chapter in one hour.

Here, then, with more than a little poetic license, is a list of Microsoft's 11 steps to designing an Exchange system:

1. Assess the needs of users in your organization.

2. Study your organization's geographical profile.

3. Assess your organization's network.

4. Establish naming conventions.

5. Select a Microsoft networking domain model.

6. Define site boundaries.

7. Plan intersite links.

8. Plan servers and internal connections to them.

9. Plan connections to other systems.

10. Validate and optimize your design.

11. Roll out the plan.

Now let's discuss each of these steps in more detail. This discussion builds upon the 11-step process presented by Microsoft in the Exchange documentation and other Microsoft publications, but it is far from a word-for-word regurgitation. Therefore, you should blame me—not Microsoft—if you encounter any problems from following the advice I give in this chapter. (Of course, if this stuff helps in any way, you should send the fruit baskets and such to *me*.)

EXCHANGE DESIGN IS ITERATIVE, NOT LINEAR

Throughout this chapter, remember that designing an Exchange system is not a linear process, it's an iterative one. You'll find yourself coming back to each of the steps to gather new information, to reinterpret information you've already gathered, and to collect even more information based on those reinterpretations. New information will likely lead to design changes and further iterations. Even after you've fully implemented Exchange, you'll return to steps in the design process as problems arise or as your organization changes.

Within reason, the more iterations you go through, the better your final design will be. But take care not to use iteration as a route to procrastination. Whatever you do, start running Exchange—if only in a limited test environment—as soon as you can.

ASSESS USER NEEDS

Here you're interested in who needs what, when they need it, and how you'll provide it. You'll want to get a handle on the programming, software, hardware, MIS systems, systems support, and training resources that will be required to satisfy user needs.

Remember that Exchange is an e-messaging package, not just an e-mail product. Users may need specific e-messaging-enabled applications. Depending on what they have in mind, application development can be a real resource hog. Also remember that, in some cases, hardware and software may require new workstations, not just new servers.

Be prepared to give users a clear idea of what Exchange can do. You don't need to get technical with most users; just give them a view of Exchange from the end user's perspective. Take another look at the first two sections of Chapter 18 to see how you might organize your presentation.

One of the biggest mistakes most people make when implementing a system is to ignore or give only passing attention to the assessment-of-user-needs step. Knowing as much as you can about what the users require up front means you'll have an easier time during implementation.

For example, imagine that you don't know from the get-go that your organization could benefit significantly from a particular custom-programmed e-messaging-enabled application. You'd go ahead and implement Exchange as an e-mail system with only the resources such an implementation requires. You'd get your Exchange system up and it would be perking along just fine when suddenly—maybe three months later—some user comes up with this great idea for an e-messaging-enabled app.

Boink! Suddenly you have to tell management that you need a few programmers and maybe more hardware to implement this—"er, um, idea nobody thought of four or five months ago." I'll leave the rest to your imagination.

NOTE

Whatever you find out in your user-needs assessment, add a fudge factor in favor of more hardware and support personnel. Exchange has so many fantastic capabilities that you can be sure your users will find all kinds of ways to challenge whatever resources you make available. Depending on your users and their ability to get away with unplanned demands for resources, fudging by as much as 25 percent is reasonable.

Suffice it to say that a user-needs assessment is the single most important part of the Exchange design process. Because it is, we'll cover it in more detail than the other 10 Exchange design steps.

Questions to Ask

There are a number of questions you'll want to answer during your user-needs assessment. Here are the major ones:

1. What kinds of users (for example, managers, salespeople, clerical staff, lawyers, doctors) does my organization have, and what do they think they want from the new Exchange system?

2. What sorts of e-messaging services are different groups of users likely to need (for example, e-mail, calendars and scheduling, public folders, specially designed applications)?

3. Which specially designed applications can be developed by users, and which must be developed by MIS personnel?

4. Do all users need every capability from day one, or can implementation be phased in—perhaps based on user groupings from question 1 above?

5. What sorts of demands are users (or groups of users) going to put on your Exchange servers? Much of the information in this category can be used with Exchange Server's Load-Sim program to simulate expected server load and thus project server hardware and networking requirements.

   ▶ How many users will there be per server?

   ▶ How many sent messages will there be per user per day?

   ▶ How many received messages will there be per user per day?

   ▶ How frequently will users send messages:

      ▶ to others on their server?

      ▶ to others in their site?

      ▶ to others at each of the other sites in your organization?

      ▶ to others outside your organization? Be sure to break this down by the different kinds of external connections you'll have (see steps 7 and 9).

   ▶ How often will users read messages in their mailboxes?

   ▶ How often will users read messages in public folders?

   ▶ How often will users move messages to personal folders stored locally and on the network?

   ▶ How often will users move messages to public folders?

   ▶ How big will the messages be? What percentage will be 1K in size, 2K, 4K, 10K with attachments, or 100K with attachments?

6. What level of message delivery service will users want and need? This should be stated in hours or minutes between the time a message is sent and received. You'll need to specify this for both internal and external communications.

7. What sorts of hardware and software resources (for example, computers, operating systems, Exchange client licenses) will different groups of users need to implement Exchange on the client side?

8. What kinds of training will be required for users or groups of users?

9. What sorts of MIS resources will be required to support user needs?

An Example: Assessing GerCom's User Needs

Throughout this chapter we'll use a set of examples based on GerCom, the fictitious little company I created for this book. Though the examples are not real, they are based on my own experience in implementing e-messaging systems, including Exchange. The examples are illustrative, not exhaustive; they don't cover every conceivable issue you might encounter in designing your own Exchange system.

Tracking through Microsoft's 11 design steps can be interesting, exciting—even exhilarating. It also can be as boring as watching glue dry. So I'll try to leaven my GerCom examples with a bit of humor. Hey, it's my company; I can do as I like with it, right? Anyway, as you read along, please keep in mind that I'm not making fun of a very important process—I'm just trying to keep an artificial example from becoming dried glue.

What GerCom Users Need to Do

In our user-needs assessment, we at GerCom uncovered several user groups with different needs. Here are some highlights of our assessment.

Our top-level execs, led by little old me, are small in number but big in ideas when it comes to Exchange. We want to do e-mail and apps based on the collaborative tools built into Exchange and both Word and Excel 2000. Our controller has this great idea about building a system in Exchange-enabled Excel that lets employees act on their stock options. This system would play against our financials, which run on an Oracle database on a UNIX server. The controller would also like to use an Exchange-Excel system to collaboratively develop annual budgets. And he and I are thinking about more elaborate, custom-programmed Exchange-enabled workflow apps for things like purchasing. Again, there would be a lot of interaction with our Oracle financials.

Our vice president of human resources is one of those power users—always coming up with ideas that no one else ever thought of. She wants to put, say, the personnel manual and all the forms we use into public folders. Then employees could read the latest copy of the manual or get a form they need. Some forms, like those for our internally administered health insurance, would be full-blown Exchange or Outlook Forms Designer forms. People would select one of these while in their Exchange client, fill it in, and send it off using the default address built into the form. Forms like all those "W-something" whatsits from the IRS would just be legal electronic copies that people can fill in, print, sign, and return by—gag—our internal snail-mail system.

WHY NOT THE INTERNET?

You might be wondering why GerCom doesn't just put all its forms and such on the Internet. Well, while I'm the last one to disparage the Web, I don't believe it's the best place for all internal business processes. People work in their e-mail all the time. They usually have to start their browsers to go after Web stuff. Not only can users easily find what they need in public folders, they can easily interact with corporate staff and processes simply by filling in an e-mail-enabled form.

GerCom execs travel a lot (too much if you ask the board of directors or other employees), so we want to be able to dial in to send and pick up our Exchange messages and use those Exchange-based applications we've come up with. There are several ways to dial into an Exchange server from Microsoft's Exchange client, using either the company's Remote Access Server or the Internet. However, the Exchange client is a bit of a disk- and RAM-resource hog for less well-endowed portable PCs. So for our road warriors, we're strongly considering standardizing on the Internet-based IMAP4 client that comes as part of Microsoft's Outlook 2000 or Internet Explorer 5 Outlook Express application. We'll also take advantage of the Web browser–based access to Exchange server that's been around since Exchange 5.

We execs want our clerical staff to do e-mail and to be able to create forms with Outlook Forms Designer. My secretary came up with a great idea for using an e-mailed form to collect personal information about employees. No, we're not one of those super-snooper kind of companies; we just like to recognize things like spouses' and kids' birthdays and such. The clerical staff also came up with the idea of using Microsoft

Outlook's e-messaging-enabled Calendar capabilities to do group scheduling and room reservations. They hate the combination of phone tag and written messages now used to set up meetings.

Our systems people expect the executive suite to be a heavy user of Exchange. I haven't seen all the numbers they've come up with from LoadSim yet, but rumor is they're considering giving us our own Exchange server. Since I know the boss intimately, I'm sure I can get him to sign off on that one.

The salespeople have some big ideas, too. They want in-office and remote e-mail like the top execs, but they also want to use Exchange for customer ordering and to keep copies of our price lists stored on customers' computers automatically updated. We're still not quite sure how we'll do it, but we do know we'll need some way of linking to those customers. The sales staff also wants to build an e-messaging-based system in which customers can place orders and pay for purchases. That would involve our Oracle-based ordering and payables systems. As president, I like that one, especially the payment part.

GerCom's marketing folks mainly want e-mail so they can send press releases to all those magazine editors who would rather never see another press release. We showed them some of the other stuff you can do with Exchange, but they couldn't seem to come up with any apps. So we told them that unless they could make a good argument for other apps over the next few weeks, they'd have to live with only e-mail for a while. They seem happy.

The manufacturing people are really excited about Exchange. I never mentioned it, but GerCom makes Enter keys—you know, the little key on your computer keyboard marked ↵. (Hey, it's a really specialized world out there.) Anyway, the manufacturing folks figure Exchange will provide a good way to link their production plans and inventory to the sales department's customer ordering system. Manufacturing wants to be able to send customers automatic updates on shipping dates. A copy will go to sales, of course. Manufacturing figures this will both keep customers happy and keep our aggressive salespeople out of their faces. We accepted this proposal, though we know it's going to take some custom programming involving our Oracle data. Of course, manufacturing also wants in-house e-mail.

For some reason, GerCom's engineering department hasn't been able to come up with a use for Exchange other than in-office e-mail. Well, what do you expect from a bunch of people who spend most of their working hours trying to improve the Enter key?

The MIS department wants in-house and remote e-mail, and it has a bunch of ideas of its own about Exchange. For example, it's tired of printing and routing all those Oracle reports most people ignore. MIS wants to develop an app that downloads electronic copies of those reports to the NT environment, puts them into specific Exchange public folders, and then sends out an electronic form telling recipients that the latest report has arrived.

Why a form and not a message? There'll be a field on the form where recipients can indicate that they don't need the report anymore. The form will be programmed to automatically remove those recipients who don't want the report from its Exchange distribution list. There'll also be a place to put ideas about changing the report or new reports. Pretty neat. The MIS people have not only eliminated a lot of increasingly expensive paper, they've also come up with a way to keep the reporting process alive and responsive to changing needs.

Supporting GerCom's User Needs

Whew! Our users have a lot of great ideas. Now we should begin laying out some specific things we'll need to support their needs. We won't go into detail on things like network connections, server hardware needs, or systems support personnel; those come later. For now, we just need to cover things like acceptable message delivery performance, end-user support personnel, and end-user hardware.

A lot of the apps we're planning are going to be pretty critical to GerCom's bottom line. We've decided we want messages to move between our offices and to our trading partners at a good speed—within ten minutes, if at all possible.

We already know it'll take about six new MIS people just to serve the needs of our 2,500 employees. Two of these will be involved in initial training and then in supporting users who want to develop their own apps. The other four will focus on programming custom apps. We've got plenty of space for these new folks, so we won't have any serious added costs on that front. We will, however, have to buy these new employees some hefty hardware. And we'll have to outfit our training rooms with beefier systems.

We've also decided to hire a corporate Exchange manager who will report to the director of MIS. The six people I mentioned above will report to the Exchange manager, as will any other Exchange-related personnel we add.

Part iv

We're also trying to decide what to do about user workstations. Someone suggested we cancel all executive travel to pay for new machines for everyone. (I can't imagine where they got that idea.) We probably won't do that, but I'm working with the controller to try to figure out how we can upgrade everyone who needs a new computer (about 75 percent of our employees) in the next year and a half. It will involve lots of bucks, but GerCom's going to gain a great deal from this system, and the Enter key business is really hot right now. That year-and-a-half time frame, by the way, ties in closely with our rollout plans, which you'll read about at the end of this chapter. Are you beginning to see why I included the sidebar "Exchange Design Is Iterative, Not Linear" in this chapter?

I'm very happy with GerCom's needs assessment. Since we started the process, I've seen the LoadSim numbers for the whole organization. Though they're just rough estimates, they look pretty good; we can refine them later. We're off to a good start.

STUDY YOUR ORGANIZATION'S GEOGRAPHICAL PROFILE

You need a list of all the geographical units in your organization. Here you should think not only in terms of cities, states, and countries but also in-city and even in-building locations. Start at the top and work your way down. At this point, diagrams are important. Draw maps and building layouts.

This is the time to gather information on the workstations and servers you've got in each location. You'll want to know how many run each of the different kinds of operating systems in your organization. Operating systems you should watch for are Windows NT Workstation and Server; Novell NetWare 3.x and 4.x Servers and NetWare IPX/SPX workstations; Banyan VINES servers and workstations; Windows 95/98; Windows 3.1x; MS-DOS; Apple Macintosh; UNIX workstations by type of operating system; and workstations used remotely. If you've got hardware and software inventories for these machines, your job will be a lot easier. If you're looking for an automatic inventorying system, check out Microsoft's Systems Management Server. Not only can you use it to gather workstation and server hardware information automatically, it can help you install Exchange clients throughout your organization. You can use all the information you collect about workstations and servers to determine who's ready for Exchange and who isn't and how many Exchange client licenses you'll have to buy.

As you gather information in other steps, begin to look at it in the context of your geographical profile. For example, you'll want to meld geographical information with what you've found out about user needs and user groupings.

MORE ON USER WORKSTATIONS

"Yes, I know that our users are working on ancient desktop computer systems. But we just don't have the money to buy them what they really need." I wish I had a dollar for every time I've heard that one; why, I'd be able to buy decent systems for most of those poor users. I've always wondered why companies that have money to burn on fancy cars and trips to expensive and often useless meetings and employee seminars can't seem to find the two or three thousand bucks it takes to upgrade a user's workstation.

I limped along for quite some time on a substandard 200MHz Pentium II workstation with 64MB of memory. Then I moved up to a 500MHz dual Pentium II processor and 512MB of RAM. Yes, 512MB of RAM. When I ran NT on my old, underpowered sleepwalker, it was all I could do to keep my word processor, a spreadsheet, and my e-mail software open at the same time. If I opened anything else, the machine started thrashing around so much between RAM and virtual memory that it slowed to a nearly useless crawl.

With my new system, I can run word processing programs, spreadsheet programs, and Exchange together without wasting precious time to switch between them. And I still have plenty of horsepower left for all those tasks I used to do with paper because I couldn't bring up the applications fast enough when I needed them. At will, I can now simultaneously open (or keep open) such apps as an accounting package and Microsoft Word, Excel, Project, Outlook, and PowerPoint. With all that computer power, I'm also no longer reluctant to run other key programs—say, Internet Web browsers or NT Control Panel applets—at the drop of a hat.

Bottom line: I've had my new system for less than a year; by my estimates, the productivity increase I've experienced in that time has already paid back the cost of the system's purchase.

CONTINUED ➡

Part iv

Maybe all of your users don't need a dual 500MHz Pentium system with NT and 512MB of RAM. However, as you start assessing user needs, don't let the dismal state of your organization's stable of workstations stop you and your users from reaching for the stars as you think about potential applications for Exchange. Who knows—you just might come up with a next-generation business-computing model for your organization. And that might get you a corporate car or a trip to Hawaii for that conference on the role of MS-DOS and the 486 PC in modern corporate computing.

You'll notice I talk here about my NT desktop system, not my Windows 95 or 98 system. I strongly urge you to consider starting with or moving to NT Workstation for desktop business computing. Sure it doesn't always let you use some of the neat pieces of hardware that no home should be without (e.g., some digital scanner or camera products). But, business is about platform stability, not trivial fun and games. If you need that other stuff, run one or two 95 or 98 machines to support it.

An Example: GerCom's Geographical Profile

As you can see in Figure 22.1, GerCom has grown by leaps and bounds since earlier chapters. It now has offices in Chicago and New York City—Figure 22.2 shows just how much we've grown. Hey, we've got two buildings in the "City of the Broad Shoulders." Now aren't you sorry you didn't buy stock when you had a chance?

GerCom's top executive staff, marketing, and most of MIS are in Los Angeles; sales has people in all three cities. Manufacturing and engineering are in Chicago, the Enter key capital of the world. We've got 1,500 people in LA, 800 in Chicago, and 200 in New York.

All but two of our network servers run NetWare 4.x. The operating system on the two maverick servers, which support our Oracle database, is Sun Solaris (UNIX). We lucked out when it comes to user workstation types and operating systems: Except for five workstations, they're all Intel-based, almost all run Windows, and all but a few are linked to our NetWare servers using either Novell's ODI or VLM IPX/SPX stack.

We have five Windows NT workstations, and three are in the executive suite. They belong to me, our controller, and our head of human resources. At my insistence, MIS started learning NT about a year ago. Two of our midlevel MIS staff use NT workstations for everything they do. All five workstations are linked to our Novell servers using NT's built-in IPX/SPX networking capabilities.

Because we're a young company, most workstations are Pentium-based or better, though a lot of the Pentium systems have only 16MB of memory. Still, as I noted in the sidebar "More on User Workstations" in this chapter, we've got a lot of upgrading to do before we can fully implement Exchange.

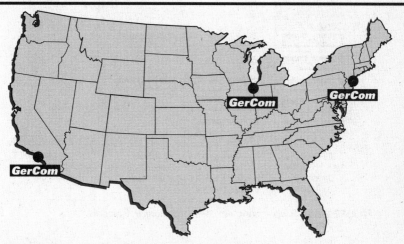

FIGURE 22.1: GerCom, an Enter key manufacturer with a national presence

Our year-to-year-and-a-half goal is to move all our users from Windows 95/98 to NT workstation. NT Workstation is a real business operating system without the system-destabilizing weaknesses of Windows 95/98. We're seeing our competition moving in that direction, and we need to go there, too. Yes, there is competition in the Enter key business.

With information from the first iteration of our user-needs and geographical assessments in hand, GerCom's MIS folks are already beginning to think about who's where, and how to structure the company's NT and Exchange hierarchy. They've also started lobbying me and our controller for user workstation upgrades.

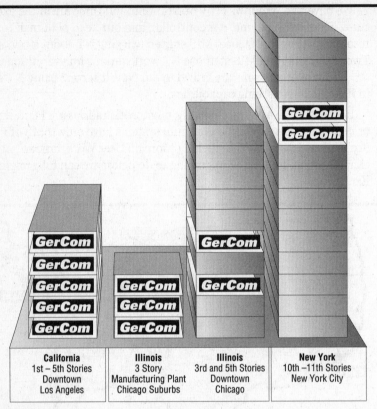

California	Illinois	Illinois	New York
1st – 5th Stories	3 Story	3rd and 5th Stories	10th –11th Stories
Downtown	Manufacturing Plant	Downtown	New York City
Los Angeles	Chicago Suburbs	Chicago	

FIGURE 22.2: Two—count 'em, two—locations in Chicago

ASSESS YOUR ORGANIZATION'S NETWORK

In this step, you just want to know what your network looks like now. This isn't the place to get into what kinds of networking you'll need; that comes later. You need to answer four key questions here: What's connected to what, and how? (If you're counting, that's two questions.) How much bandwidth have we got on each network? And, finally, how reliable are our networks?

What's Connected to What, and How?

Generally, in answering the first question, you should start at the top of your organization and work down to the domain or server level. For each link, name the physical connection, the networking topology, and the networking protocols running on the connection. For example, physical connection = local hardwire, networking topology = Ethernet, networking protocols = IPX/SPX, TCP/IP, SNA. This information, especially when combined with the information you've collected in steps 1 and 2, will prove invaluable as you start to plan for the Exchange connectivity you'll need.

In looking at your organization's network, don't forget about connections to the outside world. Do you have connections to the Internet, to X.400 messaging systems, to trading partners? If you've got such connections, pay particular attention to existing naming conventions. They may limit your choices in naming the key entities in the Exchange hierarchy.

How Much Bandwidth Have We Got on Each Network?

To assess the bandwidth on each of your networks, you'll need some help from a network monitoring tool. If your networks are NT-based, you can try using NT's Performance Monitor to get a handle on traffic. Microsoft's Systems Management Server has some pretty good network monitoring capabilities, too. For NetWare systems, try one of the many software-based network traffic monitors out there. A lot of modern network hubs, switches, and such also come with excellent network monitoring software. If you're flush with cash, go for a hardware-based monitor, such as Network General's Sniffer.

What you want here is a chart that tells you, on average, how much of a network's bandwidth is available during each of the 24 hours in a day. You'll have to take several samples to get reliable data, but it's worth it. A warning light should go on in your head if you're already using more than, say, 40 percent of the available bandwidth on any network during daytime hours and you're not already running a heavy-duty messaging system like Exchange. With that kind of scenario, you just might have to make some changes in the network before installing Exchange. We'll talk about those changes later; for now, be sure to collect this data on available bandwidth and incorporate it into your organizational maps.

How Reliable Are Our Networks?

Having a reliable network is an important issue. More and more in corporate America, there is strong pressure to centralize network servers. Centralization makes good economic sense. If all network servers are in one place, one set of staff can support and monitor them, assuring 7-day-a-week, 24-hour-a-day uptime.

That's quite true. However, a 7-day, 24-hour server availability is useless if the networks people use to get to the servers are unreliable. I've seen this little scenario play itself out in several organizations: centralize the servers, the network fails, users can't get to their now mission-critical e-mail and other data, responsible IS planners are roundly criticized, lower-level IS personnel are even more heavily criticized or fired. Grrr!

Bottom line: Don't make your users work on unreliable networks. If your networks can't come close to matching the reliability of your servers, put the servers closer to their users. The little extra it costs to manage decentralized servers is worth the access insurance it buys. Sure, get those networks up to par, but don't risk your Exchange implementation on centralized servers before the reliable network is in place to support them.

An Example: GerCom's Networks

Figure 22.3 shows the GerCom map with some higher-level connectivity information added. In Los Angeles, GerCom has a dedicated T1 TCP/IP link to the Internet. By the way, the registered Internet domain name is "bgerber.com." GerCom's four office buildings are connected in serial fashion through NetWare servers, using a networking topology consisting of non-dedicated, asynchronous dial-up lines and the Point-to-Point Protocol (PPP). We run both IPX/SPX and TCP/IP on the dial-up network.

You can see in Figure 22.4 that NetWare servers and user workstations in all GerCom buildings are linked by Ethernet and IPX/SPX. We also run TCP/IP to support workstation connections to our Sun UNIX servers, where e-mail and our Oracle databases reside.

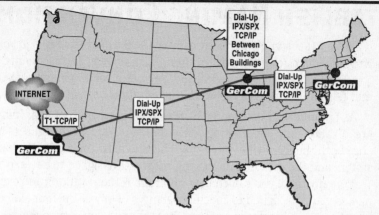

FIGURE 22.3:   GerCom's existing cross-country links

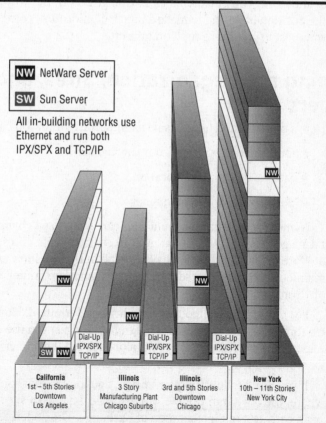

FIGURE 22.4:   GerCom's existing in-building networks

ESTABLISH NAMING CONVENTIONS

It's time to set some criteria for naming the four key elements in your Exchange hierarchy: the organization, sites, servers, and recipients. Your goal here is to establish a logical and consistent set of naming conventions that fit in well with your real-world organizational structure and culture.

As I pointed out in Chapter 19, the choices you make for Exchange organization- and site-naming conventions—at least at the outset—influence both the ease with which you'll be able to manage your Exchange system and the default e-messaging addresses assigned to users. It's true that, at any time, you can change your naming conventions and even the names you've assigned to specific instances of any of the four elements in your Exchange hierarchy. Some of these changes are easy to make, while others are much more difficult. For example, to change your organization or site name, you must reinstall Exchange Server. But why put yourself in the position of having to make a bunch of midcourse corrections? Do your best to get things right on take-off.

Naming the Organization, Sites, and Servers

Here's one easy and usually safe naming convention you can use:

▶ Organization = master company name

▶ Site = a geographical location

▶ Server = departmental names

Names for organizations and sites can be up to 64 characters long, but I'd suggest keeping them to around 10 characters out of respect for people at "foreign" sites who may have to type in these names as part of a recipient's e-messaging address. Server names are limited to a maximum of 15 characters.

For most names, almost any character is permitted. However, for organization, site, and server names I strongly suggest you use only the 26 upper- and lowercase letters of the alphabet and the numerals 0 through 9. Don't use spaces, underscores, or any accented letters.

If you don't follow this convention, I guarantee that sometime, somewhere, you'll get into trouble. For example, I named a site "LA_HOME" in an early test implementation of Exchange. The underscore became a question mark when the site name was used to construct X.400 addresses. The question mark was technically okay, but it threw users who sometimes had to give their address with an underscore and sometimes with a question mark, depending on the type of address it was. Bottom line: Don't get fancy when naming organizations, sites, and servers.

Naming Recipient Mailboxes

You'll also need some criteria for naming mailboxes. There are four key names for each Exchange mailbox: the first name, the last name, the display name, and the alias name. Exchange administrators create and modify these names in the Exchange Administrator program. You enter the first and last names, and by default Exchange constructs the display names and alias names from the first and last names. You can change the rules for constructing default display names and alias names, and you can also alter these manually once they've been created. In Figure 22.5 you can see the different names for my Exchange mailbox.

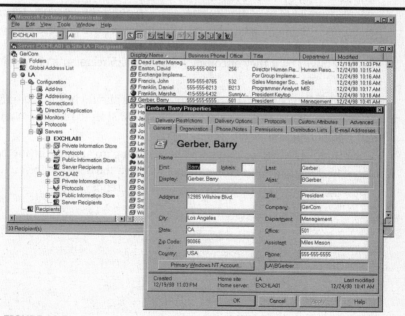

FIGURE 22.5: Exchange creates display and alias mailbox names using first and last names.

Part iv

Display Names

The Exchange client global address book shows the display name for each mailbox (see Figure 22.6). You'll need to decide on a convention for display names. You've got two basic options: first-name-space-last-name (John Smith) or last-name-comma-space-first-name (Smith, John). You can also set up custom defaults. You can change the defaults at any time, but the change applies only to newly created mailboxes.

NOTE

Fortunately, there's a fairly easy way to automatically change the display names of old mailboxes as well. See the sections on importing from and exporting to the Exchange directory in Chapter 17 of the Sybex book *Mastering Microsoft Exchange Server 5.5.*

Display names can be up to 256 characters long. Display names are only a convenience—they're not a part of the mailbox's e-message address. They are, however, the way in which Exchange users find the people they want to communicate with—so don't scrimp when setting them up. You might even want to include department names and/or titles in display names so users aren't faced with ambiguous selections, as they might be if they encountered a list of 25 recipients named John Smith.

Practically speaking, display name lengths should be limited only by your users' willingness to read through lots of stuff to find the mailbox they're looking for.

Full-blown religious arguments have sprung up around the meta-physics of display name conventions. I'll leave the decision to you (though, as you'll see, I do have my own preference).

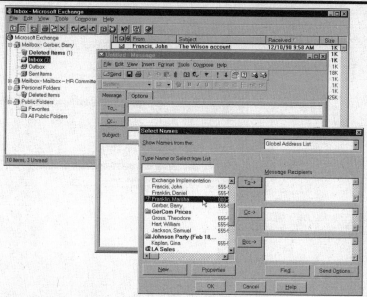

FIGURE 22.6: The Exchange client global address book shows each mailbox's display name.

Alias Names

For some messaging systems, the user's mailbox is identified by an alias name, which is part of the mailbox's address. Either Exchange itself or the gateway for the foreign mail system constructs an address using the alias. For other messaging systems the mailbox name is constructed from other information. Figure 22.7 shows the four addresses that Exchange built for me for cc:Mail, Microsoft Mail for PC Networks, the Internet, and X.400. My MS Mail and Internet addresses use the alias "bgerber." cc:Mail and X.400 addresses do not use the alias. Rather, they use the full first and last name attributes of the user.

Aliases can be up to 64 characters long. That's too long, since some people in foreign messaging systems will have to type in the alias as part of an e-messaging address. Try to keep aliases short—a 10-character alias is long enough.

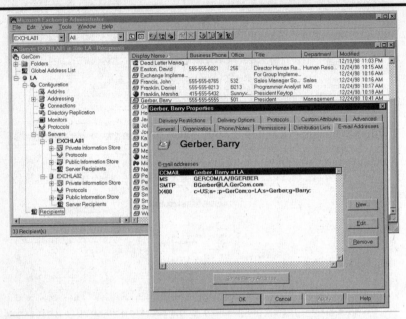

FIGURE 22.7: Exchange Server uses mailbox alias or the first and last names to construct e-mail addresses.

For some foreign messaging system addressing schemes, Exchange must remove illegal characters and shorten the alias to meet maximum character-length requirements. Remember my example about a site "LA_HOME"? It can be just as bad with aliases. Do all you can to ensure that aliases are constructed using less-esoteric characters.

As with display names, you can set default rules for the aliases that Exchange assigns newly created users. There are several options for these defaults, including full-first-name-first-letter-of-last-name (JohnS) and first-letter-of-first-name-full-last-name (JSmith).

Alias naming conventions are a religious issue, too, so you'll get no recommendations from me.

An Example: GerCom's Naming Conventions

GerCom chose to follow the simple guidelines listed above for naming its organization and sites. The organization name is "GerCom." Site naming is based on geography (cities): "LA," "NY," and "Chicago."

We did run into one problem in selecting an organization name: You'll remember from the GerCom network assessment that our registered Internet domain name is "bgerber.com." My current Internet address for GerCom is bgerber@bgerber.com. (Don't try to send anything to that address; remember that all this GerCom stuff is fake.) Given the name I chose for my organization (*GerCom*), the Internet address that Exchange will construct for me by default will be bgerber@LA.gercom.com. Take another look at Figure 22.7, if you don't believe me. We could have used "BGerber" for our Exchange organization name, but we like "GerCom" too much. There's no accounting for taste. We also could have tinkered with DNS MX records on the UNIX side to redirect mail sent to bgerber .com over to gercom.com, but since our Internet mail flow is limited right now, we decided to go whole hog and de-register the name bgerber.com and instead register gercom.com as our Internet domain name.

We nonconformists at GerCom didn't follow the guidelines for server naming, though. As I mentioned in Chapter 19, rather than create separate departmental servers at each site, my MIS department and I prefer to create one Exchange server, fill it up with users, and then set up a new one. This is a nice approach for smaller organizations that don't want to invest in lots of hardware at the outset. Many large organizations also like this approach, since there's often not much to be gained in identifying different Exchange servers with different departmental units.

GerCom servers get names based on this convention: EXCH + *SITE* + *an ordering number.* The first server in the site LA is EXCHLA01, the second is EXCHLA02, and so on.

GerCom display names use the last-name-comma-space-first-name (Smith, John) convention. Remember that the display name is what people see when they go looking for a mailbox in the Exchange client. I just think it's easier to find people by their last names (all the Smiths) rather than by their first names (all the Johns). For similar reasons, alias naming at GerCom is based on the first-letter-of-first-name-full-last-name (JSmith) convention. Since Exchange and NT security are so tightly integrated, we'll use the same first-letter-of-first-name-full-last-name (JSmith) convention for NT usernames. I should note that I had no trouble imposing these conventions on my very compliant and, it should be noted, imaginary MIS department.

SELECT A MICROSOFT NETWORKING DOMAIN MODEL

You've got four networking domain models to choose from. Which is right for your organization? Here you should think about both today and tomorrow, because it's not easy to change a domain model. Moving to a new model often involves changing server and domain names and moving users and resources to different or new domains, and neither of these is pleasant to do with NT. As with Exchange naming conventions, the best way is to get it right the first time.

Go back to Chapter 21 and take a look at the section on the four domain models. Decide how your organization is structured and pick the model that best fits that structure.

An Example: The GerCom Domain Model

At GerCom we've decided on the multiple-master domain model. Look how much we've grown in five chapters: Though we have only 2,500 employees now, we're already in three cities. We're gonna be *big,* and we need to think seriously about exceeding those users-per-domain limits I discussed in Chapter 21.

Figure 22.8 shows how we'll structure the domains. We'll have a master domain for each city, as well as a single-resource domain in each of the four buildings we now occupy. Right now only the Chicago master domain will be responsible for multiple-resource domains—one for each of our two Chicago buildings. As we add cities we'll add master domains and appropriate resource domains. As we add buildings in cities we'll add resource domains.

GerCom doesn't have a lot of NT expertise in-house. (I'm probably the most knowledgeable employee right now.) We're planning to hire an NT networking guru right away, and once that person is in place we'll determine how many more NT support staffers we'll need. With the ability to remotely manage NT, we should be able to stay light on the NT support side, at least until we get more deeply into programming Exchange-enabled custom applications. For now, the NT people will report to the Exchange manager we decided on in step 1. That's kind of unusual, but for now we primarily need NT support staff to implement Exchange.

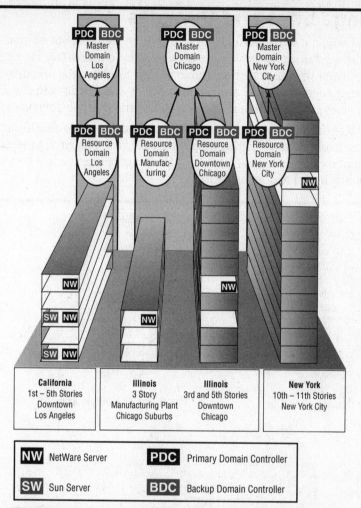

California
1st – 5th Stories
Downtown
Los Angeles

Illinois
3 Story
Manufacturing Plant
Chicago Suburbs

Illinois
3rd and 5th Stories
Downtown
Chicago

New York
10th – 11th Stories
New York City

NW NetWare Server	**PDC**	Primary Domain Controller
SW Sun Server	**BDC**	Backup Domain Controller

FIGURE 22.8: GerCom's implementation of the multiple-master domain model

DEFINE SITE BOUNDARIES

When defining site boundaries you have to remember a couple of things.
First, Exchange sites and Microsoft network domains are related. Second,
all the Exchange servers in a site must have certain networking capabilities.

Exchange Sites and Domains

One domain may include one or more sites. In addition, one or more Exchange sites can cross two or more networking domains (see Figure 22.9). If you want your Exchange system to be easy to administer and manage, I strongly suggest you stay away from multiple sites in a domain and sites that cross multiple domains. Stick with the one-site, one-domain model.

All of the Exchange servers and users in a site must be able to communicate freely, without issuing passwords each time they need to access each other. As I noted in Chapter 21, Exchange server freedom of speech is tightly linked to domain security.

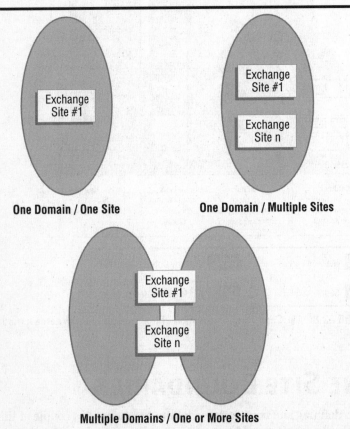

FIGURE 22.9: The three ways that Microsoft networking domains and Exchange Server sites can relate to each other

Required Networking Capabilities

With the right security in place, the moment an Exchange server starts running it automatically begins communicating with other Exchange servers in its site. You don't have to do a thing to start these communications—they just happen. The first time this happens, you'll literally jump for joy, especially if you're used to those old fashioned e-mail systems like Microsoft Mail for PCs with all their gizmo gateways, dirsync machines, and such.

When communicating with each other, Exchange servers in a site automatically swap user messages and frequently update one another's directory information. Optionally, they can also cross-replicate all or part of their public folders. As noted in Chapter 20, intrasite cross-server directory replication not only helps keep directories up to date on all Exchange servers, but it also brings a degree of fault tolerance to Exchange. As long as you have one good copy of the directory on one Exchange server, the others can reconstruct a good portion of their directories from it. Don't let this lull you into thinking you don't need to do regular backups. There is some server-specific information in each server's directory that can only be protected with a backup. It can't be reconstructed from the copies of the directory on other servers.

Frequent intrasite directory replication increases network traffic a bit. Also, since users in a site often have some affinity for each other, you can usually expect higher user messaging and folder replication traffic between servers in one site than between servers in different sites.

All of this intrasite interserver network traffic requires that Exchange servers in a site be connected by a high-bandwidth dedicated network, but high bandwidth isn't absolute. For example, from Exchange's perspective, a 155Mb/sec ATM link isn't high bandwidth if you're eating up 154.9Mb/sec sending continuous streams of video images. There are no hard and fast rules here, but any physical network that can provide Exchange with 512kbps of bandwidth most of the time should be adequate. Lower bandwidths can work in cases where directories change very little and public folder replication is nonexistent or kept at a bare minimum. Physical networks capable of delivering at least this kind of dedicated bandwidth include (in increasing bandwidth availability) faster Frame Relay and satellite, full T1, microwave, DSL, T3, Ethernet, Token Ring, Fast Ethernet, FDDI, ATM, and SONET.

Part iv

CONSIDER DSL

Digital Subscriber Line (DSL) networking is finally available in many locales in the United States. DSL is a variable bandwidth networking topology. Bandwidth ranges from as little as 64kbps through T1. Compared to most other higher bandwidth technologies, DSL is inexpensive. In the real world, I currently pay $199 per month for a 384kbps always-on DSL Internet link. This link supports my Exchange Server connection to Internet mail as well as a lot of other Internet-based functionality, like an FTP service, a Web server, and a time sync service. Always-on links have distinct advantages when you're connecting Exchange Server to the Internet using the Internet Mail Service.

Intrasite communications between servers is based on the remote procedure calls (RPCs) discussed in Chapter 21. Networks must run networking protocols that support the RPCs; these include IPX/SPX, NetBEUI, TCP/IP, SNA, NetBIOS, Windows Sockets, and Named Pipes. For the best overall performance, I've found TCP/IP is generally the best option, though NetBEUI/NetBIOS can be quite impressive in smaller, non-routed nets.

A good deal of the information that moves between Exchange servers in a site is transmitted in Exchange's native MAPI-based format. As you'll see later, when information leaves an Exchange site it isn't always possible to transmit it in MAPI format.

An Example: GerCom's Site Boundaries

As you'll remember from its geographical assessment, GerCom is located in three cities: Los Angeles, Chicago, and New York. It has more than two physical locations only in Chicago. Though you already know this from GerCom's site-naming conventions, the company will have Exchange sites in each city.

Except in Chicago, our existing Ethernet-TCP/IP-IPX/SPX networks are all we need for intrasite connectivity. We'll have to add a higher-bandwidth connection between our two buildings in Chicago, and we're planning to use a T1 connection for that. Figure 22.10 shows the GerCom building diagram with this new site boundary information imposed on it.

We plan to station an Exchange administrator at each GerCom site. These three MIS employees will be responsible for Exchange installation, testing, implementation, and management. They'll also provide NT system management backup. To do these things, we feel that the three employees must be on-site. We think that one person at each site will be enough, but we're open to adding people if more are needed. The Exchange administrators will report to GerCom's new corporate Exchange manager, mentioned in step 1.

With Exchange Server's great remote management capabilities, the Exchange administrators in each city will be able to help out at other sites when needed without leaving their offices. And when we add administrators, they won't have to be assigned to a specific site—they can remotely go wherever their Exchange administrative skills are required.

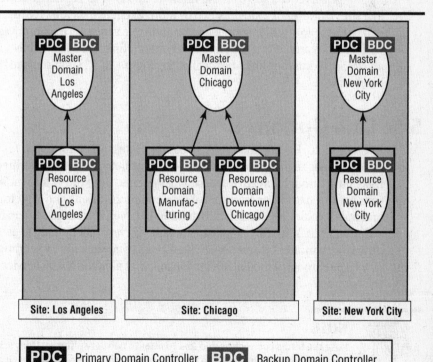

FIGURE 22.10: GerCom's site boundaries

The four end-user-oriented Exchange training and app-development staffers mentioned in step 1 will be distributed among the sites as well.

Two will be in Los Angeles, one in Chicago, and one in New York. In addition to their main responsibilities, these folks will also back up the Exchange site administrators. Because of the remote management capabilities built into NT Server and Exchange Server, the backup function won't require full knowledge of NT or Exchange Server. These folks will mainly be ready to help when a local hand is physically required.

Plan Intersite Links

As you'll remember from Chapter 20, you link sites by running one or more Exchange connectors on Exchange servers in each site. There's no need for each Exchange server in a site to run its own connectors; one Exchange server can serve all the intersite needs of all Exchange servers in a site. However, if a site has two or more Exchange servers, it often makes sense to run site connectors on multiple servers. This improves performance and, if you use different network links for each connector, allows for redundant links between sites. Figure 22.11 should make this a bit clearer.

Site Link Options

In Chapter 20, I noted that you can connect sites either *directly* or *indirectly*. Direct connections are point-to-point between servers; indirect links pass through foreign e-messaging systems. Both direct and indirect connections use messages to move user communications and directory and public folder replication information between Exchange servers in different sites. With direct connections the servers talk directly to each other. With indirect connections the servers communicate by sending messages through a mediating system, such as a public X.400 service or the Internet.

NOTE

I use the terms *connection* and *link* to refer to two very different things. In the paragraph above, they refer to the way servers *communicate* with each other, be it directly or indirectly. In other places in this book, *connection* and *link* refer to actual *physical and protocol-level networking options*, such as Ethernet, TCP/IP, and X.400. I tried without success to find another word to modify the terms *direct* and *indirect*.

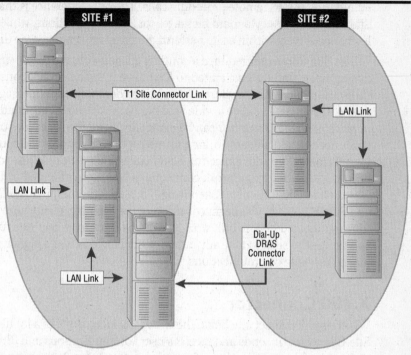

FIGURE 22.11: Making the Exchange intersite connection

When connecting Exchange sites, you get to choose between four connector options:

- ▶ Site Connector (direct link only)

- ▶ X.400 Connector (direct and indirect links)

- ▶ Dynamic RAS Connector (direct link only)

- ▶ Internet Mail Service (direct and indirect links)

Let's look at each of these in more detail.

Site Connector

Of all the Exchange connectors, the Site Connector is the fastest and simplest to set up and manage. And of all the ways to link sites, the Site Connector is most similar to the automatic, built-in links between Exchange servers in the same site. It moves messages and directory and folder replication information between Exchange sites using the Open Systems

Foundation (OSF) remote procedure calls. The only difference is that the Site Connector uses standard messages for all three functions, while Exchange servers within a site perform directory replication more directly.

The Site Connector requires a continuous network. It doesn't support dial-up links, and it's best suited to Exchange intersite connections with heavy user loads and directory and public folder replication message duties. If you already have a wide area network with adequate bandwidth in place, the Site Connector can be especially attractive, because you don't need to add any networking infrastructure to support the connector. Of course, if you're expecting heavy cross-site network loads, you'll need high-bandwidth network connections like those provided by topologies such as T1, Ethernet, Token Ring, T3, Fast Ethernet, FDDI, ATM, and SONET. When you begin considering the higher-capacity networking topologies listed here to link sites, you might want to go one step further and merge the sites to take advantage of Exchange Server's higher performance intrasite communications.

X.400 Connector

When used for direct site links, the X.400 Connector works a lot like the Site Connector. It sends and receives user communications and directory and public folder replication information as messages. It doesn't use RPCs, however. The X.400 Connector can move messages between sites in X.400 format or, like the Site Connector, in native MAPI format. If you choose to use the X.400 format, the messages will have to be translated into X.400 before they leave the originating site and then translated back into MAPI after arriving at the receiving site.

The X.400 Connector runs on top of a special physical transport stack that supports TCP/IP, OSI TP0 (X.25), and OSI TP4/CLNP networking protocols. If you're into the OSI world, these protocols will be familiar to you. If not, you can find info on them in any of a number of fine books on OSI-based networking. Like the Site Connector, in direct link mode the X.400 Connector can handle heavy intersite loads given adequate bandwidth.

The X.400 Connector is a bit slower than the Site Connector, both because it has to translate to and from X.400 format when that format is used for intersite communications, and because there's some networking overhead involved in X.400 communications. However, the X.400 Connector gives you more control than the Site Connector over a site link and what passes over it. For example, you can schedule X.400 site connections, restrict the message size, and specify which sites you'll accept messages from. The Site Connector doesn't support restrictions of this sort. The X.400 Connector allows direct server-to-server links over dial-up lines using X.25, for example. The Site Connector doesn't support dial-up links.

You can also use the X.400 Connector for indirect Exchange site links. In this case you connect each Exchange site to a public X.400 provider's network. The sites can be connected to the same provider network or to different ones. Of course, if different providers are used, they must be able to communicate with each other. You can use any of the networking protocols noted above to make these connections.

Cost considerations lead most organizations to opt for lower, sub-local area network bandwidth links to public X.400 providers. That's fine, but it means that indirect site links should be used mostly for low-traffic site connections and to provide redundant links for sites already connected by higher-bandwidth direct links.

Dynamic RAS Connector

Unlike the Site Connector and like the X.400 Connector, the Dynamic RAS Connector (DRASC) lets you link sites that don't have full-time networks between them. You can use the DRASC for ad hoc asynchronous links using voice, X.25, and ISDN physical connections. Exchange servers talk directly to each other over the DRASC, so DRASC connections support RPCs. As should be obvious from its name, the DRASC is based on NT's RAS (Remote Access Server), which I talked about in the last chapter. You'll remember that RAS provides NetBEUI, TCP/IP, or IPX/SPX protocol support on top of PPP.

With the DRASC you get many of the controls that the X.400 Connector delivers without all the complexities of X.400. Exchange data is always moved in native MAPI format, though you won't see any great speed advantage since you're connecting at ISDN bandwidths at best. So, as with low-bandwidth, indirect X.400 site links, use the DRASC for low-traffic or redundant links.

Internet Mail Service

The Internet Mail Service lets you link sites directly and indirectly. I won't spend a lot of time on these here; each gets coverage in later chapters. For now, suffice it to say that the caveats about low-speed links also apply to the use of these two connectors.

An Example: GerCom's Intersite Connections

So how about GerCom? What is that paragon of Enter key manufacturers going to do to connect its three sites? Well, as president I've had to swallow hard a couple of times, but we're going to pop for T1 links between our three sites and use Site Connectors. The main reason for this decision is the amount of cross-site traffic we expect our neat but demanding applications to generate in the form of public folder replication and cross-site movement of larger messages. Figure 22.12 shows the GerCom building diagram with our planned intersite connections in place.

Those T1 lines aren't going to be cheap, but we have high hopes that Exchange will revolutionize the way we do business. As you'll see later in this chapter, we're also planning to do some indirect links. These will add important redundancy to our Exchange network.

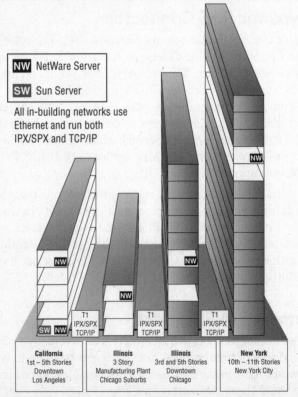

FIGURE 22.12:   GerCom's intersite connections

PLAN SERVERS AND USER LINKS TO THEM

There's quite a bit to do in planning your servers and user links. You need to decide what kinds of hardware to use for each of your Exchange servers. After that you have to figure out how to back up the servers. Then you have to make sure you've got adequate bandwidth on your local networks to keep Exchange happy; if you don't have it, you've got to decide how to get it. Finally, before you go on to the next step in the Exchange design process, you have to think about remote users and how you'll connect them to Exchange.

Designing Your Exchange Servers

The intricacies of Exchange Server design and fine-tuning could occupy a whole book; you'll have to experiment here. Install NT Server and Exchange Server, then run the optimization app that comes with Exchange Server. Next, take out that set of user-demand numbers you put together when you did your user-needs assessment. Plug those numbers into LoadSim and run it against a reasonable Exchange server machine—say, a 500MHz Pentium II with 256MB of memory and at least two 4GB SCSI hard drives. Don't run LoadSim on your Exchange server. Instead, run it on a separate 400MHz or better Pentium-based NT workstation with at least 128MB of memory. And don't try to simulate more than 200 users on one LoadSim machine. If you don't follow these guidelines, LoadSim may not be able to generate the loads you've asked it to, and you could be led to believe that your Exchange server hardware is adequate when it's not.

SCSI, NOT ENHANCED IDE

Enhanced IDE drives are nice, but for production Exchange Servers I prefer SCSI drives. They're fast and tend to be more reliable than IDE drives. If you're going to use a hardware RAID configuration, you won't have much choice other than SCSI, because SCSI drives are used in most hardware RAID products. For best performance, choose wide or ultrawide SCSI drives.

If LoadSim indicates that you've got too little computing power for your needs, start by moving Exchange's transaction logs to another disk drive. If this doesn't solve your problem, you'll need to run NT's Performance Monitor to locate any bottlenecks. (See the Sybex book *Mastering Windows NT Server 4*, by Mark Minasi, Christa Anderson, and Elizabeth Creegan, for more on using the Performance Monitor.)

Look at the obvious culprits: server hard disk capacity, memory, and CPU. Based on the results you get from the Performance Monitor, you can decide what to do. Distributing Exchange database files differently—for example, putting the server's public folders on a different drive, RAID array, or server—can significantly improve an Exchange server's performance in some situations. Adding RAM to an Exchange server can make a world of difference in performance, because it allows the server to do more work without having to waste time paging RAM segments out to disk. Adding more processors to multiprocessor machines, or moving to more powerful processors like those from Digital Equipment, can be a quick route to improved performance. However, be careful here: Focus on disk capacity and RAM before turning to CPU power. More or faster CPUs can indeed improve performance, but they're not going to fix performance problems originating from poorly optimized disks or too little RAM. If all this vertical scaling can't solve your problem, consider going horizontal and splitting users across multiple Exchange servers. Exchange makes horizontal scaling very easy.

SERVER FAULT TOLERANCE

As you're designing your servers, don't forget the whole issue of server fault tolerance. Multiprocessor machines are starting to show up with processors that can back each other up in case of failure. You'll need a version of NT that can handle this sort of processor redundancy. In addition to processor redundancy, look for systems with error-correcting memory. On the disk side, consider multiple controllers and nicely redundant RAID level 5 technologies. Remember, NT Server can do software-based RAID level 5. Many machines are now available with two or more redundant power supplies. Don't forget uninterruptible power supplies (UPSes). More about them later in this chapter. In some cases, you can swap out failed RAID drives and power supplies without even

CONTINUED ➡

bringing down your system. And, be sure to consider the new technologies like Microsoft's NT Server Enterprise Edition that lets you
set up multiple NT/Exchange servers that mirror each other, with
server A generally able to quickly and automatically replace server
B in case server B fails.

You'll need to start thinking now about how you'll manage user storage on each server. Storage management gives you more control over how
much of what is stored on Exchange server disks, and it helps you remain
within your server disk budget. There are several disk management questions you'll want to answer here, including

▶ Do you want some or all of your users to store messages in personal folders on a workstation or non-Exchange networked disk
  drives, instead of in their Exchange server-based mailboxes? (See
  Chapter 19 for more on these two options.)

▶ For those who will use their Exchange server mailboxes, do you
  want to limit the amount of storage they can use?

▶ Do you want to impose limits on the storage used by public
  folders?

▶ If you have public folders containing messages that lose value
  with time—for example, messages from Internet lists or USENET
  news feeds—do you want Exchange to automatically delete messages from these folders based on message age?

▶ Will you implement Exchange Server's ability to save deleted messages for a designated period of time? This is a neat capability,
  because users can recover messages they accidentally deleted.
  However, all those "deleted" messages can take up tons of disk
  space.

You can base your answers to most of these questions on the results of
your user-needs assessment, though you're bound to make adjustments
as you pass through iterations of the design process. And, do note that
while it's tempting to force users to store messages in personal folders on
local or non-Exchange networked disk drives to save on Exchange server
disk, you then run the risk that key user messages won't get backed up.

As the ever-present "they" say, "You pays your money and you takes your chances."

Once you're comfortable with the basic design of your servers, you need to plan for uninterruptible power supplies (UPSes). I consider a UPS to be part of a server, not an add-on. UPSes are cheap, given the peace of mind they can bring. In spite of NT's and Exchange Server's ability to recover from most disastrous events, you don't want to tempt fate and risk damage to your organization's precious e-messaging data. Get enough UPSes to serve the power needs of each server, and get a UPS that comes with software to gracefully shut down your servers if power stays off for an extended period.

Backing Up Your Exchange Servers

When you know what your Exchange servers and networks will look like, you can begin thinking about backing up your servers. You need to use backup software that is especially designed for Exchange's client/server architecture. Such software lets you back up an Exchange server's directory and information store without shutting down Exchange processes and, thus, closing off user access to the server. The software communicates with Exchange's directory and information store services to ensure that the databases they are responsible for are fully backed up.

NT's own Backup program has add-ons to do a proper backup of Exchange servers. Other NT backup vendors, such as Computer Associates's ArcServeIT (http://www.cai.com/) and Veritas Software's Backup Exec (http://www.veritas.com/), have released add-ons to their products that can properly back up Exchange Server.

You can back up an Exchange server either locally or over the network. When you back it up over the network, you can run the backup from another NT/Exchange server or from an NT-only server.

For Exchange servers with lots of disk space (5GB or more) and slow network links to potential backup servers (less than 100Mb/sec), I strongly suggest that you bypass the networked server backup option and do the backup locally on and from the Exchange server itself. You'll have to spend some money on a backup device and software for the Exchange server, but you'll get it back in available bandwidth and faster backups. Available bandwidth means that other network-dependent tasks—and there are lots of those on an Exchange network—run faster. And faster backups mean shorter periods of that awful feeling you get when important data is not yet on tape.

Whether you back up over the network or locally, don't skimp on backup hardware. You're going to *add* hard disk storage to your Exchange server, not take it away. Go for high-capacity 4mm, 8mm, or DLT tape backup systems. Think about tape autoloaders—those neat gizmos that give one or more tape drives automatic access to anything from a few tapes to hundreds of them.

Don't forget those personal folders stored on user workstations. You have to decide who will be responsible for backing them up—Exchange staff, other MIS staff, or users themselves. The technology for centralized workstation backup is readily available. For example, agents are available for most third-party NT backup products that let you back up all or part of specific user workstations.

While you're at it, don't forget NT server backup. If you have NT servers that don't support Exchange, you'll need to back them up, too. You can back up an NT server over the network, but if the servers have lots of disk space, consider the same local backup strategy for non-Exchange NT servers that I suggested for Exchange servers.

Networking Your Exchange Users

Once you've got your server design down, you'll need to think about how to connect users to your Exchange servers. It's usually a no-brainer for local connections, though you'll want to be sure you've got enough bandwidth to move the stuff that Exchange makes available to your users. For example, a message I put together with a very simple embedded color screen capture is 855K. The graphic looks impressive, and it let me make a point that I never could have made without it. Still, I wouldn't want my recipients to get it over a 33.3 or 56Kb/sec connection.

If you're concerned about LAN bandwidth, there are a couple of things you can do. First, get rid of those slower networks. Dump 4Mb/sec Token Ring and Arcnet networks. Second, segment your LANs to reduce the number of users on any segment. In this situation you might even put multiple network adapters in your Exchange server, one for each segment or group of segments. And do take a look at faster networking technologies like 100Mb/sec Ethernet; those really neat networking switches that can replace routers and significantly improve network backbone performance; and the latest in neat stuff, switched fast Ethernet hubs that bring switching to workstation connectivity. Yes, any of these options will cost your organization some bucks, but they're likely to be bucks well spent. It's just like the way it is with user workstations: Slow technologies don't get used, and the benefits of the applications you're trying to run on top of them are lost.

Don't forget remote Exchange users. Many users need to keep in touch when they're away from the office, whether at home or on the road. Remote users can connect to an NT server by way of its Remote Access Server. The RAS gives users the equivalent of a hardwired connection, so for them it's more or less like being on the office LAN. The major difference is that they probably won't stay connected all the time—they'll connect to send and receive messages, and the rest of the time they'll work offline.

Remote users also can connect to their Exchange servers by way of direct TCP/IP links through an Internet Service Provider (ISP). And don't forget the Internet-based POP3, IMAP4, and Web browser–based client options that are supported by Exchange Server. With their lighter-weight demands on workstation resources, they could be just what the doctor ordered for your remote users.

We'll talk more about how to implement remote Exchange links in a later chapter. At this point you need to think about how many users will likely need a RAS connection to each site at one time. If it's just one or two, you can set up a couple of modems on an Exchange or NT server and let users dial in to those. If you expect lots of users you might want to consider setting up a separate NT server dedicated to dial-in connections. Remember, one NT server with the right hardware can support up to 256 dial-in RAS connections.

If users will be connecting to their Exchange servers over the Internet, you'll need an Internet connection of adequate bandwidth to support them. Unless you have few users who need Internet access, think T1.

An Example: GerCom's Servers and User Links

With one exception, we GerComites are pretty sure from our LoadSim tests that the "reasonable machine" I described above—a 500MHz Pentium II with 256MB of memory and two 4GB SCSI hard disks—will work for now for each of our four Exchange servers. The exception? The LA server. With the heaviest staff load and an Internet connection to boot, we've decided to buy a four-processor capable 500MHz Pentium II machine and put 512MB of RAM and 32GB of hardware-based RAID level 5 disk space on the LA server. (We bought the LA machine with only two processors; we'll add more as needed.)

Remember how the GerCom executive suite was possibly going to get its own server? MIS overruled the idea. They really don't want the responsibility of administering two Exchange servers in LA, at least at the outset. Instead they opted for LA's special powerhouse server. Of course, as soon as it looks as if we execs (or any other group, for that matter) need it, we'll get our own Exchange server.

We'll try to limit all but select users to 10MB of mailbox storage. Select users will be those heavily involved in building, testing, or using some of those e-messaging-enabled apps we're planning to do; they'll get as much as 200MB to play with. Since most users won't have write access to public folders, at least at the outset, we're not going to impose any limits on storage there. We will, however, set Exchange to automatically delete messages older than two weeks in those public folders that contain e-mail from Internet lists and older than five days for USENET newsgroups stored in our public folders. And, we'll only let deleted messages hang around for seven days. Most users know almost immediately that they've deleted something they need. Seven days should be more than adequate for GerCom's fast-fingered Delete key pushers.

Just from thinking through all the storage issues, there's one thing we know for sure: We won't get far on the 4GB or 32GB of disk space we put in our servers. We're already planning for increased storage needs.

Each server will have a UPS with orderly shutdown software. We'll back up for now with those neat little Hewlett-Packard DDS-3 SureStore tape autoloader units (`http://www.hp.com/storage/surestore/`) that let us put six 4mm tapes' worth of storage—up to 144 compressed GB—online. We plan to put one SureStore on each Exchange server. For now, to save some money, non-Exchange NT servers acting as primary or backup controllers will be backed up by the tape units on the Exchange servers.

As you'll remember, all but one of GerCom's networks had adequate bandwidth available; only the Engineering network had less than 60 percent of its bandwidth available during most of the day. We're planning to split the Engineering network into three nets: Two will support our two CAD groups, and the other will be for Engineering's clerical and administrative staff.

For remote users, we'll run the RAS dial-in on all our servers. To start, there will be two standard voice-line-based RAS links on each server

Part iv

except the one in LA. (The large number of users in LA dictates that we start with six voice-based RAS lines.) In LA we'll also have a 128kbps ISDN RAS connection for us execs who just can't tolerate those "creepy" 56kbps modem links. We expect ISDN use at GerCom to grow considerably over the next few years, unless a better option comes along.

We decided that, for now, we can get the most reliable remote connectivity with RAS, as opposed to TCP/IP or the new Internet-based client connects. However, we'll also test Outlook client TCP/IP links through an ISP and Exchange's Internet-based Web browser and POP3 and IMAP4 clients. If they work well, we'll start moving remote users over to them. Heck, if they work well, we might even have some of our users with lower-powered workstations use them instead of the resource-hog Outlook clients.

PLAN CONNECTIONS TO OTHER SYSTEMS

As John Donne almost said, "No organization is an island." In fact, today not only is no organization an island, but no organization can *afford* to be an island. With the e-messaging decade upon us, electronic messaging will increasingly become the primary means of communicating and doing business. Consider connections to systems outside your organization to be necessities, not niceties.

Connection Options

Exchange sites can be connected directly to foreign X.400 systems, Internet mail systems, and legacy Microsoft Mail for PC and AppleTalk Networks systems and cc:Mail. Legacy system links can include not just message exchange but synchronization of Exchange and legacy address directories as well. With optional gateways from Microsoft and third-party vendors, you can connect to such systems as IBM PROFS, Verimation Memo, MCI Mail, and fax devices.

Exchange connections to foreign X.400 systems use the X.400 Connector. Such connections can be either continuous and permanent or dial-up, and they can use any of the X.400 Connector networking options listed above in step 7 (designing site links). The Internet Mail Service can use a continuous and permanent or dial-up TCP/IP link to the Internet.

Third-party gateways use a range of networking protocols; contact your gateway vendor for specifics. The Microsoft Mail Connector can run on top of almost anything, including TCP/IP, IPX/SPX, NetBEUI, X.25, voice lines, and the RAS. The Exchange Directory Synchronization Agent mentioned in Chapter 20 lets you keep Exchange and legacy Microsoft messaging systems in sync. It uses the same networking protocols as the Microsoft Mail Connector.

CONNECT OR MIGRATE?

Now is the time to decide if it's better to migrate users from legacy systems to Exchange Server or to wait and just link them to Exchange Server using various connectors, gateways, or even direct individual workstation connects in the case of Microsoft Mail for PC Networks or cc:Mail. The number of users to be migrated, the kinds of messaging systems they use, and the size of your own technical and training staff will play a big role in this decision.

If you do decide to migrate users, you need to determine exactly which messaging systems you'll be migrating your users from: Microsoft Mail for PC Networks and/or AppleTalk Networks, Lotus cc:Mail, IBM PROFS, Verimation Memo, DEC All-in-One, and so on. Next, you need to figure out what kinds of tools, if any, exist that can help you migrate users from each messaging system to Exchange. For example, Exchange includes a nice migration application for Microsoft Mail users. Once you know what kinds of migration tools are available, you have to set a timetable for migration. Finally, you have to determine whether, based on your timetable, you should link other messaging systems to Exchange before you've migrated all users in them over to Exchange.

If you choose to migrate users to Exchange, be aware that Exchange can create new user accounts from text data files. If your legacy messaging system lets you output user information to a file and you've got someone around who can write a program to assure that all the information Exchange needs is in the file in the right format and order, you should certainly consider using this nice, time-saving Exchange migration option.

In planning, don't underplay the importance of X.400 connections, especially if your company communicates with organizations outside the United States. The X.400 suite includes the Electronic Document

Interchange (EDI) standard, which supports electronic commerce by providing secure communications when you use your messaging system to, say, purchase products and services. Yes, you can secure your Internet mail communications, but X.400 is catching on, even in the United States. Keep it in mind.

As with intersite links, you need only one Exchange connector to link an entire site to a foreign messaging system. And as long as intersite links are in place, a single foreign messaging system connector can send and receive messages for an entire organization. As with intersite connections, though, you might want more than one connector to balance network traffic loads and provide redundancy.

An Example: GerCom's External Links

GerCom will stick with its T1 Internet connection, moving management of the e-mail side of its Internet domain from our Sun systems to the Exchange server in Los Angeles. For the time being, at least, domain name service will continue to be handled by GerCom's Sun systems, though we're looking seriously at the DNS software available for NT.

We're also going to set up T1 Internet connections for our other two sites—for intersite redundancy, not direct delivery of Internet mail. Internet mail will still come into the LA Exchange site and be delivered to Chicago and New York through the Exchange system. Those T1s will put us in just the right position bandwidth-wise if our tests of remote access for Exchange users via the Internet are successful and we move most users from RAS to Internet-based Exchange client links.

To support the customer purchasing and payment applications that our salespeople want to build, we'll be using X.400 connections to six of our trading partners—two inside the United States and four outside. This will let us develop the app using the X.400 EDI standard. We'll have one T1 link to a public X.400 provider in Los Angeles. (Yikes, another T1!) Figure 22.13 shows all of GerCom's external links.

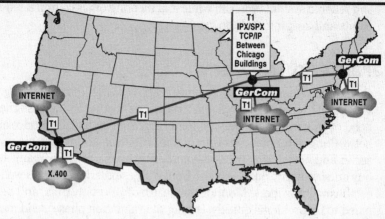

FIGURE 22.13: GerCom's connections to the outside world

We don't have any legacy Microsoft Mail systems; we've been using our Sun systems to support the Simple Message Transport Protocol (SMTP) on our UNIX system. Users have a bunch of POP mail clients for e-mail. As indicated above, we want to close down our UNIX-based mail system. So, we'll have to migrate our UNIX mail users to Exchange and deal with that e-messaging address change brought about by changing our registered Internet domain name from "gerberco" to "gercom." We'll use comma-delimited files from the UNIX system to create Exchange user accounts, so we should be able to set up all our user accounts easily. I'm less sure about migrating messages and any storage folders our users may have. We may just leave that up to users; most have reported that much of what's in their folders is no longer of use to them anyway.

VALIDATE AND OPTIMIZE THE DESIGN

Validation means ensuring you've got a system that guarantees message delivery, integrity, and security. It also means making sure the system you've designed is versatile enough to handle the range of documents, messaging formats, and applications your organization needs. *Optimization* is a balancing act in which you try to build the fastest, most stable and reliable systems you can while still meeting organizational requirements and keeping costs down.

Guaranteed Delivery

Guaranteed message delivery comes with reliable NT and Exchange servers and reliable internal and external networks. To increase the likelihood of guaranteed delivery, go for as much server fault tolerance and networking redundancy as your organization can afford. Use high-quality server and networking hardware and software inside your organization; buy outside networking services from stable, experienced, and well-established providers. Monitor the health of your networks, and be prepared to fix problems quickly. During the validation phase, send messages of all kinds through all of your connections, and then check to see if they arrive intact. When problems arise, use Exchange's own message-tracking tools to catch up with wayward messages, and take advantage of Exchange's network and system-monitoring tools to discover why a message didn't get through.

Reliability is only one side of guaranteed message delivery. You also need Exchange servers that are sufficiently fast and networks that have the bandwidth to move messages quickly enough to meet maximum delivery time parameters. If you've specified that all messages should be delivered to all internal users within five minutes, for example, now's the time to see if your Exchange system is capable of performing up to spec. If not, you have to either increase your permissible maximum delivery times or, depending on the source of the problem, come up with speedier servers and/or higher-bandwidth networks.

Message Integrity

Message integrity means that messages arrive in the same form as they were transmitted. Problems with message integrity often can be traced to mismatched binary message-part encoding and decoding. For example, a binary attachment to a message bound for the Internet is uuencoded by the sender, while the receiver expects MIME encoding. As you'll see later, there are lots of ways to set coding parameters in Exchange to help avoid problems like this.

Message Security

In Exchange 5 and greater, RSA encryption and public keys work both within a single Exchange organization and can be enabled to work across Exchange organizations. For messages defined for foreign e-messaging systems, Exchange Server implements a set of encryption and authentication standards: NTLM encryption, TLS encryption, SASL clear text authentication, and Secure MIME.

You can try to validate message security on your own or with the help of a certified electronic data processing auditor. If security is important to your organization, I strongly recommend the latter.

System Versatility

Exchange's internal message formatting, along with formatting available in X.400 and Internet Mail, means that you'll be able to send documents of almost any type, containing virtually anything from text to last night's Letterman show. But be sure to validate that everything you need is there and works.

On the applications side, you've got all the app development environments I mentioned in Chapter 18, as well as applications like Microsoft's Schedule+ and Outlook. Exchange Server is a very popular product, so plenty of Exchange-based e-messaging-enabled applications are already available from third-party vendors, and there are many more in development. Keep your eyes open for the latest "killer" Exchange apps.

Optimization

When you've done everything to ensure guaranteed message delivery, message integrity, and security, as well as system versatility, it's time for *optimization*. You optimize your design by checking out alternatives that may help improve your Exchange system. The basic question is: Can you do it better, faster, easier? For example, you might want to consider implementing support for X.400 messaging, even though your organization has no current need for it, simply because competitors are moving toward it.

Optimization can also focus on reducing costs without compromising the quality of your system. For example, you might want to come up with lower-cost options for connecting Exchange sites or for realizing network redundancy.

An Example: Validating GerCom's Design

GerCom's design validates very well. Based on tests we've done, our system seems quite reliable, and we're meeting our ten-minute message-delivery maximum. Our certified data processing auditor says our messaging security looks good.

We've covered the message format bases by including native Exchange, X.400 Mail, and Internet Mail capabilities. We've found nothing that we can't dump into a message and move through and out of our system with integrity. That includes everything from text to a full-color animated "film," complete with sound, showing our exclusive high-end, Fine Egyptian Marble Enter key in action.

On the applications side we've started working with Schedule+ and both Exchange and Outlook Forms Designer. Both are performing as expected so far. Our development people are quite happy with the custom programming APIs available in Exchange. They're sure they can put together any of the applications our users have requested so far.

We put together and evaluated one alternative networking option, using the Dynamic RAS Connector in place of a Site Connector to link our Exchange sites. I continue to worry about the cost of those T1 connections in our original plans for intersite links, but in our tests the DRASC was just too slow to handle the traffic we expect. So we're now wedded to those T1 lines.

ROLL OUT THE PLAN

Rollout doesn't mean dropping a whole Exchange system on your organization all at once. It means making Exchange available to specific systems people and users according to a carefully thought-out schedule. You should also go through a testing phase with specific users.

You might start your rollout in MIS—maybe just with yourself, if you're part of MIS. Next, you might move on to samples of users based on the groupings you uncovered in your user-needs assessment. Then move steadily onward until all users are up and running in Exchange. The key is to get Exchange out to all users as fast as possible without crashing your organization. (Here I'm referring to your *real* organization, not your Exchange organization.)

Remember that rollout is an integral part of the Exchange design process. As you step through your rollout plans, be ready to change your design. If something doesn't work, change it now. Don't let things pile up to the point that change becomes virtually impossible.

Whether you're in a test or production rollout phase, be sure to keep users in the loop. Get them committed to Exchange. Let them know if and when they're going to see the new Exchange client or other clients supported by Exchange Server. Explain to them how they can use whatever client you plan to provide them both to do what they're already doing and to get other tasks done. This is where user training comes in.

Keep MIS staff involved and informed as well. An Exchange installation and implementation is a big deal for an MIS department. Over time, I'll bet that just about everyone in MIS will get involved with Exchange. MIS staff should understand and welcome Exchange, not see it as a threat to their jobs. Train MIS personnel as data processing colleagues rather than just end users. You don't have to tell everyone in MIS everything there is to know about Exchange—they can buy this book for that purpose (hint, hint). But be sure to talk to them about both server and client basics from a more technical perspective.

An Example: The GerCom Rollout

The GerCom Exchange rollout is a two-year project, and we're about six months into it. (How time flies when you're having fun.) The rollout is a very detailed and complex process; I can only touch on key highlights here. I've got to keep that glue from drying, you know.

We decided to start with a basic Exchange installation for use by our 11 new Exchange MIS employees and the executive suite. If our executive staffers weren't so computer literate I'd never have approved this part of the rollout plan, but we execs have all lived with computers and new system rollouts for a long time, and I know we're a good and safe starting point for Exchange. And what better way to get upper management behind Exchange and the rollout?

The first phase of GerCom's Exchange rollout went pretty smoothly, though we were surprised at how poorly the Outlook 2000 client performed on anything less than a 200MHz Pentium machine with 32MB of RAM. We're pushing hard to find the resources to upgrade user workstations to at least this level.

We allowed two months for phase one of the rollout. As a condition of employment, all of GerCom's new non-Los Angeles Exchange staff had to live in LA for these two months (at great but justifiable expense, I might add). Exchange site administrators participated in the setup of the LA site and then helped bring up the servers for the Chicago and New York sites. The servers were linked by local networks for the test phase, and we were able to proof out the entire GerCom Exchange system right in LA.

During this period our Exchange training and applications development staff went through training of their own. I was happy when, to a person, they came out of training as enthusiastic as I am about end-user and MIS Exchange application development. They did remind us that we had to make a commitment to buy the latest version of Microsoft Word and Excel for our users. We did. Staff also suggested that we buy some evaluation copies of Microsoft's Access database product. We did.

When our trainers finished their own training we had them do some test training with the MIS staff. That turned out really well; everyone seemed genuinely enthusiastic. No one openly expressed opposition to Exchange or the kinds of applications we plan to develop with it. I've asked our MIS director to talk to his staff to be sure that what we saw on the surface is real.

At the end of the two-month period the Chicago and New York Exchange staff returned to their respective cities. There they set up their servers and connected them to the T1 lines we had installed. Our LA Exchange site administrator is specially skilled in Internet and X.400 connectivity, so we sent her to Chicago and New York to help with those connections. Hey, these Exchange folks are traveling as much as we execs are.

Bringing site administrators to Los Angeles worked very well. It concentrated them for training, let them learn from each other as they did real tasks, and helped them build important relationships that would make their jobs both easier and more rewarding. We'll get these folks together on a regular basis, and we'll use this same plan when we implement a new site.

With all sites up and running, the second phase of the GerCom Exchange rollout focused on bringing all of our departments into Exchange for e-mail only. This involved a lot of training and no small amount of Exchange system administration. We were able to create most of our user accounts from comma-delimited files produced on our UNIX system, but that information wasn't enough to fill in all of the blanks on those 11 property pages available in Exchange Administrator's user administration and management tool. We exported more information from our Oracle human resources database in comma-delimited files and imported it into our Exchange servers, but our Exchange administrators still had to fill in information we didn't have in electronic form. They also had to create accounts for employees who didn't have UNIX mail accounts (mostly recent hires).

During phase two we brought the LA and New York sales staffs into the loop first, because they're the biggest contributors to GerCom's bottom line. Then, in order, came Chicago Sales, LA Marketing, Chicago Manufacturing, and Chicago Engineering.

Our Exchange training/end-user application development staff was stretched to the limit a few times during phase two of the rollout. The Exchange site administrators also felt a lot of pressure as they worked to add users and tune their systems. Probably at least in part because of the LA training, they all supported each other both technically and emotionally—face-to-face, on the phone, and through our growing Exchange system.

Our hardware and networking projections are holding pretty well, though I have to tell you that our servers' disks are filling up fast. And Performance Monitor tests are indicating that we may soon need to add more processors and memory to our LA machine. (It's either that or cut back on our expectations.)

Phase two lasted four months, though we thought we could finish in three. The final phase of our Exchange rollout involves the creation of end-user and custom-programmed applications. We've allotted 18 months to complete this phase, and we're going to start it now.

We'll work on the two kinds of applications in parallel. We'll start with some of the end-user apps our controller wants to implement, then we'll move on to the human resources apps. Our first custom-programmed application will be the customer notification system that our manufacturing people came up with. Once that's in place, we'll move on to the customer ordering and payment system that the salespeople want. We figure that we should start easy and work up to the more difficult tasks.

Of course, now that we're into the implementation phase we're hearing new ideas from all quarters. I've asked MIS to work with users to quickly understand what they have in mind and determine if it can be implemented in Exchange—and if it can, what it might cost. The exec staff will look at these proposals with MIS and determine where they should fit into our current implementation plans. Of course, as you might imagine, some of our hotshot users are already coming up with their own

Exchange applications based on the user-oriented app tools we've talked about.

Because we execs and MIS worked closely together, there was no finger-pointing when these surprise apps popped up. We gave everyone an opportunity during the early phases of the design process. We told everyone that we couldn't guarantee implementation of ideas that came in late, but we quickly came up with a way to filter new ideas that surfaced during rollout. No one panicked. No one screamed. All is well.

Right now, things look good. A reasonable amount of planning, coupled with an openness to change, has gotten our Exchange rollout off to an excellent start. I can't wait to see what the system looks like in 18 months.

What's Next?

In this chapter you learned the 11 steps involved in designing an Exchange system. You also learned that the Exchange design process is an iterative one in which you constantly revisit steps to refine your design. This is true even for the final step—Exchange system rollout, where you test and modify your design in the real world. In the next chapter, you will learn about the Exchange Administrator program menus.

Chapter 23

THE ADMINISTRATOR AND ITS MENUS

his chapter walks you through lots of menus and pages for setting properties of one kind or another. I think you'll find it useful to track through everything once and set some specific Exchange Server parameters when appropriate.

Adapted from *Mastering™ Microsoft® Exchange Server 5.5* by Barry Gerber

ISBN 0-7821-2658-8   916 pages $44.99

ADMINISTRATION AND MANAGEMENT

Notice that this section of the book deals with Exchange Server administration *and* management. There's a real and sharp difference between the two terms. In a nutshell, *administration* is everything you do to set up Exchange Server, while *management* is what you do to keep the server running and its users happy.

Administration includes tasks like creating Exchange Recipients such as mailboxes and distribution lists; setting up Exchange server backups; and configuring Exchange components such as sites, servers, Message Transfer Agents (MTAs), and connectors. Management covers tasks like monitoring Exchange servers and ensuring that they keep running, backing up and restoring a server, tracking mail messages to find out why they weren't delivered, and keeping address book information current as people change offices and phone numbers.

You use the Exchange Administrator program to do both administration and management, so "Administrator" might seem like a less-than-comprehensive name for the program. But when I consider the alternatives—the sexist "AdminMan," for example—the name seems just fine.

ADMINISTRATOR WINDOWS

The Exchange Administrator takes advantage of several Microsoft Windows capabilities. For example, it lets you use multiple windows for views of one or more Exchange servers, and each window has two variable-size panes.

Multiple Windows

Figure 23.1 shows the Administrator window. Inside the window are two additional windows, both labeled in part Server EXCHLA01 in Site LA. This tells you that you're looking at two views of the server EXCHLA01, which resides in the Exchange Server organization GerCom and the site LA.

You may recall from earlier chapters that Exchange Server is object-oriented and that the Administrator is the tool you use to manipulate its objects. Also, remember that some Exchange Server objects are containers—that is, they hold other objects. Not all objects are containers, but all containers are objects.

The lower window in Figure 23.1 shows the Recipients container for the LA site, hence the name Server EXCHLA01 in Site LA—Recipients. Notice that the word "Recipients" in the left-hand pane is highlighted, telling you that the container is selected. The objects in the Recipients container—Exchange Recipients—are shown in the right-hand pane.

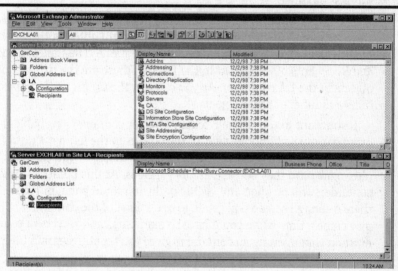

FIGURE 23.1:   Two views of the same Exchange server

Because I just finished setting up EXCHLA01 and have created no Recipients yet, the only recipient is the Schedule+ Free/Busy Connector. This connector is used to exchange Schedule+ information between Exchange sites and MS Mail post offices. This allows users in both systems to set up meetings using Microsoft Schedule+ while taking into account the schedules of potential meeting participants.

Notice the scroll bar at the bottom of the lower window. It's showing because there are more columns for the list of Recipients than can be displayed given the window's current width. Two columns aren't displayed in the lower window; these are labeled Department and Modified. Respectively, they show the recipient's department and the date and time when a recipient was last modified. To see columns that aren't displayed in a window, you can either resize the window or scroll over until the columns are visible.

While I'm talking about columns, note that you can re-sort the rows in certain lists. If a list has column title bars like the ones in the two windows in Figure 23.1, you can click some of the bars to re-sort the list by the column. Not all column title bars can be used to sort lists; for example, you can sort Recipients' lists only by display name and the date an object was last modified.

The upper window shows the Configuration container within the LA site container. The term Configuration isn't highlighted in the left-hand pane because the lower window is the current one. The Configuration and Recipients objects show in the LA site; these are the two second-level objects in the LA container. As you can see, the Configuration object contains a number of other objects.

If you want to see all the Exchange Server containers available in your organization, just double-click all the objects in the left pane until there are no objects with plus (+) signs in front of them. Or you can click all plus signs until they become minus (−) signs. At this point, all available containers will be open and visible in the left-hand pane. In Figure 23.2 there's enough screen real estate to open most of the containers. There may come a time when you'll have so many sites and servers in your organization that opening all containers gives you repetitive-strain injury, so do it now, while you've got just one site and server.

Now it's your turn. Open the Exchange Administrator. You can see what's inside any object in the Exchange hierarchy—in the left-hand pane—by clicking the object. Open your site by double-clicking its name or by clicking the plus sign to the left of the site's name. Then open another window by selecting New Window from the Window menu. Now play with the two windows, getting each to display whatever you'd like. You can open more windows or close any of them at any time.

The neat thing about these multiple windows is that you can easily have different servers or sites open in different windows. This lets you manage multiple servers in multiple sites simultaneously (if, of course, you've got the necessary rights to those servers).

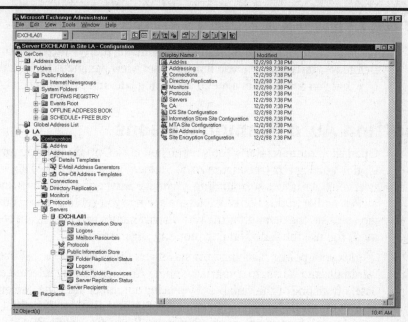

FIGURE 23.2: Almost all the containers in a new Exchange organization are displayed in the left-hand pane.

NOTE

Try to start thinking of the collection of objects you see in the Administrator as the *Exchange Directory*. A copy of the directory for an entire Exchange organization is stored on each Exchange server in the organization. As you'll see later, the directory is automatically updated and replicated across the organization. This is what makes centralized management of Exchange servers possible and extremely easy.

Manipulating the Splitbar

The left and right panes of the two windows in Figure 23.2 are divided by a *splitbar*—a bar that lets you adjust for the amount of screen real estate used by the two panes in a window.

To move the splitbar, just move your Windows pointer so that it's touching any part of the splitbar, and the pointer will turn into a crosshair. Then press and hold down the left mouse button. While still holding down the left mouse button, move the splitbar until you're happy with the size of the right and left panes.

Part iv

Preliminary Settings

We're going to cover the Administrator's menus pretty much sequentially. Before we start, however, you'll need to set a few parameters in a dialog box that you access from a menu appearing later in the sequence.

Setting Auto Naming Options

Open the Administrator's Tools menu and click Options to bring up the Options dialog box (see Figure 23.3). Remember when I talked about the near-religious issues surrounding Exchange Server display names and aliases earlier in this book? Well, here's where you get to choose your religion and set the default for the way display names and aliases are created. You use the Auto Naming property page to do this.

Pick your poison. Custom options let you use the variables %First, %Initials, and %Last to construct a name. You can display selected characters from one of the variables by placing a number after the percent sign in the variable name. (For example, %1First displays the initial character in each first name—so the first name *Barry* displays as *B*.) Click Apply, but don't close the Options dialog box.

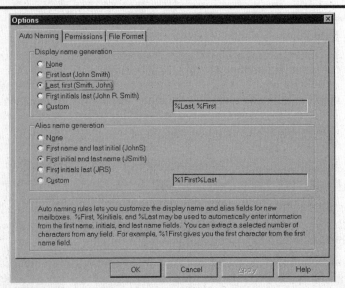

FIGURE 23.3: The Options dialog box shown with its Auto Naming property page

Setting the Domain for NT Account Selection

Keep an eye on Figure 23.4 as we move along. As I noted earlier, Exchange mailboxes are usually linked to an NT account. When you're creating a new Exchange mailbox, you can select the account you want to link the mailbox to. When you choose to do this, NT presents you with a list of accounts in a specific domain. You can use the Permissions property page on the Options dialog box to tell this copy of Exchange Administrator whether to present the user with a list of NT accounts either from the domain where the Exchange server is installed or from the default domain, which is the domain selected in the drop-down list. In our case, since there's only one domain, LA, we'd get the same domain for whichever of the two options we selected. However, if you begin to build multidomain networks, it's very likely that you may want to choose NT accounts from a domain other than the one in which you've installed Exchange Server. You can use these options to ensure that Exchange Administrator presents the most appropriate list of domain users as you create new mailboxes.

Setting Permissions Options

As you'll remember, Exchange Server security is based on NT Server security. You can give an NT account or group the permissions (rights) to administer and manage all Exchange servers in a site, as you did with your Exchange administration group in the last chapter. You can also permit different users or groups to administer different pieces of Exchange Server—even different Exchange servers. For example, you might give one group permissions to administer a specific site's Recipients, while permitting a different user to administer each of the Exchange servers in a site.

With a few exceptions, if an NT account or group has permissions to an Exchange Server container, these permissions automatically extend to all objects in the container, including nested containers. Objects within the container automatically inherit the permissions that were granted to the account or group at the master container level. For example, when we gave the Exchange administration group (Exchange Admins) permissions in the site container, those permissions were inherited by objects in the site's Recipients container. Permissions granted at the site level are not inherited by objects in the Configuration container, which is also a subcontainer of the site container.

Part iv

As we go through the Administrator's menus, it will be most helpful if you see all the permissions options for all objects, so you need to ensure that some general Administrator parameters are properly set. Click the Permissions tab in the Options dialog box. Make sure your computer account's domain is showing and that the Show Permissions Page for All Objects and Display Rights for Roles on Permissions Page boxes are selected (see Figure 23.4).

Don't worry about the whys and wherefores of these options right now; I promise that by the end of this chapter you'll be on intimate terms with both. If you've changed either of the two options, click Apply, but don't close the Options dialog box yet.

NOTE

You might not want to set separate access permissions for every little piece of Exchange Server. If you don't, you can go back and deselect Show Permissions Page for All Objects after we've gone through this chapter.

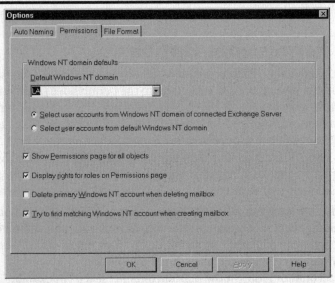

FIGURE 23.4: The Options dialog box shown with its Permissions property page

Setting the NT Account Deletion Option

Recall that you can create NT accounts while creating Exchange mail-boxes, and vice versa. When you delete an NT account in the User Manager for Domains, you're asked if you want to delete the mailbox associated with the account as well. When you delete a mailbox in the Exchange Administrator, the NT account associated with it is deleted only if you select the option Delete Primary Windows NT Account When Deleting Mailbox. If you select this option, you are alerted before the deletion and offered the opportunity to not delete the mailbox.

Setting the Option to Find a Matching Windows NT Account

As you'll soon see, when you create a mailbox, you will usually assign an NT account to it. If the account doesn't exist, you can create a new one on the spot. If you want to assign the mailbox to an existing NT account, you can either search for it manually while creating the mailbox or select Try to Find Matching Windows NT Account When Creating Mailbox. If you check this option and, while you're creating a new mailbox, the Exchange Administrator finds an NT account with a username that matches the alias you've given the mailbox, you'll be offered the option of assigning the account to the NT account.

This can save a bit of manual searching time on already established NT systems, so I suggest you accept the default check for the option. When you're finished, click OK.

Setting File Format Options

The last tab on the Options dialog box is used to set the format for data that is exported from or imported into Exchange Server. The default set-ting is for standard comma-delimited files. Unless you have a pressing need to alter this option, leave it as is.

WARNING

The settings you established above apply to the copy of the Administrator pro-gram you're running now and to the account you are logged into now. If you install and run the program on another computer or log into the same computer under a different account, you'll need to modify these settings for that com-puter or account. Be careful here. If your naming conventions aren't the same as Administrator's default, the Recipients you create will be misnamed until you properly set auto naming properties in the Options dialog box.

WARNING

The setting we're about to make applies to your Exchange site. Once set, it stays in effect for the site until changed—no matter which copy of the Administrator you use to view the setting.

Changing Site Addresses

When you installed your Exchange server, at least four special site addresses were created for your site: cc:Mail, Microsoft Mail, SMTP (Internet), and X.400. These addresses are appended to Exchange Server recipient alias names to create full MS Mail and SMTP addresses. Exchange Server uses First and Last Names along with the site addresses to create full cc:Mail and X.400 addresses. For example, as you can see in Figure 23.5, the SMTP site address for the GerCom LA site is @LA.GerCom .com. My alias name is BGerber, and my SMTP address is BGerber@LA .GerCom.com.

You can change any of the four site addresses. Use caution here, however, because any changes you make should be based on addresses you have or expect to get in the real world. For example, if you've already got an Internet domain name, you'll want to change the site's SMTP address to reflect that name.

SMTP, cc:Mail, and X.400 addresses are modified in one way (which I'll talk about in a minute). Microsoft Mail addresses are modified using the Microsoft Mail Connector dialog box. To change a cc:Mail, an SMTP, or an X.400 address, click the Configuration container for your site in the left-hand pane of an Administrator window. Then double-click the Site Addressing object, which is in the right-hand pane of the window, and click the Site Addressing tab. (See Figure 23.2 for help in locating these objects.)

In the resultant Site Addressing dialog box, click the address you want to change, then click Edit (see Figure 23.5). Edit the address using the cc:Mail, SMTP, or X.400 dialog box that pops up, then click OK to close each dialog box.

We're done with the preliminaries. Now we're ready to move on to the first menu of the Administrator: the File menu.

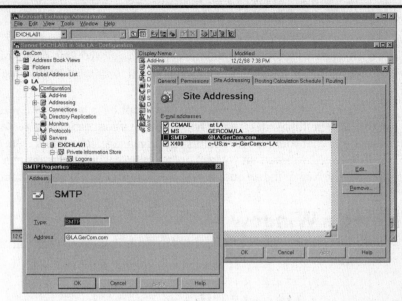

FIGURE 23.5: The Site Addressing dialog box is used to change the base e-messaging address for a site.

THE FILE MENU

As you can see from Figure 23.6, the File menu is pretty important. You use it to connect to new servers and create new Recipients and other objects, to quickly export data on your Exchange server, and to view and set object properties and duplicate certain objects, such as mailboxes.

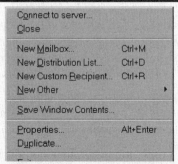

FIGURE 23.6: The Exchange Administrator's File menu

Connecting to a Server

You use the File menu's Connect to Server option to link to a server and open a new window on it. Since all servers in a site contain copies of all information for the site, you'll generally need to connect to only one server in a site.

As we'll see later, the Connect to Server option is most useful when you have multiple sites; you'll then establish a connection to a server in each site that you need to administer and manage. Remember from our little exercise above that you can open multiple windows in any site by using the New Window option in the Administrator's Window menu.

Closing a Window

The File menu's Close option is used to close any selected Administrator window.

Creating a New Mailbox

This is another exciting milestone: You're going to create your first Exchange recipient, a mailbox.

From here on, I'll assume you've already opened the Administrator. Click your site (mine is LA); your Administrator screen should look like the one in Figure 23.7. Next, from the File menu choose New Mailbox. A dialog box like the one shown in Figure 23.8 pops up to tell you that you must create new Recipients in a *site-based Recipients container*—in my case, the LA site Recipients container, since I have no other sites. I've played a nasty trick on you by having you first click your site. There is a method to my madness, however. The first time I saw the dialog box shown in Figure 23.8, I thought that something had broken. Now you know it's just a friendly reminder and the Administrator will take you to the right container. To avoid the dialog box, just click the site-based Recipients container you want to use before selecting New Mailbox. Go ahead and click OK in the warning box.

The next thing you'll see is the mailbox's Properties dialog box, shown in Figure 23.9. Note the twelve tabs on the dialog box; each lets you set a different group of attributes for a mailbox. Let's take a look at each of the eleven property pages used to administer and manage mailboxes.

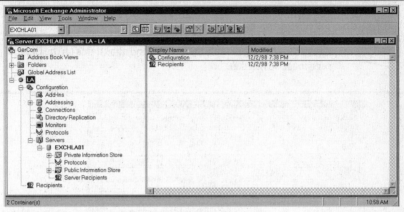

FIGURE 23.7: The Administrator with a site selected

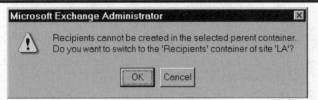

FIGURE 23.8: The Administrator's wrong container warning

General Properties

As you can see in Figure 23.9, you use the General property page to fill in all the information about a mailbox and its user. This is also where you grant the right to use the mailbox to a specific NT account.

Filling in General Information   In Figure 23.10, I've already filled in information to create a mailbox for myself on the General property page. The Display and Alias names are created automatically; the ones for your site may look different, depending on how you set your options earlier in this chapter. Now fill in the information for your first mailbox (you'll probably want to make it your own). *Don't* click OK or Apply yet.

NOTE

When creating a new mailbox, you don't have to fill in every last lovin' field on every property page—only the display and alias fields on the General property page must be filled in.

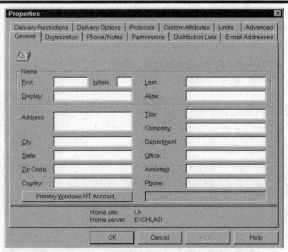

FIGURE 23.9:   The mailbox's Properties dialog box

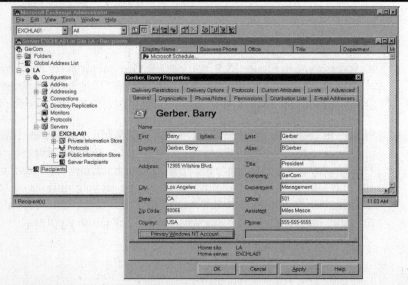

FIGURE 23.10:   Filling in the General property page of the mailbox's Properties dialog box

Granting an NT Account the Rights to a Mailbox To grant an NT account the rights to a mailbox, click Primary Windows NT Account on the General property page to bring up the dialog box shown in Figure 23.11. You can grant rights to an existing NT account or create a new account.

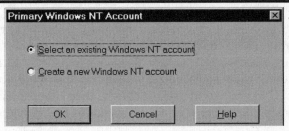

FIGURE 23.11: Granting mailbox access rights to an existing or new NT account

If access rights are to be granted to an existing NT account, click Select an Existing Windows NT Account and then click OK. This brings up the Add User or Group dialog box shown in Figure 23.12. Making sure you're in the right domain, find and click the account you want to give rights to, click Add, and then click OK.

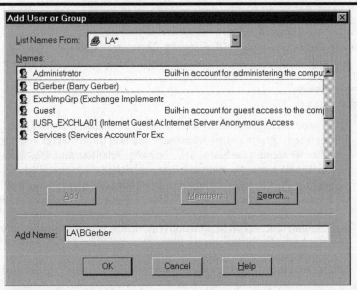

FIGURE 23.12: The Add User or Group dialog box lets you assign rights to a mailbox to an existing NT account.

Part iv

If you selected Try to Find Matching Windows NT Account When Creating Mailbox when you set the Tools/Options/Permissions options discussed above, the Administrator will look for an NT account with the same name as the alias. If one is found, you'll be given the option of using that account here. If you accept the option, you're done. If you don't, you can either locate an account with the Add User or Group dialog box or create a new account.

If you need to create a new NT account and give it rights to the mailbox you're creating, select the Create a New Windows NT Account option from the Primary Windows NT Account dialog box (see Figure 23.11) and then click OK. The Create Windows NT Account dialog box pops up (see Figure 23.13). Be sure the domain is correct, then either accept the default NT account name offered or type in a name of your choice and click OK.

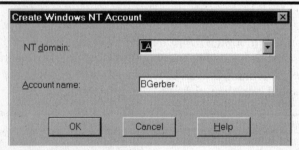

FIGURE 23.13:   Creating an NT account to be assigned rights to a new mailbox

NOTE

As you can imagine, based on the limited information Exchange Administrator has when it creates a new NT account, many of the attributes you might enter for an NT account are blank. Still, Exchange Administrator does a pretty good job. The NT account's username defaults to the Exchange mailbox's alias. The account's full name is set equal to the mailbox's display name and the password is set to blank so the user will have to change it the first time she or he logs in. If the account will be used only to access the Exchange mailbox, don't worry; this automatically-set information is sufficient. If, on the other hand, you need to further configure the account for NT access, you can do that in NT's User Manager for Domains.

Organization

Use the Organization property page to record information about the mailbox user's status in your organization's hierarchy (assuming, of course, that
the mailbox will be used by one person and not by a group of people or a
custom-programmed application). Here you can set the name of the mailbox user's manager and the names of those who report directly to the user.
You can view this information in other places in Exchange; for example, the
user of an Exchange client can open and view an Organization property
page for any unhidden mailbox in the Exchange Global Address List.

The Mailbox User's Manager   To add information to the Organization property page, first click the Organization tab. Then, to add information about the mailbox user's manager, click Modify in the Manager box.
A dialog box showing a list of valid Exchange Recipients pops up (see
Figure 23.14). This dialog box is called the *address book*. It lists all unhidden Exchange Recipients: mailboxes, distribution lists, custom Recipients, and public folders. Find the manager's name in the address book,
click the name, and then click OK in the address book. (In the figure, I've
selected myself as the manager of my Administrative Assistant, Miles
Mason. I created a mailbox for Miles while you weren't looking.)

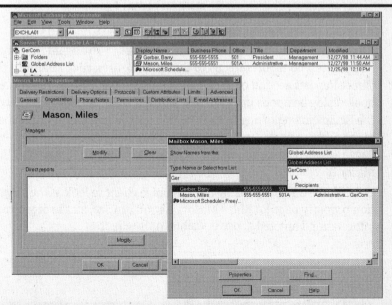

FIGURE 23.14:   Setting the name of the Exchange recipient who manages a mailbox user

THE ADDRESS BOOK DIALOG BOX

Notice in Figure 23.14 that I found myself in the address book by typing in the first three letters of my last name. As the number of Recipients in your organization grows, this is a way to quickly find the one you're looking for.

Another way to narrow down a search is to use the drop-down menu for the Show Names From The option. The menu is open in Figure 23.14; as you can see, it lets you walk down your Exchange hierarchy and pick the specific site and Recipients container to search in.

Finally, you can use the Find button. It brings up a template with fill-in-the-blank fields for things like first and last name, title, and department.

NOTE

When you're working in the Exchange client, you'll tend to think of entries in the address book as individuals, groups of individuals, or public folders. When you use the address book in the Exchange Administrator program, try to think of these real-world entities as Recipient objects. Doing so will make your life as an Exchange administrator/manager easier—I guarantee.

Recipients Managed by the Mailbox User   To add information on Recipients who report directly to the mailbox user, click Modify in the Direct Reports section of the Organization property page. The address book dialog box pops up. From the address book, select and add each of the Recipients reporting to the mailbox user. When you're done, click OK in the address book. (In Figure 23.15, I've added three Recipients—which I again created while you weren't looking—who report directly to Miles Mason.)

In Figure 23.16, I'm using my Exchange client to look at the Organization property page for Miles Mason. As you can see, all the organizational information I entered above is visible to the client.

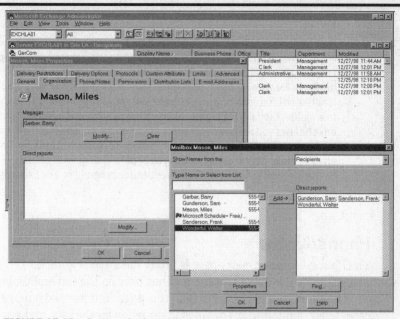

FIGURE 23.15: Setting the Recipients who report directly to a mailbox user

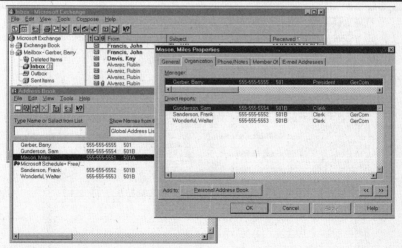

FIGURE 23.16: An Outlook client user views a mailbox's Organization property page.

NOTE

Before viewing Miles Mason's Organization property page with an Exchange client, I had to use the Exchange Administrator program to apply the changes I made to his mailbox. If I hadn't done this, the changes would not have been available for viewing by an Exchange client. Remember this when you change mailbox attributes on any property page: Until you apply changes you've made to a mailbox (by clicking Apply or OK in the mailbox's Properties dialog box), any changes you make will not be available to the Administrator program or to Exchange client users. This rule applies to modifications you make to any Exchange Server object. When you apply a change, you are saving it to the Exchange directory, where the Administrator program or any Exchange client can access it.

Phone/Notes

The Phone/Notes property page is pretty basic (see Figure 23.17). The phone number you enter for the mailbox user on the General property page is automatically carried over to this page. You can add a range of other telecommunications-oriented information for the user, and you can also add notes about the user. All this information will be visible to Exchange clients. Go ahead and fill in the page for the mailbox you're creating.

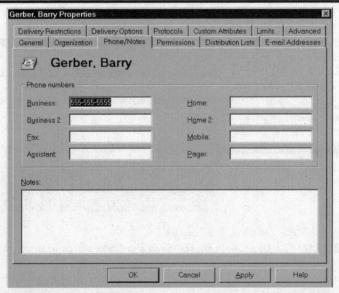

FIGURE 23.17: Entering telecommunications and other information for a mailbox user

Permissions

You use the Permissions property page to establish or change rights for the mailbox.

NOTE

If you don't see the Permissions property page, or you don't see the Roles and Rights boxes at the bottom of the page, you've been messing with those options we set back at the beginning of the chapter. To make things right, close the mailbox's Properties dialog box by clicking OK; then open the Tools menu, select Options, tab to the Permissions property page, and be sure that Show Permissions Page for All Objects and Display Rights for Roles on Permissions Page are selected. Click OK in the Options dialog box, then reopen the Properties dialog box for the mailbox you were creating by double-clicking it in the Recipients container. Whew!

Accounts with Inherited Permissions   Notice in Figure 23.18 that the permissions of two Windows NT accounts (LA\Administrator and LA\Services) and one NT group (LA\Exchange Admins) have been inherited by mailbox objects. The accounts and the group have permissions at the site level. These permissions are inherited by the Recipients container and all objects in it—individual mailboxes, in this case.

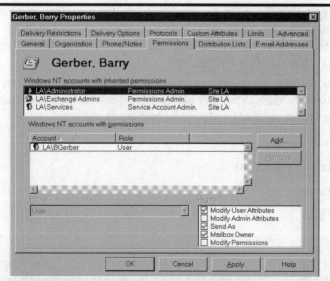

FIGURE 23.18:   Controlling access to a mailbox

LA\Administrators is the account I used when I installed Exchange Server, so it was granted organization-wide rights by default. I gave permissions to run Exchange services in the LA site to the LA\Services account. Like LA\ Administrators, it got organization-wide permissions when I installed Exchange Server.

You can't remove permissions on a mailbox from accounts and groups listed in the Windows NT Accounts With Inherited Permissions box; you have to remove the permissions for these accounts or groups at the appropriate container level. (All of this container-level stuff will become clearer as we move along.)

Granting Permissions to Other Accounts or Groups   When an NT account is made the Primary Windows NT account for a mailbox on the General page, it is automatically given permissions on the mailbox. As you can see in the Windows NT Accounts With Permissions box in Figure 23.18, BGerber was given permissions for the mailbox.

You can add to this list of NT accounts or groups with permissions on a particular mailbox. You can also limit the role that any account or group with permissions can play. This lets you do a number of things, including creating multiuser mailboxes or assigning a group to perform certain administrative tasks on one or more mailboxes without giving the group full administrative rights or access to all mailboxes.

To give an NT account or group permissions on a mailbox, click Add in the Permissions page and use the Add Users and Groups dialog box that pops up to choose an account or a group. You've used this dialog box before, so I'll let you take it from here.

Each account or group with permissions on a mailbox must have a *role*. Essentially, roles expand or limit what an account or group can do to a mailbox. There are five role types for mailboxes:

- ▶ Admin
- ▶ Permissions Admin
- ▶ Send As
- ▶ User
- ▶ Custom

Notice that BGerber's role is that of User. You use the Roles dropdown menu to pick a role for an account or group (see Figure 23.18). You won't see the Custom role here, and I'll explain why in just a bit.

Each role type is defined by the rights it has. These rights are listed in the lower right-hand section of the Permissions property page (see Figure 23.18). There are five mailbox rights:

▶ *Modify User Attributes* permits changes to the mailbox's user-modifiable attributes ("attributes" is another name for properties). For example, in an Exchange client, a user can delegate to other NT accounts or groups certain access rights to his or her mailbox.

▶ *Modify Admin Attributes* permits changes to any mailbox attribute that is modifiable in the Exchange Administrator. For example, those manager and direct-reports attributes you set on the Organization property page can be modified by those with Modify Admin Attributes rights. You certainly wouldn't want users to change their place in the organizational hierarchy, even if it's only in Exchange, would you?

▶ *Send As* allows the NT account or group granted the right for a mailbox to send messages from other mailboxes to which they have rights. With this feature, it appears that the messages came from the Send As mailbox. This right can be useful when, for example, you want an administrative aide to send messages from their own mailbox that appear to have come from a corporate mailbox (e.g., President at GerCom). Send As rights should be granted with care because they can be dangerous in the wrong hands, like when a disgruntled employee sends out a nasty message that appears to have come from some innocent person's mailbox.

▶ *Mailbox Owner* can log into the mailbox and send, receive, read, and manipulate messages.

▶ *Modify Permissions* can change permissions for the mailbox—that is, the entries on the mailbox's Permissions property page.

If the box in front of a particular right is checked in the Rights area of the Permissions property page, the role includes that right. Take a look at the rights for the different roles by selecting each role from the drop-down Roles menu.

There is no preset Custom role. To set up a Custom role, just check off the boxes for the rights you want an account or group to have. If the rights you choose don't match those for a particular role, Custom shows in the drop-down menu as the role type for that account or group.

Distribution Lists

You can add mailboxes to distribution lists using the Distribution Lists property page (see Figure 23.19). You don't have any distribution lists yet, so you can't do it now, but I'll add my mailbox to a distribution list I sneakily created while you were otherwise occupied.

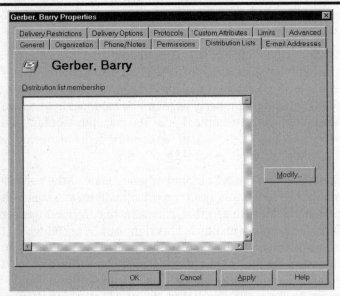

FIGURE 23.19:   The Distribution Lists property page

To do this, I click Modify in the Distribution Lists property page to bring up the dialog box shown in Figure 23.20. Then I click the distribution list to which I want to add my mailbox (LA Sales, the only list I have) and click Add. Finally, I click OK in the dialog box. My mailbox has now been added to the LA Sales distribution list.

You can also add a mailbox to a distribution list by using the configuration dialog box for a particular distribution list. This method is easier, since you don't have to open every mailbox you want to add to the list. I'll show you how to do this when we get to distribution lists.

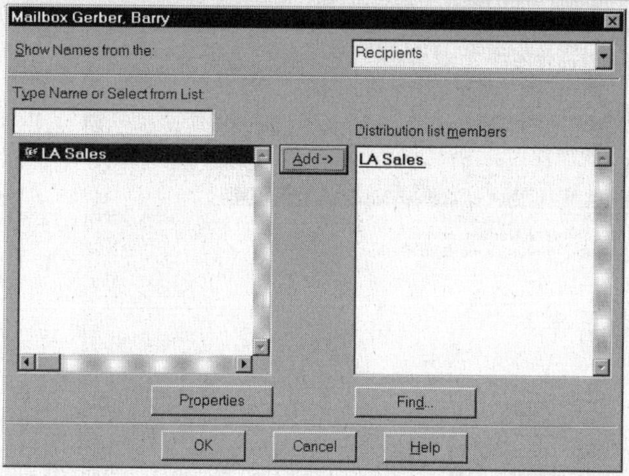

FIGURE 23.20: Adding a mailbox to a distribution list

E-mail Addresses

The E-mail Addresses property page shows a mailbox's addresses for different types of e-messaging systems. Four addresses are created by default: cc:Mail, MS Mail, SMTP, and X.400 (see Figure 23.21). Addresses for cc:Mail and MS Mail are created only if you've installed the cc:Mail Connector and MS Mail Connector, respectively.

Using this property page, you can manually change a specific user's address or add a new address for a user. For example, I sometimes give certain users a second SMTP address that includes their specific department. Adding or changing addresses manually is fun, but not for those new to Exchange Administrator, because it's usually not enough to just change the address. You'll also have to do some things in other areas in Exchange Administrator and maybe even in external systems.

If you wish, Exchange Administrator can regenerate addressing entries on this and all other recipient property pages when you change an e-mail addressing default for an entire site. If you add a gateway for another e-messaging system (fax, for example), the appropriate new gateway address can be added automatically to each recipient's E-mail Addresses property page.

Part iv

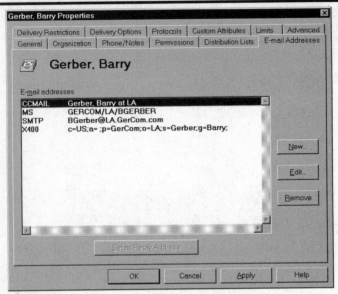

FIGURE 23.21: Use the E-mail Addresses property page to display, create, and modify addresses for a mailbox.

Delivery Restrictions

If, for whatever reason, you want to let only certain Recipients send messages to a particular mailbox, you use the Delivery Restrictions property page. As you can see in Figure 23.22, you can specify who can and who can't send messages to the mailbox.

You add Recipients to the Accept Messages From or Reject Messages From lists by clicking the appropriate Modify button; you'll see the address book dialog box shown back in Figure 23.14. Select the Recipients you want to add or exclude and then click OK in the Recipients list dialog box. To record your restrictions, click either OK or Apply on the Delivery Restrictions property page.

When a restricted recipient tries to send a message to an off-limits mailbox, the system will return the message (see Figure 23.23).

(I love the Send Again button; you can send the message again until you're blue in the face and you'll keep getting these rejection notices.)

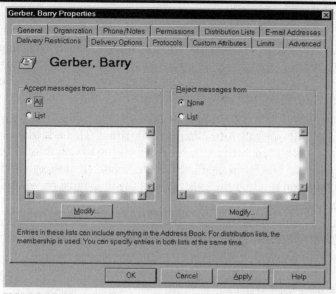

FIGURE 23.22: Use the Delivery Restrictions property page to specify which Recipients can send messages to a mailbox.

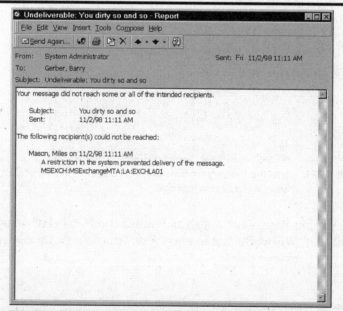

FIGURE 23.23: A system message tells restricted Recipients when they've tried to send a message to an off-limits mailbox.

Delivery Options

You use the Delivery Options property page to give other Recipients rights to the mailbox. You do this when a mailbox owner wants another mailbox owner or group to manage his or her mailbox—for example, when a secretary is assigned to watch a boss's mail, or when people go on vacation and need their mailboxes monitored.

In Figure 23.24, I've given Send On Behalf Of permissions to my mailbox to Miles Mason, my Administrative Assistant. This lets Mason send new messages and reply to messages for me using my mailbox as the return address. The From field in Send On Behalf Of messages identifies both the person sending the message and the individual on whose behalf the message was sent.

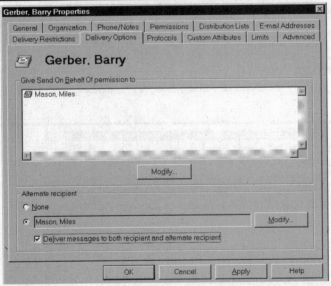

FIGURE 23.24:   Use the Delivery Options property page to give other Recipients special rights to a mailbox.

Can you imagine going through and setting Send On Behalf Of options for each user? Whew! But not to worry: Users can do it for themselves using their Exchange clients.

NOTE

The Send On Behalf Of permission is different from the role right Send As, which you set on the Permissions property page for a mailbox. Remember, Send As lets the user of one mailbox send a message as though it came from another mailbox, without any hint that the other mailbox didn't send the message itself. If you worry about users sending embarrassing messages that look like they came from another user, then Send On Behalf Of is a far safer option than Send As. If both options are granted to a user, Send As will override Send On Behalf Of.

At the bottom of the Delivery Options property page, I've indicated that messages to me should be delivered to an alternate recipient, Miles Mason. If I hadn't selected the Deliver Messages to Both Recipient and Alternate Recipient option, messages would have been redirected to Mason without a copy being sent to me.

The Alternate recipient option can be used in league with Send On Behalf Of to keep up with incoming mail when an employee is out of the office for one reason or another, or when she or he stops working for the organization. It can also be used to monitor an employee's use of Exchange messaging, since mailbox owners have no idea that messages for their own mailbox are also being sent to another mailbox.

Protocols

Exchange 5.5 comes with a bunch of new Internet-oriented features. You use the Protocols property page to enable five of these features for a mailbox. Here I'll give you the most basic of introductions. Follow along, referring to Figure 23.25 as I discuss the Protocols page.

Following are the five new protocols supported by Exchange Server:

- ▶ *HTTP (Web)* lets mailbox users access their Exchange server with an Internet browser, for example, to read their e-mail. *HTTP* is an acronym for Hypertext Transfer Protocol.

- ▶ *IMAP4 (Mail)* provides access to Exchange server messages and folders through the Internet Message Access Protocol v4.

- ▶ *LDAP (Directory)* allows a mailbox user, or even a non-Exchange user, to access the Exchange directory (e-mail addresses, phone numbers, etc.) using a Lightweight Directory Access Protocol (LDAP)–compliant client. This is a neat way to get e-mail addresses when using a non-Exchange client such as a POP3 or IMAP4 client, or to find information about an Exchange user with an LDAP client.

▶ *NNTP (News)* gives a mailbox user access to Usenet newsgroups stored in Exchange Server's public folders. *NNTP* stands for Network News Transfer Protocol.

▶ *POP3 (Mail)* support lets a mailbox user read and, with the help of the SMTP e-mail protocol, send mail through her or his Exchange server using a Post Office Protocol version 3 (POP3)–compliant client like Microsoft's Outlook or Outlook Express or Qualcomm's Eudora.

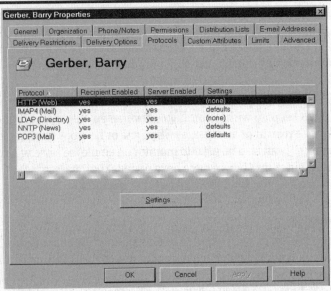

FIGURE 23.25: Using the Protocols property page to enable and modify the Internet-oriented features available to an Exchange mailbox user

Each of the five protocols can have up to three sets of attributes. These are represented by the columns in the table in Figure 23.25: Recipient Enabled, Server Enabled, and Settings. If "yes" appears in the Recipient Enabled column for a particular protocol, the protocol service is available to the user of the mailbox you're working on. If the Server Enabled column is marked yes, then you know that support for the protocol has been enabled on your Exchange server. The Settings column tells you if there are parameters you can set for a protocol and, if there are parameters, whether the current settings are defaults or custom.

Custom Attributes

You can create up to ten custom fields to hold information about Recipients. For example, you could create a custom field to hold an employee ID number for each recipient. Custom fields are created at the site level and apply to all Recipients in the site.

Use the Custom Attributes property page to fill in custom fields for a mailbox. For example, imagine that you've created a custom attribute called Employee ID for all Recipients. You enter the specific Employee ID for the user of a specific mailbox on that mailbox's Custom Attributes property page. Since we haven't yet created any custom attributes, there's nothing much we can do here.

Limits

You use limits to save disk space on your Exchange server. In a world where gigabytes of storage are never enough, limits judiciously used are most welcome. However, be careful not to overly limit user storage or you're likely to find the cost of fixing problems related to too little storage more expensive than adding more disk storage.

Deleted Item Retention Time   Exchange 5.5 includes a nifty new feature. You can tell Exchange Server to hold on to items that are deleted from users' Deleted Items folders. Prior to Exchange 5.5, once a user or automatic process deleted items from the Deleted Items folder, they were gone forever. With Exchange Server, you can set a default number of days that messages are retained in the information store before real, final, that's-it deletion. You can use the mailbox Limits property page to override the information store default.

Information Store Storage Limits   Use the Information Store Storage Limits options to either accept the mailbox's default maximum size limits that were set elsewhere or set your own maximum limits for the mailbox. As shown in Figure 23.26, you can use any or all of three options when setting your own limits. The mailbox user gets a warning when the first limit is reached and then on a specific schedule thereafter until storage drops below the limit. The warning message schedule is set on the Site Warnings schedule page on the Information Store Site Configuration object (in the Configuration container). When the second limit is reached, the mailbox can no longer send mail. It still can receive mail, however, since you might not want those who send messages getting a bunch of bounced message notifications just because a mailbox user is a resource hog. The third limit prevents reception as well as sending of messages. This option is useful when a user will be out of the office for an extended period and you don't want their mailbox to fill with gobs of unanswered messages.

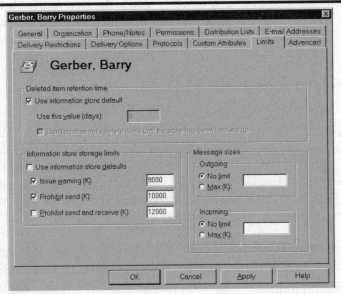

FIGURE 23.26:   The Limits Property page helps control Exchange Server storage.

Message Sizes   The Message Size Limits field lets you set maximum sizes for outgoing and incoming messages from and to a mailbox. With Message Size Limits, you can refine that setting for an individual mailbox. Use the Max (K) field for either incoming or outgoing messages, and type in the message size limit in kilobytes.

Advanced Properties

The Advanced property page is fun (see Figure 23.27). It's where you can do a lot of interesting but often esoteric things.

Figure 23.27 shows the Advanced property page for my mailbox. I've filled in a few fields, but your page should look pretty similar. Starting at the top left-hand corner of the property page, we'll move more or less from left to right, inching our way downward as we go.

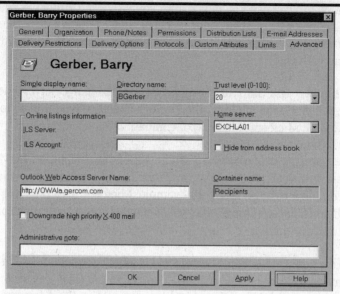

FIGURE 23.27:   The Advanced property page for a mailbox

The Simple Display Name   The Simple Display Name field is especially useful in certain multilingual Exchange environments. Exchange clients and the server's copy of the Administrator program show the simple display name when the full display name can't be properly displayed. For example, if a full display name is stored in a double-byte character set like Kanji, and a particular copy of the client or the Administrator program isn't set to display the character set, the simple display name is shown in place of the full display name.

The Directory Name   Directory names are unique identifiers for objects stored in the Exchange directory. Generally, you're offered a default directory name for any kind of object, and although you can change the name while creating the object, you can't change it afterward.

For a mailbox, the default directory name is the alias constructed by Exchange Server when you filled in the new mailbox's General property page. In Figure 23.26, the alias for my mailbox, BGerber, is offered as the default directory name. You can change the directory name while creating a mailbox, but you can't change it after you've clicked either OK or Apply in the mailbox's Properties dialog box. The only way to change a directory name after you've gone this far is to delete the object and re-create it, so name with care.

Trust Level   Use the Trust Level field to tell Exchange Server whether it should include the mailbox when it does directory synchronization with cc:Mail, Microsoft Mail 3.2, or compatible systems.

Online Listings Information   Microsoft's Internet Locator Service (ILS) server can be used to locate an Exchange Server mailbox owner and set up online meetings, using, for example, Microsoft's NetMeeting software. If an ILS server is available, you can enter the server's name and account names here.

Home Server   The Home Server field is where you specify which server the mailbox is to be created on; it's the place where messages for the mailbox are stored. If you change the home server on the Advanced property page, Exchange Administrator asks if you want to move the mailbox to the server you've just chosen. Answer yes, and the mailbox is moved. (There's another way to move a mailbox to another server. We'll get into that method in a later chapter.)

Hide from Address Book   Select Hide from Address Book to prevent a mailbox from showing up in the various address lists in the Exchange address book (not just Global Address List). Generally, you'll want to hide a mailbox from the address book to protect a particular mailbox's privacy or when it is used by custom-programmed applications rather than by human users.

X.400 Priority   Check the box next to Downgrade High Priority X.400 Mail to prevent the mailbox from sending X.400 mail at high priority. If the mailbox user attempts to send a message destined for an X.400 system at high priority, the Exchange Server downgrades the priority to Normal.

Container Name   Use the Container Name option to set the name of the Recipients container that will hold the mailbox. As you'll soon see, you can have multiple Recipients containers in a site. To change the name of the Recipients container, click Modify; this brings up a little tree that shows you the Recipients containers available in the site where you're creating the mailbox. You can't pick a container outside this site, and once you've clicked Apply or OK for the mailbox you're creating, you can't change the Recipients container assigned to it. After that point, you won't even see the Modify button. That's why the Modify button isn't displayed in Figure 23.27. My mailbox had already been created by the time I captured the screen for the figure.

Outlook Web Access Server Name   Outlook Web Access lets you get to your Exchange Server messages and calendar as well as Web-based forms with an Internet Web browser, such as Netscape's browser products or Microsoft's Internet Explorer. If you choose to use a POP3 or IMAP4 Internet mail client to access your messages, how do you get to your calendar and the Web forms? If you set the name of an Outlook Web Access Server on the Advanced property page of your mailbox, you can use your Internet mail client to access messages and access your calendar and the Web forms with a Web browser through Outlook Web Access. You can set this value for all mailboxes on a server on the General properties page of the Private Information Store for the server.

Downgrade High Priority X.400 Mail   Select this option to prohibit this mailbox from sending high priority messages through X.400 connectors. Messages bound for X.400 sites are automatically downgraded to a priority status of normal.

Administrative Note   The Administrative Note field is a place where you can type in up to 1,024 characters of descriptive text about the mailbox or its user. This information is visible only in the Administrator program.

That covers as much about mailboxes as we need to cover for now. Let's continue with the next option on the Administrator's File menu, New Distribution List.

Part iv

RECONFIGURING AN EXISTING MAILBOX

To reconfigure an existing mailbox, just locate it in the Recipients container and double-click it. You'll get the same Properties dialog box you've been using to create new mailboxes. Now just edit as you wish and click OK or Apply to save your changes.

Follow these same directions to modify any existing recipient, whether mailbox, distribution list, custom recipient, or public folder.

Creating a New Distribution List

As you'll remember, distribution lists are another form of Exchange recipient. To create a new distribution list, click New Distribution List in the Exchange Administrator's File menu. This pops up the Distribution List Properties dialog box shown in Figure 23.28.

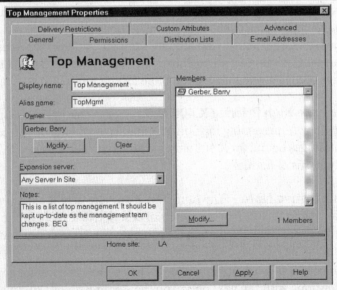

FIGURE 23.28: The General property page of the Distribution List properties dialog box

An Exchange Server distribution list has most of the properties of a mailbox, except that five property pages are missing—Organization, Phone/Notes, Limits, Delivery Options, and Protocols—none of which make much sense for a distribution list. The other seven pages are either exactly like or very similar to their mailbox-based cousins. I'll emphasize the differences here and refer you back to the mailbox property pages for the similarities.

General Properties

Let's look first at the items on the left-hand side of the General property page, then at the items on the right.

Display and Alias Names   You need to fill in a Display name and an Alias name. The Display name will show in the address book; the Alias will be used in creating e-mail addresses for the address list.

Owner   The name in the Owner field is the person to whom users should forward requests to be added to or removed from a distribution list. By default, the list owner is given rights to add and delete users from within an Exchange client. Since my GerCom list will include the company's top management, and since I'm the president of this mythical company, I've assumed ownership responsibilities. (I don't want anyone but a top exec involved in decisions about whom to admit to this list.) To set an owner for a distribution list, click Modify in the Owner box to bring up a standard address book dialog box like the one shown back in Figure 23.14. Select the owner and click OK.

NOTE
Only one Exchange recipient can own a distribution list. A distribution list cannot own another distribution list.

Expansion Server   Distribution lists must be *expanded*—that is, the members of the list must be identified and an efficient route to each member must be determined. Expansion is done on an Exchange server in a site; if a distribution list is large (with thousands of users), you may want to specify an expansion server for it that is less busy. For smaller lists, you don't have to change the Any Server in Site default.

Notes   Put anything you like in the Notes field of the distribution list. This information will be displayed for users when they look at the properties of the list using an Exchange client.

Members   Finally, add list members. Click Modify in the Members area and select members from the address book dialog box that pops up. Click OK when you're done.

Click Apply if you want to record your work so far, but don't close the distribution list's properties dialog box yet.

Permissions

The distribution list's Permissions property page looks and behaves almost exactly like the one for a mailbox—the only thing missing is the Mailbox Owner right, which is irrelevant for a distribution list. So, refer to mailbox permissions if you have any questions about the Permissions page for the distribution list.

THOSE NO ACCOUNT DISTRIBUTION LISTS

Unlike mailboxes, distribution lists don't have Primary NT accounts. You can see this by comparing Figure 23.10 (for a mailbox) with Figure 23.28 (for a distribution list). Figure 23.10 includes the Primary Windows NT Account button, while Figure 23.28 doesn't.

NOTE

If you want to take away a distribution list owner's right to add and remove the list's members while using an Exchange client, remove the Modify User Attributes right from the owner's role. Similarly, if you want to give other users the right to modify a distribution list, add their NT accounts to the Permissions page for the list and assign their accounts the Modify User Attributes right.

Included Distribution Lists

Distribution lists can include other distribution lists. You use the Distribution Lists property page to optionally add your new list to selected existing distribution lists. Click Modify in the Distribution Lists property page to bring up a dialog box showing existing distribution lists (see Figure 23.29). Use the dialog box to add your new list to existing lists and click OK when you're done.

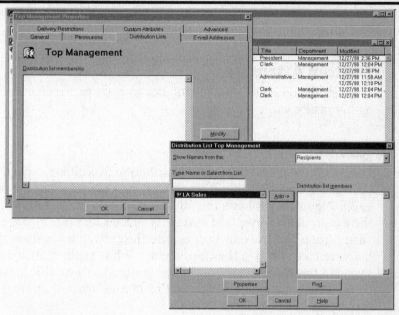

FIGURE 23.29:   Adding a new distribution list to existing distribution lists

E-mail Addresses

Exchange Server distribution lists have their own e-mail addresses. Among other benefits, this allows users of foreign e-messaging systems to send messages to the distribution lists. Except for different addresses, the distribution list's E-mail Addresses property page looks exactly the same as the one for mailboxes.

Delivery Restrictions

The Delivery Restrictions property page for distribution lists is a carbon copy of the one for mailboxes, pure and simple. You'll probably use this page more often than the one for mailboxes because it lets you specify which mailboxes, additional distribution lists, and custom Recipients can easily send one message to large groups of users. For example, you can prevent a slew of mass mailings—those advertising everything from cars for sale to apartments for sublet—by giving only a narrow set of mail-boxes the rights to send messages to large distribution lists such as those containing all Recipients in a department, a site, or an entire Exchange organization.

Custom Attributes

The distribution list's Custom Attributes property page is identical to the one for mailboxes.

Advanced Properties

The Advanced property page for distribution lists differs enough from the one for mailboxes that it's worth taking a quick look at the differences. Figure 23.30 shows the Advanced property page. First note that there is no Home Server field as there is for a mailbox (see Figure 23.27). Distribution lists live only in sites, and their attributes (names, members, etc.) are stored in the site directory. While mailbox attributes are stored in the site directory, mail itself is stored on a specific home server, so it's reasonable to say that mailboxes live both in sites and on servers.

Message Size Limit   You'll notice that, unlike the Limits property page for mailboxes, distribution lists don't have size-limit options for both incoming and outgoing messages; instead, they have a Message Size Limit setting. Distribution lists receive messages; they usually don't send them; though by giving a list Send As rights, you can use it to send messages. The limits you set on the Advanced property page are for incoming messages only.

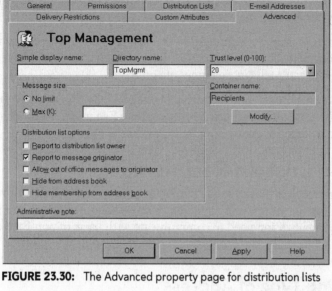

FIGURE 23.30:   The Advanced property page for distribution lists

Distribution List Options   Let's look at Distribution List Options in the Advanced property page one at a time. I've already talked about the Hide From Address Book option, so I won't cover it again.

▶ *Report to Distribution List Owner* sends notification to the owner of the distribution list when a message sent to the list has requested a delivery notification message or when the message is undeliverable.

▶ *Report to Message Originator* sends delivery notification or un-deliverable message information to the message originator for each member of the list. If this option is not selected, delivery notifications and non-delivery messages are sent to the message originator for the list as a whole. If a list member is hidden from the Address Book, to protect the secrecy of hidden members, delivery notification and undeliverable information messages are sent for the list, not its individual members.

▶ *Allow Out of Office Messages to Originator* sends to the originator of the message individual out-of-office messages from all list
members who have active out-of-office messages.

▶ *Hide Membership From Address Book* protects the privacy of the
members of a distribution list. Even if the list itself isn't hidden,
users can't tell whose names are on it.

Now that you are familiar with distribution lists, you're ready to move
on to the next option on the Administrator's File menu, New Custom
Recipient. Refer to Figure 23.6 for a view of the File menu.

Creating Custom Recipients

You'll remember that custom recipients are essentially aliases for recipients in foreign e-messaging systems. They're helpful when a lot of people
in your organization need to communicate with users of non-Exchange
systems.

Setting Type of Address

To create a custom recipient, click New Custom Recipient in the Exchange
Administrator's File menu. This brings up the dialog box shown in
Figure 23.31. Select the type of address for the custom recipient and then
click OK. (In the figure, I've chosen to create a custom recipient with an
Internet address.)

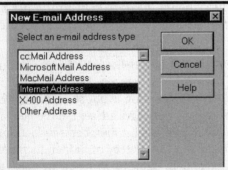

FIGURE 23.31: Selecting the type of address for a new custom recipient

The E-mail Address Type Properties Dialog Box

The next thing you'll see is a dialog box for entering the custom recipient's e-messaging address. Figure 23.32 shows the dialog box for the new Internet-based custom recipient I want to create. If you're creating a custom recipient for a different type of messaging system, you'll see a dialog box with fields appropriate to that system. When you're done entering the address, click OK.

The Internet Address Properties dialog box contains a second tab. See Figure 23.32. It's used to modify the way messages are coded before being sent out across the Internet.

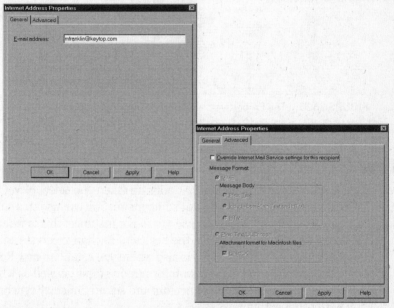

FIGURE 23.32: The Internet Properties dialog box

Standard Property Pages

Next you'll see the Properties dialog box for Custom Recipients. It looks very much like the one for a mailbox configuration, except that it's missing the Delivery Options and Limits property pages, which are not of much use here anyway (see Figure 23.33). If you think of a custom recipient as a sort of mailbox–distribution list hybrid, nothing in these property pages should surprise you. That said, I'll leave the rest of custom recipient configuration to you.

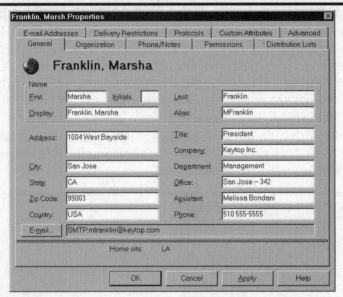

FIGURE 23.33: The Properties dialog box for Custom Recipients

New Other Options

Figure 23.34 shows the menu that pops up when you select New Other from the Exchange Administrator's File menu. You can use this submenu to create a variety of objects and services. For instance, this is where you create new monitors that watch the health of Exchange servers and links to other sites and systems. This is also where you establish new Recipients containers for a site and new information stores, as well as where you create Exchange Server connectors and set up directory synchronization with other systems.

You won't be able to use many of the New Other options until you've got more than one server or site. Other options are a bit advanced for our needs right now. So, I'll focus here on server monitors and Recipients containers.

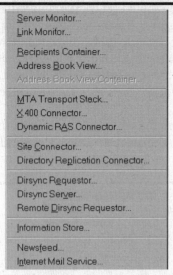

FIGURE 23.34: The New Other options menu

PUBLIC FOLDERS ARE RECIPIENTS, TOO

Public folders are the fourth type of recipient. However, they're created by users, not by Exchange Server administrators; that's why there's no New Public Folder option on the Exchange Administrator program's File menu.

Configuring a Server Monitor

Server monitors are really impressive. They watch over Exchange servers, their clocks, and the services running on them. One server monitor can operate on one or more of the servers in a site. You can set up multiple monitors in a site or even in an organization. You can also set up a monitor so that it notifies you if a service shuts down or never starts, if clients can't connect to the server, or if the server disappears from the network. Server monitors are also able to restart computers or services and synchronize server clocks.

Part iv

Server monitors are important; you should get comfortable with them right away. Let's create one for your server. From the Administrator's File menu, select New Other, then select Server Monitor. Since monitors are created in the Monitors container for a site, Exchange will warn you if you're not in one of these and will offer to take you there, just as it does if you're not in a site Recipients container when you create a mailbox.

General Properties When you see the server monitor's Properties dialog box shown in Figure 23.35, you're ready to go. I've already filled in the General property page for my server EXCHLA01.

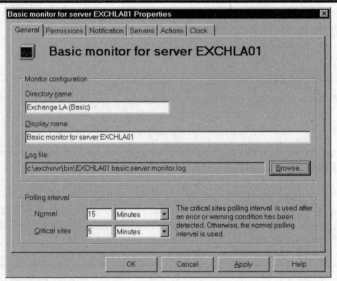

FIGURE 23.35: Configuring the General property page for a Server monitor

You can set several options on the General property page:

▶ *The Directory Name*, as with all standard directory names, cannot be changed after you create the server monitor.

▶ *The Display Name* is what you see when you look into the Monitors container. It can be up to 256 characters long.

▶ *The Log File* specifies the file in which the server monitor puts information about its activities. Even if a monitor can watch over many servers, I generally store its log file on the server that the monitor will run on. That way, if the network goes down, the monitor will still be able to write to its log file. Click Browse to set the directory and filename.

▶ *The Normal Polling Interval* is the time period the monitor waits before checking to see that all is running properly on the server. The default is fifteen minutes, which is just about right in most situations.

▶ *The Critical Sites Polling Interval* is the time period the server monitor waits before checking servers that are in trouble and that it is trying to fix. ("Sites" in this context actually refer to Exchange servers, not Exchange sites.) The default polling interval is five minutes. As you'll see in a bit, reviving a dead service or server can involve two or three cycles, each of which will require a wait equal to one critical sites polling interval. You'll have to decide on the best interval for each server monitor you create. For now, accept the default setting.

Permissions   The list of role rights is a bit different on the server monitor's Permissions property page than on other permissions pages you've worked with. The only right you haven't seen before is Delete, which is the right to delete the server monitor. If you give monitor access rights to other accounts or groups, grant the Delete right with caution.

Notification   Use the Notification property page to tell the server monitor whom to contact (and how to do it) when a problem arises. Click New and the New Notification dialog box opens (see the lower right-hand corner in Figure 23.36). You're offered three options in the New Notification dialog box:

▶ *Launch a Process* starts a program. For example, it can start a program that sends information about the problem to an alphanumeric pager.

▶ *Mail Message* sends a mail message about the problem to a specific recipient.

▶ *Windows NT Alert* sends a standard network message about the problem to a specific computer.

Click the Notification option you want and then click OK in the New Notification dialog box. The Escalation Editor dialog box for the option you've chosen pops up. This dialog box looks pretty much the same for all three options; Figure 23.37 shows how it looks when the Mail Message option is chosen. For the other two options, the Mailbox to Notify field is replaced by other fields appropriate to the particular notification action you're setting up.

To fill in the Escalation Editor dialog box for mail message notification, enter the time interval that the monitor should wait before issuing notification when it detects a problem. (The default is fifteen minutes, but in many cases you'll want more immediate notification.) As you can see in Figure 23.37, you can set the time unit to minutes or hours.

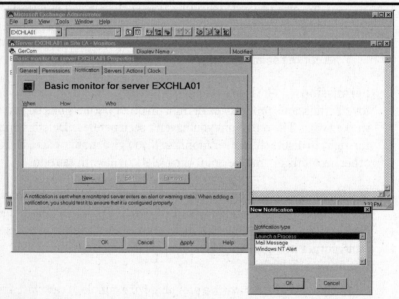

FIGURE 23.36: The New Notification dialog box

If you select Alert Only in the Escalation Editor dialog box, the monitor sends notification to this recipient only when actual problems exist. If you *don't* select Alert Only, then the monitor notifies the recipient about warnings and potential problems, as well as actual problems. This is a nice option: You can tell the monitor to notify certain people both when a problem starts brewing and when it reaches a critical level, while notifying others only when things actually go wrong.

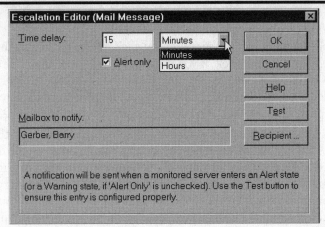

FIGURE 23.37:   Using the Escalation Editor (Mail Message) box to configure notifications

Finally, click Recipient to select any recipient from the resultant address book dialog box. (I probably don't need to remind you that the recipient here can be any valid Exchange recipient, mailbox, distribution list, or custom recipient.) If you've got a fax or pager gateway in place, of course, you can send the message to Recipients accessible through the gateway as well.

When you've finished selecting a recipient, click Test. Exchange will run a check to ensure that you've picked a valid and reachable mailbox. If you don't get an error message, click OK in the Escalation Editor dialog box. You'll get a warning telling you that notifications will not be sent until the next polling interval after the notification time (the delay you just entered) has passed. Click OK again and you'll now see your notification listed on the Notification property page.

With all this mail message notification experience behind you, you should have no trouble setting up one of the other two notification processes. So let's move on to the next property page for the server monitor.

NOTE

You can set up as many kinds of notifications as you want. Just click New in the Notification dialog box and fill in the New Notification and Escalation Editor dialog boxes with your information.

Servers   You use the Servers property page to choose the servers and services you want monitored (see Figure 23.38).

Click the name of your server and then click Add to put it into the Monitored Servers scroll box. If you want to include more than one server in this monitoring operation, add it here. If you have access to other sites, you can add servers from them by choosing another site from the Site drop-down menu in the lower left-hand corner of the Servers property page.

Now select your server in the Monitored Servers scroll box and then click Services, just below the right-hand scroll box, to bring up the dialog box shown in Figure 23.39. By default, three of the four core Exchange services are listed in the Monitored Services scroll box: the directory, the information store, and the MTA. (The System Attendant isn't automatically included because it's largely responsible for all monitors; if it dies, active monitors die with it.)

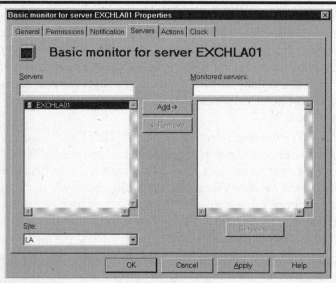

FIGURE 23.38: Selecting a server to monitor

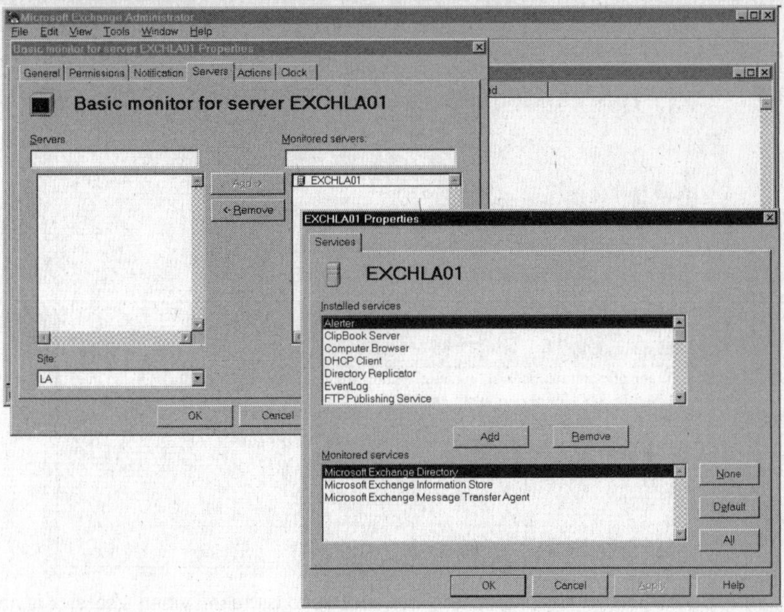

FIGURE 23.39:   Selecting services to be monitored on a server

Leave the default settings for now and click OK in the Services dialog box. You can come back later and add any service you'd like, whether it's an Exchange Server service or not.

NOTE

As should be pretty obvious from what we've just done, a server monitor can watch different services on each of the servers it monitors.

Actions   You use the Actions property page to tell your server monitor what to do when a service is not running (see Figure 23.40). What you put on this page applies to all the servers being monitored. In the figure, I've already selected options and filled in fields on the page.

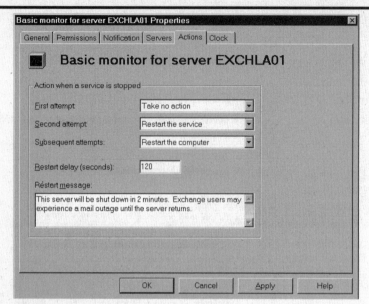

FIGURE 23.40:   Setting options for actions to be taken when a service is not running

You have three options when a service is not running: Take No Action, Restart the Service, or Restart the Computer. As you can see, I've instructed the monitor to do nothing on the first attempt, to restart the service on the second attempt, and to restart the computer on subsequent attempts. Timing for these actions is based on the polling intervals that were set on the General property page. When you request a computer restart, you can set a delay time before it restarts and include a message that will be sent to users logged in to the computer. I've selected a 120-second delay. The default is 60 seconds.

NOTE

An Exchange Server client is almost always able to survive the disappearance of its Exchange server or servers without your having to restart it or reboot your workstation. This is true whether the disappearance is due to a server outage or a network problem. If you're responsible for administering an MS Mail installation or any of the other file-based e-messaging systems out there, I bet you'll consider this little feature of client-server messaging alone to be worth the price of an Exchange system.

Clocks The Clock property page deals with keeping Exchange server clocks synchronized. We'll come back to it later when we have more than one installed Exchange server.

Starting a Server Monitor When you're through setting parameters, click OK in the server monitor's Properties dialog box. You'll see your monitor in the Monitors container for your site. Double-clicking the server monitor reopens the Properties dialog box, which you can use at any time to change the monitor's properties.

Now you have to start the server monitor. Click the monitor name and then select Start Monitor from the Tools menu. Next, you're asked what server you want to run the monitor on. After you answer, the monitor's window opens, indicating that your server monitor is now up and running and ready to act as you instructed should anything go wrong (see Figure 23.41).

If you double-click the line in the monitor that displays the monitor's name (see Figure 23.41), a dialog box pops up that lets you see how things are going. Try it. When you no longer need to see the monitor, minimize its window for better access to other Administrator windows.

Server monitors continue running when you exit the Administrator and resume when a server is rebooted. To stop a server monitor, close its window.

To test your server monitor, double-click the Services applet in your Exchange server's Control Panel, then halt a core Exchange Server service, such as the MTA. The monitor should restart the service just fine.

For a really serious test, disable the service by clicking Startup in the Services dialog box and selecting Disabled. The monitor will now be unable to restart the service—so if you've specified a computer restart, your Exchange server will be rebooted after any polling and service restart intervals have passed. Since you've disabled it, of course, the service won't start on reboot, either, so change the service's startup status back to Automatic after the reboot. The monitor will now be able to restart the service. (Remember to give the monitor enough time to go through the polling and restart delays you've set.)

Part iv

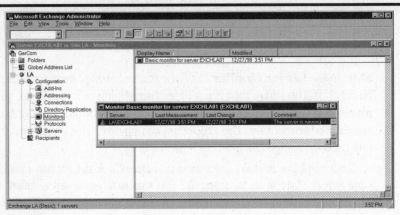

FIGURE 23.41: A server monitor up and running

Creating a New Recipients Container

You can put all the Recipients in a site into one container—the default container named Recipients—or you can create separate containers to hold specific kinds of Recipients. You can use multiple Recipients containers to more easily manage different types of Recipients. For example, you could set up separate containers to hold the Recipients used by specially programmed messaging-enabled applications or put all distribution lists in a single container.

You can't move existing Recipients once they've been created in a specific Recipients container, so plan additional Recipients containers carefully before you start adding Recipients to one container or another.

You can create a new Recipients container in a site or in an existing Recipients container. First highlight either the site or an existing Recipients container, then select Recipients Container from the New Other options menu under the Exchange Administrator's File menu. A Properties dialog box like the one in Figure 23.42 pops up.

General Properties   On the General property page for the Recipients container, fill in the display and directory names and add an administrative note if you want, as shown in Figure 23.42.

Permissions   The Permissions property page for the new Recipients container has one new role right on it: Add Child. An NT account or group with Add Child rights can create subcontainers under the master container. For now, accept the defaults and click OK in the Properties dialog box for the container.

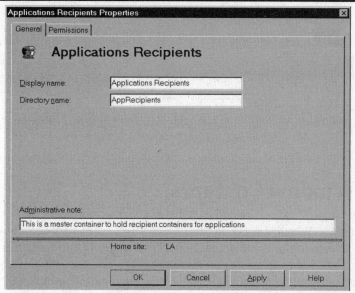

FIGURE 23.42:   The Properties dialog box for a new Recipients container

The New Container   In Figure 23.43, you can see the new Recipients container I created to hold Recipients containers for different custom-programmed messaging applications. Because I created it while the Recipients container was selected, the new container is a subcontainer of the Recipients container.

That's it for the New Other menu for now. Let's move on to the remaining options on the Administrator's File menu. Refer to Figure 23.6 for a reminder of the File menu.

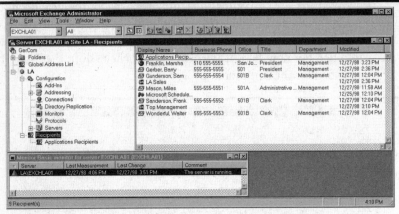

FIGURE 23.43: A container to hold other Recipients containers for custom-programmed messaging-enabled applications

Save Window Contents

Exchange 5.5 adds a neat and useful item to the File menu, Save Window Contents. When you choose this item, a select set of attributes for the Recipients in the Window (container) you're currently viewing (for example, the Recipients container) is exported to a file. For each recipient, Save Window Contents exports all of the attributes represented by the columns shown in the Window. In Figure 23.43, for example, Display Name, Business Phone, Office, Title, Department, and [Date] Modified would be exported.

After you select Save Window Contents, you're offered a chance to name the file to hold the export. The file is saved in the default format for your specific copy of Exchange Administrator. Unless you change it, the default file format is comma delimited.

Exchange allows you to do complex exports and imports of recipient attributes. However, for now, consider this a quick and easy way to export a limited number of key attributes. You can use files created with Save Window Contents in a number of ways. For example, they can be used to create import files that modify all or selected Recipients, or even as a kind of container backup that lets you restore lost Recipients by importing all or part of a file created by Save Window Contents. In the latter situation, however, exercise caution. Recipient objects usually have far more attributes than those showing in the display window.

Properties

Properties, of course, are what you've been setting on all those property pages. You can view the properties of any Exchange object either by clicking the object and then selecting Properties from the Exchange Administrator's File menu or by holding down the Alt key while pressing the Enter key. For objects other than containers, you can also see properties by double-clicking the object in the right pane. However, this won't work with containers since clicking once, twice, or a million times on a container only shows you what's inside.

Duplicating Objects

You can duplicate any non-container object. For example, you can duplicate a mailbox and then use the copy to set up a new mailbox with similar properties.

To duplicate an object, click it and select Duplicate from the Administrator's File menu. This brings up a standard Properties dialog box for the object with all the properties of the original intact, except that blanks replace the information that makes the original object unique. For example, all four fields are blank in the Name area on the General property page for a duplicate mailbox. (Look back at Figure 23.10 for the location of the Name area.)

THE EDIT MENU

The Exchange Administrator's Edit menu is pretty plain-vanilla. It includes all the usual items: Undo, Cut, Copy, Paste, Delete, and Select All. 'Nuff said.

THE VIEW MENU

Figure 23.44 shows the Exchange Administrator's View menu. Use this menu to indicate which Exchange objects are to be shown and how the views of Exchange's hierarchy are to be formatted. You can also use it to move the splitbar and to toggle on and off both the toolbar (below the menu bar on the Administrator window) and the status bar (at the bottom of the Administrator window).

Part iv

FIGURE 23.44: The Exchange Administrator's View menu

What to View

Most of the time, I like to see all Recipients in the Administrator, so I select All on the Administrator's View menu. To view only certain Recipients, select the ones you want using the View menu; to view Recipients you've hidden, select Hidden Recipients.

You can also select the recipient types you want to view from the drop-down menu in the toolbar, as shown in Figure 23.45. Notice that hidden Recipients aren't listed in the drop-down menu; the only way to view hidden Recipients is by using the View menu.

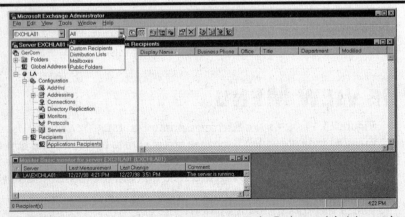

FIGURE 23.45: Selecting Recipients to view using the Exchange Administrator's toolbar drop-down menu

Recipient Attributes and Views

Exchange Recipients can have a plethora of attributes or properties; Figure 23.46 shows some of these. A number of recipient attributes are used for column heads when you view a list of Recipients in a Recipients container. Note that the attributes shown in the right-hand scroll box in Figure 23.46 are the titles of the column bars for the Recipients listing in Figure 23.47.

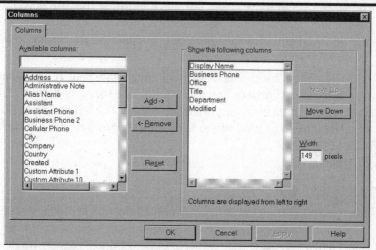

FIGURE 23.46: Some of the attributes of Exchange Recipients

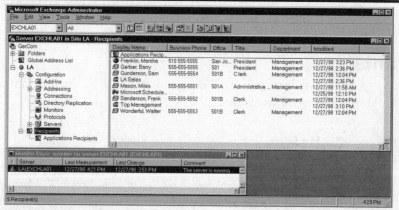

FIGURE 23.47: Recipient attributes are displayed as column heads in a recipient listing.

To change the attributes (columns) used in a display of Recipients, select Columns from the Administrator's View menu. This brings up the Columns dialog box shown in Figure 23.46. Use the dialog box to add and remove attributes to be displayed. The topmost attribute in the right-hand box in Figure 23.46, Display Name, is the leftmost column in the Recipients list in Figure 23.47. The second attribute, Business Phone, is the second column in the Recipients listing, and so on.

To change the column display order, highlight a column title and use the Move Up and Move Down buttons to position the title as you wish (see Figure 23.46). To set the column width for an attribute, click the attribute and enter the measurement (in pixels) in the Width box. Each column has its own width setting.

To resize the Recipients display columns, place your Windows pointer on the little line between any two column title bars (see Figure 23.47). The pointer turns into a crosshair. Hold down the left mouse button and move the crosshair until you're happy with the real estate that each column occupies.

Sorting Lists

You can sort certain Exchange Server lists—Recipients lists, for example—by column headings. The Sort By option on the View menu lets you select a default sort column. There are two options: Display Name (the default) and Last Modified Date.

Remember, you can change the sort order for any list by clicking the column title bar you want to sort by. If you're permitted to sort by that column, the list will be resorted.

Fonts

Use the Font option on the View menu to change the display font used by the Exchange Administrator.

Move Splitbar

The Move Splitbar option on the View menu is another way to set the splitbar on an Administrator window. Select it and your Windows pointer is automatically placed on the splitbar of the current Administrator window. At that point, you can move the splitbar as you wish, changing the real estate occupied by the two panes in the window.

The Toolbar

As you already know, you can use the toolbar, which is located below the menu bar, to set the type of Recipients you want to view. The toolbar also lets you select the Exchange server you want to focus your attention on. More about this capability later.

Finally, the toolbar contains buttons for performing various Administrator functions. You can see these in Figure 23.47. Here's what the buttons do in the order they appear from left to right:

- ▶ Move up one level in the Exchange hierarchy
- ▶ Show or hide the container tree view in the left-hand pane of an Administrator window
- ▶ Create a new mailbox
- ▶ Create a new distribution list
- ▶ Create a new custom recipient
- ▶ Show the properties of an object
- ▶ Delete an object
- ▶ Move to Configuration container
- ▶ Move to Servers container
- ▶ Move to Connections container
- ▶ Move to Recipients container

You don't have to worry about memorizing these functions. Just hover over the button you're interested in with your mouse pointer, and in a second a standard Windows tooltip will pop up telling you the button's function.

The Status Bar

The status bar is in the bottom area of the Administrator screen. In Figure 23.47, the status bar displays "9 Recipient(s)" to tell you that there are nine objects (Recipients) in the currently selected container. Keep the status bar turned on—it doesn't cost you anything.

THE TOOLS MENU

The Exchange Administrator program's Tools menu is chock-full of interesting functionality (see Figure 23.48). The first four items on the menu make it easier to create mailboxes en masse. The items fit nicely into the category of advanced Exchange Server administration.

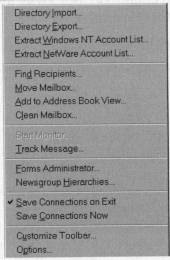

FIGURE 23.48:   The Exchange Administrator's Tools menu

Finding Recipients

The Find Recipients option gets more and more valuable as the number of Recipients and servers in your Exchange organization grows. To search for a recipient, select Find Recipients from the Tools menu. If you're asked which server you want to connect to, click Browse, find your server, and click OK in the Connect to Server dialog box. The Find Recipients dialog box will pop up (see Figure 23.49).

You can search on attributes such as first name and last name, as shown in Figure 23.49. And by clicking the Custom button, you can perform a search on custom attributes. Clicking Container brings up a dialog box that lets you select the site and Recipients container to search in.

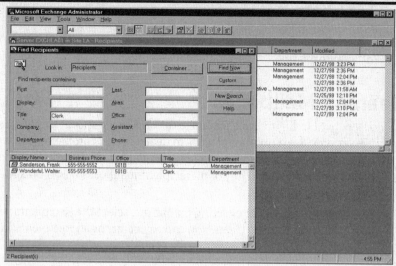

FIGURE 23.49:   Finding specific Exchange Recipients

When you've filled in the appropriate fields in the Find Recipients dialog box, click the Find Now button. When the searching is finished, you'll see a list of all Recipients that meet the criteria you entered. (In Figure 23.49, I searched for all the Recipients in GerCom's LA site with a title of Clerk.)

Recipients are listed by the columns set under the Columns option of the Administrator's View menu (see Figure 23.46). You can use the list of found Recipients pretty much as if it were a Recipients container. For example, you can double-click any found recipient to edit its Properties dialog box.

Moving a Mailbox

When users move to new locations, or when you need to move a mailbox for administrative reasons, it's nice to be able to move mailboxes from one Exchange server to another. The Tools menu's Move Mailbox option makes this easy. You can move mailboxes only within a site, however.

Adding to an Address Book View

You might have noticed that the New Other menu includes an option that lets you create different views of the Exchange address book. (Refer

Part iv

back to Figure 23.34.) The address book is used to find e-mail and other information stored in the Exchange directory. Having various views of the address book can make it easier for users to find specific addresses or other information.

Cleaning Mailboxes

Users tend to fill up their mailboxes at breakneck speed, so Exchange Server provides a number of ways to deal with this problem. One way is to set limits on the amount of storage available to mailboxes; another is to remove messages from any or all recipient mailboxes based on specific criteria.

To set up criteria for cleaning mailboxes, select the Recipients whose mailboxes you want to clean. You can select any or all Recipients in the following:

▶ The Global Address List

▶ Any site's or server's recipient containers, including those you've created yourself

▶ A found Recipients list created using the Find Recipients option on the Tools menu

Use the standard Windows list-selection keys to select the Recipients. For example, to select a noncontiguous group of mailboxes, hold down the Ctrl key while clicking each mailbox you want to clean. Once you've selected the Recipients, click Clean Mailbox on the Tools menu; this brings up the dialog box shown in Figure 23.50.

Everything in the dialog box should be pretty easy to figure out except for Sensitivity, which is a privacy-based attribute that's set by the person sending a message. Select all of the criteria you want and click OK to start the mailbox-cleaning process immediately. This is a powerful little tool; use it with care.

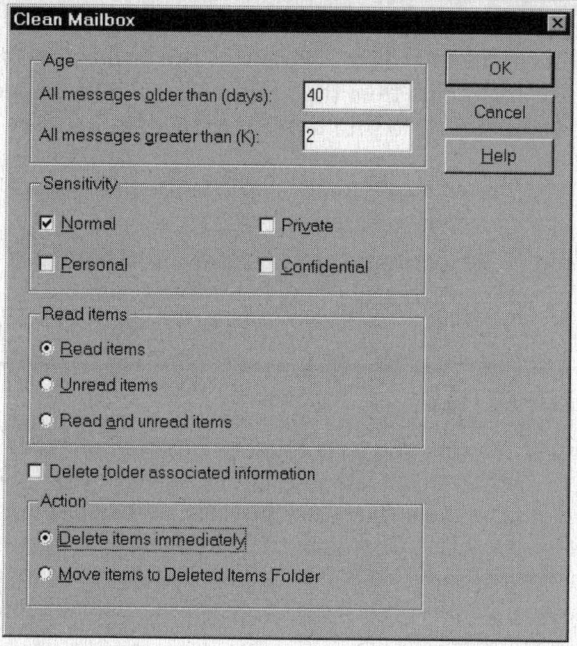

FIGURE 23.50: Specifying criteria for cleaning mailboxes

Starting a Monitor

You've already used the Start Monitor option to start the server monitor you created earlier in this chapter, so you already know what this option is for and how it works.

Saving Connections

You can save the Administrator's connections to Exchange servers upon exiting from the Administrator or at some other time. When you come back into the Administrator, the connections are automatically reestablished. To save connections upon exit, select that option. To save connections at any time, select Save Connections Now.

Customizing the Toolbar

You can add to or subtract from the Administrator's toolbar. Just select the Customize Toolbar option from the Tools menu and use the friendly interface to tailor the toolbar to your own special needs.

Options

You already used the Options option way back at the beginning of this chapter, so we've now covered everything in the Tools menu.

RAW PROPERTIES

I can't resist showing you a well-hidden little capability of the Exchange Administrator. It lets you start up Administrator in such a way that you can examine and modify every last bloody property available for any object. When you start the Administrator this way, you're in what Microsoft calls "raw mode." Even if you never use raw mode, you should check it out to see how absolutely detailed the object properties can get.

To start the Administrator in raw mode, open a DOS Command Prompt window. At the command prompt, go to the disk drive where you installed Exchange Server. Then change to the directory C:\exchsrvr\bin and type **admin/raw**. Or you can click the NT Start menu, select Run, type **<*drive*>\exchsrvr\bin\admin –r** and click OK. <*drive*> is the hard disk drive where you installed Exchange Server, usually your C drive.

That's it. When the Administrator starts, highlight any object and open the File menu. You'll find a new option on the menu, Raw Properties, located just below Properties. Click it and play to your heart's content. One warning: Use your mouse, and keep your hands off your keyboard so there's no chance you'll change anything. You're not ready for that kind of stuff yet.

The graphic included in this sidebar shows some of the raw properties or attributes for the mailbox I created earlier in this chapter.

CONTINUED →

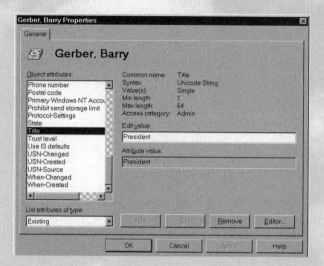

The Title attribute is selected, and my title—President—is listed and can be edited in the Edit Value box. Notice that the Access category for Title is Admin. This means that only NT accounts or groups with Admin role permissions for the mailbox can change this property.

WHAT'S NEXT?

In this chapter, you learned about the Exchange Administrator program and how to use it and its menus to do a number of administrative and management tasks. In the next chapter, you will learn how to avoid making one of the biggest mistakes organizations make when deploying Microsoft Exchange Server. You will learn to adequately plan a proper foundation for Exchange, considering the consequences of site and organization design and choosing reliable hardware. Don't act hastily. Read Chapter 24 and get it right the first time.

PART V
EXCHANGE SERVER ADVANCED TOPICS

Chapter 24

EXCHANGE ORGANIZATION DESIGN

Perhaps one of the biggest mistakes organizations make when deploying Microsoft Exchange Server is that they don't adequately plan a proper foundation for Exchange; they don't consider the consequences of site and organization design, and they don't choose reliable hardware. Time and time again, I find myself assisting someone who has deployed Exchange in great haste, only to find that they need to upgrade their server platform, add hard disk space, or restructure their Exchange organizational design structure. I don't know about you, but I really hate to do something over again; I prefer to get it right the first time.

Exchange Server 5.5

24 seven

The Essential Resource for Systems Administrators

Adapted from *Exchange Server 5.5 24seven™* by Jim McBee
ISBN 0-7821-2505-0   657 pages $34.99

Why are some Exchange deployments less than a stellar success? What are some of the mistakes I see made time and time again?

- Organizations don't employ a consistent naming standard between sites (and this can get ugly!).

- Exchange site design is often left to chance. Care must be taken to ensure that Exchange servers are grouped according the organization's WAN or administrative model.

- Exchange server hardware is chosen that is either insufficient or unreliable.

- There is no testing of new software, service packs, or hot fixes. Further, practicing for disaster recovery, which requires equipment that can be dedicated at least part of the time to a test lab and/or cold standby equipment in the event of server failure, is neglected.

- Operational plans and assignment of responsibilities are afterthoughts.

- Little or no thought is given to system maintenance and disaster prevention.

While planning your Exchange organization foreseeing many disasters is impossible, but there are things that you can do to minimize the impact of most catastrophes. When you are making design decisions, there are six simple things to consider: consistency, reliability, usability, maintainability, security, and performance.

BUILDING A SOLID FOUNDATION

Before your first Exchange server is installed, you must have a solid foundation for Exchange. And believe it or not, much of this is going to be on paper. This foundation will include your standards and design document, a good server design, and recommendations for operations and administration.

Standardizing Your Naming Conventions

The Exchange Server global address list (GAL) is replicated to every single site in an organization. In order for this to occur (and for it to *not* look like a mishmash of names), you must have a naming convention in place for the many different types of names that are used in the Exchange directory.

Exchange Organization/Site/Server Naming

Prior to deploying Exchange, your organization must have agreed upon a naming standard for the organization, sites, and server names.

Organization name must be *exactly* the same for all sites. This name can be up to 64 characters in length, though I recommend keeping it to 16 characters or fewer so that it will match the X.400 PRMD field, which is limited to 16 characters.

Site name must be unique for the entire organization and can be up to 64 characters in length. I recommend using something that is descriptive of the Exchange site. Spaces, dashes, and underscores are permitted, but avoid the spaces and underscored characters if you want the site name to match the DNS name.

Server name is, of course, the Windows NT server's NetBIOS name. This name is limited to a maximum of 15 characters and should be unique for your entire organization. I suggest using some sort of naming standard that identifies the server type and location as well as assigning it a unique number. Something like HNLEX001 identifies a server in Honolulu (HNL) that is an Exchange server (EX) and has a unique number of 001. (HNL is the airport code, which I like using, but not always useful in a city with several airports.) Avoid using the "_" (underscore) character, because many versions of DNS do not support that character. Though this has little bearing on Exchange, I also avoid using the "-" (hyphen), because SQL Server does not recognize that character in an SQL Server name.

TIP

Are the organization and site names case sensitive? I have never found a situation where case sensitivity mattered with Exchange. However, Microsoft continues to insist that the names should be treated as though they are. Thus I consider it a good practice to use all uppercase letters in my organization and site names.

DNS or WINS Server

"Should I use a WINS server or should I use a DNS server?" If your clients are using DNS, then the Exchange server's NetBIOS name should be entered into your DNS zone. For example, if the server name is HNLEX0Ø1 and the domain name is Somorita.com, then clients should be able to do a DNS lookup (or just a simple PING to HNLEX0Ø1.Somorita.com).

Further, all clients and servers should have their TCP/IP DNS Domain Name fields entered as Somorita.com, as shown in Figure 24.1.

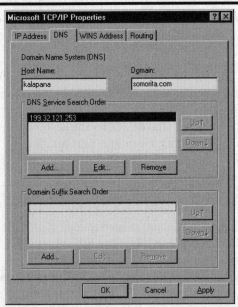

FIGURE 24.1: TCP/IP DNS domain name properties

Part v

Exchange Server, Exchange Administrator, the Exchange client, and all versions of the Outlook client are *not* NetBIOS applications. Their preferred method of resolving a host name to an IP address is not the standard NetBIOS name resolution method.

Mailbox and Custom Recipient Names   When creating an Exchange Server mailbox or custom recipient, there are a number of property fields that you have the option of filling out. Only a few of these are required. Figure 24.2 shows the fields that are available for an Exchange mailbox in a typical installation of Exchange. Of these fields, only Display Name, Alias, and Primary Windows NT Account are required. On the Advanced tab, the Directory Name field is required (and cannot be changed once the mailbox is created); if you do not provide data for the Directory Name field, it is copied from the Alias field.

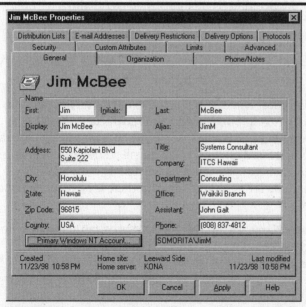

FIGURE 24.2:   Property fields available on the General tab of an Exchange mailbox

Many of the Exchange mailbox fields that you should consider standardizing are found on the mailbox's property page. They include:

Display Name is the field shown in the global address list and is displayed in the To field of the Outlook clients. It can be a maximum of 256 characters, though you should keep it shorter than that; I limit my display names to no more than 64 characters. Standardizing how this field is displayed is extremely important; if one administrator enters names one way and another does it differently, then the global address list does not appear cohesive. Following are some examples of how names are displayed:

> McBee, Jim
> Last Name, First Name—my favorite
>
> McBee, Jim (Honolulu - Systems Admin)
> Last Name, First Name, location and job information
>
> N6503–Mr. Jim McBee (Hawaii)
> Job Code followed by salutation, name, and location which is common in government and military installations

Alias is a short name identifying this mailbox. Many administrators like to limit this field to eight characters, though you can use up to 64 characters. Some legacy mail systems (such as PROFS and SNADS) don't allow e-mail addresses longer than eight characters. I personally like matching the e-mail alias to the Windows NT account name, but there is no requirement to do this.

Directory Name is found on the Advanced tab and can be up to 64 characters long. This name is used internally by the Exchange directory service and is part of the DN (Distinguished Name). The directory name is also sometimes called the RDN (Relative Distinguished Name). It defaults to the same as the alias when the mailbox is created, but it cannot be changed once it is created.

First Name is a 16-character field for the user's first name.

Last Name is a 40-character field for the user's last name.

Primary Windows NT Account is the field that contains the Windows NT user account that is allowed to access this mailbox. You can also assign Windows NT global and local groups to access a mailbox rather than individual accounts. Additional accounts and groups can be given access to a mailbox through the Permissions property page.

MAILBOX PROPERTIES

Why should I fill in all the property fields for a mailbox? Well, if you are in an organization of 20 people, I am betting you don't need to. Suppose, though, that you are in an organization of a couple hundred (or a few thousand or even tens of thousands) people. Have you ever needed a phone number, fax number, or shipping address of someone in your own company? Install Exchange Server and—voila!—instant company-wide phone directory.

Is keeping the character case of mailbox directory entries important? People tell me that I am being picky when I do this, but, yes, I think it certainly is important. You have gone to the trouble of setting standards for how names will appear in the global address list; take it just a bit further and make sure your administrators enter people in the correct case (upper or lower). The global address list will look a lot more professional and credible.

Distribution Lists

Exchange Server distribution lists are used for a couple of things. The obvious use is, of course, sending messages to many users at once. Distribution lists are also used for assigning permissions to public folders. Distribution lists are an organization-wide resource and will be seen throughout the organization in the global address list. Here are a few hints for making your life with distribution lists a little easier:

▶ Restrict the list membership size to less than 5,000 recipients. You can always nest large distribution lists if necessary.

▶ Create a distribution list for all mailboxes in each site. These site-level distribution lists can then be added to organization-wide distribution lists (this is called nesting). Site-wide distribution lists can also be used when assigning permissions to public folders that only the users in a specific site need access to.

▶ Assign an owner to the distribution list. The owner can assign and revoke membership in the list through Outlook. The Exchange Administrator program only allows you to assign one "official" owner, but using the Permissions tab, you can give others the User role, which will allow them to control membership just like the owner.

▶ For large distribution lists, set delivery restrictions so that only specific people can send to a distribution list. This does not stop a determined person, but it sure makes it harder to send to everyone in the entire company!

▶ I like to put an underscore (_) or ampersand (&) character in front of my distribution lists so they all sort to the top of the global address list. (Most any special character will work.) In larger organizations, I like to also put a blank distribution list at the top of the list. My global address list, including distribution lists, would look like Figure 24.3. For companies that want all their distribution lists to sort to the bottom of the global address list, put a zz_ in front of the distribution list display name.

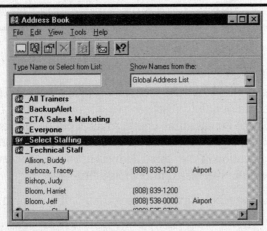

FIGURE 24.3:   A global address list with a few distribution lists sorted to the top of the list

Part v

RESTRICTING ACCESS AND PROVIDING A BLANK DISTRIBUTION LIST

A company I know made heavy use of distribution lists. Unfortunately, anyone could send to any of these lists. One user displayed the address list to select her friend's name. She inadvertently also selected a distribution list. She sent a rather long message detailing her love-life woes to over 1,000 people. The MIS director, mail administrator, human resources manager, and several other people spent the better part of the morning in a panic attack trying to figure out how to remove the message.

The moral of the story: By restricting who can use large distribution lists and by putting a blank distribution list at the top of the directory, you can help prevent accidental distribution list usage.

Using Recipient Containers

A *recipient container* is quite simply a receptacle in which you can put recipients (mailboxes, custom recipients, public folders, and distribution lists). Recipient containers are created at the site level. Currently, once an object is created in one recipient container, it cannot be moved to another.

So if recipients cannot be moved from one container to another, then what's the use? If you plan containers correctly, you can still find a number of good uses for them. Here is a list of recipient containers I create and what each is used for:

Mailboxes is actually the original recipients container. I rename the Display Name property from Recipients to Mailboxes so that it more accurately describes what is in the container.

External Users is a container that holds all custom recipients such as users with SMTP addresses.

MS Mail Users and similarly named containers are used for recipients on other mail systems from which you are synchronizing directories.

Public Folders contains a list of public folders. Don't forget to change the default directory location of public folders in Configuration > Information Store Site Configuration > Public Folder Container. This ensures that any public folders created (hidden or not hidden) will be displayed in the Public Folders container.

Distribution Lists contains all distribution lists.

Resources contains a list of mailboxes that are actually resources such as conference rooms, projectors, and so on.

Other recipient containers might include containers for other organizations with which I manually replicate my directory.

NOTE

Recipient containers are created and named per site, not for the entire Exchange organization. Each site should follow a similar naming convention.

EXCHANGE@WORK: I LOVE MY RECIPIENT CONTAINERS!

At one company, the Exchange administrator fell in love with recipient containers. He created one for every department in his company. Sure enough, problems started arising when people transferred from one department to another, which happened quite often. The administrator could not move a recipient from one container to another, so he had to delete the mailbox and re-create it. This required moving all the user's messages to a PST file, deleting the mailbox, re-creating the mailbox, deleting the user's Outlook profile, and re-creating the Outlook profile.

All of this extra work could have been avoided if the administrator had a better understanding of how to use recipient containers. If he had known that recipient containers were not as flexible, he would not have created departmental containers in the first place.

WARNING

All objects have a Distinguished Name (DN) that is a combination of the organization, site, recipient container, and directory name of the object; Exchange refers internally to this name as the Obj-Dist-Name. Exchange uses the DN to route messages within a single Exchange organization. For example, user Reid Shigeoka's directory name is RShigeoka; he is in the Somorita Surfboards organization, the Hilo Region site, and the Recipients container. His DN will be /o=Somorita/ou=Hilo Office/cn=Recipients/cn=RShigeoka. You should plan your organizational naming standards so that this name does *not* exceed 256 characters.

Part V

Public Folders

Once the directory replication connector is set up between two sites, the names of public folders from all sites will be visible in the Exchange public folder hierarchy. This is not a very big deal for smaller organizations (fewer than 1,000 mailboxes) that may only have a few dozen public folders. However, for large organizations with hundreds of public folders, searching a huge list of meaningless public folders for one or two commonly used folders will be a waste from a user's perspective.

One of your administrative challenges will be to organize your public folder hierarchy in a manner that makes sense to all users in all sites. A few of my own approaches include creating root public folders for each site, each location, or each specific department. Another option is to make each location's public folder visible only to the users in that location.

Don't forget to create a public folder for organization-wide use. Figure 24.4 shows a public folder hierarchy based on a root folder being created for each site name. Each site can then create as many subfolders as desired. This makes navigating the public folder hierarchy much more user friendly.

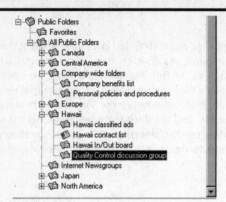

FIGURE 24.4:   This public folder hierarchy gives each site (or location) a root
folder specifically for that site.

Address Book Views

Address book views solve an organization-level naming issue. They were
introduced in Exchange 5 to help give a more hierarchical structure to the
global address list. The address book view feature allows you to create
"virtual" address books based on one of 18 recipient properties: city,
company, country, department, home server, site, state, title, and any of
the 10 custom attribute fields.

NOTE

So why am I bringing up address book views in the context of a naming standard? Because address book views are an organization-wide resource; if you
create one for your site, it is visible in all sites. Address book views need to be
part of the deployment plan, and all administrators need to know that they can't
start creating views without affecting what the other sites will see.

Organization Forms Libraries

Another organizational item, though not directly related to naming, is
the Organization Forms Library. The Organization Forms Library gives
you the ability to store forms for purposes of collaboration and workflow,
and to help move toward the ultimate paperless office. <grin> These

forms are stored in system-level public folders, and you can have one forms library folder for each language and each Exchange organization you are supporting.

By default, a Forms Library created in one site is not accessible from other sites. This kind of defeats the purpose of an "Organization" Forms Library, doesn't it? The Organization Forms Library should be created in one site and then made available to other sites through public folder replication or public folder affinity. Once replication or affinity is set up, users can use the forms, and individuals with the proper permissions can install forms into the library from any site.

Site-Level Details Templates

The site-level Details templates are quite useful when customizing the templates that your users see. Figure 24.5 shows the Find dialog box that is available from the Outlook client when a user needs to search for a mailbox in the global address list. The properties necessary to build and display the Find dialog box are stored in the Exchange directory.

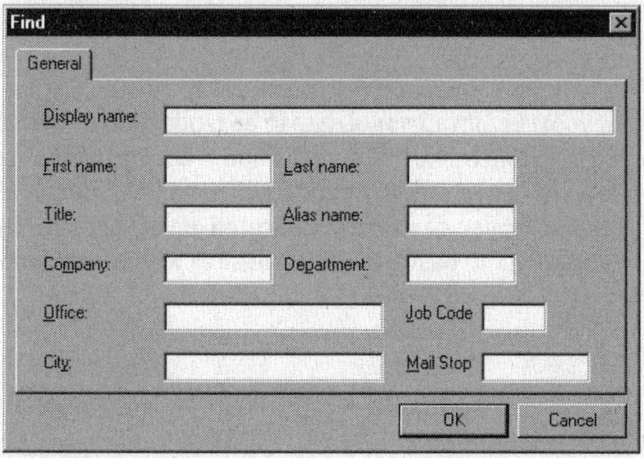

FIGURE 24.5: A slightly customized Find dialog box includes fields for searching based on Job Code or Mail Stop.

If you have seen this dialog screen before, then you may also notice that there are two additional search dialog boxes: Job Code and Mail Stop.

The issue that you need to keep in mind during the planning phase is that Details templates are modified on a per site basis. If you want all users in all sites to see the same custom Details templates, you must modify them in each site. The templates do not replicate between sites.

Custom Attributes

I just showed you a neat feature of Exchange-the ability to modify the Details templates to further customize your Exchange installation. In Figure 24.5, you may have noticed the Job Code and Mail Stop fields. These are not exactly built-in fields, but rather custom attribute fields. For example, I renamed the Custom Attribute 1 to Job Code. I then incorporated that field into my customized Find template, as you saw in Figure 24.5.

The data contained in the custom attribute fields are replicated to all sites by default. However, the custom attribute field names themselves are not replicated to other sites. For example, if another site decided to change the name of Custom Attribute 1 to Date Of Birth, whenever anyone looked at my Date Of Birth field in their site, they would see my Job Code *data* instead; my renamed field would not be replicated, but its data would.

This is another example of the necessity of careful coordination and planning when deploying Exchange. The custom attribute fields should be part of your design document as well.

TIP

If you don't want your custom attribute data to be replicated to other sites, this can be controlled from *Site Name* ➤ Configuration ➤ DS Site Configuration. On the Attributes tab, choose Inter-Site Replication in the Configure field and deselect any attributes that you don't want replicated out of your site. You cannot control this on a site-by-site basis; it affects all sites with which you are replicating directory data.

SMTP Address

If you are connecting to the Internet or an SMTP network, you must decide what your SMTP address will be for all users. This value is set for each site in the Site Addressing tab; go to *Site Name* ➤ Configuration ➤ Site Addressing. All sites can use the same SMTP address, or certain sites can use their own. The deciding factor is which sites are going to host inbound Internet Mail Services.

If several sites are going to host inbound Internet Mail Services and they want their mail delivered directly to their site from the Internet, then they must have a separate Internet domain name. A DNS server must set the appropriate MX and A record entries in the DNS zone database.

Developing a Standards and Design Document

By now you have been planning furiously, right? You've been to meetings, formed committees, talked to the bosses, and all of your colleagues in all branches of your company are in agreement! Now that you've also got your naming conventions down, you need a *standards and design document* that is going to detail everything that you and your fellow administrators have agreed upon. Everyone should have a copy of this document and agree to follow it to the letter when they deploy their piece of the Exchange puzzle. Everyone must sign off on this plan and follow it.

What should be in this document? Table 24.1 shows a sample of some of the more critical elements that I recommend you include.

TABLE 24.1: Somorita Surfboards Exchange Standards

ITEM	VALUE	EXPLANATION
Organization name	SOMORITA	All sites will use this value when installing their Exchange servers.
Site name	HAWAII for the Hawaiian Islands offices	Use the value for your particular region.
	NORTHAMERICA for offices in the continental U.S.	
	JAPAN for the Tokyo and Osaka offices	
	EUROPE for the Germany, France, Spain, and Italy offices	
Server names	Use your nearest airport code, followed by EX, followed by three unique numbers. For example: HNLEX001, SFOEX001, LAXEX002	Register your server's names and IP addresses with the Exchange Coordinator so that they can be entered into the DNS database.

TABLE 24.1 continued: Somorita Surfboards Exchange Standards

ITEM	VALUE	EXPLANATION
Alias name	Use the Windows NT Account Name.	
Display name	Last Name and First Name followed by "(Office Name, Job Title)"; for example: Suzuki, Makoto (Tokyo, Sales) McBee, Jim (Honolulu, Trainer)	Follow these standards exactly. Case counts; don't use all uppercase or all lowercase.
Mailbox fields to be filled in	Fill in all address, phone, title, and departmental information.	This has to be followed carefully or you won't be able to replace your company phonebook application.
Recipient Containers	External Recipients	For your site, you are required to create these four containers. Put mailboxes only in the recipients container.
	Distribution Lists	
	Public Folders	
	Resources	
Address book views	By Department By City	The corporate MIS staff will create address book views. Do not create your own address book views.
Custom attributes	CA 1 → Date Of Birth CA 2 → Hire Date CA 3 → Hobbies	Rename your site's custom attributes as shown. When creating recipients, enter the appropriate information for each. Enter dates in the U.S. fashion (such as 03/09/1963).
SMTP address	@SOMORITA.COM	Set this in site addressing. All inbound mail will be delivered to the same domain name.

I cannot emphasize enough the importance of all system administrators agreeing to this standards document. Having someone of great importance within your company (the CEO, the director of IS—someone who can affect other people's paychecks) sign off on this document and declaring that all the organization's sites, offices, and locations will follow this document is also helpful.

EXCHANGE@WORK: BEWARE THE ROGUE SITE!

Several organizations I have worked with have experienced rogue installations of Exchange. This happens when a particular office, department, or division decides they won't wait for the standards and pilot tests to be completed. They deploy Exchange and use their own standards.

In fact, I know of one very large company that had two competing divisions deploying Exchange; both divisions were racing to see who could get their division completely migrated first. Both believed that if they "won," someone up the food chain would eventually make a decision and name them to be the de facto standard.

Now they are stuck with two Exchange organizations whose directories are not very interoperable. Even the organization name is different, so they can't participate in Exchange directory replication. Users are now asking for address lists of people who are in the other division; they want to share public folders and to deploy a couple of standardized forms. Neither division's MIS department will bend, and the director of IS is afraid to make a decision because the situation has become so politically charged.

One suggestion is to use the Microsoft Exchange Move Server Wizard (also known as Pilgrim). Pilgrim has many uses, but I will warn you now: Pilgrim is not a magic wand. You can't wave it and magically merge two distinctly separate organizations. There are a lot of issues to address.

Planning and standardization must be done before anything is deployed, even in a pilot project. All implementers must agree to adhere to the organization-wide standards. The standards and design document needs to be created, agreed upon, and followed.

SITE DESIGN

Many issues affect the decision to break organizations up into multiple sites. The following sections discuss two major factors: available network bandwidth between server locations, and the administrative responsibility of the mailboxes and servers.

NOTE
You may also consider connecting sites as part of your organizational design.

Bandwidth between Servers

Bandwidth between servers is the biggest issue to consider when deciding how many sites to have in your organization. All servers within a single Exchange site communicate with one another using Remote Procedure Calls (RPCs), a communication mechanism that expects full-time, high-speed connections; at least this is the official Microsoft rule. However, no one ever bothers to define exactly what "high-speed" connectivity is. Is it a T1 line? Is it a 28.8 modem? Is it a minimum of Ethernet speeds?

My own rule of thumb: When separating two servers by a WAN that are in a single site, there should be a minimum of 64Kbps *available* bandwidth. For every additional server, add an additional 64Kbps. Is this a perfect rule? Not even close. However, it is a good place to start. Some network managers report that they are able to operate perfectly well with far less than 64Kbps available bandwidth. Some of my students have told me I should have the words "It depends" tattooed on my forehead because I say that so often.

How much bandwidth is required between Exchange servers greatly depends on the situation. Within a single site, things to ask to help figure out how much bandwidth is enough include:

▸ What types of and how much data is being transferred between servers?

▸ How often is the directory database being updated?

▸ How often are messages being sent from one server to another?

▶ Does the public folder hierarchy change often?

▶ Are you employing public folder content replication? If so, how often is the public folder data being replicated and changed?

DIAL-ON-DEMAND ROUTERS AND EXCHANGE

Several people have asked me recently if they can put several servers in a single site but have them separated by dial-on-demand routers. This seems to be an especially popular idea with the ISDN aficionados. Unless you live in an area where you are not charged every time ISDN dials out and you are not charged per-minute surcharges, you will be unpleasantly surprised when you get your first ISDN bill.

Within a single site, there is a lot of chatter between Exchange servers. The MTA delivers messages as soon as they arrive in the MTA queues; the directory service sends any changes between servers every five minutes. There are also public folder replication (content and hierarchy) messages, link monitor messages, and knowledge consistency checks every three hours. With this amount of traffic between servers in a single site, dial-on-demand routers will stay "off the hook" quite often during the course of a regular business day. In most cases, you will find Frame Relay to be a cheaper option.

Site Services Accounts

All Exchange servers in a single site must share a common site services user account (the user account you assigned to the first server in the site during installation). It is used to validate all the services on an Exchange server upon startup and when one server's message transfer agent (or directory service) connects to another server using RPCs. This means that any domain with an Exchange server in it must have a trust relationship to the domain that contains the site services account.

Site Administration

The decision to break an organization up into several sites is not purely technical. Administrative requirements may also determine site boundaries. Administrative responsibility is assigned by site; an administrator of one site does not necessarily have permissions to another site. Organizations with centralized MIS will benefit from the ability to manage one large site, but organizations with very decentralized MIS will benefit from a site model based on their administrative model.

SERVER DESIGN

One of the biggest problems that I experience in the field is improper or insufficient server hardware. Nearly 50 percent of the Exchange servers I have installed over the last year and a half have been upgraded to better (faster, stronger, higher capacity) servers since they were installed. The reasons given for upgrading or replacing servers include insufficient disk space, slow response time for clients, movement towards a standard server platform, and unreliable original server platform.

TIP

I have a tendency to overestimate the amount of server hardware and disk space I believe I am going to need. This approach gives me room to grow. I also operate under the philosophy that it is easier to ask for money for hardware up front than it is to come back six months later and ask for upgrade money.

Super Servers versus Off-the-Shelf Servers

It is always exciting to go shopping for the new breed of super servers. They have four, eight, or more processors, a few gigabytes of RAM, and cool-looking enclosures. These servers hold the promise of supporting thousands of mailboxes on a single machine. Table 24.2 lists some advantages and disadvantages of today's super servers.

Part v

TABLE 24.2: Advantages and Disadvantages of Super Servers

ADVANTAGES	DISADVANTAGES
Centralized management	If the super server fails, then many users are unable to access their e-mail
Reduced cost for server software licenses for Windows NT and Exchange	Difficult to back up or restore quickly due to the size of the information stores
	Often proprietary
	Expensive
	More users on a single Exchange server means the MTA will be transmitting fewer messages between servers

But before you rush out and put your entire organization on a single machine, consider the advantages of using off-the-shelf equipment (servers that can easily be ordered through your friendly neighborhood systems integration company). Though the super servers are pretty cool, my personal preference is to use several less powerful, off-the-shelf servers rather than one or two super servers. Table 24.3 lists advantages and disadvantages of off-the-shelf servers that are widely available.

TABLE 24.3: Advantages and Disadvantages of Off-the-Shelf Servers

ADVANTAGES	DISADVANTAGES
Distributed workload	More difficult to manage
Failure of a single server does not affect many users	More costly server software licenses, because you have to run more servers to support the same number of users
Information store backs up (and restores) more quickly since it is smaller	More servers to maintain

EXCHANGE@WORK: TO SUPER SERVE OR NOT TO SUPER SERVE

I recently spent several weeks with a client who was in the middle of Exchange design and planning. Before I came on board, they had decided to purchase a single super server to support 1,200 mailboxes and an identical super server to serve as a cold standby in the event of hardware failure. (Both servers were four-processor Pentium II 200MHz systems with 1GB of RAM.) They were also going to use this extra server for testing and doing practice disaster recovery restores. They had a very high-tech DLT tape loader system on a server on their backbone that could back up remote servers at a rate of about 2GB per hour. Furthermore, each user mailbox was going to be limited to 50MB.

Using the estimated size that the database would grow to over the first year, we calculated that a full private information store backup (or restore) would take 30 hours. Database repairs could take even longer. If there was a database corruption on this system, it would affect 1,200 users for many hours.

Was this acceptable? No, not even close. This company, like many others, found that messaging has become an integral business process.

Instead of one super server, we decided on five off-the-shelf servers (Pentium II 300Mhz systems, each with 256MB of RAM and its own DAT tape unit). Four of the servers were put into production supporting roughly 300 mailboxes per server, and the fifth machine is now a cold standby. We estimated that full backup (or restore) time could be reduced to around two hours.

The cost to move from two super servers to five moderately-configured servers was virtually the same. The super server was a major single point of failure and this was eliminated. Each server can be backed up completely each night on a single tape. In addition, this company's user community is split up across two major locations, so this design allowed us to place the servers closer to the users they served.

Server Configuration and Hardware Decisions

How much storage space do you purchase? Should you get many different types of servers or try and standardize with one brand and model? How much RAM should you start with? How should the machine be configured? What processor type should you use? These are all questions that you need to have coherent answers for before entering the server design phase.

Disk Storage Space

How much disk space do you need to purchase? The age-old question. My metric is to estimate about 50MB per user for the private information store. A lot of people's mouths fall open when I tell them this, but you will be surprised how quickly your power users will approach this amount. Some users will never reach 50MB, yet others will need to go way past the default limits I impose.

Estimating the amount of disk space required for the public information store is going to be much more difficult if you don't already have a good idea of what you are going to be storing there. If you don't know, then take the amount of disk space you are going to use for the private information store and double it to come up with an approximation of the total disk space you will need.

Table 24.4 shows a quick calculation for a server that will host both a public and private information store. There will be 450 mailboxes on the server.

TABLE 24.4: Estimated Database Storage Requirements for a Server Hosting 450 Mailboxes and Public Folders

DATABASE STORAGE	ESTIMATED SPACE
Private IS	(50MB × 450) = 22.5GB
Public IS	22.5GB
Extra space	25GB
Total database storage required	70GB

"Wow, 70GB of storage, just for e-mail?!" Have you heard that from your boss before? It is not just e-mail, though. The mailbox stores e-mail, calendar items, sent items, journal information, contact items, and any collaborative types of data that you may be routing using Exchange. Don't forget that you may also be integrating faxing or other systems that will keep data in the private information store.

What about that "extra space" of 25GB that I allocated? It is always a good practice to have an area of free space available on any server that is at least as large as the largest database you have. This allows you to perform offline database maintenance locally. There are other reasons why we need the extra space; I cover these in Chapters 25 and 28.

TIP

Don't ever sell yourself short on disk space. Disk drives are cheap compared to the downtime costs associated with upgrading a server with new disk drives.

EXCHANGE@WORK: AN EXTERNAL DISK ARRAY

One of my friends operates four Exchange servers to support almost 1,500 mailboxes. Rather than purchase twice the amount of disk space that he actually needs (my recommendation), he purchased one external disk array with 20GB of usable storage. If he needs to perform database maintenance on any of his servers, he shuts the server down (make sure you do this!), plugs in the external drive array, and powers the system backup. Ta da! An instant extra 20GB of disk space to rebuild or defragment a database. Though he does have to contend with the minor hassle of moving the external storage from one machine to another, this approach works well for him and saves his company a pretty good chunk of money.

RAM Requirements

Another good question: How much RAM is required? The best answer: RAM is cheap, so don't skimp on it. I consider 128MB to be a good starting point. For servers that are going to support more than 150 users, I move the RAM requirements up to 256MB. For servers that are going to support more than 400 users, I increase the RAM to 512MB. (Keep in mind that any Pentium II-based server with 512MB of RAM or more should also have 1MB of Level II cache.) Additional memory will almost always improve performance of any Microsoft BackOffice product.

WARNING

Only use RAM recommended and provided by the server manufacturer. Using slower or substandard SIMMs can cause Windows NT to be unstable.

Hardware Standardization

Picking a server hardware vendor can be one of the most critical decisions you will make during the design phase, but you can save yourself a fair amount of stress if you standardize on a particular hardware vendor. If at all possible, try to standardize on the same server family and model. Pick a vendor that not only has a good reputation for building quality hardware, but also is experienced in supporting Windows NT installations. I am still groggy from tracking down bizarre problems on a no-name brand late last night.

Disk Configuration

The disk subsystem on any system is always broken up into two major components: the disk controller and the disk drives themselves. Don't skimp on these either. I highly recommend using hardware-based RAID 5 drive arrays to increase the level of disk fault tolerance. I further recommend using SCSI disk drives; the best drives widely available today are the fast ultra-wide SCSIs.

TIP

An emerging technology that is becoming more affordable is fiber channel disks and controllers. Fiber channel can significantly improve the throughput of your disk subsystem.

TIP

Use RAID 5 and SCSI disk drives that are recommended by the server manufacturer. Even better, use controllers that will allow "hot swapping." Provided there is redundancy built into the disk array, a failed disk can be replaced while the server is in production.

When I configure a server for any type of application, I use hardware-based RAID 5 drives in an enclosure that supports "hot swapping." If a drive fails, I don't have to schedule downtime in order to replace it; I simply make sure I have a recent backup and then replace the failed drive.

NOTE

Should you use disk controllers with write caching enabled? Microsoft's official position on this is that you should leave write caching disabled. I have found performance to be enhanced considerably when write caching is used, but you should make sure that the controller has a battery backup system and that your data can be recovered off of the memory chips on the RAID controller. Inquire with your hardware manufacture about recovering data from memory chips on your RAID 5 controller.

Figure 24.6 shows a drive configuration for my ideal server, on which I would comfortably support more than 500 mailboxes. I am putting Windows NT software, Exchange software, and the page file on a 2GB, NTFS C drive, the log files on a 2GB FAT D drive, and the Exchange databases on a larger RAID 5 drive array formatted as an NTFS E drive.

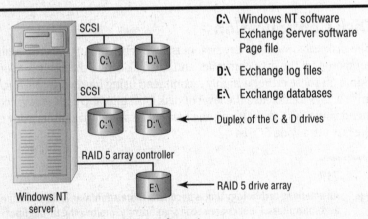

FIGURE 24.6: Server drive configuration

There are many different options for configuring disk drives. On a typical server supporting mailboxes, I would make sure that the log files are on a separate physical disk drive from the disk that has the database files on it. For a server operating as a messaging hub or bridgehead server, I would put the MTA working files on a separate disk.

Do the disks that contain log files and MTA working files need fault tolerance? Not in the strictest sense of the word, but I consider fault tolerance to be of paramount importance on any system. Which component in any PC-based system fails the most often? The disks. Regardless of which disk fails, you don't want it to affect the operation of the server. Disk fault tolerance, more than anything else, will help keep your server up and running.

Does the file system matter? You can give yourself another boost in performance by formatting the disk that holds log files with the FAT file system. FAT disks provide better performance for sequential writes. Formatting a server drive with the FAT file system does make some security specialists a little nervous, though there is no reason that any directory on a disk that holds the log files should be shared.

Processors

What speed processor should you use? The fastest processor you can purchase. There, that was simple, wasn't it? Any server you are buying today should have a minimum of a 300MHz Pentium II processor. If the server is expected to support more than 500 simultaneous clients, consider a dual-processor system. If the system is expected to support more than 1,000 clients, consider a four-processor system.

Other Server Options

When you are making out your shopping list for Exchange Server and server peripherals, here are some essential items to add:

▶ Uninterruptible power supply, monitoring software, and remote shutdown capabilities. You don't want a power failure to cause the sudden failure of your Exchange server and possibly corrupt one of the database files.

▶ A CD-ROM drive. Any Windows NT server you build should have one.

▶ A fast tape drive capable of backing up the entire system, preferably on one tape. I would prefer to use the exact same tape drive (and tape software) on all my Exchange servers so that my tapes are interoperable between servers.

TIP

Keep your servers simple! In my personal experience, the more software that is installed on a Windows NT platform, the more unstable the software and the operating system become. If you have the option, separate your Exchange Server software from other BackOffice server products. In addition, install Exchange Server onto member servers, not domain controllers.

EXCHANGE@WORK: PLUG IT IN AND MAKE SURE IT RUNS FOR THE NEXT THREE YEARS!

I have been working with a client for many years who is finally upgrading to Exchange Server; she has been operating a Microsoft Mail shop for years. I sat down with their Exchange project manager recently to develop a budget for server hardware. The system has to support 500 simultaneous users, be highly reliable, and provide some room for growth (no more than five percent per year). Further, my client told me that she is leasing the server equipment for three years and does not want to spend one additional penny on upgrades for leased hardware later on, so we should attempt to plan a server that will last for three years without upgrades. Her words were something like, "I want to turn on the power switch and have it run for three years without interruption." She and I both know this may not be possible, but it is a great goal to shoot for.

Though I urged her to split the load up across two servers, the company was intent on purchasing a single server. So we configured a Compaq Proliant 5500 server with two Pentium II 333MHz ZEON processors and 1MB of Level II cache. The server has a RAID 5 drive array with 75GB of usable storage and a 35/70 DLT tape unit installed in it. On a separate SCSI controller, there are two 4GB disks, one for the Windows NT operating system and one for the Exchange Server log files. There is an identical SCSI controller and drives that mirror the log files and the operating system. Though I would have preferred to see her go with two servers just to split the load up between two Exchange servers (for redundancy), this server configuration will be more than adequate for her new Exchange organization.

Server-Based Message Storage versus PST Storage

Where are messages stored? This is a decision you will be required to make. You have two primary options: Users can keep their messages on the server, or Outlook can automatically move messages from the server to a personal folder (PST). Naturally, if users are storing all their messages in a personal folder, you won't be needing any 70GB disk drives for the private information store.

The important factor is who is responsible for backing up the data. If the user message data is moved off the server and to a personal folder that is on a local hard disk, then who is responsible for that? I know, we warn users repeatedly to back up their hard disks, but they don't. Still, they blame their friendly neighborhood administrator when their hard drive fails and they lose data.

To help you decide which option is better for you, Table 24.5 shows some of the characteristics of server-based message storage and PST-based message storage.

TABLE 24.5: Server-based Message Storage versus PST-based Message Storage

SERVER-BASED MESSAGE STORAGE	PST-BASED MESSAGE STORAGE
Messages are backed up when the server is backed up.	Messages are only backed up if someone backs up the PST file.
Can take advantage of deleted item recovery.	Cannot take advantage of deleted item recovery.
Difficult to restore a single mailbox.	If the PST file is backed up, mailbox restoration is simple.
Permits single instance message storage.	For each recipient, there is a copy of a mail message stored in a separate personal folder.
Message only stored once on the server.	Two copies of each message are stored in the PST file, an RTF version and a plain text version.

TABLE 24.5 continued: Server-based Message Storage versus PST-based Message Storage

SERVER-BASED MESSAGE STORAGE	PST-BASED MESSAGE STORAGE
Only administrators and the user can access server-based messages.	Anyone who can access the file can access a personal store. If it is password encrypted, this password can be broken with tools from the Internet.
Outlook Web Access feature is available.	Since messages are removed from the server when they are transferred to a PST file, moved messages are not available to users using Outlook Web Access.

Grouping Your Users Together by Server

If you have more than one Exchange server, on which server should you place which mailboxes? The main factor in deciding where to place a mailbox is "Who does the user send messages to most often?" Though this can vary from organization to organization, usually the answer is users within the same department or group. You can further optimize Exchange by making sure that departments that often send messages to one another are grouped together on the same Exchange server. This will reduce the messaging load on your network and the message transfer agents (MTAs).

TIP

Don't put all the users with executive decision-making abilities on the same server (such as directors, vice presidents, CEOs, and so on), even though they might be grouped together logically, because they frequently send messages to one another. You don't want all the people with the power to get upset because their e-mail is not available. <grin>

Part v

EXCHANGE@WORK: PREPARING YOUR WINDOWS NT SYSTEM FOR EXCHANGE

Windows NT Server is the basic platform for all Microsoft BackOffice products. This platform needs to be solid; otherwise, any BackOffice product you run on it will be subject to the whims of a flaky Windows NT installation. Here are some steps to follow when configuring Windows NT to support Exchange Server:

1. Start with a clean installation of Windows NT.

2. Install network-related services and protocols. Ensure that you have the latest device drivers for network adapters, disk drivers, video drivers, and so on.

3. Partition and format the remaining disk partitions. If possible, format the disk that will contain the log files using the FAT file system.

4. Set the correct DNS domain name in the TCP/IP properties. Test TCP/IP connectivity and host name resolution (using NSLOOKUP).

5. Increase the initial size of the system page file to 125MB plus the amount of RAM and increase the maximum size to 250MB plus RAM. If possible, make sure the page file does not occupy the same physical disk on which the log files are stored.

6. Apply the latest Windows NT service pack. I recommend using Windows NT 4 SP4, because it includes many security fixes only found in post-SP 3 hot fixes. If you are in the United States or Canada, contact Microsoft to get the North American edition of the SP4 CD (128-bit encryption). Order part number 236-01176 from (800) 370-8758. Check with Microsoft for recent releases of service packs and hot fixes that may affect Exchange.

7. Install Windows NT Option Pack services and Internet Explorer *only* if you plan to use them in the future. If you require products from the Option Pack CD, install Internet Explorer 4 and then install the Option Pack products. If you have installed SP4, you will get a message warning you that SP4 has not been tested with the Option Pack. This is okay.

CONTINUED ➡

8. Reapply the Windows NT 4 Service Pack 4.

Once you have the basic platform installed, you are then ready to progress to installation of Exchange Server. Once Windows NT is installed, there are a few simple rules you can follow to ensure that Windows NT remains stable:

- After any upgrades, blue screens, or new software installations, run the CHKDSK /F command.

- Keep an updated copy of your Emergency Repair Disk, especially after making system or disk configuration changes.

- Make sure you have a recent system backup.

- After installing software and Windows NT system services, re-apply any service packs and hot fixes.

- Never install beta software on production servers.

- Do not use OpenGL screen savers on servers; they seriously impact performance.

- Reboot after any software updates or installing new service packs.

- Be careful of Windows 16-bit and DOS applications; poorly written applications can degrade performance.

WARNING

Do not install unnecessary services; they take up memory and disk space. Unnecessary services can contribute to system instability and pose potential security risks.

WARNING

Never use NTFS file compression to compress the Exchange databases, log files, or working directories. This could result in decreased response times and, if the database exceeds 4GB, possible database corruption.

Microsoft Cluster Services

With the release of the Windows NT Server 4 Enterprise Edition, Microsoft introduced the concept of clusters to the Windows NT family. This is by no means a new concept—Digital Equipment Corp. brought clustering to the VAX/VMS family nearly 20 years ago.

In my own humble opinion, Windows NT clustering is still very much a 1.0 product. Not that it is going to stay that way, but it is a first-generation product from the perspective of Windows NT. Figure 24.7 illustrates a two-node cluster running Exchange services. Currently, Windows NT Server is only capable of supporting a two-node cluster.

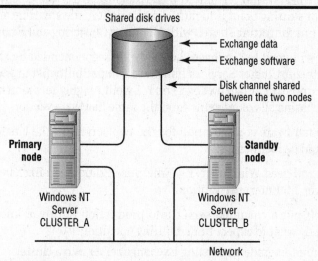

FIGURE 24.7: A two-node Windows NT cluster

The cluster appears as a single Exchange server. Though there are two nodes in the cluster, Exchange services are only active on a single machine at a time. Both nodes in the cluster share a set of disks where the databases, working directories, and log files are located.

What Does Clustering Protect You From?

Clustering protects you from hardware failures. It does not protect against a database failure, because there is only one copy of the Exchange databases (on the shared disk). There is always the chance that the active node in the cluster will corrupt the database when it fails.

In a clustered environment, Exchange does not provide instantaneous failover. When failover from the active node to the secondary node in a cluster occurs, some services on the active node may have to be shut down. Database transactions may have to be rolled forward from the logs to the databases. The exact time that is required to transition between one node and the other will vary based on the server hardware and the software configuration, but I can assure you that if it occurs during a busy period of the day, your user community will take notice of the failure.

Installing Exchange on Microsoft Cluster Services

What is the best way to get started with Exchange in a clustered environment? Your starting point is to purchase the right hardware. Here are a couple of tips for getting started with Microsoft Clustering and Exchange:

▶ You will need to purchase the hardware recommended by the Microsoft Cluster Services hardware compatibility list at www .microsoft.com/hwtest/hcl. I would highly recommend purchasing all components from the same hardware vendor.

▶ The hardware configuration for the two servers in the cluster should be identical.

▶ You will need Windows NT 4 Enterprise Edition and Exchange Server 5.5 Enterprise Edition.

▶ Don't put a clustered server into production until you know exactly what to expect from it during operation.

You cannot upgrade an existing Exchange server into a cluster. Though there is a way to move the databases onto a newly installed cluster server, I recommend installing a new cluster server and moving all the mailboxes to the new machine.

Before you deploy clusters in your environment, you should have tested your new hardware thoroughly. The cluster-testing phase provides you with an excellent opportunity for you to play with the cluster, testing failover and learning more about what to expect once you put it into operation.

Exchange Services That Support Clustering Microsoft Clustering is a new technology and is only supported for certain Exchange services. These services are:

▶ System Attendant

▶ Directory Service

▶ Information Store

▶ Message Transfer Agent

▶ Internet Mail Service

Automatic failover for the Internet News Service, Microsoft Mail connector, Lotus cc:Mail connector, Lotus Notes connector, IBM PROFS connector, SNADS, and the Key Management Server services are not supported; in many cases, however, you can configure these services and manually restart them on the secondary cluster node.

NOTE

Tony Redmond (from Compaq in Dublin, Ireland) is one of the best-known people in the Exchange community. He has a very good discussion of clustering in his book *Microsoft Exchange Server 5.5 Planning, Design, and Implementation* (Digital Press, 1998).

BUILD A TEST LAB

I strongly recommend having an extra server standing by in case one of your production servers fails. This server's hardware should be identical to your production servers'. This way, bringing any failed server up can be as simple as moving the disks from a server that may have failed over to the standby server and powering the system backup.

Some of the most successful Exchange administrators I know have taken their extra server and built a test lab, often with a few additional servers and workstations. They use this test lab to test new service packs, handle mailbox restoration (in case of deletion), and practice disaster recovery.

An Overview of the LoadSim Utility

Microsoft offers a utility called LoadSim that you can download from www.microsoft.com/exchange. (Microsoft does not support this utility.) This utility simulates user load on an Exchange server by actually generating e-mail messages, calendar access, and public folder access. You control the number of users, the type of user (light, medium, or heavy), and the length of the test.

During the test, LoadSim records average response times. You then use a utility called LSLOG to report on the average response times for various types of activities. The combination of LoadSim and LSLOG lets you determine how a particular server platform will behave under various loads.

Though not the intended function of LoadSim, my favorite use of this utility is to generate large databases so that I can test activities such as backup, restore, and disaster recovery. In a few hours time, I can create a 2GB private information store.

I also use this utility to test upgrades and service packs on my test lab server prior to deploying the server into production. I will set up an Exchange server, run LoadSim to generate some activity, and then apply the service pack or hot fix. Then I will run LoadSim again for several hours (or days). This method is not guaranteed to find obscure bugs in service packs or hot fixes, but it certainly can help pinpoint any show-stopping bugs that might be specific to my environment.

NOTE

From January to April of 1998, *Windows NT Magazine* published a series of articles on the LoadSim utility. These articles were all titled "Understanding and Using LoadSim" and are available on the *Windows NT Magazine* Web site at www.winntmag.com.

PLANNING EXCHANGE OPERATIONS

As system administrators and engineers, our first responsibility is to keep our systems up and running. Therefore, a solid plan for operations should be in place and clearly defined expectations should be published. Some of the many items to consider include:

- ▶ Plan a maintenance window so that the user community will know exactly when they can expect the system to be unavailable.

- ▶ Publish a Service Level Agreement (SLA) to clearly outline the type of performance and response the user community can expect from both the messaging system and the support organization.

- As part of the SLA, end users should be required to sign an Acceptable Use Agreement that details what is considered acceptable use of the company's computers and what is not.

- Technical support and help desk responsibilities should be clearly outlined so that no one steps on another person's toes and to make sure that everyone understands who is responsible for what.

Publish a Maintenance Window

Even if you don't believe you are going to need it, publish a weekly or biweekly *maintenance window*. This is a time each week or month that your user community should expect to have limited networking services (or possibly no network services at all). This will provide you with an opportunity to perform any sort of scheduled maintenance.

Not everyone can publish a time that her system can be down. Many organizations expect the system to be available all the time. As you will see in Chapter 25, there are few operations tasks that truly require that the server be taken completely offline.

How long should your maintenance period be? I would ask for two separate types. Every night, say from 11:30 until midnight, I would ask for 30 minutes that I could use for a reboot or other quick maintenance. I would use this time interval only if necessary.

For the second period, I recommend a weekly maintenance window long enough to allow for an offline defragmentation of the private information store (or the public information store, whichever is larger). I don't do this every week, but I would like the option of having that much time.

Did your request for a maintenance window get turned down? If you can't get a nightly or weekly slot, then at the very least publish one six-hour window each month (such as the second Saturday night of each month) that will enable you to take your servers offline. I try to avoid the very first and last of any month due to deadlines and activities that tend to come at the end and beginning of each month, such as sales closures, accounting end-of-month processes, and so on.

NOTE

Are you curious about what you may be required to do during these maintenance windows? Chapter 25 has recommendations for daily, weekly, and periodic maintenance activities.

EXCHANGE@WORK: DEFINE YOUR MAINTENANCE WINDOWS EARLY IN THE DEPLOYMENT

On a site I worked on a few years ago, we made a fatal mistake by not publishing a maintenance window as the LAN was being rolled out. The users were already conditioned to expect that the computer system would be unavailable; our three minicomputers were unavailable from 9:00 P.M. until 6:00 A.M. every day of the week.

At first, the LAN did not need a maintenance schedule, so we never requested one. Yet over time, little tasks started popping up that needed to be done on a monthly or even weekly basis—minor software upgrades, database re-indexing and defragmentation, printer driver updates, and so on. However, our user community had gotten used to the LAN servers being available 24 hours a day, 7 days a week. Even at midnight, there would always be a few people working. We asked for a maintenance window during which we could perform these tasks, and the request had to go all the way to the CEO. Department managers raised a little holy heck when we tried to shut the system down. Eventually, we got our maintenance window; it was from midnight Saturday night until 6:00 A.M. on Sunday morning. We would start announcing the shutdown to our users at 11:30 P.M. on Saturday, and the help desk lines would inevitably light up with a couple of users who "had to keep working."

In our case, the tail was wagging the dog. If we had merely defined a schedule when the system was deployed a year before, we probably could have gotten away with Saturday mornings from 8:00 A.M. until noon, or some other more reasonable schedule. But our users got used to working on the system whenever they wanted to, so we were reactive rather than proactive.

Publishing a Service Level Agreement (SLA)

Upper-level management wants to see better returns on their investments in Information Services. Driven by poor end-user support and frequent system failures, end-user communities are asking for (okay, demanding) guarantees that the system will be available when they need it. Information Services departments need a mechanism to set expectations. To that end, *Service Level Agreements* (*SLAs*) are becoming more and more important and common in today's corporate and government world.

An SLA is a document detailing a level of service that the end users can expect from their computer system. Further, SLAs demonstrate to management a strong commitment on the part of IS team to deliver quality service. Finally, the SLA gives the IS team certain levels of service to live up to.

What should your SLA contain? Here are a few suggestions:

- ► A statement of expected up time, system availability, and maintenance windows.

- ► Expected system response times and projected message delivery times within the site and throughout the organization.

- ► Help desk availability and expected responses to basic questions as well as problems that affect usage.

- ► Promise and availability of advanced training.

- ► Planned future functionality and expected deployment dates.

- ► Promise to provide a location for users and managers to review system statistics, such as a Web site or public folder. These statistics could include average local and remote delivery times, volume of messages processed per month, average number of users supported each day, and storage utilized.

Naturally, if I were writing an SLA, I would put a few clauses in it to make sure that no one holds me to a certain level of service if the local volcano is erupting or an earthquake has destroyed the computer room. However, this document is an excellent and extremely important way to set reasonable expectations.

NOTE

Keep in mind that the SLA is an agreement of realistic goals between the IS support organization and the user community. Compromise will always be necessary.

Acceptable Use Policies

Running parallel with creating an SLA to set expectations of what the IS team will provide, organizations should also have a policy of acceptable use that outlines the limits of the e-mail system's usage. There are many boilerplate agreements available today, but I would make sure that anything my user community agrees to includes these elements:

▶ Users must understand that all messages are subject to monitoring and auditing by the proper authority. Management can request the content of any mailbox at any time. The rule of thumb I suggest to my users is "Don't put it in an e-mail if you would mind your boss reading it."

▶ Detail policies regarding acceptable language usage in electronic communication of any kind. Users should be cautioned not to use profanity or anything that would suggest sexual harassment. Naughty graphics, jokes, and other material of a questionable nature should be considered unacceptable.

▶ Different companies have varying views on personal e-mail. My own view is that as long as the e-mail system is not abused, a few personal e-mail messages per day are acceptable.

▶ Passwords, private keys, or access devices should never be shared or written down.

▶ Computers and terminals must never be left unattended without first locking down the computer or logging out.

▶ Misuse of passwords, browsing directories or public folders, or other activity not related to a user's job is grounds for termination.

▶ Users must understand that any commercial activity other than that related to the operation of the company paying for the e-mail system is prohibited.

Users must understand that violation of any of these policies is grounds for termination. Prior to asking employees to sign or to agree to anything, the company lawyer and/or human resources specialist should review and approve the acceptable use policies.

NOTE

Attorney Michael R. Overly has written a book called *E-Policy: How to Develop Computer, E-mail, and Internet Guidelines to Protect Your Company and Its Assets* (Amacom, 1998). This guide is a must for anyone developing an acceptable use policy for his or her messaging system.

Assigning Administrative and Technical Support Responsibilities

Who is responsible for what? Regardless of the size of your Exchange organization, responsibilities need to be clearly defined. Larger organizations can break up administrative levels into a couple of categories; smaller organizations may have one person who handles all of these tasks.

Frontline support or help desk support handles Outlook user support, debugging connectivity, public folder issues, and profile problems. These people may also be given permission to update recipient attributes such as phone numbers, addresses, and so on.

Recipient administrator is responsible for creating new mailboxes, custom recipients, and distribution lists. This person may also be responsible for adding Windows NT accounts.

Server administrator is responsible for tape backups, ongoing maintenance, reviewing event and security logs, looking for stuck queues, checking performance data, and handling escalated tech support calls. This person should not be in direct contact with the user community but rather work with the help desk or recipient administrator.

Exchange security manager is responsible for managing permissions on objects (such as mailboxes) in the Exchange directory. In an environment where Exchange Advanced Security is in use, this manager would also be responsible for handing out public and private key pairs. Only a few people within the organization should have this level of access.

Exchange architect is responsible for the big picture of Exchange organization, including server design, connectivity, analyzing performance data, and handling technical support incidents that have been escalated from the server administrator. In some organizations, this person may actually work for the systems integrator or vendor.

EXCHANGE@WORK: MAINTAINING A STABLE SYSTEM

One of my big beefs with the microcomputer world is our relative nonchalance with our server hardware and software. I am not picking on anyone except myself, because I am as guilty of this as anyone else. The original platform that I worked on (in the early 1980s) was the DEC VAX/VMS. (When I mention VMS, everyone has to get up, bow to the west, and chant thrice.) Back then, we would never dream of loading a new device driver during the business day. Operating system upgrades and patches were scheduled weeks in advance and only done with a DEC employee on site. Software upgrades were only done with the software vendor on site or, at the very least, on the phone. And we did not experiment with new software no matter how cool it sounded.

Yet I constantly find myself tempted to load unnecessary software onto production Windows NT servers. If you have the same urges, you should stifle them! Experimenting with a production system is a recipe for disaster.

Here are a few tips to help you make sure you run without unexpected incidents:

- Don't apply Windows NT or Exchange service packs and hot fixes unless you know for certain that they fix problems you are having or that they are going to add functionality that you need immediately.

- Nothing should occur on your production servers without first being scheduled and tested in a lab environment.

- Do not add new functionality to your servers without first testing it; this includes virus protection, message scanning, fax servers, and any other third-party solutions.

- Avoid beta software like the plague. Beta software has no place in a production environment unless you are part of an early adopters program and will have immediate technical support for problems you are experiencing. Even then, your user community should be conditioned to expect problems.

CONTINUED ➡

Some of these items may make your job a little more difficult. But think about how much more difficult your job is going to be if 500 people can't read their e-mail messages because a device driver has conflicted with a new service pack, and then your server blue screens upon startup. Your entire messaging system will be down, and your job will be more than a little difficult. <grin>

WHAT'S NEXT?

This chapter explained how you can make solid organizational design decisions that include planning a proper foundation for Exchange, considering the consequences of the design, and choosing reliable hardware. The next chapter will introduce you to the database technology that Exchange Server uses and the tools you will need to test and repair your Exchange public information store, private information store, and directory service databases. It then discusses the types of backups that are available and recommends types of maintenance that you should perform. Also, you will learn some tips and ideas for helping to prevent disasters on your Exchange servers.

Chapter 25
MAINTENANCE PROCEDURES

I have a theory on system operations: The more prepared you are for a disaster, the less likely it will be that the disaster will occur. A very important part of your battle to prevent disasters is ongoing maintenance.

This chapter introduces you to the database technology that Exchange Server uses and the tools you will need to test and repair your Exchange public information store, private information store, and directory service databases. It then discusses the types of backups that are available. I make a series of recommendations on the types of daily, weekly, and periodic maintenance that you should perform. At the close of the chapter, I discuss some tips and ideas for helping to prevent disasters on your Exchange servers.

Adapted from *Exchange Server 5.5 24seven™*
by Jim McBee
ISBN 0-7821-2505-0   657 pages $34.99

EXCHANGE REQUIRES LESS DATABASE MAINTENANCE!

I was a Lotus cc:Mail administrator for several years. While I loved cc:Mail, the maintenance drove me nuts. The post offices had to be shut down in order to be backed up, there was often no indication of problems until there was serious data corruption, and database diagnostics and disk space reclamation had to be run often. Though there are maintenance tasks that you should perform with Exchange Server 5.5, I have found them to be minimal compared to cc:Mail and other legacy systems.

EXCHANGE DATABASE TECHNOLOGY: AN OVERVIEW

Exchange Server uses a database technology that Microsoft calls ESE (Extensible Storage Engine); this technology is a modified version of the JET (Joint Engine Technology) database engine. Ultimately, the current Exchange database technology is a distant cousin of the technology used by Microsoft Access. In reality, however, it is much more similar to modern relational database technologies such as SQL Server. The version of the database that is used with Exchange 5.5 is sometimes called JET Blue; it is highly optimized for use with Exchange.

In order to ensure that the database files are available and correct, the Exchange technology borrows concepts from the minicomputer and mainframe relational database world. This includes the use of log files to record all transactions prior to the transaction being committed to the database file. In the 1970s, database transaction technology was defined and measured by the database ACID test (Atomicity, Consistency, Isolation, and Durability).

▶ All operations on an Exchange Server database are *atomic*, meaning all transaction data are either committed to the database or rolled back. Exchange Server log files record data in the form of transactions and commit these transactions to the database once complete.

Part v

- In order to ensure *consistency*, the database is always transformed from one known, valid state to another. The atomicity of the transactions and the use of the transaction log ensure that the database always stays in a valid state.

- All transactions are serialized and *isolated*. This prevents simultaneous activity from interfering with any specific transaction.

- Transaction results are *durable*; they are permanent and capable of surviving system failures.

EXCHANGE@WORK: MUCH ADO ABOUT TRANSACTIONS AND LOGS

A *transaction* is a sequence of information exchange and related steps that are treated as a single operation. In order for the transaction to be considered finished, all steps have to be completed.

For example, let's say that your bank has a database with two tables of data: checking data and savings data. You call the bank's customer service and ask that $100 be transferred from your checking account to your savings account. The transaction will consist of two steps: subtracting $100 from your checking account and adding $100 to your savings account.

What if the system fails right in the middle of this operation? Did it finish, or are you out $100?

In the relational database world (and in Exchange Server), both operations are recorded to a *transaction log* first. Once all the operations that make up the transaction are complete, the operation work is performed on the database. If the system fails in the middle of performing the "subtract" step on the database, when the system restarts, the database software detects an incomplete transaction. If all the information required to complete the transaction is located in the transaction log files, the transaction is "rolled forward." If not, the transaction is "rolled back" or returned to a valid state.

Database Circular Logging

By default, a feature called *circular logging* is turned on. This feature is enabled for the directory database and the information store databases, and it is designed to minimize the amount of space consumed by the transaction log files.

If you can answer "yes" to all the following questions, be sure to keep circular logging enabled:

▶ Are you going to perform a normal (full) backup every night?

▶ Will you not require incremental or differential backups?

▶ Are the log files and the database files on the same disk drive?

If you answered "no" to any of these questions, plan to turn off circular logging as soon as possible. To do so, the information store and directory services must be stopped and restarted, so plan to do this during one of your regularly scheduled maintenance periods. Further, you must disable circular logging on each server. Begin by locating the server object, and then display the server object's properties and select the Advanced tab (see Figure 25.1). In the Database Circular Logging section, remove the check mark from both Directory and Information Store. When you click OK, you will be asked if this is really OK, because if it is, the information store and the directory will have to be restarted.

FIGURE 25.1: Disable circular logging on a server's Advanced tab.

TIP

I highly recommend disabling the circular logging feature for all servers.

Once circular logging has been disabled, Exchange Server will keep all old log files until a normal or incremental backup is done. Disabling circular logging allows you to back up just the log files instead of the entire database when using incremental or differential backup. Given that all the log files are on the drive since the last normal backup, up-to-the-minute recovery can be performed.

Exchange Database Files

Exchange uses database, log, and other files to store messages and make sure that the data is stable. Though the actual disk drive locations may vary based on the system, I am going to assume that the data locations are the same as the ones found in Table 25.1. You should have documentation similar to this for each of your servers that tells you which disk is used for each database, transaction log, and working file. In addition to sample locations, Table 25.1 lists estimated disk sizes that a server might have.

TABLE 25.1: Sample Data File Locations

Data File	Disk Format	Disk Size	Location
Private information store database	NTFS	50GB	E:\exchsrvr\ MDBdata
Public information store database	NTFS	50GB	E:\exchsrvr\ MDBdata
Directory database	NTFS	50GB	E:\exchsrvr\ DSAdata
Information store transaction logs	FAT	2GB	D:\exchsrvr\ MDBdata
Directory transaction logs	FAT	2GB	D:\exchsrvr\ DSAdata
Information store working path	NTFS	4GB	C:\exchsrvr\ MDBdata
Directory working path	NTFS	4GB	C:\exchsrvr\ MDBdata

Part v

All transactions are committed first to memory, then to the log file, then finally to the database file. As transactions are being written to the log files, they are written sequentially; transactions and other database operations are random. Servers that have the log files and data files on separate physical disks will experience up to a 40 percent improvement in performance.

WARNING

Never compress any of the Exchange working directories, database files, or transaction log files. Performance will suffer, and any Exchange database that surpasses 4GB in size *will* experience database corruption. This will become noticeable when you start seeing errors in the Windows NT event log such as event ID 116, "Synchronous read page checksum error –1018."

Information Store Data

In the `E:\exchsrvr\MDBdata` directory, you will find two files: the `pub.edb` and the `priv.edb`. They contain all the information from the public information store and the private information store, respectively. These files can grow to 16GB using Exchange 5.5 Standard Edition and 16TB using Exchange 5.5 Enterprise Edition.

Directory Service Data

In the `E:\exchsrvr\DSAdata` directory, you will find the `dir.edb` file; this file contains the directory service database. The `dir.edb` file is specific to the Exchange server that it was installed on and cannot be moved to an Exchange server with a different name. I consider it prudent to occasionally make an offline backup of this file.

Transaction Logs

In the `D:\exchsrvr\MDBdata` and `D:\exchsrvr\DSAdata` directories, you will find the data transaction logs. All transaction log files are 5,120KB in size; any other size for a log file may indicate corruption or that the file is not an Exchange log file. The public and private information store databases share a common set of log files.

The active log file in both of these directories is the `edb.log`. When this file fills up, it is renamed to `edb00001.log`, and a new `edb.log` is created. When the newly created log file fills up, it is renamed to edb00002.log, and another new edb.log is created. If you view either of these directories, you will see a collection of these old log files.

If circular logging is enabled (default), generally only four previous log files are stored in the directory. On a server that has circular logging turned on, the previous logs might look like edb00009.log, edb00010.log, edb0001a.log, and edb0001b.log. Once a new log file is created, the oldest log file is automatically deleted, and the new log file list would be edb00010.log, edb0001a.log, edb0001b.log, and edb0001c.log.

NOTE
If the server is heavily loaded, it is normal to have more than four log files in this directory.

If circular logging is disabled, the log files in the directory will continue to collect. It is not uncommon to see dozens of log files in this directory. Yet when a normal or incremental online backup is performed, Exchange purges these old log files.

WARNING
Never delete log files manually. The Exchange server should manage these files itself. If the number of log files continues to grow, make sure that you are performing a normal online backup periodically.

The log file directories also have two reserved log files, res1.log and res2.log. Reserved logs are used in case Exchange runs out of disk space when it tries to create a new edb.log file. If this occurs, the reserved files are used instead; any transactions in memory are flushed to the reserved log files, and Exchange will shut down the affected services. You must correct the disk space problems before you can restart Exchange.

Checkpoint Files

In both the C:\exchsrvr\DSAdata and C:\exchsrvr\MDBdata directories (this is the location of the information store working path and the directory working path), you will find a file called the checkpoint file, edb.chk. This file is always 8KB in size.

A checkpoint is a place marker; it points a location in the log files. All transactions before the checkpoint have been committed to the database; all transactions after the checkpoint have not been committed to the database. The checkpoint is stored in the edb.chk file.

Other Files

There are a few other files that you may see periodically in the Exchange data and log directories. On the disk that hosts the information store and directory working paths, you may see a tmb.edb file. This file is used to store transactions that may not be able to be written to the disk immediately when online maintenance is occurring.

WARNING

Do not delete this tmb.edb file! Exchange Server will manage its creation and usage.

An additional log file may appear from time to time, depending when you look at the log file directory; it is called edbtmp.log. It is a temporary file used when creating a new log file. The process of converting edb.log to an edbxxxxx.log file requires a new edb.log file, hence edbtmp.log is created while the edb.log is renamed to edbxxxxx.log.

During an online backup, you will see patch files created. Each database that is being backed up has its own PAT file: priv.pat, pub.pat, and dir.pat. During an online backup, transactions can still be committed to the database files. However, if the transaction is committed to a part of the database that has already been backed up, the transaction is also written to the corresponding PAT file. When the database is completely backed up, the PAT file is backed up and then deleted.

NOTE

If you see a PAT file in either the \DSAdata or the \MBDdata directory, that indicates that the server is currently undergoing an online backup. If this file grows extremely large (more than a few hundred megabytes), make sure that there is not a backup running that has hung up or is waiting for an additional tape.

Database Tools

Microsoft provides two tools for checking, repairing, and defragmenting Exchange databases. These tools are `isinteg.exe` and `eseutil.exe` (this tool was named `edbutil.exe` in Exchange 4 and 5).

WARNING

Do not attempt to run an `edbutil.exe` on a newer Exchange database, and do not run `eseutil.exe` on an older Exchange database. Each tool is specific to its version of the Exchange database and cannot be used for other versions.

WARNING

Prior to running *any* database utilities, you should perform a full, complete (normal) backup of all Exchange databases. If you cannot perform an online backup, run an offline backup. Microsoft recommends running these utilities only when advised by Microsoft Product Support Services.

The ESEUTIL Program

The `eseutil.exe` program is located in the `C:\WinNT\System32` directory. This tool is a database repair utility; it understands the structure of the Exchange databases and repairs, checks, and compacts Exchange 5.5 database files. It also understands the underlying structure of the database, tables, indexes, and records, but it does not understand the Exchange data that is placed in those tables and records. In short, it is a database tool for database errors.

ESEUTIL is a command-line tool. The information store and/or directory services must be stopped in order to run this utility. Table 25.2 has some of the common command-line options for the ESEUTIL program.

TABLE 25.2: Common Command-Line Options for the ESEUTIL Program

Option	Operation
/?	Displays ESEUTIL options.
/DS	Selects the directory database.

TABLE 25.2 continued: Common Command-Line Options

Option	Operation
/ispriv	Selects the private information store.
/ispub	Selects the public information store.
/D	Performs offline defragmentation/compaction on the selected database.
/G	Performs integrity check on the selected database.
/P	Performs repair operations on the selected database. Used for a damaged database file. Data may be lost.
/R	Performs a recovery bringing selected database into a consistent state.
/U	Upgrades the selected database (not normally used by an administrator).

WARNING

Command-line switch order is important. You should always put the switch that is setting up the type operation first, i.e. /R, /D, /G, and /P. (Example: ESEUTIL /D /DS.)

Database Defragmentation/Compaction ESEUTIL can perform an offline defragmentation/compaction of the public information store, private information store, and directory databases. Defragmentation takes the existing database file and builds a new temporary database file (tempdfrg.edb by default) from it by copying the records from the old file to the new one. This process cleans up any "white space" (unused storage) in the database, makes the storage contiguous, and reduces the overall size of the database file. When the temporary database is successfully created, the original database is deleted, and the temporary database is renamed to the original database name. If ESEUTIL discovers an error while copying records from the original database to the new temporary database, it will stop and display the error.

There are a few optional command-line switches that you should be aware of when running the ESEUTIL command with the defragmentation option.

Option	Operation
/T <*path\dbname*>	Redirects the temporary database to another location other than the default (the current drive). This can prove very useful, and you can direct the temporary database across the network, which can slow the process considerably. Consider installing an extra disk or disk array and redirecting to a local disk instead of to the network.
/L <*path*>	Specifies the location for the log files.
/B <*path\dbname*>	Makes a backup copy of the database before starting the defragmentation procedure.
/P	Defragments/compacts the database to a new temporary database, but does not delete the original database when complete. They call this the "don't instate" option.

When running ESEUTIL with the /D option, consider these useful tips:

▶ Always make a normal backup immediately before running any sort of database utility.

▶ As soon as the defragmentation is complete, make another normal backup. This is because after the database is reorganized, it gets a new log file signature. The old log files are no longer usable. (See Knowledge Base article Q183380 for more information.)

▶ Make sure that at least one disk has free disk space equal to 110 percent of the size of the database to be defragmented (or 210 percent if you plan to use the /B option). If you don't have this kind of space available locally, you can direct the temporary or backup database to another server, though this will considerably slow down the defragmentation operation.

▶ Your actual mileage will vary greatly, but on a moderately configured system, plan for one hour for every 3 to 5GB of database size. This time depends on the speed of your hardware as well as the complexity of the message database.

NOTE

Should you defragment the Exchange databases often? Keep reading! The section titled "Should You Perform Database Maintenance?" later in this chapter will help you to answer this question (though, I'm betting the answer is no).

EXCHANGE@WORK: DEFRAGMENTATION/COMPACTION EXAMPLES

Here are a couple of examples of using ESEUTIL that may be helpful.

To defragment the private information store and redirect the temporary files to another server (LAXEX002), type **ESEUTIL /D /ISPRIV /T\\LAXEX002\temp\temppriv.edb**. If you do not specify the /T parameter, the temporary database will be created in the current directory.

To run a simple defragmentation on the public information store when you have adequate disk space on the current drive, type **ESEUTIL /D /ISPUB.**

NOTE

Whenever you run ESEUTIL with the /D option, ESEUTIL always performs a soft recovery first to make sure the database is in a consistent state. This is equivalent to running ESEUTIL with the /R option.

Database Consistency Check   A database is consistent if it has been shut down normally; a flag is set in the database when the database is shut down correctly. ESEUTIL uses the /M option to dump the status of the database files. This allows you to determine if the database is in a consistent or inconsistent state. I recommend redirecting the output of the ESEUTIL /M command to a text file like this:

```
ESEUTIL /MH \exchsrvr\MDBdata\priv.edb > priv.txt
```

The output from the command is redirected to the file priv.txt; it should include the line State: Consistent. If you see this, you can be assured the database is consistent. However, if you see the word inconsistent and the information store service will not start, then you may be on your way to restoring the database. You can attempt recovery using the ESEUTIL /R command (as described below); as long as there are no problems with the database, this should run quickly. As an absolute last resort (no backups available), run the ESEUTIL /P command.

Database Recovery   If you encounter an inconsistent database, you should consider running the ESEUTIL /R command before attempting a repair of the database. You could save yourself several hours of repair time.

TIP

Prior to running the any ESEUTIL options, you should make backup copies of the database, .log, and .chk files. You will need them if you need to return the database to its original state later.

The ESEUTIL /R command performs a soft recovery, bringing the database to a consistent state by rolling forward transactions, rolling back transactions, and fixing the files located in the directory specified by the Registry for the private, public, and directory databases. When running ESEUTIL to perform a soft recovery of log files, checkpoint files, and database consistency, you should specify which database this will be performed on. It would look something like this: **ESEUTIL /R /ISPRIV**. This command returns the database to a consistent state and ensures recovery will ensue.

In normal circumstances, the IS and DS would run this recovery. In the event the database is a very bad state or "has torn pages," as we say, you may be restoring from a backup and restoring your last set of log files. You did back up the log files like I said in the last section before you ran this tool, right?

Database Integrity Check   ESEUTIL also provides an option (ESEU-TIL /G) to check the integrity of the database. It is a "non-destructive" option, meaning it makes no changes at all to the database file. If there are problems, such as damaged or unreadable records, the utility will report them. ESEUTIL creates a small working file in the current directory (integ.edb) file; I have never seen this file grow above 50MB in size, though. Depending on your hardware configuration, you can expect to process between 6 and 10GB per hour running the integrity check option.

Using ESEUTIL with the /G option provides you with a few additional command-line options that might prove useful.

Option	Operation
/T <*path\dbname*>	Redirects the working database to another drive and directory
/V	Outputs all messages (verbose) and performs more detailed tests
/X	Outputs detailed error messages

To run the integrity check option of the ESEUTIL utility on the private information store, type **ESEUTIL /G /ISPRIV.**

Database Repair: A Last Resort   When all else fails, ESEUTIL offers an option (ESEUTIL /P) to repair a damaged database file (sometimes called a "hard repair"). This option should be considered a last resort. If you are performing backups regularly and have circular logging turned off, you will be able to restore your last backup more quickly than you can run a database repair. Moreover, ESEUTIL "fixes" the database, which means that any database pages it considers bad or torn will be deleted, including attachments and messages. You won't know what information was deleted until a user complains.

Depending on your server hardware and the complexity of the database, the /P option can process anywhere from 1 to 3GB per hour. Take 25 percent of the size of the database that you are repairing and plan to have at least that amount of disk space available on the disk that will hold the temporary file.

TIP
Prior to running ESEUTIL /P, try running the ESEUTIL /R command. This latter option runs very quickly and may fix your problem.

Refer to the previous section for information on the /R option. On a finer note, be sure to back up the current log files and checkpoint files to a backup directory. If the /P option fails, you can still attempt to recover the database and log files from backup and try another option.

If you don't have a good backup or you are just feeling adventurous, run ESEUTIL with the /P option. It has several command-line options you should be aware of.

Option	Operation
/T <*path\dbname*>	Redirects the temporary database to another drive and directory
/D	Scans for errors, but doesn't actually make any repairs
/V	Generates verbose output and performs more detailed tests
/X	Generates detailed error messages

To perform a repair on the public information store and direct the temporary database file to another disk drive, type **ESEUTIL /P /ISPUB /TG:\temp\tempdb.edb.**

TO REPAIR OR NOT TO REPAIR?

Microsoft asserts that you *never* run the ESEUTIL /P option unless at the recommendation of a Microsoft PSS (Product Support Services) Engineer. Despite this warning, I have had a few problems where I did indeed need to run this utility, and it fixed my problems. The problem was fixed, but some messages were lost. If you have a database that you cannot use, try this method (*only* if you are comfortable with self-medicating):

▶ First rule of data recovery: Do no further harm. Or at the very least, make sure you can get back to the point you were when the problem started. This means taking a full, offline backup.

▶ Research any error messages you are receiving with the Microsoft TechNet and Knowledge Base.

▶ Run ESEUTIL with the /MH option to make sure the database is consistent.

▶ Run ESEUTIL with the /R option to see if you can bring the database to a consistent state. If this succeeds, try to start the information store or directory service.

▶ Run ESEUTIL with the /P option and perform the repair.

▶ Delete the log files and checkpoint file.

CONTINUED ➡

> ▶ Run ESEUTIL /R a second time.
>
> ▶ Open a technical support incident with Microsoft PSS; they may have some additional tricks up their sleeves.
>
> This method has worked for me in the past. If you are the slightest bit uncomfortable with these procedures, you should probably skip to the big finish and get Microsoft on the phone as soon as possible. Experimenting with these utilities can lead to worse problems than you are currently experiencing!

The ISINTEG Program

In contrast to ESEUTIL, which understands generic database files, the information store integrity checker (ISINTEG) knows all about Exchange messages, attachments, access control lists, folders, rules, deleted items, and so on. ISINTEG understands the data in the database file.

ISINTEG fixes problems where users cannot access messages or folders. It should also be run if you have had to repair a database using ESEUTIL. It can be used to "patch" the information store after an offline restore.

NOTE
The directory service must be running to use ISINTEG.

The isinteg.exe utility generates a small temporary database when it is analyzing the selected database. (I have never seen this database grow to more than 10 percent of the total size of the database being fixed.) This utility can take a few minutes or many hours to run, depending on the number of tests that you select. If I have to run the entire battery of tests on a database, I plan for about 1 to 3 hours per GB.

Table 25.3 lists ISINTEG command-line options that you should be aware of.

TABLE 25.3: Command-Line Options Available for ISINTEG

OPTION	OPERATION
-?	Displays online help.
-pri	Selects the private information store.
-pub	Selects the public information store.
-fix	Fixes problems if they are found. The default is to only check for problems and report them. Microsoft recommends running the -fix option only upon the advice of Microsoft PSS.
-detailed	Performs additional tests beyond the tests covered by the default testing mode.
-verbose	Output in verbose mode.
-test	Specifies test name(s). Refer to the document isinteg.rtf file on the Exchange Server CD for specific test names and test definitions.
-L <log filename>	Specifies an alternative log filename and location. The log files are text files, and their default names are isinteg.pub and isinteg.pri.
-T <temp database location>	Specifies the location of the temporary database that ISINTEG uses when it checks the public or private information store database. The database it creates is called refer.mdb. Specifying another disk drive can improve performance, but specifying a network drive will hinder performance.
-patch	Patches the GUIDs (discussed below) found in the information store, directory service, and Registry after an offline restoration.

The ISINTEG "Patch" Option Every object in the public and private information store has a unique, 64-bit hexadecimal string assigned to it. This string is called the *globally-unique identifier (GUID)* and is used to uniquely identify items in the information store databases. Information about the current GUIDs is stored in the Registry and in the directory service. After an offline restore of the public or private information store, the different locations that contain GUIDs will no longer agree with each other, and the information store will not know which GUIDs have been assigned already. (This is automatically corrected during an online restore.)

NOTE

If the GUIDs are not correct, the information store service will not start. If the information store service does not start, scan the application event log for event ID 1087, 1089, 2083, and 7202.

If you have performed an offline restore of the public or private information store, from the \exchsrvr\bin directory, run ISINTEG –patch. This operation should only take a few seconds, but no more than a minute or two. The System Attendant and the directory service must be running in order for the –patch option to work.

TIP

If your Exchange server is in a Microsoft cluster, you need to set an environmental variable prior to running ISINTEG. If the cluster server's network name is BOSEX001, type SET_CLUSTER_NETWORK_NAME=BOSEX001 at the command prompt, then run ISINTEG. It is a good idea to set this variable in the Control Panel; choose System, open the Environment property page, and select the System Variables list. This way, the environmental variable is always set regardless of who is logged in at the server.

INFORMATION STORE INTEGRITY CHECKER EXAMPLES

Here are a couple of examples of using the ISINTEG program.

To run an integrity check (but not to fix anything) on the private information store, report all details of the test, create a log file called pri-log.txt, and run all tests, type **ISINTEG –pri –verbose –lpri-log.txt –test alltests**.

To run ISINTEG to check and fix errors in the public information store for folder and message tables only, type **ISINTEG –pub –fix –verbose –test folder,message**.

To redirect the temporary database file to another disk while fixing messages in the private information store, type **ISINTEG –pri –fix –TG:\temp –test message**.

Should You Perform Database Maintenance?

Should you perform any sort of periodic database maintenance? To quote one of the more active contributors of the Exchange administrator's mailing list: "Just leave Exchange alone."

This is somewhat alien advice for me, but I have taken it to heart. In the late 1980s, I ran a large Lotus cc:Mail installation, and weekly and monthly maintenance were just part of our operations. This was also true to a great degree on some larger installations of Exchange 4; with monthly defragmentation, I found Exchange 4 to be much more stable (no errors or corruption).

Exchange 5.5, on the other hand, requires very little database maintenance. Many Exchange administrators have told me that "we just keep an eye on Exchange and let it do its thing." They perform very little in the way of database maintenance tasks and "Exchange hums along just fine." Over the life of Exchange 5.5, I have come to adopt this strategy as well. If it ain't broke, don't fix it.

All versions of Exchange Server performed information and directory database cleanup and management while online. Exchange Server 4 and 5 were not as efficient at this as Exchange Server 5.5 is. Exchange Server 5.5 is able to defragment and reuse 99 percent of the white space in the database.

Is There Ever a Time for Offline Defragmentation?

I used to feel that offline defragmentation was important to do at least every two or three months. This is, of course, the remnants of the cc:Mail administrator in me talking. For most Exchange installations in the world, there is never a reason to perform an offline defragmentation.

However, there are situations in which you might want to perform an offline defragmentation. One instance is if you have just deleted many mailboxes and you want to compact the size of the private information store database back down. Another possibility is if a large number of messages have been deleted recently, and now that space is freed up. In this case, offline defragmentation/compaction will reduce the overall size of the database files.

Event ID 1221 is generated each time online defragmentation occurs on the public or private information store. This event will tell you how much space can be recovered. Figure 25.2 shows an example of event ID 1221. Notice that the database has 147MB of free space available.

The total size of this particular database is about 890MB (though you cannot see that in Figure 25.2). This means that about 17 percent of the database's total size is unused. However, when new messages are stored, this space will be used.

Some paranoid Exchange administrators still run an Exchange offline defragmentation once every four to six months. Though I don't believe this is necessary, if you have good backups and the time to bring your server down to do this, go for it.

TIP

Always perform a full backup before and after an offline defragmentation/ compaction!

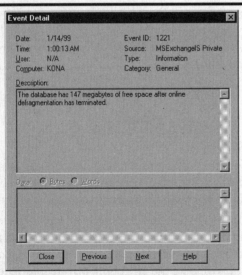

FIGURE 25.2: Event ID 1221 shows the total amount of white space available in the private information store.

EXCHANGE@WORK: DOUBLE PARANOIA

I know an Exchange administrator who takes his information store integrity concerns to the extreme. Once every two months, he shuts down his information store and directory databases for several hours to perform a couple of tests. First he runs an integrity check on all the database files:

```
ESEUTIL /G /ispriv >C:\Logs\esepriv.txt

ESEUTIL /G /ispub >C:\Logs\esepub.txt

ESEUTIL /G /DS >C:\Logs\eseds.txt

ISINTEG -pri -test alltests

ISINTEG -pub -test alltests
```

Then he checks the output of each of these database integrity checks for any potential problems.

Though I have not found this procedure to be worth my time and effort to come in late at night and run, it makes both my administrator friend and his boss feel much better about the integrity of their Exchange system.

Note: If you redirect the output of commands to a file using the > option, be patient—you will not be able to see the progress indicator for ESEUTIL nor ISINTEG.

DISK DEFRAGMENTATION

Recently, someone asked me about using disk defragmentation software on disks that contain Exchange databases. I answered off the top of my head that using such tools is probably not a good idea since the Exchange database files are always open and in use. I was slightly uncomfortable with the thought of a background process rearranging database files that are being used by another process. Still, the thought of defragmenting the disks that the Exchange databases are located on stuck with me. Surely the database and log file drives would become fragmented, just like any other disk drive. Reading from a disk that is badly fragmented will not be nearly as efficient as reading from a disk where the files are all contiguous and will naturally benefit from defragmentation.

Microsoft does not provide any soft of disk defragmentation tools for Windows NT 4, so I contacted a friend at one of the companies that makes disk defragmentation tools and discussed the merits of running their tools on Exchange servers. An Exchange server hard disk can become badly fragmented and require the disks to be defragmented from time to time. In researching this issue, I found a couple of interesting facts and, based on them, offer the following defragmentation tips:

▶ First, check with the software company from which you are purchasing disk defragmentation software. Make sure that they support running disk defragmentation on the same disks that host Exchange Server databases. Ask them if they recommend scheduled defragmentation. Also ask them for references of customers that are successfully using their software.

▶ Test the defragmentation software on your standby server. During my own testing, I used the load simulator utility (LoadSim) to generate a large load on a test server. I then installed the disk defragmentation software and analyzed the drive for fragmentation. The program reported that the disk drive that contained the Exchange databases and transaction logs was seriously fragmented. I kept the load simulator running and fired up the defragmentation program to run on a continuous schedule. Using the Windows NT Performance Monitor, I noticed that the percentage of disk utilization and the total percentage of processor utilization was quite high and stayed that way for the next 24 hours.

▶ Once you are confident that the disk defragmentation software will be stable in your environment, I recommend defragmenting the disk the old-fashioned way prior to installing the new software; the old-fashioned way involves backing up, reformatting, and restoring. You do this so that the disk is already defragmented when you install the new software. The software will only have to work at keeping the disk defragmented and will not have to work extra hard for several hours (or days) to initially defragment the disk.

WARNING

Technical Editor Joshua Konkle noted that if each of the databases is on a dedicated disk drive, database fragmentation will not be a problem. However, the log file disks can still become badly fragmented because log files are continually being created and deleted.

BACKING UP AND EXCHANGE

The most important daily task you are going to perform is making sure that you have good backup copies of your Exchange databases. Neither RAID 5 drive arrays, clustered servers, nor mirrored disks are fault-tolerant enough to get you out of performing daily Exchange backups. There are too many things that can go wrong with both your hardware and software.

Backup Hardware and Software

The first step in a successful backup plan is to get quality backup media and software. I am approaching this from the traditional *tape* backup perspective, though there are many in the Exchange community who feel other forms of backup (such as optical) are coming of age.

Purchase a tape drive system that is easily and quickly capable of backing up your entire messaging system. My own preference is to locate the tape drive hardware on the same machine that hosts the Exchange server. The costs are generally a little more, but the backups run quickly. When purchasing tape backup hardware, I also purchase the same tape drive type for all servers. This allows my tapes and my tape hardware to be more easily interchangeable.

When you install Exchange Server, a special version of the Windows NT Backup program is installed. This version is capable of backing up the Exchange server online. The Windows NT Backup program does have its limitations, but it's free. I prefer one of the third-party backup programs available, such as Seagate's Backup Exec, BEI International's UltraBac, or Cheyenne's ArcServe. These utilities have job scheduling, tape management, and better cataloging.

TIP

When purchasing tape backup software, make sure that you also purchase the Exchange Agent; this option is not usually included in the base price of most third-party utilities. The Exchange Agent is required for backing up Exchange while it is online. On a side note, the third-party tools are faster.

I Feel the Need for Speed

A determining factor in how many users and how much data you can fit onto a single Exchange server is how long it takes to back up that data. I have seen vendors talking about backup rates of 25GB per hour. I can assure you that a typical production system backup utility cannot accomplish such a speed; this rate is only achievable with very specialized backup hardware (RAID 5 tape arrays and special tape array controllers).

Recent backup and restore rates that I have been able to achieve range from 2.5GB per hour (with an HP SureStore 5000 DAT tape drive) to 10GB per hour (with a Compaq 7000 DLT tape drive). Both of these were on Pentium systems with no active users, PCI SCSI adapters, ample memory, and Seagate Backup Exec.

Online Backups versus Offline Backups

Should you use the Exchange Server online backup feature? Yes, absolutely, certainly, for sure! Though many of us feel comfortable with the old, tried and true file-level backup, online backups are much better for Exchange for several reasons:

- ▶ The online backup allows you to back up the database even if it is in use.

- ▶ Online backups back up the database files "page by page." As the page is transferred to tape, Exchange Server does a cyclic redundancy check (CRC) on the data to make sure that it is valid. If there are problems with the page of data, the backup stops and an event is logged to the Windows NT Event Viewer application log. If you were performing offline backups, you would not be aware of this.

- ▶ Online backups permit the use of incremental and differential backups (backing up only the log files) which occur much more quickly than normal backups.

- ▶ Online backups are easier to schedule, because the information store and directory service does not have to be shut down.

Exchange Backup Options

Software that is capable of backing up Exchange can perform three backups: normal, incremental, and differential. You need to fully understand what each of these options is doing so that you can select the right backup type for your organization.

A *normal* backup will back up the entire information store or directory database. The normal backup then backs up the transaction logs and the .PAT files. When the log files and the .PAT files are backed up all log files that have been committed to the database are purged from the disk.

An *incremental* backup selects and backs up only the Exchange server transaction logs. Once the logs are backed up, the log files are purged. A tape that had incremental backups put on it will have only the log files since the last full or incremental backup.

A *differential* backup selects and backs up only the Exchange server transaction log files. The log files are not purged after the backup, meaning they will continue to accumulate until an incremental or normal backup is performed.

NOTE

In order for an incremental or differential backup rotation strategy to work properly, circular logging must be disabled. This ensures there are log files to back up and recover.

CIRCULAR LOGGING, TRANSACTION LOG FILES, AND BACKUPS

If you have disabled circular logging, the transaction logs will accumulate until either an online normal backup or an online incremental backup occurs. Online differential and offline backups do not purge transaction logs. Here is what happens during a normal backup:

▶ The backup program selects and starts backing up the specified database. During this process, any transactions that are written to parts of the database that have already been backed up are also written to a patch file.

▶ After the database has been backed up, the patch file is backed up.

CONTINUED ➡

> ▶ The patch file is purged from the system.
>
> ▶ The checkpoint file is consulted, and any log files that were completely committed to the database and/or patch file are purged. These files are not necessary, since the transactions in these files have already been committed to the database.
>
> During an incremental backup, only the log files are backed up. Based on information in the checkpoint file, transaction log files completely committed to the database and/or patch file are purged.

Performing a Server Backup

For me, a nightly backup consists of the information store and directory service databases. In addition, I want to make sure that there is a good backup of the Windows NT Registry, the Exchange software, and the domain database that contains my users (especially the site services account).

For me to feel warm and fuzzy about the procedure, I set the backup to perform a verification pass when it is finished; this usually doubles the amount of time required. Further, I check the backup log files each day. The ultimate in warm and fuzzy backup procedures is to periodically perform trial restores to a standby server. This not only guarantees that the tape really contains the data, but it also helps keep me familiar with my disaster recovery procedures.

The Exchange Server Key Management Server database and the Exchange Server Directory Synchronization (used for MS Mail, PROFS directory sharing) databases do not get backed up during an online backup. These files are in use by their respective services. In order to back these databases up, you need to shut down their respective services and back them up offline.

The Key Management Server data is stored in the \exchsrvr\KMS-data directory, and the Directory Synchronization database is stored in the \exchsrvr\DXAdata directory. When backing up the Key Management Server database, care must be taken. This database contains the escrowed private keys and should be stored in a secure location.

You may also want to include all the files in the \exchsrvr directories. This will include the MTA database, IMS archive, and log files as well as the Exchange Server and connector software.

Here are some other tips for implementing a successful Exchange server backup plan:

► Rotate your tapes; don't use the same tape every night, and don't use a tape for more time than the manufacturer recommends.

► Protect your tapes. Store them in a location that cannot be accessed by just anyone. Always keep a copy of a recent backup stored in a location other than near your computer room. In the event of a disaster that destroys the primary tape storage location, you will have a copy of your data elsewhere.

► Examine your backup log files and application log daily to ensure that the backups are running and that there are no errors.

► Clean your tape drives according to the schedule recommended by the tape manufacturer.

► Perform a trial restore to your standby server periodically.

By default, each day from 1:00 A.M. until 6:00 A.M., the information store service runs scheduled maintenance. This includes removing online defragmentation, cleaning up indexes, expiring old messages from public folders, and making sure that space formerly taken up by deleted messages is returned to the pool of available space. This should run at least once per day for both the public and private information stores.

WARNING

The online defragmentation process will not run if the tape backup is running. Make sure that the tape backup *does not completely overlap* the IS maintenance schedule. Each morning, sometime between 1:00 A.M. AND 6:00 A.M., you should see an event ID 180 generated by ESE97; you should see one of these for both the private and public information stores.

Backing Up Other Messaging-Related Data

Even though you may be performing a normal backup of your Exchange server data, Registry, SAM file, and Exchange Server software, there may still be other messaging-related data that you should consider when making backup plans.

Does your user community have PAB files (personal address books), PST files (personal folders), SCD files (Schedule+ data), and other data that is related to the messaging system? Outlook offers a useful feature called AutoArchive that will automatically archive older message data to an `archive.pst` personal folder file. By default, this file is on the user's local hard disk. Be sure it is being backed up.

Sample Rotations

I prefer to back up everything every night. I have had too many incidents where I was unable to get something off of a tape for one reason or another. I have developed a mistrust of tape systems in general, though PC-based tape systems are generally much more reliable today than they were 10 years ago. However, I also recognize that many organizations don't have the luxury of performing a full (normal) backup every night. Here are examples of both daily and weekly backup rotations; choose which is suitable for your situation.

Daily Rotation

My daily rotation requires a normal backup each day. I put together a rotation of tapes that will enable me to have two weeks' worth of back-ups, plus a month's worth of Friday backups. I label my tapes as follows:

Tape Label	Used On
Monday/Even	Monday the 2nd, 16th, etc.
Monday/Odd	Monday the 9th, 23rd, etc.
Tuesday/Even	Tuesday the 10th, 24th, etc.
Tuesday/Odd	Tuesday the 3rd, 17th, etc.
Wednesday/Even	Wednesday the 4th, 18th, etc.
Wednesday/Odd	Wednesday the 11th, 25th, etc.
Thursday/Even	Thursday the 12th, 26th, etc.
Thursday/Odd	Thursday the 5th, 19th, etc.
Friday/First	First Friday of the month
Friday/Second	Second Friday of the month
Friday/Third	Third Friday of the month

Friday/Fourth	Fourth Friday of the month
Friday/Fifth	Fifth Friday of the month

This rotation strategy can be extended to include a Saturday and Sunday backup as well. You should consider performing weekend backups if you have staff working on the weekend or if you have a tape autoloader system. If you have many users who send and receive mail on the weekends, you should *definitely* perform weekend backups. In many situations, I also include a monthly or bimonthly tape backup that is archived for an entire year.

For each day of the week, I schedule a backup to start at some point in the evening after the majority of my users are gone. The backup type is normal, so the entire information store and directory service should be on each tape.

EXCHANGE@WORK: A LITTLE EXTRA BACKUP PARANOIA

I know several folks who are extra paranoid about their Exchange server backups. They perform a normal backup each night, and then every two hours during the day, they run a differential backup and append a backup of the transaction log files to the end of the normal tape.

Though their log files are on a separate physical disk from the database files, this still protects them from a catastrophic server failure. If the server experiences a catastrophe where all hard drives fail, the most data they will lose is two hours' worth.

Weekly Rotation

Though I much prefer running a normal backup each night, I don't always have that option due to time constraints, database size, or capacity of the tape drive hardware. In such cases, I revert to differential backups. The schedule consists of a normal backup one day a week and differential backups on the remaining days. Here is a sample set of tapes for a weekly backup:

Tape Label	Used On
Normal/1	First Friday of the month
Normal/2	Second Friday of the month

Normal/3	Third Friday of the month
Normal/4	Fourth Friday of the month
Normal/5	Fifth Friday of the month
Differential/Monday	Monday night
Differential/Tuesday	Tuesday night
Differential/Wednesday	Wednesday night
Differential/Thursday	Thursday night

I schedule a normal backup for Friday night and have a different Friday tape for each week. Since each Friday night tape will have a complete backup of the server, I don't see much need in having even/odd tapes for the weekly differentials; however, you may decide that you want to put those into your rotation.

When you need to restore a server, restore the most recent normal backup tape first, and then restore the most recent differential tape. The differential tape will contain all the log files created since the last normal backup.

WARNING

The differential backup does not purge the log files. Watch the disk space on your transaction log drive to make sure that the log files do not accumulate and exhaust all available disk space.

Brick-Level Backup

Many Exchange 4 and 5 administrators have cried mournfully, "I hate restoring a single mailbox!" The principal reason a single mailbox has to be restored is that a user deleted some important messages or folder. Microsoft has responded to the "Oops, I deleted a really important message" statement with the Deleted Item Recovery feature.

However, deleted item recovery will not help you if the entire mailbox gets deleted. If this is the case, you must restore the entire information store (usually to your standby server) and recover the contents of the mailbox to a PST file.

Third-party vendors such as Seagate (`www.seagate.com`) and Cheyenne (`www.cheyenne.com`) have addressed this with a feature called *brick-level backups* (a.k.a. single mailbox backup and restore).

Part v

While normal backups back up the information store databases a page at a time, a brick-level backup opens each mailbox separately and backs up the folders and messages.

The advantage of this feature is that you can now restore a single mailbox or even a single folder within a mailbox. The *dis*advantage is the amount of time that the backup takes to run and the space required on the tape. By some estimates, the backup can take up to ten times longer than a standard backup.

Here is an example of a typical backup time using a standard, normal Exchange backup versus a brick-level backup. The hardware is a single processor P/60 clone system with 128MB of RAM, two SCSI hard disks, and an HP 5000 SureStore tape unit. Software includes Exchange Server 5.5 with SP2 and Seagate Backup Exec 7.2 with the Exchange Agent loaded. The private information store is 1.1GB, and there are 350 mailboxes on this server. A standard information store backup of the private information store (all mailboxes) only took 42 minutes. A brick-level backup of the private information store took 5 hours and 10 minutes.

EXCHANGE@WORK: IS A BRICK-LEVEL BACKUP USEFUL?

With Exchange 4 and 5, I primarily had to restore entire Exchange servers in order to recover a few items that a user accidentally deleted from his mailbox. (Normally, the person carried a certain amount of weight with the information services department.) Since the release of Exchange Server 5.5 and the advent of deleted item recovery, I have not had to restore a single Exchange server due to accidentally deleted messages.

The main use now for a brick-level backup would be to restore a mailbox that was accidentally deleted. Though I think this is a great feature, the brick-level backups I have tested take anywhere from four to ten times longer to perform than a regular Exchange backup and usually take up considerably more tape space. Here are some steps that some Exchange administrators have taken to eliminate the need to do a brick-level backup and restore:

▶ Implement deleted item recovery with enough time for people to recover any items they deleted. Recommendations range from 10 to 30 days. The longer you retain deleted items, the larger the information store must be, but most Exchange administrators believe the increase is worth it.

CONTINUED ➡

- Implement a policy of not deleting mailboxes right away. This may mean not deleting the mailbox for 60 or 90 days.

- Implement a mailbox deletion policy similar to the following procedure:

  1. Do not delete the mailbox right away.

  2. Disable the associated Windows NT account.

  3. Assign mailbox ownership permissions to the departed user's manager. This will let the manager access any messages in the user's mailbox.

  4. Rename the Display Name to something like "zz_McBee, Rebecca–Delete after 9/15/99".

  5. On the Advanced tab of the mailbox's property page, hide the mailbox from the global address list.

  6. Remove all e-mail proxy addresses except for the X.400 address from the mailbox's E-mail Addresses list.

  7. In the Notes field, enter the date you made the changes and the reason the mailbox should be deleted.

  8. Scan the directory periodically for hidden mailboxes that are ready to be deleted. If you have renamed the Display Name to something like I have recommended, any mailboxes that need to be deleted will be sorted to the bottom of the list and stand out with the date you have entered in the Display Name, which indicates the date after which the mailbox can be deleted.

DAILY MAINTENANCE TASKS

What should you do on a daily basis to keep your Exchange server healthy and happy? What can you do so that you can sleep well each night? Here is a checklist of things that you should perform daily on your Exchange servers:

- Backing up your server is the most important activity. Make sure that the backups are running and completing. Review your backup log files. Make sure that tapes are rotated.

▶ Examine the application and system logs for error (red) and warning (yellow) events. See the list of events that should catch your eye in the next section, "Event IDs to Watch Out For."

▶ Check all hard disks to make sure that ample disk space is available.

▶ Check the message queues, including the MTA queues and any connector queues. If there is an unusual number of messages backed up, find out why.

▶ Check the transaction log file directories to make sure that there are not a large number of transaction logs accumulating. If you are using a rotation that incorporates differential backups, it is not uncommon to see dozens of log files. Busier systems could see a couple of hundred log files if a normal backup has not been performed recently.

▶ If running server monitors and link monitors, review their respective log files or status screens.

Event IDs to Watch Out For

On your daily scan through the application and system event logs, there are some events that you should watch out for. In general, any error events (red) should catch your eye and should be investigated *immediately* to find the cause. Warning events (yellow) should also be looked into. Though yellow events are generally not as critical as red events, they may indicate a problem that will become critical later.

Table 25.4 lists some event IDs that you will want to be familiar with when looking at events generated by Exchange Server. This is by no means a complete list—when reviewing daily events, you will see dozens.

TABLE 25.4: Common Exchange Server Events Found in the Event Viewer Application Log

EVENT ID	SOURCE	MEANING/DESCRIPTION
104	ESE97	The database engine has stopped, indicating that a backup has completed. This is good.
9411	MSExchangeMTA	The MTA has terminated due to low disk space on the disk where the MTADATA directory is located.

TABLE 25.4 continued: Common Exchange Server Events

Event ID	Source	Meaning/Description
179 and 180	ESE97	The online defragmentation process has completed a pass on the private or public information store. This is a good event, and you should see this at least once per night for both the public and private information stores.
1221	MSExchangeIS Private, MSExchangeIS Public	This message will include a description letting you know how much free space is available in the database file.
1112	MSExchangeIS	The Exchange database has reached its maximum size and the Exchange server is shutting down. Make an offline backup and perform an offline defragmentation (ESEUTIL /ispriv /D or ESEUTIL /ispub /D). Once the information store restarts, clean up as many mailboxes as possible.
M105, 112, 116, 117, 118, 135, and 184	ESE97	Some type of database corruption has occurred. Make sure you have a good backup. If the corruption occurs during backup, you may have a serious problem. The event log may suggest restoring from the last good backup. You can ask users to copy all their messages to a PST file or perform an offline backup. At this point, I would check the Knowledge Base or call Microsoft and report the error.
1000 or 1001	MSExchangeSA, MSExchangeDS, MSExchangeIS Private, MSExchangeIS Public	Indicates that the respective service is starting. If you see this event, make sure it corresponds to a time when the server was officially restarted. If the server is starting at a time when you were not aware of it, there may be software problems, or unauthorized work may be being performed on the Exchange server.

Table 25.4 offers a small sample of the error codes that you may see in the description portion of an event. Others include −1018, −1022, and −510. If you see these numbers, there is a good chance that there is a disk hardware or device driver problem.

When you see an error or warning event in the application event log, you need to take immediate steps to find out what it means. The best starting point is the Knowledge Base. If you see any event that indicates database corruption of any kind, consider bringing Microsoft into the picture, especially if you are uncomfortable with troubleshooting database-related problems.

TIP

If you would like the entire list of Exchange event messages, locate the Back-Office Resource Kit (Second Edition) CD and search for the exmsgref.xls file. It contains a list of event IDs, sources, and messages.

Part v

Event Log Monitoring Tools

There are two utilities supplied with the Microsoft BackOffice Resource Kit that can assist you in gathering information from the event logs: evtscan.exe and elf.exe. These utilities are found on the BackOffice Resource Kit CD in the \Exchange\WinNT\I386\Eventlog directory.

The ELF (Event Log Filter) tool allows you to collect certain types of entries from multiple servers. You can specify event IDs that you wish to scan for, and the ELF program will monitor for these on multiple servers.

The EVTSCAN (Event Scan) tool can be used to monitor event logs for specific events. If a specified event occurs, EVTSCAN can launch an application, send an e-mail message, send an alert message, or stop/restart a service. This tool is especially useful if you want to monitor for certain events that you suspect might occur. The EVTSCAN tool requires that a configuration file containing the events and event sources to monitor be created along with an action that needs to be performed if that event occurs. This configuration file should contain a single line for each type of event. The format for the file looks like this:

```
EventID;Source;Action;Alert list;Mail list;Command line;
Comment string
```

Each configuration entry may only have a few of these items. Here is a list of the configuration entries for this file and what each is used for:

Configuration Entry	Use
EventID	The Event Viewer's event ID.
Source	The source name for the event.
Action	Action to take if this event occurs. The options are Restart and Stop. You can leave this field blank.

Alert List	A list of computers or users to send a network pop-up message to if the event occurs. You can specify more than one computer by separating them with commas.
Command Line	Specifies a command to execute if the event ID occurs.
Comment String	Specifies a comment string that will appear in the network pop-up messages.

Here is a sample EVTSCAN configuration file. This file will monitor for three different event IDs. The first one, event ID 1221 from the source MSExchangeIS Private, will send a mail message to mailbox BenjaminC; the second event is 104 from the source ESE97 and will send a message to the computer WS-HELPDESK; the final event sends a mail message and alert message if event 9411, source MSExchangeMTA, appears.

```
1221;MSExchangeIS Private; ; ;BenjaminC; ;Report on available
space in the IS
104;ESE97; ;WS-HELPDESK; ; ; Tape backup has completed
9411;MSExchangeMTA; ;WS-HELPDESK;BenjaminC; ;MTA has shutdown!
```

Next, I save this file as important.cfg. Now I have to run the EVTSCAN program to use this file and send the appropriate notifications; in order to run EVTSCAN, I must be logged in. The EVTSCAN has several command-line options:

Option	Use
-F <config file>	Specifies the name of the configuration.
-U <profile name>	Specifies a messaging profile to be used if the event needs to send a mail message. Avoid spaces in the profile name.
-P <password>	The password used for the messaging profile.
-T <delay>	The interval (in seconds) between event log scans.

Launch EVTSCAN with a list of servers to monitor and any necessary command-line options required. A sample command would look like this: **EVTSCAN –F important.cfg –U notification_profile –P profile_ password SFOEX001, LAXEX001, HNLEX001, HNLEX002**. This command will run EVTSCAN using the configuration file I created (important.cfg) and scan the servers SFOEX001, LAXEX001, HNLEX001, and HNLEX002 every 120 seconds.

NOTE

If you want EVTSCAN to send mail messages, make sure that there is a messaging profile created. The configuration file should be in the same directory as the evtscan.exe program.

EXCHANGE@WORK: IS THE PROBLEM HARDWARE OR SOFTWARE?

Everyone has heard this joke: How many software engineers does it take to change a lightbulb? None, that's a hardware problem! I often agree with this punch line, yet when a database becomes corrupt, I tend to blame the software—and not consider that the problem could be related to hardware.

One of my clients started having error messages pop up in the application event log. "Event ID 23. Description: MSExchangeIS ((455)) Direct read found corrupted page error -1018 ((1:251563) (0-2295758), 251563 379225672 381322824). Please restore the database from a previous backup."

Not very pretty, eh?

Twice within a three-month period of time, we had to restore the database from a previous backup. After the first time, we made sure we had the latest service pack and hot fixes. Only after the second time did we notice there had been SCSI errors in the system event log that closely corresponded to the database failures. We replaced the SCSI controller and the problem did not recur.

What is the moral of the story, kids? Don't be so quick to blame the software and check your system event logs daily!

Part v

NOTE

−1018 and −1811 errors in the application event log (in the event description, not the Event ID) indicate some type of database corruption, yet the cause is almost always linked back to failing hardware or buggy device drivers. An exception to this would be where NTFS compression is enabled on the Exchange databases.

WEEKLY MAINTENANCE TASKS

About once a week, I have an additional series of checks that I like to run on each of my Exchange servers:

▶ Check the Windows NT Performance Monitor to ensure that the server is not running out of memory or exceeding other resources such as the capacity of the disk system or processor.

▶ If message tracking is enabled, check the message tracking log directory (\exchsrvr\tracking.log) to make sure that the older log files are indeed being purged by the system attendant service.

▶ Confirm that directory replication is occurring between sites within your organization and to external mail systems such as Microsoft Mail and Lotus cc:Mail.

▶ Check the public folder replication properties to make sure that the public folders are being replicated and are up-to-date.

▶ View the public information store's public folder resources container and the private information store's mailbox resources container to make sure that user mailbox and public folder disk resources are in line with expectations.

▶ If necessary, archive the application event log. Though I don't keep copies of the old event logs, many administrators archive event logs (especially the security logs) for later review.

▶ If applicable, run mailbox cleanup routines.

▶ Clean your tape drives according to the manufacturer's recommendations (usually weekly).

PERIODIC MAINTENANCE TASKS

In addition to daily and weekly procedures, there are several tasks that I perform on a periodic basis. Some of these might be performed as often as every month, while others are done less frequently (possibly as little as every six months).

NOTE

Some of the tasks on the periodic maintenance list may not apply to your environment. For the most part, this is not a list of things to do to the server, but rather a list of things to watch out for so that the server continues to do its job.

▶ Perform a test restoration to validate that your tapes are good and that your disaster recovery plan is functional.

▶ Audit the Exchange permissions to make sure that the actual permissions granted are in line with expectations.

▶ Delete any mailboxes or other directory objects that are no longer in use and that exceed the "holding" period for your company.

▶ Archive and remove any organizational forms and public folders that are no longer in use.

▶ Apply service packs and hot fixes that you have ascertained that you need. Do this only after testing them on your standby system and reviewing the Knowledge Base for any potential problems that could affect your environment.

▶ Using the Windows NT Performance Monitor, create a log of critical counters during a typical operation period. This information can be compared to previous logs to project system growth.

▶ Test the UPS hardware that is connected to the server every few months. Don't forget that the batteries in a UPS are only good for about three years.

▶ Every six months, verify that the firmware and ROM revisions in your server equipment are up to the current revisions. Many hardware manufacturers provide tools to upgrade the firmware and ROM.

▶ Run the RDISK command monthly to make sure that you have a backup copy of the Registry on an Emergency Repair Disk (ERD). On the PDC, run the RDISK /S command to make sure that you have an updated copy of the Windows NT security database (the SAM file) on the ERD. This disk should be stored in a secure location.

▶ Every four to six months, perform an offline backup followed by a CHKDSK.

Though I have come to believe that the following tests are not necessary, some particularly cautious administrators run them in addition to those above:

▶ Perform a semi-annual offline backup.

▶ Run the ISINTEG -tests alltests option on both the public and private information stores.

▶ Run the EDBUTIL -G integrity check option on the information stores and the directory database.

TIP

If you feel you must run these tests but don't want to do it on a production system, perform a test restore to your standby server and run the tests on the standby server. Restoring the database to a standby server is also excellent disaster recovery practice.

DISASTER PREVENTION TIPS

Disaster prevention is one of my favorite subjects; I can spend hours discussing ways to make Exchange (and other BackOffice products) more stable and less susceptible to failure and downtime. Deep down, I believe that this has something to do with being inherently lazy; I hate being awakened in the middle of the night to come in and fix a down server or restore a database. Therefore, the more things I can do ahead of time to prevent disaster type situations from happening, the better off I am.

Preventing disasters and keeping Exchange Server up, running, and healthy are the primary reasons I am writing this book, and I'll bet they are the primary reasons you are reading it. One of the most useful activities I participate in is spending time with other administrators and system engineers, listening to them talk about their systems and the problems they have experienced and solved.

When I started working on this book, I talked to several dozen experienced Exchange administrators and asked them, "What tips can you pass on to other administrators to keep your Exchange servers running twenty-four hours a day, seven days a week? What types of things do you do to make your job easier?" Here is a list of tips from those who took an interest in sharing what they had learned (in no particular order of importance):

- Enable the Deleted Item Recovery feature for both the public and private information stores. This will decrease the likelihood that you will have to restore data from tape if a user deletes something important from their mailbox or a public folder.

- Use a separate physical disk for the database transaction logs; this will dramatically improve your chances for recovering data up-to-the-minute in case of a database failure.

- Perform regular online backups, check your tape logs, and perform periodic trial restores.

- Standardize the tape backup hardware, software, tapes, and tape rotations you are using.

- Install a UPS and UPS-monitoring software on your servers, hubs, and other network infrastructure devices, such as switches and routers.

- Scan your event logs daily for critical errors.

- Never use NTFS file compression to compress Exchange databases and logs.

- Restrict mailbox disk space.

- Have a disaster recovery plan and a disaster recovery kit. The kit should contain a written copy of the plan, system documentation, and all software required to rebuild any server in your site or organization. Practice disaster recovery and database restoration a few times a year.

- Restrict usage of large distribution lists.

- Run a Windows NT CHKDSK periodically and after any system upgrades.

▶ Take Windows NT and Exchange Server training classes early on in your Exchange deployment. Learn as much as you can about both products.

▶ Install Exchange Server on a member server or backup domain controller (BDC).

▶ Don't delete mailboxes right away; wait 30 days or longer to delete mailboxes.

▶ Subscribe to Microsoft TechNet—and use it whenever something comes up that you don't understand!

▶ Run Exchange database maintenance utilities to repair the database only as a last resort.

▶ Keep your user community informed.

You will find some of these tips explained in much more detail in this chapter; this list is just the "sound bites" version of them.

Inevitably, disaster will strike when you least expect. Chapter 29 covers disaster recovery and what to do when that fateful moment arrives.

FOR FURTHER INFORMATION

To learn more about some of the topics presented in this chapter, here are some resources that may prove helpful:

▶ Microsoft Consulting Services has put together two excellent documents called MS Exchange Disaster Recovery Part 1 and Part 2. These documents can be found on the Microsoft Web site at www.microsoft.com/exchange. You should download these documents and read them. They provide excellent information relating to database technology, backups, restores, and of course, disaster recovery.

▶ On the Exchange Server CD-ROM, there is a document in the \server\support\utils\ folder called isinteg.rtf that includes a list of all the ininteg.exe tests that you can specify with the −test options along with a description of the tests.

CONTINUED ➡

▶ Executive Software has a product called Diskeeper, which I have found to work well with Exchange Server. You can download a 30-day evaluation version of Diskeeper on the Web at www .execsoft.com.

▶ Consult the Microsoft BackOffice Resource Kit for more information on the ELF and EVTSCAN event log monitoring tools.

▶ Consider third-party monitoring tools for medium to large size businesses. I recommend NetIQ (www.netiq.com) for 90 percent of the installations I work on. They have two white papers on monitoring Exchange with their tools.

WHAT'S NEXT?

In this chapter you learned how ongoing maintenance can prevent serious Exchange disasters. The chapter introduced database technology that Exchange Server uses and the tools you will need to test and repair, as well as backups that are available. The next chapter will provide some tools that Exchange administrators can use to monitor and report on Exchange Server activities.

Chapter 26

MONITORING AND OPTIMIZING EXCHANGE

As an Exchange administrator, I have come to think of myself as being similar to an air traffic controller, with the Exchange server being the pilot and airplane. As long as I monitor the skies around the airplane and provide basic services, the airplane flies along without incident. All Exchange administrators have certain tasks they have to perform to make certain the skies stay clear around their Exchange servers.

In Chapter 25, I reviewed not only system backup procedures and a little theory on the database operation, but I also recommended some operational tasks. Here, in Chapter 26, I take a closer look at some tools that you can use to keep the skies clear. Microsoft provides some excellent tools through both Exchange Server and Windows NT, and numerous third parties provide tools for monitoring and reporting on Exchange Server activities.

Adapted from *Exchange Server 5.5 24seven™*
by Jim McBee

ISBN 0-7821-2505-0   657 pages $34.99

WHY MONITOR YOUR EXCHANGE SERVERS?

A clear understanding of what is happening in your Exchange (and Windows NT) environment is important. As an administrator or systems engineer, you have to be able to react to changing resource needs accordingly. A network manager once joked to me that he had the cheapest network management system available. He pointed to the telephone, indicating that when there were problems, he didn't find out about them until his users called.

How many administrators really like to hear about their network problems from the users? I sure don't.

However, as an administrator, you should be performing certain monitoring tasks to ensure that Exchange is available and delivering messages in a timely fashion. Further, you should be able to easily determine if Exchange Windows NT or your network infrastructure is coming close to exceeding the allocated resources. Finally, you may be required to provide weekly or monthly usage statistics. This may be a requirement of a Service Level Agreement (SLA) or simply to satisfy your own curiosity.

EXCHANGE SERVER PERFORMANCE OPTIMIZER

The first tool in my arsenal of performance monitoring and optimization tools is the Exchange Server Performance Optimizer or Performance Wizard (`perfwiz.exe`). This tool allows you to tweak many Exchange Server software settings. When you run the tool, it stops all Exchange services, so it cannot be run while the Exchange system is in production. Based on information about your organization and your hardware, the Performance Optimizer makes decisions about memory buffer allocation; the number of threads for the services; and the optimal disk location for the transaction logs, databases, and working directories. Figure 26.1 shows Performance Optimizer's system parameters dialog box.

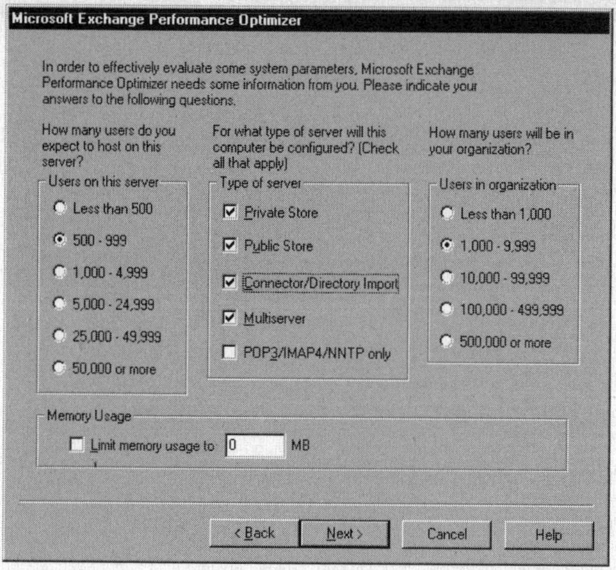

FIGURE 26.1: Performance Optimizer's system parameters dialog box

You may notice that the Performance Optimizer has no clue as to what role the server is playing; it does not know if the server has 50 mailboxes or 5000, nor does it know the total size of the organization. Performance Optimizer is depending on you to make the appropriate changes.

Performance Optimizer will analyze the processors and available memory in an effort to decide how many threads to allocate to each service. When finished, if there is more than one logical disk drive, Performance Optimizer will recommend on which disk drives to locate the Exchange databases, transaction logs, and working files.

By placing the transaction log files on a separate disk drive from the Exchange databases, you can realize as much as a 40 percent performance improvement over a system that has the transaction logs on the same physical disk.

When the Performance Optimizer is finished, it creates (by default) a log file called perfopt.log in the C:\WinNT\System32 directory. This log is a simple text file (shown in Figure 26.2) and contains a summary of the Performance Optimizer activities. Each time Performance Optimizer runs, it appends to the log file. The log file only lists the changes that are made to the Exchange configuration.

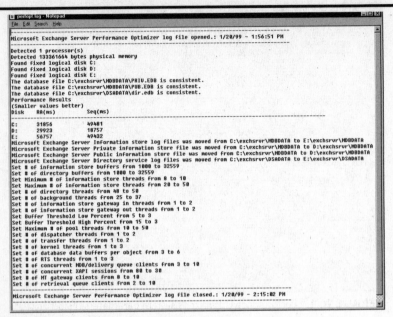

FIGURE 26.2: Performance Optimizer log file

Notice in Figure 26.2 that Performance Optimizer did the following:

▶ Inventoried the processors, memory, and logical disk drives.

▶ Checked to make sure that the Exchange databases were consistent.

▶ Ran random access and sequential performance tests on the logical disk drives.

▶ Moved the information store databases to the D drive and the information store and directory transaction logs to the E drive. Performance Monitor will always ask you whether it is okay to move the files and will show you its recommendations, which you can override.

▶ Set the directory store and information store buffers to 32559.

▶ Set the number of threads for various services and threads.

WHERE ARE ALL THOSE BUFFERS GOING?

You may have noticed that the total number of buffers for directory service and information store was set to 32559 for both. 32559 buffers $\times$ 4096 bytes per buffer = 133361664 bytes. This is also the total amount of physical memory in the server. This would have been a serious oops if this were Exchange 5. Older versions of the Exchange services immediately allocated all the memory that was available and did not release that memory.

Exchange Server 5.5, however, introduced a new memory management feature called Dynamic Buffer Allocation (DBA). DBA allows Exchange services to allocate memory as required and release unused memory if another service requires it. Thanks to DBA, Exchange is much friendlier with other services that are running on the same Exchange server.

The Performance Optimizer does give you the option of restricting the total amount of memory that Exchange will allocate (see the bottom of the screen shown in Figure 26.1). This is not necessary for servers that are dedicated exclusively to Exchange.

When to Run Performance Optimizer

The Exchange Performance Optimizer should be run any time there is a change in the server's hardware or role. Here are a couple of situations where you should run Exchange Performance Optimizer:

- ▶ If there is an increase or decrease in the Exchange server's physical memory.

- ▶ If new disk drives are installed and you want to move databases, working directories, or transaction logs to a new drive. Performance Optimizer is the best way to do this.

- ▶ If new or faster disk controllers or caching controllers are installed.

- ▶ If there is a change in the organization size (more items in the directory) or the Exchange server is supporting more mailboxes than originally configured.

▶ If there is a change in the server's role. For example, if it is now supporting public folders, connectors, or is part of a multi-server site.

EXCHANGE@WORK: IMPORTING AND MIGRATION

One administrator reported to me how handy Performance Optimizer is during migration. For one weekend's worth of mailbox migrations, the server was set so that it did not support Connector/Directory Import because there were no connectors installed on it. The migration and import of nearly 250 Microsoft Mail users took almost 25 hours.

The next weekend, this administrator ran Performance Optimizer prior to beginning the migration process, and he chose the Connector/Directory Import option under Type Of Server (see Figure 26.1). He then ran another import of about 250 Microsoft Mail users; this time it took only about four hours. Quite an improvement!

Tweaking Exchange through Performance Optimizer

The Exchange Performance Optimizer actually can make over 125 separate changes to the Windows NT Registry as it is optimizing Exchange memory, disk, and thread parameters. You see almost none of the fine-tuning that goes on in the background when Performance Optimizer runs. However, if you run the Performance Optimizer with the –V parameter (verbose), Performance Optimizer will reveal nearly 50 additional settings. Figure 26.3 shows one of the seven additional screens you will see during a verbose session.

If the Exchange binaries are on the C drive, for example, type **C:\exchsrvr\bin\perfwiz –V** to run the Performance Optimizer in verbose mode. After the Exchange services stop and you see the standard system parameters screen (Figure 26.1), you will then see the seven additional parameter screens. In Figure 26.3, the Prev. Value column allows you to see the previous value of each parameter, and the New Value column allows you to see the value that Performance Optimizer is recommending. You can override the recommended value by entering your own value in the New Value column.

Microsoft Exchange Performance Optimizer

Based on your system's hardware, the following system parameters are being set to recommended values. If you don't want to use these values, you can change them by typing in new values.

Parameter	Prev. Value	New Value
# of information store buffers	32605	32605
# of directory buffers	32605	32605
Minimum # of information store threads	10	10
Maximum # of information store threads	110	110
# of directory threads	50	50
Maximum # of concurrent read threads	10	10
# of background threads	51	51
# of heaps	4	4

< Back   Next >   Cancel   Help

FIGURE 26.3: One of the seven additional screens you will see running Performance Optimizer in verbose mode

The various items in verbose mode are simply values in the Registry for the DS, IS, and MTA. If you want to know more about a particular setting, consult Appendix C in the Sybex book *Exchange Server 5.5 24seven* or the BackOffice Resource Kit (Second Edition). Both contain a Registry reference for Exchange Server. On a final note, considering how many "options" are stored in the Registry, be sure you back it up!

WARNING

Tread lightly with the verbose option of Performance Optimizer! You can significantly degrade the overall performance of your Exchange server if you do not understand exactly what you are doing. If you must make changes in verbose mode, make a small change and then judge the effect of that change before making another. I recommend only changing items based on recommendations from either Microsoft PSS or a Knowledge Base article that specifically details what you need to accomplish.

USING PERFORMANCE MONITOR WITH EXCHANGE

Does your Exchange server need more RAM? Is the CPU fast enough? Are the disk drives too slow? *Everyone* believes that their servers and workstations are too slow, but how can you quantify that?

Microsoft shipped an incredible tool with Windows NT, the Windows NT Performance Monitor. If you have not used this utility, you should become familiar with it. Not only can you monitor high-level information such as processor utilization and memory usage, but you can look right down to the details of individual processes and threads. Any product written to work with Windows NT can be extended to report counters and objects to Performance Monitor.

When Exchange Server is installed on a Windows NT system, 10 new objects and 350 new counters are added to Performance Monitor's monitoring abilities. The Exchange-related objects include the following:

Database provides file, logging, and caching counters for directory service and information store service database operations.

MSExchange Internet Protocols provides message size, queue length, and connection information for the POP3, IMAP4, NNTP, and LDAP Internet protocols.

MSExchangeDS provides search and replication statistics for the directory service.

MSExchangeES provides event-processing information for the event service.

MSExchangeIMC provides queue, connection, and message transfer information for the Internet Mail Service.

MSExchangeIS provides connection and request information regarding usage of the information store service.

MSExchangeIS Private provides message delivery statistics for the private information store.

MSExchangeIS Public provides message delivery statistics and replication counters for the public information store.

MSExchangeMTA provides general information about the message transfer agent usage.

MSExchangeMTA Connections provides specific information about each connection that the MTA is configured to handle.

Using a combination of these Exchange-specific performance counters and the standard Windows NT performance counters, you can answer your performance questions with hard facts.

NOTE

The Windows NT Workstation Resource Kit has several chapters on using the Windows NT Performance Monitor.

A Few Words about Monitoring

When monitoring Exchange Server or any other type of system, there are some basic pointers to keep in mind:

- ▶ Don't get monitoring tunnel vision! Don't monitor a specific resource and decide that resource is the bottleneck without taking a broader view of monitoring. For example, if the CPU looks over-tasked, check to make sure there is sufficient memory.

- ▶ Make sure you know the scale that is being used when using the Performance Monitor chart view. Some values are percentages, so the range naturally goes from 0 to 100 percent. Other values are actual measurements such as bytes free, RAM used, milliseconds, and so on. Though they are plotted on the graph from 0 to 100, a value near the top of the scale does not indicate that the resource is exhausted.

- ▶ Monitor activity during typical periods of activity. The system will definitely look underused if you monitor at midnight.

- ▶ Don't sweat the peaks. Look for sustained activity throughout the life of your monitoring session. Spikes in activity such as CPU and disk usage are normal.

- ▶ Establish a baseline for your system. Monitor it when there are no active users to see how the system components (memory, disk, processor, and network) behave when the system is idle. Then monitor it as your system's load increases. Save the log files so that you can look back as well as project system growth.

Any performance monitoring should include objects that represent the four main "subsystems" within a Windows NT server: memory, processor, network, and disk.

Useful Performance Monitor Counters

I have categorized several Performance Monitor counters that may prove useful when performing system performance analysis. My categories include counters for monitoring basic Windows NT performance, counters for monitoring Exchange server objects, and, finally, some counters that may provide useful information about your Exchange environment but don't relate specifically to performance.

MISSING OBJECTS AND COUNTERS WITH ZERO VALUES

By default, there are several objects that do not appear in Performance Monitor, or, if they do appear, their values register only zero values. Here is a list of objects that you might be looking for and how to get them to appear:

▶ Before disk counters (physical or logical) can be monitored, they must be activated using the DISKPERF −Y command (DISKPERF −YE for systems with RAID 5 disks). If this is not done, these counters will register only zero values.

▶ The TCP/IP objects (IP, ICMP, TCP, and UDP) and the Network Interface object will not appear unless the SNMP Service is installed. If you install the SNMP Service, make sure that you use a SNMP community name besides public.

▶ The Network Segment object will not appear unless the Network Monitor Agent has been installed.

Monitoring the Performance of the Windows NT Server

Before you start monitoring Exchange-specific counters, you need to look at counters that will let you know if your basic system resources are overtasked. These counters are your first clue that you need more hardware resources or that your software configuration needs to be changed.

Table 26.1 shows a list of Windows NT counters that you should monitor, which values to watch for, and how to improve those counters.

TABLE 26.1: Basic Counters for Monitoring Your Server's Performance

Object ➤ Counter	Explanation	Desired Value	How to Improve
System ➤ %Total Processor Time	Total real work being performed by all system CPUs.	Less than 70 percent.	Get a faster CPU or more CPUs.
Memory ➤ Pages/Second	The number of 4k pages written to or read from the paging file.	Less than 5–15 4k pages per second. Sustained larger values can indicate a low memory situation.	Add RAM.
Memory ➤ Available Bytes	Amount of memory available after all processes and caching memory have been allocated.	Should not ever drop below 4,000,000 bytes (4MB).	Add RAM.
Logical Disk ➤ % Disk Time	Percentage of time that a logical disk is used for both reads and writes.	Ideally, should be less than 60 percent on a sustained basis.	Add additional physical disks, faster disks, or faster disk controllers.
Logical Disk ➤ Avg Disk Queue Length	The average number of pending read and write requests for a specific disk.	Should be less than 2.	Add additional physical disks, faster disks, or faster disk controllers.
TCP ➤ Segments Retransmitted per second	The number of TCP segments retransmitted per second as a result of network problems.	In a perfect world, should be zero; regardless, it should be less than 10 percent of the TCP ➤ Segments Sent/sec counter.	You have a network problem. Your network is too busy or there is an unreliable link.

TABLE 26.1 cont'd: Basic Counters for Monitoring Server's Performance

Object ➤ Counter	Explanation	Desired Value	How to Improve
Network Segment ➤ %Network utilization	The percentage of network bandwidth used on this segment.	The ideal value for this counter will vary from network type to network type, but should be below 30–40 percent on an Ethernet network. I have seen healthy, switched networks run much higher.	Break your network into small pieces or implement switching technology.

The counters found in Table 26.1 are only a few of the many that are available to any Windows NT installation, but they are the ones that I consider critical to locating system bottlenecks and determining if a single resource is overburdened. The desired values are my own; I have derived these from a combination of a dozen books and white papers I have read, as well as personal experiences. These counters and desired values can apply to any Windows NT system, including those running Exchange Server services.

When monitoring a system, you need to take a holistic approach; never perform system monitoring with blinders on. Look at the critical memory, processor, disk, and network counters. Performance monitoring is not an exact science; rather, it's an art form.

Exchange-Specific Performance Monitoring

Now that you have looked at your basic Windows NT system counters, you can enhance your knowledge of what your server is doing on the Exchange side by monitoring some of the Exchange-specific counters. Table 26.2 lists some of the more useful counters (not all of them—remember, there are over 350 of them!). These counters are useful when monitoring Exchange Server performance and response times.

TABLE 26.2: Exchange-Specific Counters for Monitoring Performance and Response Times

OBJECT ≻ COUNTER	EXPLANATION
MSExchangeMTA ≻ Messages	The number of messages that the MTA sends and receives each second. Lower values are desired, but higher values indicate a server that is transmitting and receiving a lot of messages.
MSExchangeMTA ≻ Work Queue Length	The number of messages queued for delivery to the local and other servers. Lower values are desired. Higher values indicate the system is getting backed up delivering messages. Compare this with Messages/Sec.
MSExchangeIS Private ≻ Average Time for Delivery	Average time (in milliseconds) that the last ten messages waited before being delivered to the MTA. (High values could indicate the MTA is operating too slowly.) I do not like to see this value climb above 1500 milliseconds.
MSExchangeIS Private ≻ Average Local Delivery Time	Average time (in milliseconds) that the last ten messages waited before being delivered to recipients on the same server (local delivery). High values could indicate the Information Store service is very busy. I don't like to see this value climb above 1000 milliseconds.
MSExchangeIS Private ≻ Send Queue Size and MSExchangeIS Public ≻ Send Queue Size	The number of messages waiting to be delivered by the information store. During busy times this value may spike, but on average it should be very near zero. Non-zero values indicate the information store is not keeping up with the load that has been placed on it.
Database ≻ Cache % Hit (monitor both the information store and the directory instances)	This is the percentage of database file page requests that were serviced by the database cache rather than having to go to the disk. If this value is less than 95 percent, add memory and run the Performance Optimizer again.

Other Useful Performance Monitor Counters

Table 26.3 lists some other counters that provide useful and interesting insight into an Exchange server, particularly when watching trends. These are not directly related to performance optimization, but they are useful when correlating activity to other variables such as the number of users connected.

TABLE 26.3: Performance Monitor Counters

OBJECT ≻ COUNTER	EXPLANATION
MSExchangeIS ≻ User Count	The total number of connected client sessions.
MSExchangeIS ≻ Active User Count	The total number of users that have generated any activity within the previous ten minutes.
MSExchangeIS Private ≻ Messages Submitted/Min and MSExchangeIS Public ≻ Messages Submitted/Min	The number of messages that have been submitted to the private (or public) information store. This does not include the total number of recipients per message.
MSExchangeIS Private ≻ Total Size of Recoverable Items and MSExchangeIS Public ≻ Total Size of Recoverable Items	The amount of space used by deleted items in the private (or public) information store database.
MSExchangeIS Private ≻ Total Count of Recoverable Items and MSExchangeIS Public ≻ Total Count of Recoverable Items	The number of messages used by deleted items in the private (or public) information store database.
MSExchangeIS Private ≻ Single Instance Ratio	The average ratio of mailbox "pointers" to each message in the information store. Many organizations consider themselves lucky if this value is above 1.8. This value will change over time as users delete "their" copy of a message (in the Sent Items folder) that was sent to many mailboxes. A very low value indicates a lot of the messages sent and received are coming from and going to points beyond the Exchange server.
MSExchangeIS Private ≻ Messages Submitted and MSExchangeIS Public ≻ Messages Submitted	The total number of messages submitted to the private (or public) information store database since the information store service was started.
MSExchangeMTA ≻ Message Bytes/sec	The number of message bytes being processed by the MTA every second. Divide this value by the Messages/sec counter to get the average message size.
MSExchangeMTA ≻ Outbound Messages Total	The total number of messages the MTA has delivered off the server since the MTA service was started.
MSExchangeMTA ≻ Inbound Messages Total	The total number of messages the MTA has received since the MTA service was started.

Part v

NOTE

Refer to the BackOffice Resource Kit help file eperfmon.hlp for a complete listing of the Exchange-related Performance Monitor counters.

MTA Connection Counters   Each messaging connector that is established from a server is listed as a separate instance under the MSExchangeMTA Connections Performance Monitor object. In the list, you will see an instance for the Microsoft Private MDB and Microsoft Public MDB; in addition, you will see instances for any connector you have installed including X.400, Microsoft Mail, the Internet Mail Service, and the site connector. If you have the site connector configured to connect to any server in a remote site, you will see an instance for each server in the remote site.

The MSExchangeMTA Connections object and the instances of each connector provide you with the unique ability to monitor the amount of message traffic that is flowing through each of your messaging connectors. Table 26.4 lists some interesting counters that I like to watch.

TABLE 26.4: MSExchangeMTA Counters

COUNTER	MEANING
Associations	The number of associations between the two servers. A single connector can open multiple associations, but it will do so only if the first association is becoming backlogged based on "threshold" levels for creating additional associations.
Inbound Bytes Total	The total volume of messages in kilobytes that has been received from this connection since the MTA was initialized.
Inbound Messages Total	The total number of messages that have been received through this connection. Inbound Bytes Total divided by Inbound Messages Total will give you the average message size received through this connector.
Oldest Message Queued	The amount of time in seconds that the oldest message has been queued up and waiting to be delivered. Naturally, you want this to be low (less than a few minutes, perhaps).
Outbound Bytes Total	The total volume of messages in kilobytes that has been sent from this connection since the MTA was initialized.
Outbound Messages Total	The total number of messages that have been sent through this connection. Outbound Bytes Total divided by Outbound Messages Total will give you the average message size received through this connector.

TABLE 26.4 continued: MSExchangeMTA Counters

COUNTER	MEANING
Queue Length	The number of messages waiting to be transferred.
Queue Bytes	The total volume of messages in bytes that is waiting to be transferred.
Received Bytes/sec	The rate in bytes at which messages are being received per second.
Received Messages/sec	The total number of messages that are being received per second.
Sent Byte/sec	The rate in bytes at which messages are being sent per second.
Sent Messages/sec	The total number of messages that are being received per second.
Total Recipients Inbound	The total number of recipients specified in all messages that have been received since the MTA was initialized. This is provided since each message received may be addressed to more than one recipient.
Total Recipients Outbound	The total number of recipients specified in all messages that have been sent since the MTA was initialized. This is provided since each message received may be addressed to more than one recipient.
Total Recipients Queued	The total number of recipients specified in all messages currently in the queue for this connection.

When Should I Monitor?

Plan to perform system monitoring after any changes to your system, such as new hardware, new software, or additional users. New hardware and software may also affect your baseline data.

As far as the time of day to monitor, unless you are taking a baseline measurement, you should monitor your system during typical periods of activity. For many Exchange environments, the first hour of the workday is the busiest, so you may want to isolate and analyze that part of the day separately from the rest of the business day. This allows you to know when your system is the busiest as well as what resources are the most used (or possibly when the system bottlenecks appear) during this period.

Viewing and Capturing Performance Data

Now that you know a few of the counters to follow when monitoring a Windows NT server running Exchange, let's take a brief look at different ways to track these counters. Performance Monitor provides you with the ability to view and capture data in four different ways. These views are chart, alert, log, and report. The optimal view to use will depend on the information you are trying to track and how you want to report on that information.

The Performance Monitor Chart View

By far, the most impressive way to view performance data is the Performance Monitor chart view shown in Figure 26.4. The chart view allows you to see data in real-time; chart view is the default view when you launch Performance Monitor.

Note a couple of areas on the Performance Monitor chart. The left side of the graph (the y-axis) is the scale; the default is 0 to 100, but you may change this depending on the types of data you are charting. Directly below the graph is a line that gives you the statistics (Last, Average, Min, and Max) for the currently highlighted counter.

Though this is difficult to view on paper, in Figure 26.4, I noticed that my %Processor Time counter was pegged at 100 percent. I noticed that my Work Queue Length was quite long (122 was the last reported value). I did a quick check of the MTA queues and noticed that there were a large number of messages queued up for the private information store. There was plenty of memory in this system (28MB available) and no paging. This suggests either a disk bottleneck or a CPU bottleneck. The log file disk (E) was about 35 percent busy, and the database disk (D) was less than 10 percent busy. Since this system actually only has a P/60 processor, I can be pretty confident that the processor is the bottleneck.

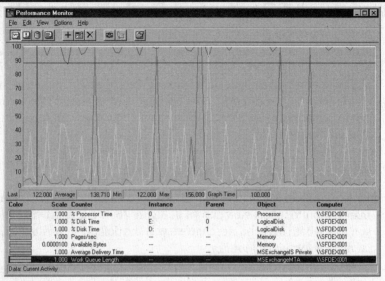

FIGURE 26.4: The Performance Monitor chart view showing typical Exchange and Windows NT system counters

Creating a Performance Monitor Chart   To add counters to a chart, click Edit ≻ Add To Chart. From the Add To Chart dialog box, you can choose:

Computer to select another Windows NT computer to monitor. You can select counters from up to 25 different computers.

Object to view a list of counters for any two dozen or more objects. The number of objects available will vary from Windows NT systems depending on the software that is installed on that particular computer. For example, an Exchange server will have an additional 10 objects related to Exchange.

Instance to select which instance of a particular object. Some objects will only have one instance, such as Memory, while other objects such as Processor, Logical Disk, and Physical Disk may have several instances.

Counter to select one or more counters for the object/instance you currently have highlighted.

Color, **Width**, and **Style** to change the appearance of the line as it appears on the chart.

Scale to change the scale of the line on the chart.

Explain to turn on a small text box on the bottom of the Add To Chart dialog box that offers a definition of the currently highlighted counter. I love this feature, since I rarely remember exactly what most of these counters do.

Highlight as many of the counters as you wish and click the Add button so that they appear on the chart. I caution against putting too many on a single chart, however, because the chart becomes difficult to read.

When reading a chart with many counters on it, you can highlight the currently selected counter so that it stands out on the chart. To do this, highlight the counter in the list of counters on the bottom of the Performance Monitor chart window and press the Backspace key (or Ctrl+H). The line corresponding to that counter will be emphasized, and the line will appear white.

The Performance Monitor Report View

Figure 26.4 showed you some counters from an Exchange server that was experiencing a CPU bottleneck. While the chart view is impressive and cool to look at in real-time, the data that chart view provides is difficult to interpret. The report view often provides you with more readable data, but you have to remember that it is reporting a snapshot in time.

To create a report view, switch the Performance Monitor view to report from the View menu. Add the appropriate counters to the report. Figure 26.5 shows a sample report view from a server that is experiencing a CPU bottleneck.

The actual figures in Figure 26.5 are much easier to read than they were in chart view, even on paper! This particular report view took a snapshot of the system every 30 seconds. Notice the %Processor Time is at 100 percent and the system is paging 13.2 times per second (a little high!). The Work Queue Length and the MSExchangeMTA Connections ➤ Microsoft Private MDB ➤ Queue Length are both a little high. The log file drive (E) was 94.2 percent busy (very busy in my view), and the database drive (D was 52.3 percent busy). If you watch this activity in chart view (as I did in Figure 26.4), you will notice the activity on the database disk (E) spikes every few seconds. This occurs every time transactions are committed from the log files to the database files.

I generated this load using the LoadSim utility. I used LoadSim to create a bunch of users that all use distribution lists frequently; then I fired up the simulation. The simulation created more messages than the existing system resources could keep up with.

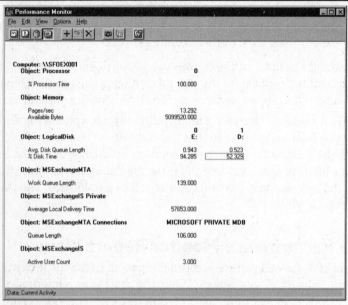

FIGURE 26.5:   Report view from Performance Monitor

The Performance Monitor Log View

Though the chart view is useful and interesting to watch and the report view is easy to read, in the long run, the log view has got to be one of the most useful views in the Performance Monitor. The log view allows you to capture Performance Monitor objects you want to track to a log file. You can later analyze this log file from the Performance Monitor chart or report views. From the View menu, select Log to initiate a logging session.

To create a new log file, first select which objects you are going to monitor. For logging, you select an entire object (all instances), not a single counter. To add objects to the log, click Edit ➢ Add To Log. From the

Add To Log dialog box, select all the objects you wish to monitor. For basic Windows NT troubleshooting and system analysis, I choose at a minimum:

- ▶ Logical Disk (I prefer Logical Disk over Physical Disk since Logical Disk lets me view each individual logical drive letter)
- ▶ Memory
- ▶ Process
- ▶ Processor
- ▶ Server
- ▶ System

Next, you need to set the log filename and the interval at which Performance Monitor will take a snapshot of the system. Choose Options ➤ Log to see the Log Options dialog box. Set the name and location of the log file. Unless you are going to be manually taking measurements, make sure that the Periodic Update button is selected and a reasonable value is entered in the Interval box.

What is a reasonable interval value? The default is 15 seconds, but this interval is far too often in my opinion. The counter values that are collected are actually an average between the last collection interval and the current collection interval. Do you really need to collect this data every 15 seconds?

As an example, if I were going to collect data for my system's activity from 8:00 A.M. until 11:00 A.M., I would choose a value about every 120 seconds. Over a three-hour period of time, that is still going to give me 90 separate measurements. The log file will grow to considerable size with only 90 measurements. Even with just the objects I recommended above (and none of the Exchange counters), a log file with 90 separate measurements in it will be over 1MB in size.

Viewing Logged Data   One of the great mysteries of Performance Monitor data logging is: "How do I see the data that I have logged?" When viewing data in chart view, you are normally viewing data in real-time (or Current Activity). From any Performance Monitor view, you can select to view data from a log file instead. Select Option ➤ Data From to see the Data From dialog box. Two radio button options here give you the option of viewing data from Current Activity or a Log File.

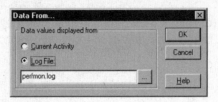

Simply select the Log File option and click the radix button (the button with the three periods in it) to browse the file system for the log file you want to view. Once you have selected the log file and clicked on OK, create your chart or report as you would if you were viewing data from current activity. You can create a log from a log, called *relogging*, for purposes of creating new logs or reducing the size of existing log files.

Automatically Creating Performance Monitor Logs   Suppose you want to create a Performance Monitor log a few times per week. You estimate that the busiest time of the day for your servers is 9:00 A.M. and 11:00 A.M., so you want to log activity during these times. If you are like most system administrators, you probably don't have time every morning to start and stop the Performance Monitor at the exact times required. The Windows NT Resource Kit includes two programs that can assist you in automatically creating the logs you wish to create. These two utilities are collectively referred to as the data logging service.

To set up the data logging service, make sure that the datalog.exe and monitor.exe programs that come with the Windows NT Resource Kit are copied to the \WinNT\System32 directory. Then type **MONITOR SETUP** at the command prompt. This will install the Performance Monitor service (you will see a new service in Control Panel ➤ Services called Monitor Service) and configure the appropriate Registry values. The default startup type will be set to manual startup mode.

Next, you need to create a Performance Monitor workspace that specifies the objects you are going to collect in the log and the log file you are going to create. To do this:

1. Start Performance Monitor and switch to the log view.

2. Add the objects you wish to monitor. Remember when creating a log that you have to capture the entire object, not specific counters.

3. In the Log Options dialog box (Options ➤ Log), set the Periodic Update interval to a reasonable value (somewhere between 300 and 900 seconds). Also, enter a filename (e.g., C:\dailylog.pmw) that you want the data to be logged to, and click Save (not Start Log).

4. On the Performance Monitor main menu, choose File ➤ Save Workspace and create a workspace file in the C:\WinNT\System32 directory (e.g., dailylog.pmw).

Next you need to specify the file and start the service. Since you want this to occur automatically, use the Windows NT Scheduler server and the Windows NT AT command to schedule two commands to run daily. The first command will run every day at 9:00 A.M. and will start the monitor service; the second will run at 11:00 A.M. and stop the monitor service.

Create two batch files, one called startlog.cmd and one called stoplog.cmd. These batch files will be placed in the C:\PERFDATA directory. The startlog.cmd is easy—all it has to do is set the correct workspace for the monitoring service to use and then start the service. Here is a sample:

```
@ECHO OFF
REM STARTLOG.CMD file starts the logging service
REM Change current directory to C:\WINNT\SYSTEM32
CD \WINNT\SYSTEM32
REM Set the Monitor Service to use the DIALYLOG.PMW workspace
MONITOR DAILYLOG.PMW
REM Start the Monitor Service
MONITOR START
```

Next, use the Windows NT Schedule service to launch this every weekday at 9:00 A.M. The command to do this is:

```
AT 9:00 /EVERY:MONDAY,TUESDAY,WEDNESDAY,THURSDAY,FRIDAY
C:\PERFDATA\STARTLOG.CMD
```

This command will cause the monitor service to start every weekday at 9:00 A.M. It will create the log file you specified in the workspace file (C:\PERFDATA\dailylog.log). You need to write a batch file that will stop the logging service and rename your log file. I use a shareware utility called dateset.exe that sets the current date to an environmental variable; you can find many utilities like this on the Web. To rename your dailylog.log file to the current date:

```
@ECHO OFF
REM STOPLOG.CMD stops the logging service and renames the log
file
```

```
REM Stop the logging service
MONITOR STOP
REM Set the current date to the environment
C:\PERFDATA\DATESET
REM Rename the file to the current date
REN C:\PERFDATA\DAILYLOG.LOG C:\PERFDATA\%DATE%.LOG
```

NOTE

The Windows NT Resource Kit program WINAT is a graphical version of an AT command utility and it is much easier to use than the AT command utility.

Running a Performance Monitor session every day might be excessive. Instead, you might want to monitor only on specific days or maybe even only once a week. The data logging service and the Schedule service make it easy for you to automate this process.

TIP

The Windows NT Performance Monitor is not very intrusive and will have little impact on the system being monitored. However, I still prefer to do my performance monitoring from my workstation rather than from the server. The network traffic created can also be monitored if necessary, though it is minimal.

The Performance Monitor Alert View

The fourth view provided by the Performance Monitor is the alert view. This view allows you to set specific values for Performance Monitor counters. If the counter goes above or below that value, an event can be logged to the Event Viewer application log and a network message can be set.

Let's say that you want to set up an alert view that notifies the administrator and generates an application log entry if any of the following are true:

- ▶ The disk space on your database and information store disks drops below 15 percent.

- ▶ The MTA Work Queue exceeds 40 items.

- ▶ The Internet Mail Service's Total Messages Queued exceeds 50.

- ▶ The X.400 to Hawaii connector has more than 25 messages.

Switch Performance Monitor to the alert view and add the appropriate counters to the alert view. You will notice that the Add To Alert dialog box (shown in Figure 26.6) has two additional options.

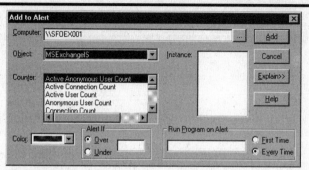

FIGURE 26.6:   Alert thresholds on the Add To Alert dialog box

In the Alert If section, you can set a value and choose whether to alert if the counter goes over or under that value. There is also an option to Run Program On Alert either the first time the alert occurs or every time it occurs. This program can send you a mail message, generate a pager alert, or run some other notification type program.

Once the alert thresholds are set, you can specify the update time and whether to send a network message or generate an event in the application log using the Alert Options dialog box found at Options ➤ Alert.

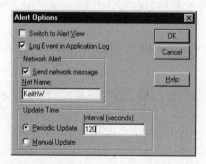

The resulting Performance Monitor view will look like Figure 26.7. The only alert that has been generated in Figure 26.7 is for the Work Queue Length counter. Notice that the values reported were 212, 216, 223, and 225.

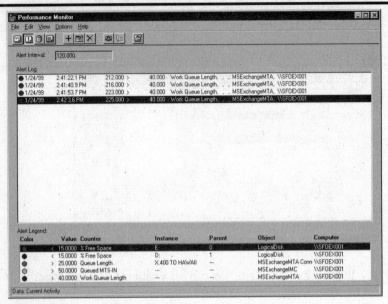

FIGURE 26.7: Performance Monitor alert view

TIP

The alert view of Performance Monitor can be saved and run automatically as a service in the background using the Performance Monitor service found on the Windows NT Resource Kit. Follow the same procedures found in the section titled "Automatically Creating Performance Monitor Logs," but create settings for the alert view instead of the log view. Save the PMW file, specify that the monitor service will use that file, and start the monitor.

Saving Performance Monitor Settings to Use Later

So you have worked and slaved over Performance Monitor all day and have finally found the counters that you want to monitor. You have configured chart, logging, reporting, and alert options, and you *don't* want to do it again. To save the Performance Monitor setting from the Performance Monitor menu, choose File ➢ Save Chart (or Log, Report, Alert) settings. If you have not previously saved these settings, you will be asked to provide a name for them.

To save the settings found in all four Performance Monitor views, select Save ≻ Workspace and provide a name for your workspace if it has not been previously named. These settings can now be retrieved for later use or they can be used with the data logging service found on the Windows NT Resource Kit.

Built-in Performance Monitor Charts

During Exchange Server installation, the Setup program includes eight pre-built Performance Monitor charts. These charts are stored in PMW (Performance Monitor workspace) files in the `C:\exchsrvr\bin` directory. For convenience's sake, these charts are also on the Microsoft Exchange menu (choose Start ≻ Programs ≻ Microsoft Exchange). These charts are designed to track critical activity on your Exchange server. They include:

▶ The Server Health chart, which tracks CPU usage for all the Exchange core services including the directory service, MTA, information store, and System Attendant. It also displays the total CPU usage and the Memory Pages/sec counter. Figure 26.8 shows the Server Health chart. This chart is updated once a second.

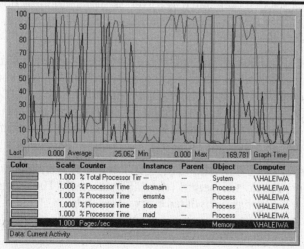

FIGURE 26.8: The Server Health chart shows the CPU usage for core services and pages per second.

▶ The Server History chart tracks the total number of users that have connected to this server, the memory object's Pages/sec counter, and the message transfer agent's Work Queue. This chart is updated once every 60 seconds.

▶ The IMS Queues chart displays the messages waiting to be transferred to and from the Internet Mail Service (stored in the information store) and the messages queued up at the IMS, both inbound and outbound. This chart is updated once every second.

▶ IMS Statistics show the total messages sent out and received inbound via the Internet Mail Service. IMS statistics are updated once every 30 seconds.

▶ The IMS Traffic chart displays messages passing through the information store going to the Internet Mail Service (through the IMS mailbox MTS-IN and MTS-OUT queues) as well as the total number of connections. This chart is updated once every second.

▶ The Server Load chart is used to track the total load on the server by tracking statistics on the number of messages submitted and delivered per minute, the number of address book reads, and the number of RPCs (Remote Procedure Calls) per second. This chart also tracks activity generated by servers in the same site by tracking the Adjacent MTA Associations counter. This chart is updated once every 10 seconds.

▶ Server Queues display the number of messages that are stored in server queues and are waiting for processing. Naturally, you want these numbers to be low. The counters charted include the MTA's Work Queue Length and the Send and Receive queues for the public and private information stores. Server queues are updated once every 10 seconds.

▶ The Server Users chart shows the total number of users that have a connection to the server (the MSExchangeIS User Count counter). This chart is updated every 10 seconds.

TIP

If you work with any of these supplied counters, you will notice that these Performance Monitor charts have no pull-down menus and often no legend. You can resize these charts with your mouse and close it by pressing Alt+F4. And, if you absolutely have to see a menu, press the Enter key while the chart is the active window.

SERVER AND LINK MONITORS

Microsoft provides two tools that function as part of the Exchange Administrator program. These tools are the Exchange server monitor and link monitor. Server monitors are used to monitor the status of services on one or more Exchange servers placed throughout your organization. Link monitors are used to send what I like to call a "ping" message to other mail servers; it then measures the amount of time it takes to get a response.

Both of these tools can be used to help maintain your organization and to make sure that you know that a server or link has failed before your user community has a chance to call you. This type of monitor is critical if you want to stay one step ahead of the ringing phone.

The server monitor and the link monitor allow you to specify different polling intervals and escalation notifications. The *polling interval* choices are normal and critical. You may want to poll sites that are operating normally (with no problems) less frequently than a site that has started experiencing problems (critical sites).

You can further specify an *escalation interval* that is different for sites that have experienced a minor delay (warning) versus sites that have been designated as critical. Critical sites are sites where the problem has not been resolved within a certain amount of time.

Server Monitors

Any service on a Windows NT server that has Exchange Server running on it (not limited to the Exchange services) can be monitored by the Exchange server monitor. The server monitor is configured to monitor the service and notify the administrator if the service fails. The server monitor can also attempt to restart the service or the entire server, if so configured.

By default, only three services are monitored by a server monitor: the directory service, the information store, and the MTA. The services to be monitored are specified on the Services tab of each Exchange server's properties. In Figure 26.9, this server is configured so that the Backup Exec Job Engine, Exchange Directory, Exchange event service, Exchange information store, Exchange Internet Mail Service, and Exchange message transfer agent are monitored.

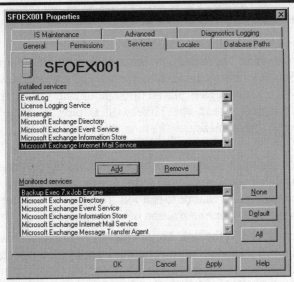

FIGURE 26.9: Services on server SFOEX001 configured to be monitored by a server monitor

Creating a Server Monitor

Server monitors are created and run from within Exchange Administrator. To create a server monitor, choose File ➢ New Other ➢ Server Monitor. The server monitor has five tabs: General, Notification, Servers, Actions, and Clock.

General On the General tab, you must provide a directory name and a display name for the monitor. You can also specify a log filename where status information and notifications are kept.

At the bottom of the General tab, you can specify a normal polling interval and critical sites polling interval. The *normal polling* interval (15 minutes) is used for servers whose services are all functioning and whose clock is not off by more than a specified interval (specified on the Clock page).

If a server does not meet the criteria for a normal polling interval, it will be polled at the *critical sites* interval instead. The default for critical servers is every 5 minutes. Polling intervals can be set as frequently as a few seconds or as infrequently as a few hours. The defaults work quite well in most environments; polling too frequently will generate excessive network traffic, whereas polling infrequently may mean you are not notified of service failures for a long period of time.

Notification   The Notification tab (shown in Figure 26.10) is used to specify how notifications should occur if a server or service enters either a warning state or an alert state. A server will enter a *warning state* if the server clock is off by more than the number of warning seconds you specify on the Clock tab. A server or service will enter an *alert state* if a service does not respond to the server monitor or if the server clock is off by more than the alert amount specified on the Clock tab.

You can set a server monitor to deliver notifications to administrators or computers via an e-mail message or a Windows NT alert. You can also configure the server monitor to launch an application if a warning or alert occurs.

To specify a type of notification, click the New button on the Notification tab; you will see the Escalation Editor dialog box. This dialog box is slightly different for different types of notifications. The mail message notification box is shown in Figure 26.10. When you specify a notification type, you may also specify a time delay; the default is 15 minutes. The Time Delay is the amount of time that the server monitor waits after a warning or alert is generated before it sends out a notification.

TIP

When configuring notification types, e-mail is a great way to send notification messages. This is, of course, provided that the e-mail server that is causing problems is not yours. To make sure you receive critical server monitor messages, configure Windows NT alerts in addition to mail message alerts. The Windows NT alert option allows you to specify a computer or user to notify.

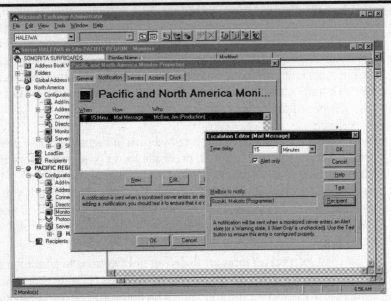

FIGURE 26.10: A server monitor's Notification tab, including the Escalation Editor dialog box

Servers   The server monitor's Servers tab is where you specify which servers you want to monitor. A server monitor can monitor any server within the organization, as long as the monitor has RPC connectivity to the servers it is monitoring. Servers listed in the Monitored Servers column will be monitored by the server monitor.

By highlighting a server in the Monitored Servers column and clicking the Services button, you are able to configure which services are monitored for that particular server. You can also configure the monitored services on the Services tab of the server's property page (shown in Figure 26.9).

Actions   The Actions tab allows you to specify what action the server monitor will take if an Exchange service is stopped or does not respond. You can specify a first attempt, second attempt, and subsequent attempts to take corrective action. The three options for corrective actions include Take No Action, Restart The Service, and Restart The Computer. If you specify the Restart The Computer option, you can specify a restart delay and a restart message.

NOTE

When configuring a server monitor to take corrective action, the Windows NT user who is running the server monitor must have server operator rights or greater on the destination servers.

Clock   The Clock tab allows you to set a warning and alert interval for monitored Exchange servers whose clocks differ by more than a specified interval. The computer that is running the Exchange server monitor is used as the baseline for correct time. The Synchronize check box option allows you to specify that you want the server's clock to be synchronized with the monitoring computer. Windows NT tracks time internally in UCT (Universal Coordinated Time); you see the local time displayed. If the monitored servers are in different time zones, the server monitor still sets their local time correctly.

Part V

Using Server Monitors

Exchange server monitors are operated as part of the Exchange Administrator program, which must be operating in order to start a server monitor. To start a monitor you have created, locate the monitor in the Monitors container (*Site Name* ➤ Configuration ➤ Monitors) and highlight it. From the Tools menu, choose Start Monitor. You are asked for a specific server to connect to; when you select the server and click OK, you will see the monitor window.

In Figure 26.11, you can see a server monitor called WorldWide Monitor that is monitoring 14 Exchange servers around the world. Notice that the ATLANTA (in the North America site) server's time is off by a little over five minutes, and the RIO (in the South America site) server's MTA service is not available. The VANCOUVER server (in the North America site) has an X next to it, meaning that it is currently undergoing maintenance. If you have configured the monitor to take corrective actions (such as restart a service or synchronize the clock), both of these issues will be addressed automatically.

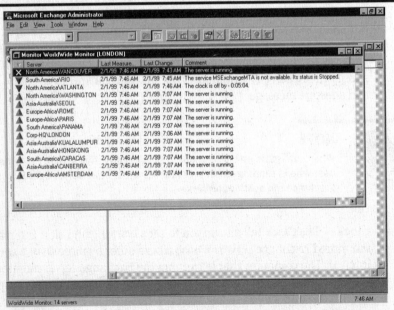

FIGURE 26.11: WorldWide Monitor monitoring 14 servers; two of the servers are in an alert state, and one is in maintenance mode.

The server monitor window will display one of five symbols to indicate the current status of the server. These symbols are used for both server monitors and the link monitors.

Symbol	Meaning
Blue question mark (?)	You will usually see this right after the monitor starts; this means the state of the monitored server is unknown.
Green triangle	All services are operating normally.
Red exclamation point (!)	The link or the server is in a warning state.
Red upside-down triangle	The link or server is in an alert state.
Black X	The server is currently undergoing maintenance.

In Figure 26.11, notice that the RIO server has a problem with the message transfer agent service. You can highlight this line in the server monitor and display its properties (File ➣ Properties, or just double-click). Figure 26.12 shows the RIO server's property page.

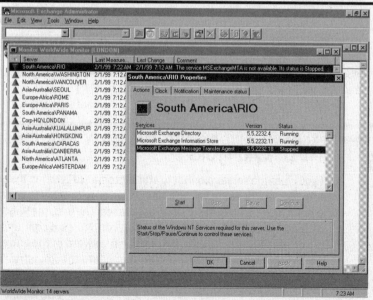

FIGURE 26.12:   RIO server's property page

There are four tabs on this dialog box. The Actions tab allows you to see the status of the monitored services. You can also stop and start these services. If the service supports the pause and continue functions, you can perform those functions as well.

The Clock tab shows you the current clock offset and the server's time zone information. The Notification tab shows who has been notified and how they were notified (through e-mail or network pop-up message). The Maintenance Status tab displays the server's current maintenance status, who made the modification, and when it was made. The Clock, Notification, and Maintenance tabs are read-only; you cannot change any of the values.

Automatically Starting Server Monitors   You can start Exchange server monitors from a command prompt or a batch file using Exchange Administrator's startup switches. The monitor startup switches for Exchange Administrator include the /M and /S switches. The /M switch allows you to specify a specific server monitor; the /S switch allows you to specify which server to connect to during startup.

To automatically start the WorldWide Monitor found in the Corp-HQ site, type **C:\exchsrvr\bin\admin /mCorp-HQ\WorldWide Monitor\London**.

Notice that you have to specify \London also; the server name is required for connecting to the server for reading monitor information and for any operations requiring a home server, such as sending e-mail messages. You can also specify multiple monitors to start in the same command line.

EXCHANGE@WORK: AUTOMATICALLY STARTING SERVER AND LINK MONITORS

If you want the server monitor to start automatically when the computer boots, there are two utilities provided with the Windows NT Resource Kit that may be of some assistance. The first, the Windows NT Auto Logon Setter (autolog.exe), configures a computer to automatically log in. It asks you for the password of the currently logged on user and puts this information into the Registry. From this point forward, the computer will automatically log in as the user

CONTINUED ➡

you have specified. This is somewhat dangerous, because that password is now stored in the Registry and the computer automatically logs in. Make sure that this computer is physically secured if you do this.

The second utility is called Applications As Services (srvany.exe). This utility will configure any application to start as a service. If you configure a server or link monitor to run as a service, you will not be able to see the server monitor status screen, but notifications and corrective action events will still take place. This is a more secure option than the AUTOLOG option.

Putting a Server in Maintenance Mode

If you are going to take a server down for maintenance, ask yourself, "Is there a server monitor that is currently monitoring this server?" If you have implemented server monitoring, make sure that you put the server into maintenance mode prior to starting any maintenance, especially if the server monitor is performing notification or taking corrective actions.

I speak from experience. On more than one occasion I have stopped Exchange services to perform maintenance, only to find the services automatically restarting. In one instance, I disabled a service so that it would not restart. Within a few minutes, the server monitor that was monitoring that server was rebooting the server. I had no way to stop it from rebooting.

To put the server in maintenance mode, use the Exchange Administrator command-line switch /T. You run this command at the server console of the server you are about to take down for maintenance. Here are a couple of examples of how to put a server into maintenance mode and the function that it provides.

Command	Function
Admin /T R	Suspends repair, but notification will still be generated.
Admin /T N	Suspends notifications, but repairs will still be performed if the monitor finds problems.

Admin /T NR   Suspends both notifications and repairs.

Admin /T   Resets the server to normal mode. Repairs and
               notification will resume normally.

If you use the switch /T feature, don't forget to use the /T command to
put the server back in normal mode.

Link Monitors

Server monitors are used to verify the availability of Exchange servers and
services. Link monitors are used to verify that messages are actually being
transmitted between two Exchange servers or between an Exchange
server and an external mail system. For Exchange to Exchange link monitor tests, the System Attendant service generates an e-mail message and
sends it to the System Attendant on another server. The System Attendant on the other Exchange server replies as soon as it gets the message.
When the message is returned to the originating server, the System
Attendant determines how long it took for the round-trip and if that time
is within specified norms.

For Exchange to non-Exchange systems link monitor tests, the System
Attendant sends a message to a custom recipient that represents a user
on this non-Exchange system. The other system must be either able to
recognize and automatically reply to the message or it must be able to
send a non-delivery report.

Link monitors are excellent tools to use if you need to determine if
your message delivery times are acceptable.

Creating a Link Monitor

Link monitors are created and displayed in the same Monitors container
in which server monitors are held. To create a server monitor using
Exchange Administrator, choose File ➢ New Other ➢ Link Monitor.
The link monitor has five tabs: General, Notification, Servers, Recipients, and Bounce.

General   The General tab (shown in Figure 26.13) contains the link
monitor's directory and display names. In addition, you can specify a log
file (this file is in ASCII text) to which all link monitor activity is written.
The Polling Interval box allows you to specify how often both normal
operation and critical sites are polled.

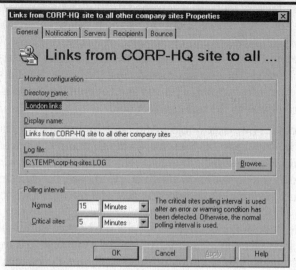

FIGURE 26.13:   Link monitor for the CORP-HQ site

The default polling interval is every 15 minutes for a server that is operating normally and 5 minutes for sites that are considered critical. I would not set these values below this level, because doing so increases the number of messages that have to be transferred between servers. If the messaging system is very busy, frequent link monitor messages will interfere with the regular messaging traffic.

Notification   The Notification tab behaves exactly like the Server Monitor tab described earlier in the chapter. From here you can set network pop-up messages and e-mail message notifications, as well as specify a program launching a process.

Servers   The Servers tab allows you to specify which servers in *your own* Exchange organization you want to send link monitor messages to.

Recipients   The Recipients tab gives you a place to put custom recipients for addresses that exist on external systems. When you create this custom recipient, you will most likely want to create a custom recipient that does not exist on the foreign system. If you specify a real recipient, you probably won't receive a reply right away unless that recipient has an automatic reply rule on its mailbox. After I create a recipient and set up the link monitor, I prefer to hide these recipients so they are not visible to the global address list.

When a non-delivery message is returned, the link monitor does not read the contents of the message, but rather the message subject. You have one of two columns you can use for custom recipients; these two columns represent the typical reply types. The left column (Message Subject Returned From) is the one you should most likely use. It is for systems that have an automatic reply feature and that put the original message subject text into the reply subject field.

The right column (Message Subject And Body Returned From) is used when you do not know how the foreign system will return the subject. Systems that return the message body are less efficient because they generate more overhead. If you do not know which one to choose, try choosing the Message Subject Returned From selection first and seeing if it works.

Bounce   The Bounce tab is where to specify the bounce duration. This means the longest acceptable round-trip time for a message to travel between two systems. This duration is used for all servers and recipients configured for this link monitor. If you have different bounce times for different systems, you will need to configure multiple monitors.

You have two bounce duration-time options. Enter Warning State After determines how long to wait for a return message before entering a warning state. This time should indicate messages that are late. Enter Alert State After determines how long to wait for a return message before entering an alert state; the alert state is for messages that are considered very late.

To calculate how long to set these values for, you will need to take into consideration your message topology and typical times to send messages between servers and sites. I always consider the longest acceptable times during the busiest parts of the day; that way, I do not get a lot of false alarms just because the system is busy.

Using Link Monitors

Link monitors are started the exact same way that server monitors are started; this was described earlier in this chapter. The Exchange Administrator program's command-line switches can also be used to automatically start a link monitor.

Once you start the link monitor, you will see the link monitor status screen. This screen will be similar to the one shown in Figure 26.14,

which shows the list of servers and custom recipients to which you have
established link monitoring.

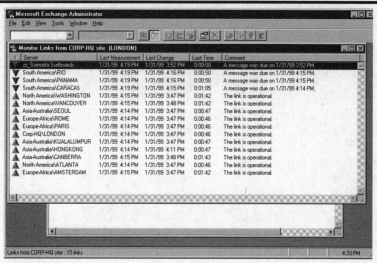

FIGURE 26.14: Link monitor status; notice that all three servers in the South
America site are overdue.

Notice the columns in Figure 26.14 that tell you the last time that a
measurement was taken, the last time there was a change, and the total
time it took for the last message to be returned. This link monitor is running in the London office; notice that it took one minute and 42 seconds
for a message to travel to and from the WASHINGTON server in the
North American site.

Also, notice that there are four servers from which this monitor
expected a response but did not received one. The top one in the list is a
custom recipient that was created for an SMTP user. Notice that the Last
Time figure is 0:00:00; this means it has never received a reply.

Another fact we can disseminate from this status screen is that this
link monitor is expecting a response from all three servers in the South
America site. This may well be indicative of a failed WAN link.

If you highlight any of these servers or recipients in the list, you can
display its properties. Figure 26.15 shows the details for the CARACAS
server in the South America site.

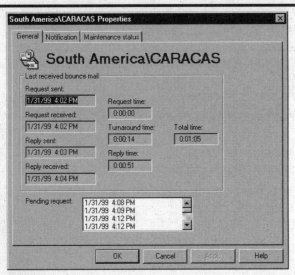

FIGURE 26.15: Property page of the CARACAS server

On the General tab, you can see the statistics for the request and reply messages. The Notification tab shows the notifications that have occurred, and the Maintenance Status tab shows whether the server is in maintenance mode or not.

Good Monitoring Practices

When you are planning your server monitors and link monitors, avoid the temptation to have multiple administrators all monitoring the same servers. While this is not detrimental, it can result in a situation where unnecessary monitoring traffic is being generated. You can, however, have problems if you have more than one monitor configured to take corrective actions.

Don't monitor too frequently, either. You need to find a good balance between getting up-to-date information and not saturating your network and servers with monitor requests. For me, that means starting with the default monitor settings and making small adjustments based on those defaults.

NOTE

The Microsoft BackOffice Resource Kit provides a tool called Exchange Monitor Report Generator. This tool is used to scan server monitor and link monitor log files and create a report of problems and downtime. This tool can be found on the CD-ROM in the \Exchange\WinNNT\I386\Admin\EMRG directory.

THE MICROSOFT NETWORK MONITOR

Microsoft provides a tool with both Windows NT Server and Systems Management Server (SMS) called the Network Monitor. This tool is indispensable when solving tricky network problems. This program listens to the network and can intercept and decode data that is traveling over the network. This is nothing new; for years, Network Associates (formerly known as Network General) have had a very high-end product called the Sniffer, which does the same thing.

NOTE

Before you can install the Network Monitor program, you must install the Network Monitor Agent (Control Panel ➤ Network ➤ Services ➤ Add). You do not have to activate the agent, but it must be installed.

Microsoft ships two flavors of the Network Monitor. The version that ships with Windows NT Server is capable of capturing only the traffic that is being sent to and from the server on which it is running. The SMS version is capable of capturing any traffic on the subnet that the server (or workstation) is running on. This is not always the case in switched networks, though, since not all traffic reaches all ports of a switched network. The SMS version also allows administrators to connect remote Network Monitor agents, which can collect the traffic on a remote network and relay it back to the Network Monitor program.

This is a big deal for many reasons. If you do not already realize this, any information that is passed over the network in "clear text" format can be captured and decoded. This means that a person with Network Monitor can capture the text of most any SMTP message as well as passwords for POP3, NNTP, and IMAP4 users. Figure 26.16 shows a sample capture from Network Monitor. In the bottom pane of the Network

Monitor you will see the decoded SMTP message. Notice the sender is asking the receiver never to divulge the fact that they have been given an additional 15 percent discount. Oops! So much for confidentiality over the Internet!

Notice also in Figure 26.16 that the Network Monitor screen is broken up into three panes. The bottom pane shows both the hexadecimal and the ASCII decoded information. The middle pane shows the protocol information (such as IP addresses, TCP or UDP port numbers, and so on), and the top screen is a summary of each frame. Anyone who can put Network Monitor on the network wire anywhere between the sender and receiver will be able to see this information without problems.

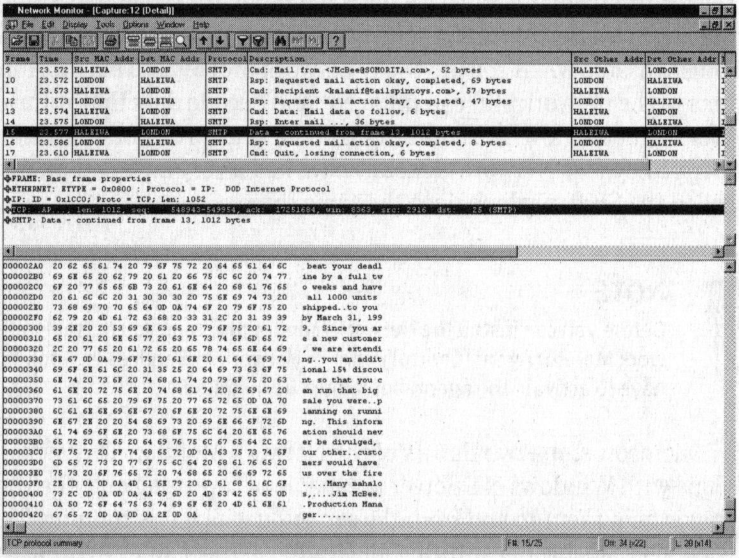

FIGURE 26.16: A capture SMTP message using Network Monitor

That is the bad news. The good news is that most of the information between one Exchange server and another is encrypted. The data between the Exchange and Outlook clients and the Exchange server can also be encrypted. With proper preparation, a great deal of the data that you transmit over the Internet can also be encrypted.

The other big deal about using Network Monitor is that you can use this tool to diagnose network problems. Even if you simply use the summary screens, such as the one shown in Figure 26.17, to see the network's general statistics this tool can come in handy.

The Network Monitor screen shows you real-time statistics while it is in capture mode, including the total % Network Utilization, Frames Per Second, and Bytes Per Second, as well as summary statistics for each machine that the Network Monitor finds on the network. When the monitor finds a new machine on the network, it initially displays the machine's MAC address, but it can also learn the machine's name. You can also enter the machine name and MAC address information into the address list manually.

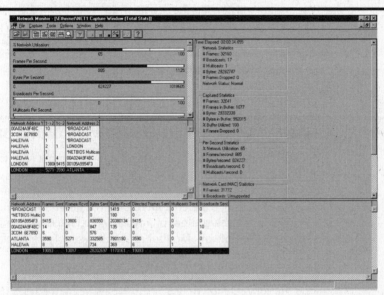

FIGURE 26.17:   Network Monitor in capture mode showing general network statistics

Additional Parsers

The Network Monitor does its magic in part due to DLL files called parsers (which are what I typically call decoders). A *parser* contains the definitions for a specific protocol; the parser is what allows Network Monitor to figure out what type of data is being transmitted and to decode it into a more humanly readable form. The Network Monitor program includes parsers for the Microsoft protocols such as SMB, NetBIOS, Netlogon; protocols such as HTTP, SMTP, SNMP; and others.

If you are an old hand at network monitoring, then you are ready to progress to the next level. The BackOffice Resource Kit includes additional parsers for ISO X.400 and TP4.

NOTE

The Network Monitor is an extremely sophisticated and powerful management tool. Naturally, it is not simple to use. You cannot just point the Network Monitor at your network and say, "Thar's problems in them there hubs—sniff 'em out!" The monitor will do a fine job of sniffing them out, but we are still faced with the challenge of interpreting what the analyzer says. As a matter of fact, the Network Monitor is just about as close to "network rocket science" as most of us non-programmers will ever get. Don't be discouraged. You *can* learn enough about the Network Monitor for it to be useful to you.

EXCHANGE@WORK: USING THE NETWORK MONITOR

The Network Monitor has come in handy for me a number of times when dealing with Exchange. The Outlook/Exchange-client-to-server and Exchange-server-to-Exchange-server connectivity are all RPCs-based and thus are encrypted past the point of allowing mere mortals to see the content of any individual network frame. In these cases, the Network Monitor is useful in simply determining that the client and the server are actually exchanging data.

Network Monitor really shines when you can see (and understand <smile>) the conversation that is occurring between two systems.

For example, a client was having problems sending SMTP mail to one specific Internet domain; all other Internet mail was transferred correctly. I contacted the Exchange administrator for the company (in another country) and quite politely asked if we could work together to figure out the problem. The Exchange administrator quite directly (okay, okay, quite rudely) stated that his system was operating perfectly.

I loaded the Network Monitor program on the client's Exchange server and captured all data going between the Exchange server and their router (to the Internet). I then sent a message to the problem domain and viewed the capture. The SMTP conversation looked

CONTINUED ➡

perfectly normal, much like the one seen in Figure 26.16. The Cmd: Mail from, Cmd: Recipient, Cmd: Data, and Cmd: Quit SMTP commands indicated that the mail transfer was taking place. As a matter of fact, their server accepted every message I sent to it. I monitored a normal conversation with a domain I knew worked just to make sure I was interpreting the results correctly.

I called the administrator back and told him that I would e-mail him the Network Monitor trace file (from another mail system). He still did not believe me, but I went ahead and e-mailed it to him. Magically, in about two days their domain started receiving messages properly. Though I never found out the exact reason, the rumor was that they had an Internet Mail Connector configuration problem.

Exchange Logging and Reporting

Exchange Server does a tremendous amount of logging and reporting. Some of this information is easily obtainable, while other information is a little more time-consuming to retrieve. Monitoring this information can sometimes be tedious, but it is your first line of defense when solving problems or preventing small problems from becoming big problems.

The Windows NT Event Viewer

The Windows NT Event Viewer program should be one of the biggest tools in your toolbox. In Chapter 25, I recommended that you check the event logs daily. I also discussed a few of the events you should regularly watch for. As you learn more about Exchange, you will find many more events that are relevant to your installation.

> **EXCHANGE@WORK: DON'T BE AFRAID TO CHECK THE EVENT LOGS!**
>
> A few years back, I was troubleshooting a message transfer agent problem. Every time I restarted the MTA, it automatically stopped within about five minutes. I ran the MTACHECK program, I restarted the server—you name it, and I was trying it. After nearly an hour of troubleshooting, I was at the end of my rope.
>
> As a last resort, I checked the Event Viewer. There was an error (red) event generated by the MTA: Event ID 9411, Source MSExchangeMTA "The MTA is terminating because the disk where MTA-DATA is located has less than 10MB of space, or an error occurred while trying to check for free space on the disk." I still blush when I think about this, because I did not check the application event log first thing.
>
> The moral of the story: At the first sign of trouble, *always* check the Windows NT Event Viewer.

Turning on Diagnostics Logging

There are a number of places that you can turn on diagnostics logging for the components in your Exchange server. All services and most connectors have a Diagnostics Logging tab; the connectors that do not have their own Diagnostics Logging tab can be logged through the MTA Diagnostics Logging tab. Services and connectors that have Diagnostics Logging tabs include:

- ► Message transfer agent
- ► Public information store
- ► Private information store
- ► Directory service
- ► Microsoft mail connector
- ► Directory synchronization
- ► Lotus cc:Mail connector

One of the more central places to turn on diagnostics logging is on the Diagnostics Logging tab for each server. Figure 26.18 shows the Diagnostics Logging tab for an Exchange server called HALEIWA.

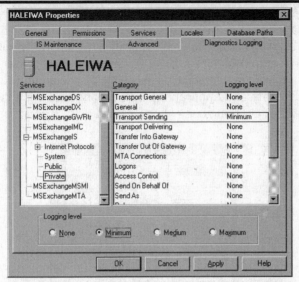

FIGURE 26.18: Diagnostics Logging tab for the HALEIWA server

There are four levels of logging for each of the categories for which you can turn on logging. The first level, None, is pretty self-explanatory. Minimum provides only the bare necessities of information, basically just letting the administrator know that the event occurred. Medium provides a little more detail, and Maximum provides a great amount of detail. Unfortunately, there is no hard and fast rule for the logging levels that will let you know exactly what each level will provide. The services and categories are documented quite well in the Microsoft Exchange Books Online. Some good rules to follow when using diagnostics logging include:

▶ Follow the general rule of turning on only the categories you need.

▶ Start with the Minimum logging level to see if that provides you with the information that you require. Excessive logging will only serve to fill your event log up with extraneous and useless information.

▶ When you have diagnosed the problem or found the information you need, set the logging level back to None if you no longer require information from that category.

Tweaking the Windows NT Log Files

The default maximum size of a Windows NT event log file is 512KB. A log file of this size will become full quite quickly. Further, the default is to overwrite only events older than seven days. One of the first things I do when I install a new Exchange server is to change this default for all three logs (System, Security, and Application). This is done from the Windows NT Event Viewer by choosing Log ➤ Log Settings.

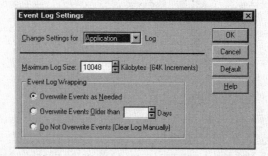

In the Maximum Log Size window, I change it to about 10MB (since the display is in kilobytes and is set in 64KB increments, I have to set it to 10048KB). Further, I change the Event Log Wrapping to Overwrite Events As Needed. In high security installations, this setting is often switched to Do Not Overwrite Events (Clear Log Manually); this is so the security officer has an opportunity to view each log. I change these settings for all three log types.

Archiving Logs

The Windows NT Event Viewer gives you the ability to archive the log you are currently viewing. You can archive the event log to an EVT file that can be later retrieved back into the Windows NT Event Viewer, to a comma-delimited text file, or to a simple ASCII text file.

To archive the current event log, choose File ➤ Save As and provide a filename and path. I usually save event logs as EVT files because they are easy to retrieve and read through Event Viewer. However, some administrators I know think it is important to keep this information in a database and thus require the comma-delimited text format.

Viewing Event Logs from Remote Computers

If you connect to an Exchange server from a remote computer, the remote computer will not have the Registry keys and files that are required by the Windows NT Event Viewer to display the correct descriptions for the Exchange-related errors. You may see the message:

```
The description for Event ID (104) in Source (ESE97) could
not be found.
```

If this is the case, you need to populate the local Registry with the appropriate Registry keys and copy the appropriate files to your local computer. The BackOffice Resource Kit has a tool called the Initialize Event Log tool that can do this for you.

Exchange Error Numbers

Exchange Server has several hundred error numbers that it may display in the application and system event logs. Sometimes the Event Viewer program will have an excellent description of the event; other times it will not.

On the Exchange Server CD-ROM there is a tool called `error.exe` that will look up an error message if you provide it with the error code. The tool is in the `\Server\Support\Utils\I386` directory of the CD-ROM. You supply the error number (including the dash, if the error code has one), and `error.exe` will give you the error message. For example, if you're seeing the error number –1018, you can type **ERROR –1018**, and it will reply with `Error –1018 (0xfffffc06) = JET_errRead-VerifyFailure`.

Okay, it's not much, but at least it is one more piece of information you can use when searching the Knowledge Base or TechNet.

Logging MTA Events When Queues Reach a Specified Size

Starting with Exchange Server 5 SP2 and all versions of Exchange 5.5, there is a set of four new Registry values that allow you to set an alarm level to log MTA events when the outbound queue or the MTA work queue has more than a specified number of messages waiting to be delivered. These settings can be useful if you want to track each time the work queue or any outbound queue exceeds a certain size. These values only monitor the X.400 connectors and the site connectors, since the MTA manages these two connectors. All of these parameters are set in the move Registry key.

```
\HKLM\System\CurrentControlSet\Services\MSExchangeMTA\Parameters
```

Two of these Registry values control event logging if the MTA work queue exceeds a specified size. These values are:

```
Work queue alarm on
Work queue alarm off
```

Note that the spaces are required and the values *are* case-sensitive. When you add these, choose the data type REG_DWORD. For the Work Queue Alarm On value, specify in the data field a number that you want an event logged if the queue size exceeds. The Work Queue Alarm Off value allows you to specify a number at which the MTA will log another event to let you know that the work queue has dropped below that size. If you do not enter a Work Queue Alarm Off value, then half the value of the Work Queue Alarm On value is used. If you set the Work Queue Alarm Off value to 0, then the event will not be logged until the work queue is completely empty.

The other two Registry values control event logging for outbound MTA queues (this includes X.400 and site connectors). These values are:

```
Outbound queue alarm on
Outbound queue alarm off
```

These are also case-sensitive and require the spaces; they also use the data type REG_DWORD. If any outbound queue exceeds the number specified in the Outbound Queue Alarm On value, an event is logged. Another event is logged when the number specified in the Outbound Queue Alarm Off value. If no Outbound Queue Alarm Off value is specified, one half of the Outbound Queue Alarm On value is used. If 0 is specified in the Outbound Queue Alarm Off value, the event is not logged until the queue is cleared.

Figure 26.19 shows the Parameters key of the MSExchangeMTA section of the Registry. The Outbound Queue Alarm settings are near the top, and the Work Queue Alarm settings are near the bottom. I set both On settings to 100 (0x64 in hex) and the Off settings to 25 (0x19 in hex).

In Figure 26.19, if any outbound queue exceeds 100 messages waiting to be delivered, event ID 659 will be logged to the application event log. The description will tell me which queue has surpassed the 100 mark and how many messages are waiting. When the queue drops below 25, a second event (event ID 660) will be logged telling me that the queue has dropped below 25.

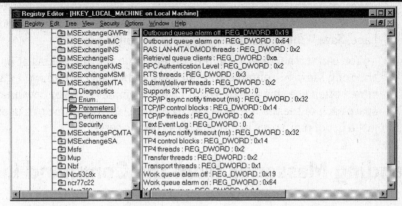

FIGURE 26.19: New Registry settings to log events when the MTA work queue size or any outbound queue exceeds 100 messages

If the MTA work queue has 100 or more messages waiting to be processed, event ID 666 will be logged to the application event log. The description will note how many messages are waiting to be processed by the work queue. Once the number of messages drops below 25, another event will be logged.

NOTE

The MTA work queue is the message queue to which all outbound messages are delivered when the MTA receives the messages from the information store or inbound queues.

Saving Window Contents

One feature that I use all the time is the Save Window Contents feature found in the Exchange Administrator program. Though it provides a very simple ability, it is certainly worth mentioning. I am often asked whether it is possible to print out the content of the Mailbox Resources container or a Recipients container. You can't directly print out the content of these containers, but you can save them to a comma-separated value (CSV) file and retrieve that file into a program such as Excel. The Save Window Contents feature also lets you save the data as a simple ASCII text file.

To do this, highlight the container you want to take a snapshot of in the container pane (left-hand pane) of the Exchange Administrator program. Then, highlight one of the objects in the content pane (the right-hand pane); once you have done this, the Save Window Contents option will be visible on the File menu. If you have not highlighted an object in the right pane, Save Window Contents will be grayed out.

You can further customize the content pane you are looking at by choosing View ➤ Columns and selecting additional columns you want to view. I often use this feature when I need a simple report of how much space each of the mailboxes is taking up, the last login time of a user, or just a list of mailboxes in the site on a specific server.

Sending Messages from the Command Line

Do you have a message to send, but you need to do it from the command prompt? Would you like to find a way to automatically e-mail a report or file to someone? The Microsoft BackOffice Resource Kit (Second Edition) includes a utility called the MAPIsend tool (mapisend.exe). This tool used to be called the Command-Line Mail Sender Tool (sendmail.exe). This tool allows you to send messages and attachments from a command prompt or through a batch file from computers running Windows NT Workstation and Windows NT Server.

You can create a batch file that creates and e-mails reports such as disk space usage, tape backup logs, and other noteworthy system events. Then you can use the Windows NT Scheduler to automate the batch file so that it runs periodically.

Installing and Using MAPIsend

Installing the MAPIsend program is simple. Copy the mapisend.exe file from the BackOffice Resource Kit directory (usually \BORK\Exchange) or CD-ROM (\Exchange\WinNT\I386\Admin\MAPIsend) to a directory in the computer's path such as C:\WinNT.

To use MAPIsend, you need to be aware of several command-line options:

Option	Explanation
-U	The message profile that contains the Exchange server name and mailbox name that MAPIsend will use.
-P	Specifies the password; MAPIsend requires that a password is specified, even if it is a dummy password.

-R   Specifies the recipient or recipients of the message
            MAPIsend is sending. Separate multiple recipients with
            semicolons.

-C   Specifies cc recipients. Separate multiple cc recipients
            with semicolons.

-S   The message subject provided in quotes.

-M   The text of the message in quotes.

-F   Specifies file attachment. Separate multiple attachments
            with semicolons.

When specifying command-line options, there must be a space
between the command-line option and the parameter. A password must
be provided, though it is not required if the currently logged-on user has
ownership or Send As permissions to the mailbox. You can provide anything as a password. Make sure that the recipient that is specified in
the -R option is unique. If it is ambiguous, MAPIsend will not send the
message.

The best way to illustrate how to make MAPIsend work is to give you
an example of how I have used it. Every night, the Windows NT Backup
program creates a log file in the C:\WinNT directory called
backup.log. I want to automatically e-mail this backup report to a mailbox whose alias is HelpDesk.

I already have a batch file that runs every night and backs up the
Exchange server. It runs as a scheduled job under the Windows NT
Scheduler service. If I had not already done this, I would need to create a
new Windows NT user account called BACKUP and make it a member of
Account Operators.

I then need to select the Schedule service in Control Panel ➤ Services
and change the Log On As account to the user account BACKUP and provide BACKUP's password. I set the service to start automatically. I have
to do this because the Scheduler service will kick off the backup, and the
job will run under the Scheduler's security context. Therefore, the user
that Scheduler logs in as needs to have Backup Operator group membership.

Now I need to create a mailbox that will be used to send the nightly
tape backup reports. I call the mailbox BACKUP and assign the Windows
NT user BACKUP as the Primary Windows NT Account. I will give it a
display name of something like Tape Backup System. The BackOffice

Resource Kit documentation says you can give the Domain Users group ownership to this mailbox because it does not matter who uses it, but I feel uncomfortable if everyone in the domain has permission to send messages as this mailbox. There is no point in asking for trouble.

Next, I need to log in at the server (or wherever the Scheduler service is running) as the BACKUP user and create a messaging profile. I will call the profile BackupReport.

Finally, I am going to add the following command to the batch file that Schedule service runs nightly:

```
MAPISEND -u BACKUP -p boguspw -r HelpDesk -s "Nightly tape
backup report" -m "Tape Backup Report is attached." -f
c:\winnt\backup.log
```

This is just one example of how you can put this neat program to use. Consult the Microsoft BackOffice Resource Kit documentation for additional information.

Third-Party Reporting Tools

There are a number of tools that will help you when reporting on usage and activity within a large Exchange organization. Microsoft includes a limited copy of Seagate Crystal Reports with the Microsoft BackOffice Resource Kit. Crystal Reports can create quality reports using data from message tracking logs, address books, and e-mail messages.

NetIQ Corp. has a system called AppManager that is a comprehensive monitoring and reporting platform for Windows NT and NT-based applications such as Exchange Server. AppManager is a powerful tool to use if you are providing data to backup support levels specified in an SLA. AppManager provides features that allow an administrator to track end-to-end response time, identify top messaging system users, monitor queues, check sizes of queues, and report on general Windows NT performance.

EXCHANGE SERVICES

When an application is written, the programmer's name for it is often quite different than the name that the application is given in the documentation. Table 26.5 has a list of the common Exchange Server services, the short service name, and the executable filename.

TABLE 26.5: Exchange Server Services and Various Names Associated with Them

SERVICE NAME	SHORT NAME	EXECUTABLE NAME
Microsoft Exchange System Attendant	MSExchangeSA	mad.exe (short for Mailer Administrative Daemon)
Microsoft Exchange Directory	MSExchangeDS	dsamain.exe
Microsoft Exchange Information Store	MSExchangeIS	store.exe
Microsoft Exchange Event Service	MSExchangeES	events.exe
Microsoft Exchange Message Transfer Agent	MSExchangeMTA	emsmta.exe
Microsoft Exchange Internet Mail Service	MSExchangeIMC	msexcimc.exe
Microsoft Exchange Internet News Service	MSExchangeINS	exchins.exe
Microsoft Exchange Connector for cc:Mail	MSExchangeCCMC	ccmc.exe
MS Mail Connector Interchange	MSExchangeMSMI	mt.exe
Microsoft Exchange Directory Synchronization	MSExchangeDX	dxa.exe
MS Schedule+ Free/Busy Connector	MSExchangeFB	msfbconn.exe
Microsoft Exchange Key Management Server	MSExchangeKMS	kmserver.exe
Microsoft Exchange Connectivity Controller	MSExchangeCoCo	lscntrl.exe

NOTE

Most of the executable files in Table 26.5 are found in the \exchsrvr\bin directory, but some of the programs relating to connectors and gateways can be found in the \exchsrvr\Connect directory structure.

Service Dependencies

Before Exchange Server services can start, there are a number of Windows NT services that must be started, including Event Logging, NT LM Security Support Provider, Remote Procedure Call (RPC) Locator, Remote Procedure Call Service, Workstation, and Server.

Once the basic Windows NT services are started, the core Exchange Server services are started in this order:

1. Exchange System Attendant

2. Exchange directory service

3. Exchange information store

4. Exchange message transfer agent

5. Exchange event service (if installed)

6. Additional components as required

All Exchange services depend on the successful startup of the four Exchange Server core services (System Attendant, directory service, information store, and message transfer agent). All the core services depend on the System Attendant service.

EXCHANGE@WORK: SHUTTING DOWN THE EXCHANGE SERVER

Does it take a long time to shut down your Exchange server? Don't feel like you are alone if it does! I have seen Exchange servers that took as long as 10–20 minutes to shut down.

What is happening during this time? Well, in my experience, a lot of nothing. Don't get me wrong, there are things happening. When you execute a request to shut down Exchange Server, the Exchange services have to flush all buffers to disk, and all transaction logs need to have any outstanding transactions committed to disk. However, a lot of the long delay between when you order an Exchange server to shut down and when it actually shuts down is the old "hurry up and wait" syndrome. Here is what I suspect is happening.

CONTINUED ➡

Buried deep in parts of the Windows NT Registry that I don't care to visit or alter, there is a Registry value called WaitToKillService in the \HKLM\System\CurrentControlSet\Control key. The default for this value is 20000 milliseconds (20 seconds). Windows NT uses this value to specify how much advanced notice it is going to give system services before the system shuts down. This delay gives the service time to clean up before Windows NT shuts down. This also lets Windows NT shut the system down (and abort non-responsive services) without any guilt; Windows NT can say, "Gee, Mr. Service, I warned you I was shutting down. You should have hurried."

Once you install Exchange Server on a Windows NT server, this value is changed to 600,000 milliseconds (10 minutes). Microsoft increased this value for Exchange servers for a very specific reason: to allow all Exchange services time to flush data from memory, commit pending transactions, clean up, and shut down properly.

Several Exchange administrators I know advocate reducing this value back down to a lower value, such as 300,000 milliseconds (or about 5 minutes).

I remain skeptical about changing this value, and I would not change it on a server that supported more than 300 or 400 users or a server that had more than 256MB of RAM. This is due to the volume of transactions that might be in the logs and the potential amount of data that could be cached in buffers. Many people have reported to me that Windows NT 4 SP 4 improves shutdown times. This is supposedly due to an improved version of the service.exe program included with SP4.

So What Is the Best Practice for Shutting Down an Exchange Server?

I have found the fastest and most efficient way to shut down an Exchange server is to use the Control Panel ➤ Services application. Highlight the Microsoft Exchange System Attendant service and click the Stop button. You will be informed that, in order to stop the System Attendant, you must also shut down additional services. Click the OK button to initiate the shutdown.

CONTINUED ➡

Part v

If you wish to automate this process, you can stop these services from a command prompt. Here is a sample batch file that will shut down all the core Exchange services. You may have to add additional Exchange services from Table 26.5; you may use the service's full name or its short name. The long name must be in quotes:

```
@ECHO OFF
REM EXDOWN.CMD
REM Batch file to shutdown Exchange services
NET STOP MSExchangeIMC /Y
NET STOP MSExchangeES /Y
NET STOP MSExchangeMTA /Y
NET STOP MSExchangeIS /Y
NET STOP MSExchangeDS /Y
NET STOP MSExchangeSA /Y
```

Once an Exchange server begins its shutdown process, *never* power off the system until the shutdown process is complete. You risk corrupting the database files.

FOR FURTHER INFORMATION

For additional and more in-depth information about the topics covered in this chapter, check out these resources:

▶ You can refer to the Microsoft Windows NT Server Resource Kit and the Microsoft BackOffice Resource Kit (Second Edition).

▶ Microsoft Certified Technical Education Centers (CTEC) offer an excellent class called Windows NT 4.0 Enterprise Technologies, which covers the Network Monitor, Performance Monitor, Windows NT troubleshooting, and Windows NT domain design.

▶ You can learn more about Seagate Software's Crystal Reports on the Web at www.seagate.com.

▶ You can find more information about NetIQ Corp.'s AppManager product at www.netiq.com.

WHAT'S NEXT?

This chapter discussed the tools available for monitoring and reporting on Exchange Server activities. The next chapter explains the interoperability issues to keep in mind when configuring connections that will send messages out of your Exchange organization and into the world of SMTP or X.400.

Chapter 27

Exchange Internet Interoperability

I n 1990, I was working for a systems integration company in Northern California; our clients were just beginning to install LAN-based e-mail systems. After a few months of usage, the clients all wanted to know "Who else can we send e-mail to using our mail system? Can we send mail to vendors and customers?" At that time, the standard in messaging interoperability was X.400. We installed a number of MCI Mail and AT&T Mail (both X.400 networks) gateways for our clients so that they could e-mail the world. As a matter of fact, it looked like X.400 was going to take over the messaging world.

Adapted from *Exchange Server 5.5 24seven™*
by Jim McBee
ISBN 0-7821-2505-0   657 pages $34.99

Interest in sending e-mail over the Internet was still only a distant light on the horizon. Customers were not interested in global messaging as much as they were interested in sending mail only to a few select customers. Both MCI Mail and AT&T Mail would let you do this, but the address was not pretty. X.400 addresses were long, difficult to remember, and easy to mistype.

In 1992, interest in the Internet began to take hold. This was much to the chagrin of many people who had been using the Internet for e-mail for nearly 10 years already. However, the interest in using the Internet for general business mail was not widespread until late 1993 when the first Web browsers began to become popular and more people began to get their own e-mail addresses.

Within a few short years, SMTP had replaced X.400 as the de facto standard in business messaging for most of the world. As a result, Exchange Server was designed tightly around SMTP and X.400 environments and integrates quite well in both.

There are a few interoperability issues to keep in mind when configuring connections that will send messages out of your Exchange organization and into the world of SMTP or X.400. These topics are the focus of this chapter and include:

- E-mail and recipient addressing
- Advanced features of the Internet Mail Service (IMS)
- Preventing junk mail
- Security features of the IMS
- Avoiding garbage and unknown attachment types in messages
- IMS management tips

E-MAIL AND RECIPIENT ADDRESSING

For each connector installed on a server, a proxy address generator is installed that is used to create recipients' e-mail addresses. The rules that the proxy generators use to create e-mail addresses for a mailbox are found in the Site Addressing object (shown in Figure 27.1) at the site level; choose *Site Name* ➤ Configuration, open the Site Addressing object property page, and view the Site Addressing tab.

You can edit the e-mail addresses seen in Figure 27.1 to change how new addresses are created; if you edit or disable any of these addresses, you will be asked if you wish to update that address for all recipients. If you answer yes, a process starts updating the particular address type you have changed. The System Attendant service is responsible for generating the proxy addresses.

You can edit the X.400 address's country (c), administrative management domain (a), private management domain (p), and organizational unit (ou) fields, but you cannot change which fields are used for the surname (s), given name (g), or other X.400 fields.

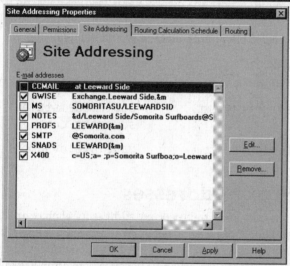

FIGURE 27.1: Site addressing properties; only SMTP and X.400 addresses are required.

However, you can edit the address defaults for many of the addresses including the SMTP connector. In Figure 27.1, all SMTP addresses created are going to be `alias@Somorita.com`. There are several fields that you can use instead of the alias by substituting another field. If there are spaces or illegal characters, they are removed. Here are some substitutions that you can make:

Substitution	Meaning
%d	Use the display name of the user
%s	Use the surname of the user
%g	Use the given name of the user
%m	Use the mailbox name (alias) of the user
%i	Use the initials of the user

Further, you can place a number in front of the substitution value if you want only so many characters from that substitution. For example, if you created a mailbox with the display name Dodie Edelstein, first name Dodie and last name Edelstein, some examples that would be generated if you edited the SMTP address would include:

Substitution	Result
%2s %g@somorita.com	EdDodie@somorita.com
%g.%s@somorita.com	Dodie.Edelstein@somorita.com
%1g %s@somorita.com	Dedelstein@somorita.com

Secondary Proxy Addresses

Each mailbox has only one primary proxy address for each connector type that is installed. If you wish to generate additional proxy addresses (called *secondary* proxy addresses), you must do so manually. I hope this changes in a future release of Exchange, because I am often asked how to do this.

Creating secondary proxy addresses can be done on a per-mailbox level, or you can export your addresses to a comma-separated value (CSV) file, insert the addresses in that file, and then import the file once again. Figure 27.2 shows the E-mail Addresses tab for a mailbox. The address that is in bold is the primary proxy address, or the Reply To address. Notice that there are additional SMTP addresses for this mailbox.

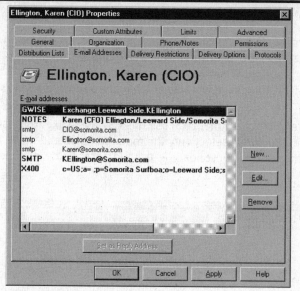

FIGURE 27.2:   E-mail addresses for Karen Ellington's mailbox

EXCHANGE@WORK: ADDING SECONDARY PROXY ADDRESSES IN BULK

Suppose I have to create secondary proxy addresses for all of my users. Well, I can go through the directory one mailbox at a time and add the addresses, but that is going to be a major pain if I have to do more than 10 or 20 mailboxes. To illustrate a way to do this, I'll use a procedure that I do quite often.

Let's say that Somorita Surfboards has just consolidated their North American operations into the Exchange organization, and they want all Internet mail to be addressed to Somorita.com. However, the folks in North America have had their own Internet domain name (NAmerica.Somorita.com) for a couple of years, and they want to continue to receive messages from their old addresses for a while.

CONTINUED ➡

Well, first of all, on the Site Addressing property page (shown in Figure 27.1), I set the North America's SMTP site address to @Somorita.com. When new mailboxes are created, this will be their default address; it will also be everyone's Reply To address.

Next, I use the Header.exe utility from the BackOffice Resource Kit to create a header file; I will use this CSV file to export aliases from the directory. I select only the required fields and the Alias Name, then add the Secondary-Proxy-Addresses fields, as shown here:

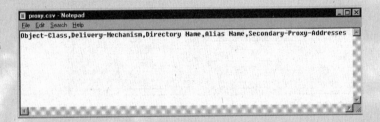

(I selected the alias since that is the name in the e-mail address, regardless of whether it was the old address or the new address. Of course, it could be different, but I am keeping it simple for this example.)

Using the Exchange Administrator, I export all my mailboxes to the CSV file I have just created (Tools ➢ Export). Though I could edit it using Notepad, it will probably be easier to do using Excel or a database program since I have to make many changes at once. I want to be able to handle the changes using a macro or script.

In the following window, you see that I have retrieved the CSV file into Excel 97. Notice that mailbox KEllington already has some values in the Secondary-Proxy-Addresses field; I had manually added these earlier. As a matter of fact, this mailbox has several secondary proxy addresses, all separated by a percent sign (%).

CONTINUED ➡

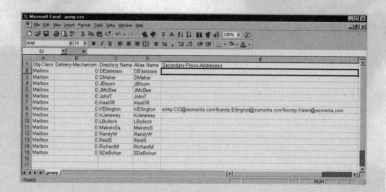

Part V

While in Excel, I can manually edit each of the fields and insert the new SMTP addresses, or I can run an Excel macro on the file and create new secondary addresses for all the users. Once the file is updated to contain the secondary addresses, I can use the Exchange Administrator program to import (Tools ≻ Import) the file back into the Exchange directory.

ADVANCED FEATURES OF THE INTERNET MAIL SERVICE

Originally, Microsoft shipped Exchange Server 4 with a connector called the Internet Mail Connector (IMC). When Microsoft began to realize the importance of the Internet and Internet technologies, they began improving Exchange Server's Internet Mail Service (IMS). It became more tightly integrated with the information store service—and much more efficient. With Exchange Server 5, Microsoft renamed the Internet Mail Connector to Internet Mail Service. (You can still see traces of the IMC lying around, such as the service short name MSExchangeIMC and the program name msexcimc.exe.)

I was recently working on an Exchange Server 4 IMC and was surprised by how many new features are now available in the Exchange 5.5

IMS that I had just taken for granted. These features that take the IMS beyond just simple Internet mail transfer include:

▶ Anti-spam tools to help prevent junk mail

▶ Tools to allow mail retrieval that may be stored at an ISP so that you don't have to have a full-time connection to the Internet to receive Internet mail

▶ Better controls for message content and message conversion

▶ Greatly improved IMS security features to better control who you can send mail to and the security of those messages during transfer

NOTE

The Exchange Server IMS acts as both an SMTP client and server. However, products such as Outlook Express, Netscape Communicator, and other IMAP4/POP3 products are only SMTP clients.

Preventing Unsolicited Commercial E-mail

Every day I get between 10 and 15 pieces of junk mail, more commonly known as unsolicited commercial e-mail (UCE) or spam. And I don't get as many as some people I know; one friend counted 50 junk messages in a single day! One of the challenges facing messaging administrators is preventing these messages from using up your Internet bandwidth and disk storage.

Figure 27.3 shows a message of questionable taste and content that I received recently. The left side of Figure 27.3 shows the message, and the right side shows the Internet headers (View ➢ Options in Outlook 98/2000). Upon first examination, the URL and IP address in this message looks bogus, but it's not. The address is called a *dotless IP address* because the IP address in binary has been converted to one large number rather than the dotted decimal address (for example, 192.168.54.10) that you are used to seeing. This can be a potential security hole as it may fool your Internet Explorer into believing that the address is on your intranet. See Microsoft Security Bulletin MS98-016 for more information.

The above message could have gone out to thousands or even millions of people, wasting bandwidth, disk storage, and people's time. You can see why people who send these things are the lowest of the low pond scum on the Internet.

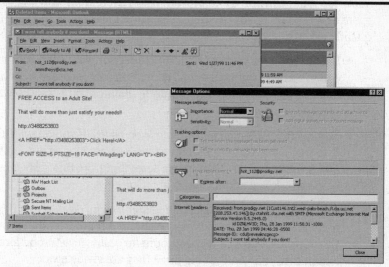

FIGURE 27.3: A sample UCE message and the message's Internet headers

How Did This Happen to Me? I'm Really a Nice Guy!

Typical spam messages advertise stock deals, pager services, get-rich-quick schemes, miracle weight loss programs, cures for baldness, cheap vacations, adult Web sites, and more. The fact that I did not ask for any of this garbage makes it unsolicited. It makes me wonder, "How did they get my e-mail address? What have I done to deserve this?"

Well, for starters, I quite frequently post on the Usenet newsgroups. I used to use my real e-mail address; now I use something like JMcBee@Somorita.Com.NoSpam (newsgroup-savvy users will realize what my real address is if they want to send me a message directly). The folks who collect these addresses scan newsgroups looking for addresses; they call this "harvesting." My e-mail address is also posted on several Web sites, and spam companies will often scan Web pages looking for the `<a ref="mailto:jmcbee@somorita.com">` HTML tag.

Stopping Spam

What can you do to prevent spammers from getting your e-mail address? What can you do to prevent advertisers from wanting to use spam as a method of advertising? Here are some answers to these frequently asked questions:

- ▶ Don't configure your newsgroup reader software with your real e-mail address; put your e-mail address in your message signature instead. (Good newsgroup etiquette dictates you should always identify yourself when you post.)

- ▶ Don't put your e-mail address on Web pages. If you do, disguise it so that it is easy for a human to see, but hard for an automated process to decipher. I like to use something like this: "My e-mail name is JMcBee and my domain is Somorita.Com."

- ▶ Avoid filling out surveys and "register to win" Web pages if you don't know the company whose Web site you're currently viewing. Or set yourself up a Hotmail account for online registration forms, just in case you win that big prize they are giving away.

- ▶ Don't be tempted to reply to the message; it will either go nowhere, or the reply will be automatically accepted, confirming that your address is good and can be used again. Many spam messages tell you that they will remove you from their list if you reply with the word "Remove" in the subject or body. I have seen my volume of spam increase dramatically when I have tried this. Remember that these people have no Internet etiquette.

- ▶ Complain to the advertisers, not the spammers. If the message contains an 800 number, call it and complain. I know a few people who have used demon dialers to call those 800 numbers hundreds or thousands of times. I don't recommend this approach, but it does seem like poetic justice.

Understanding SMTP Headers

The SMTP header is the part of a mail message that defines not only who the message is sent to and from, but also information such as the subject, sending message system type, date sent, and MIME information. The Received field identifies the hosts that the message crossed during its journey through the Internet. Quite often, you will only see a single

Received entry. However, some messages can have several Received fields. A sample of an SMTP header looks like this:

```
Received: from emh.Misawa.AF.MIL ([132.20.128.128]) by
ctahn11.cta.net with SMTP (Microsoft Exchange Internet Mail
Service Version 5.5.2448.0)
id FA030TY4; Wed, 17 Feb 1999 17:14:46 -1000
Received: from gw5.misawa.af.mil (gw5.Misawa.AF.MIL
[132.20.123.35])
by emh.misawa.af.mil (8.8.8/8.8.8) with SMTP id KAA25253
    for <JMcBee@cta.net>; Thu, 18 Feb 1999 10:43:32 +0900
Received: from Misawa-Message_Server by gw5.misawa.af.mil
with Novell_GroupWise; Thu, 18 Feb 1999 11:39:52 +0900
Message-Id: <s6cbfc08.080@gw5.misawa.af.mil>
X-Mailer: Novell GroupWise 4.1
Date: Thu, 18 Feb 1999 12:39:29 +0900
From: "SrA Benjamin D. Craig"
<Benjamin_Craig@gw5.misawa.af.mil>
To: JMcBee@cta.net
Subject: Exchange Service Level Agreements
Mime-Version: 1.0
Content-Type: text/plain
Content-Disposition: inline
```

Notice that there are three Received fields. The ultimate originating host of this message was a host called gw5.misawa.af.mil. However, this host handed the message off to a host called emh.misawa.af.mil, which delivered it to ctahn11.cta.net. The example shown in Figure 27.3 actually originated from a node on uu.net's network, which may or may not be part of Prodigy's network. If I were reporting the spam messages to someone, I would start with the administrators at uu.net.

TIP

If you are tracking down the originating point of a spam message, make sure you give the headers a careful look. The originating point of the message can be deceptive.

Filtering Junk Mail Using the Internet Mail Service

Exchange Server's Internet Mail Service allows you to filter and reject mail based on two criteria: the source IP address and the originator's address. Neither of these is extraordinarily effective, because one rarely receives an unsolicited message from the same address twice. However, these tools are certainly better than no tools at all.

Message Filtering   Exchange Server 5.5 introduced *message filtering*, which allows you to reject messages based on either the originating domain name or the originator's full e-mail address. This is configured for each IMS that you have installed. To edit or view the list of restricted domains and senders, display the IMS properties and choose the Connections tab, then click the Message Filtering button.

NOTE
The Message Filtering button only appears with Exchange Server 5.5 SP1 or greater. If you do not have this service pack installed, review the readme at the root of the Exchange Server CD.

The Message Filtering dialog box (see Figure 27.4) allows you to configure which senders and domains the IMS rejects. The IMS simply accepts the message and deletes it; no non-delivery notification is generated. To reject messages from an entire domain, in the Prevent These Domains And Users dialog box, make sure the @ sign is in front of the domain name (such as @Prodigy.net). Every time you add new domains and users to this list, restart the IMS for your changes to take effect.

The Delete Messages Instead Of Moving To The Turf Directory check box is used to automatically delete messages instead of saving them. It is possible to set up a directory to collect these messages in case you want to inspect them prior to deletion. To do this, clear the check box and create a directory such as C:\TURFDIR.

Edit the Registry to point the IMC to this directory. Locate the \HKLM\System\CurrentControlSet\Services\MSExchangeIMC\Parameters Registry key and add a new value called TurfDir with a data type of REG_SZ. In the string dialog box, type in the path to the directory you created, such as **C:\TURFDIR**. Restart the Internet Mail Service for the change to take effect.

Each time an inbound message is "turfed," you will see event ID 4142 generated by the MSExchangeIMC service, which will tell you why the message was not delivered and the name of the file if you want to view it.

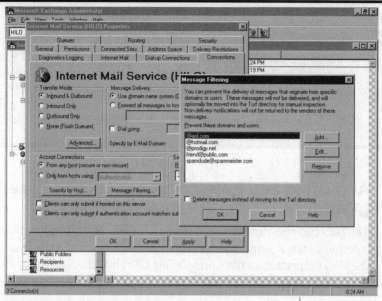

FIGURE 27.4: IMS Message Filtering dialog box

EXCHANGE@WORK: REJECTING MAIL FROM THE BIG SPAM DOMAINS

You may have noticed in Figure 27.4 that the list of restricted domains included @prodigy.net. This is becoming prevalent as junk mail becomes more common. Companies are rejecting junk mail from the "big spam" domains such as Hotmail, Prodigy, and America Online.

I communicate daily with people who use these services for their legitimate e-mail addresses, so I can see the point of messaging administrators. Junk mail senders are often using these services to send large quantities of mail. But the address you see in the From field is usually spoofed, so the message may not really have come from Hotmail after all. However, I still feel that the administrators of these big messaging systems should do more to control users sending large numbers of the same message through their system.

CONTINUED ➡

Part of the problem is that there is very little authentication or verification that happens when one host sends another host an e-mail message—but this is changing. Many SMTP mail systems now will not accept a message from another SMTP system unless the sender's DNS address record (the A record) matches the name found in the reverse lookup table (the PTR record).

Accepting and Rejecting Connections Based on IP Addresses

The IMS can also examine each inbound IP address and determine whether or not it wants to accept the connection. This is configured from the IMS properties on the Connections tab; click the Specify By Host button to see the Specify Hosts dialog box (see Figure 27.5).

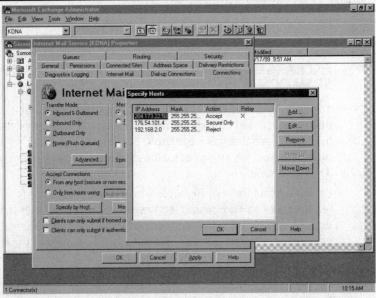

FIGURE 27.5:   Use the Specify Hosts dialog box to control which hosts are accepted by the IMS.

From within the Specify Hosts dialog box, you can control which hosts are accepted and rejected based on their IP address. You can specify which hosts to accept messages from and whether or not that host is a mail relay host. Further, you can specify hosts from whom you will reject messages as well as IP addresses that can only connect to this IMS if they are using authentication and/or encryption.

In Figure 27.5, all connections from network 192.168.2.0 (all hosts on this network) will be rejected, connections from IP address 176.54.101.4 will be accepted only if they are authenticated and/or encrypted, and connections from IP address 204.173.22.50 will be accepted. Host 204.173.22.50 is marked as a relay host, so messages from many domains will be relayed through this host.

Using the IMS without a Full-Time Internet Connection

Many smaller companies cannot afford a full-time connection to the Internet. Unfortunately, SMTP was originally designed under the assumption that all SMTP servers will be online all the time (or at least most of the time). Later, a new command for SMTP was developed called TURN, but it was implemented only with limited success, partially due to security concerns.

RFC 1985 now defines the SMTP command ETRN (Enhanced TURN), which allows an SMTP client to connect to an SMTP server that has been queuing mail for the client and issue the ETRN command. The SMTP server will then deliver any queued messages to the SMTP client.

Sound good? Sure, ETRN works great, but there are some things to keep in mind as you configure it. On the Exchange side, you must be running Exchange 5 SP1 or later. If the host that is queuing mail for you is Unix-based, it must support sendmail 8.8.x or later.

Configuring ETRN

There are a number of steps involved in getting ETRN working; you will have to work closely with your Internet Service Provider (ISP) or whoever is going to be queuing your mail until you connect. To show an example of how to configure ETRN, I am going to use my favorite pseudo-organization, Somorita Surfboards. Somorita wants to get connected for Internet mail, and they have an Exchange server with the IMS configured on it.

Let's begin our journey by exploring the steps the ISP must take in the configuration process.

Configuring ETRN at the ISP   The ISP must first allocate a static IP address on a dial-in modem or ISDN port. Usually, this means that the ISP has given (well, rented) a dedicated telephone line to Somorita that will be theirs and theirs alone. Let's say they assign Somorita 204.175.131.45; this is an IP address on one of their 56K modems. They take the telephone number for that modem and give it exclusively to Somorita.

Next, the ISP has to make some entries in the DNS server that contains the Somorita.com data files. (I am assuming the same ISP manages Somorita's DNS server; if not, whoever manages the DNS server will have to make these entries.) The entries will look something like this:

```
Exchange.Somorita.com. A  204.175.131.45
Somorita.com      MX 10     Exchange.Somorita.com
Somorita.com      MX 20     mailrelay.ispname.com
```

The first entry identifies the IP address (A) record of the Exchange server. The second line is a message exchange (MX) record and says that all mail that is sent to the domain Somorita.com should be directed to the host Exchange.Somorita.com. The number 10 is a preference or weighting; the preference controls which host the sender will try first. The third line indicates that if the host Exchange.Somorita.com is not available (which it usually will not be since it is a dial-up), deliver the mail to the host mailrelay.ispname.com, which in this case is the ISP's mail relay server.

The ISP may also have to configure its Unix system to store mail for your domain. Exchange Server 5 SP1 and later can be configured to queue messages for ETRN clients; if the ISP is using Exchange Server and the IMS, they can configure the IMS to queue mail for your domain. This is done on the IMS Connections property page; click the E-mail Domain, then click Add. Enter the domain name, and then click the Queue Messages For ETRN check box.

Configuring ETRN on the Exchange Server   Once your ISP has configured its side, you must first configure the Dial-Up Networking software on the Exchange server that's running the IMS. If you have not previously installed the Dial-Up Networking software, don't forget to reinstall the Windows NT service pack. Once you have the Dial-Up Networking software installed, create a dialing entry for your ISP using the telephone number they provided for you. Test this entry and make sure you can connect to the Internet while dialed in; my litmus test is whether or not I can browse the Internet using Internet Explorer (and Fully Qualified Domain Names, not just IP addresses).

Next, the IMS needs to be configured to reflect that it is going to have to relay all outgoing mail to a mail relay host and pick up mail queued for it.

On the IMS Connections property page, the Message Delivery section has a radio button called Forward All Messages To Host. In the case of the Somorita Surfboards example, I would click this radio button and enter **mailrelay.ispname.com** (if I knew the IP address, I could use that as well) in the box directly below the check box. This will cause the IMS to deliver *all* outgoing mail to the mail relay server at the ISP.

Then, on the IMS Dial-Up Connections property page, I need to configure the dial-up connection properties. Figure 27.6 shows the Dial-Up Connections property page on the left and the Mail Retrieval dialog box on the right. The Mail Retrieval dialog box is opened by clicking the Mail Retrieval button on the Dial-Up Connections property page. The Mail Retrieval button specifies how the SMTP client will retrieve mail from the SMTP server.

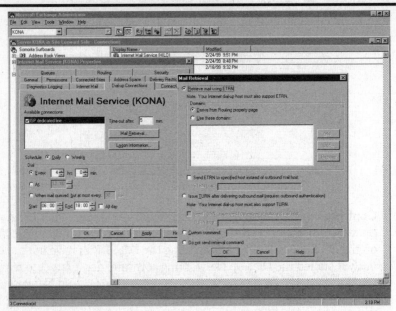

FIGURE 27.6: The IMS Dial-Up Connections tab and Mail Retrieval dialog box

The Dial-Up Connections property page has quite a few options:

The **Available connections** list allows you to select the Dial-Up Networking connection for your ISP. This must have been created and tested prior to configuring the IMS.

The **Time-out after** box is the amount of time to keep the RAS connection open after all the outbound mail has been sent. This should be long enough to give the system to which your server issued the ETRN command enough time to start transmitting queued messages. If you set this value too high, though, it is possible that the connection will never hang up. Somewhere between five and ten minutes should be sufficient.

The **Mail Retrieval** button opens the Mail Retrieval dialog box which is used to configure the connection for ETRN or TURN.

The **Logon Information** button allows you to specify the user account and password information at the ISP.

The **Schedule** radio buttons allow you to determine whether the ISP connection will be made every day (Daily) or only certain days of the week (Weekly). If you choose weekly, you will have additional check boxes for Monday through Friday and the option of disabling the connection on the weekend.

The **Dial** section is used to determine how often to connect to the ISP. Within the Dial section, you have several different options:

Every specifies that the connection is made at specified intervals regardless of whether or not there is outgoing mail. For most installations, I would use this selection and specify a value of two hours.

At specifies the connection will be made only at a certain time of the day. This is useful if you want to connect only once per day.

When mail queued, but at most every selection specifies that a connection will be made every time there is mail waiting to be transferred outbound. However, the outbound connections will not occur more often than the specified number of minutes.

The **All Day** check box, when selected, means those connections will be made 24 hours a day. If you clear the All Day check box, you can specify the times when connections will be made and when they will not be made.

For most installations, once the Internet Mail Service is set to retrieve messages using ETRN and to route all outgoing messages to the ISP, and the dial-up connection is configured, there are usually few additional options you need to set. However, the Mail Retrieval dialog box allows you to further customize mail retrieval. The options found in the Mail Retrieval dialog box have the following functions:

Retrieve mail using ETRN causes the ETRN command to be issued to the host listed in the Forward All Messages To Host box on the Connections tab.

The **Domains** section allows you to specify the domain names that will be requested when the ETRN connection is made. By default, the domain names are found on the Routing tab, but you can specify your own list.

Send ETRN to specified host instead of outbound mail host allows you to override which host the ETRN command is sent to. The IMS assumes that the same host that it sends all out-bound mail to is the same one that queues messages for retrieval.

Issue TURN after delivering outbound mail allows you to use the TURN command instead of ETRN.

Custom Command can be used to issue a mail retrieval command for systems that do not support ETRN.

ETRN and Dial-on-Demand Routers

While the easiest way to configure ETRN is using Dial-Up Networking, it is also possible to use a dial-on-demand router. If you have configured a dial-on-demand router, messages will be sent out anytime they need to be delivered to the host designated in the Forward All Messages To Host option on the Connections tab.

However, since Dial-Up Networking is not used, the ETRN command will not be issued when outbound messages are sent. You can configure the IMS to always use the ETRN command when it connects to an SMTP host. This configuration must be made through the Registry.

To do so, locate the \HKLM\System\CurrentControlSet\ Services\MSExchangeIMS\Parameters Registry key and create a new value called AlwaysUseETRN with a data type of REG_DWORD. In the data field, enter **1** to set the IMS to always send the ETRN command or **0** to never send the ETRN command.

NOTE

This solution works great as long as messages are being sent outbound, but what happens if no messages are going to the outbound mail relay host? You need to create some type of process that will periodically generate a bogus message and send it out to the Internet. You can do this with the Exchange link monitor functionality, or you can create a scheduled job using the Windows NT schedule service and the mapisend.exe utility from the BackOffice Resource Kit.

Message Interoperability

Users are often going to call you and ask about a particular attachment on a message that originated from the Internet. This is probably because the transmitting system did not properly convert the message into a format that your mail clients can understand. As an act of good Internet etiquette, you don't want to send users messages that contain unknown attachment types or attachment types that are not usable.

Within an Exchange site or organization, messages are transported using a Microsoft encoding format called Messaging Database Encoding Format (MDBEF). The message remains in this format as long as the message is being transported using RPCs, the site connector, the dynamic RAS connector, or the X.400 connector, and it is staying within the Exchange organization. When a message leaves the Exchange organization, it has to be converted to a format that the receiving system can understand.

If a message is to be delivered via SMTP, or if it is being read by an IMAP4, NNTP, or POP3 client, an information store process called IMAIL converts the message to the appropriate format. IMAIL is also responsible for converting messages that have been delivered via SMTP or NNTP before they are stored in the information store. Messages are always stored in the public and private information store database in MDBEF format.

When messages are transported across a non-Microsoft connector, such as the IMS, the messages are converted to another encoding format called Transport Neutral Encapsulation Format (TNEF). Messages transported using TNEF have an extra attachment associated with them that describes all the rich text formatting such as bold, italic, font changes, and so on that may be in the message text. When a message arrives at its destination, the mail client must understand how to reassemble the messages back to its original appearance. If the mail client does not understand this formatting, then an extra attachment will appear on the message. This attachment will often appear as an unknown file type, though its MIME content type is *application/ms-tnef*. If non-Microsoft clients receive messages with unknown or application/ms-tnef attachments, you can bet that someone sent them a message formatted with rich text.

Inbound Internet Messages

Messages that are delivered to the IMS are automatically converted from the standard Internet message formats to an Exchange MDBEF message. The IMS recognizes MIME and uuencode.

If a message arrives that has unknown attachment types, then it is quite possibly the sending system that did not convert the message properly. Alternatively, the problem might be that the sender is sending you a

MIME type that your IMS does not recognize and therefore does not associate the correct extension with.

Figure 27.7 shows the MIME Types tab of the Protocols container. From this page you can create, edit, and delete MIME types.

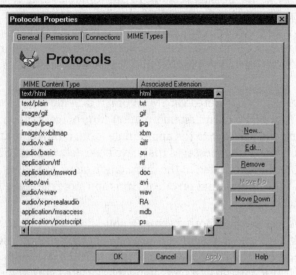

FIGURE 27.7: The Protocols container's MIME Types tab

You can configure MIME types for the entire site (*Site Name* ➤ Configuration ➤ Protocols Container properties ➤ MIME Types tab) or for each individual server (*Site Name* ➤ Configuration ➤ Servers ➤ *Server Name* ➤ Protocols Container properties ➤ MIME Types tab).

Resetting the MIME Database Okay, for some reason you've trashed your Exchange server's MIME settings; this can happen if you accidentally delete or edit an item. It can also happen if you install Internet Explorer 4 *after you have already installed Exchange Server.*

There is a utility on the Exchange Server CD-ROM that resets the MIME database to its defaults. The utility filename is `reset.inf`, and it is found in the `\Server\Support\MIMEDB` directory of the CD. To reset the MIME database, locate the file, right-click it, and choose Install.

Outbound Internet Messages

Unfortunately, the IMS cannot automatically determine the correct format to convert a message to when transferring a message to another host. By default, the Exchange IMS sends all messages out as plain-text, MIME messages. The IMS Internet Mail property page has a section called Message Content that controls what default message type is used when sending out an SMTP message.

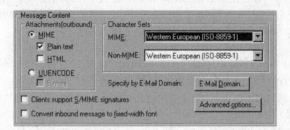

I recommend leaving the default attachment type as MIME; it is now the de facto standard for SMTP messaging, and all modern systems support it. If you need to support MHTML or MIME Encapsulated HMTL, select the HTML check box under the MIME radio button. MHTML allows HTML attachments to be encapsulated in MIME messages and allows the format of HTML pages to be preserved.

The E-mail Domain button allows you to override the default attachment, character set, and other message options on a per domain basis.

On the Message Content section of the Internet Mail property page, there is an Advanced Options button. Clicking this button opens the Advanced Options dialog box:

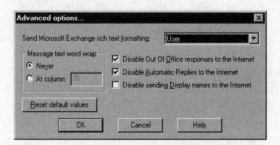

From the Advanced Options dialog box, you can specify whether or not the IMS will send out messages as rich text. The default is user-specified, but you can override this by specifying Always or Never in the

Send Microsoft Exchange Rich Text Formatting drop-down list box. I recommend leaving this selection at User. You can override this per domain.

The Advanced Options dialog box also allows you to specify whether or not Automatic Replies and Out Of Office messages are always sent out to the Internet. This feature should probably be left disabled except in special cases; for most people who send me messages, I don't want to advertise the fact that I am on vacation. However, keep this tidbit in the back of your mind, because if automatic responses to the Internet are disabled, then no client or public folder rules will be allowed to automatically send responses back to the Internet.

User-Specified Rich Text Formatting   If a user wishes to send an Internet recipient messages using rich text formatting, she can specify this when she addresses the message or in her Outlook Contacts folder. To do the latter, the user locates the SMTP address either in the To field or in the Outlook Contacts folder, right-clicks the SMTP address, and chooses Properties. The SMTP Address property page opens; the user then clicks the check box that says Always Send To This Recipient In Microsoft Outlook Rich-Text Format.

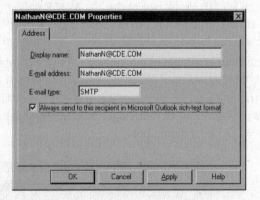

As an administrator, you can also specify to send rich text messages to custom recipients. On the Custom Recipient object's Advanced property page, enable the Allow Rich Text In Messages option.

EXCHANGE@WORK: OVERRIDING MESSAGE TYPE BY DOMAIN

XYZ Corporation made heavy use of its Internet Mail Service to many customers and vendors. When XYZ Corporation began doing a lot of business with Company CDE, they exchanged a lot of e-mail messages. Company CDE was also using Exchange Server and the Outlook 98 client.

The messages that traveled back and forth between the two companies were highly formatted, but the users at XYZ were forgetting to specify to send rich text formatting to users at CDE. Users complained that they couldn't always remember to select RTF when sending the message or to make the changes in their personal address books. Further, users in both companies wanted to be able to have Out Of Office messages and automatic replies sent between the two companies.

XYZ and CDE administrators to the rescue: They decided to create an exception to the standard user-defined rich text formatting. They did this by using the E-mail Domain button on the Internet Mail tab of the IMS property page. By clicking Add, they were able to add new domains to this exception list.

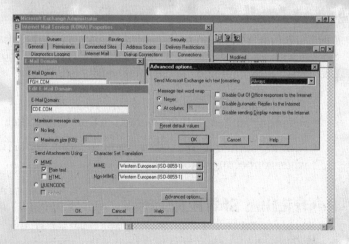

On the Edit E-mail Domain dialog box, the XYZ administrator specified CDE.COM in the E-mail Domain box, then clicked the Advanced Options button. In the Advanced Options dialog box, the XYZ administrator cleared the Disable Out Of Office Responses To The Internet

CONTINUED ➡

and the Disable Automatic Replies To The Internet check boxes and set the Send Microsoft Exchange Rich Text Formatting drop-down list box to Always.

Once the Internet Mail Service was stopped and restarted, the users at XYZ no longer had to remember to specify rich text formatting for addresses at CDE.COM. And Out Of Office and Automatic Replies will be sent to addresses at CDE.COM.

XYZ Corp later used the same feature again except this time it was to send all mail to a specific domain using uuencode. Older SMTP gateways and clients do not handle MIME messages; messages were being delivered to a company that had clients that did not support MIME, but they were getting MIME messages. Well, the message was formatted as a MIME message, but the user saw a lot of garbage characters.

So the ability to override message types sent to specified domains can be quite useful in a number of different ways.

Internet Mail Service and Security

Microsoft first introduced basic security features into the Internet Mail Service with Exchange Server 5. With Exchange 5.5, the security capabilities have greatly improved. These new security features include:

- ▶ Restricting SMTP relay
- ▶ Requiring authentication/encryption from SMTP clients
- ▶ Sending authentication/encryption requests to SMTP servers when connecting outbound

Restricting SMTP Relay

The Exchange IMS is capable of acting as a relay server; this means that it will deliver any message that is submitted to it regardless of the message's origin or where it is to be delivered. This capability is required if you have IMAP4 and POP3 clients. The IMAP4 and POP3 protocols are "retrieve only" protocols, meaning that these protocols can only be used to retrieve messages from a message store. IMAP4 and POP3 clients

Part v

deliver their outbound messages to an SMTP server, which in turn relays the messages to their ultimate Internet destination.

Figure 27.8 shows the IMS Routing tab for Somorita Surfboard's Exchange server. The Reroute Incoming SMTP Mail radio button is selected.

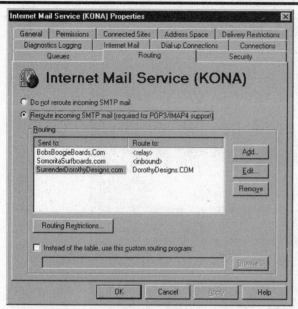

FIGURE 27.8: The server highlighted here will relay any message submitted to it.

The IMS in Figure 27.8 is wide open as far as mail relay is concerned; anyone can submit a message to this server for delivery, including someone who wants to use your server to send 10 million spam messages. The solution is to turn off mail relay using the Do Not Reroute Incoming SMTP Mail radio button. From that point forward, the IMS will only accept or relay messages for the domains specified in the Routing box. You can add, edit, and delete domains that will be accepted as inbound or relayed.

WARNING

If your IMS permits SMTP relay from anyone, you are inviting unscrupulous spammers to use your server for mail relay.

However, turning off mail relay will break any IMAP4 or POP3 clients that were using this Exchange server to relay mail. A new feature was included in Exchange 5.5 that allows you to restrict which IP addresses your IMS will reroute messages for. If you click the Routing Restrictions button on the IMS Routing tab, the Routing Restrictions dialog box will appear (see Figure 27.9).

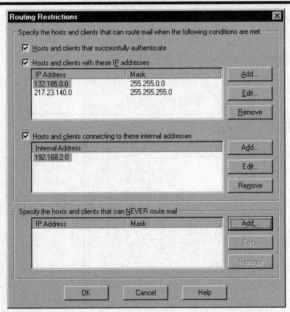

FIGURE 27.9: The IMS Routing Restrictions dialog box

From the Routing Restrictions dialog box, you can enable only certain clients or IP addresses for which the IMS will relay messages. The options on this dialog box include the following:

Hosts and clients that successfully authenticate requires a IMAP4, POP3, or SMTP client that supports authentication, such as Outlook Express on the IMAP4 and POP3 side and other Exchange Internet Mail Services on the SMTP side.

Hosts and clients with these IP addresses is quite useful if you want to restrict SMTP relay only within your own network, but not the outside world. Many ISPs have such restrictions turned on for their SMTP systems.

Hosts and clients connecting to these internal addresses allows you to specify the IP addresses through which a client can connect to the IMS and have messages relayed. This is useful if the Exchange server is multihomed and you want only hosts on your internal network to be able to submit messages for SMTP relay.

Specify the hosts and clients that can NEVER route mail is pretty self-explanatory. If your IP address is on this list, you are not going to be able to submit messages to the IMS for message relay.

NOTE

These restrictions only affect SMTP clients. They do not affect Outlook clients (MAPI clients), which submit messages to the information store service, not the IMS, for delivery.

Requiring Authentication and Encryption from Clients

Under many circumstances you many need to require some or all SMTP clients to authenticate and possibly encrypt their data during transmission. This is enabled on the Connections tab of the IMS property page in the Accept Connections section.

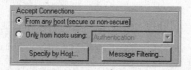

The default choice is to accept connections From Any Host (Secure Or Non-Secure). For an Exchange IMS that is connected to the Internet for general usage, you should keep the default setting. If you select the Only From Hosts Using radio button you can select Authentication, Encryption, or Authentication and Encryption.

If you select a choice that includes Authentication, you must create a Windows NT account and password and provide this information to the administrator of the SMTP server. They must then configure their SMTP server to authenticate using that user ID and password.

TIP

If you are going to send Windows NT accounts and passwords over a public network, you should require encryption as well as authentication.

The Specify By Host button allows you to specify only specific IP addresses for which you require authentication and encryption. This was discussed earlier in this chapter.

Connecting to SMTP Hosts Using Authentication and Encryption

If you wish to connect to another SMTP server using authentication or encryption, you must configure this on the Security tab of the IMS property page. The Security tab and the Edit E-mail Domain Security Information dialog box are shown in Figure 27.10.

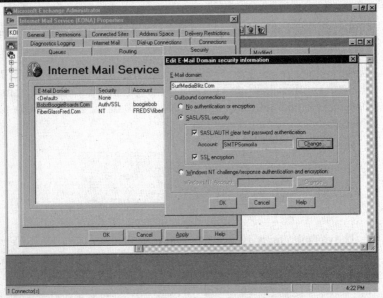

FIGURE 27.10:   The E-mail Domain Security Information dialog box specifies the type of security required for a specific domain.

You have three options for outbound connection security:

No authentication or encryption causes connections to the listed domain to be neither encrypted nor authenticated.

SASL/SSL security uses Simple Authentication and Security Layer (SASL) for clear text authentication and Secure Sockets Layer (SSL) for data encryption. In order to use the SASL/AUTH Clear Text Password Authentication option, you must have been provided with a user ID and password on the remote system, and the remote system must support SASL. In order to use SSL, the remote system must have set up SSL.

Windows NT challenge/response authentication and encryption uses a Windows NT challenge/response for authentication, and the data is encrypted. The destination server *must* be an Exchange 5 or later server with Exchange IMS and must provide you with a Windows NT domain name, user account, and password.

NOTE

The encryption algorithm by the Internet Mail Service for Windows NT challenge/response authentication and encryption as well as SASL/SSL is RSA RC4; for the North American edition of Windows NT (and service packs), the encryption key is 128 bits. Outside of North America, the encryption strength is only 40 bits.

Protocol Logging and Internet Message Archives

The IMS has two useful diagnostic logging categories found on the Diagnostics Logging tab of the IMS property page. These are the SMTP Protocol Log and the Message Archival categories.

SMTP Protocol Log

The SMTP Protocol Log keeps information about all SMTP conversations in text files located in the \exchsrvr\IMCdata\log directory. The current log is named L0000000.log, and previous logs are renamed L0000001.log, L0000002.log, and so on.

If the SMTP Protocol Log category is set to Minimum, only basic connection information is logged to the protocol logs. If the logging level is set to Medium, the entire SMTP conversation is recorded in the log file except for the message data. Figure 27.11 shows a sample of an SMTP protocol log set to the Medium logging level. Figure 27.11 shows the EHLO, MAIL FROM, RCPT TO, DATA, and QUIT commands, but it does not show the actual message content.

```
L0000002.log - Notepad
File  Edit  Search  Help
2/18/99 3:06:04 PM : A connection was accepted from rug.ukcore.bt.net.
2/18/99 3:06:04 PM : <<< EHLO relay1.bt.net
2/18/99 3:06:04 PM : >>> 250-exchange1.cta.net Hello [rug.ukcore.bt.net]
250-XEXCH50
250-HELP
250-ETRN
250-DSN
250-SIZE 0
250-AUTH LOGIN
250-AUTH=LOGIN
250-STARTTLS
250 TLS
2/18/99 3:06:07 PM : <<< MAIL FROM:<owner-msexchange@insite.co.uk> SIZE=6997
2/18/99 3:06:07 PM : >>> 250 OK - mail from <owner-msexchange@insite.co.uk>; can accomodate 6997 bytes
2/18/99 3:06:07 PM : <<< RCPT TO:<EXCHTECH@cta.net>
2/18/99 3:06:07 PM : >>> 250 OK - Recipient <EXCHTECH@cta.net>
2/18/99 3:06:07 PM : <<< DATA
2/18/99 3:06:07 PM : >>> 354 Send data.  End with CRLF.CRLF
2/18/99 3:06:08 PM : >>> 250 OK
2/18/99 3:06:08 PM : <<< QUIT
2/18/99 3:06:08 PM : >>> 221 closing connection
```

FIGURE 27.11: A sample SMTP protocol log at the Medium logging level

If the logging level is set to Maximum, the SMTP commands and the message content will be recorded in the log files. These files can get quite large on a busier IMS server, and they can pose a security risk if someone gets access to them and can read the message data.

Message Archival

If the Message Archival category is set to either Medium or Maximum, a text file copy of all incoming messages is saved to the \exchsrvr\ IMCdata\in\archive directory. All outgoing messages are saved to the \exchsrvr\IMCdata\out\archive directory.

These text files contain the message header and message contents. While this is useful for troubleshooting and some companies require records of all Internet messages to be kept, this can take up a tremendous amount of disk space very quickly. If you are using this feature, consider turning on NTFS compression for both \archive directories, and don't forget to archive these files often. These directories should also have restricted NTFS permissions, because all inbound and outbound Internet messages are stored in these directories, and the data can be viewed by anyone who can connect to the Exchange server's hard drives.

Bad Messages in the MTS-IN and MTS-OUT Folders

The Internet Mail Service has its own mailbox in the information store on the server that the IMS is installed on. This mailbox has a folder called MTS-IN that stores messages being transferred into the information store from the IMS and a folder called MTS-OUT that stores messages being transferred out of the information store.

You can see this IMS mailbox in the *Site Name* ➢ Configuration ➢ Servers ➢ *Server Name* ➢ Private Information Store ➢ Mailbox Resources container; the mailbox is listed as Internet Mail Service (*Server Name*). In a normal state, this mailbox should always be empty. However, I have seen a number of situations where this mailbox contained hundreds of messages and megabytes of data. There is also a rare circumstance where a malformed message has been transferred into this mailbox and causes the information store service to crash. If either of these situations occurs, you may need to open this mailbox and delete the offending messages.

This is not a simple process. A special MAPI profile must be generated that is capable of accessing this mailbox. There is a utility available from Microsoft called `profinst.exe` that will create this profile for you. It is available on the Web at `support.microsoft.com/support/downloads/lnp244.asp`.

Once you have the `profinst.exe` utility, you must create the profile on the server that is running the IMS. Open a Windows NT command prompt and, to change to the directory that the `profinst.exe` utility is located in, type **profinst /service=msexchangeimc /name=IMS / type=gateway**.

Next you need the Microsoft Exchange MDB Viewer Utility from the Exchange Server CD-ROM; this utility is located in the `\Server\Support\Utils\I386` directory. From this directory, copy the `MDBVU32.exe`, `XVPORT.dll`, `TBLVU32.dll`, `STATVU32.dll`, and `PROPVU2.dll` files to a directory on the server.

The `MDBVU32.exe` program is not simple to use, but it is very revealing. It allows you to see the folders and messages in raw form.

To open and examine the IMS mailbox, follow these steps:

1. Run the `MDBVU32.exe` program.

2. At the first dialog box you see, click the MAPI_Explicit_ Profile check box and click OK.

3. Select the profile that you created in the previous step (I called my example IMS) and click OK.

4. From the MDB menu, select Open Message Store.

5. You should now see the Store Display Name dialog box. Select Mailbox ➤ Internet Mail Service (*Server Name*) and click Open.

6. From the MDB menu, select Open Root Folder.

7. You should now see the MTS-IN, MTS-OUT, Bad, and other folders.

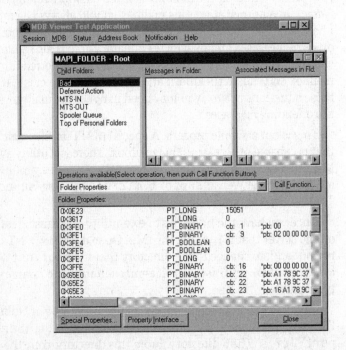

You can now highlight any of the folders to see if the offending message or messages are listed. Most commonly, when the information store mailbox resources indicate there are messages waiting in the IMS mailbox, the messages are in the Bad folder.

To delete a message from one of these folders:

1. Select the message in the Messages In Folder list.

2. In the Operations Available drop-down list box, select IpFLD
    ≻ DeleteMessages().

3. Click the Call Function button and click OK to confirm the
    operation.

The offending message should now be deleted. When you are finished,
click the Close button to return to the main MDB Viewer Utility menu
where you can then click Session Menu and Exit.

WARNING

The MDB Viewer Utility is a powerful tool. Treat it with the same respect and
caution that you use with the Registry Editor.

USING AN SMTP RELAY HOST OUTSIDE A FIREWALL

Firewalls have become commonplace as more businesses and organizations get hooked up to the Internet and need to protect their internal
data from the evils that lurk there. Hand in hand with using firewalls is
the use of an SMTP host outside that firewall. This host acts as a relay
host, accepting messages for an organization and relaying them through
the firewall to an Exchange IMS. The firewall is configured to allow
SMTP traffic between only the relay host and the IMS. SMTP traffic
directly from the Internet to the IMS is not allowed. The major advantage
of this approach is securing your IMS running on the internal Exchange
server. This type of solution becomes more critical if your IMS and pub-
lic/private information store databases share a common Exchange server.
For most of us, downtime due to a mischievous hacker is not acceptable.

There are different approaches to building a relay host, and among
them are many combinations with varying costs and benefits.

ISP Relay Hosting with ETRN

This approach allows you to release all Internet security support to the
ISP. The Exchange server has to periodically connect to the ISP to pick up
mail that has been stored there. In this situation, you configure your IMS
to deliver all mail to a specific host using the Connections tab; that host
would be the ISP's host that is queuing your mail. While connected to

that host, you configure your IMS to issue the ETRN command and retrieve any waiting messages using the Registry's Always Use ETRN setting.

Your ISP would configure their SMTP system to queue mail for your domain using the ETRN methodology. Benefits include easing security issues on inbound mail and putting the burden on the ISP to deliver the outgoing mail to the final SMTP host.

Some possible disadvantages include working with the ISP to get the configuration functioning, delay in mail retrieval, and possible support issues from the ISP.

Integrated SMTP on Firewall

This approach allows you to release all security to your firewall. It is similar to the ISP, but you are in control. In this situation you would configure your Exchange server's IMS to deliver all Internet mail to the firewall; the firewall acts as the SMTP relay host. The firewall would be configured to accept messages from the internal system and deliver them to the destination SMTP host.

Benefits include controlling security internally and learning about attempted attacks on your mail by monitoring the firewall. The firewall can be configured to forward requests from certain IP addresses to the internal IMS for extranet connectivity, authentication, encryption, and SSL connections. The firewall can also attach declarative statements (disclaimers) to e-mail about company and employee relationships.

Disadvantages include the cost of purchasing firewall, added support requirements, internal management, and the overhead of the firewall supporting SMTP.

INTERNET MAIL SERVICE TIPS

Here are some tips that will be helpful when managing your Internet Mail Service:

> ▶ Use the Internet Mail Service's diagnostic logging capabilities only when required for troubleshooting or for analyzing trends. Otherwise, keep all diagnostic logging levels at None. A busy IMS can generate tens of thousands of application event log messages

per day and fill the application event log quickly. Heavy use of the IMS diagnostics logging feature also makes it harder to find critical or important events.

▶ The default timeout period for a message waiting to be delivered to another host is 48 hours. I recommend bumping the time up to 72 hours (three days). If the destination SMTP system is offline because of some hardware, software, or internetwork problem, this gives the destination's manager one more day to get the problem corrected. You set the timeout period on the Connections tab of the IMS property page; click the Time-outs button to set message timeouts for Urgent, Normal, and Non-Urgent messages.

▶ If you have specified a host to deliver outbound mail to (on the Connections tab of the IMS property page), that hostname *must* be available when the IMS starts. Otherwise the service will not start. If the IMS fails to start and you notice event IDs 4032, 4057, and 4014 in the application event log, this is why.

▶ You can use the IMS Pickup directory to submit messages that are formatted as RFC-821 messages. This can be useful for automating message delivery of maintenance or system maintenance. This path for this directory is `\exchsrvr\IMCdata\ Pickup`.

NOTE

See Microsoft Knowledge Base article Q201314 for more information on the IMS Pickup directory.

FOR FURTHER INFORMATION

For more information on topics discussed in this chapter, here are some resources:

▶ The Coalition Against Unsolicited Commercial E-mail (CAUCE) has a good Web site containing an overview of anti-spam resources: www.cauce.org.

▶ Mail Abuse Prevention System (MAPS) is a non-profit company dedicated to stopping spam; they have an interesting Web site and links to other anti-spam efforts: maps.vix.com.

CONTINUED ➡

▶ See Microsoft Knowledge Base article Q185216 for a list of common mail abuse phrases and their definitions.

▶ Exchange gurus Simpler-Webb have put together an Exchange resource Web page that includes some great tips and resources for connecting Exchange to an ISP. This site is especially useful if you don't have a full time connection. Check them out at www.swinc.com.

MAXIMIZING USE OF SMTP

Organization RST makes heavy use of SMTP and always has, even before they deployed Exchange Sever and the Internet Mail Service. When they began deploying Exchange Server to their various locations, they had to choose a messaging connector to connect their Exchange sites together. Though they had virtually no security previously using a Unix-based SMTP mail system, one of the strong selling points for Exchange was better security.

The first choice was the X.400 connector, since it handles low bandwidth situations very well and the connector administrator can restrict not only who uses the connector and the maximum message size, but also the times when the connector operates. However, many of RST's offices were connected through the Internet, and the lack of security using X.400 over TCP/IP troubled RST's Information Services team.

RST evaluated the Exchange site connector. Though the site connector was easy to install and configure, RST found that it did not work well on some of their lower speed links, which were quite often saturated during the business day. The site connector did not permit the connector to be scheduled so that it would operate only during specified hours, nor did it allow restriction of large messages on which users could use the connector.

Since neither the X.400 connector nor the site connector completely satisfied RST's requirements, they selected the IMS as their inter-site messaging connector.

CONTINUED ➡

To ensure the security of data being transferred between RST's Exchange sites over SMTP, each site had a bridgehead server installed that operated the IMS. SASL/SSL was enabled for each of these IMS servers, and the IMS servers were configured to use authentication and encryption. In each domain, a Windows NT account was created for each of the Exchange sites. This account was used by the respective IMS servers for authentication to the other sites; a single account could have been used for all sites, but the company's IS group wanted each site to have its own user account and password.

The IMS servers were also configured so that SSL was required between all the company's internal IP addresses to further guarantee that SSL was used for all intra-organization message transfer. In order for SSL to be supported on each of the IMS bridgehead servers, Internet Information Server 4 was installed. A CSR (Certificate Signing Request) file was created using the IIS Key Manager application. This CSR file was sent to VeriSign where it was signed and returned. The purpose of sending the certificate to VeriSign is to get the certificate signed by a known and trusted certificate authority.

Once the official certificate was signed by the trusted signing authority and returned, the certificate was installed onto the appropriate IIS server. Certificates are created specifically for one server, so each server that was to support SSL had to have a certificate created for it.

RST had the certificates signed by VeriSign so that they would be recognized and trusted by entities outside of RST. Many of RST's customers and vendors had expressed an interest in sending messages securely with RST. SSL was selected as the encryption method of choice by RST because SSL is widely accepted and supported.

Previously, each geographic region accepted and processed its own SMTP mail. In order to simplify all e-mail addresses, a single IMS was designated as the primary host to accept SMTP mail for all of rst.com, rather than for each subdomain that previously existed (e.g. chicago.rst.com, newyork.rst.com, etc.). All MX records for the subdomains that previously pointed to the old SMTP systems now point to the main IMS primarily and point to an additional IMS as a backup.

WHAT'S NEXT?

This chapter discussed interoperability issues in the messaging world. In the next chapter, you will learn how to troubleshoot, diagnose problems, and solve mysteries related to Exchange Server operations.

Chapter 28

DIAGNOSING SERVER PROBLEMS

What do you do first when Exchange Server services fail to start or when a service suddenly shuts down? When a user calls you and claims that the messages he is sending are not getting through, what steps to you take to verify this claim? There are problems with the directory service or the message transfer agent; where do you look first?

Adapted from *Exchange Server 5.5 24seven™*
by Jim McBee

ISBN 0-7821-2505-0   657 pages $34.99

This chapter covers troubleshooting and diagnosing problems related to Exchange Server operations, including these topics:

▶ The basic troubleshooting steps

▶ Investigating Exchange database problems

▶ Solving the mysteries of disappearing messages

▶ Fixing directory service problems

▶ Solving problems related to the message transfer agent

▶ Working with an Internet Mail Service that won't deliver messages

▶ Unraveling the mysteries of Outlook Web Access problems

NOTE

When troubleshooting Exchange Server software problems (especially those related to performance), don't forget the Windows NT Performance Monitor. Performance monitoring and Exchange Server are discussed in detail in Chapter 26, "Monitoring and Optimizing Exchange."

TROUBLESHOOTING BASICS

At the first hint of trouble with an Exchange server, there are several basic things to check that will help you isolate the problem. Before you start troubleshooting more complicated scenarios, perform these steps to verify that the basic potential problem areas are not causing the problem(s):

▶ Check the system and application event logs using the Windows NT Event Viewer for any error (red) or warning (yellow) events that may have been generated recently.

▶ Check Control Panel ➢ Services to make sure that all Exchange Server services are started. The four core Exchange services (System Attendant, directory service, message transfer agent, and information store) must be started for basic Exchange services to happen.

▶ Confirm that there is sufficient hard disk space available on all disk drives that Exchange Server is using. I am uncomfortable if any disk drops below 100MB (or 10 percent, whichever is lower) of free disk space.

   ▶ If circular logging is turned off and disk space is low, run a normal or incremental backup as soon as possible. The normal and incremental backup procedures purge the old transaction logs.

   ▶ Check the \exchsrvr\IMCdata\in\archive, \exchsrvr\IMCdata\out\archive, and \exchsrvr\ IMCdata\log directories for Internet mail archives and logs that can be purged.

   ▶ When message tracking is enabled, the log files can take up a considerable amount of disk space. Check the \exchsrvr\tracking.log directory to make sure the log files are being purged accordingly.

▶ Verify network connectivity. Make sure that the server can be pinged and that it can ping others. Also verify that you can connect to the server's shared folders.

▶ Verify the server can be pinged using the RPC Ping tools. The Exchange servers communicate using the RPC session protocol.

If you have indeed found that a service is stopped, a database is corrupt, or you are having communications problems, this chapter discusses some solutions to these common problems.

SOLVING DATABASE PROBLEMS

If the Event Viewer's application event log indicates that there is a problem related to the public or private information store databases, the first step you should take is to perform a backup. This will ensure that if things get worse, you can always go back to where you were prior to your troubleshooting. If the server is currently online, attempt an online backup. If the services will not start, perform an offline backup. (These methods are discussed in Chapter 25, "Maintenance Procedures.")

If the application event log is generating errors that indicate a corrupted database, you are probably going to be better off immediately restoring the database from the last normal tape backup. However, it does not hurt to make sure that the database is actually in good shape before doing so.

TIP

The golden rule of disaster recovery is "Do no further harm." Prior to beginning any sort of database maintenance or operations, perform a full backup.

Checking the Database

If the database is experiencing problems, the two main ways to check for problems are to run a consistency check and to verify the database integrity.

WARNING

All ESEUTIL and ISINTEG options must be performed with the information store service stopped.

Database Consistency Check

A consistency check lets you know if the database service was shut down properly and if all outstanding transactions have been committed to the database. To check and make sure the database is consistent, use the ESEUTIL command with the /MH option, which dumps the header of the specified database. You must explicitly refer to the filename using the /MH option.

To check the consistency of the private information store database that is on the E drive, type **ESEUTIL /MH E:\exchsrvr\MDBdata\ priv.edb >priv.txt**. This redirects the results of the /MH option to the priv.txt file. Examine this file for a line that contains **State:**. If all is well, this line should say **State: Consistent**. If it says **State: Inconsistent**, then the database is in an inconsistent state.

Restarting the information store service should correct consistency problems. However, sometimes when the services restart, the consistency problems don't always get fixed automatically. It may be possible to fix these problems using ESEUTIL /R /ispriv or ESEUTIL /R.

Running ESEUTIL /P /ispriv or ESEUTIL /P /ispub can also adjust consistency problems, but you should run this utility only as a last resort.

Database Integrity Check

The database integrity check examines the low-level database structure and pages. This ensures that the database file is actually in good shape.

To perform an integrity check on the private information store database, at the command prompt type **ESEUTIL /G /ispriv >priv.txt**. Examine the content of the priv.txt file for errors with the database. If you find errors, Microsoft recommends that you contact their PSS folks for assistance in fixing the problem. The first question they'll ask you is whether or not you have a recent backup, and then they'll ask you to check if circular logging is disabled. Chapter 29, "Disaster Recorvery," covers database recovery from tape and some of the options you have available.

The problem with attempting to recover a database that has damaged pages is that you don't know the extent of the damage or the number of pages that are unrecoverable. It is likely that you will waste many hours attempting to recover a database file that is unrecoverable, or that you will lose most of the data in it, anyway. It is important to remember this data or these pages equate to "e-mail and attachments." You may not notice the missing e-mail for some time. My point is that sometimes it is better just to revert back to the most recent normal tape backup.

If you do not have a recent backup, then ESEUTIL offers a few options that may help return the database to a usable state. For example, if the private information store database will not start, run the ESEUTIL /P /ispriv >priv.txt command. Examine the priv.txt file for reports of problems that may have been fixed, and then start the information store service.

If this is unsuccessful, then try the ESEUTIL recover option; run the ESEUTIL /R /ispriv >priv.txt command. If this option fails to recover the database, then there is very little that can be done if you do not have a good tape backup. Consult with Microsoft PSS for more information.

TIP

Anytime you have to run the ESEUTIL /P or ESEUTIL /R options, you should run the ISINTEG program with the –fix option. Refer to Chapter 25 for usage information.

Table 28.1 lists information store–related event IDs and a recommended course of action for each. I am assuming that the source of the event ID is the MSExchangeIS Private source. If you have one of these events generated from the MSExchangeIS Public source, use the –pub option rather than the –pri option specified in the table.

TABLE 28.1: Event IDs and Recommended ISINTEG Commands

Event ID	Recommended Command
1025	Isinteg –fix –test search
1087	Isinteg –patch
1089	Isinteg –patch
1131	Isinteg –patch
1186	Isinteg –fix –test acllistref or Isinteg –fix –test aclitemref
1198	Isinteg –fix –test folder
2083	Isinteg –path
7200	Isinteg –fix –test mailbox or Isinteg –fix –test folder
7201	Isinteg –fix –test folder,artidx or Isinteg –fix –test rowcounts,dumpsterref
7202	Isinteg –patch
8500 or 8501 or 8502	Isinteg –fix –test message
8503	Isinteg –fix –test message*
8504 or 8505	Isinteg –fix –test folder*
8506 or 8507	Isinteg –fix –test folder,message*
8508 or 8509	Isinteg –fix –test attach

*For a complete listing of the functions that each test performs, consult the ISINTEG.RTF document on the Exchange Server 5.5 CD-ROM.

TIP

The ESE (Extensible Storage Engine) database that Microsoft implemented with Exchange 5.5 is remarkably stable. If you are consistently experiencing database problems, look toward possible disk hardware or device driver problems.

NOTE

After completing any database maintenance operations, a normal online backup should be run as soon as the services are restarted and you know that the system is stable.

NOTE

The ISINTEG and ESEUTIL programs are discussed in further detail in Chapter 25.

MISSING MESSAGES

A user reports to you that her messages are not being delivered. She swears that she has sent the message several times, but it is simply not arriving. Exchange's message tracking facility allows you to monitor the progress of a message through the entire organization. To track a message, the message tracking options must be turned on for each site and each connector across which you want to track the message.

The Enable Message Tracking option needs to be checked for the MTA Site Configuration object and the Information Store Site Configuration object in each site configuration container (choose *Site Name* ➤ Configuration). Each connector that you have installed should also have an Enable Message Tracking option available; this includes the Internet Mail Service (IMS), the Microsoft Mail connector, and the Lotus cc:Mail connector.

The System Attendant service maintains the tracking logs and keeps them for seven days. This value can be changed on each server by displaying the properties of the System Attendant. Go to *Site Name* ➤ Configuration ➤ Servers ➤ *Server Name*, then select System Attendant object properties.

A shared directory on each Exchange server allows an Exchange administrator to connect to that server and read its message tracking logs. (The Exchange Administrator automatically connects to this shared directory transparently; the shared directory must be available.) The share name is `tracking.log`; the logs are stored in the `\exchsrvr\tracking.log` directory. By default, these files are stored on the drive onto which Exchange was installed, but this location can be changed in the Registry.

Tracking a Message

Now you need to determine what is happening to the disappearing messages. Let's say that user Jill Johnson has sent a message to user Les Iczkovitz, but the message is not getting through to him. Jill needs to tell you when she sent the message, and then you can use Exchange Administrator to track the message:

1. Within Exchange Administrator, choose Tools ➤ Track Message.

2. A dialog box appears asking you which server you want to connect to. Make sure a server is displayed and click OK.

3. The Select Message To Track dialog box appears. In the From field, select Jill Johnson, and in the To field, select Les Iczkovitz. Leave the 0 in the Look Back box (you are looking for a message that was sent today). Then click the Find Now button.

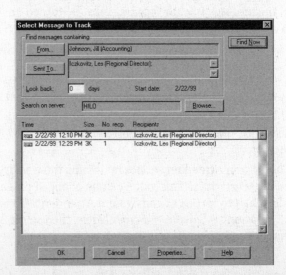

4. A list of messages that meet the search criteria is displayed. Select the message that you are interested in tracking and click OK.

5. The Message Tracking Center dialog box appears. Click the Track button.

6. The Message Tracking Center will display the route that the message took to get to its destination or wherever it is currently stopped (see Figure 28.1).

Behind the scenes, Exchange Administrator follows this message on its course of Exchange servers and connectors. Notice in Figure 28.1 that Jill submitted the message, then the HILO server's MTA delivered it to the KONA server. (There are two entries for MTA transfers, one from the HILO server's perspective and one from the KONA server's perspective.)

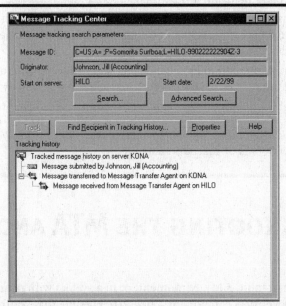

FIGURE 28.1: Message Tracking Center for a message that originated on the HILO server

Now, the strange part about the message tracking information seen in Figure 28.1 is that there seems to be no trace of where the message went after it arrived at the KONA MTA. A little investigation reveals that Les Iczkovitz's mailbox is on the KONA server. That MTA routed the message to the correct server, but there should be an entry saying that the message was delivered to Les's mailbox. Checking the KONA server's MTA discloses that Jill's message is still waiting in the private information store queue. Upon further investigation, checking the Exchange services shows that the information store service is stopped.

Most of the message tracking you are doing will probably not uncover such a dramatic problem, but it will provide a revealing look at message flow though the Exchange organization.

EXCHANGE@WORK: OTHER USES FOR MESSAGE TRACKING

Company NEM uses the Exchange message tracking feature for a completely different use than finding stalled messages. NEM's Exchange messaging infrastructure includes a number of redundant routes between sites. They use the Exchange server monitor and link monitors to ensure that servers are available and that messages are being delivered in a timely fashion.

One administrator periodically sends messages to administrators located in other sites to confirm that messages are taking their expected path through the Exchange messaging connectors. In at least once instance, this pointed out that a WAN connection had failed and the messages destined for the site connected by the WAN connection were taking an alternate path.

TROUBLESHOOTING THE MTA AND QUEUES

In a multi-server or multi-site environment, or in a system with connectors, the MTA is a critical component. I like to tell people that "nothing leaves the server without the MTA touching it." When the MTA stops working, the problems may not be noticeable immediately, but the severity of the problem will grow as more and more messages fail to be delivered.

A good approach to solving MTA problems is to be proactive about MTA management. The first step in this process is checking the queues daily to make sure that messages are not stacking up.

However, an even better approach is to implement Exchange server and link monitors. For administrators who want an up-to-the-minute status of each queue, you can create a Windows NT Performance Monitor chart that plots the number of messages queued (Queue Length) for each connection.

NOTE

See Chapter 26 for a detailed discussion of monitoring and optimization tools that will help you be proactive when working with the MTA.

As Exchange has matured over the last few years, the MTA software has become more and more robust. Still, regardless of how proactively you manage your MTA, an occasional flaw is going to slip through and trip up your server. I have seen MTA problems caused by large numbers of messages, corrupt messages, and corrupt queue databases.

TIP

Remember that the MTA can usually keep up with most WAN links. If an MTA queue to another site is backing up, check to make sure that the bandwidth to that site is not saturated.

NOTE

A known MTA bug in Exchange 5 and 5.5 produces a memory leak that causes a very busy MTA to become unable to create additional connections. This will manifest itself by generating event ID 9156, and the message queues will start backing up. Exchange 5.5 SP2 fixes this problem. You can also stop and start the MTA service to clean things up temporarily.

The Message Transfer Agent Databases

The MTA stores all queued messages in a series of database files in the \exchsrvr\MTAdata directory. In this directory, you will find a series of message queue database files starting with DB000001.DAT, DB000002.DAT, and incrementing upwards in hexadecimal. These files are used as temporary storage for messages being routed through this MTA, internal indexes, and other MTA message queue items. Collectively, these files are referred to as the *MTA database*. You will see a minimum of about 40 files in this directory, but it is perfectly normal for it to have dozens or even upwards of a hundred .dat files. Some of these files may be only one byte in size; this is a feature, not a bug. After a message that is contained in a DAT file is delivered, the data is cleared out, but the DAT file remains and can thus be reused quickly for future messages. This is a performance enhancement and does not affect day-to-day operations.

In addition, you will see a series of additional files in the MTA database that end with the extension .TPL and .XV2. These files are templates that represent the different types of encoding information that the MTA may need to generate messages. These files should *not* be deleted.

WARNING

On servers responsible for moving a lot of message traffic (hundreds or thousands of messages an hour), the number of files can grow to be very large. I have seen \MTAdata directories on Exchange bridgehead servers with over 3,000 files. This server was very backlogged due to WAN problems, and this was not a normal occurrence, but the drive that holds the MTA working directory *must* be located on an NTFS partition. MTA performance will suffer dramatically if the \MTAdata directory is on a FAT partition.

The MTACHECK Utility

Microsoft provides a utility with Exchange called MTAcheck.exe, which is located in the \exchsrvr\bin directory. This utility is designed to fix corrupt MTA database files, remove orphaned files no longer needed by the MTA, delete any objects it believes are corrupt, and remove system messages from the MTA queues.

If the MTA software detects problems with any of the queues, the MTACHECK utility is run automatically. You can run the MTACHECK utility manually, but the MTA service must be stopped. Table 28.2 lists some command-line options that can be used with the MTACHECK program.

TABLE 28.2: MTACHECK Command-Line Options

Option	Meaning
/V	Report errors verbosely (in as much detail as possible)
/T logfile.txt	Create a log file called logfile.txt

TABLE 28.2 continued: MTACHECK Command-Line Options

OPTION	MEANING
/RL	Remove any link monitor messages from the queues
/RP	Remove any public folder replication messages from the queues
/RD	Remove directory replication messages from the queues

If a WAN link or MTA has been offline for more than several hours, it is possible that many hundreds of messages could queue up for a particular connection. This includes system messages such as link monitor messages, public folder replication messages, and directory replication messages.

You can clear up the queue so those user-generated messages are processed and the system messages are deleted. To do this, stop the MTA service and type **MTAcheck /RL /RP /RD /V /F logfile.txt**.

NOTE

If there is a large number of files (500 or more), the MTACHECK process could take an hour or more.

I use the /RD option sparingly because I don't want to have to remember to force directory replication manually. If you use the /RD option, once you are certain that the MTA has caught up with transferring mail messages, force an update on your directory replication connectors to other sites and ask the administrators in the adjoining sites to do the same.

If the MTACHECK program detects any corrupt message queue data files, it will move them to the \exchsrvr\MTAdata\MTAcheck.out directory. Each file moved into this directory represents a message that was queued. The BackOffice Resource Kit includes a utility called MTAview.exe that allows you to view these files, but the information that it displays is in a pretty raw format.

TIP

The first thing I do when I start experiencing problems with messages backing up in the MTA queues is stop and restart the MTA service. You can safely do this while users are logged in and working.

Fixing a Corrupt MTA Database

I have seen a few instances where the MTACHECK program could not fix a corrupted MTA database. In this case, here is what I recommend you do to solve the problem yourself:

1. Copy all the DAT files in the `\exchsrvr\MTAdata` directory into a backup directory.

2. Delete all the DAT files from the `\exchsrvr\MTAdata` directory.

3. Copy all the files from the Exchange Server CD-ROM `\Server\Setup\Platform\bootenv` directory to the `\exchsrvr\MTAdata` directory. This replaces the current MTA database with the original MTA database.

4. Start the MTA.

There is a procedure for making sure that all the files you removed from the `MTAdata` directory are delivered, but it is very time-consuming. Get Microsoft PSS involved if you decide to rescue any messages that have not been delivered.

MTA Communications Problems

The Exchange MTA has to be able to communicate with other servers in order to transfer messages. If you notice that an MTA queue is starting to grow, suspect the possibility of a network communications problem. You can test client-to-server communications and server-to-server communications.

One of the most misunderstood features in Exchange is how Exchange resolves IP addresses based on the host's name. Though not the most elegant solution, I will often put a HOSTS file on each Exchange server with the IP addresses and names of all the other Exchange servers. This guarantees that the Exchange server will be able to quickly resolve the IP addresses of the other Exchange servers.

DIRECTORY SERVICE PROBLEMS

Directory replication within Exchange is a powerful and complicated feature. It does a great job of keeping all the servers and objects synchronized properly, yet every once in a while there may be a need to perform troubleshooting tasks on your directory database. Some of the more common ones include:

- ▶ Running the DS/IS consistency adjuster
- ▶ Removing orphaned objects
- ▶ Re-homing public folders

Part v

TIP

Keep in mind that directory replication between sites depends on your messaging connectors delivering updates to the directory. If directory updates are not going through, check your messaging connectors to make sure that messages from the directory service are not queuing up.

The DS/IS Consistency Adjuster

Information about mailboxes—such as users' telephone numbers, addresses, e-mail addresses, and permissions—are stored in the directory. The same is true for public folder information such as ownership, home site, and permissions. However, the information store must also have this information, such as which users have permissions to access a folder or mailbox. So to share this information, each object in the information store has a corresponding object in the directory database.

In rare situations, this information can fall out of synchronization. This problem can be reconciled using the DS/IS (directory service/ information store) consistency adjuster. For example, you would run the adjuster after:

- ▶ *Permanently* removing a server or site from your organization
- ▶ Recovering a server from tape
- ▶ Moving a database to a new Exchange server
- ▶ Accidentally performing a raw delete on a mailbox object or an object that also exists in the information store

NOTE

You do not need to run the DS/IS consistency adjuster on any scheduled (weekly, monthly, yearly) interval.

The DS/IS consistency adjuster process can be started from any Exchange server using Exchange Administrator. To do so, choose *Site Name* ➤ Configuration ➤ Servers, view the server's properties, select the Advanced tab, and click the Consistency Adjuster button. The DS/IS Consistency Adjustment dialog box appears (see Figure 28.2).

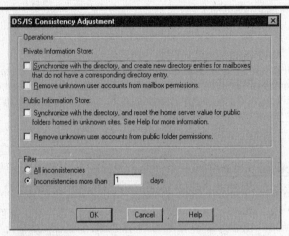

FIGURE 28.2: The DS/IS Consistency Adjustment dialog box

As you can see in Figure 28.2, the DS/IS Consistency Adjuster corrects four types of inconsistencies:

▶ It scans the private information store database for mailboxes that do not have a corresponding directory database entry. If a mailbox is found that is not in the directory, a directory entry is created for it. Even though this mailbox is created, it does not have a primary Windows NT account associated with it.

▶ It reviews mailbox permissions lists for any user accounts that do not exist. If it finds any, it removes them from the list.

▶ It scans the public folders looking for any that are homed in an unknown site. If it finds any of these public folders, it changes the home server value of these folders to the server that is running the DS/IS consistency adjuster.

▶ It looks at public folder permissions and removes any mailboxes from the permissions list if the mailbox no longer exists.

In this dialog box, you can choose also to have the tool adjust inconsistencies that are older than a certain number of days or to adjust all inconsistencies immediately.

Danger, Will Robinson, Danger!

The DS/IS Consistency Adjuster should be run only when deemed *absolutely* necessary. "Why? What is so dangerous about it?" Well, three of the options are not all that problematic (inspecting the private information store, the private information store permissions, and the public information store permissions). The adjustment that causes the problems is synchronizing the public folders with the directory and resetting the public folder home server value.

Though you would not think that this need to synchronize is common, it happens quite frequently. When public folders are re-homed by accident, they have to be put back the way they were manually. I have heard numerous horror stories of how hundreds of public folders had to be re-homed manually (one at a time) after an accidental and unintentional DS/IS consistency adjustment.

EXCHANGE@WORK: AVOID RE-HOMING PUBLIC FOLDERS

JWM Corporation has six regional Exchange sites spread throughout the U.S. Their directory replication architecture consists of their two primary sites, Boston and San Francisco, replicating to one another. Two additional sites in the western part of the U.S. connect to San Francisco for directory replication data, and two additional sites in the eastern U.S. connect to the Boston site. This creates a dual-hub and spoke directory-replication architecture.

During a major leased-line upgrade, JWM's Exchange administrator decided to switch from the X.400 connector to the Exchange site connector because the site connector is faster and more efficient as long as the bandwidth is sufficient. He also decided to redirect the local directory replication bridgehead servers in the Boston and San Francisco sites.

CONTINUED ➡

Then one day the X.400 and directory replication connectors were deleted. Due to a problem in the San Francisco office, the site connector could not be reconfigured. Everyone agreed that messaging could wait until the next morning to resume, so they decided to fix the problem the next morning.

The administrator in Boston arrived early the next morning and mistakenly decided that, since the directory replication connector had been deleted, it would be a good time to run the DS/IS Consistency Adjuster. Though he did not fully understand the implications of this selection, he configured the DS/IS Consistency Adjuster to re-home any public folders that were located in an unknown site. Unfortunately, all the public folders in the directory that were located in the three western U.S. sites were then re-homed to the server in Boston!

Once directory replication was re-established later that day, the damage became evident. The western U.S. public folders were no longer homed in their respective sites and could not be administered anywhere but from the Boston site.

Though the folders were organized by site, the western sites had nearly 80 folders. Each of these folders had to be re-homed back to its original server using the PFADMIN utility. The home folders for many of the servers were not known, so a recovery server had to be built in order to determine this.

The entire process took nearly two days to complete. This entire problem could have been avoided if the administrators all had a better understanding of the DS/IS consistency adjustment process.

Re-homing Public Folders

The procedure to assign a new home to a public folder requires that you assign the new home in the correct order. If a public folder inadvertently becomes homed in a site where it does not belong (such as an accidental DS/IS consistency adjustment), you can re-home it. This procedure is not as simple as pointing and clicking to reassign the home server to the way it was before someone accidentally ran the DS/IS consistency adjuster.

You are going to need some information, some software, and some preparation, including:

▶ The original home server name for any public folder that you wish to re-home. If you don't have this information, you will have to restore the public information store from a backup. This should be a copy of the original server prior to the accidental DS/IS consistency adjustment on a recovery server, not in the production system. (Chapter 29 will review restoring the information store databases to a recovery server.) Once the database is restored, you can create a report of the original public folder hierarchy. I recommend you use the PFINFO utility from the BackOffice Resource Kit to generate a report on all the public folder configurations.

▶ The PFADMIN utility from the BackOffice Resource Kit. One of the many things this utility does is re-home public folders. (Make sure you have the latest version of this software.)

▶ A user account that has the Service Account Admin role on both the source server (the server that the folder is now homed on) and the destination server (the server to which you want to re-home the folder, or the original server).

▶ Create a mailbox whose primary Windows NT account is the one that has the service account role on the two servers in this home/re-homing project.

▶ Create a messaging profile (avoid spaces in the profile name) for the mailbox you just created. This profile should be created on the server on which you are going to run the PFADMIN tool. (Yes, this tool should be run from the Exchange server.)

▶ Ensure that directory replication is working between all sites in the organization before attempting to fix this problem (remember, that was partly what broke it in the first place).

NOTE

If the source server and the destination server are not available on the same intranetwork (i.e. the remote site is accessible only through Dynamic RAS), PFADMIN will not work for re-homing folders. You must move all the public folder data into a PST file, delete the public folder, allow time for the data to replicate back to the original site, re-create the public folder, and copy the data back into the folder.

Once you are set up to re-home these public folders, here is the procedure you need to follow:

1. On the source server (the current home of the public folders that need to be re-homed), display the instances of public folders listed on that server. To do so, choose *Site Name* ➢ Configuration ➢ Servers ➢ *Server Name*, view the public information store properties, and select the Instances tab.

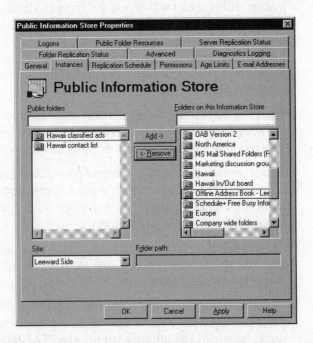

2. Make sure that the folders you are about to move are listed in the Folders On This Information Store list. If they're not, locate the folder name in the Public Folders list on the left-hand side of the screen and click Add.

3. For each public folder you want to re-home, type **pfadmin /e5** *Profile_Name* **rehome** *Folder_Name Site_Name\Server_Name* **/NO** at the command prompt.

4. When all public folders have been re-homed, run the DS/IS consistency adjustment on each server that has had a public folder re-homed to it. Select the Synchronize With Directory And Reset The Home Server Value For Public Folders Homed In Unknown Sites check box.

Run the DS/IS consistency adjuster only when you are sure that all directory replication connectors are working properly and that the replicated data is up-to-date.

Here is an example using PFADMIN to re-home public folders. The folders are called Hawaii Folders, and they are being re-homed to server HNLEX001 in the PACIFIC site.

```
pfadmin /e5 ServiceProfile rehome "Hawaii Folders"
PACIFIC\HNLEX001 /YES
```

In this command, the /YES option tells PFADMIN to re-home the Hawaii Folders folder and *all* subfolders. The /e5 option tells PFADMIN to send the results to a log file, but instead you can specify a /e3 option, which will send the results to the application event log.

Orphaned Objects in the Directory

Each copy of the Exchange directory database has copies of all objects found in all sites in the organization. However, only objects created in a site can be edited or deleted by an administrator of that site. An object that originated in one site is set to read-only when it is replicated to other sites. This is normally not a major issue; if you need to edit an object, you must connect to a server in that object's home site.

However, this becomes a major issue when an object is deleted in its home site, but the replication message instructing the other sites to delete the object is not received (possibly because MTACHECK /RD was run). The result is an *orphaned object* in the other sites; this object cannot be deleted because the home site had the only read-write copy.

Cleaning up orphaned objects is a major pain in the neck. There are several methods for doing so (see KB articles Q183739 and Q179573), but the easiest and most reliable way is to display the raw properties of the object and locate the Obj-Dist-Name using Exchange Administrator's raw mode feature (admin /R), as shown in Figure 28.3. The Obj-Version number below Obj-Dist-Name needs to be noted as well.

The object in Figure 28.3 is an orphaned mailbox object, and its Obj-Dist-Name attribute is /o=Somorita Surfboards/ou=Leeward Side/cn=Recipients/cn=REsmond. To delete this orphaned object, the administrator in the Leeward Side site needs to recreate this mailbox (in the Leeward Side site) so that its Obj-Dist-Name is exactly the same. Then, she needs to modify the object several times so that its Obj-Version number will be higher than that of the orphaned object. She then needs to give the newly created object time to replicate to all sites.

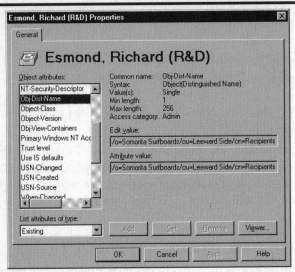

FIGURE 28.3: The Obj-Dist-Name as seen from Exchange Administrator's raw mode

Once the object replicated to all sites, the Leeward Side site administrator can delete the object. As long as directory replication is working properly, the message to delete the mailbox object will be replicated to all sites.

Avoiding Orphaned Objects

Well, I fibbed a little bit when I said that a message would be replicated to all sites instructing them to *delete* the object. The object is not really deleted immediately, but that is a simple way to think about it. Rather than risk a visit by Phil, Prince of Insufficient Light, I will give you the real scoop.

Each object in the directory has a property commonly called a *tombstone* (the raw mode attribute name is Is-Deleted). If you delete an object, the tombstone is set, and that change is replicated to all copies of the directory. An item with a set tombstone is kept in the directory (you just can't see it anymore) for 30 days by default. This is configured at the site level on the General tab of the DS Site Configuration object (see Figure 28.4).

Every 12 hours, a process runs on each server's directory service that is called *garbage collection* (also configured on the DS Site Configuration object). Any objects whose tombstones are older than 30 days are removed from that copy of the directory database.

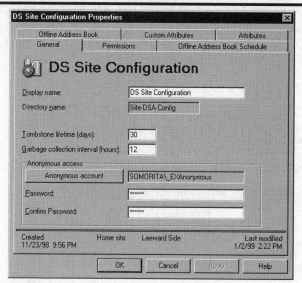

FIGURE 28.4:   DS Site Configuration object's General tab

So how do you avoid those little orphaned objects? Here are two suggestions to keep you orphaned-object free:

▶ Don't use the MTACHECK /RD to remove directory replication messages.

▶ Do not adjust the tombstone lifetime value seen in Figure 28.4; 30 days is more than sufficient.

COMMON IMS PROBLEMS

Though I generally experience very little trouble with the Internet Mail Service on a regular basis, I do have some troubleshooting tips that prove useful when the IMS is causing problems. These include the following:

▶ Monitoring for errors

▶ Confirming that name resolution is working properly

▶ Cleaning up corrupt files

Monitoring for Errors

Your first line of defense against IMS errors is the Windows NT Event Viewer. To monitor errors generated by the IMS, you first need to turn on diagnostic logging. To do so, display the Diagnostics Logging tab of the IMS; choose *Site Name* ≻ Configuration ≻ Connections, view the Internet Mail Service (*Server Name*) properties, and select the Diagnostics Logging tab.

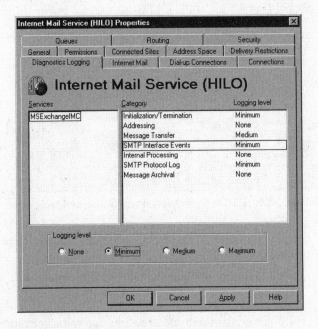

There are seven IMS diagnostics logging categories. Their names and functions are listed in Table 28.3.

TABLE 28.3: IMS Diagnostics Logging Categories

CATEGORY	DESCRIPTION
Initialization/Termination	Logs events related to the IMS starting and shutting down.
Addressing	Logs events related to the generation of proxy addresses and directory lookups.
Message Transfer	Logs events related to incoming and outgoing messages and message queue operations.

TABLE 28.3 continued: IMS Diagnostics Logging Categories

CATEGORY	DESCRIPTION
SMTP Interface Events	Logs events involving connections between two SMTP hosts, such as the initiation of a connection.
Internal Processing	Logs events that relate to the operation of the IMS service.
SMTP Protocol Log	Creates SMTP protocol log files in the \exchsrvr\IMCdata\log directory. Setting the level to Minimum logs only basic SMTP protocol information. Setting the level to Medium logs the SMTP conversation except for the message data. Setting the level to Maximum logs the entire SMTP conversation, including the message data.
Message Archival	Creates a separate file for each message transferred if set to Medium or Maximum. Inbound messages are stored in \exchsrvr\IMCdata\in\archive, and outbound messages are stored in \exchsrvr\IMCdata\out\archive.

Part v

Generally, the higher the logging level, the more detailed the generated information is. I start at the Minimum logging level to see if it gives me the information I need; if not, I increase to Medium, then to Maximum.

NOTE

Don't forget to turn off logging if you no longer need the extra information that is being generated.

NOTE

A common problem that is caused by the IMS is turning on the SMTP Protocol Log and Message Archival categories and leaving them running. On a busier IMS, these can quickly use a lot of disk space.

Using the IMS in Console Mode

Sometimes the Internet Mail Service can generate some interesting information to the console. This feature is not well-documented, but you can actually view the IMS as a console application. When it is operating in console mode, the IMS displays errors, statistics, and message processing information on the screen.

Here is what you need to do to run the IMS in console mode. The first step is to create a Registry entry that will tell the IMS to log errors and statistics to the console window. Locate the `\HKLM\System\Current-ControlSet\Services\MSExchangeIMC\Parameters` Registry key. Add a new value called `DisplayErrsOnConsole` with a data type of REG_DWORD. In the data field, enter a value of 100 and make sure that the Hex radio button is selected. When you enter the data, it should appear as 0x100.

In the same Registry key, locate the `ConsoleStatFrequency` value. This controls how often data is updated to the console screen. The default is 20 (decimal) seconds (0x14, in hexadecimal), but you can adjust this to suit your own needs.

Stop the IMS and open a command prompt. Change to the IMS software directory, usually located in `\exchsrvr\connect\msexcimc\bin`. From the command prompt, type **msexcimc –console** and press Enter. The IMS is now in console mode, and you will see a screen similar to this:

Close this window and start the IMS normally.

Confirming Name Resolution

In order to deliver SMTP messages to the correct host, the IMS depends on being able to resolve mail exchange records and host names. The Exchange server first does a special type of DNS query looking for a mail exchanger (MX) record for the domain to which it is about to send mail. There is a utility on the Exchange Server CD-ROM called RESTEST that will show you the results of an MX query. (This utility is in the CD's `\Server\Support\Utils` directory.) If there is no MX record, the Exchange server then resorts to standard host name resolution and assumes that the name it is querying is a host name instead.

For example, assume the IMS is attempting to deliver a message to `JonasG@microsoft.com`. The IMS will do an MX query to the DNS for all MX records at `microsoft.com`; if there is more than one host, the hosts will be listed in their order of preference. If the SMTP host with the lowest preference value is not available, the IMS will attempt to deliver to the SMTP server with the next highest preference value. You can use the RESTEST utility to see this list of MX records. Here is a sample querying `microsoft.com`:

```
D:\Temp>restest microsoft.com.
Microsoft (R) Name Resolution Test Utility (5.5.1960.3)
Copyright (C) Microsoft Corp 1986-1997. All rights reserved
host[0] = '131.107.3.124'
host[1] = '131.107.3.122'
host[2] = '131.107.3.125'
host[3] = '131.107.3.123'
host[4] = '131.107.3.121'
D:\Temp>
```

Similar results could be obtained by typing **NSLOOKUP –Q=MX MICROSOFT.COM**.

But suppose there is not an MX record. For example, the IMS is attempting to deliver a message to `Mike@mail.backman.com`. The IMS will first assume that `mail.backman.com` is a domain name and will generate a query for any hosts that will accept messages for `mail.backman.com`. If that query fails, the IMS will resort to standard host name resolution and see if there is an address record or alias (CNAME) for `Mail.Backman.com`. When creating MX records, don't use an IP address in the MX record; use an A or CNAME record for the Exchange IMS.

Cleaning Up Corrupt Files

Chapter 27, "Exchange Internet Interoperability," has some information on cleaning up corrupt files once they are stored in the IMS mailbox on the information store. However, corrupt files can also be stored in the IMS working directories, and these files can cause the IMS to fail or to not start.

If this occurs and the IMS generates an event ID 4037, it is possible that there is a corrupt message in either the `\exchsrvr\IMCdata\in` or the \exchsrvr\IMCdata\out directory. To correct this problem, follow these steps:

1. Move all the files in the exchsrvr\IMCdata\in directory to a backup directory.

2. Delete the exchsrvr\IMCdata\queue.dat file.

3. Start the IMS and test it. If it stays on, it is working normally. If the IMS stops again, repeat the process for the exchsrvr\IMCdata\out directory.

NOTE

If the IMS does not work after cleaning out both the IN and OUT directories, the corrupt message is probably in the IMS mailbox in the information store. There is a procedure in Chapter 27 that covers how to open the IMS mailbox and remove bad messages from it.

If the above procedure works and you were able to reliably restart the IMS, you can still deliver the messages that you moved to the backup directory. Here is how to recover those messages:

1. Stop the IMS and delete the exchsrvr\IMCdata\queue.dat file.

2. Copy about half of the messages you moved to the backup directory back into the \in (or the \out directory).

3. Start the IMS and see if the messages are delivered. If the IMS stops again, you know that the bad message is in the list of messages that are currently waiting in the queue. Though slightly time-consuming, you can use the process of elimination to figure out which message is causing the problem.

TIP

If the IMS is locked up, you may be able to find out which message caused the lockup. Before killing the IMS service, attempt to copy all the messages out of the \in or \out directories. If you get a "file in use" message, chances are good that it's the message file that caused the problem.

Other Internet Mail Service Problems

Here are some problems that I commonly see when working with the IMS, as well as some tips for troubleshooting them.

▶ If the TCP/IP host name and domain name are missing, the IMS will not start. You must make sure these fields have valid values. To do so, go to Control Panel ≻ Network, select the Protocols tab, click TCP/IP Properties, and select the DNS tab. Confirm that the Host Name and Domain Name fields are correct.

▶ When the IMS starts, it checks to make sure that it can resolve IP addresses for hosts specified as relay hosts. If any of these hosts are not resolvable , the IMS will not start. This can be checked on the IMS Connections tab and the Specify E-mail By Domain selection under the Forward All Messages To Host box. You may need to add the relay host to the hosts file or use and IP address. It is important to make sure that the relay hosts are specified properly.

▶ The IMS will shut down if disk space becomes too low (less than 15MB available). Check the \log, \in, and \out\archive directories for files that can be deleted.

▶ If the IMS becomes seriously backlogged with hundreds or thousands of messages to deliver, you can set the Transfer Mode on the IMS Connections tab to None (Flush Queues). The IMS will not accept any new inbound or outbound messages; this will allow time for it to deliver all the messages that have stacked up in the queues.

▶ You can use the IMCSAVE utility from the BackOffice Resource Kit to save the configuration of the IMS or to restore it to another machine.

NOTE

See Chapter 27 for more information about advanced features of the Internet Mail Service.

Troubleshooting Internet Protocols

If you have IMAP4, NNTP, POP3, or LDAP, here are some trouble-shooting tips and techniques that may prove helpful. While basic troubleshooting for these protocols is the same as for the Outlook client, there are some additional elements that come into play.

When troubleshooting an Internet protocol, first make sure the protocol is enabled. It can be enabled at the site level, at the server level, or per mailbox. If the protocol is enabled at the site level but disabled either at the server or at the mailbox, then the user will not be able to use it. Also, if the protocol is disabled at the server level but enabled at the site and at the mailbox, the protocol is still disabled.

Telnet Troubleshooting

Many people don't realize that if you need to check and make sure that a protocol is working, you can use the Telnet utility to converse with the respective information store. To do so, you must specify the correct port number for the Internet application you are using. Do this either on the command line after the server name or in the Port field in the Connect box of the Windows Telnet program.

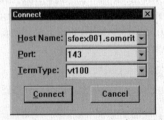

To check IMAP4, type **Telnet** *Server_Name* **143** and press Enter. If the IMAP4 is enabled and responding, you should receive a message similar to this:

```
* OK Microsoft Exchange IMAP4rev1 server version 5.5.2448.8
(sfoex001.somorita.com) ready
```

To check NNTP, type **Telnet** *Server_Name* **119** and press Enter. You should see a response that looks similar to this:

```
200 Microsoft Exchange Internet News Service Version
5.5.2448.8 (posting allowed)
```

To check POP3, type **Telnet** *Server_Name* **110** and press Enter. You should see a response similar to this:

```
+OK Microsoft Exchange POP3 server version 5.5.2448.8 ready
```

If you know the actual protocol commands, you can read messages and post news articles. The protocol commands are documented in the RFC for each Internet protocol.

NOTE

You cannot Telnet to the LDAP port (389) and discern any useful information.

Internet Protocol Logging

The IMAP4, NNTP, and POP3 Internet protocol logs can enhance the information you get through diagnostics by logging anywhere from basic information as the connection records, to protocol command conversations, and possibly including actual message data. They give you the ability to log detailed information and to create protocol logs similar to the SMTP protocol logging option. You can enable diagnostics logging for the IMAP4, NNTP, and POP3 protocols at the server level; choose *Site Name* ➣ Configuration ➣ Servers, view the server's properties, and select the Diagnostics Logging tab (see Figure 28.5). Under the Services list, open MSExchangeIS and Internet Protocols to reveal the IMAP4, NNTP, and POP3 categories.

Diagnostic logging for LDAP is enabled on the same screen as that in Figure 28.5, but under the MSExchangeDS service. Enable the category called LDAP Interface for LDAP diagnostics logging.

NOTE

The protocol logs are created through the Registry; all the Registry keys discussed in the protocol logging section are found in the \HKLM\System\ CurrentControlSet\Services **Registry key.**

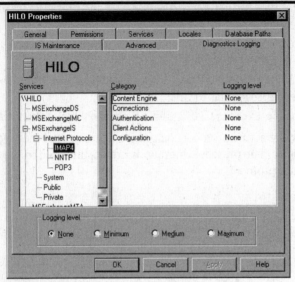

FIGURE 28.5: IP logging categories for IMAP4

Further, I recommend creating a directory to hold all of the log files. This way the log files are not created in the default directory.

NOTE

The protocol logs are continuously locked open. To delete them, set the logging level to 0. The next time the information store restarts, the file will no longer be locked, and you can delete it.

IMAP4 Protocol Logging

To enable IMAP4 protocol logging, locate the `\MSExchangeIS\ ParametersSystem` Registry subkey. Then locate the `IMAP4 Protocol Logging Level` Registry value and set the data to 0 for no logging, 1 for minimum logging, or 5 for maximum logging (including message data). Next, locate the Registry value `IMAP4 Protocol Log Path` and change the data to `C:\Logs`. Stop and restart the information store service for these changes to take effect.

NNTP Protocol Logging

To enable NNTP protocol logging, locate the \MSExchangeIS\Parame-tersSystem Registry subkey. Then locate the NNTP Protocol Log-ging Level Registry value and set the data to 0 for no logging, 1 for minimum logging, or 5 for maximum logging (including message data). Next, locate the Registry value NNTP Protocol Log Path and change the data to C:\Logs. Stop and restart the information store service for these changes to take effect.

POP3 Protocol Logging

To enable POP3 protocol logging, locate the \MSExchangeIS\Parame-tersSystem Registry subkey. Then locate the POP3 Protocol Log-ging Level Registry value and set the data to 0 for no logging, 1 for minimum logging, or 4 for maximum logging (including message data). Next, locate the Registry value POP3 Protocol Log Path and change the data to C:\Logs. Stop and restart the information store service for these changes to take effect.

LDAP Authentication Problems

If you have LDAP enabled for authenticated access only, the LDAP client must provide the Exchange server with a user ID and password. This sounds easy enough, but it is a little tricky. When you provide the user account name, it must be in a format that includes the Windows NT domain—but not the format you are probably used to. LDAP usernames must be passed to the directory service using Distinguished Name format.

Let's say that user JoshuaK (in the Somorita Windows NT domain) is entering his user account name. He must enter it in this format: **cn=*user-name*,cn=*domain*** or **cn=JoshuaK,cn=Somorita**. Figure 28.6 shows an LDAP directory service entry for the Outlook Express client.

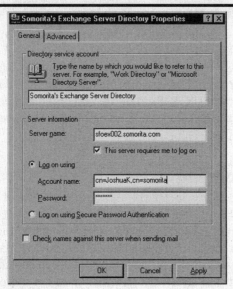

FIGURE 28.6: JoshuaK's LDAP directory service in Outlook Express

Notice the Account Name field? The username is preceded by a **cn=**, and there is a **cn=** for the Windows NT domain name as well.

NOTE

The Windows NT account must have permissions to the Exchange directory.

TROUBLESHOOTING OUTLOOK WEB ACCESS

Troubleshooting Outlook Web Access involves a whole new area of trouble-shooting. Though OWA seems like an Exchange component, it is really an Internet Information Server component that accesses the Exchange server much like any other MAPI client.

In a nutshell, a Web client connects to an IIS server and the Exchange page (i.e. `internal.somorita.com\Exchange`). The IIS server requests that the user authenticate. Then, through a series of scripts, IIS opens the user's mailbox, retrieves the mail, formats the mail as HTML messages, and sends them to the user's Web browser software. At no time is the Web client in communication with the Exchange software (or even the Exchange server if the Exchange server and IIS are on different hardware!).

What can go wrong here? Well, quite a few things, actually. The IIS server can fail to contact the designated Exchange server to perform a directory lookup. The IIS server may not authenticate the user properly. The user may not enter his username or mailbox name correctly. Here are a couple of steps to take to troubleshoot IIS and OWA:

▶ Make sure that the latest Windows NT service pack and any hot fixes related to IIS are installed.

▶ Make sure that the latest Exchange Server service pack is installed on the OWA/IIS server. Yes, the service packs must be installed on the OWA/IIS server even though Exchange server is not running on that machine.

▶ If the client is using the Netscape browser, make sure that the IIS server is capable of handling clear-text passwords.

▶ On the IIS server, make sure that OWA is looking for a valid Exchange server. This is controlled in the `HKLM\System\Cur-rentControlSet\Services\MSExchangeWeb\Parame-ters\Server` Registry setting.

▶ Make sure that the HTTP protocol is enabled. HTTP is only configurable at the site level; go to *Site Name* ➣ Configuration ➣ Protocols ➣ HTTP (Web) Site Settings, and select the General tab.

▶ If the user is being prompted for a user ID and password by his Web browser, make sure that he enters his user account name as *Domain\Username*, such as SOMORITA\GiovanniR.

NOTE

If you have access to the OWA server (with Exchange 5.5 SP1 or later), Microsoft has included a Web page with common problems and their solutions. You can get to this Web page by entering this URL: `OWA_Server_Name\Exchange\tshoot.asp`.

FOR FURTHER INFORMATION

To find out more information about some of the topics discussed in this chapter, check out the following resources:

▸ Knowledge Base article Q153188 has detailed information about the MTA diagnostics logging options.

▸ *The MTA Troubleshooting Guide* by Paul Bonrud is available on Microsoft TechNet. This guide contains a lot of detail on troubleshooting MTA-related problems.

▸ Microsoft has published *The Troubleshooting Guide: Microsoft Exchange Internet Protocols* by Peter Baggiolini, which can be found on TechNet and in the online Knowledge Base.

▸ When working with Outlook Web Access, an excellent resource for troubleshooting is the *Troubleshooting Guide for Outlook Web Access*, which is available on TechNet and the Knowledge Base.

WHAT'S NEXT?

In this chapter, you learned how to troubleshoot and diagnose problems related to Exchange Server operations. However, in spite of these preventive measures, an event will eventually occur over which we have no control. In the next chapter, you will learn how to focus your energy and resourcefulness on recovering from it. The chapter reviews some of the more common Exchange disasters and how you can recover from them.

Chapter 29

DISASTER RECOVERY

> "Anything that can go wrong will go wrong."
> —*Murphy's Law*

> "Any event you are completely prepared for will probably never happen."
> —*McBee's Axiom to Murphy's Law*

The day that you have been dreading has finally come. The information store is reporting database errors and will not start. Windows NT generates a blue screen upon startup. Little smoke spirals are coming out of your server, a disk drive has failed, there is no redundant disk, and you have just accidentally deleted the CEO's mailbox.

Some of you reading this book will never experience a disk failure or any other sort of catastrophic event that will cause your Exchange server to be unavailable. However, I'm betting that an equal number of you will have a few war stories over the next couple of years that you'll share when you gather around the watercooler with the other Exchange administrators.

Adapted from *Exchange Server 5.5 24seven*™
by Jim McBee

ISBN 0-7821-2505-0   657 pages $34.99

It seems the more prepared I become for some catastrophe, the less likely it is that the catastrophe will occur. Thus, Chapters 25 and 26 reviewed some of the important operational and maintenance items that you should perform and listed some tips from other Exchange administrators on how best to prevent disaster and keep your system running. Additionally, Chapter 24 included information on how best to design your server hardware to keep disasters from happening.

Despite these preventive measures, sometimes we have to face the fact that an event has occurred over which we have no control, and then we have to focus our energy and resourcefulness on recovering from it. This chapter reviews some of the more common Exchange disasters and how you can recover from them. Topics in this chapter include the following:

- Running an occasional fire drill to make sure you know exactly what you need to do in the event of a server or disk failure

- Preparing a disaster recovery kit that contains everything you need to recover from a catastrophic event

- Recovering from the accidental deletion of a single (important) mailbox

- Recovering from a complete Windows NT systems failure

- Recovering from the failure of the disk that contains the database files or a corrupted database file

- Recovery using offline backups

Disaster Recovery 101

Rule number one: Don't panic! When disaster strikes, keep your wits about you. To successfully recover from any sort of significant failure, you must have a plan and be familiar with what you need to do each step of the way. Here are some tips that will help your disaster recovery go more smoothly:

- Keep your system's standards and design document handy so that you can quickly refresh your memory on the standards that your organization is using.

Part v

▸ Document the hardware and software configuration of all Windows NT servers and any customizations that have been made to Exchange.

▸ Have a written disaster recovery plan.

▸ Keep a disaster recovery kit that includes your system documentation, software, CD-ROMs, and service packs.

▸ Nothing will help speed your recovery along like solid knowledge of what to do next. To gain this knowledge, practice your worst-case disaster recovery situations.

Here are some general disaster recovery steps to take for any type of disaster:

1. Identify the cause of the failure (disk, CPU, power supply, corrupted file, and so on).

2. Determine your course of action (restore from tape, rebuild server, or run database utilities).

3. Estimate the time needed to complete the recovery action and inform management and your user community of when service will be restored. (You might want to give yourself a little extra time when estimating recovery times.)

4. If Exchange is currently online, make an online backup of it prior to going any further. If Windows NT is running but Exchange is not, perform an offline backup.

5. Perform the actual recovery.

6. Test to ensure that the recovery was successful.

TIP

As soon as a problem strikes, create an outline based on these general disaster recovery steps. You should be able to refer back to this outline as the recovery progresses. During the recovery process, a lot of people are going to be asking questions, making suggestions, and screaming about downtime. If you get distracted by the commotion, you will need to be able to pick up easily where you left off.

We Don't Need No Stinkin' Plans!

If you think you don't need a disaster recovery plan, just wait until you have a significant problem and watch your team running around not knowing what to do next. *Have a disaster recovery plan in place.* It does not matter if you are supporting 100 users or 100,000. You and your co-workers must know what to do next. During a major problem is not the time to be figuring out the next step.

What should your disaster recovery plan include? For large organizations, this plan may be many hundreds of pages and include contingencies such as off-site recovery, earthquakes, hurricanes, alien invasions, and the release of the next Pauly Shore movie. But for many of us, this plan will not be quite so detailed and may include only more likely scenarios. Here is a list of things that should be included in any disaster recovery plan:

- A current phone contact list, which should include the following:

  - Information Systems employees' information such as home, pager, and cellular phone numbers. Special notes should be made for employees who have critical passwords such as the Administrator account password and the Exchange site services account password.

  - Contact names, support contract numbers, and account numbers for vendors and support organizations. Don't forget phone numbers and circuit numbers used to report problems with WAN links.

  - Contact information for the people who provide power, air conditioning, and electricity.

  - Contact information for department heads and management along with names of those who should be notified in the event of major outages.

  - Contact information and procedures for retrieving off-site backup information.

- A job responsibilities list that outlines what areas of the network and the software each IS employee is responsible for and who each person's backup is.

- Procedures for retrieving backup data from off-site storage.

▶ Location of and person responsible for spare hardware such as cold standby servers, extra disk drives, and so on.

▶ A printed copy of the MS Exchange Disaster Recovery documents.

▶ Instructions for common disaster-type events that may occur, including the following:

> ▶ Failure of environmental services such as power or air conditioning
>
> ▶ The occurrence or prediction of a natural disaster such as an earthquake, hurricane, snowstorm, flood, tsunami, tornado, volcanic eruption, and so on
>
> ▶ Detection of a hacker break-in in progress
>
> ▶ On the Exchange side, the failure of your bridgehead server, a server that supports mailboxes, or a server that supports critical public folders

WHAT WOULD *YOU* DO?

What would you do if you walked into your computer room and found that the racks supporting the 40-file server, print server, gateways, and backup systems that run your network had collapsed, and all the components had crashed to the floor; Computer cases were open, pieces of monitors and network hardware littered the entire room, and chaos reigned?

This is exactly what I asked myself minutes after the 1989 San Francisco earthquake. Our LAN computer room had almost completely self-destructed. The rocking motion of the building (we were on the 22nd floor) was too much for the metal racks, and when they collapsed, all our components were sent crashing to the floor.

The steps that we went through to recover from this disaster could fill a book—we were not prepared. Do you have a plan that would dictate what to do in the event of the complete destruction of your computer room?

Part v

Does Anyone Know Where the Exchange Server CD-ROM Is?

How many times have you set out to install something, only to find that you spend most of your time looking for software, service packs, and system documentation? Twice in the past two months I have been called in to the middle of someone else's disaster. Both times I spent the better part of a day tracking down things like an Exchange CD-ROM, Windows NT CD-ROM, and device drivers for a SCSI controller. Not to mention the time I spent and phone calls I made to find out things like IP addresses, disk configurations, and system passwords. Why? Because the customers did not have the software and information close at hand when it was needed most.

I like to create a *disaster recovery kit* that contains everything I need to rebuild a server from the ground up (well, except for the actual hardware). My disaster recovery kit contains the following:

▸ The printed copy of the disaster recovery plan along with all the important phone numbers and service account numbers.

▸ System documentation for the Windows NT Server and the Exchange Server software configuration. This should be updated as necessary.

▸ CD-ROMs necessary to re-create the system including Windows NT Server, Exchange Server, Windows NT 4 Option Pack, Exchange Server service packs, Windows NT service packs, third-party software that is installed on the server, and hot fixes that have been applied.

▸ CD-ROMs and floppy disks provided by the manufacturer of the server hardware that include device drivers and supporting software for the server hardware.

▸ Windows NT Server Emergency Repair Disks.

As your software versions are upgraded and service packs are applied, make sure that you update your disaster recovery kit.

TIP

Once you have created the disaster recovery kit, don't "loan out" pieces of it such as CD-ROMs and floppy disks. Loaned items tend to disappear—and you won't realize that an item's gone until you need it.

Practice Makes Perfect

Throughout this book I have been referring to your cold standby server; this is the extra piece of hardware that is configured identically to your other Exchange servers with respect to disk space, disk controllers, and RAM. I am also a strong advocate of performing periodic Exchange Server restores to your standby server.

Every few months, randomly pick one of your servers and pretend that it has had a catastrophic failure and conduct a fire drill.

Start your stopwatch.

Separate the standby server onto an isolated network and begin the restoration process. You will probably have to build the Windows NT server and apply all the necessary service packs. Reinstall the Exchange Server software and the service packs, and restore the Exchange databases. Reconfigure the Exchange connectors that this server supported (you probably won't be able to confirm that the connectors are working since this server is on an isolated segment). Do anything else necessary to prepare the server to allow users to log back in.

Stop your stopwatch.

How long did it take? Granted a lot of the time was probably spent watching software installation screens or tape restore progress indicators. Yet the time that it took is important, because it can be used in Service Level Agreements and, in the case of a real emergency, it can be used to inform your users of approximately how long it will take to restore the system to a usable state. (I usually give myself an additional 30 to 50 percent on my test restoration times, just for some slack.)

Evaluate your own performance during the test restoration. Was there anything that you could have done to make the restoration go faster? (Yes, we would all like faster hardware and tape drives.) Did you have all the software and documentation you needed nearby?

NOTE

Restoration of an Exchange server is a complex process. It is not something that you want to try for the first time while 500 users are waiting. It is absolutely critical that you become familiar with the backup and restore procedures *before* you need to know them. I cannot emphasize enough the importance of thoroughly understanding the restoration process.

EXCHANGE@WORK: PRACTICING DISASTER RECOVERY AND VERIFYING DATABASE INTEGRITY

The management at GHI Corporation expects the messaging system to be available 24 hours per day. The GHI Exchange administrator is responsible for two Exchange servers that support almost 850 mailboxes. She has one maintenance window of six hours per month that she uses to restart the servers, apply service packs, and perform a bimonthly offline backup. Her Exchange servers have circular logging disabled, and she performs a normal backup at 11:00 P.M. daily followed by two differential backups, one at 10:30 A.M. and one at 3:00 P.M. Each server's normal backup takes approximately three hours, and the differential backups take an average of about ten minutes.

During the design phase of her Exchange organization, the administrator was able to convince her superiors to purchase a third server identical to her two production servers. She uses this server as a cold standby and for practicing disaster recovery. Every three months, she picks one of the two servers and builds a recovery server on an isolated network. She then restores the server with the normal backup tape from the evening before and the most recent differential tape. Her time to restore the larger of her two servers (approximately 500 mailboxes and about 20GB of data) is just under four hours.

When the restoration process is finished and she is comfortable with the fact that the users could go back to work if necessary, she takes this recovery a step further. The only way to completely verify that a database is free of corruption is to perform an offline defragmentation. So on the *recovery* server, the administrator stops the directory and information store services and runs ESEUTIL /D with the /ispriv, /ispub, and /DS options to make sure that each of the three databases is truly free of corruption. This is merely done for the sake of testing and quality assurance; these compacted databases are never put back into production.

Though this process is time-consuming, GHI Corp's administrator is assured that the Exchange databases are corruption free, and she has an excellent understanding of the recovery process.

Disaster Recovery Tips

No amount of tips and hints is going to make your disaster recovery a positive and enlightening experience. Each time you have to recover from some type of system failure, you are going to learn a lot more. However, there are some things that may prove helpful in making the disaster recovery go a little smoother:

▶ Keep your user community informed of how long you expect to be offline. You will be surprised how cooperative they can be if you just give them a straightforward, honest answer.

▶ Keep your boss and the help desk appraised of your progress. Your boss is your first line of defense against management pressures, and the help desk is your first line of defense against angry end users. If there are major problems, your boss and the help desk are going to find out anyway; it is best if you let them know rather than waiting until they ask. If you *are* the help desk, change your outgoing message on your voicemail to give your users an update to the current situation.

▶ If you are trying to solve a database corruption problem, know when to quit and do a restore from tape. Restoring from tape is the preferred way to recover from database failures. The database repair tools (ESEUTIL and ISINTEG) should be considered viable options only if you have no recent backup.

▶ Ask for at least two separate phones in your computer room. One of these should have a hands-free headset, which should either be cordless or have enough cord so that you can access the consoles of all your servers.

▶ Prior to starting a disaster recovery, reread the relevant parts of the MS Disaster Recovery document.

DISASTER RECOVERY SCENARIOS

This section reviews some common disaster recovery scenarios that may cause you to lose some sleep. Some of these scenarios are easier to recover from than others, and the amount of data that you will lose will vary from situation to situation.

NOTE

For these scenarios, there are many types of Exchange-aware tape backup and restore software packages you can use. Further, the actual screens and restore options may be significantly different for your software. Consult your software documentation.

Building a Recovery Server

Many sites I work on have an identical cold standby server sitting beside their production systems. If the problem is hardware-related, the Exchange administrator can simply move the disk drives from the failed system to the cold standby system and restart. However, if you do not have an identical system, the first step toward restoring an Exchange server is getting the recovery server built.

TIP

If you have an identically configured standby server and a production server fails (memory, CPU, power supply, disk controllers), the first thing the IS team does is move the drive arrays over to the cold standby system and attempt to bring the disks back up on new hardware.

Most of the skills required are going to be drawn from the Windows NT side of your brain rather than the Exchange side. There are two types of rebuilds, and you should base your choice on the result you want to achieve. Are you attempting to recover a mailbox or test your disaster recovery procedures? Or are you attempting to restore your Windows NT system after a complete Windows NT server failure?

Building an NT System for Mailbox Recovery and Disaster Recovery Testing

When you restore Exchange Server databases to new server hardware, the Exchange server will need access to the original site services account. If the server you are restoring to is used only for recovering messages from the public and private information stores, or if it is used just for test restores (fire drills), the server name does not need to be the same as the original Exchange server. (This is not true if you are trying to restore the server.)

However, this server does need access to the original Windows NT domain database. I know a few administrators who use a Windows NT member server that is a member of the original Windows NT domain as their recovery server, but I am uncomfortable doing disaster recovery near the production system.

For this reason, when I install the recovery Windows NT system, I make it a Backup Domain Controller (BDC) as part of the original domain first. Then, once the server is fully installed and the domain database has synchronized, I move the server to an isolated network and promote it to be a Primary Domain Controller (PDC).

An alternative to this approach is to run the RDISK /S utility on the original PDC and store a backup of the SAM database on the Emergency Repair Disk (that is what the /S option of RDISK does). You then can install your recovery server in an isolated environment. Once installed and the appropriate service packs are installed, you can use the Windows NT Setup boot disks to perform a repair option on the recovery server. Insert the Emergency Repair Disk and instruct the repair process to inspect the Registry and restore only the SAM from the ERD. This will make this machine a PDC in the original domain (don't put the recovery server on the production network).

Building an NT System to Restore the Original Server

Some circumstances, such as a meltdown of the entire Windows NT system, may require that you completely rebuild the original Windows NT server. For example, if the system disk fails, Windows NT has to be completely rebuilt as it once was. The server name must be the same, and it must be a member of the same domain.

This type of situation emphasizes the need for complete and total documentation of not only Exchange Server, but also the underlying Windows NT platform.

Failure of an Exchange Database Disk Drive or Database File

Chapters 24 and 25 discussed the importance of placing the Exchange transaction logs on a physical disk separate from the disk that contains the Exchange database. Though the server's performance will be improved quite a bit, the main reason for this is for disaster recovery (provided you have disabled the server's circular logging feature). If you have not disabled the circular logging feature, then you will not have the old transaction log files necessary to rebuild a database from the last full backup.

If circular logging is disabled, the transaction log files are retained until after a normal (full) or incremental online backup is performed. For example, if it is Wednesday and you have not performed a normal or incremental backup since Sunday night, the log file disk will still have all the transactions since Sunday night. Though these transactions have all been committed to the database, they are kept until the next backup.

Recovery with Circular Logging Disabled

Retaining the log files will help with recovery in two situations: if the disk that contains the Exchange database files fails, or if an Exchange database becomes corrupt. Recovery from the latter situation is quite simple. (If the disk has failed, of course, you will have to replace the failed disk drive.) In this example, I am assuming that the Exchange software and transaction log files are on disks that did not fail. In addition, the logs on the disk have been accumulating since the last normal backup; hence, circular logging is turned off.

1. The first law of data recovery is to do no further harm. Since the Exchange Server services are probably going to be offline, you should make a full offline backup, which will include the Exchange Server software and the Exchange Server transaction log files. While you may not need this, mistakes can be made during restoration that could cause the recent log files to be purged and replaced with the older log files from the tape.

2. Once the full offline backup is performed, start the Exchange Server System Attendant service. This is required for the backup software to be able to contact and restore data to the Exchange server.

3. Restore the databases from the last normal backup tape, but make sure that you tell the restore software *NOT* to erase existing files. If it does, there go your recent log files.

4. Start the directory service and information store services.

5. Watch the Windows NT Event Viewer's application log for event ID 71 from the source ESE97. This event indicates that a transaction log has been committed to the database. This process can take between three and five minutes per transaction log, and it is not uncommon for a busy server to have several hundred transaction logs.

6. Connect to the Exchange server as a user and verify that the mail data has been restored. (At this point, you might want to use the `Logon Only As` Registry key to prevent your users from logging in until you have completed your testing. This will keep your users from logging back in before you are ready.)

7. Confirm that the connectors that were previously installed on the server are still installed and configured. Send at least one message that will use each connector on the server, and have someone on the other side of the connector send a message back to you.

8. Let the users log back on to the system. (If you added the `Logon Only As` Registry key, don't forget to delete it and restart the information store service.)

The data that the users see should be very close to the most recent data that was saved before the disk or database failure.

What If Circular Logging Is Enabled?

If circular logging is still enabled for the server that has lost its databases, the log files that are on the system will be of no use, because they will not contain all the transactions that have occurred since the last normal backup. You are still able to restore the database from the last normal backup, but you will lose any messages that have been sent or received since that time.

The restore procedure is identical to that above except that in step 3 you instruct the backup software to erase the existing files. There will be no indication of event logs being committed to the database because there will be no new event logs.

What If I've Done Incremental or Differential Backups?

In many organizations, a normal backup cannot be accomplished on a daily basis. There may be several reasons for this, including limited tape backup time for each day or limited personnel resources. As I have mentioned before, if you disable the Exchange Server circular logging feature, Exchange Server will keep all the transaction log files even after the data from that log file has been committed to the database files.

To briefly review what was discussed in Chapter 25, remember that when circular logging is disabled, the only time log files are purged is when a normal or incremental backup is run. Naturally, the types of backups you are performing will affect the type of restore that you do.

WARNING

Transaction log files should only be removed using the normal and incremental backup processes. Do not delete these files manually; this is bad for the general health of your Exchange server.

When restoring incremental and differential backups, you must perform the normal restore documented in the steps in the "Recovery with Circular Logging Disabled" section. Step 3 (restoring the databases) assumes that the log files already exist on the system. You will only need to restore the differential or incremental backups if the original transaction files are lost.

Restoring Incremental Backups   Once you have completed step 3 in the "Recovery with Circular Logging Disabled" section, you will need to restore each of the incremental backups since the last normal backup. Restore the oldest incremental backup first, and then restore each subsequent incremental backup until you reach the most recent one. The exact restoration procedure will depend on the type of Exchange backup software you are using.

Once you have restored all the incremental log files, continue with step 4 in the "Recovery with Circular Logging Disabled" section.

Restoring Differential Backups   Once the normal backup data has been restored, you need to restore only the most recent differential backup tape. This tape will contain all the transaction log files since the last normal backup. The exact procedure for restoring the differential data will depend on the type of Exchange backup software you are using.

Continue with step 4 in the "Recovery with Circular Logging Disabled" section once you have successfully restored the differential backup data.

Failure of a Single Information Store Database

If either the public or private information store database fails, but not both, you can still restore the database that needs to be restored. For this example, I am assuming that you are only going to restore the latest version of the public information store database but not the log files. Since the log files will not be replayed, you can delete them.

1. Shut down the MTA, information store, and directory services.

2. Remember the first rule of data recovery? Do no further harm. Make a complete offline backup of the Exchange server.

3. Confirm that the database that you will be keeping is consistent. Do this from the command prompt in the \exchsrvr\ MDBdata directory by typing **ESEUTIL /MH priv.edb > check.txt**. Scan the check.txt file that was created for a line that reads "State: Consistent." If the file is not consistent, use ESEUTIL /R /ispriv to correct it.

4. In the directory that contains the Exchange information store transaction log files (\exchsrvr\MDBdata), delete all the .log files and the edb.chk file.

5. Using the most recent normal backup, restore the public information store. Make sure that you specify in the restore parameters to restore *only* the public information store. The backup should be allowed to restore the log files from the tape. (At this point, you might want to use the Registry key Logon Only As to prevent your users from logging in until you have finished testing. This will keep your users from logging back in before you are ready.)

6. Start the MTA, information store, and directory services.

7. You will see messages in the application event log generated by the source ESE97 stating that recovery has started. You may also see an event indicating that the private information store was not recovered. This is normal because it did not need recovery.

8. Connect to the Exchange server from a client and make sure that the public folders have the data in them that you were trying to restore.

9. The log file numbering will have changed, so immediately run a normal backup. The old backups will not be usable with the current transaction logs.

10. The server is now ready to use again. (If you added the Logon Only As Registry key, don't forget to delete it and restart the information store service.)

What If the Information Store Does Not Restart After a Restore?

When the information store restore operation starts, a new Registry key is created called \HKLM\System\CurrentControlSet\Services\ MSExchangeIS\RestoreInProgress. When the restore is finished, this key should be deleted. However, I have seen instances where this was not the case. After the restore is complete and you attempt to restart the information store, you may see errors such as these two:

```
5000 Unable to initialize the Microsoft Exchange Information
Store service. Error 0xc8000713
1081 Unable to recover the database because error 0xc8000713
occurred after a restore operation.
```

If you see either of these two errors, it is possible that the above Registry key has not been automatically deleted. Start the Registry Editor and delete the RestoreInProgress key, and then try to restart the information store service.

Catastrophic Server Failure

At some point, you may experience a complete systems failure. This is usually a result of the system disk failing, which renders the Windows NT operating system unable to start. In this case, you will have to completely rebuild Windows NT as described earlier.

Once you have reinstalled Windows NT, you need to install Exchange Server and any service packs and hot fixes that you were previously running. Don't upgrade the recovery server to a later version of a service pack until the recovery is completed.

If you are restoring the server, here is a quick (but by no means exhaustive) list of items to make sure have been completed prior to continuing with the Exchange portion of the installation:

▶ Windows NT Server, any service packs, the option pack (if necessary), and hot fixes have all been installed as they were prior to the failure.

▶ The Windows NT server has the same server name, protocols, IP addresses, and network services installed.

▶ The disk configuration is sufficient to reinstall the Exchange data.

▶ If the tape backup software is locally installed on the Exchange server, reinstall the tape backup software and re-catalog the most recent Exchange server backup tapes.

Once you are sure that the Windows NT server is ready, the next step is to get the Exchange software installed and ready for the database restoration.

1. Set up the Exchange Server with the SETUP /R command. This will install the Exchange software, but it neither creates the information store databases nor starts the services. When prompted, choose to create a new site. Do not join an existing site. Enter the exact organization name, site name, site services account, and site services account password that was used with the original server. Remember to use the exact same upper- and lowercase letters when creating the organization and site names.

2. If the original server had a service pack installed on it, install the service pack with the UPDATE /R command.

3. Run the Exchange Performance Optimizer program and make sure the parameters, working directories, database, and log file location files are set correctly. Also make sure you document the location of the working directory, database, and log files locations (and make sure the locations have sufficient disk space to accommodate the data that is about to be restored).

Part v

4. If circular logging was disabled on the original server, it must be disabled on the recovery server. Make sure that this is set correctly.

The Exchange server is now ready to have the databases restored. The exact procedures will vary for different tape backup systems. Depending on how you perform Exchange server backups, there are two possible restoration options: online restores and offline restores.

NOTE

If you receive software through the Microsoft Select program, the Exchange Server 5.5 Standard Edition Setup program is srvmin.exe, and the Enterprise Edition Setup program is srvmax.exe instead of setup.exe.

Online Exchange Restoration

If the original Exchange server was backed up using an online backup, you'll perform an online Exchange restoration. Online backups are performed while the Exchange server is in production using Exchange Server–aware backup software. To restore Exchange data using the online Exchange agents for your backup software:

1. Make sure that the Exchange System Attendant service is started.

2. Locate the most recent normal backup and insert it into the tape drive.

3. Direct the tape backup software to restore the directory and information store databases to the Exchange server that you are rebuilding.

4. Do not start Exchange server yet. If you need to restore the incremental or differential backup tapes, restore those in the correct order. Incremental backup tapes should be restored in order, with the oldest first and the most recent last. Only the most recent differential backup tape should be restored. (When the restoration is complete, it might be a good idea to use the Logon Only As Registry key to prevent your users from logging in until you are ready.)

Part v

5. Once all incremental or differential backups are restored, start the Exchange directory, MTA, and information store services. Wait until all the outstanding transactions have been committed to the databases.

6. Using Exchange Administrator, confirm that the mailboxes and directory information (such as first name, last name, address, phone number, primary Windows NT account name, and so on) have been restored.

7. Log in to the Exchange server as a typical user and confirm that the user's messages, calendar entries, and contacts are available. Also confirm that the contents of public folders stored on the recently restored server are available.

8. Check the connectors that used to be installed on this recently rebuilt server. Some connectors such as the IMS and Microsoft Mail connectors will probably have to be rebuilt, yet others such as the X.400 and site connectors store their configuration in the Exchange directory. Double-check the configuration of all connectors because connector data is often stored in the Registry.

9. Once the connectors are rebuilt, send a few test messages, which should cross those connectors and have their delivery confirmed.

The Exchange server should now be ready to use. (If you used the Logon Only As Registry key, don't forget to delete it.)

TIP

If you have restored existing transaction log files, the information store service will take longer to completely initialize because each transaction log has to be recommitted to the information store. Confirm that this process is complete using the Windows NT Event Viewer's application log.

Offline Exchange Restoration

For normal operations, I highly recommend performing online backups, though there may come a time when you have performed an offline backup and need to restore the offline backup data. Offline backups are done file-by-file and are performed with the Exchange server directory and information store services stopped. These backups can be done to tape, but I have performed offline backup-and-restores a number of times by copying all the Exchange data to a shared directory on the network. If I am actually physically replacing one server with another, I recommend performing an offline backup-and-restore simply to guarantee that the data does not change after the backup is complete.

To restore an Exchange server from an offline backup:

1. Make sure you know the location of the Exchange server databases and transaction logs. If there are any data in these locations currently, rename the directories and create empty directories.

2. Restore the public, private, and directory databases using the mechanism you used to back them up (such as using tape or copying from a shared disk on the network). The log files should not be necessary because all transactions are committed to the database when the Exchange server is shut down. However, if you have separate backups of more recent log files, restore those to the log file directories.

3. Start the Exchange System Attendant and directory service. The directory service must be available for the next step.

NOTE
If the directory service doesn't start, you may need to run ESEUTIL /R /DS. This tool will create basic log data, edb.chk, and reserved log files. You shouldn't need to run this if you are restoring transaction log files along with the database.

4. At the command prompt, change to the \exchsrvr\bin directory and type **isinteg –patch** to adjust the globally-unique identifiers.

5. Start the information store service.

6. In the application log, confirm that the information store has started without errors.

7. When the information store service starts, continue with step 6 in the "Online Exchange Restoration" section earlier in this chapter.

Restoring Other Databases

Depending on the configuration of the Exchange server configuration, you may have other Exchange-related databases that need to be recovered. If the server supported the Exchange directory synchronization service, you should reconfigure directory synchronization, and the database will automatically be rebuilt. In a larger organization, this resynchronization can take 24 to 48 hours.

If the Exchange server is running the Exchange Key Management Server (KMS), the KMS software should be installed as normal. Once the KMS is installed, stop the KMS service and restore the KMS database to the \exchsrvr\KMSdata directory and restart the service.

Recovering the Exchange Directory Database

Though the Exchange public and private information store databases can be restored to a different server than the one from which they were backed up, the Exchange directory service database is specific to the machine on which it was created.

Restoring the directory database from a recent backup tape should solve any corruption problems. This is generally true for the public and private information store databases as well. However, you can run utilities such as ESEUTIL and ISINTEG on the public and private information store databases if there is ever a situation where there is not usable tape backup. Database utilities should *not* be run against this directory database file because that may cause the file to become out of synchronization with the other copies of the directory database on the other servers in the site.

Some administrators keep a backup copy of each server's original dir.edb file just in case there are corruption problems with this database. If this file becomes corrupted and a backup copy is not available, the administrator can delete all the files in the \exchsrvr\DSAdata directory (back them up first!), copy the original dir.edb file back into the directory, and restart the directory service. The directory service uses a process called *backfill* to determine if one copy of the directory is missing data and, if it is, to re-replicate that copy with the other directory databases in the site.

Without a backup tape version of the Exchange directory or an offline backup copy of the dir.edb file, the only way to recover from a corrupted directory database is through a full disaster recovery. The server would have to be reinstalled, and then the information store databases would have to be restored. Once the Exchange server was reinstalled, the DS/IS consistency adjuster must be run to recreate all the mailbox and public folder objects that are missing from the directory. You will lose most of the information stored in the directory for the mailboxes (phone numbers, mailing addresses, proxy addresses, and so on). You may also lose custom recipients and distribution lists.

NOTE

To make an offline copy of the basic dir.edb, stop the Exchange directory service, copy the \exchsrvr\DSAdata\dir.edb file to a backup directory, and restart the directory service.

ACCIDENTAL MAILBOX DELETION

Using Exchange 4 and 5, I found myself restoring quite a few mailboxes simply because someone important had deleted a message or a folder. Exchange 5.5 introduced the Deleted Item Recovery feature, which I consider to be one of the most important new features of Exchange. However, you must enable this feature because it is not enabled by default.

Deleted Item Recovery saves you from having to recover the entire information store database if a user deletes an important message. However, this does not protect you against the occasional accidental mailbox deletion by an administrator. Though deleting a single mailbox is not considered a disaster in most parts of the world, if that mailbox happens to belong to your boss, you are going to have to treat it like a disaster.

Recovering a single mailbox is going to cost you a lot of pain and time, but it is an excellent way to become familiar with Exchange restoration procedures. You have two avenues to pursue to restore a single mailbox: restoring the entire server to a standby server or restoring from a brick-level backup if available. If you have configured all users to use an offline store (OST file), you will have a third avenue available to you—recovering mailbox data from an OST file, which is discussed later in this chapter.

Recovering a Mailbox from a Standby Server

Since Exchange Server stores all private messages in the same database file, (i.e. a brick wall of mailboxes) you are going to have to restore the entire information store if a mailbox is deleted. Remember that standby server I keep extolling the virtues of having? Here is another situation in which that standby server will be useful. To restore a single mailbox that has been accidentally deleted, follow these steps:

1. A Windows NT recovery server will need to be built as described earlier in this chapter. This server does not need to have the same name as the original server, but it does need to have access to the original domain database because the original Exchange site services account must be used.

2. Install Exchange Server on this server using SETUP /R. This will install the Exchange software, but it neither creates the information store databases nor starts the services. When prompted, choose to create a new site. Do not join an existing site. Enter the exact organization name, site name, site services account, and site services account password that was used with the original server. Don't forget to match the case of the letters in the organization and site name.

3. If the original server had a service pack installed on it, install the service pack with the UPDATE /R command.

4. Run the Exchange Performance Optimizer program and make sure the parameters, working directories, database, and log file location files are set correctly. Also make sure you document the location of the working directory, database, and log files locations (and make sure the locations have sufficient disk space to accommodate the data that is about to be restored).

5. Make sure that the Exchange System Attendant service is started.

6. Using the most recent normal backup tape, restore the information store to this server. The directory service database is not necessary. If there are incremental or differential backups, restore those as well.

7. Start the directory store and information store services.

8. Check the event logs to make sure that the information store service has started correctly.

9. Using Exchange Administrator, run the DS/IS Consistency Adjuster: go to *Site Name* ➤ Configuration ➤ Servers, view the server's properties, choose the Advanced tab, and click the Consistency Adjuster button. Select all the check box options for the public and private information stores, click the All Inconsistencies radio button, and click OK.

10. Highlight the mailbox in the recipients container that you wish to recover and display its properties.

11. On the General tab, click the primary Windows NT account and select the Administrator user (or whomever you are currently logged in as).

12. Either from the server or from a workstation, create a Mail (or Mail And Fax) profile for this mailbox.

13. Launch Outlook and connect to the mailbox you want to recover on the recovered Exchange server.

14. Either export the entire mailbox to a PST file using the File ➤ Import And Export feature or copy the messages you wish to recover to a PST file. If you are trying to recover the entire mailbox, the former procedure is much easier to use.

15. Copy the recovered PST file to the production system and import the recovered messages in the PST into the newly created mailbox.

This is a time-consuming process because you have to completely build a recovery server if you did not already have one, and you have to wait for the information store database to be restored. Further, the recovery server must have enough hard disk space to hold the private and public information store databases.

NOTE

This same procedure can be used to recover a deleted public folder. Instead of recovering the mailbox data, you simply export the public folder data to a PST file and import it back to the production system. If you have enabled Deleted Item Recovery for the public information store, you can recover a deleted public folder from the Deleted Items cache.

Part v

Brick Restores

Chapter 25 reviewed a new feature being incorporated into the newest version of Exchange-aware backup software packages called a brick-level backup. Simply put, the software opens each mailbox and backs up the messages and folders in that mailbox. This is much slower than a standard Exchange database backup and usually uses more space on the tape. However, if you have just deleted an important mailbox and need to restore it, the brick-level backup software is going to save you a tremendous amount of time.

For most software packages that are capable of doing this, you simply locate the mailbox name you want to restore, select it, and click the Restore button. You may even have the option of only restoring a single folder within a mailbox, depending on the software product you are using.

Recovery Using Offline Store Files

The Exchange and Outlook clients support a special type of local message storage called an offline store (or an OST file). This file contains a complete mirror image of a mailbox's Calendar, Contacts, Deleted Items, Drafts, Inbox, Journal, Notes, Outbox, Sent Items, and Tasks folders. Additional mailbox folders can be synchronized to this file by selecting the Synchronization tab on the folder's property page and choosing the When Offline Or Online radio button in the This Folder Is Available section. Public folders can also be synchronized to this file if the folder is placed in the Favorites folder first; then the user can set its synchronization properties.

By default, the items are synchronized manually, but the user (or the administrator) can set them to be synchronized automatically on exit or periodically while the user is working. Outlook 98 and 2000 will synchronize in the background.

There are two major advantages to using OST files. The first is that when the client launches Outlook and attempts to connect to Exchange, the user can work offline if the Exchange server is not available. She will have her old messages with which she can work offline and they can prepare new messages (but the new messages will not be delivered until the server is back up).

The second advantage is that, if the mailbox is ever accidentally deleted from the server, there is still a local copy of the mailbox data.

Recovery is not tricky, but you have to perform the steps in the correct order.

If a mailbox has been accidentally deleted, do not re-create it immediately. Instead, have the user start Outlook in Work Offline mode. The user then needs to copy all her messages to a PST file. You can export the entire Exchange mailbox using the Outlook Import And Export Wizard found on the File menu; simply choose Export To A in the Choose An Action To Perform dialog box and export the entire mailbox to a PST file. Then delete the original OST file because it will no longer be usable once the mailbox is recreated.

Once the offline version mailbox is exported, you can re-create the mailbox and have the user reconnect. Import the data from the PST file back in using the Outlook Import And Export feature on the File menu.

Recovering Many Deleted Mailboxes

Let's say that one of your administrators accidentally deleted an entire container of users with, say, 500 mailboxes (and of course, he confirmed that this is what he really wanted to do). The Exchange Administrator program took the administrator seriously and deleted all the mailboxes. The Exchange directory service now notifies all the other servers in the site (and the organization) that these mailboxes have been deleted.

Well, luckily, these items don't get deleted out of the directory immediately. As a matter of fact, the default is that they remain hidden in the directory for 30 days. These entries are marked with a tombstone (as discussed in Chapter 28). When the tombstone reaches a certain age, the item will be deleted from the directory database on that server. By default, the garbage collection process runs every 12 hours and cleans up any directory item with a tombstone older than 30 days. These values are controlled by choosing *Site Name* ➢ Configuration, viewing the DS Site Configuration object properties, and selecting the General tab.

The first answer to your deleted-mailbox dilemma is to restore the entire server from backup (unless you want to recover 500 mailboxes using the single-mailbox recovery techniques). Take the most recent backup tape and restore the directory database and public and private information store databases. This solves the problem of the deleted mailboxes. Or does it?

When a server is restored, the directory on the restored server is considered to be more out of date than the other replicas of the directory in the organization. The other directories in the organization will eventually "backfill" information to the server that has been restored and instruct it to delete those directory entries once again.

The solution is to run a program called `authrest.exe`, which is found on the Exchange Server CD-ROM in the `\Server\Support\Utils\I386` directory. However, if you have a backfill problem, I highly recommend bringing Microsoft PSS into the picture as soon as possible just to make sure you don't make any mistakes while trying to correct this situation.

FOR FURTHER INFORMATION

If you would like more information on the topics covered in this chapter, here is some essential reading:

▸ Microsoft publishes two documents called "MS Exchange Disaster Recovery Part 1 and Part 2." The current version of this document is 4.00 and is available on Microsoft's Web site at www.microsoft.com/exchange/55/whpprs/disaster.htm. You should download this document and keep it in a notebook. And don't just download it, print it out, and forget it—read it.

CASE STUDY: LOOK CLOSELY AND KEEP AN OPEN MIND!

BAM Corporation supports nearly 5,500 users across five Exchange servers running Exchange 5 SP1. During a daily scan of the Windows NT event logs, the Exchange operator noticed event IDs 2197 and 2191 appearing in the application event log of one of the servers. The MTA was also stopped on that server. The operator could not get the MTA to restart, so the incident was immediately escalated to the Exchange administrator.

The Exchange administrator's first action was to attempt to restart the MTA herself. Upon confirming the messages in the event log, she checked the Microsoft Knowledge Base and found that these errors were known issues with Exchange 5 SP1, and that SP2 fixes the problem. She applied SP2, and everyone thought that the problem had been resolved.

CONTINUED ➡

However, the following morning, the event logs indicated an –1811 error stating that the backup had failed. At the end of the day, the server was shut down, an offline backup was performed, the log files were moved to a backup directory, and the PAT file was deleted (that was left over from the backup that failed). The Exchange services were restarted, and everything looked like it was going to work properly. An online backup was started but failed with the same error message.

The Exchange server was shut down again, and another offline backup was run. The logs were removed, and the administrator tried to run the EDBUTIL /MH priv.edb command (remember, this is Exchange 5 which uses EDBUTIL rather than ESEUTIL) to verify that the database was in a consistent state. EDBUTIL refused to run. The Microsoft Knowledge Base indicated that the problem was related to insufficient permissions. However, the Exchange administrator and the site services account had full control over the directories with the database files in them. In addition, the administrator knew that EDBUTIL /MH priv.edb worked because she had used it in the past.

The administrator decided that there may be a problem with the information store database, so she ran an ISINTEG –fix –pri –verbose to attempt to repair the private information store. This program ran, but it would not finish. On the first pass through, ISINTEG indicates that it fixed problems, but it failed after test number eight. A second pass using ISINTEG also failed at test number eight.

At this point, the administrator had just about decided that the database would have to be restored from tape. The major problem was that the most recent backup had failed, which meant that the users would lose all their messages for the past 24 hours. The curious thing was that everything with the users' mailboxes seemed to be fine—or at least no one had complained.

The Exchange administrator decided at this point to move as many of the important mailboxes as possible to other servers. BAM Corp had a dedicated bridgehead server that functioned as a connector server to other sites as well as running the IMS. Since this server had adequate storage, the administrator decided to move all the

CONTINUED ➡

mailboxes from the server that was having problems to the bridge-head server. All the mailboxes moved without incident. Later, all public folders that had replicas located on this server were moved to other servers.

Backups continued to fail on the problem server (even though there were now no mailboxes or public folders on it). Since all the data was now safe and sound on another server, the Exchange adminis-trator had the luxury of a little additional time on her side. She placed an incident with Microsoft Product Support Services (PSS). The PSS engineer surprised the Exchange administrator with his diagnosis: –1811 errors are almost always related to hardware prob-lems, specifically SCSI-related problems.

The Exchange administrator then opened up an incident with the hardware manufacturer and learned fairly quickly that there was a known bug with certain versions of their SCSI device drivers which could generate such errors. The SCSI device driver was upgraded, and the Exchange server was reinstalled. Once the server was rein-stalled, the mailboxes and public folder data were slowly moved back to the original server, and the problem did not recur.

The BAM Exchange administrator learned an important lesson dur-ing this saga—one that most of us often forget. Don't be so quick to blame Exchange for your problem, for Exchange Server may merely be exhibiting symptoms of a larger one.

PART VI

EXCHANGE SERVER COMMAND-LINE REFERENCE

Chapter 30
EXCHANGE SERVER TOOLS
BY JOSHUA KONKLE

The following reference describes some of the lesser known command-line tools available to Exchange administrators. The purpose here is to open the Pandora's box of possibilities. This reference is best used for perusing and viewing the descriptions. It is also helpful for looking up a tool to find valuable usage information.

ADMIN.EXE

Description

The ADMIN.EXE is the executable for the Exchange administrator tool. This admin tool has the potential to automate imports to the Exchange directory. In addition, the ADMIN.EXE tool allows access to the directory in its most raw state.

Installing

ADMIN.EXE is an integral part of the Exchange administration tools. When installing Exchange Server, you must choose the Custom/Complete option, then deselect all components except Books Online and the Exchange Administrator Program.

Usage

The ADMIN.EXE program has many command-line usage options. They are as follows.

/e   This option allows you to use the administrator program to perform bulk directory exports. A command-line export must be done in order to extract information on various object classes. This will allow an administrator to use the extracted data to generate a template that can then be used to modify any given connector via directory import. This can be very helpful if you have a complex connector configuration and want to save it for later use or if you need to delete and re-create the connector while troubleshooting.

The following is an example of the command-line syntax used in directory export:

```
Admin /e <export file> /o <option file>
```

The option file used should look like the following example:

```
[export]
ExportObject=All
Subcontainers=Yes
Basepoint=/o=<Your Org Name>/ou=<Our Site
Name>/cn=Configuration/cn=Connections
```

Full declaration of the export file contents is listed below.

The `export.csv` file can contain any or all of the following connector-related fields in the header:

- Obj-Class
- Delivery-Mechanism
- Directory Name
- Home-MTA
- Home-Server
- Accept messages from
- Accept messages from DL
- Activation-Schedule
- Activation-Style
- ADMD
- Can-Preserve-DNs
- Computer-Name
- Connected-Domains
- Country-Name
- Deliv-Ext-Cont-Types
- Deliverable Information Types
- Diagnostic-reg-key
- Encapsulation-Method
- Export-Containers
- Export-Custom-Recipients
- Home-MDB
- Import-Container
- Import-Sensitivity
- Incoming message size limit
- Issue warning storage limit

- Line-Wrap
- MDB-Unread-Limit
- Obj-Container
- PRMD
- Reject messages from
- Reject messages from DL
- Routing-List
- Supported-Application-Context
- Transfer-Retry-Interval
- Transfer-Timeout-Non-Urgent
- Transfer-Timeout-Normal
- Transfer-Timeout-Urgent
- Translation-Table-Used
- Trust level

NOTE

Please see the header.exe command syntax to learn more about generating your own header files for bulk exporting/importing. Each field above should be on a single line, separated by a comma, creating comma-separated values (or a CSV file).

Export Options File Contents

```
[export]
DirectoryService=<DS server name>    (default=NULL)
HomeServer=<server name>   (default=NULL)
Basepoint=<DN of basepoint object>   (default=NULL, which
  indicates the organization)
Container=<RDN of container object>   (default=Recipients)
ExportObject=[Mailbox, Remote (custom recipients), DL,
  Recipients (all recipients), All (all object types)]
  (default=Mailbox)
InformationLevel=[None, Minimal, Full]   (default=Minimal)
BasepointOnly=[Yes, No]   (default=No)
RawMode=[Yes, No]   (default=No)
Hiddenobjects=[Yes, No]   (default=No)
```

```
Subcontainers=[Yes, No] (default=No)
CodePage=[-1,0,code-page-ID] (Default=0)
ColumnSeparator=<ASCII value of column separator character>
  (Default=44) (",")
MVSeparator=<ASCII value of multivalue separator character>
  (Default=37) ("%")
QuoteCharacter=<ASCII value of quoted value
  delimiter>(Default=34) (")
```

NOTE

If you are after hidden objects, then use the HiddenObjects=Yes entry in the export.ini file.

/h or /?   This option will start the administrator program and open up the associated help file. The information listed on the default page will include the command-line options that follow. Use by typing **Admin /?** or **Admin /h**.

/i   This option allows you to import a CSV file. For example, you could have modified your export file and now want to import the changes that were made.

WARNING

It is recommended that you practice your imports on a pilot system before taking them to a production Exchange site. See also MS Knowledge Base Article Q155414.

Use by typing **Admin /i <import file> /o <options file> /n**. To turn off the progress bar, type **/n**. This is helpful if you are running the import in unattended mode using the AT command.

/d allows you to specify a directory server, but you may prefer to identify the directory server in the options file. In some cases you can name the file server.ini to help identify what server is being used.

Import Options File

```
[Import]
DirectoryService=<DS server name>    (default=NULL)
Basepoint=<DN of basepoint object>    (default=NULL, which
indicates the local site)
Container=<RDN of container object>    (default=Recipients)
InformationLevel=[None, Minimal, Full]    (default=Minimal)
```

Part vi

```
RecipientTemplate=<DN of default mailbox>    (default=none)
NTDomain=<NT domain where accounts will be created>
(default=none)
OverwriteProperties=[Yes, No]    (default=No)
CreateNTAccounts=[Yes, No]    (default=No)
DeleteNTAccounts=[Yes, No]    (default=No)
ApplyNTSecurity=[Yes, No]    (default=Yes)
GeneratePassword=[Yes, No]    (default=No)
RawMode=[Yes, No]    (default=No)
CodePage=[-1,0,code-page-ID] (Default=0)
ColumnSeparator=<ASCII value of column separator character>
(Default=44) (",")
MVSeparator=<ASCII value of multivalue separator character>
(Default=37) ("%")
QuoteCharacter=<ASCII value of quoted value
delimiter>(Default=34) (")
```

/m   This command-line option is helpful when you want to start an Exchange Administrator program to monitor several systems. The /m command allows you to specify which monitors will be started when the Admin program opens up. You must also specify a server where the monitors will be running. By default, the server site is the one checked for the monitor name. The monitors container in the site configuration object is checked for the name of the monitor you specify in the command.

Use this option by typing **Admin /m [site] [monitor/server]**. [site] is totally optional and normally not included. [monitor/server] is a combination of the directory name of the monitor (found on the general page on the monitor) and the server that will host the monitoring.

NOTE

It is especially important to know which server is hosting the monitoring functions, especially if you are using a link monitor.

/r   This option allows the Administrator program to be run in raw mode. This mode gives direct access to the directory attributes that may normally not be accessible. In addition, you can access the Exchange Server schema using the View/Raw Directory menu option.

As an example you may want to assign a department name to a distribution list. You cannot do this in the interface, but in raw mode you can view the extended attributes of an object by using Shift+Enter when the object is selected. You can then view all attributes and set the department value to something of value. This can be helpful when generating address book views by department.

/s This command is useful when you want to connect to a specified server. By default, the Administrator program will provide you with the local server's name unless you've specified another server as the default server to connect to in Admin. It is sometimes helpful to simply type the command-line option. Use this command by typing **Admin /s [server]**. [server] is the host name of the Exchange server to which you want to connect.

/t This option is especially helpful if you are monitoring a server that is going to go offline for maintenance. The /t option allows you to temporarily disable notifications resulting from a monitor determining problems with a monitored service or link. The usage is quite simple. Highlight the monitor you want to suspend in the Administrator program; then go to the command line and type **admin /t nr**.

NOTE

The *n* and *r* options allow you to disable *n*otifications and *r*epairs. Notifications would be things like e-mails or NT alerts, and repairs would be attempts to restart a server or the service. It is important to use these options correctly. In very few instances would you disable repairs and not notifications (possibly for logging purposes).

The screen may blink slightly and you may see no noticeable difference in the monitor, except that the last checked time will not change until you run **Admin /t**. Within a few minutes the last checked time will change.

CALCON.EXE

Description

CALCON, or the Calendar Connector, is shipped with Service Pack 2 of Exchange Server 5.5. This utility extends the calendar interoperability features of Exchange Server, building upon previously released connector enhancements that allow meeting requests to be sent among Exchange Server, Lotus Notes, and OfficeVision/VM. Group scheduling in a mixed-product environment is improved by support of queries for free/busy information among Exchange Server, Novell GroupWise, Lotus Notes, and OfficeVision/VM.

Part vi

Installing

CALCON is an executable included with Exchange Service 2 and higher.

Usage

The CALCON service can be started in console mode. This may be useful for troubleshooting and diagnosing problems related to the Calendar Connector.

To start CALCON in console mode, perform the following steps:

1. Ensure that the Calendar Connector service is not running.

2. Locate `calcon.exe` in the `Exchsrvr\Connect\Calcon` directory.

3. Type **calcon.exe** at an MS-DOS command line, or double-click the file from Windows Explorer to start the Calendar Connector in console mode. It may be a good idea to expand the properties of the MS-DOS window to view more information.

To stop the Calendar Connector, press Ctrl+Break to end the task. In some cases, you may have to kill the task to end it.

DUPPROXY.EXE

Description

The Duplicate Proxy tool enables you to search for directory entries that contain duplicate proxy addresses. In most cases, duplicate proxies are prevented from being created, but in scenarios where replication occurs, duplicate proxy entries can be created in different sites.

Installing

The DUPPROXY.EXE tool can be found on the Back Office Resource Kit with the Exchange tools.

Usage

To use the command-line Duplicate Proxy tool, you must have lightweight directory access protocol (LDAP) configured on your computer.

To search the Microsoft Exchange Server directory for entries with duplicate proxy addresses, follow these steps:

1. At the command prompt, switch to the directory where `dupproxy.exe` is installed.

2. The correct syntax, with the flags as described below, is: `Dupproxy <Microsoft Exchange Server computer name> <proxy type> <proxy value>`.

3. Type **dupproxy** with one of the following variable options:

TABLE 30.1: DUPPROXY Parameters

OPTION	DESCRIPTION
<Microsoft Exchange Server computer name>	The name of the Microsoft Exchange 5.0 Server computer with LDAP configured where you want to run the query.
<proxy type>	The e-mail address type of the proxy you are searching for—for example, simple mail transport protocol (SMTP) or X.400.
<proxy value>	The value you are searching for—for example, username@microsoft.com.

For example, you may want to periodically search for any object with a proxy of type SMTP with the prefix characters of a user's alias. To perform a search of this type, you can use the following syntax:

```
Dupproxy aoxomoxoa SMTP username*.
```

DSEXPORT.EXE

Description

DSEXPORT is a tool that uses the Directory Application Programming Interface or DAPI. Its primary function is to export information from the Microsoft Exchange Server directory service at the command line.

Installing

To install DSEXPORT.EXE, you will need to install Programming Library from Visual Studio or Microsoft Developer Network (MSDN).

Usage

The DSEXPORT tool has several command-line parameters that can be helpful to the Exchange administrator.

TABLE 30.2: DSEXPORT Parameters

OPTION	DESCRIPTION
/FILE=	Gives the name of the file to receive exported information.
/SERVER=	Restricts exports to objects on this server.
/DSA=	Specifies the Microsoft Exchange server on which to perform the directory export options.
/BASEPOINT=	Gives the starting point in the directory where the export begins to look; this is in the form of a Distinguished Name (DN).
/CONTAINER=	Gives the starting container beneath the basepoint where DSEXPORT exports data; this is in the form of a Relative DN.
/ONLY_BASEPOINT=	This may be used in place of /basepoint and /container to specify that you want DSEXPORT to export objects *only* at the *basepoint*.
/ALL_RECIPIENTS=	Exports all recipient objects (Mailbox, DLs, Custom Recipients) beneath the fully qualified DN created by the /basepoint + /container or specified directly by the /only_basepoint option.
/DIST_LIST=	Exports only distribution lists at the fully qualified DN created by the /basepoint + /container or specified directly by the /only_basepoint option. The default option is NOT to export only distribution lists but all recipient objects as specified by the /all_recipients option.
/MAILBOX=	Exports only mailboxes at the fully qualified DN created by the /basepoint + /container or specified directly by the /only_basepoint option. The default option is *not* to export only mailboxes but all recipient objects as specified by the /all_recipients option.
/REMOTE_ADDRESS=	Exports only custom recipients at the fully qualified DN created by the /basepoint + /container or specified directly by the /only_basepoint option. The default option is *not* to export only custom recipients but all recipient objects as specified by the /all_recipients option.
/CLASSES=	This is one of the most powerful options of the DSEXPORT tool. This allows you to specify a class from the schema, such as "computer," that you would like to export. The upcoming example will find all Exchange servers in your organization using the specified "computer" class as a /classes option.
/ALL_CLASSES	This option, similar to the /classes option, exports all objects of any type at the DN specified by the basepoint options.

TABLE 30.2 continued: DSEXPORT Parameters

OPTION	DESCRIPTION
/HIDDEN	This option simply allows DSEXPORT to export data on all hidden objects at the DN specified by the basepoint options.
/SUBTREE	This option allows the DSEXPORT tool to traverse all subcontainers of the container specified using the basepoint options. This is used primarily when enumerating *all* objects in a site or *all* objects in the organization.

You may want to enumerate all the Exchange servers in your organization for reporting purposes or for running a script. In some cases, such as message journaling, you must set register parameters on every Exchange server in the organization to have a complete message journal for the company. It would be necessary to retrieve all server names so you could process a registry change on each. The following is an example of how to use DSEXPORT.EXE to retrieve all Exchange server names in the organization.

```
dsexport /file=d:\output.csv /dsa=ServerName /server=""
/classes=Computer /basepoint=/o=ORGName /subtree
```

The output.csv file can be viewed in Excel as cell data. From here you can extract all the server names and place them into a file called exservers.txt.

NOTE

It would be a good idea to learn how the NT command FOR works so that you could use the server names in a FOR script. In the example, "FOR /F %I IN (SERVERS.TXT) DO <command> %I," %I becomes the server name from servers.txt, and the FOR command steps through each line of the file to process the <command>.

ESEUTIL.EXE

Description
ESEUTIL is the Microsoft Exchange Server database management tool. ESE stands for Extensible Storage Engine, and the UTIL is for utility.

This tool is commonly pronounced "E-Z UTIL." It is important to note that this tool manages the database, not the data internal to the database. The data (your messages and attachments) will be of no concern to this utility during a repair.

Installing

This tool is installed as a part of every Exchange server. If you run ESEU-TIL anywhere in the Windows NT system, this tool will run. The tool is installed in the c:\winnt\system32 directory by default. The older version of the tool (EDBUTIL) was installed in the \exchsrvr\bin directory; the change caused a bit of confusion. You may now run the tool from any path in the command line. However, as you will see in the following section, it's important to identify the location of the Exchange server files.

Usage

/d   This option is one of the safer switches. It allows for an offline compaction of the databases. When Exchange Server runs its normal IS maintenance, it reports the amount of free space in the databases; this is referenced as Event ID 1221, which you should see twice (one for MS-ExchangeIS Priv, one for MSExchangeIS Pub). Use this event ID to determine if you need to use the /d option. It is generally unnecessary to use the /d command to reclaim unused database space on disk. However, you should check Event ID 1221 weekly to determine the amount of free space in the databases. You will use the following:

  ▶ <database name> is the filename of the database to compact, or one of /ispriv, /ispub, or /ds.

  ▶ /l<path> is the location of log files (default: current directory).

  ▶ /s<path> is the location of system files (e.g., checkpoint file) (default: current directory).

  ▶ /b<db> is used to make a backup copy under the specified name.

  ▶ /t<db> is used to set them temporary database name (default: TEMPDFRG.EDB).

  ▶ /p is used to preserve the temporary database (i.e., don't instate).

  ▶ /o is used to suppress logo.

NOTE

The switches /ispriv, /ispub, and /ds use the registry to automatically set the database name, log file path, and system file path for the appropriate Exchange store.

NOTE

Before defragmentation begins, soft recovery is always performed to ensure that the database is in a consistent state.

NOTE

If instating is disabled (i.e., /p), the original database will be preserved uncompacted, and the temporary database will be the defragmented version of the database.

/r The soft recovery option is traditionally run "automagically" by the database tools. In most cases an administrator will not need to run this tool. However, in the event an administrator does a file copy backup of the databases, it will be necessary to run the ESEUTIL in recovery mode. This tool regenerates the `edb.chk` and `edb.log` files for the databases. You will use the following:

- ▶ /is or /ds
- ▶ /l<path> as the location of the log file (default: current directory)
- ▶ /s<path> as the location of system files (e.g., checkpoint file) (default: current directory)
- ▶ /o to suppress logo

NOTE

The special switches /is and /ds use the Registry to automatically set the log file path and system file path for recovery of the appropriate Exchange store(s).

/g Integrity checking mode does not require any additional space to complete its work. This option is primarily used during the early phases of database checking. It simply reads from the database and checks the integrity of the database, not the data therein. You will use the following:

- ▶ <database name> is the filename of the database to verify, or one of /ispriv, /ispub, or /ds.
- ▶ /t<db> is used to set temporary database name (default: INTEG.EDB).
- ▶ /v stands for verbose.
- ▶ /x will give detailed error messages.
- ▶ /o is used to suppress logo.

NOTE

The consistency checker performs no recovery and always assumes that the database is in a consistent state, returning an error if this is not the case.

NOTE

The special switches /ispriv, /ispub, and /ds use the registry to automatically set the database name for the appropriate Exchange store.

/u   This option allows you to upgrade a database without having to allow setup to process it for you. If you are using this command, you need the original install CDs for the server you are upgrading. You will use the following:

- ▶ ESEUTIL /u <database name> /d<previous .DLL> [options].
- ▶ <database name> is the filename of the database to upgrade.
- ▶ /d<previous .DLL> are the path and filename of the .DLL that came with the release of Microsoft Exchange Server from which you are upgrading. This filename is edb.dll; you should consider renaming it after copying it to the system. Rename based on the version and service pack (i.e., edb.dll from 40sp2 would be edb40sp2.dll).

Zero or more of the following switches can be used, separated by a space:

- ▶ /b<db> is used to make backup copy under the specified name.

▶ /t<db> is used to set the temporary database name (default: TEMPUPGD.EDB).

▶ /p preserves the temporary database (i.e., don't instate).

▶ /o is used to suppress logo.

NOTE

This utility should only be used to upgrade a database after an internal database format change has taken place. If necessary, this will usually only coincide with the release of a major, new revision of Microsoft Exchange Server.

NOTE

Before upgrading, the database should be in a consistent state. An error will be returned if otherwise.

NOTE

If instating is disabled (i.e. /p), the original database is preserved unchanged, and the temporary database will contain the upgraded version of the database.

/m This option is used primarily to troubleshoot. As with the /g command, the /m command is used to diagnose potential problems with the databases. Its primary function is to dump the header data of the database file, checkpoint file data, or log file. I like to use this tool to determine the last full backup, incremental backup, or differential backup and to see if the database is consistent. You will use the following:

▶ ESEUTIL /m[mode-modifier] <filename> [options].

▶ [mode-modifier] is an optional letter designating the type of dump to perform.

Valid values are:

▶ h, the dump database header (default)

▶ k, the dump checkpoint file

▶ l, the dump log file

▶ s, the dump space usage

Part vi

► <filename> is the name of the file to dump. The type of the file should match the type of dump requested (e.g., if using /mh, then <filename> must be the name of a database). If using /mk it must be the edb.chk file.

/p   This option fixes the database corruption. Since the database is fixed irrespective of the actual mailbox data, this tool will delete user data. This tool is designed to fix the database, not to get the information store working. ISINTEG is the tool most often used to help with IS problems. In many cases the /p option is a last-ditch effort to clear things up by an administrator who forgot to do backups regularly.

NOTE
A dialog box will appear when you attempt to run the /p option; this means that this option should not be taken lightly.

You will use the following:

► ESEUTIL /p <database name> [options].

► <database name> is the filename of the database to repair, or one of /ispriv, /ispub, or /ds.

You will use zero or more of the following switches separated by a space:

► /t<db> is used to set the temporary database name (default: REPAIR.EDB).

► /v is for verbose output.

► /x gives detailed error messages.

► /o is used to suppress logo.

NOTE
The switches /ispriv, /ispub, and /ds use the registry to automatically set the database name for the appropriate Exchange store.

/z   An additional switch was added to ESEUTIL with Exchange 5.5, Service Pack 2. ESEUTIL /z will perform the zeroing of unused database pages in the same manner as explained above, by running an offline command-line database utility. It will also detect and zero orphaned long values.

NOTE

For more information about orphaned long values, see Microsoft Knowledge Base article Q185271, XADM: Orphaned LV Errors Running ESEUTIL Consistency Checker.

You will use the following:

▶ PARAMETERS: (database name) is the filename of the database to compact, or one of /ispriv, /ispub, or /ds.

▶ The switches /ispriv, /ispub, and /ds use the registry to automatically set the database name for the appropriate Exchange store.

If you do not want to bring the server down on a regular basis, then modify the following suggested registry subkey:

```
HKEY_LOCAL_MACHINE\SYSTEM\CurrentControlSet\Services\
MSExchangeIS\ParametersSystem
```

Add the following entry:

```
Data "Zero Database During Backup" (without quotes)
Type: REG_DWORD
Value: 0x00000001
```

This will allow the IS maintenance to run a zeroing process on the database, whereby all information that had been deleted will be zeroed out.

EVENTS.EXE

Description

EVENTS.EXE is the executable used to provide the Event Scripting service in the Exchange 5.5 environment. Traditionally this tool runs silently and happily in the background. However, from time to time you may need to take advantage of the tool's command-line parameter. This tool is primarily run because of corrupted event_config folders in the system folders of an Exchange server site.

Installing

If you have installed the Event Scripting service and are having problems with the event_config folders (i.e., you have two sets of folders for the same server), then this command will be available in the `\exchsrvr\bin`.

Usage

`Events.exe/c:servername` has a special feature of cleaning up duplicate event_config folders for the same machine in the enterprise.

WARNING
You must be logged on as the Exchange Service Account for that site.

GUIDGEN.EXE

Description

A Microsoft Developer Network (MSDN) GUID Generation utility that is used to help rebuild site folders if the first server in the site is removed without following the steps in the Microsoft Knowledge Base Article Q152959.

It may be necessary to rebuild the site folders (that is the Offline Address Book, Schedule+, Free/Busy Information, and Organizational Forms) if the first server in the site is removed without following the procedures in the Knowledge Base Article Q152959.

Installing

This tool is only available as a part of MSDN. It may be possible to retrieve a copy from Microsoft Support.

Usage

1. Run GUIDGEN and select option 4, Registry Format.

2. Click New GUID.

3. Copy or write down the new GUID number from the Result box. This number will be needed in step 10.

4. Run the Microsoft Exchange Administrator program in raw mode. To do this, go to the command line, change to the Exchsrvr\Bin directory, and type **admin /r**.

5. Select the configuration container of the site you want to rebuild and highlight the Information Store Site Configuration object.

6. Select File, Raw Properties.

7. In the Object Attributes window, scroll down to the Site Folder GUID attribute and select it.

8. Click Editor.

9. Replace the existing GUID number with the one generated in step 2 (the value should be entered in hexadecimal), and then click OK.

10. Press the Set button. After doing this, make sure the Edit Value and Attribute Value are the same.

11. Click OK to close the dialog box.

12. Stop and restart the Information Store service with the Services icon in Control Panel.

IMCCOPY.EXE

Description

IMCCOPY is used to copy and potentially restore the IMC (now known as the Internet Mail Service, or IMS) configuration. It should be noted that quite a bit of the IMS configuration is stored in the registry, so this tool helps keep copies of the specific registry settings for a given IMS.

Installing

IMCCOPY is a utility available on the Exchange Server CD. It can be found under the Support directory on the CD. Simply copy it to your exchsrvr\bin directory or place it in a Utilities directory.

Part vi

Usage

IMCCOPY is a utility that must be used locally on an Exchange server. The following parameters are supported.

TABLE 30.3: IMCCOPY Parameters

Option	Description
-save	Saves the tabs specified by the options below
-restore	Saves the configuration specified by the options below
general	Specifies the General tab
security	Specifies the Security tab
domain	Specifies the domain-specific information on the Internet Mail tab
mime	Specifies the mime database information in the registry
routes	Specifies the Routing tab
all	Saves all the above information
filename	Identifies the file where the output file will be saved

IMCSAVE.EXE

Description

The IMCSAVE, or Internet Mail Connector Save, was designed to move the IMC from one server to another. In the early days of Exchange 4.0, administrators installed the IMC, or Internet Mail Connector. When upgrading or retiring services on certain systems requires you to consolidate the services, this tool helps move existing Internet Mail Services/Connectors.

Installing

Traditionally the IMCSAVE tool has been available on any of the Back Office Resource Kits, and you can still find it there.

Usage

IMCSAVE performs the following actions when executing on your server:

▶ Inspects the registry to determine the working directory location of the IMCDATA. It must then create a `backup` directory in the `imcdata` directory.

> **WARNING**
>
> If the process already ran or if there is a directory called imcdata\backup, the tool will halt immediately.

▶ After generating the backup file, the tool begins to copy configuration information from the registry. The configuration information is copied to a file called `imcsvc.reg` in the `imcdata\ backup` directory (specified earlier).

▶ The IMS, like Outlook, logs on to the Exchange server information store. Therefore, the IMS has a profile used to communicate with the Exchange server. This service profile registry information is copied to a file called `imcpro.reg` in the `imcdata\ backup` directory.

▶ In addition to the registry, the IMS stores configuration in the Exchange directory. It is crucial that this data be exported using the standard Exchange directory access API or DAPI. The data exported from the Exchange directory is stored in a file called `imcobj.csv` (a comma-separated value file format).

▶ The IMS could potentially have unsent messages in queues when it was shutdown to begin the IMCSAVE process. The IMCSAVE tool interacts with the Exchange server in the same way the IMS does. The tool logs on to Exchange as the IMS to interact with the IMS data in the Exchange IS.

▶ The IMCSAVE tool is in the process of collecting the e-mail stored in the IS and the IMCDATA\OUT. To ensure that no more data will enter the IMS to be delivered inbound or outbound, a flag is set to disable e-mail activity using the IMS.

▶ IMCSAVE is responsible for extracting the data in the IMS connector queue, which is stored in the IS. This is composed of the MTS-OUT folder and MTS-IN folder. These folders are hidden in the Exchange IS from normal administrative use. Please see mdbvu32.exe for more information. The IMCSAVE copies all data from these internal IS folders to a directory in the Transport-Neutral Encapsulation Format (TNEF). The directories are called imcdata\backup\mtsout and imcdata\backup\mtsin, respectively.

▶ The IMCSAVE tool needs all of the files to restore the IMS to its state when it was saved. To provide this functionality, the IMC-SAVE tool generates a type of packing list and places the list into a file called imcfls.ini. This file is used to ensure that the files are used as a whole.

The following list describes the commands IMCSAVE utilizes to provide the above services.

-output SaveDir saves all output under the specified directory (SaveDir) in a subdirectory named Backup. If not specified, output will be stored under the IMC root directory in a subdirectory named Backup.

-save Item [Item]... saves the specified output items:

Reg[istry] is the IMS registry configuration.

Dir[ectory] is the IMS directory service configuration.

MTSI[n] is the MTS-IN IS connector message queue.

MTSO[ut] is the MTS-OUT IS connector message queue.

Bad is the queue for dumping bad messages.

Con[tentConversionFailed] dumps the ContentConversion-Failed message queue.

Work is the IMS working queue message queue.

-delete deletes messages in the queue. Can be used with the above options.

-help displays help.

ISINTEG.EXE

Description

This tool is designed for the Exchange Server system. It is used to fix the information store database as it pertains to Exchange data. ISINTEG.EXE is sensitive to the data and tries to save portions of the database without deleting data.

Installing

This tool is installed when you install the Exchange server. There are no special installation requirements for this tool.

Usage

TABLE 30.4: ISINTEG Parameters

Option	Description
-pri	private information store
-pub	public information store
-fix	check and fix (default: check only)
-detailed	detailed mode (default: non-detailed mode)
-verbose	report verbosely
-l filename	log filename (default: .\isinteg.prilpub)
-t refdblocation	default: the location of the store
-test testname,...	folder message aclitem mailbox (pri only) delfld acllist rcvfld (pri only) timedev rowcounts attach morefld oofhist(pri only) global searchq dlvrto namedprop (-detailed mode only) peruser artidx(pub only) search newsfeed(pub only) dumpsterprops
	Ref count tests: msgref msgsoftref attachref acllistref aclitemref newsfeedref(pub only) fldrcv(pri only) fldsub dumpsterref
	Groups tests: allfoldertests allacltests
	Special tests: deleteextracolumns
-patch	repair information store after an offline restore
–pri -pub -dump [-l logfilename]	verbose dump of store data

ISSCAN.EXE

Description
In the past year Microsoft responded to customer demand for virus exoneration by providing a solution to existing customers who need to eradicate file-borne viruses. The tool is designed to cleanse Exchange server databases that have messages or attachments with viruses. The tool will scan the database's message and/or attachment table and extricate the infected messages and/or attachments.

Installing
ISSCAN.EXE is a tool that must be downloaded from the Microsoft FTP site. The following versions are available:

- ▶ ftp://ftp.microsoft.com/bussys/exchange/
  exchange-public/fixes/ENG/Exchg5.5/ISSCAN/
  ISSCANA.EXE for the DEC Alpha platform.

- ▶ ftp://ftp.microsoft.com/bussys/exchange/
  exchange-public/fixes/ENG/Exchg5.5/ISSCAN/
  ISSCANI.EXE for the Intel x86 platform.

After downloading, unzip and follow the instructions in the readme. ISSCAN is also available as a part of Exchange Server Service Pack 3.

Usage
When using ISSCAN.EXE, you must stop the Microsoft Exchange Server Information Store service. After stopping the IS you can then run ISSCAN.EXE. You will use the following:

```
ISSCAN -fix {-pri | -pub} -test badmessage or badattach -c
<criteria file>
```

- ▶ The -fix is used to remove infected files that match the specified criteria.

- ▶ The -pri | -pub determines against which database, public or private, the -fix or -test parameter performs its actions.

- ▶ The -test badmessage will remove all messages from the database whose subject begins with "Important Message From" and have a creation time after 03/01/99.

- ▶ The -test badattach or badattach2 will remove all attach-ments from the database whose filename is list.doc and whose file size is between 40KB and 60KB.

- ▶ The -c <criterion file> option provides the user with other options pertaining to what messages and/or attachments are searched for and destroyed.

When using the criterion file option, the ISSCAN tool will read the file for the entries used in the scan. The file can contain entries for messages and attachments. The file format is tab delimited, meaning that each entry should be separated by a tab. The criterion entry formats are very specific. The attachment entries are specified as follows:

```
Attach filename <tab> minimumsize <tab> maximumsize
```

The message entries are specified as follows:

```
MSG start of subject <tab> yyyy/mm/dd
```

In most cases you will want to scan for multiple infected files or mes-sages. When scanning for the file attachment, include a search option for the file's short filename. Short filenames, 8.3, are stored to for backwards compatibility with Windows 3*x*– and Windows for Workgroups–based applications.

```
ATTACH infected1.doc 50000 60000
ATTACH infected2.doc 45000 60000
ATTACH issacnew10.doc 30000 40000
MSG Good Times 2001/03/01
MSG ID ten T errors 2005/02/29
```

There are two ways to express the file names in the Exchange IS. The long name and the short truncated filename. It may be prudent to create a criterion file that holds both short and long names. The following is an example:

```
ATTACH bigtxfile.exe 50000 100000
ATTACH bigfil~1.exe 50000 100000
```

Using the ISSCAN tool will generate log files. The filenames are depen-dent on the types of scans completed. When you run the tests against the public information store database, the log file is isscan.pub, and it is isscan.pri when run against the private information store database.

Interpreting the log files is simple. When deleting attachments with -test badattach an entry for the deleted attachment name will be in the log file. If you use -test badattach2 you can view the attachment, the sender, and the receiver of the e-mail message involved in the infected attachment. Be forewarned that badattach2 takes longer because it is querying the sender/receiver of messages and looking at attachments. If you are deleting messages using -test badmessage, then you will see the name of the sender of the message in the log file.

TIP

The ISSCAN tool is designed to clean an already infected database. It is not designed to perform prevention of inbound virus attachments or messages.

MGMTLIST.EXE

Description

The Management Chain List tool enables you to specify a user's e-mail address through the command line and returns a formatted list of the management chain from the user's level up to the CEO.

Installing

There are no special installation instructions. This tool is available as part of the Back Office Resource Kit Second Edition.

Usage

To use this tool, type **MGMTLIST [/p Profile] [/s Server [/i Site [/e Enterprise]]] Name [Name]...**

Blanks are optional between switches and their values (e.g. /pProfile). Use single or double quotes to input values containing blanks, such as a profile name with spaces.

NOTE

Server, Site, and Enterprise are ignored if Profile is given.

TABLE 30.5: MGMTLIST Parameters

PROFILE	MAPI PROFILE NAME (DEFAULT = DEFAULT PROFILE)
Server	Server to logon to (default = Local server)
Site	Site to logon to (default = REDMOND)
Enterprise	Enterprise to logon to (default = MICROSOFT)

The name specified at the command line is the user for whom you want the manager's list. The output format is in the form of comma-separated values. It is recommended to pipe this information to a file for easy review. Output includes the following information: Display Name, Alias, Title, Department, Phone [or Phone2] listed for the user, the user's manager, the manager of the user's manager, 3rd level manager, etc.

MAPISEND.EXE

Description

The MAPISEND tool is used to send messages with optional file attachments through Microsoft Exchange Server from a Windows NT workstation or Windows 95 command prompt. MAPISEND.EXE was formerly known as the Command-Line Mail Sender Tool (SENDMAIL.EXE). This program is also available in the Microsoft Mail Resource Kit.

NOTE

The tool was renamed because the original name conflicted with an existing SMTP mailer server that was used very heavily in the Unix world.

NOTE

Microsoft Exchange administrators can run this program automatically by using the AT Scheduler in Windows NT or the winat.exe program included in the Windows NT Resource Kit.

WARNING

Programs scheduled with the Windows NT AT Scheduler are run by the Windows NT Schedule service. To send mail to a Microsoft Exchange mailbox with the MAPISEND.EXE program, you must use a domain account to start the Schedule service. By default, the service starts by using the LocalSystem account.

Installing

MAPISEND.EXE requires no special installation. It is installed as a part of the Back Office Resource Kit. You can copy this file to any machine where you need it.

Usage

This tool is best used if you need to send a reminder on a regular basis and would prefer to automate the sending rather than sending it manually.

MIGRATE.EXE

Description

The Source Extractor for Unix Mail tool automates the transfer of user accounts, messages, and associated information from a Unix e-mail system to Microsoft Exchange Server. The Source Extractor tool extracts the data to migration files, which can then be imported to Microsoft Exchange Server. To import data to Microsoft Exchange Server, you can use the Microsoft Exchange Migration Wizard Import from the Migration Files option.

Because many organizations with Unix RFC822–based messaging systems require the rich content capabilities provided by Microsoft Exchange Server, the extractor provides a way to extract messages from the mail spooler as well as messages filed in private folders.

Note Source Extractor for Unix Mail imports mail messages without attachments from Unix Mail to Exchange 5.0 or Exchange 5.5. To read attachments, a mime client is also required.

The following list defines terms you should be familiar with:

Pine   Text-based Unix e-mail client written and owned by the University of Washington

DAPI   Microsoft Exchange Directory Import/Export

Elm   Text-based Unix e-mail client that is included in most standard UNIX distributions

RFC822   The standard for the format of Advanced Research Projects Agency (ARPA) SMTP messages

Installing

You can install this tool when you run the Microsoft Back Office Resource Kit, Second Edition Setup program, or you can use the following procedure to install the Source Extractor for Unix Mail tool:

1. From the `Exchange\Samples\UnixSE` subdirectory on the Microsoft Back Office Resource Kit, Second Edition CD, copy the Unix source code to your computer.

2. Because the Source Extractor for Unix Mail is provided as source code, a C-compiler on the host computer or a compiler capable of compiling to the host computer is required to produce the migrate file. For more information, see the compiler documentation for your version of Unix.

Usage

Before attempting to use this utility, you should be familiar with the RFC822 standard.

NOTE

The migrated files will be named `mmddhhmm.pk1`, `mmddhhmm.pri`, `<loginID>.pri`, and `<loginID>.sec`. The `mmddhhmm.pri` file will only contain the directory section. If a file exists with the same time, the minutes value (mm) will be incremented by one minute.

Use the following syntax to begin the migration process:

```
migrate [-u<User File>] [-r] [-a] [-m] [-d<path>]
[-p</path/Parameter File>] [-? | -h | -H]
```

The following list gives the command-line options available in the Source Extractor for Unix Mail tool and their functions:

-u<file name> indicates a file containing a list of the users to be migrated.

NOTE

Note that a filename must be present. The file can be in password file format (/etc/passwd), as seen in File 1 below, or as a list of logon IDs with one logon ID per line (see File 2 below). This file will be used to obtain the necessary information (such as the user ID, info section, and home directory) if the line contains six colons; otherwise the password file will be used. This overrides the lowest UserID variable in the Parameter file.

File 1:

jones:x:173:175:M jones:/usr/bin/jonesj:/bin/csh

billlp:x:175:110:Z Billlp:/usr/mktg/Billlp:/bin/csh

Steelee:x:176:110:S Steelee:/usr/bin/steelee:/usr/local/bin/tcsh

File 2:

annemcp

johne

-r creates custom recipients in Microsoft Exchange (does not create accounts or mail).

-a create accounts in Microsoft Exchange (does not migrate mail).

-m migrates mail to Microsoft Exchange (assumes custom recipients or mailboxes exist).

-d\<path> overrides the default location where the extracted data will be located. The default location is the current directory.

-p is the fully qualified path to the parameter file including the filename. Use the parameter file to indicate additional parameters. The parameter file can be located anywhere with any name (the current directory is the default).

-?, -h, -H displays command-line help.

TIP

The -r, -a, and -m commands migrate only the specific type of information indicated. However, if they are used together they will migrate all of the types.

MSEXIMC.EXE

Description

The Internet Mail Service was first introduced as a connector in Exchange Server 4.0. Thus its name became MSEXIMC.EXE. The Internet Mail Connector was later changed to the Internet Mail Service. The service itself is very powerful and offers many solutions to the business world. However, time and again it does not perform quite as expected. It will undoubtedly perform inversely to your preparation for problems. That is why it is important to know this tool offers a troubleshooting method unlike the other services in Exchange.

It is possible to run the MSEXIMC in a console window on the Exchange Server system. This allows you to get updates on the system as they are occurring or at set intervals. Sendmail, MSEXIMC's Unix counterpart, has since its creation provided logging to the stdout (standard out)—thus printing status messages to the screen.

Now you will know how to configure your IMS to provide you with detailed console reporting on a blow-by-blow basis. Sometimes this is necessary because it really feels like Exchange is trying to knock you out!

Installation

Running the IMS in console requires you to complete the following steps:

1. Open the Registry Editor (regedt32.exe).

2. Go to the following registry key: HKEY_LOCAL_MACHINE\
SYSTEM\CurrentControlSet\Services\MSExchangeIMC\
Parameters.

3. Choose Edit and select Add Value from the list of options.

4. In the Add Value dialog box, type the following in as the value name: DisplayErrsOnConsole.

5. In the Data Type drop-down list, select REG_DWORD.

6. In the Dword Editor Data field, enter 100 (or any value greater than 10).

7. In the Radix section, select HEX.

Usage

1. Open Control Panel and double-click Services. Stop or insure that the Internet Mail Service is not started.

2. Open a command window (cmd.exe), and change directories to <%Exchange Install Directory\Connect\ MSExcImc\Bin.

3. Type the following while in the \connect\mseximc\bin directory: **MSEXCIMC -console**.

4. You could increase the frequency of the on-screen logging to the console by decreasing the value for the following key by using HKEY_LOCAL_MACHINE\SYSTEM\CurrentControl-Set\Services\MSExchangeIMC\Parameters\ ConsoleStatFrequency.

5. The default rate is 14; lower this to a rate that meets your needs.

NOTE

If you have installed Services for Unix v1 you could telnet in and run mseximc –console during a telnet session and monitor it remotely.

MTACHECK.EXE

Description

This utility is designed to fix corrupt MTA database files, remove orphaned files no longer needed by the MTA, delete any corrupt objects, and remove system messages (such as directory replication messages) from the MTA queues.

Installing

Microsoft provides a utility with Exchange called MTACHECK.EXE, which is located in the \EXCHSRVR\BIN directory.

Usage

If the MTA software detects problems with any of the queues, the MTA-CHECK utility is run automatically. You can also run the MTACHECK utility manually, but the MTA service must be stopped. The following is a list of options that can be used with the MTACHECK program.

/v reports errors verbosely (in as much detail as possible).

/t creates a log file called `logfile.txt`.

/rl removes any link monitor messages from the queues.

/rp removes any public folder replication messages from the queues.

/rd removes directory replication messages from the queues.

NET [stop] and [start]

Part vi

Description

These commands allow you to stop or start an NT service from the command line. Remember that all services that have spaces in their names must be enclosed in quotation marks for the command to work correctly. In the list below we use the shortened registered names that are derived from the HKEY_LOCAL_MACHINE\SYSTEM\CURRENTCONTROLSET\SERIVICES\MSEXCHANGE* registry keys.

Installing

No installation is necessary. The net commands have been built into the Windows NT Server Operations System since it first debuted on the OS scene in 1993.

Usage for [stop]

- ▶ MSExchangeSA for Microsoft Exchange System Attendant
- ▶ MSExchangeIS for Microsoft Exchange Information Store
- ▶ MSExchangeDS for Microsoft Exchange Directory
- ▶ MSExchangeMTA for Microsoft Exchange Message Transfer Agent

- MSExchangeMSMI for MS Mail Connector Interchange
- MSExchangeDX for Microsoft Exchange Directory Synchronization
- MSExchangeIMC for Microsoft Exchange Internet Mail Connector
- MSExchangeFB for MS Schedule+ Free/Busy connector
- MSExchangeES for Microsoft Exchange Event Service

Usage for [start]

- MSExchangeSA for Microsoft Exchange System Attendant
- MSExchangeIS for Microsoft Exchange Information Store
- MSExchangeDS for Microsoft Exchange Directory
- MSExchangeMTA for Microsoft Exchange Message Transfer Agent
- MSExchangeMSMI for MS Mail Connector Interchange
- MSExchangeDX for Microsoft Exchange Directory Synchronization
- MSExchangeIMC for Microsoft Exchange Internet Mail Connector
- MSExchangeFB for MS Schedule+ Free/Busy connector
- MSExchangeES for Microsoft Exchange Event Service

NEWPROF.EXE

Description

NEWPROF was designed to aid administrators and desktop application managers in configuring Outlook's mandatory MAPI Profile. NEWPROF helps create new profiles for the Outlook program.

Installing

No special installation is required. This tool is available on any machine where Outlook has been installed. The new profile generation tool requires a file called default.prf when using default settings. This file can be found in the Windows directory.

NOTE

Please see the Office Resource Kits for more on the semantics of the profile file `default.prf`.

In the default state, NEWPROF does not require any parameters. It relies instead on hardcoded defaults to avoid any interaction, by default. This behavior can be changed.

Usage

In a specialized environment you will want modify the default new profile generation behavior. The following are acceptable commands.

```
NEWPROF [-P <Path to .PRF file\profile.prf>] [-S] [-X] [-Z]
```

TABLE 30.6: Acceptable Commands for NEWPROF

Option	Description
-P	<Path to .PRF file>\profile.prf is the path and the filename used by NEWPROF.EXE when generating a new profile.
-S	Forces NEWPROF.EXE to enter into a user interaction mode. One reason is to select the `profile.prf` file by hand. The option also helps when troubleshooting a NEWPROF.EXE command.
-X	Allows for onscreen monitoring when used in conjunction with –S and –P <Path to .PRF file\profile.prf>.
-Z	Verbose logging of the MAPI errors experienced when using the NEWPROF.EXE tool. Allows for easy debugging of a failed NEWPROF script when and only when used with the –S key.

WARNING

It is important to note that NEWPROF does not generate any log files, but will simply report to the screen.

NTBACKUP.EXE

Description
NTBACKUP is the built-in backup program used in Windows NT Server 4.0.

Installing
There are no special requirements to install the NTBACKUP.EXE utility. However, if you intend to back up an Exchange server remotely, you must install the Exchange Administrator program (ADMIN.EXE) on the machine where the backups will be performed.

Usage
When you want to back up the databases with little intervention of the GUI, you can use command-line switches with NTBACKUP.

NOTE

If you use a batch file, please limit the command-line length to 256 characters. If this limit is exceeded, it may result in files not being backed up. Additionally, the backup process may stop without warning.

The following parameters enable command-line backups of the Microsoft Exchange Server databases using the NTBACKUP:

Path specifies the component and the server.

DS \\server IS \\server is used when backing up Exchange. "Server" is the name of the Exchange server. "DS" indicates that you are backing up the directory, and "IS" indicates that you are backing up the information store.

```
Ntbackup backup DS \\Server_A IS \\Server_A DS \\Server_B /v
\t:normal
```

The command line syntax is:

```
Ntbackup operation path [/v][/r][/d"text"][/b]
[/t{option}][/l"file name"][/e]
```

The following list gives an operation and then specifies what you want to do:

Path specifies the path if you were backing up files; however, you use DS or IS since you are backing up Exchange.

/v is used after backing up the databases so that you can verify the data on tape against what is on disk.

/r is used to restrict or restore the backup set to the account backing up.

/d "text" is the friendly tape name written to the header when it is necessary to name the tape. This is not stored on the outside of the tape, but is readable by the backup program so you can identify the tape at a later time.

/b is used to back up the registry—a critical operation when backing up Exchange servers, as much of the config also resides in the registry.

/t {option} specifies the backup type. Option can be one of the following: normal, copy, incremental, differential, or daily.

Normal (aka Full) means that databases, transaction logs, and patch files are backed up. Transaction logs are purged and backup date and time are written to the header of the database, viewable using ESEUTIL.

Copy means that databases are backed up, but the transaction logs are not purged and the database header is not modified to indicate that a backup occurred. This is useful when attempting to do some proof of concept testing and you need a quick copy of your database.

Incremental backs up on the log files. This type of backup is disabled if circular logging is turned on (default). However, if circular logging is off, incremental backups will back up only the day's log files and purge what is on disk. You must perform at least one normal backup prior to using incremental; otherwise you will receive an error.

Differential is similar to incremental backups, but differential does not purge the log files. It only backs up the log files since the last successful normal or incremental backup that purged log files. You must have one successful normal backup prior to using differential.

Daily has no use when backing up Exchange.

/l "file name" is used when backing up the databases; it is recommended that you create a backup log using this option. Give it a name without spaces and use MAPISEND to e-mail it yourself.

/e requests that only exceptions be placed into the log since keeping the backup log small is the goal for some administrators.

ONDL.EXE

Description
The ONDL tool is a Microsoft Win32 command-line utility that displays the members of a Microsoft Exchange Server distribution list (DL). This tool can also display the Microsoft Exchange distribution lists that a user is a member of.

Installing
No special instructions are required. The ONDL tool is installed with the Back Office Resource Kit, Part 2.

Usage
Exchange command-line DL member/member of utility.

```
ONDL [/A] [/h | /?] [/m] [/p "Profile"] [/Q] [/r] [/s] [/u]
[/V] AliasName
```

The following list of options are used with this utility:

/a is a modifier switch. If used, output includes only the alias name of any recipients displayed. Default format is AliasName, DisplayName.

/h displays the help screen.

/m is a modifier switch. If used, AliasName is interpreted as a message recipient, and all of the distribution lists that AliasName is a member of will be displayed.

/p is the profile switch. Use MAPI profile with the name "Profile." If the profile name contains spaces, it must be enclosed in double quotes.

/q is used for quiet mode. Informational headers and footers are suppressed. Only member (member of) output is displayed.

/r recursively expands the membership list of nested DLs. This switch is ignored if used with output modifier switches /a, /m, or /s.

/s is the alias stream mode. Output is a stream of semicolon-delimited alias names. Implies /a switch behavior.

/u is used for a different MAPI profile. Do not piggyback on an existing session, but instead prompt for a profile to use.

/v signifies verbose output. This command displays all diagnostic output.

AliasName is the target alias name for the DS query. Normally considered to be the alias name of a DL whose membership is to be displayed. Behavior is changed by use of the /m switch. It piggybacks on the existing MAPI session, if one has been established. Otherwise the standard MAPI logon prompt is displayed.

OUTLOOK.EXE

Description
OUTLOOK.EXE is the main executable for Outlook.

Installing
No special requirements; you just need to install Outlook.

Usage
Usage varies depending on the version of Outlook, as described below.

TABLE 30.7: Available Options for Outlook 97/98

Option	Description
/CleanFreeBusy	Cleans up free and busy information on Exchange Server.
/CleanReminders	Cleans up reminders in Outlook and rebuilds reminder notices.
/CleanSchedPlus	Exonerates all Schedule + 1.0 settings, i.e. permissions, .cal file, published free and busy information. Used primarily in reparation of errors in a mixed Outlook and Schedule + environment as it pertains to calendaring and meeting requests.
/CleanViews	Deletes all users' customized views and restores the default view settings for all applications, i.e. Inbox, Outbox, Calendar, Journal, etc.
/Regserver	Replenishes Outlook's global settings in the registry (i.e., it will replace all HKEY_LOCAL_MACHINE settings). Additionally, all file associations and CLSID references in the HKEY_CLASSES_ROOT section of the registry are replaced. Optionally, you could run Outlook setup with the /y parameter. The oulook.srg file maintains the registry replenishing information; if it is missing or corrupt, this option will fail.
/ResetFolders	Resets all default Outlook folders, i.e. Calendar, Contacts, Inbox, Journal, Notes, Outbox, Sent Items, and Tasks.
/ResetOutlookBar	Rebuilds the Outlook bar so that if you change PST files or move from an Exchange server to a PST file type, storage on the Outlook bar can be fixed to point to the new location. The items in the Outlook bar are simply links to specific storage locations.
/Unregserver	Removes Outlook global settings in the registry (i.e., it will replace all HKEY_LOCAL_MACHINE settings and all file associations and CLSID references in the HKEY_CLASSES_ROOT section of the registry). Optionally, you could run Outlook setup with the /y parameter. The oulook.srg file maintains the registry replenishing information; if it is missing or corrupt, this option will fail. Run this prior to running /regserver.

NOTE

OUTLOOK.EXE is the base component of the Outlook e-mail program. The Outlook executable allows several command-line options that help repair a user's Outlook and possibly mailbox corruption on the Exchange server.

TABLE 30.8: Available Options for Outlook 2000

OPTION	DESCRIPTION
/CheckClient	Asks users if they would like Outlook 2000 to control all aspects of Internet mail, news, and contact databases.
/CleanFreeBusy	Cleans up free and busy information on Exchange Server.
/CleanReminders	Cleans up reminders in Outlook and rebuilds reminder notices.
/CleanSchedPlus	Exonerates all Schedule + 1.0 settings, such as permissions, .cal file, published free and busy information. Used primarily in reparation of errors in a mixed Outlook and Schedule+ environment as it pertains to calendaring and meeting requests.
/CleanViews	Deletes all the user's customized views and restores the default view settings for all applications, such as Inbox, Outbox, Calendar, Journal, etc.
/NoPreview	Disables all use of the preview pane in Outlook. Additionally, the option for the preview pane is removed from the tool options. Additionally used when companies want to ensure that users double-click a message to read it. Savvy users can read mail and not generate a read receipt by using the preview pane.
/ResetFolders	Resets all default Outlook folders, such as Calendar, Contacts, Inbox, Journal, Notes, Outbox, Sent Items, and Tasks.
/ResetOutlookBar	Rebuilds the Outlook bar so that if you change PST files or move from an Exchange server to a PST file type, storage on the Outlook bar can be fixed to point to the new location. The items in the Outlook bar are simply links to specific storage locations.

TABLE 30.9: Additional Outlook 2000 Switches

OPTION	DESCRIPTION
/c <messageclass>	Creates a new item using the specified message class. Classes always begin with IPM. For example, IPM.CONTACT would generate a new contact item. IPM.APPOINTMENT, IPM.CONTACT, IPM.MESSAGE, IPM.TASK, and IPM.ACTIVITY are default message classes.
/Cleanprofile	Expels profile data stored in the registry. Profiles are stored on a per user basis. This option is similar to creating a new profile for a user then deleting the old one, while ensuring the old settings are in the new profile. A time-consuming, arduous task that once required a desktop visit, now it is done over the phone!

Part vi

TABLE 30.9 continued: Additional Outlook 2000 Switches

OPTION	DESCRIPTION
/Cleanpst	It is impossible to get Outlook 2000 to use a new PST when in Internet mail mode, unless you use this option. In corporate/workgroup mode you can create and delete personal stores at will. However, you do not have this option in Internet mail mode. This switch allows you to create a new personal store.
/Embedding <filename>	This is the option assigned to the right-click menu for desktop uses. For example, when you right-click and choose to send to a mail recipient, this command-line option is used, thus allowing you to attach any document to the default message type. Consider using this option with the /c option and a custom form.
/Explorer	Outlook will start as the Explorer browser essentially starting in file system–browsing mode. Click Other Shortcuts while in Outlook to browse the file system otherwise.
/Folder	Starts Outlook in folder view only. No Outlook bar or folder tree view, just a folder. By default it is the Inbox.
/Profiles	Use this to force the profiles dialog box to pop up, regardless of the number of profiles or the default setting in tool options.
/Profile	Starts Outlook using the profile specified in the command line. Use this to avoid the pop-up box if you run multiple profiles for testing, etc.
/Safe	Starts Outlook with the default tool bars, default add-ins, and no preview pane. Used primarily when troubleshooting profiles or creating a kiosk.
/s <filename>	Allows a user to load a specified favorites file. Outlook users who use the Outlook bar frequently have a rather arduous task of re-creating the bar if something goes amiss. This command option allows you to use a specified favorites file for your needs.

WARNING

The above commands should only be used after ample testing in a proof-of-concept environment.

PEWA.EXE

Description

PEWA, or Password Expiration Warning Application, was designed at the request of users. Its primary goal is to provide users on non-Windows machines a way to change their password associated with the primary user account on their mailbox. All Exchange mailboxes have primary NT accounts. However, on non-Windows machines those users do not know when their password is going to expire. Hence, they are e-mailed a notification of password expiration when their account is within seven days (default) of expiring. Primary beneficiaries of the PEWA tool include all who use Outlook Web Access as their primary e-mail client.

NOTE

A simple, yet thorny, caveat of the PEWA tool is that users of Windows-based systems will receive a pop-up notification when they log on suggesting they change their password prior to expiration. After receiving this notification, they will receive yet another notification (even if they did change their password). Therefore, it is recommended that you modify the file used for password expiration notification.

NOTE

PEWA is for use in an Exchange environment only. It is not designed for use in other message systems.

PEWA's functions are simple and based on ADSI (Active Directory Services Interface). PEWA identifies all accounts whose passwords will expire in the default of seven days (placing this list into memory). The account information or SID is compared against the GAL (global address list of Exchange). Each mailbox has a primary NT account. If the SID in the password expiration list matches the primary NT account of a mailbox in the GAL, then an e-mail is sent to the mailbox. Very simple, yet effective.

TIP

Large domains require special care when using this tool since large amounts of memory and processor time could be used.

Installing

To install PEWA from the `Exchange\<operating system\platform>\ Security\PEWA` directory on the Microsoft Back Office Resource Kit, Second Edition CD, copy the `Pewa.txt` and `Pewa.rtf` files to the same directory on the hard drive of your computer.

Follow these steps to set up your server to use the Password Expiration Warning Application:

1. In User Manager, create a Windows NT user account for the Microsoft Exchange Server profile that PEWA is to use.

WARNING

The account should not expire, and the user account should not have to change password.

2. Create a Microsoft Exchange Server mailbox for the Windows NT user account you have just created. Name the account PEWA.

3. Create a Microsoft Exchange Server profile for PEWA on the computer on which PEWA is to be run. Use the profile defaults. Consider calling the profile PEWA.

NOTE

Only one Windows NT user account and one Microsoft Exchange Server profile are required for PEWA, regardless of the number of Windows NT domains involved.

Usage

PEWA must be run on a computer in the domain where the accounts exist or on a trusted domain. Additionally, for PEWA to run correctly the following requirements must be met:

▶ A copy of PEWA must run against the domain controller of each domain that has Microsoft Exchange Server mailboxes.

WARNING

You can run copies of PEWA for multiple domains on the same machine, but you should schedule them to run at different times.

▶ The actual text in the body of the e-mail message sent by PEWA is the RFT file named `Pewa.rtf`; you should modify this file.

▶ To run PEWA, type the following at the command prompt:

```
pewa -d \\<server name> -u <profile name> -z <days>
```

> ▶ -d is the name of a domain controller in the domain where the accounts are located. (-d must always be present and precede the profile name, as well as the number of days to expiration.)
>
> ▶ -u is the Microsoft Exchange Server profile name without spaces.
>
> ▶ -z is the number of days to expiration; the default number of days is seven.

NOTE

If you do not specify a profile, PEWA uses the default Microsoft Exchange Server profile or the profile in use at the time; this is called piggybacking. Use quotation marks if there is a space in the profile name. (Profiles without spaces are recommended, not required.)

The following example shows the Windows NT user accounts that are to expire within six days on the MyCompanyDC domain controller.

```
PEWA -d \\MyCompanyDC -u "PEWA" -z 6
```

NOTE

Running PEWA will have an adverse effect on a production domain controller or Exchange Server. Thus, you should run PEWA during low production hours using the Windows NT Scheduler.

PHONE.EXE

Description

PHONE.EXE is a nifty little tool that allows you to quickly get the phone number of an Exchange server user. If you have been using your Exchange server to store some basic white pages information, then you can utilize this tool immediately.

Installation

There are no special requirements for this tool. It is a part of the Back Office Resource Kit and can be copied to any machine without any special modifications or dlls.

Usage

The following procedures outline how to perform specific functions with the Phone Book Search tool, including searching by e-mail alias and searching by phone number.

TIP

Microsoft Exchange Server computers index for phone numbers; therefore this search could be time-consuming. Adding an index on the phone number attribute speeds up this task.

Servername is the Exchange server name.

Alias is the user's alias name as specified on the general tab.

Extension is the user's phone number.

To search by e-mail alias at the command prompt, switch to the directory where PHONE.EXE is installed. Type **Phone <Microsoft Exchange Server computer name> <e-mail alias>** (for example, Phone Exchange1 joshuak).

TIP

You can also use wildcards to search for multiple phone numbers (for example, Phone Exchange1 joshua*).

To search by phone number at the command prompt, switch to the directory where PHONE.EXE is installed. Type **Phone <Microsoft Exchange Server computer name> <phone number>**.

PROFINST.EXE

Description

This is the profile installer for gateway profiles. This is primarily used to create IMS profiles for use with MDBVU32.EXE. MDBVU32.EXE is used to view the IMS MTS-IN/OUT folders in the information store during troubleshooting.

Installing

If you intend on using this tool you will need to download it from the Microsoft support site, or get a copy from the Back Office Software Development Kit. Here's where you can go to download it:

    http://support.microsoft.com/support/downloads/LNP244.asp

Usage

TABLE 30.10: Required Options

OPTION	DESCRIPTION
/SERVICE=	Service name (MSExchangeIMC or MSExchangeCCMC)
/NAME=	Profile name
/TYPE=	Profile type (GATEWAY or AGENT)

TABLE 30.11: Optional Parameters

OPTION	DESCRIPTION
/DELETE	Delete profile
/HELP or /?	Display help

Part vi

REGSVR32.EXE

Description

REGSVR32 is a tool used to register or un-register Dynamic Link Libraries into the Class ID database in the registry. Once done, the library is available to the OS. If the library registration database gets corrupted or if an entry is missing, this spells bad news for administrators and users alike.

Installing

REGSVR32 is bundled with NT Server. No special installation is required.

Usage

REGSVR32 accepts command-line parameters. The most common usage is: REGSVR32 <path to DLL>\some.dll

TABLE 30.12: REGSVR Parameter Options

OPTION	DESCRIPTION
/u	Un-registers a dll.
/s	Used during registration or un-registration. This option works well if you are using the REGSVR32 tool in a login script.
/i	Calls dll install, passing it an optional [cmdline]; when used with /u it calls dll uninstall.
/n	Do not call DLLRegisterServer; this option must be used with /i.

Examples If you install Outlook 97 (version 8.03) on an Exchange Server 5.5 computer, Outlook Web Access does not perform as expected. To solve this problem, run REGSVR32.EXE after installing Outlook. This utility resets the affected registry settings by re-registering cdo.dll (regsvr32 systemroot\system32\cdo.dll).

If you install an Outlook 2000 client on the same computer as Exchange Server and then un-install that client, you must run the REGSVR32 command on the `esconf.dll` file, as shown here:

```
regsvr32 drive_letter:\exchsvr\bin\esconf.dll
```

NOTE

REGSVR32.EXE comes in handy in many Exchange Server situations. As an example, you will be using the REGSVR32.EXE tool in Exchange 2000 to load the Schema Manager component.

INDEX

Note to Reader: In this index, **boldfaced** page numbers refer to primary discussions of the topic; *italics* page numbers refer to figures.

About the Contributors

Some of the best—and best-selling—Sybex authors have contributed chapters from their books to *Exchange Server 5.5 and Outlook Complete*.

Gini Courter and **Annette Marquis** are co-owners of TRIAD Consulting, LLC, a firm specializing in computer applications training and database development, including customized solutions using Microsoft Outlook and Microsoft Exchange Server. Courter and Marquis are the authors of numerous books, including *Mastering Microsoft Office 2000*, *Microsoft Office 2000: No Experience Required*, and *Mastering Microsoft Outlook 98*, all from Sybex.

Barry Gerber is an IS consultant focusing on communications systems, networking, and advanced database technologies. He has worked in a variety of fields, including finance, medicine, law, and academia. A founding editor of *Network Computing Magazine*, he has served as Director of Social Sciences Computing at UCLA, Vice President of Distributed Data Processing at a major insurance company, and Computing Director for a federally funded health-care program.

Jim McBee, MCSE+Internet and MCT, is a consultant and trainer based in Honolulu, Hawaii. He specializes in Exchange deployments and has worked for many Fortune 500 customers, as well as on the Defense Messaging System for all branches of the U.S. Department of Defense. He has taught Windows NT and Exchange Server courses throughout the United States and the Pacific Rim.

Cynthia Randall is a veteran technical writer and the author of several computer guides. In addition, she has written numerous articles for publications such as *Microsoft Magazine* and various online magazines. Randall has a degree in journalism from the University of Washington.